QANOON-E-ISLAM,

OR THE

CUSTOMS OF THE MOOSULMANS OF INDIA;

COMPRISING A

FULL AND EXACT ACCOUNT

OF

THEIR VARIOUS RITES AND CEREMONIES,

FROM THE

MOMENT OF BIRTH TILL THE HOUR OF DEATH.

QANOON-E-ISLAM,

OR THE

CUSTOMS OF THE MOOSULMANS OF INDIA;

COMPRISING A

FULL AND EXACT ACCOUNT

OF

THEIR VARIOUS RITES AND CEREMONIES,

FROM THE

MOMENT OF BIRTH TILL THE HOUR OF DEATH.

BY

JAFFUR SHURREEF,

(A Native of the Deccan):

Composed Under the Direction of, And Translated By

G. A. HERKLOTS, M.D.

SURGEON ON THE MADRAS ESTABLISHMENT

GYAN

Published by

Gyan Publishing House
5, Ansari Road
Daryaganj, New Delhi-110002
Phone: 011-47034999, 9811692060
E-mail: books@gyanbooks.com

Distribution Network
gyanbooks.com
India, USA, Canada, UK, Australia, France

ISBN : 978-81-212-3927-1 (PB)
First Published, 1832

2nd Impression 2020

Printed at: Gyan Press, Delhi.

The book at your disposal is the edition of an old book originally published long back. The Text quality of this book may not be at par as compared to our other books but many readers approached us to reprint this important book so that it could satiate their hunger. We request all the readers of this book to help us to improve its quality by providing the necessary text of those pages which are not properly visible. Your valuable support in this case will be highly appreciated and acknowledged and our future readers will be benefitted immensely.

QANOON-E-ISLAM,

OR THE

Customs of the Moosulmans of India;

COMPRISING A

FULL AND EXACT ACCOUNT

OF

THEIR VARIOUS RITES AND CEREMONIES,

FROM THE

MOMENT OF BIRTH TILL THE HOUR OF DEATH.

By JAFFUR SHURREEF,

(A Native of the Deccan):

COMPOSED UNDER THE DIRECTION OF, AND TRANSLATED BY

G. A. HERKLOTS, M.D.

SURGEON ON THE MADRAS ESTABLISHMENT.

LONDON:

PARBURY, ALLEN, AND CO.

LEADENHALL STREET.

M.DCCC.XXXII.

R. Martin, sculp.t 124, High Holborn

London, Parbury, Allen & Co. September 1833.

AN INDIAN WOMAN DECKED OUT IN HER JEWELS.

TO

THE HONOURABLE

THE CHAIRMAN, DEPUTY CHAIRMAN,

AND

COURT OF DIRECTORS

OF THE

United East-India Company,

THIS WORK,

PUBLISHED UNDER THEIR KIND AND LIBERAL PATRONAGE,

RELATING TO

AN IMPORTANT AND INTERESTING CLASS OF BRITISH SUBJECTS
UNDER THEIR GOVERNMENT,

IS, WITH PERMISSION,

MOST RESPECTFULLY DEDICATED

BY

THEIR VERY OBEDIENT AND HUMBLE SERVANT,

G. A. HERKLOTS.

TRANSLATOR'S PREFACE.

THE manners, customs, social habits, and religious rites of nations, have ever been esteemed an object of rational and interesting inquiry; hence, with this view, travellers have explored the remotest regions, and antiquaries pushed their researches into the farthest verge of recorded history. The toils of the journey, the uncongeniality of climate, the savage character of the inhabitants, have not been able to deter the progress of the former; the labour of solitary study, the scantiness of materials, or the dark mists of antiquity, have failed to damp the ardour of the latter. The adventurous foot of man has penetrated the dark forests of America, crossed the burning deserts of Africa, and ascended the lofty snow-clad summits of the Himalaya; his ships have swept the ocean and visited the most sequestered shores, from the dreary abodes of the torpid Esquimaux to the tepid isles of cheerful Otaheita and the inhospitable coast of the cannibals of New Zealand: and though nature, inanimate and irrational, has not escaped his notice, yet his own species under every variety of form has chiefly attracted his attention and engrossed his reflections ; feeling, in the words of the poet, that

"The proper study of mankind is man."

If the manners and customs of other tribes of men be worthy of our study, certainly not less so are those of the Mohummudan natives of India. They are the immediate descendants of the race of conquerors who exercised supreme dominion over the greater part of that vast country for so many centuries, until it fell into British hands. As their successors in Indian rule, we must naturally feel a curiosity regarding the character and habits of our predecessors in power; now, our subjects. And it is not a topic of philosophical speculation merely, but a matter of real practical utility, to understand thoroughly a people with whom we have constant transactions and daily intercourse, in the relations of public officers, soldiers, and subjects, in administering the government of the country.

The utility of a work directed to this object is so obvious, that it appears to me a matter of no small surprise something of the kind has not hitherto been undertaken. On the history, religion, manners, customs, &c. of the *Hindoos*, ample information may be obtained from valuable works already before the public; such as Mill's History of British India; Moor's Hindoo Pantheon; Ward's History, Literature, Mythology, Manners and Customs of the Hindoos; Coleman's Mythology; the Abbé Dubois on the Manners and Customs of the Hindoos, and others. But, as far as my knowledge extends, no similar work exists, giving a methodical account of the *Mohummudan* branch of the Indian population which embraces the various subjects comprehended in this, or which treats of them individually with sufficient precision and accuracy. From the comparative simplicity and rationality of the Mohummudan system of religion, its followers are less accessible to the influence of conversion, and may have therefore attracted less attention from Christian missionaries, (who are the closest observers of a people among whom they pursue their pious labours); while few other Europeans could have acquired the minute and curious information requisite for composing such a work; and learned natives did not think of describing, to their own countrymen, matters which they knew from daily observation and practice.

But whatever may have been the cause of the almost total neglect of this interesting field of inquiry, I shall here proceed to explain the object of the following sheets. It is to give a detailed account of all the customs adopted and observed in India, more particularly in the Duk'hun, (vulgarly written Deccan: *i. e.* the Peninsula or Southern part of India), by the followers of the Arabian Prophet, in addition to the duties inculcated on them in the *Qoran* and *Huddees.** Among the customs described, not a few will be discovered to have been borrowed from the Hindoos; and although the work professes to treat on the *customs* of the Moosulmans, it will be found interspersed also with observations on their *manners*.

To guard against misconception on the part of those who have a partial knowledge of India, it may here be remarked, that many of the customs described in this work are peculiar to the Duk'hun; and some of them are only observed at certain places; not throughout every part of that division of India; far less in remote quarters of the country, such as Bombay, Bengal, and Upper Hindoostan; yet, a very great general resemblance will be found in the manners and customs of the Mohummudan inhabitants in all parts of it.

The following is the plan which the author has followed in describing his countrymen. He traces an individual from the period of birth (and even before it), through all the forms and ceremonies which religion, superstition, and custom, have imposed on the Indian Moosulman. The account begins with the ceremonies observed at the seventh

* The *Huddees* comprises the traditional sayings attributed to Mohummud.

month of the mother's pregnancy; details the various rites performed by the parents during the several periods of the lives of their children as they grow up to maturity, and the almost endless ceremonies of matrimony. Then follow the fasts, festivals, &c. which occur in the different months of the year. These are succeeded by an account of vows, oblations, and many minor subjects, such as the pretended science of necromancy, exorcism or casting out devils, detecting thieves, determining the most auspicious times for undertaking journies or other enterprizes, all of which are matters of almost daily occurrence: and the whole concludes with an account of their sepulchral rites, and the visiting of the grave at stated periods during the first year after death. For a fuller view of the extent and variety of subjects discussed, and the order of arrangement, I must refer to the Table of Contents.

The persons to whom I conceive the work will prove most acceptable and useful are, in the first place, gentlemen in the service of the Honourable East-India Company generally; and in particular, all military officers serving in India, more especially those on the Madras establishment. For example, how often during the year do we find the Moosulmans of a native regiment apply for "leave," or exemption from duty, to celebrate some feast or other, when the commandant to whom such request is submitted, being unacquainted (as frequently happens) with either the nature of the feast or the necessity of attending it, cannot be certain that, in granting the application, he is doing justice to the service, or that in refusing it he would not infringe upon the religious feelings of his troops. If an officer be more endowed than others with a spirit of inquiry, he may ask after the nature of the feast for which the holiday is solicited. The only reply he obtains is some strange name, which, though to a native it may be very expressive and quite explicit, is to him, as a foreigner, altogether unintelligible. Should he inquire farther, his want of sufficient knowledge of the language prevents him from understanding the explanations offered ; and these are often rendered still more dark by the ignorance of the informers themselves, of whom few even know the origin and nature of the feast they are about to celebrate. This want of knowledge the present work is intended to supply ; and how far the author has succeeded, I leave to the judgment of the reader.

Having myself felt the want of such a work, ever since my arrival in India I set about collecting all the intelligence procurable relative to the various subjects comprised in these pages. To accomplish this object, it must be admitted, was no easy task, in a country where the natives, as is well known, are very reluctant to impart information respecting their religious rites, ceremonies, &c. This arises, perhaps, from an unwillingness to expose themselves to the ridicule of persons of totally different national customs and religious faith; or from a wish simply to keep Europeans in the dark, under a vague apprehension that frankness would ultimately prove to their own detriment. I had succeeded, notwithstanding, in accumulating a pretty extensive stock of the requisite materials, when I accidentally became acquainted with the liberal-minded author of these sheets. At my particular request he composed, in the Duk'hunee language, the treatise now presented to the public; while I acted merely as a reviser, and occasionally suggested subjects which had escaped his memory.

Though the enlightened English reader will smile at some of the notions gravely propounded by an Oriental writer, yet I must do my author the justice to say, that in all my intercourse with natives of India, I have seldom met with a man who had so much of the European mode of thinking and acting, or who was so indefatigable in the pursuit of knowledge. He was penetrating and quick of comprehension; and, according to my professional judgment, a skilful and scientific physician.

I have made the translation as literal as the different idioms of the two languages would admit of, bearing in mind, that though a free translation has often more ease and elegance, a close version is more characteristic of the original. And I considered this the more important, as I have some intention of publishing, hereafter, the Oriental version of the work; and conceive that the close correspondence between the two will be of great advantage to the young Oriental student.

As my object has been to give a complete and precise idea of the things described, I have, by a full and minute description, avoided the obscurity which often arises from vagueness of language and brevity of expression. During the progress of the work and researches connected with it, a large quantity of useful miscellaneous information has come into my hands. Part of this I have comprised in an Appendix, under the heads of Relationship, Weights and Measures, Dresses of Men and Women, Female Ornaments, Mohummudan Cookery, Musical Instruments, Fireworks, Games and Children's Plays.

I have followed the example of several eminent writers on India (such as Mr. Mill in his History, and Colonel Tod in his Annals of Rajast'han), in not attempting to preserve any theoretic system of writing Indian terms in Roman characters. In the spelling of the words, I have been guided by the ear; and the following letters representing the sounds contained in the words, are given as examples, respectively—*a*, as in "art;"—*ai* (when medial) and *ay* (when final) as in "sail" and "day;" —*aee*, as the word "eye;"—*e*, as in "emery;"—*ee*, as in "bee;"—*g*, as in "good;"—*gh*, as in "g'haut;"—*j*, as in "jest;"—*o*, as in "bold;"—*oo*, as in "moon;"—*u*, as in "bust;"—*y*, as in "fly;" —*kh* (for خ) as *ch* in the Scotch word "Loch;"—Roman g (for غ), like the Northumbrian provincial sound of R,—the French r. grassié;—*Q* (for ق) as in "quoit." The Arabic *futha* (or *zubur*) is generally represented by *u*, sometimes by *a*, when initial or final with a silent *h* (ه). The *kusr* (or *zayr*) by *e* or *i* when followed by two consonants; and sometimes by *ay*, which must not always be considered as long. The *zumma* (or *paysh*) by *o* or *oo*.

For the sake of the European reader, and those unacquainted with the current native language of India, I have subjoined a copious Glossary of all the Oriental words occurring, and which have not been already explained in the body of the work, or in the Index, in which it was found more convenient to insert the Oriental terms expressive of such subjects as are particularly treated of in the work. All the Oriental words are put in italics; and this will serve an an intimation to the reader, that every word so distinguished will be found explained in the Glossary or Index.

Since this work was prepared for the press, I have had an opportunity of consulting two recent publications which throw considerable light on the subject; *viz.* the correct and interesting "Observations on the Mussulmauns "of India," by Mrs. Meer Hassan Ali, 1832; and the learned and curious "Mémoires sur les Particularités de la "Religion Mussulmane dans l'Inde," (Paris 1831,) by that ingenious and profound Orientalist the professor of Hindoostanee to the French Government, Monsieur Garcin de Tassy.

I have carefully compared their labours with the following sheets, and whenever I found anything of interest or importance in them, which had been omitted, or otherwise stated by my author, I have supplied the omission, or marked the difference in notes and a few Addenda, so as to render this work, as far as possible, complete.

I may now therefore, I think, venture to say, that it embraces an account of all the peculiarities of the Moosulmans, worthy of note in *every part* of India.

I would remark, that any one at all conversant with the Mohummudans or their faith, will instantly perceive that the first work alluded to above embraces the opinions of a *Sheeah*, and that of my author the doctrines of a *Soonnee* (or orthodox Moosulman). The two works thus develope the conflicting opinions of the two great sects, who entertain the most inveterate hatred towards each other; and combined, afford as complete an insight into the national character of that race as can be reasonably desired or expected. Barring the difference of their religious notions, the general descriptions given of their manners, customs, &c. accord so entirely, that so far from one at all detracting from the merits of the other, the statements of the English Lady and the Indian Moosulman will be found to afford each other mutual support and illustration.

G. A. H.

LONDON,
1*st September* 1832.

CONTENTS.

CHAPTER I.

Page

Concerning, 1st. The rite *Sutwasa*, or "the seventh month," (*i. e.* of pregnancy).—2d. The situation of the *Juch-chee*, or lying-in-woman, during the puerperal state, *viz.* for forty days after her confinement.—3. The ceremonies observed on the *birth* of children.—4th. The mode of *naming* children; the subject leading to the consideration of, 1. The division of Mohummudans into the four great classes of *Syed, Sheikh, Mogol,* and *Putt'han*; 2. The two principal sects of *Soonnee* and *Sheeah*; and the subsects *Nu-wa-ay-tay* and *Gyr Muhdee*; 3. The casting of the nativity; 4. The influences of the planets 1

CHAPTER II.

Concerning the ceremonies of *Puttee* and *Ch'hutthee* 23

CHAPTER III.

Concerning, 1st. *Chilla*, or the fortieth day (*i. e.* after child-birth).—2d. *Uqeeqa*, or sacrifice.—3d. *Moondun*, or shaving.—4th. Placing the infant in a *Guhwara*, (or swinging cradle) .. 27

CHAPTER IV.

Concerning, 1st. *Luddoo-bandhna*, (or the child's folding hands). 2d. *Chuttana*, or the causing the infant to lick; (*i. e.* weaning). 3d. *Dant-neekulna*, or teething.—4th. *Moott'hee-bandhna*, or crawling on all fours.—5th. *Kan-ch'haydana*, or boring the ears .. 33

CHAPTER V.

Concerning *Dawut*, or invitation; comprising, 1st. The sending of *Eelachee* (or cardamoms), with verbal invitations.—2d. The bringing or taking of *Nay-oo-ta*, alias *Munja* (or presents carried in state), by the guests 35

Page

CHAPTER VI.

Concerning the custom of forming the *Sal-giruh*, or *Burrus Ganth* (lit. annual knot); *i.e.* the observance of the Birth-day Anniversary 38

CHAPTER VII.

Concerning the custom of teaching the child *Bismilla* (or pronouncing the name of God), and the mode of doing it 39

CHAPTER VIII.

Concerning *Khutna*, alias *Soontan* (or circumcision) 43

CHAPTER IX.

Concerning the *Huddeea* (or conclusion of the child's reading) of the *Qoran*, and the making of presents to the tutor; including the subject of *Eedee* (or feast-gifts) 47

CHAPTER X.

Concerning the period of Virginity, and the Ceremonies observed on the occasion 51

CHAPTER XI.

Concerning the age of Puberty or Maturity in Males; and the observance of the religious duties required of them after reaching manhood 53

CHAPTER XII.

Concerning the real foundation of Mohummudanism; comprising five divine commands, *viz.*; 1st. *Kulma purna*, or Confession of Faith; 2d. *Numaz kurna*, or Prayer; 3d. *Roza ruk'hna*, or Fasting during the month *Rumzan*; 4th. *Zukat dayna*, or alms-giving; 5th. *Mukkay ka huj ko jana*, or Pilgrimage to Mecca 54

CHAPTER XIII.

Concerning *Numaz*, or Prayer; embracing, 1st. *Wuzoo* and *Tyammoom* (or Ablutions before Prayer); 2d. *Azan*, or Summons to Prayer; 3d. Forms of Prayer 72

Page

CHAPTER XIV.

Concerning Marriage, which comprises eleven sections, *viz.* 1st. Concerning the looking out for a suitable partner; the ascertaining by the science of astrology whether the match will prove a propitious one; and the offering of proposals, and arranging matters for the ceremonies;—2d. Concerning Betrothment; including, 1. *K'hurray pan bantna*, or the distributing of betel-leaves standing; 2. *Shookrana* (prop. *Shukur-ana*), or the bringing of sugar; 3. *Mangnee*, or the asking (in marriage); 4. *Pooreean*, (or a kind of patties); 5. *D'hayleez k'hoondlana* (or treading the threshold); 6. *Numuk chu-shee* (or tasting the salt).—3d. The application of *Huldee* (or turmeric), to the Bridegroom and Bride, alias *Munja bythana* (or sitting in state), and *Puttee*, *Juhaz*, and *Mudar ka ch'handa*, alias *Bhundara*.—4th. Concerning the carrying of *Huldee* and *Maynhdee*, from the Bridegroom's to the Bride's; and *vice versâ*.—5th. *Paoon-minut*, alias *Paoon-mayz*, or the measuring for the Bride and Bridegroom's wedding dresses.—6th. Concerning the ceremonies observed on the *Shub-gusht* day; viz. 1. The custom of depositing the *Kulus kay mat* (or water-pots) under the shed; 2. The method of painting the *Tail-g'hurray*, (or oil-pots); 3. The fashion of making the *Mundway kay Beebeean*, (or Ladies of the Shed); 4. The forms attending the conveyance of the Bridegroom's *Burree* (or wedding gifts) to the Bride; including a description of a Moosulman *zeeafut*, or dinner-party; 5. The mode of carrying the Bride's *Jayhez*, (or bridal paraphernalia) to the Bridegroom's house; 6. The ceremony of *Jhol p'horana*, (or breaking open the pots); 7. The manner of beating the *Put kay chawul*, (lit. virgin-rice); 8. The observance of the rite *Tail churhana*, (or raising the oil-pots); 9. The performance of *Shub-gusht*, (or nocturnal perambulation).—7th 1. *Neekah*, (or the solemnization of matrimony); 2. *Joolwa*, or the first interview of the new married couple.—8th. *Kunggun k'holna*, or untying the *kunggun* (or wedding bracelets), from the wrists of the bride and bridegroom.—9th. 1. *Hât burtana* (or the resumption of the use of the hands); 2. *Joomayee*, or the giving of entertainments on five successive Fridays (the Mohummudan Sabbath), during the honey-moon; 3. *Kulus kay mât oot'hând*, or removing the before-mentioned waterpots.—10th. 1. The number of wives authorized; 2. Relatives whom it is unlawful to marry; 3. The subject of divorce.—11th. The postponing and expediting the performance of the matrimonial rites 83

Page

CHAPTER XV.

Concerning the *Mohurrum*, (or the first month); it comprises three subjects, *viz.*—1st. The *Mohurrum kee Eed*, or Feast.—2d. The cause of the Martyrdom of their Highnesses *Eemâm Hussun* and *Hosein*, (may God reward them!).—3d. The ceremonies observed during the *Ashoora*, or first ten days of the month *Mohurrum*; including a description of the *Ashoor-khanas*, and *Emambaras*; *Allawahs*; *Ullums* and *Neezas*; *Taboots* or *Tazeeas*; *Shah-nusheens* or *Dad mahals*; *Booraqs*; *Mohurrum-Fuqeers*; *Lunggur neekalna*; *Mohurrum Nuzur-o-Nyaz*, (vide p. 269); *Shub-gusht* or *Shuhur-gusht*; *Shuhadut ka roz*; *Run ka dola*, or *Run ka taboot* 148

CHAPTER XVI.

Concerning the *Tayra Tayzee*, (or the first thirteen evil days); and the *Akhree Char Shoomba* (*kee Eed*, or Feast) held on the last Wednesday of the second month *Sufur* 229

CHAPTER XVII.

Concerning *Bara Wufat*, or the Death of the Prophet on the 12th day of the third month *Rubbee-ool-awul* 233

CHAPTER XVIII.

Concerning his excellency *Peer-e-Dustugeer Sahib's Geearween* on the 11th day of the fourth month *Rubbee-oos-Sanee*, and the putting on of the *Bayree* (Fetters), *Towq* (Collar), or *Buddhee* (Belt). 237

CHAPTER XIX.

Concerning *Zinda Shah Mudar's Churagan* (or lamps), and *Buddhee*, *Dhummul koodana* and *Gaee lootana*, observed on the 17th day of the fifth month *Jummadee-ool-Awul* 241

CHAPTER XX.

Concerning *Qadir Wullee Sahib's Oors*, observed on the 11th day of the sixth month *Jummadee-ool-Akhir* 243

CHAPTER XXI.

Concerning, 1st. *Rujub Salar's Kundoree*; 2d. *Syed Jullal-ood-Deen's* (of Bokhara) *Koondon*; 3d. His holiness Mohummud Moostuffa's (the peace and blessing of God be on him!) *Mayraj* (or Ascension), observed in the seventh month *Rujub* 249

Page

CHAPTER XXII.

Concerning the *Shaban* feast; *viz. Shub-e-Burat*, held on the 14th, and its *Arfa*, on the 13th day of the eighth month *Shaban* 251

CHAPTER XXIII.

Concerning 1st. The *Rumzan ka Roza* (*i. e.* the *Rumzan* Fast, or Lent); 2d. The *Turaweeh kee Numaz* (or the *Turaweeh* Prayers); 3d. *Aytaykaf bythna*, (or constantly praying in the mosque); 4th. *Lylut-ool-qudur's Shub-bay-daree*, (or the nocturnal vigils on the night of Power,) observed in the ninth month *Rumzan* 255

CHAPTER XXIV.

Concerning *Eed-ool-Fitr*, or *Rumzan kee Eed* (or breaking the Fast), held on the 1st day of the tenth month *Shuwal* 261

CHAPTER XXV.

Concerning *Bunday Nuwaz's Churagan* (or lamps, *i. e.* illuminations), observed on the 15th day of the eleventh month *Zeeqaeda* 265

CHAPTER XXVI.

Concerning the *Buqr-eed* (*qoorbanee*, or sacrifice), alias *Eed-ool-Zoha*; its *Arfa* and *Eed* (or feast), held on the 9th day of the twelfth month *Buqr-eed* or *Zeehuj* 266

CHAPTER XXVII.

Concerning *Nuzur-o-Nyaz*, or vows and oblations 269

CHAPTER XXVIII.

Concerning *Tureequt*, or the Path (*i. e.* to Heaven). It comprises three sections; *viz.* 1st. The becoming a *Mooreed* (disciple); 2d. The manner of making a *Fuqeer* (*Durwaysh*, or devotee), and the investiture with the *Kheelafat* (deputyship); 3d. The austerities requisite to be practised in order to become a *Wullee* (saint, or a performer of miracles) 281

Page

CHAPTER XXIX.

Concerning the science of *Dawut* (or exorcism), comprehending four sections: 1st. The rules necessary to be observed, and the articles required by the exorcist; 2d. The giving of *Nissab, Zukat,* &c. of the *Isms,* and the manner of reading the *Dawut;* 3d. The commanding the presence of genii and demons; 4th. The casting out of devils 303

CHAPTER XXX.

Concerning the method of establishing friendship between two persons, and of captivating the hearts of members of assemblies 341

CHAPTER XXXI.

Concerning the causing of enmity between two individuals, and the effecting the death of one's enemy 345

CHAPTER XXXII.

Concerning the science of *Tukseer* (or numbers), comprising the art of constructing *Taweez* (amulets), and *Puleeta* (charms); the uses to which they are applied; and in the name of the sick to consult horoscopes and predict future events 347

CHAPTER XXXIII.

Concerning the ascertaining of unknown things by the viewing of *Unjun* (or lamp-black, *alias* the Magic Mirror), or by the viewing of *Hazirat,* (or the flame of a charm-wick); the giving of the *Purree kay Tubuq,* (or Fairy-Tray); and the performing of *Nahown,* (or the Fairy-Bath). 376

CHAPTER XXXIV.

Concerning the art of detecting thieves 390

CHAPTER XXXV.

Concerning travelling 395

CHAPTER XXXVI.

Concerning the hour and day of the month most propitious for undertaking any particular business 402

Page

CHAPTER XXXVII.

Concerning the measuring for, and wearing of new clothes; the preserving of the beard, mustachios, hair of the head, &c.; the custom of bathing and shaving, and of eating and drinking, &c. 403

CHAPTER XXXVIII.

Concerning the administering consolation to the dying, and the shrouding and burial of the dead 407

CHAPTER XXXIX.

Concerning the *Teeja*, alias *Zeearut*, or *P'hool-churhana* of the dead, or the visiting the grave on the third day after burial 421

CHAPTER XL.

Concerning the *Fateeha* (or offerings to the dead) on the tenth, twentieth, thirtieth, and fortieth day after the demise; and the quarterly, half-yearly, nine-monthly, and annual-*Fateeha* .. 422

ADDENDA, including a Summary of the Moosulman Saints of India 428

APPENDIX, comprising an account, 1st. of relationships; 2d. of weights and measures; 3d. of dresses; 4th. of female ornaments; 5th. of Moosulman cookery; 6th. of games; 7th. of children's plays, and 8th. of fireworks i

GLOSSARY of Oriental Terms lx

INDEX ciii

THE AUTHOR'S PREFACE.

Lord, Prosper Work with { In the name of GOD, the Merciful and Compassionate! } and finish this thy blessing!

Glory be to that God who has, out of a drop of fluid, created such a variety of creatures, rational and irrational! Adored be that Creator, who has established such a variety of forms, statures, and vocal sounds among them, though their origin is the same pure, liquid, and genuine spirit!

In Praise of the Prophet (i. e. Mohummud).

A thousand thousand salutations and benedictions are due to his sublime holiness Mohummud Moostufa* (the blessing and peace of God be with him!) through whose grace the sacred *Qoran* descended from the Most High! How inadequate is man justly to praise and eulogize him! Salutation and blessing, also, to his companions and posterity!

My object in composing the present work is this: I, Jaffur Shurreef, alias Lala Meea*n*, son of Allee Shurreef (who has received mercy†), of the Qoreish tribe, born at

* Moostufa, *i. e.* "the chosen."

† "The late," or as we should say, "who is now in heaven."

Nagore (may God illuminate his tomb, pardon his iniquities, and sanctify his soul!) a native of Ooppoo Elloor (Ellore), have for a considerable time been in attendance upon English gentlemen of high rank and noble mind (may their good fortune ever continue!), and under the shadow of their wings have nourished both my soul and body; or, in other words, my office has been that of a teacher of language.

Gentlemen of penetration used often to observe to me with the deepest interest, that if a concise work were written in a familiar style, and in the genuine Dukhunee language, containing a full account of all the necessary rites, customs, and usages observed by Moosulmans, Europeans would not only read it with pleasure, but would derive much useful information from its perusal. However, hitherto, owing to want of leisure, this humble individual* has not been able to undertake any thing of the kind. But, in the present instance, at the earnest request of (a possessor of favour and kindness, a man of great learning and magnanimity, a mine of humanity, a fountain of generosity, a just appreciator of the worth of both high and low, well versed in the mysteries of philosophy, a Plato of the age, in medicine a second Galen, nay, the Hippocrates of the day), Dr. Herklots (a man of virtue, an ocean of liberality, may his good fortune ever continue and his age increase!)† I have endeavoured, to the extent

---

* Literally "this know-nothing;" one of the many expressions of humility which Oriental writers are accustomed to use in speaking of themselves; such as "this sinner;" "this beggar;" "this slave."

† At the very earnest solicitation of the author, the translator has been prevailed upon (very much against his own inclination) to allow the above hyperbolical eulogiums to remain, though conscious of his being little entitled to them. He has been induced to accede to the author's

of my poor abilities, to arrange this work under different heads, and entitled it "QANOON-E-ISLAM,* *i. e. The Customs of the Moosulmans.*"

Although various Hindoostanee authors have occasionally adverted to similar subjects, yet no work extant contains so full an account of them as has been given here.

I have also included in it, local customs which have been superadded to the laws prescribed by the sacred *Qoran* and *Huddees*, observed by Moosulmans, in order that the liberal-minded Englishman should not continue ignorant of, or remain in the dark as to any rite or ceremony observed by Moosulmans.

Although the author (who deems himself no wiser than a teacher of the A B C) be somewhat acquainted with the science of divinity (*i. e.* the knowledge of the interpretation of the *Qoran* and the *Huddees*, precepts of Mohummud), as well as with law and medicine, he has confined himself merely to a narration of the established and indispensable *customs* commonly observed by Moosulmans in the Dukhun, and to an idiom of language calculated to be understood by even the most illiterate.

Of him who can judge of the state of the pulse of the pen (*i. e.* estimate the beauty of composition), and is likewise erudite, I have this request to make, that should he observe any errors in it, he would kindly consign them to oblivion, by erasing them with his quill.

---

author's wish, more particularly to shew the remarkable proneness of this class of people to flattery. In their epistolary correspondence, as well as in their intercourse with each other, they are equally lavish of praise. A somewhat similar specimen will likewise be found at the conclusion of the work.

* More strictly "rules (canons) of the Mohummudan religion."

This work was completed Anno Hijræ* 1248, corresponding with Anno Domini 1832.

---

* *i. e. Sun-e-Hijree*, or the year of the flight. It is generally, simply called the *Hijra*, or flight; *i. e.* the flight of Mohummud from Mecca to Medina, which happened on the 16th of July, A.D. 622, whence the Mohummudan æra commences.

QANOON-E-ISLAM.

CHAPTER I.

Concerning, 1st. The rite *Sutwasa*, or "the seventh month," *i. e.* of pregnancy.—2d. The situation of the *Juch-chee*, or lying-in-woman, during the puerperal state, or for forty days after confinement.—3d. The ceremonies observed on the birth of children.—4th. The mode of naming children; which leads to the consideration of, 1. The division of Mohummudans into the four great classes of *Syed*, *Sheikh*, *Mogol*, and *Putthan*;—2. The two principal sects of *Soonnee* and *Sheeah*, and the sub-sects *Nuwa-ay-tay* and *Gyr Muhdee*;—3. The casting of the nativity;—4. The influences of the planets.

SECT. 1. *The rite* sutwasa, *observed when a woman arrives at the end of the seventh month of her pregnancy.*

ON this occasion, her parents invite her to their house, and regale her with all kinds of delicacies; and, should Providence have blessed them with the means, they put a new suit of clothes on her, perfume her with *uttur* and *sundul*, adorn her with flowers, and amuse themselves the whole of that day and night with music, singing, and all kinds of merry-making.

At this ceremony they perform a certain experiment, from the result of which they predict the sex of the expected offspring; that is, they press out a few drops of the woman's milk on a piece of yellow cloth; and if, when dry, it leave a white stain, they conjecture that the child will be a girl; but if a yellow mark, they suppose that it will be a boy.

Again, on entering her ninth month, all the female relatives and neighbours assemble; and as the pregnant woman was not allowed to wear fine clothes or jewels from the seventh to the ninth month, they now adorn her with them. In the course of the day they have *sanuk fateeha* (vide Glossary) performed by some learned man, in the name of her highness Beebee Fateema (the daughter of Mohummud), and fill the woman's lap with such fruits and vegetables as are in season. After this, they keep *rutjugga*, or nocturnal vigils, and make great rejoicings.

Among the great this ceremony is observed at every lying-in; while among the poor it is kept only on the first confinement.

SECT. 2. *The situation of the lying-in woman during the puerperal state, or for forty days after confinement.*

Among the generality of the people, it is the custom for the first accouchement to take place at the house of the woman's parents; but among the very poor and needy, she is confined at her husband's house.

When the period of parturition approaches, the female relatives, friends, and neighbours assemble, and choose a warm apartment for the accouchement. The woman is then brought to bed by the assistance of the family *Daee junnaee* (or accoucheuse).* After she has been delivered, all the women, except her mother and sister, who still continue to attend upon her, return home.

* The professional fee of a midwife varies from hundreds (nay thousands) of rupees, to a few pice, each one rewarding her according to his means.

The moment that the woman is delivered, they cause her to swallow a *dumree* or *rooa*, or any small piece of copper, with the view of facilitating the expulsion of the placenta. As soon as that object is accomplished, they administer to her some assafœtida,* to prevent her catching cold. A handkerchief is then tied on her head and a fit roller round her abdomen, and she is laid in bed, or on a sheet spread on the ground, in a warm apartment, enclosed by curtains or screens; and by the side of her bed are deposited a lemon, some *neem* leaves, and a *kuthar* (or dirk), a knife, or any other weapon, to ward off the influence of misfortune and apparitions. They then give her a parcel of *betel* leaf, with the addition of *bol* (myrrh) as a medicine, to chew.

The drink she is allowed for forty days after her confinement is water boiled, in which a red-hot horse-shoe, or any other piece of iron, has been slaked, and allowed to cool.

In some countries, the woman-in-the-straw gets nothing to eat or drink whatever for the first three days.

Among some of the people, her food on the first day consists of a kind of caudle called *uchwanee*† (*i. e.* a boiled preparation of sugar, a little coarse wheaten flour [*ata*], and *ajwaeen*,) made of a thin watery consistence; on the next day, of *hurreera*, i. e. a mixture of wheaten meal or flour (*ata* or *myda*), sugar and *ghee* boiled to a paste; and on the third and some following days, wheaten *t'hoollee*,† i. e. a pudding or dumpling composed of *kunkee*,† sugar, and *ghee*.†

But, among the generality of the people, for the first six

* Assafœtida is considered by the natives a powerful stimulant; and as it is an antispasmodic, it proves likewise beneficial in relieving after-pains. It is not unfrequently an ingredient in curries, to give them a flavour.

† Vide Glossary.

days, they give the mother nothing to eat but caudle (*uchwanee*) and *suthwara** (vulgo *suthoora*) or only the former. After that, *khooshka* (or a dish of boiled rice), made of *oobala chawul,** or of old raw rice (i. e. not boiled in the husk), with black-pepper *chutnee.*

After the tenth or twelfth day, the woman resumes her accustomed diet of animal food, vegetables, &c., being regulated in the choice of them by what agrees best with her constitution.

Among some of them, the woman does not oil, or comb her hair, for forty days after child-birth, but wears a handkerchief tied on her head; and some do not permit her to leave her bedroom, except for the purpose of bathing on the *ch'huttee* (p. 24.), and *chilla* days (p. 27.), and that of counting the stars. (These ceremonies will be described hereafter.) During those days, whenever a stranger, male or female, comes into the room, they throw some *ispund** on the fire, that no evil influence, which may have accompanied the visitor, may hurt the mother or child; and some place a *kalik ka tuwa,*† and a broom, in a corner, which remain there constantly, until the *chilla*-day, in order that no evil spirit may approach the house. Great care is taken that no dog or cat enter the room, in order to ward off the misfortunes which their presence might occasion; and even the very name of a cat is not allowed to be mentioned, as it is considered a witch.

---

* Vide Glossary.

† *Kalik ka tuwa,* the iron or earthen plate on which wheaten cakes are toasted or baked; in this case used for collecting *kalik.*—Vide *kalik,* note p. 23.

SECT. 3. *The Birth of the Child and the Ceremonies attending it.*

On the birth of the child,* the midwife demands something shining, such as a *fanam*, a piece of silver, or a *rupee;* and having touched the navel-string with it, she divides it, and appropriates the glittering substance, under the pretence that in the absence of the illuminating power of some such sparkling object she could not possibly see to operate. She then puts the after-birth into a *lota* (a large) or *hundee* (a small earthen pot), together with a *pice*,† and a *betel*-leafparcel, and buries it in a corner of the room or on one side of the *compound*, (*i.e.* the area or enclosure round the house), in a cool place, where pots of water are usually kept; and the knife by which the umbilical cord had been divided is not used for any purpose, but left near the lying-in-woman until the *chilla*-day, when *kajul* (or lamp-black) is collected on it, and applied to the child's eyelids. Whenever the child is bathed, or taken out of the house, the knife is carried along with it; and when they are brought in again, the knife is deposited in its former place near the mother; and on the *chilla*-day they must, with the self-same knife, sacrifice a sheep or a cock.

After the infant is born, and after he has been properly washed with warm water and bound in swaddling-clothes,

---

* "The birth of a boy is greeted by the warmest demonstrations "of unaffected joy, in the houses both of the parents of the bride "and bridegroom. When a female child is born, there is much less "clamorous rejoicings."—"The birth of a son is immediately an-"nounced by a discharge of artillery, where cannons are kept; or "by musketry in the lower grades of the native population, even to "the meanest peasant, with whom a single matchlock proclaims the "honour as effectually as the volley of his superiors."—*Mrs. Meer*, vol. ii. p. 2, 3.

† A copper coin in value equal to two farthings.

he is carried by the midwife to the assembly of male relatives and friends met on the occasion. There the *azan* (or summons to prayer) is uttered aloud in his right ear, and the *tukbeer* (or Mohummudan creed) in his left.—This is done by the *Khuteeb* (or preacher), or any other person present, though more commonly by a boy, who is instructed and desired to repeat the words *Allah-ho-akbur* (God is great), into the ears of the babe; for which he is rewarded with a few *pice*, or a little sugar.

It is customary among some people (more frequently among the literati than the nobility or the poor), for a man of true piety and erudition, such as a *Mushaekh* (patriarch), or the *Moorshud* (religious instructor of the family), if present, to dip his finger in honey, or chew a little of the date-fruit, or the grape, and insert a small quantity of it, thus masticated, into the infant's mouth, before he is put to the breast, in order that the wisdom and learning of the sage may be imparted to him.

This ceremony being ended, and *fateeha* (or prayers) offered, in the name of the Prophet, over some sugar and *betel* leaves, they are distributed to all the connexions and friends, both absent and present.

As soon as the friends and relatives of a woman receive the intelligence of her having been brought to bed, they repair to her house in a body, carrying with them a blade, or a few blades tied together, of fresh or green grass. On reaching the place, the head of the party sticks the tuft of grass into the hair of the husband's head, and after they have all paid their congratulatory compliments on the joyful occasion, they demand of him the usual *gote* (or present), in order that they may celebrate the happy event. When they have received it, they give an entertainment in the house of one of the party, or in some neighbouring garden, and eat, drink, and enjoy themselves with their own vocal and instrumental performances, while such as can afford it, hire dancing-girls for the purpose. The observance of this custom is very common among the lower orders of the community.

The infant is bathed mornings and evenings, and fumigated with the smoke of *ispund* and *ood*, and they tie round his neck or legs *puchar* leaves, or assafœtida, to prevent people's sight, or shadow, from falling upon him. Whenever the child is bathed, they take some red or yellow dye, made of *choona* (quick-lime) and turmeric, add to it a few pieces of charcoal, and the midwife having waved it three times over the child, it is thrown away: or she takes merely some water in a vessel (*lota*), waves it over the infant, and pours it on her own feet; as much as to signify, "May all the child's misfortunes be on me;" and a common mode of expression for this act is, "All the child's misfortunes have beset the midwife."

SECT. 4. *The Naming of Children.*

The naming of the child takes place, either on the day of its birth, or, as in some parts of the country, on that day-week; for the most part, however, on the former: as, until the child is named, the woman is not even indulged with a draught of water, be she ever so thirsty; much less are the usual luxuries of *betel*, *myrrh*, &c. allowed to be given to her, which they consider as forbidden till the ceremony of naming has been performed.

Among the better ranks of society, after the name has been given, and the before-mentioned *fateeha* performed over the *betel* and sugar, or *butasha* (sugar-cakes), they are sent along with music, &c. to the absent relatives and friends. It is the province of the midwife to superintend these, and which she accompanies with or without carrying a dish of sugar in her own hands. On delivering them, it is customary for her to receive a douceur of two or four *pice*, or a little unboiled rice, from each family.

The offspring of Moosulmans invariably belong to their father's tribe,* consequently if the new-born be the son of

---

* Mohummudans are divided into four great classes, distinguished by the appellations *Syed*, *Sheikh*, *Mogol*, and *Putt'han*. The *Putt'hans* are sometimes also termed *Afgans*. The origin of these are as follows. It is said that originally they were all *Sheikhs;* not even the prophet Mohummud Moostuffa (the blessing and peace of God be on him!) excepted.

According to one tradition, on a particular day, as his holiness Mohummud Moostuffa (the blessing and peace! &c.) was sitting in company with his son-in-law Allee, and his daughter Fateema, together with his grandsons Hussun and Hosein (the blessing and peace of God be on them!), the angel Jibbreel (Gabriel—peace be unto him!) descended from heaven with the divine Revelation, and holding a blanket or sheet (or rather an *aba*), as a curtain of honour over the heads of the *punjatun* (or the five) as they are called, exclaimed, "O "Mohummud! the Almighty showers down upon thee the abun- "dance of his rich blessing, and declares, that ye who are at present "in the shade of this canopy, as well as the offspring of the four† "sitting with thee, and who believe in thee, shall henceforth be "*Syeds*."

The meaning of *Syed* is a lord, a prince, a noble. Hence, it has become a title of honour.

Another oral saying among some is, that his holiness Mohummud Moostuffa (the blessing, &c.) on giving his daughter Beebee Fateematooz Zohura (may God reward her!) in marriage to Allee (may God reward him!), he supplicated of heaven that the descendants from the womb of Fateema and of the seed of Allee, (may God! &c.) might be *Syeds*.

Allee's race by Fateema, *i. e.* Hussun and Hosein (may God reward them!) and their descendants, are denominated *Syed Hussunee* and *Syed Hoseinee;* while his progeny by his other wives are termed *Syed Alleewee*.

The

---

† Not including the future descendants of the Prophet, who, as we shall presently observe, continued to be *Sheikhs*, and therefore the Prophet is considered as belonging to both classes.

a *Syed*, the first word attached to his name is *Syed* or *Meer;* such as *Syed Allee* or *Meer Ahmud.* But although,

---

The *Sheikhs* are of three varieties:

1st. *Sheikh Qorayshee*, of which class are, the prophet Mohummud Moostuffa (the blessing! &c.) and all his companions and descendants.

2d. *Sheikh Siddeeqee*, also descendants of Aba Bukur Siddeeq.

3d. *Sheikh Farooqee*, of his highness Oomur.

The word *Sheikh*, among various other significations, means a chief.

The prophet Is'haq (Isaac) in blessing his son Ees (Esau), declared that all his race would be monarchs. Accordingly, they became of royal blood. Then those of his lineage formed a *gol* (or society) among themselves, and would pay no respect or honour to any one; they were designated as a people belonging to the *gol;* which term some corrupted into *mogol*. In the course of time, the former became obsolete and the latter was confirmed.

Moreover, on one occasion of obtaining a victory over the enemy, the Prophet (on whom be the blessing of God!) in issuing his orders to Balbug (a *Mogol*), addressed him with the title of *Beg;* since which period his descendants have retained that surname, *beg* signifying a lord.

The *Mogols* (Moguls) are of two kinds, depending upon the country which gave them birth; *viz.*

1st. *Eeranee*, or Persian, who are all *Sheeahs;* and

2d. *Tooranee*, or Turkish, who are all *Soonnees*.

This brings me to the consideration of the two great sects, *Sheeah* and *Soonnee*, into which all the four classes of Mohummudans are divided; the latter constituting by far the greater number.

The *Sheeahs* are likewise termed *Tu-Sheeah, Muzhubee, Eeranee* and *Teen-Eearee.*

The *Soonnees* are also called *Soonnut-Jumma-ut, Tussunoon*, and *Char-Eearee.*

Between these two sects exists the most inveterate enmity.

The *Sheeahs*, out of hatred, call the *Soonnees, Kharjee* (*i. e.* schismatics), because, as they opprobriously affirm, they reject his high excellency Ameer-ool-Momeeneen-Allee, the son of Aboo-talib (may God reward him!). So far is this from being the case, that all the *Soonnees* place the utmost faith in his excellency Allee-oon-Moortooza. It is from pure motives of enmity and reproach that they assert such a thing. Moreover they call them *Kafirs* (or infidels).

Independently of the *Tussunoons* being unjustly denominated *Kharjees* (or schismatics), there are some real ones of that description which may be classed under a third head, and unfortunately they are so from their mother's womb; and they utterly abhor his excellency Allee according to this rule, the child at its birth had received the name of Meer Golam Hyder, or Syed Sufdur Allee, it

---

Allee-oon-Moortooza. Therefore, to nickname *Soonnees*, *Kharjees*, clearly evinces a spirit of ill-will, and a wish to slander.

The *Soonnees*, on the other hand, maliciously term the *Sheeahs*, *Rafzees* (*i. e.* heretics, rejectors, or abusers); because they reject the following three companions of the Prophet; *viz.*

1st. His highness Ameer-ool Momeeneen Aboo Bukur Siddeeq, the son of Quhafa (may God reward him!), his highness the prophet's (the blessing and peace of God, &c.) father-in-law, the father of Beebee A-ay-sha (may God reward her!).

2d. His highness Ameer-ool Momeeneen Oomur, son of Khuttab (may God reward them!), also the prophet's (the blessing, &c.) father-in-law, and the father of Beebee Hufusa.

3d. His highness Ameer-ool Momeeneen Oosman, the son of Afan (may God reward them!), his highness the prophet's (the blessing, &c.) son-in-law, and the husband of Beebee Rooqeea. On the demise of Rooqeea, the prophet gave him in marriage a second daughter named Oom-e-Koolsoom; and owing to this circumstance, Mohummud Moostuffa (the blessing, &c.) named Oosman, Zin Noorrain, signifying 'be thou master of two lights (*i. e.* lights of his eyes) *alias* daughters.

The *Sheeahs* consider the three above-mentioned worthies, and many of the other companions of the prophet, as wicked men, and hold them in the utmost contempt; and in speaking of them, make use of such mean expressions as does not become me to mention.

Some of them, in their arithmetical calculations, never utter the number four; and others, instead of using a country cot (or bed) with four legs (called *charpaee*, which means literally four-legged), have one with six, and name it *ch'hay-paee* (or six-legged).

Others again, should they ever have allowed the word four inadvertently to escape their tongue, instantly go and gargle their throats; or in meeting a *Soonnee*, should they have kissed his hands (which they do agreeably to their mode of saluting a friend), they perform *wuzoo* (or ablutions, *vide* chap. xiii. sect. 1.) immediately after.

In some countries they write the names of the three companions on a piece of paper and wear it on the soles of their feet, as the most marked token of disrespect and contempt that they can shew towards them.

Real *Rafzees* and *Kharjees* are guilty of many base acts.

Among various others, it is customary with the former to celebrate in the month *Buqur Eed*, a feast called *Gudeer;* on which occasion they form three hollow images of dough composed of wheaten flour, and fill is not uncommon for them, as they grow up, to drop the surnames Meer and Syed, and merely to call themselves

---

fill their cavities with honey; then, using severe terms of abuse, they thrust a knife, first into the body of the one they have named *Aboo Bukur Siddeeq;* and, in like manner, they stab the second, called *Oomur;* and lastly, poor *Oosman* suffers the same fate; and while the honey flows from the wounded bodies of these dolls, the *Sheeahs* sip a little of it, as emblematic of drinking the blood of their enemies; and eat a small bit of the paste, in allusion to the devouring their flesh in rage.

The fact is, the *Sheeahs* assert that his highness Mohummud Moostuffa (the blessing! &c.) before his death bestowed the *kheelafut* (or sovereignty) on Allee; but that immediately after his demise, the other three companions convened a meeting of the nobles and grandees, and with the aid and assistance of men of talents and worth among the Arabs, assigned the right of succession, first, to Siddeeq-e Akbur; then to Oomur-e Adil; next to Oosman-e-*G*unnee; and lastly, to his highness Allee. Whereas, his highness Allee was the first legal successor to the royal dignity; and it is for this reason that the *Tusheeahs* hold the three usurpers (as they call them) in such abhorrence.

The *Tussunoons*, on the other hand, deem all this to be mere slander and falsehood; for if, say they, his high excellency Allee was really so brave, that God called him his "lion," how came he to lose his courage when he had to encounter opposition, and actually through fear of the above-mentioned people, to stand behind the priest,* and among the congregation, when his actions were said to be governed by the divine will? Moreover, if his highness Mohummud Moostuffa (the peace, &c.) did, during his life, appoint him his successor, why did he not risk his life in the service of his God, and stand up for the defence of his religion, and take by force what was his right? He must have been perfectly well aware of the blessing pronounced upon those who engage in such a warfare; for the text of the sacred *Qoran* saith, "He that dies fighting for his religion, though he be dead, yet "doth he live in the presence of God."

Independently of this, numerous rewards and blessings promised to such, are to be found in the chapters of the *Qoran* relating to martyrs and heroes.

Thus, by their own mouths they would seem to condemn Allee.

May the Lord preserve us from such folks, and may the Almighty protect

---

* Or in other words, to act in the capacity of a clerk.

by the names of Golam Hyder, or Sufdur Allee. It is, therefore, only by enquiring after their tribe, that it can be learned such a one is a *Syed*.

---

protect every Moosulman from such evil and temptation, which it is highly dishonourable to assert of such respectable characters.

To the writer of these pages (this humble teacher of the alphabet), the following seems to be the position of the argument worthy of belief; *viz.* that, since the present period is the termination of the 1248th year of the *Hijree* (or flight) of his holiness Mohummud Moostuffa (the blessing! &c.), and to this day no doctrine has been inculcated at Mecca or Medina, save that of the sacred *Shurra* (or precepts of Mohummud), and no religion professed, except that of the *Soonnut-e-Jummaut*, we may justly infer that there will be no other.

But to return from this digression.

The *Putt'han* caste has descended from the prophet Yaqoob (or Jacob). Its origin is thus recorded in a work entitled *Syer*. It is there said, that the prophet Mohummud Moostuffa (the blessing! &c.) in a particular battle, ordered ten officers of rank to take the field. After all these had been killed, he desired his people to choose a brave and skilful individual from among themselves, as their leader. Accordingly, they selected one from among the family of Khalid-bin-wuleed (a descendant of the prophet's), and prepared themselves for action. That intrepid warrior having gained the victory, returned with his forces to the prophet (the blessing! &c.); and the latter, on seeing him, honoured him with the title of *Futt'han* (*i.e.* a victor or conqueror). In progress of time, the word *Futt'han* became corrupted into *Putt'han*.

Moreover, at a particular battle, the prophet (the blessing, &c.) addressed Khalid the son of Wuleed as *Khan*. Hence, the origin of that surname. *Khan*, as well as *Beg*, are honorary titles, signifying brave or valiant. The *Putt'hans*, thereafter, became of various descriptions, according to their descent; *viz.*

1st. *Yusoof Zuee;* from Yusoof (or Joseph).

2d. *Lodee;* from Lodee (or Lot), and so on; they are exceedingly numerous.

Among all the four classes of Moosulmans, there is to be found a fifth, denominated *Nuwá-ay-tay*, which has had its origin after the days of the prophet (the blessing, &c.); and their history is as follows. In the holy (lit. illuminated) city Medina, the inhabitants of a part of the town having formed the project of conveying the illustrious corpse (*i.e.* of the prophet) to some distant country, to collect there the crowd who go to worship at his shrine, were employed in digging a mine under ground; and the subterranean passage was nearly completed, when

If he be the son of a *Sheikh*, then at the beginning or end of his name is added one of the following surnames,

---

when the servants who had charge of the tomb, were warned by the prophet in a dream, that the people of such a district had excavated a gallery even to the foundation of the walls of the sacred mausoleum, and were further directed to apprehend and banish them out of the city. Early the next day, having caught the villains, they expelled them from the place. On their arrival at the next village, the inhabitants, on hearing of the circumstance, likewise beat them and drove them out. Thus wherever they went, they met with a similar reception. The ignorant part of the inhabitants used to ask of the others who the strangers were, and where they were going: from whom they invariably received the reply, that they were *Nuwá A-ay-t'hay* (or new comers), and that they were flogged and sent out. Thus, wherever they went, they got the name of *Nuwá A-ay-t'hay*, which term was afterwards corrupted into *Nu-wá-ay-tay*.

Tippoo Sooltan, however, on one occasion, when several of his noblemen of this tribe were present, affirmed that this class was a most abominable one; since they were the descendants of a woman to whom *Now A-ay-thay* (or nine came), and consequently on the birth of her child, each would have it named after himself, as being the father: but the court decreed, that since nine had her, the infant should receive the name of *Now A-ay-thay* (or nine came); which term has been changed into *Nuwá-ay-tay*.

He observed moreover, that the word *nashood* ناشد or "should not be," should not exist under his government; meaning the four tribes of which this word comprises the initial letters (though he afterwards eulogized that race, observing, they were in fact notwithstanding, a clever, sensible, and intelligent class of people, expert in all sorts of business), *viz.*:—

ن or *N.* for *Nu-wa-ay-tay.*

ا or *A.* for *Afghan* (or *Putt'han*).

ش or *Sh.* for *Sheeah* (or *Rafzees*).

د or *D.* for *Daeeraywalay* (or *Gyr Muhdee*), who are all *Putt'hans*, but constitute merely one-tenth of that tribe, and are only to be met with in Hind'h (Hindoostan), there being no *Gyr Muhdees* in Cabul, Candahar, Persia, or Arabia. Their origin (according to Ferishta) is dated from Anno Hijræ 900. They differ a little in their forms of worship from the others: such as in the mode of burying their dead, in not raising up their hands in prayer (*numaz*), nor in making use of supplications (*doa*).

Some

viz. *Khoaja*, *Golam*, *Mohummud*, *Deen*, *Bukhs*, *Allee*, *Sheikh*, *Abd*, or *Allah* (pronounced *Oollah*), *e. g. Khoaja, Yusoof*, *Golam Nubee*, *Mohummud Hosein*, *Shums-ood-Deen*, *Hussun Bukhs*, *Ruzza Allee*, *Sheikh Mohummud*, *Abd-ool-Qadir*, *Fusseeh-Oollah*. These names, however, do not invariably indicate the individual to be a *Sheikh*, since the generality of *Syeds* call themselves by these, leaving out their own surnames *Meer* and *Syed; e. g.* if you ask a *Syed* what his name is, he replies, *Golam Nubee*, or *Mohummud Allee*, whereby one is left in the dark as to whether the person is a *Syed* or *Sheikh*. Such being the case, it is solely by enquiring after their tribe, as we have said before, that one can ascertain whether he be a *Syed* or *Sheikh*.

If he be the son of a *Mogol*, his name commences or terminates with the words *Mirza*, *Beg*, *Aqa*, or *Aga*; for instance, Mirza Ahmud, Ismaeel Beg, Aqa or Aga Jaffur. As *Syeds* and *Sheikhs* are in Persia frequently addressed

---

Some among this sub-sect say, that there was an individual of the *Qoreish* tribe, whose name was Naet, نايط and consequently his descendants inherited that appellation; whom his majesty Haroon-oor-Rusheed banished from his dominions.

A second report current among them is that it is a title, and means "chosen;" and consequently, in their correspondence they invariably write the Arabic word *Naet* نايط (and not *Nuwaet* نوايت), which has that signification. Whereas other Moosulmans say, it means "driven away."

However, they are *Sheikhs*, and in every respect adhere to the precepts of the prophet; and in learning, in all arts and sciences, and in commercial pursuits, very much superior to the other classes of Moosulmans. Hence the latter esteem them as much as Hindoos do Brahmins. They are no soldiers.

Independently of this class, there is among the *Soonnees* another, called *Gyr Muhdee*. Between the *Soonnees* and them exists the most inveterate enmity, as will be particularly described when we treat of the *Rumzan* fast.

by the names Aga, Aqa, and Mogol (words signifying lord or master), it is requisite to ask, in order to ascertain to what tribe a person belongs.

It appears that the word *Mirza* was originally *Meerza*, (i. e. born of a *Meer*), the name having been adopted from the circumstance of the mother being a *Syed* (the males of which class obtain the name of *Meer*), and the father a *Mogol;* but that in the course of time it has been contracted into Mirza.

If the son of a *Putt'han*, the word *Khan* invariably occurs at the end of his name; thus Buhadoor Khan, Mudar Khan, Hosein Khan.

We, however, frequently find *Sheikhs* and *Syeds* with the word *Khan* attached to their names; thus Golam Ahmud Khan, Meer Allee Nuqee Khan, Buhadoor Beg Khan; but in these cases it is bestowed upon them by their masters as an honorary title.

To the above rule the following are exceptions; viz.

Should the father be a *Sheikh* and the mother a *Syed*, the word *Shurreef* is usually added to the beginning or end of the child's name, e. g. Jaffur Shurreef or Shurreef Jaffur. This appellation it is customary, with some people, to add to the names of all the members of the family; as Jaffur Shurreef, the son of Allee Shurreef, the son of Shurreef Hummeed, the son of Moostuffa Shurreef.

In most places, however, when the mother is a *Syedanee* and the father a *Sheikh*, they leave out the word *Shurreef*, name themselves Sheikh Nasir, or Sheik Mohummud, and call themselves of the *Sheikh* caste. In other countries, again, they add the word *Khoaja* to such a one's name, as Khoaja Buha-ood Deen, Khoaja Nusur Oollah.

When the father is a *Mogol* and the mother a *Syedanee*, their offspring get the name of *Khoaja-zaday* (i. e. of the

Khoaja tribe). In general, *Syeds* are also called *Khoaja*, as are also *Peers* and *Moorshuds*; the term *Khoaja* signifying gentleman. *Syeds* are thus called solely out of respect, as they are in like manner termed *Meerza* (an abbreviation of Meer-zada, meaning the descendant of a Meer or chief).

Others again, of all the four castes, are sometimes in the habit of subjoining the words *Sahib*, *Meean*, or *Jan* to the names; as for example Daood Sahib, Lalla Meean, Ammoo Jan. This, however, is not an established practice in any tribe, but parents are accustomed to call their children by these familiar names out of love and affection for them, so that as they grow up to manhood the names take such deep root, that the real ones are not unfrequently altogether forgotten.

The following are the surnames given to females, added to the beginning or end of their names:

Among the *Syed* women *Begum*, *Beebee* or *Bee*, *Nissa*, and *Shah*, e. g. Rooqeea Begum, Zynub Beebee, or Beebee Zynub, Sukeena Bee, Khyrool Nissa Begum, Fazilla Shah. To the names of *Sheikh* girls they only add the words *Ma*, *Bee*, or *Beebee*, viz. Shureefa Ma, Humeeda Bee, Jumeela Beebee; except in the cases of children of noblemen, to whose names, as a mark of dignity, they add the word *Begum*, such as Koolsoom Begum. This is also the case with Mogols and Putt'hans.

Among the females of the Mogol tribe, the word *Khanum* is commonly added to the end of their names, such as Izzut Khanum.

Among the *Putt'han* women, to the end of their names is added *Khatoon*, *Khatoo*, or *Bano*; such as, Fateema Khatoon, Ruhmut Khatoo, Larlee Bano. Among the last-mentioned class the following is an exception, *viz.* that all illegitimate daughters invariably get the word *Baee* subjoined to their names, as Jumeela Baee, Humeeda Baee. It is customary with nobles and grandees to bring up other people's daughters, have them taught dancing and singing, and such are called *gaeenen* (or singers), to the end of each of whose names they add the word *Baee*, such as Rutun Baee, Zaybun Baee; and when they make a favourite of one, they, from affection, honour her with the title of *Khanum*, and if they are devotedly attached to her, dignify her further with the appellation of *Begum*. Their slaves in like manner they call first *Booboo*, and when they cohabit with such a one, honour her with the titles *Baee*, *Khanum*, or *Begum*.

There are two kinds of Moosulman dancing girls, *Ramjunnee* and another;* the former have the words *Baee* and *Koon-ur* subjoined to their names, such as Ram Baee, Chunda Baee, Khoosh-hal Koo*n*-ur, Raj-Koo*n*-ur. The latter have the word *Bukhs* added to their names, *e. g.* Fyz Bukhs, Rahut Bukhs, &c.

There are five different modes of naming children:

1st. The infant obtains the name of some one of the family, as that of the parent's father,† grandfather, great-grandfather, or of the tutelary saint venerated in the family.

2d. At an auspicious hour,‡ (eight or ten) learned men, assembled for the purpose, fix upon the first letter of the first line of any page of the sacred *Qoran*, opened at random, as the one with which to begin the name; *e. g.* should it be an *alif* (or *a*) the first letter of the alphabet, a name applicable to the station in life of the individual is, after

* The term, at present, not in the author's recollection.

† It is not customary among Moosulmans to give their own names to their children.

‡ To ascertain which, consult the horoscope, p. 20 and 22.

due consultation, selected from among the various ones that commence with *a*; as Ahmud (most praised), Asud (a lion), Amjud (most great), Arshud (most upright).

3d. A few tickets, on which different names are inscribed, are rolled up, and deposited on a plate, or put into a cup, which is covered with a handkerchief, and turned up and down, or shaken about in the hands, and scattered on the floor. Any little child present is then desired to take out or pick up one of them, and the name which the drawn ticket contains is the one adopted.

4th. Among some people it is customary to choose a name from among those that begin with the same letter which is found at the commencement or termination of the name of the planet in whose hour the child is born.* For example, if born on Sunday morning, between six and seven o'clock, on reference to the table, we discover that it is the planet *Shums* (the sun) who rules at that hour; consequently, the first letter being *sheen* (or *sh*), he obtains a name that begins with *sh*, such as Shums-ood-Deen, Shurreef-allee, Shuja-ut-Beg, Shah-baz-Khan: the last letter of

---

* In order to ascertain this, it is requisite to consult a horoscope of nativity, of which the following is a description:

The planets, seven in number, *viz.* The Sun, Venus, Mercury, the Moon, Saturn, Jupiter, and Mars, are supposed to preside over the twenty-four hours of the day and night; thus,—

From 6 to 7 A.M. on Sunday, is considered the hour of the Sun.

7	,,	8	....	Venus.
8	,,	9	....	Mercury.
9	,,	10	....	the Moon.
10	,,	11	....	Saturn.
11	,,	12	....	Jupiter.

And so on; but as it would be tedious to enumerate them all in this way, we shall arrange them in the form of a table, by reference to which the stars that reign during the several hours of each of the days of the week may be readily ascertained.

The

shums being an *s*, with it begins Sirraj Soob-han Bukhs Soolaymân Beg. Suleem Khan. In short, in this way,

---

The form of the geneathliacal scheme is as follows:—

Day of Saturday or Night of Wednesday.	Day of Friday or Night of Tuesday.	Day of Thursday or Night of Monday.	Day of Wednesday or Night of Sunday.	Day of Tuesday or Night of Saturday.	Day of Monday or Night of Friday.	Day of Sunday or Night of Thursday.
Saturn. *a. m. a. m.* 6 to 7	Venus. *a.m. a.m.* 6 — 7	Jupiter. *a.m. a.m.* 6 — 7	Mercury. *a.m. a.m.* 6 — 7	Mars. *a.m. a.m.* 6 — 7	Moon. *a.m. a.m.* 6 — 7	Sun. *a.m. a.m.* 6 — 7
Jupiter. 7 — 8	Mercury. 7 — 8	Mars. 7 — 8	Moon. 7 — 8	Sun. 7 — 8	Saturn. 7 — 8	Venus. 7 — 8
Mars. 8 — 9	Moon. 8 — 9	Sun. 8 — 9	Saturn. 8 — 9	Venus. 8 — 9	Jupiter. 8 — 9	Mercury. 8 — 9
Sun. 9 — 10	Saturn. 9 — 10	Venus. 9 — 10	Jupiter. 9 — 10	Mercury. 9 — 10	Mars. 9 — 10	Moon. 9 — 10
Venus. 10 — 11	Jupiter. 10 — 11	Mercury. 10 — 11	Mars. 10 — 11	Moon. 10 — 11	Sun. 10 — 11	Saturn. 10 — 11
Mercury. 11 — 12	Mars. 11 — 12	Moon. 11 — 12	Sun. 11 — 12	Saturn. 11 — 12	Venus. 11 — 12	Jupiter. 11 — 12
Moon. 12 — 1	Sun. 12 — 1	Saturn. 12 — 1	Venus. 12 — 1	Jupiter. 12 — 1	Mercury. 12 — 1	Mars. 12 — 1
Saturn. 1 — 2	Venus. 1 — 2	Jupiter. 1 — 2	Mercury. 1 — 2	Mars. 1 — 2	Moon. 1 — 2	Sun. 1 — 2
Jupiter. 2 — 3	Mercury. 2 — 3	Mars. 2 — 3	Moon. 2 — 3	Sun. 2 — 3	Saturn. 2 — 3	Venus. 2 — 3
Mars. 3 — 4	Moon. 3 — 4	Sun. 3 — 4	Saturn. 3 — 4	Venus. 3 — 4	Jupiter. 3 — 4	Mercury. 3 — 4
Sun. 4 — 5	Saturn. 4 — 5	Venus. 4 — 5	Jupiter. 4 — 5	Mercury. 4 — 5	Mars. 4 — 5	Moon. 4 — 5
Venus. *p.m. p.m.* 5 — 6	Jupiter. *p.m. p.m.* 5 — 6	Mercury. *p.m. p.m.* 5 — 6	Mars. *p.m. p.m.* 5 — 6	Moon. *p.m. p.m.* 5 — 6	Sun. *p.m. p.m.* 5 — 6	Saturn. *p.m. p.m.* 5 — 6

The use of the above table is threefold;
1st. It is used in the giving of names, as just described.

2dly.

according to the initials or terminals of the planets, the names are kept.

2dly. It is had recourse to in ascertaining what day or hour is propitious, or otherwise, for the performance of any particular business: such as, for example, during the hour that Saturn governs, no good work is on any consideration to be undertaken; *viz.*

Saturn ...	unpropitious, being the celestial	Eunuch.
Sun......	indifferent	Cook.
Venus ...	propitious	Prostitute.
Mercury..	propitious	Moonshee (or Teacher).
Moon	indifferent	Messenger.
Mars	unpropitious	Executioner.
Jupiter ..	propitious	Judge.

3dly. Having ascertained from this table under the reign of what particular planet a person is born, they cast his nativity, and thereby predict his future destiny. For instance, should an individual be born on Sunday at half past twelve or a quarter to one A.M. (which according to the Mohummudans would be Sunday night, they calculating their days from six P.M. to six P.M. and nominally from sun-set to sun-set), the planet who is sovereign at that hour being Venus, her influences will be exerted on him, and he will be "fond of music and singing, of dress and perfumes," &c. For further particulars on the disposition of the planets read what follows:

The seven planets are supposed by astrologers to exert many favourable and unfavourable influences on the human race; but as they are too numerous to be all inserted, I have selected here a few as specimens of them.

1. The Dispositions of the *Sun*. He that is born during the reign of the Sun, whether male or female, will have the following good and evil qualities inherent in him. He will be wealthy, sensible, passionate, easily irritated, generous; he will acquire much property; his word will be much respected; partial to black and red clothes; amorous; addicted to drinking; a scoffer; little formed for pious works; annually indisposed; his birth will be auspicious to his parents, but he will outlive them both (*i. e.* live to a great age).

2. The Dispositions of *Venus*. Fond of music and singing, and still more of dress and scents; partial to sweet and savoury dishes; amorous; beautiful; accomplished; amiable; delighting in always making himself appear neat and spruce; constantly contriving to enrich himself at the expense of others; not disposed to disclose his own secrets; never without perfumes; voice harmonious; a great songster; a pleasant speaker; of agreeable conversation; eloquent; numbers of men and

The fifth mode is to give the child one of the names contained in the following list, *viz.*

---

and women will be charmed and enraptured with his delightful converse; he will maintain not only his parents, but also his brothers and sisters.

3. The Dispositions of *Mercury*. A man of wisdom and learning; a transcriber; versed in several of the sciences; an ingenious painter; endowed with an admirable memory; nay, a Hafiz, or one who knows the whole *Qoran* by heart; a poet; wealthy; a perfect master of arts; many will derive advantage by cultivating his society and friendship; he will never be solitary, but invariably surrounded by people who will ever be subservient to his will; an arithmetician; of uncommon penetration; affectionate. If favourably disposed towards a person, he will exert his utmost to exalt him to the highest honours; if, on the contrary, he be displeased with any one, he will avoid the very sight of him.

4. The Dispositions of the *Moon*. A gambler; goodlooking; a drunkard; a great traveller; addicted to falsehood; a gabbler; a man of reputation in the assemblies of the great; subject every half year to diseases arising from debility and cold; having a natural dread of water; his life in danger in travelling; a blessing to his parents and friends.

5. The Dispositions of *Saturn*. Of a swarthy or dark complexion; long-lived; thin habit of body; black eyes; a flatterer; of a bilious temperament; a loud voice; courageous; a brave warrior; goodlooking; of a hasty disposition; perverse; tyrannical; fond of chastising; unkind; liberal; capricious; will detest flattery; mind pure; without malice; very forgetful.

6. The Dispositions of *Jupiter*. His daily food ever abundant; he will be goodlooking; a Hafiz; a man of science; a judge; learned; a governor; a monarch; a Nuwwab; by some means or other he will distinguish himself in science and politics; he will have many enemies, but always overcome them; none of them will ever be able to hurt him; he will be of mild address; of a sweet voice; in handicraft, drawing, and writing an elegant hand, will stand unrivalled; he will be sensible; a counsellor; charitable; firm in mind; of a delicate constitution; high-spirited; extremely persevering in all undertakings.

7. The Dispositions of *Mars*. Tyrannical; of ruddy complexion; a quick talker; kind; one easily irritated and vexed; fond of white apparel and perfumes; acquainted with several of the arts and sciences; earnestly desirous of acquiring general knowledge; much inclined to deprive his neighbour of his money, and hoard it up for himself; most ambitious.

If on the day or night of *Sunday* a boy be born, he is named Ibrâheem, Soolayman, Dâood, Moosa, I-yoob, Hashim, or Imran; if a girl, she is named Huleema, Hubeeba, Zynub, or Khodayja.

If on *Monday*, a boy is named Mohummud, Ahmud, Muhmood, Qasim, Qadir; a girl, Fátema, Ameena, Humeeda, Rafea, Rooqea, Zureena, Rábea.

If on *Tuesday*, a boy is named Ismaeel, Is-haq, Aba Bukur, Eeleeas, Yâsin; a girl, Huneefa, A-ay-sha, Koolsoom, Shureefa, Sukeena.

If on *Wednesday*, a boy is named Oosmân, Allee, Haroon, Hussun, Hosein, Oomur, Salayh; a girl, Rabea, Azeeza, Jumeela, Fazila, Nujum, Khoorsheid, Sitara.

If on *Thursday*, a boy is named Yusoof, Hummeed, Moostuffa, Moortooza, Sujjad, Baqur, Askurree, Ruzza, Jaffur, Mohummud Gowz; a girl, Maree-yum, Asea, Hajira, Zuleekha, Suffoora, Khyrun, Wajida, Wasila, Gufoor, Maroof.

If on *Friday*, a boy is named Salayh, Eesa, Anwur, Noor, Hydur, Akurum, Adum, Sooltan, Hubbeeb-oollah, Hufeez-oollah, Kureem-oollah, Ruhmut-oollah, Aleem-oollah, Qoodrut-oollah, Abd-oollah, Zeea-oollah; a girl, Mayher, Mah, Zohura, Mahboobah, Ameera, Ruttun, Bano, Khatoon, Nissa, Huwa, Arefa, Mama.

If on *Saturday*, a boy is named Abd-ool-qádir, Abd-ool-kureem, Abd-oor-ruzaq, Abd-ool-wuhab, Abd-oos-Suttar, Abd-oos Shookoor, Abd-ool Lutteef, Shums-ood-Deen, Nizzam-ood Deen, Sirraj-ood Deen, Mookurum, Siddeeq; a girl, Nazook, Mamoola, Luteefa, Bilqees.

CHAPTER II.

Concerning the rites of *Puttee* and *Ch'huttee*.

*Puttee** is a custom observed on the third day† after the woman's confinement; when the females assemble, dress the mother and infant in red clothes, tie a red handkerchief on the head of the former, and, holding a red cloth as a canopy over their heads, apply *kajul*‡ or *kalik*§ to their eyelids. After that, they fill first the mother's lap and then those of the other women with *sontana*|| and *pan-sooparee*|| (betel). The guests after this, having applied a little *huldee* (or turmeric) to the mother's face, and having deposited their *rukhtunee* (i. e. some money, which becomes the midwife's perquisite), take their departure.

From the birth of the child to the *ch'huttee*, they celebrate the days with as much festivities and rejoicings as their means will admit of.

---

* Literally signifies the division of a woman's hair, which is combed towards the two sides and parted by a line in the middle. Why the term is applied to this ceremony I have not been able to learn.

† According to Mrs. Meer, "on the fourth day after the birth of a "son, the friends of both families are invited to share in the general "joy, testified by a noisy assembly of singing-women, people chattering, smell of savoury dishes, and constant bustle; which to any other "females in the world would be considered annoyances, but in their "estimation are agreeable additions to the happiness of the mother, "who is in most cases screened only by a curtain from the multitude "of noisy visitors assembled to rejoice on the important event."—Vol. ii. p. 5.

‡ *Kajul*, or lampblack; procured by holding any metallic substance (generally a knife) over the flame of a lamp.

§ *Kalik*, the soot which collects under the bottom of earthen pots, or any vessel that has stood on the fire.

|| Vide Glossary.

Ch'huttee should be observed on the sixth, but takes place more generally on the seventh or ninth day of the accouchement.* When frequent deaths occur among the children in a family, in order to change the luck, they perform *ch'huttee* on the third, instead of the sixth day; but the proper *ch'huttee*-day is the sixth, whence the origin of the term, meaning the sixth.

Early on the morning of the day fixed upon for the observance of the ceremony, the midwife washes and besmears the floor of the house with yellow or red earth, or cow-dung, and then goes home.

At eight or nine (lit. eight or ten) o'clock of that day, the *women* (men having no part in this ceremony) despatch the following articles to each of their female friends and relations, on a large platter carried on the head of the midwife, and each individual's portion parcelled out, *viz.*

Sik-kay-kaee (mimosa abstergens, Roxb.), or *reetha* (sapindus emarginatus, Vahl.), with which they wash and clean the head.

---

* By Mrs. M. H. Ali's account, this custom would appear in Upper Hindoostan to be observed on the last-mentioned day. She observes: "on the ninth day the infant is bathed—I cannot call any of its previous ablutions a bath,—then its little head is well oiled, and the fillet thrown aside, which is deemed necessary from the first to the ninth day. The infant from its birth is laid in soft beaten cotton, with but little clothing until it has been well bathed; then a thin muslin loose shirt, edged and bordered with silver ribands, and a small skull-cap to correspond, comprises their dress. Blankets, robes, and sleeping dress are things unknown in the nursery of a *zunana*.

"The infant's first nourishment is of a medicinal kind, composed of *amultas* (cassia fistula, Lin.) a vegetable aperient, with sugar and distilled water of anniseed; this is called *gootlee*, and the baby has no other food for the first three days, after which it receives the nurse's aid. After the third day a small proportion of opium is administered, which practice is continued daily until the child is three or four years old."—Vol. ii. p. 6.

Gingilie oil (ol. sesam. oriental. Lin.), to rub over the body previous to the application of the *chicksa* (vide Glossary).

Chiksa powder, mixed with water, to apply to the body, and therewith perfume it, after the oil has nearly evaporated.

Lamp-black, on a bit of stick, to apply to the eye-lids.

Pan-sooparee, or betel (vide Glossary).

Pun-jay-ree, or caudle given to puerperal women (Glos).

After the child has been washed, a *koorta*, made of any old article of dress that had been worn by some great personage who had lived to a considerable age, is the first dress put on the child (hitherto having worn only a pinafore tied round the neck, and covering the chest and abdomen), in order that he may also attain to as great an age. Should the midwife be an old woman, she makes up a *koorta* of some of her old clothes, and brings and puts it on the child. Then all the female relatives in the house and neighbourhood bathe themselves, and wear the fine clean dresses brought by the washerman for the mother and friends; for it is the usual practice for him to lend for that day to poor people, on such an occasion, clothes which belong to his employers, for which he is suitably rewarded. Such suits of clothes are termed *purrud* (or borrowed).

This being done, they place the lying-in woman on an Indian cot, and bathe her with a decoction of aromatic herbs, *viz.* of a handful of *neem* (or margosa leaves*), and *shumbalee* (or leaves of the chaste tree†). At this time it is usual to give a present to the midwife of some ready money. On this day, the *kuleejee*, as it is called, of a

* Melia azadirachta. Lin.

† Vitex negundo. Lin.

sheep (*viz.* the heart, liver, lungs, spleen, and kidneys), are invariably dressed and served up with *k'hichree.* A portion is likewise transmitted to all absent relatives, and the night is spent in singing, music, and all kinds of merry-making. These ceremonies are observed not only on the *ch'huttee*-day of the first-born, but also on that of every child.

In the evening, a plate of *k'hichree* or *polaoo*, with two or three kinds of curries and other things, according as they can afford them, are kept over-night. This is in order that, when the child grows up, he may not eye and covet every article of food he sees. Should his parents not keep these things, and he afterwards turn out a *gourmand*, people are apt to say that it is very probable his *b'handa* (as this dish is called) was not sufficiently filled with many choice viands; and in the centre of this dish, a lamp, made of flour paste, having four wicks, is occasionally placed and lighted. The friends of the puerperal woman, on seeing this bright luminary, drop into it something in the shape of money, according to each one's means, and it is kept burning all night; but next morning the midwife carries it off.

The dish of food is termed *ch'huttee ka b'handa*, as also *rut-jugga*, and by the vulgar *ch'huttee-mah* (or sixth-day mother), because they suppose that *Ch'huttee* (whom they consider an angel that writes people's fates) comes and writes the child's destiny upon it.

The ceremony of *ch'huttee* is commonly kept by the lower orders of society; while the higher classes usually substitute the rite *Uqeeqa* (vide next chapter) in its stead.

CHAPTER III.

Concerning, 1st. *Chilla,* or the fortieth day.—2d. *Uqeeqa,* or sacrifice.—3d. *Moondun,* or shaving.—4th. Placing the child in the *Guhwara,* or swinging cradle.

SECT. 1. *Chilla, or the fortieth-day.*

CHILLA is a rite observed by both rich and poor on the fortieth day after parturition, and is esteemed by them an important festival; for, agreeably to the *Shurra* (or precepts of Mohummud), until that day the mother is not allowed to pray or fast, touch the sacred *Qoran,* or enter the *Musjid.* It was the custom originally to refrain from these as long as the woman had any issue upon her; but the foolish as well as the wise among the female sex have equally fixed upon the fortieth day as the boundary of self-denial.

On this day, as well as on that of *ch'huttee* (and also by the generality of people on the twelfth, twentieth, and thirtieth, called the monthly *chilla,* when they also cook *kheer, k'hichree, bhajee,* according to their means), the female relatives and neighbours assemble, and have the lying-in-woman and infant bathed and dressed out in fine clothes. *Kheer* and *k'hichree* having been cooked, and *fateeha* offered in the name of his holiness Mohummud Moostuffa (the blessing! &c.), are, in the forenoon, eaten and distributed, and sent to the males and females.

The female acquaintances are invited for the evening; and when the period of assembling approaches, *dooloos* are despatched for them.

The guests, on coming to the feast, necessarily bring

some *nayoota* (or present) always along with them, every one according to his ability; such as a red cloth *koorta*, or a *topee* (cap) edged with lace, or of brocade; a gold or silver *huns-lee* or *kurray*, for the baby,* and for the mother a *saree*, *peshwaz*, *orhnee*, *cholee*, and a set of *bungrees*, *pan-sooparee*, flowers, sweetmeats, and *sundul*; moreover, some also bring for the father a *sayla*, *pugree*, or some other dress. These are either brought with them on some kind of tray, such as a *tubuq*, *khoan*, *kishtee*, *soop*, or in baskets, (just as they can afford it), or sent for afterwards.

If any of the women are so poor as not to be able to afford any thing valuable, they content themselves, on beholding the infant's countenance, with putting a rupee or two into its hands.

On this occasion, it is customary for the child's maternal grandmother, maternal grandfather, maternal aunt, and other relatives on the mother's side, to bring with them for the child a present (according to their means), of a gold, silver, or wooden cradle; some ready money, a pair of *kurray*, *torray*, a gold or silver *hunslee*, with *k'hichree*, sugar and other eatables, jewels, clothes, &c.: and this is called *k'hichree kee russum* (or the *k'hichree* ceremony.)

The whole of that day is spent in amusements of various descriptions; such as music, vocal and instrumental, &c.

In most cities, on the *ch'huttee* and *chilla* days, they engage *hijray* (eunuchs); or these come of their own accord, to dance, sing, and play. It is customary for

* Also "*taweezes* of gold and silver; these are tablets on which "engraved verses from the *Qoran* are inscribed in Arabic charac- "ters; they are strung on cords of gold thread, and suspended, when "the child is old enough to bear their weight, over one shoulder, "crossing the back and chest, and reaching below the hip on the "opposite side."—*Mrs. Meer H. Ali*, vol. ii. p. 9.

eunuchs to go and search about the lanes, calling out, "where is a son born?" and when a boy is born any where, they dance at the house of the parents, and exact money from them, according to their means. If a girl be born, they do not get much—in fact, most people give nothing, nor are they themselves at all importunate in their demands. On the birth of a son, should they not be sent for, they contrive to find him out, go to his house and dance. Should they be suitably rewarded agreeably to the rank of the individual, well and good; if not, they raise a clamour and noise, and load him with curses. In short, they do not leave the house until they obtain something.

Their mode of dancing is as follows: A good looking person among them is selected to dance, and the rest play on the *dholuk* and *munjeeray* and sing. Towards the conclusion of the dance, the dancer makes an artificial increase in the size of his abdomen, by inserting a cloth pad under his dress to represent a woman with child. After a little while, the dancer, as if in actual labour, screams and roars out lustily, and ultimately drops the pad as if bringing forth the infant. Then the pretended mother rocks it in a cradle, or dandles it in her arms. After dancing and singing awhile, they take some *betel* and unboiled rice, and depart.

In the evening about six or seven o'clock, the male relatives and friends are likewise invited to a separate entertainment; when, after they have offered *fateeha* over *polaoo* in the name of all the prophets, or of his holiness Mohummud Moostuffa (the blessing! &c.), it is served up to them.

It is customary among some, on the *ch'huttee* or *chilla* night, to take the mother out into the open air with the infant in her arms, and make her count a few stars. After this they shoot a couple of arrows into the air.

Sect. 2. *Uqeeqa, or Sacrifice.*

Among some people, either on the *ch'huttee* or *chilla*, or any other convenient day, the rite *uqeeqa** is performed. It consists in a sacrifice to God, in the name of the child, of two he-goats, if the new-born be a boy; and of one, if a girl. The he-goat requires to be above a year old, and *suheeh-ool-aza* (or perfect and without blemish); he must not be blind of one or both eyes, or lame, and is to be skinned so nicely that no flesh adhere to his skin, and his flesh so cut up that not a bone be broken. It being difficult to separate the flesh from the smaller bones, they are boiled and dressed with the flesh remaining; while in eating, the people are enjoined to masticate and swallow the softer bones, and the meat is carefully taken off the larger ones without injuring the bone The meat is well boiled, in order that it may be more easily separated from the bones. This is served up with *manda*, *chupatee*, or *rotee*.† While they are offering it, an Arabic sentence is repeated; the signification of which runs thus: "O Almighty God! I offer in the stead of my "own offspring, life for life, blood for blood, head for head, "bone for bone, hair for hair, and skin for skin. In the "name of God do I sacrifice this he-goat." It is meritorious to distribute the food to all classes of people, save to the seven following individuals, *viz.* the person on whose account the offering is made, his parents, and his paternal and maternal grandfathers and grandmothers; to whom it is *unlawful* to partake of it.

---

* *Uqeeqa* properly implies, both the ceremonies of the sacrifice and the shaving of the child's head; but to this latter operation, the people of this country have given the name of *Moondun*. The former is a rite directed to be observed in the *Huddees*.

† Different kinds of bread.

The bones, boiled or unboiled, skin, feet, and head, are buried in the earth, and no one is allowed to eat them.

SECT. 3. *Moondun, or Shaving.*

Among the respectable and wealthy, *Uqeeqa* is first performed; and *Moondun* on any day afterwards. Though most people have the child's head shaved on the *uqeeqa* day, the lower classes of people only observe the latter ceremony; and those who are very poor, moreover, to save expense do it on the same day with one of the preceding, *viz. ch'huttee* or *chilla*, while the rich perform them all on different days.

On this occasion, the child's head is shaved, and the ceremony is denominated *Moondun;* from *moondna,* to shave. Those who can afford it have it performed with a silver-mounted razor, and use a silver cup to contain the water; both of which, after the operation, are given in a present to the barber, together with one and a quarter *seer* of rice, some *pan-sooparee*, a couple of wreaths of flowers, a nosegay, and some cash.

After the head is shaved, among the nobility a solution of saffron, and among the poor *sundul* embrocation is applied on it. The hair is then weighed, and its weight in silver being distributed among the religious mendicants, it is tied up in a piece of cloth, and either buried in the earth or thrown into the water.

Those who can afford it have the hair taken to the water-side, and there, after they have assembled musicians and the women, and offered *fateeha* in the name of Khoaja Khizur* over the hair, on which they put flour, sugar, *ghee*, and milk, the whole is placed on a raft or *juhaz*, (a

---

* Khoaja Khizur.—*Vide* chap. xxvii.

ship, ch. xiv. sect. 3.) illuminated by lamps, the musicians singing and playing the whole time, they launch it on the water.

Some people at the time of *moondun* leave *choontees* (or tufts of hair unshaved) in the name of particular saints (*vide* chap. xxxii.), and take great care that nothing unclean contaminates them. A few, vowing in the name of any saint, do not perform *moondun* at all, but allow the hair to *grow* for one or even four or five years; and, either at the expiration of the appointed season, or a little before or after, proceed to the *durgah* (or shrine) of that saint, and there have the hair shaved. Should it happen that they are in a distant country at the time, and have not the means of repairing to his shrine, they perform *fateeha* in his name, and have the hair shaved at the place where they may happen to be. Such hair is termed *jumal choontee*, or *jumal bal*. This ceremony is, by some men and women, performed with great faith in its efficacy.

SECT. 4. *Placing the infant in the Guhwara or Cradle.*

On the fortieth day, or usually on some previous day, the infant is placed in a *guhwara* (*i.e.* a swinging-cradle).

At the time of the ceremony of putting it in the swing (observed in the evening), the females having assembled, apply *sundul* to the four legs of the cradle, and ornament them with red thread. Then having placed four cocoanuts on the four corners within the cradle, and put some boiled *chunna** (or Bengal horse-gram), together with *maleeda* and *pan-sooparee* on a platter, placed on the floor near the swing, or held in the hand, they lay the child down in the cradle, and sing some customary song for lulling babies asleep; after which, for the sake of amusement, they scramble for the eatables.

---

* Cicer arienatum. Lin.

They sit up the whole night amusing themselves with singing, music, &c. Sometimes they perform the parts themselves, and play on the *d'hol* and *munjeera;* at other times employ hired *domneea*n (professed female musicians) to play and sing to them. These ceremonies belong peculiarly to the female department.

CHAPTER IV.

Concerning, 1st. The child's *Luddoo bandhna*, or making *Luddoo*, (alias folding hands).—2d. *Chuttana*, or causing the infant to lick, *i. e.* weaning.—3d. *Dant neekulna*, or teething.—4th. *Moott'hee bandhna*, or crawling on all fours.—5th. *Kan ch'hay da-na*, or boring the ears.

SECT. 1.—*Luddoo bandhna*.

When the child is about four months old, in playing with his hands he frequently clasps them together; this action is construed into the child's forming *luddoos;* consequently *luddoos* (a kind of round sweetmeat) are immediately ordered for the occasion; and after they have invited the nearer relatives, and offered *fateeha* on them in the name of the Prophet (the blessing, &c.), they are distributed to them, and after this they make merry.

SECT. 2.—*Chuttana*.

On the child's attaining the age of seven months, the nearer relatives, male and female, are invited to a feast; on which occasion they cook *polaoo* and *feernee* or *kheer*, and having offered *fateeha* in the blessed name of his holiness Mohummud the Chosen, (on whom, &c.), they take a little of the *feernee* with the fore-finger, and apply it to the child's tongue (hence its name *chuttana*, i. e. causing to lick). This is repeated twice; and may with greater propriety be termed weaning,* since previous to the performance of this ceremony the child tasted nothing but its mother's milk; but from this day he is allowed other kinds of food.†

On this occasion, as on all similar ones when females are entertained, the *d'hol* and *munjeeray* are necessarily present; and they amuse themselves in singing and playing on them.

SECT. 3.—*Dant neekulna.*

Frequently termed *dant ghoongnee;* because on the first tooth making its appearance, they prepare *ghoongneea*n of wheat or *chunna* (Bengal horse-gram), that is, boil them whole with sugar; and having offered *fateeha*, distribute them among the relations, friends, and neighbours. Those who can afford it have an entertainment in the evening.

SECT. 4.—*Moott'hee bandhna.*

Moott'hee bandhna (or closing the fists), and *rengna* (or crawling), are names given to the ceremony, when the child shuts his fists and begins to crawl on all fours. On this occasion they prepare *moormoora* (parched rice), mixed up with syrup of *goor*, and made in the form of *luddoos* (or balls), dispense them among the invited relations and friends, and spend the night in amusing themselves with singing and music.

SECT. 5.—*Kan ch'haydana.*

When a girl attains to the age of one or two years, the lobes of her ears are bored. Having put into the lap of the operatrix two *khopras* (or dried half-kernels of the cocoa-nut)

---

* The child does not discontinue sucking, frequently, till he is three or four years old.

† The first food they give consists of milk mixed with *ghee* (or clarified butter).

and *pan-sooparee*, and applied *sundul* to her neck, they employ her to make the holes. By degrees other holes are bored along the whole edge of the ear, and even in the centre part of it, till, when the child has reached the age of two or three years, she has thirteen holes in the right ear and twelve in the left. Some have only a hole bored in each lobe of the ear, a second in the middle projecting part over the orifice of the ear, a third above, and a few others here and there. In the Deccan it is considered vulgar by most people to bore holes uniformly all round the edges of the ears, as that practice is mostly adopted by low-caste people, such as *kunjurs* and butchers.

CHAPTER V.

Concerning *Dawut*, or invitation; comprising, 1st. The sending of *Eelachee* (or cardamoms with verbal invitations).—2d. The bringing or taking of *Nay-oo-ta*, alias *Munja* (presents carried in state), by the guests.

SECT. 1.—*Invitations.*

The custom of sending *eelachee* (or cardamoms) is a form of invitation in common use among the female sex. Men generally invite their friends by letter.

When any affair of importance is about to take place in a person's house, such as a nuptial ceremony or an entertainment, and it is requisite to invite ladies on those joyful occasions, this is done by the transmission of cardamoms to each person, as follows:

Any woman in the habit of going about the street, lane, or bazar,* is employed for this purpose; and being superbly

* Meaning, one not immured.

decked out, is despatched on her errand, attended by musicians playing, and carrying in her hand a brass plate containing *sundul, pan-sooparee ka beereean,* (betel-leaf parcels), together with sugar-candy and cardamoms enveloped in red paper, separately arranged in each one's name.

The woman sent with the cardamoms approaches the lady with the utmost respect, and having made her obeisance,* delivers her message in these terms: "Such or such "a lady (naming the person) sends her best compliments "and embraces to you; and says, that as to-morrow there "is a little gaiety about to take place in my house, and I "wish all my female friends by their presence to grace "and ornament with their feet the house of this poor individual, and thereby make it a garden of roses, you "must also *positively come,*† and by remaining a couple "of hours, honour my humble dwelling with your company."

Should she accept of the invitation, the cardamon-bearer applies a little of the *sundul* to her neck, stomach, and back, and puts her share of sugar-candy and cardamoms into her mouth, or they are handed to her along with the betel-leaf parcel.

Should the lady not be willing to go, *sundul* is only applied, and a *pan ka beera* (without any of the cardamom and sugar-candy) handed to her.

Having, after this fashion, been at all the houses and returned the message (with compliments), of their intention of coming, next day a *doolee,* accompanied by a maid-servant, is despatched for them. But if the hostess be poor,

* For the different forms of salutation, depending upon the rank of the individuals, *vide* Glossary.

† A common mode of saying, do *not decline* doing so.

she sends her own women to escort them to the house a little before daybreak.*

On their arrival, the lady of the house advances to the gate to meet them, and embracing and welcoming them with smiles, takes them by the hand into the house, and seats them on the carpet.

On many minor occasions women are similarly invited by the sending of such a messenger; but she is unattended by music, and does not carry any cardamoms, *sundul*, &c.

SECT. 2.—*Presents made.*

The guests, in going to the house, must bring with them some *nay-oo-ta* alias *munja* (i. e. presents), and in so doing, they are guided by the consideration of the nature of the feast, as well as by a regard to their own means.

The presents usually brought on the celebration of the ceremonies of *Ch'huttee* and *Chilla* have already been mentioned; *viz.* a *hunslee*, *kurray*, *koorta*, *topee*, *saree*, *cholee*, *pan-sooparee*, *p'hool* and *sundul*.

On the occasion of the child's being taught *bismilla*, the presents consist of a small gold or silver plate of the weight of eight *annas* or one *tola*,† suspended by a red thread, together with a piece of velvet sufficient to make a *cholee*, *pan-sooparee*, flowers, *sundul*, and sweetmeats.

If the present be intended for a wedding-gift, it consists of a shawl, a piece of muslin, a *saree*, *pugree*, or *cholee*, with *pan-sooparee*, flowers, and *sundul*, or some delicious viand or *muleeda*, (a kind of cake), or sweetmeats, or merely betel, plantains, and cocoa-nuts. These are either brought along with them, or, as among the great, are after

* Literally, when two *ghurrees* of the night are still wanting.

† A *tola* (or rupee) weighs exactly three drams.

their arrival carried thither by the men in great pomp and state.

It is expected that those in low circumstances should make a present of at least a velvet *cholee*,* with some sweetmeats, *pan-sooparee*, flowers, and *sundul*, according to their means.

Should they not have brought any *munja*, they are required to put a rupee or two, or half a rupee, into the hands of either the child or the mistress of the ceremony.

CHAPTER VI.

Concerning the custom of forming the *Sal giruh* alias *Burrus ganth*, or annual knot, *i. e.* the Observance of the Birth-day Anniversary.

This custom is observed on the anniversary of the child's birth-day: it is commemorated with great rejoicings. Having cooked *polaoo*, and invited all the relatives and friends for the evening, they are entertained sumptuously. Along with the *polaoo* are deposited sometimes *k'hullee* and sugar, and over them *fateeha* is offered, either in the name of his holiness the Prophet, or *Nooh* (Noah, the peace of God be upon them!) This being ended, some old dame secretly or openly ties a knot on the red thread brought for the occasion. This is observed annually by way of record of the age of the individual. The women amuse themselves all night with singing, playing, eating, and drinking.†

This is a custom very common among the nobility; less so among the lower classes of people.

---

* Value about a rupee, or two shillings.

† Though in public they, as well as the men, drink only such beverages as water, *shurbut*, milk, &c., it is not uncommon for them in private

Some are in the habit of giving first the entertainment; and after dinner is ended, the *fateeha* on the *k'hullee* and sugar, or sugar alone, with the above-mentioned red-thread, in the name of his holiness Noah (peace be unto him!)

The reason why *fateeha* is offered in the name of Noah (peace be unto him!) is, that since he lived to an incalculable age (some say five hundred, others a thousand years), it is to be hoped that by imploring his blessing the child's age will likewise prove long.*

CHAPTER VII.

Concerning the custom of teaching the Child *Bismilla*, (or pronouncing the name of God,) and the mode of doing it.

The ceremony of *bismilla* is observed when the boy or girl has attained the age of four years four months and four days.†

Two or three days previous to it, the child is decked out from head to foot in *yellow clothes*, has some *chiksa* applied by *sohagin* women, and is seated in a separate room appropriated for the purpose; has a cloth ceiling erected over his

---

private to take strong drink, although it be prohibited in the *Qoran;* excusing themselves by saying that there is no harm in the use of the juice of a fruit, (meaning the grape).

* The girl's years are numbered by a silver loop or ring being added " yearly to the *gurdonee*, or silver neck-ring. These are the only " methods of registering the ages of Mussulmaun children.

" The *sal-giruh* is a day of annual rejoicing through the whole " house, of which the boy is a member; music, fireworks, toys, and " whatever amusement suits his age and taste are liberally granted to " fill up the measure of his happiness."—*Mrs. M. H. Ali*, vol. II. p. 10.

† If a daughter, the *pulgoond'hun*, (or plaiting of the little girl's side locks,) is likewise first performed with the *bismilla*.

head, and coloured cloth curtains suspended from it all round, to represent a throne. Every morning and evening while they are rubbing the *chiksa* over his body, musicians continue singing and playing, and the child is not allowed to go about. This is denominated *munja bythna* (i.e. sitting in state).

The day before that of the ceremony, the females are, as above related, invited by the sending of *eelachee* (or cardamons), and the male relatives and friends by letter, in the following form:

" To (such a one) the obliger of friends, greeting,

" At this poor individual's dwelling, his son (or daughter, " as the case may be), is this evening to be taught *bismilla-* " *khwanee* (or to repeat the name of God), I beg you will, " by becoming one of the party, kindly grace and orna- " ment the assembly with your presence, and joyfully " partake of something; for by so doing, you will afford " me peculiar pleasure.

" The letter of (so and so) a *Moonshee* or *Mowluwee*."

Among the illiterate poor, instead of a note, a verbal message is sent to the above effect, by a person usually employed on such errands.

On the *bismilla* day, the females assemble among themselves, and the men meet together at the appointed hour in the evening.

The child having been bathed in the afternoon, and all the *chiksa* washed well off his body, they exchange his *yellow* garments for *red* or *white* ones of superior quality; such as *tash*,* *badla*,† *mushroo*,‡ or *kumkhwab*,§ (accord-

* *Tash*, or cloth interwoven with gold or silver thread.

† *Badla*, or brocade of silken stuff variegated.

‡ *Mushroo*, or stuffs of silk and cotton.

§ *Kumkhwab*, silk interwoven with gold or silver flowers.

ing to their means); then having suspended on the child's neck the gold or silver plates tied to a red thread, which some may have brought, they apply *sundul* to his neck, *uttur* and other scents to his clothes, throw a garland of flowers round his neck, put *gujray* (or flower-bracelets) on his wrists, and crown the whole with a *sayhra* (or wreath of flowers, or of gold-wire) over his forehead. In short, they adorn him in every way possible.

Thus bedecked, he is seated in the presence of his family-teacher, or in front of some learned and respectable person, as a *mushaekh* (or divine), &c.

Near them are placed a couple of trays, containing *luddoos* (two large ones being pasted over with gold or silver-leaf), together with flowers, a *nosegay*, *sundul*, a small gold or silver plate, a pen and inkstand (the two last also sometimes of gold or silver), betel leaves, and cloth of some kind, for a present to the teacher.

The tutor, after offering *fateeha* over the eatables in the name of his highness Mohummud Moostuffa, (the peace! &c.) writes on the plate with the pen dipped in the *sundul*, or a solution of saffron in water, the words *bismilla hirruhman-nirruheem*,* and makes the child lick it off. He then puts the two ornamented *luddoos* into the hands of his pupil for the purpose of tempting him to go through his task with pleasure. It is also customary to write the *soora-e-alhumd* (or the first chapter of the *Qoran*, which is a very short one), on red paper; and those who can afford it, on a gold or silver plate, and give it into the hands of the boy or girl, and desire him or her to repeat, first the words *bismilla hir-ruhman-nirruheem*,* then the *soora-e-fateeha*, (or the first chapter, called also by this name), afterwards, from the *Iqra*

* In the name of God, the merciful, the compassionate.

or *soora-e-ulluq*, (96th chapter of the *Qoran*), the following verses or sentences,* the literal translation of which is as follows: "Read, in the name of thy God; for He it is who "hath created all mankind out of a lump of coagulated "blood.† And He is likewise that Almighty Being, who "has blessed us with the voice of utterance, and taught us "the use of the pen."

The above being the sentence of the sacred *Qoran*, which was the very first that was revealed to Mohummud-the-chosen, (the blessing! &c.), it is conceived to be one of great excellence, and consequently is taught to children.

The repetition of the verse being concluded, a wreath of flowers is thrown round the neck of the tutor, the bouquet handed to him, *sundul* applied to his neck, and the piece of cloth intended for him, together with the abovementioned plate, pen, and inkstand, are presented to him.

After this, the child rises from his seat and makes his obeisance to his master and the company; the latter offer their congratulations to the parents, and some of the nearer relatives, when the child pays his respects to them, put a rupee or two, or a *gold-mohur* into his hand.

Then the *luddoos* over which *fateeha* was offered, are either by themselves, or afterwards with *polaoo*, various descriptions of *curries*, *kubabs*, &c. placed on the *dusturkhwan* (or cloth spread on the floor), each one's share being accompanied by a nosegay; and the friends set down to the repast. Dinner being ended, betel-leaves, flowers and *uttur*, are offered to the company; and a few minutes after, they retire.

---

* Qoran, chap. xcvi. 1—5, called *Iqra*.

† Alluding to the fœtus in embryo.

Should dancing-girls, *bhand*-bhugteeay,*† or singers, be in waiting, they likewise amuse the company for half an hour or so with their performances.

The females are similarly entertained among themselves, and sit up all night—*domneeans* (or female musicians) singing and playing to them.

Next day, the ladies are dispatched to their houses in *doolees*; and, if the landlord be a man of property, he dismisses them with presents of *cholees* and *bungrees*. If not, on the occasion of any such joyful celebration at any one of their houses, he in return takes suitable presents to them.

After this ceremony, the child is sent to school.

CHAPTER VIII.

Concerning *Khutna* alias *Soontan* (or circumcision).

Circumcision among Moosulmans is directed to be performed between the age of seven and fourteen years; though occasionally, it is done either before or after that period.

Should an adult of a different persuasion be desirous of embracing the Mohummudan religion, but at the same time dread undergoing the operation, it is not essentially neces sary that he should be circumcised. It is the divine command, however, that he should be initiated into the tenets of their faith.

The ceremonies attending this rite are as follows: On the

---

* *Bhand*, a mimic, an actor.

† *Bhugteeay*, a dancing-boy, dressed up as a dancing-girl.

appointed day *polaoo* or *muleeda* is prepared, and *fateeha* being offered over it in the name of the prophet Mohummud Moostuffa (the peace! &c.), it is distributed among the friends. Should Providence have blessed them with the means, they put on him a new suit of clothes; and for a few days before, some people apply *huldee* and make him *munja bythna* (or sit in state), as described above.

On the day appointed for the ceremony, they deck out the child in fine red or yellow clothes, or brocade, and having decorated him with abundance of flowers (denominated *p'hool peenana*, or the adorning with flowers), and applied *meesee* to his teeth (the only occasion on which males use *meesee*), accompanied with people letting off fire-works, and carrying artificial flowers, trees, &c., (termed *araish*), as well as musicians, they perform *shub-gusht* (or nocturnal-perambulation) and bring him home to be operated upon.

Others again, postponing the preliminary ceremonies of dinner, sitting in state, and perambulating the city, till after the operation is performed and the wound healed (which is generally about a week after), bathe the patient, let him sit in state for a few days, and then have the grand nocturnal-perambulation.*

On this occasion, likewise, the ladies and gentlemen are invited and entertained as before related.

The mode of performing the ceremony of circumcision is as follows.—The boy is seated on a large new earthen pot inverted (or on a chair) with a red handkerchief spread

---

* "At Lucknow," Mrs. Meer observes, "we see, almost daily, "processions on their way to the *Durgah* (before described), where "the father conveys the young Mussulmaun to return thanks and "public acknowledgments at the sainted shrine. The procession is "planned on a grand scale, and all the male friends that can be col- "lected attend in the cavalcade to do honour to so interesting an "occasion." Vol. ii. p. 12.

over it, having swallowed, about a couple of hours before, some *majoon*, or sweetened *bhung*, or *subzee*, which is administered with the double view of intoxicating him, so as to prevent his crying much, and of acting as an anodyne to mitigate his sufferings.

At the time when the operation is to take place, a few friends and relatives are invited, and some of them hold the boy firmly, while the barber, (whose office it is,) with a sharp razor performs the operation. The moment it is over, the child is desired to vociferate aloud, three times, the word "*deen*," (religion); and, by way of coaxing the boy, they direct him to slap the operator for having put him to so much pain. Besides, they get one of the nearest and most respectable relations to chew some betel leaves (which colours the spittle red), and spit on the wound the instant it is made, in order to make the boy believe that the red fluid is spittle, and not blood; and they endeavour to quiet him by assuring him that it is such a one who has merely spit upon him. After that, the boy, through shame, remains quiet; or, if he be mischievous, he loads him with abuse.

After the operation, the barber applies some suitable dressing to the wound, which heals in the course of a week. He then receives his professional fee of a rupee or two. While the ceremony is performing, some rice or ready money, together with a couple of chaplets of flowers, *pan-sooparee* and *sundul*, are placed near them. After all is over, the wreaths of flowers are thrown over the barber's head, some *sundul* is applied to his neck, the rice, the earthen pot, and red handkerchief are given to him in a present. Should, however, the boy have been seated on a chair, the latter is not given away.

When a boy is circumcised, if his parents are poor, they give him nothing to eat save *rotee* or *muleeda*, and sometimes *hurreera;* if rich, he is daily fed on chicken broth and *roteerow-gundar* (or wheaten cakes with plenty of *ghee* in it) until such time as the wound heals, in order to support strength; and nothing besides. No such flatulent diet as *dal,* &c., is allowed; for these retard the cure, by occasioning a superabundant suppuration.

It is customary with some women, (for others have no faith in it,) never to have a child circumcised *alone,* but always along with another to make an even number; consequently, when they have one or three of their own to undergo this rite, they get some poor woman's son to be circumcised with theirs. Should they not succeed in procuring one, they substitute an earthen *budhna* (or a pot having a spout); in the mouth of which, they insert a *pan ka beera* (or betel-parcel), and place it near them: and, after circumcising the boy, they cut off the *pan ka beera* (or betel-parcel); which is to represent a second circumcision. They consider it favourable, if the boy, during the operation, or soon after, void urine; as it prevents the blood from getting in and coagulating in the urethra. They guard the boy against the contact of dogs, cats, and other defilements—such as women who are *unwell;* for it is supposed, that to see them or receive their shadow is unlucky; and they are also afraid, lest the smell of blood should induce these animals to bite off the part. They likewise guard against ants—if poor, by putting ashes all round the child's bed; if rich, by placing the legs of the bed in stone-basins containing water; which prevents ants from approaching the patient: for these insects are generally attracted by the smell of blood. They moreover tie a peacock's feather, a copper *ch'hilla* (or ring) by means of a blue thread, to the neck, wrist, or ankle of the child, and burn *ispund.*

CHAPTER IX.

Concerning the *Huddeea* (or conclusion of the child's reading of the *Qoran*), and the making of presents to the Tutor,—including the subject of *Eedee*.

After the boy or girl has read the sacred *Qoran* completely through, a propitious day is fixed upon (*vide* horoscope, page 19), for the purpose of making presents to the teacher, as well as for the purpose of causing the child to exhibit in public, his proficiency in reading.

The day before, the females are invited by the sending of *eelachee* (cardamoms), and the males by letter or a verbal message.

In the evening, the *Qoran*-reader, decked out in superb apparel, is seated in presence of his master in the male assembly, with the *Qoran* in his hands; near them are deposited for the tutor, a robe of honour, and some money according to the person's means, and betel, flowers, *sundul* and sweetmeats in trays; a small cup with some *ajwaeen* (bishop's-weed seed), and a little salt.

The master then desires the child, after reading the *soora-e-fateeha*, alias *alhumd* (the praise, or first chapter), and a few sentences of the *soora-e-buqr*, alias A. L. M. (second chapter), to read the two chapters of the sacred *Qoran*, named *Ee-a-seen* (chap. 36.), and *Ruhman* (chap. 55.), in which, in elegant and figurative language, the unity of the Deity is beautifully described. Accordingly, the child reads them in the assembly, with a distinct and audible voice.

When concluded, the school-master having offered *fateeha* in the name of his highness Mohummud Moostuffa (the blessing, &c.) over the eatables, desires his pupil to breathe on the bishopsweed-seed and salt; and, after blessing him, says, "I forgive all the trouble I have had in teaching "thee the knowledge of the sacred *Qoran*, and do now, in "the presence of this assembly, with my whole heart and "soul, freely bestow* on thee what I have taught thee."

The discerning scholar then, with the most profound reverence, makes his obeisance to his preceptor, and offers to him the contents of the trays, the dress, money, &c. intended for him, together with some of the bishop's-weed-seed and salt.† To every individual of the assembly, some of the sweetmeat, with a little of the bishopsweed-seed and salt, as sacred‡ relics, are distributed. In some cities it is not customary to bring the *Qoran* along with the boy to the assembly, but they make the boy repeat the *punjaet* (viz. *lillahay mafis summawatay wallurzay*, &c. to the end), and some other chapter. Indeed some people have nothing read; and instead of bishop's-weed-seed and salt, they place *d'han-kay-k'heeleean*, and *butasha* (swollen parched rice and spungy sweetmeat), and each member of the assemblies of males and females give to the boy a rupee or two according to their means, which becomes the tutor's perquisite.

The obligations, however, on the part of the school-boy towards his master, do not terminate with the giving of these presents; but invariably at every feast, marriage, dinner-party, &c. the teacher's dues are to be rendered. In short he should be honoured as one's own father, for people in the world are said to have four fathers, *viz.* 1. Their own father (properly so called;) 2. Their preceptor; 3.

---

* *i. e.* the benefits of the knowledge of it.

† An excellent remedy for gripes.

‡ Rendered so by its having had the contents of the whole *Qoran* blown on it.

Their father-in-law; and 4. Their *moorshud* (spiritual guide).

Besides, the Prophet has assured us, that if any person at his daily devotions repeats the *doa-e-masoora* (or supplication for the remission of sins), for his parents and teachers, the Almighty will undoubtedly hear and answer his prayers.

For such children as go to school, the master usually writes *eedee* (*i.e.* a verse of something relating to the *eed*, or feast), or a blessing on the child, on coloured or *zur-afshanee* (illuminated) paper,* which he desires him to take and read to his parents. On witnessing the progress that their child has made in reading, they send by his hands some rupees, or a few *pice*, by way of a present to the master.

There are four *eeds* (or feasts) in the year, on which occasions, by distributing these *eedees* among the scholars, the masters exact presents from their parents, *viz.* at the feasts *Akhree char shoomba* (ch. xvi.), *Shaaban* (p. xxii.), *Rumzan* (ch. xxiv.), and *Buqur eed* (ch. xxvi.) †

In the sacred *Qoran* there are thirty *joozes* (or sections); on the commencement of the perusal of each of which it is customary to observe *huddeea*. Among these, there are four principal ones; *viz.*, at the conclusion of the reading of a quarter, of a half, of three-quarters, and of the whole of the sacred volume; and of these, again, the last is the most important.

---

* *Zur-afshanee* is paper sprinkled over with gold-dust. Whereas, *mozurriq* is paper on which are pasted devices in gold leaf.

† There are five *eeds*, or feasts, held annually. The two principal ones are the *Rumzan* feast or *eed ool fitr* and the *Buqr-eed;* which are *Furz* and *Soonnut*, (*i.e*, commanded to be observed both by God and the Prophet); the other three are, *Mohurrum*, *Akhree char shoomba* and *Shub-e burat*, which are only *soonnut*, (or commanded, *viz.* by the Prophet).

Independently of these, whenever the scholar commences a new book, it is necessary to entertain the master in a similar manner, and to observe what is called *huddeea*: *viz*. sweetmeat, betel, *sundul*, *choorway* (parched rice), and toasted *chunnay* (Bengal horse-gram), called *poothanee*, with money, such as a rupee or two, according to each one's means, are sent by the parents, and placed before the teacher in the school-room, over which the latter having offered *fateeha* in the name of his holiness Mohummud Moostuffa, (the peace, &c.) and the author of the book, distributes the sweetmeats, *poothanee*, &c. among the school-boys. He applies *sundul* to the necks of all the scholars, and sometimes a little to his own, or he takes a little *sundul* in his hand, and smelling its fragrant odour, repeats the *durood* (blessing), and having heard their lessons, and given them new ones, dismisses them for the other half of the day.

If the number of scholars be great, and too many holidays would be the consequence, the master defers the *fateeha* till Thursday (the established day for the half-holiday), and then having performed it over two or three pupils' *huddeeas*, converts the two or more holidays into one.

In short, they embrace every opportunity to compliment the tutor; for a blessing from his auspicious mouth is equivalent to perusing a hundred books; since, while his curse rests upon any one, the study of a hundred volumes will profit little: nay, he should be esteemed equal to, if not greater than one's own father and mother; inasmuch, as he makes one acquainted with the laws and writings of God and his messenger, and explains the doctrines of religion. While the natural parents nourish the body with temporal food, he provides it with spiritual.

CHAPTER X.

Concerning the period of Virginity, and the Ceremonies observed on the occasion.

When a girl has her menses for the first time, it is called *balig hona* (arriving at the age of puberty or discretion); *pyhlee sir myla hona* (the head becoming dirty for the first time); or *burron men-milna* (reaching the age of womanhood; literally, mixing with the grown-up).

At the lunar periods, the circumstance is denominated *hyz-ana* (the approach of the menses); *nuhanee ana* (the arrival of the season for bathing); *sir myla hona* (head becoming filthy; a handsome excuse for bathing); *bay-numazee ana* (become unfit for prayers); or *napak hona* (becoming unclean).

Among Moosulman girls the period of virginity is from ten to fourteen, generally about twelve years of age.*

At a girl's first menstruation, seven or nine married women of the house and neighbourhood meet in the afternoon, and each applies a little *chiksa* to her body, adorns her neck with a couple of garlands of flowers, anoints her head with *phoolail ka tail* (odoriferous oil), and confines her to a private apartment. The women having spent awhile in singing, music, &c. depart to their own homes.

For seven days the poor girl is shut up in the room, not allowed to go out, engage herself in any employment whatever, or bathe; and, during all that time, her diet consists

* Mrs. Meer (vol. ii. p. 349.) observes, "Girls are considered to "have passed their prime when they number from sixteen to eighteen "years; even the poorest peasant would object to a wife of eighteen."

solely of *k'hichree*, *ghee*, bread, and sugar: all fish, flesh, salt and acid food being prohibited.

On the seventh day she is bathed. The above-mentioned women, having assembled in the morning, hold a red-coloured cloth over her head in the form of a canopy, take a small earthen *budhnee*,* either plain or nicely painted over, and having fastened to its neck a *betel*-leaf parcel by means of a red thread, and dropped into it four or five *hurla*† and *bhurla*,‡ each woman pours warm water with it twice on her head.

Before these women commence the superintendance of the ablutions, their laps are filled with *muleeda*§ and *betel*,§ and *sundul* is applied to their necks.

In the evening an entertainment is given to the relatives of both sexes; when the girl, according to her means, is decked out in new and elegant attire, and adorned with *bungrees*, (glass bracelets,) &c. All that day and night they amuse themselves in eating, drinking, singing, and playing.

If the girl be married, and has not already consummated the rites of wedlock (which is more than probable), the husband leads his wife home to enjoy her; leaving the company to amuse themselves. On the day when a girl has attained the age of virginity, her parents generally make their son-in-law a present of a new suit of clothes, according to their means; and having seated their daughter and son-in-law together in one place, they adorn them with flowers.

But to allow such an indecent occurrence to become

---

* *Budhnee*, a kind of pot with a spout like an ewer.

† *Hurla*, Chebulic myrobolan; Terminalia chebula, Willd.

‡ *Bhurla*, Belleric ditto; Terminalia bilirica, Roxb.

§ These they receive in their clothes, the fore-part of the *saree* which is tucked up on one side.

public is only the custom among the lower classes of people; the higher and more polished ranks of society never expose such an indelicate circumstance when it takes place in the family.

CHAPTER XI.

Concerning the age of Puberty or Maturity in Males; and the observance of the religious duties required of them after reaching manhood.

When a boy, on arriving at his twelfth, thirteenth, or fourteenth (some at the fifteenth, sixteenth, seventeenth, or eighteenth) year, experiences a *pollutio nocturna*, it becomes his indispensable duty thereafter to conform strictly to the fundamental principles of his religion, *viz.* confession of faith, prayer, fasting, alms-giving, and pilgrimage. This is equally applicable to girls.

Previous to this period, *i. e.* during their childhood, all their good and evil deeds were laid to the charge of their parents; but after this, they are themselves responsible for their own actions.

When the youth is overtaken by a *pollutio in somno*, it becomes absolutely necessary for him to bathe on the morning following; for, until he has purified himself by so doing, it is unlawful for him either to eat, pray, touch the *Qoran*, or go to the mosque.

These rules extend likewise to other ablutions, directed to be observed by divine command. Of these there are four, termed *gosool*, or bathing, *viz.* 1st. after *pollutio nocturna*; 2d. after *menses*; 3d. after *coitus*; 4th. after *puerperium*.

The period to which the first and third bathing may be

delayed, is nine or ten o'clock next morning. The second, from the seventh to the tenth day. The last cannot be resorted to, with propriety, until the discharge has ceased; but a parcel of ignorant women have fixed the fortieth day of child-bed for it.

The manner of bathing is as follows: After slightly wetting the body, and reading some short prayers which are appointed for this purpose, he gargles his throat three times, then bathes; thoroughly wetting his whole body, uttering the following sentence in Arabic: "I desire by "this ablution to purify my body for prayer, and to re-"move all my inward filth and corruption."

Some of the uneducated among the vulgar throw first three pots of water on the head, then three on the right shoulder, afterwards three on the left, and having taken a little water in the hand, either after reading *durood* (thanksgiving), or without it, they sprinkle it on the clothes, in order that they also may be purified.

CHAPTER XII.

Concerning the real foundation of Mohummudanism.

Mohummudanism comprises five divine commands, *viz.*

1st. *Kulma purhna* (or confession of faith).—2d. *Numaz kurna* (or prayers).—3d. *Roza rukhna* (or fasting).—4th. *Zukat dayna* (or almsgiving).—5th. *Mukkay ka huj ko jana* (or pilgrimage to Mecca.)

SECTION I. *Kulma purhna* (*or Confession of faith*).

That is "*La-il-la-hah, Il-lul-la-ho Mohummud-oor,* "*Russool Oollahay,*" which signifies, "There is no other

" God except the one true God, and Mohummud is the " prophet (or messenger) sent by God."

SECTION 2. *Numaz kurna (or Prayer).*

There are five seasons for prayer prescribed by the divine law, *viz.*

1. *Fujur kee numaz*, or morning prayer, from five A.M., or dawn of day, to sun-rise. Should this hour unavoidably have passed by without prayer having been offered, the same prayers are to be repeated at any other convenient time; and although the same blessing will not attend a prayer that has been omitted at the appointed period, it is nevertheless to be performed, and not to be altogether omitted.

2. *Zohur kee numaz*, or mid-day prayer, between one and three P.M.

3. *Ussur kee numaz*, or afternoon prayer, from four to half past five P.M., or till sun-set.

4. *Mugrib kee numaz*, or sun-set prayer, at six P.M., *i. e.* immediately after sun-set: not to be delayed beyond that time; for it is a very delicate season.

5. *Aysha kee numaz*, or prayer on retiring to bed, between eight P.M. and midnight. Should a person, however, by business or amusement be unavoidably kept awake beyond the limits of this season, he may perform this devotion any time before daybreak.

Independently of the above prayers denominated *furz* (of divine origin), there is a variety of others termed *soonnut* and *nufil*, in which the more religious and devout are engaged, as for instance,

1. *Numaz-e-ishraq*, or prayer at half-past seven A.M.

2. *Numaz-e-chasht*, or prayer at nine A.M., or if there be

not leisure then, it may be performed at any time before sun-set.

3. *Numaz-e-tuhujjood*, or prayer at midnight, or at any time before daybreak.

4. *Numaz-e-turraweeh*, or prayer offered daily at eight A.M.

SECTION 3. *Roza rukhna, or Fasting during the month Rumzan, (immediately after the Aysha prayers).*

Numerous are the blessings promised to those who fast during the month *Rumzan* (the ninth month).

Among others, the prophet Mohummud-the-chosen (the peace, &c.) has said, that those who fast shall be the only privileged persons who at the last day will have the honour of entering the celestial city by the portal termed *Ryan* (one of the eight gates of Heaven), and no other; and that the effluvia proceeding from the mouth of him that fasteth is more grateful to God than the odour of roses, ambergrise, or musk.

During the fast, eating, drinking, and conjugal embraces are interdicted, as also chewing betel-leaves, smoking, and snuffing. If, however, the observance of any of these rules be inadvertently neglected, the fast still holds good; but if intentionally omitted, the individual so transgressing, must expiate his guilt by the manumission of one *golam* (or male slave) for every day that he broke fast; if he cannot afford that, he must feed sixty beggars; and if that be likewise out of his power, he must, independently of fasting during the month *Rumzan*, fast for sixty days together any time after for every day that he has broken fast, and add one day more for the day itself on which he broke it, and then he will receive the reward of his fast.

Those who observe this fast breakfast between the hours

of two and four A. M. (this meal is denominated *suhurgahee** and *suhur**), and take food again in the evening, immediately before evening prayer.

During the period allowed for the *suhurgahee* they play in the *musjids* on the *nuqara*, and in large cities the *nowbut*, in order that those who fast may, by hearing it, speedily arise and eat. And some *fuqeers*, during that time, by way of craving charity, proceed to the houses of *Moosulmans*, repeat verses containing admonition and advice with a loud voice, that the sound of it may arouse them from sleep. On getting up, they sometimes give the *fuqeers* something to eat, and on the *khootba*-day make them a present, according to their means, of a rupee or two, or some clothes.

On the first day of the tenth month, *Shuwal*, the *Rumzan kee eed* (or *Rumzan* feast, vide Chap. xxiv.) takes place; when it is requisite for every one who fasts, to offer, previous to going to the *eedgah* to prayèrs, *roza ka fittra* (or fast, offering), which consists in distributing among a few *fuqeers* (religious mendicants) two and a half *seers** of wheat, barley, dates, grapes, *jaree*‡ rice, or other grain commonly eaten; for until he has offered the above alms, or dispensed their equivalent in money among the *fuqeers*, the Almighty will keep his fastings suspended between heaven and earth.

Every one that fasts is obliged to bestow the above portion in alms, for himself as well as for every member of his family, if he has any (not even excepting slaves), but not for his wife or grown-up sons; since the former is to give it out of her marriage-portion, and the latter out of their own earnings.

---

* These terms signify dawn of day, or daybreak.

† Two and a-half seers equal to five pounds.

‡ Or great millet (holcus saccharatus, Lin.).

SECT. 4. *Zukat dayna, or alms-giving.*

It is the divine command to give alms annually of five things: *viz.* of money, cattle, grain, fruit, and merchandise; and that, provided they have been in one's posession a whole year, and exceed the annual expenses.

1. Money.—If one is a *sahib-e-nissab*, that is, has eighty rupees in his possession for a year, he must give alms annually at the rate of one rupee in every forty, or 2½ per cent.

2. Cattle.—Should one's property consist of sheep or goats, he is not obliged to give alms until they amount to forty.

From 41 to 120 inclusive, he is to give 1 sheep or goat.

121 — 200 .... 2 do.

Above that, a sheep or goat for every 100.

Alms for camels is as follows:

For every 5 to 25 he is to give 1 sheep or goat.
From 26 — 35 .... 1 yearling female camel.
36 — 45 .... 1 two-year old do.
46 — 60 .... 1 three-year do.
61 — 75 .... 1 four-year do.
76 — 90 .... 2 two-year do.
91 — 120 .... 2 three-year do.

121 and upwards, either a two-year old female camel for every 40, or a three-year old female camel for every 50.

Alms for property in cows or bulls:

If 30 cows, a one-year old calf is to be given.

40 do. a two-year do. do.; and so on, a one-year old for every 10.

Should one, however, possess a thousand cows (as these animals live in this country only to the age of fourteen or fifteen years), as many cows are to be given as will, by their combined ages, make up one hundred years.

Alms for buffaloes, male or female, are the same as that for sheep.

For horses, the rate is similar to that for camels; or instead of it, as it is enacted in the sacred *Huddees*, a *deenar** is to be given for every horse whose value exceeds 100 rupees.

For animals used in riding, and for beasts of burden, no alms are required to be given.

3 and 4. For grain and fruits, watered by rain, a tenth is to be given; if watered by drawing water from a tank or well, a twentieth part.

5. For articles of merchandise, for the capital, as well as the profits, alms are to be annually rendered, at the above rate of one rupee in forty, provided he be a *sahib-e-nissab* (man of property to a certain amount.)

For gold bullion, half a *mishqal*† for every 20 *mishqal*‡ weight: for silver bullion, at the rate of 2½ per cent; provided it exceeds the weight of 50 *tolas*; §—not otherwise.

For whatever is found in mines, if the value of it be upwards of 240 *dirrums*,|| a fifth is to be given; and if that money be laid out in traffic, alms are to be given on the profits.

The following are the classes of people on whom it is lawful to bestow the legal alms, *viz.* 1st. Such pilgrims as have not the means of defraying the expenses of the pilgrimage. 2dly. *Fuqeers* (*i. e.* religious mendicants) and beg-

---

* A Persian coin, in Hindoostan considered equivalent in value to two and a-half *rupees*.

† A *muishqal* is = 67½ grains.

‡ Twenty *do.* = 7½ *tolas* (or rupee weight) = 2 ounces 6 drams and 30 grains.

§ A *tola* = 3 drams or 180 grains.

|| A *dirrum* = 52½ grains, and 240 *dirhum* = 2lbs. 2 ozs. 2 drams.

gars. 3dly. Debtors who have not wherewith to discharge their debts. 4thly. Champions in the cause of God. 5thly. Travellers who are without food. 6thly. Proselytes to Islamism.

It is only the very poorest of these who are entitled to the *zukat*; religious mendicants otherwise, conceiving it unlawful to receive these, never accept of them.

Alms are not to be given to *Syeds** unless they particularly desire them; nor to the opulent, to near relations, or to slaves.

SECT. 5. *Huj ko jana, or going on Pilgrimage.*

It is the divine command for those men and women to undertake the journey once in their lives, who have sufficient to meet the exigencies of the road, and to maintain their families at home during their absence. Should a person be really desirous of going on the pilgrimage, and possess every thing necessary for the journey, but owing to indisposition, or through fear of an enemy, be unable to proceed, if he appoint a deputy, and furnishing him with all the requisites, request him to undertake it for him in his name, and the latter putting on the pilgrim's habit, travel in his behalf, the former will obtain all the blessings attendant on the pilgrimage. Or, if a rich man or a prince, without any excuse, dispatch another person to perform the pilgrimage in his name, he earns the merit of it.

Though the poor are not obliged to perform it, I have frequently observed whole families of them on their pilgri-

---

* Because they are "of the Prophet's blood, and are not to be in-" cluded with the indigent, for whom these donations are generally " set apart. The *Syeds* are likewise restricted from accepting many " other charitable offerings. *Sudqa* (q. v.) for instance."—Mrs. Meer. Vol. i. p. 252.

mage, chiefly from Bengal and Islamabad, (or Chittagong,) where Moosulmans are very numerous. Fortunately for these poor people, the charitably disposed and opulent natives at Tellicherry, Cananore, Bombay, and other sea-port towns have, for the sake of God, ships named *fyz-e-billah* (*i. e.* God's grace, or bounty-ships), on which, after supplying each traveller with food and drink for the voyage, and a couple of pieces of cloth, (each five cubits long,) they have them transported thither, and brought back.

The manner of performing the pilgrimage is as follows: On arriving near Mecca, or while still on board, it is necessary to put on the *ehram* (or pilgrim's habit). On the day on which the pilgrim intends adopting this new dress, he bathes himself, reads two *rukat* prayers,* and puts on the two wrappers-without-seam, which constitute the sacred dress. One is wrapped round the waist; the other thrown loosely over the shoulders and body, the head being kept uncovered. *Khurranwan* (or wooden pattens) may also be worn. These are not to be dispensed with until he has sacrificed the victim at Meena Bazar (p. 67), and shaved and bathed himself. Nor is he in the interim to commit any of the following acts: anoint his head with oil, *ghee*, (or clarified butter,) perfume his clothes, shave any part of his body, pare his nails, put on clothes that are sewed, wear boots,† hunt, quarrel, speak or do evil, for by so doing, he makes himself liable to death; and, as an atonement, must sacrifice a sheep, and distribute it among the poor; but on no account is he to eat any part of that meat himself.

There are five noxious animals, however, which there is

---

* For the meaning of *rukat*, *vide* note, p. 79.

† Because they are sewed.

no harm in killing, *viz.* a kite, a crow, a scorpion, a mouse, and a mad dog.

Should a person, after putting on the pilgrim's habit, indulge himself in sexual intercourse, or even kiss his wife, the whole object of his pilgrimage will be frustrated.

Some put on the sacred habit (by which is properly meant the interdicting themselves all worldly enjoyments) a month or fifteen days before they reach Mecca, while others defer it until the last day or two; each one according to his power of self-denial.

There are five fixed places where, on arriving, if the pilgrims dare to advance a step farther without putting on the sacred habit, they become deserving of death and must sacrifice the above-mentioned victim (p. 61). The places are:

1st. For the inhabitants of Yemen* and Hindoostan, if they journey by land, a village called Yelmullum;† if they travel by water, a sea-port town, Ibraheem Murseeah.‡

2d. For those of Mudeenah (Medina), Zool-khuleefah.§

3d. For those of Sham (Syria), Huj fah. ||

4th. For those of Erraq (Babylonia or Chaldea), Zât-e-Erq.

5th. For those of Nujud (Nedsjed), Qurrun. ¶

On entering Mecca and visiting the Kaabah.

Immediately on their arrival at Mecca, the pilgrims having performed *wuzoo* (or the ablutions), proceed to the

* *Yemen*, or Arabia Felix.

† *Yelmullum*, a small place near Mecca.

‡ *Ibraheem Murseeah*, a small place near Mecca.

§ *Zool khuleefah* (*D'hulholeifa*), the name of a place between five and six miles from Medina.

|| *Hujfah*, a place between Mecca and Medina.

¶ *Qurrun*, the name of a village near Tayet.

musjid ool huram (or the sacred mosque),* kiss the *Hujr-ool-uswud*† (or black stone), and encompass the *Kaabah*‡ seven times; commencing on the right, leaving the *Kaabah* on the left, they perform the circuit thrice with a quick step, and four times at a slow pace. They go then to the *Qudum-e-Ibraheem* § (or Abraham's feet), repeat *doganah* (two *rukat*) prayers, and come and kiss the black stone again. Owing to the innumerable throng, they are sometimes obliged to content themselves with merely touching the stone, and then kissing the hand.

After that, they go out of the temple by the gate leading to Suffa,|| which they ascend; then go up Murwa,||

---

* "Within the confines of the holy house life is held so sacred, that "not the meanest living creature is allowed to be destroyed; and if "even by accident the smallest insect is killed, the person who has "caused the death is obliged to offer in atonement, at the appointed "place for sacrificing to God, sheep or goats, according to his "means."—Mrs. Meer. Vol. i. p. 213.

† *Hujrool uswud*, signifies literally a black stone. It was originally white, but by the constant touching and kissing of it by the numerous pilgrims, its surface is become perfectly black; and hence its name. It is set in silver and fixed in the wall of the *Kaabah*. This stone is said to possess the singular property of floating on water. It is highly venerated; for whoever undertakes the pilgrimage and kisses this stone, obtains forgiveness of all his manifold transgressions:—yea, they fall off him like the withered leaves do off the trees in autumn.

‡ The *Kaabah* is a square stone building situated in the centre of the *Byt-oollah* (or house of God), another name for the sacred temple of Mecca. The rain-water which falls on its terrace runs off through a golden spout on a stone near it, called *Rookn-e-yemenee* (or alabaster stone): it is as white as snow, and stands over the grave of Ismaeel (the peace! &c.).

§ *Qudum-e-Ibraheem.* This is situated near the *Kaabah*, where was Abraham's (the friend of God) station for prayer. It is a stone on which is the impression of Abraham's feet; hence its name. It is held sacred, and pilgrims are directed, on visiting the temple, to pray near it.

|| *Suffa* and *Murwa* are two mountains near Mecca.

running from the summit of the one hill to that of the other* seven times backwards and forwards. On reaching the top of each, they stand for a few minutes with open hands raised up to heaven, and supplicate the Almighty for whatever their hearts desire, for their prayers on this occasion will undoubtedly be heard and answered.

The origin of the custom is as follows. When Bebee Hajrah (Hagar) brought forth Ismael (peace be unto him!) in the wilderness of Mecca, there being neither water nor habitation in the vicinity, she, in the utmost distress, left the babe, ran frantic from hill to hill in search of water, and returned frequently to her offspring, lest he should be devoured by jackals, dogs, or foxes. While the mother was thus employed, the child, through the grace and blessing of divine Providence, happened in the act of crying to strike his heels against the ground, which instantly occasioned a chasm in the sand, whence water gushed out. Hajrah perceiving this, began digging there, and formed the place into a sort of a well,† and purified herself and infant by bathing

* In imitation of Hagar's running for water to give her son.

† This well (called also Hagar's well) is situated near the *Qudum-e-Ibraheem*. It is called in Arabic, *Beer-e-zumzum*; in Persian, *Chah-e-zumzum* (and is so named from the murmuring of its waters); pilgrims esteeming the water of it most holy, on their return from Mecca bring away some of it in leaden *guglets* (or bottles), or in cotton dipped in it. On breaking fast in Lent they commence with first drinking a little of this water‡ (by this time doubtless highly concentrated by absorption) and drink it, that their sins may be forgiven, and apply a little also to the eyes to brighten vision. They also drink it at other times, considering it a meritorious act; and when they cannot procure much of it, they mix a small quantity of it with a large quantity of common water and drink it.

‡ Or they dip the cotton into common water and squeeze out (as it were the very essence of) the holy water.

in it. This spring exists to this day within the walls of Mecca.

There is another reason also assigned for running between Suffa and Murwa: It is said that in former days, a man and a woman were converted into stone for committing fornication within the temple. The *Qoreish* tribe placed one of them on Mount Suffa, the other on Mount Murwa, and used to worship them. The Prophet (on whom, &c.) not approving of the practice, prohibited them; but, finding his injunctions not attended to, he permitted them to visit these hills, in the hope that this example of God's vengeance would deter others from being guilty of a similar crime.

On the eighth day of *Zeehujja*, (called *Turweeah*), the people assemble at Meena, where they read their prayers and spend the night.

On the ninth day of the twelfth month *Zeehujja* (alias *Buqr eed*), before they proceed to Mount Aarfat to read prayers with the *Eemâm*, they read two *rukat* prayers in the name of each of their relations (except their father*) and friends, dead or living, supplicating heaven to vouchsafe a blessing on them.

Then, after the morning prayer, they rush impetuously towards Jubool Aarfat (Mount Aarfat), where, having read two *rukat* prayers with the *Eemâm*, and heard the *khootbah*, they remain on the Mount until sunset; when they run

---

it. It is likewise administered to sick people on the point of death, either by itself or made into lemonade. (Vide ch. xxxviii.)

There are other virtues ascribed to this water. It is said that, if a person experience any difficulty in pronouncing the Arabic tongue, he has only to sip a little of this water, and it will immediately become easy.

* The father is excluded on the ground that no one is certain who his real father is.

quick towards Moozdu-lufah,* where having read evening prayers, they stop all night.

Next morning, (the tenth,) they start for the *Meena Bazar*. On their arrival at *Muzar-ool-hurum*† (or the holy monument), they stop and offer up supplications to God.‡ Before sunrise, they proceed quickly by the way of *Butun-e-Muhasurah* (or the valley of Muhasurah) till they come to three places, marked by three pillars, called *Jumra*. At each of these, they pick up seven small stones or pebbles, and having read some particular prayer over each and blown upon it, they throw it at these marks, and repeat the same ritual with the rest. This ceremony is denominated *rummee ool jummar* (or the throwing of gravel).

The origin of it is this:—As his highness the prophet Abraham (peace be unto him!) was taking his son Ismaeel§ to Mecca, to sacrifice him, Satan (curses be on him!) appeared to Ismaeel in a human form, and addressed him thus: "Boy, thy father is leading thee for the purpose of offering thee a sacrifice to idols; do not consent to go." On Ismaeel's immediately relating the circumstance to his father, he observed: "Oh! my child, that individual is no other than the cursed Devil himself, who comes to tempt and deceive thee; do thou repeat *lakowl*|| and throw seven stones at him, and he will instantly be gone."

---

* Or *Muzdulifah*, a place or oratory between Aarfat and Mina.

† *Muzar-ool-huram*, the name of the mountain in the farthest part of *Muzduleefah*, more properly called *Kuzah*.

‡ Agreeably to the *Qoran*, chap. ii.—(Vid. Sale, ed. 1825, p. 34.)

§ The Mohummudans do not allow it to have been *Is'haq* (Isaac) the son of Sarah, whom Abraham was about to sacrifice; but Ismaeel, the son of *Hajrah* (Hagar).

|| *La howl o la qoow-wut*, &c. "There is no power or strength but in God." The commencement of a Mohummudan invocation, like our *Nisi Dominus frustra*.

After this fashion, Satan appeared to him at three different places, and each time Ismaeel having repeated *lahowl* over seven stones, threw them at him. Ever since, this custom has been established; and even to this day, pilgrims arriving at these places, in like manner repeat *lahowl*, and throw seven stones.

Having thrown pebbles at the three places, they repair to the *Meena bazar* to perform the *qoorbanee* (or sacrifice), which those individuals who are obliged to give *zukât* (or the legal alms) are enjoined to do. They are required to offer a ram or he-goat for each member, old or young, of the family; or for every seven persons, a female camel or cow. The flesh of such victim is divided into three portions: one is for the person's relations; the second distributed among *fuqeers* (devotees and beggars); and the third reserved for his own use.

The above sacrifice derives its origin from the following circumstance. When Abraham (the peace of God be on him!) founded Mecca, the Lord desired him to prepare a feast for him. On Abraham's (the friend of God) requesting to know what he would have on the occasion, the Lord replied, "Offer up thy son Ismaeel." Agreeably to Jehovah's command, he took Ismaeel to the *Kaabah* to sacrifice him, and having laid him down, he made several ineffectual strokes on his throat with the knife, on which Ismaeel observed, "Your eyes being uncovered, it is through pity "and compassion for me you allow the knife to miss: it "would be advisable to blindfold yourself with the end of "your turban, and then operate upon me." Abraham, greatly admiring the fortitude and wisdom of the youth, pronounced a blessing upon him with kindness and affection, and acted agreeably to his advice. Having repeated the words *bismillah allah ho akbur* (in the name of God, who is great!) he drew the knife across his neck. In the meanwhile, however, the archangel Gabriel snatching Ismaeel from underneath the blade, substituted a broad-tailed sheep in his stead. Abraham, on unfolding his eyes, observed to his surprise, the sheep slain, and his son standing behind him. Then he and his son joined in prayer, blessed God for this miraculous escape, and read two *rukat* prayers; which prayers every one going to Mecca is commanded to read; not even excepting Mohummud, and all his followers.

After the sacrifice they get themselves shaved, their nails pared, and burying the hair and nails in the same place, bathe themselves. They then take off the pilgrim's habit, and consider the pilgrimage as finished.

The act of shaving and bathing required to be performed in the *Meena bazar* is attended with much inconvenience, owing to the scarcity of water and barbers. However, many of the rich, who are likewise obliged to observe these customs, out of charity have the poor shaved and bathed at their own expence. Instead of a thorough shaving, one or two gentle strokes made with the razor, or a small quantity of hair clipped with a pair of scissors, answers all the purpose. In bathing also, if only a cup of water be thrown over the head, it is sufficient; or if water cannot be got, *tyammoom** (purification with sand or dust) may be substituted.

On this (the *Meena*) market-day very many hundred thousands *lakhs* of rupees' worth of merchandize are brought and sold there. I have understood from pilgrims that the merchants in the *Meena* market are so completely absorbed in their commercial pursuits, that they have no leisure to attend to their devotional exercises; and that with the view

---

* *Tyammoom.* Vide ch. xiii. sect. 1.

of protecting their goods, they remain in their shops, and wholly omit the pilgrimage.

The day after the *Ayyam-e-nuhur* (or season of sacrifice), the people remain at *Meena*, and therefore it is called the *Ayyam-e-qur* (or day of rest).

Some of them halt there during the eleventh, twelfth, and thirteenth of the month, and these days are denominated *tushreek* (days of communion).

On leaving it they revisit the *Kaabah* to take their final leave of it, throwing on their way thither pebbles at each *jumra* as they pass, and perform the farewell circuit as before described.

After encompassing the *Kaabah*, it is necessary to proceed to the illustrious Medina, and there pay a visit to the blessed tomb of his august highness Mohummud Moostuffa (the peace, &c.). He that performs the encompassing of the *Kaabah* and does not visit Medina, will defeat the object of his pilgrimage.

I hear from my much esteemed friends the *Mowluwees*, *Mushaekhs*, and *Hafizes*, that the pilgrims from Hindoostan go to such extremities in their veneration of this holy tomb of the Prophet, as even on approaching it to perform *sijdah** (or prostration) to it, while a few of them make *tusleem* or *koornish*.† The Arabian *Khadeeman* (servants who have charge of the tomb) become highly enraged at this, and strictly enjoin them not to do so, observing to them, that since the Prophet has not commanded *sijdah* to be offered to him, much less to any other, such homage being the sole prerogative of the Deity, a person doing it not only commits an unlawful act, but becomes highly culpable.

* Vide p. 79.

† Modes of salutation. Vide Glossary.

Some silly people at the time of the *Mohurrum*,* by bending their bodies make *sijdahs* and *tusleems* even to *taboots** and *ullums*,* as also to the tombs of apostles. Such only display their extreme ignorance and folly; for it stands to reason, that when it is improper to pay such homage to the Prophet, it will be equally so to do it to his inferiors. It is the duty, however, of *Mushaekhs* to perform what is called *sijdah-tyh-ut* to the Prophet; of *moorshuds* to their parents; of slaves to their masters; and of subjects to their king. The *sijdah-tyh-ut* consists in stooping forwards (as in *rookoo*)† while in a sitting posture with the knees touching the ground, and with hands resting closely fisted on the ground, and in that position the thumbs extended are to be kissed.

Few of the *Sheeahs* ever perform the pilgrimage, for two reasons: First. Because on Mount Aarfat, after reading the *khootbah* and offering up adorations to God and eulogiums on the Prophet, they praise the three companions; *viz*. 1st. Siddeeq-e-Akbur; 2d. Oomur-e-adil; 3d. Oosman-e-gunnee (may God reward them!), and last of all, Allee-oon-Moortooza (may God, &c.). This circumstance displeases them to such a degree, as to induce them to dispense with the journey altogether: they would have it that Allee should be praised first.

Besides these, there are six other companions, whose names are as follows: Tulhah, Saad, Saeed, Abee Obydah, Zoobayr, and Abdoor-ruhman-bin-aoof.‡ They cannot

---

* Vide *Mohurrum* festival, ch. xv. sect. 3. † Vide Glossary.

‡ These six, with the preceding four, formed the ten companions who followed the Prophet's example, when, at the desire of the angel Gabriel, he turned his face in prayer from the north towards the west (or Mecca), and of whom the Prophet declared, that they had by that act secured heaven to themselves.

bear to utter the names of these last six companions, and should they do so, they would be obliged to offer *f teeha* at their tombs.

Secondly. Because on entering the *Kaabah* each one is interrogated as to what sect he belongs to previous to his admission into the temple, (the *Soonnut jummaut* being the only ones allowed to enter the sanctuary). Some, however, concealing their own sect, and calling themselves *Soonnees*, contrive at times to gain admission; but they never venture near the illuminated Medina, since there, near the tomb of his highness Mohummud Moostuffa (the blessing, &c.) are those of Aba-Bukur-e-Siddeeq and Oomur-e-farooqee (may God reward them !)*

Many live for years in the joyful anticipation of being one day able to perform the circuit of the *Kaabah;* nay, very many never have the idea of it out of their minds.

To this day much has been said on the numerous blessings attending the performance of the pilgrimage. Among others it is stated, that at every step a person takes *Kaabah*-wards, he has a sin blotted out, and that hereafter he will be highly exalted. Should any one happen to depart this life on his way to Mecca, he will obtain the rank of a martyr, (the reward of his pilgrimage being instantly recorded in the divine book of remembrance), and in the day of judgment he will rise with the martyrs.

Indeed there are various ways in which, if people die, they become martyrs; for example,—1. If a man expire in the act of reading the *Qoran;* 2. if in the act of praying; 3. if in the act of fasting; 4. if on the pilgrimage to Mecca;

---

* The tomb of Oosman, as well as that of Beebee Fateemah and Hussun, are at *Buqeea* (the suburbs of Medina). Hosein's tomb is where he was killed in action at *Kurbulla* (or the plain of *Iraq*—ancient Babylonia or Chaldea).

5. if on a Friday (the Mohummudan sabbath); 6. if in the defence of his religion; 7. if through religious meditation; 8. if he be executed for speaking the truth; 9. if he endure death by the hands of a tyrant or oppressor with patience and submission; 10. if killed in defending his own property; 11. if a woman die in labour or child-bed; 12. if murdered by robbers; 13. if devoured by tigers; 14. if killed by the kick of a horse; 15. if struck dead by lightning; 16. if burnt to death; 17. if buried under the ruins of a wall; 18. if drowned; 19. if killed by a fall from a precipice, or down a dry well or pit; 20. if he meet death by apoplexy, or a stroke of the sun.

CHAPTER XIII.

Concerning *Numaz* (or Prayers); embracing, 1st. *Wuzoo* and *Tyammoom* (or Ablutions before Prayer);—2d. *Azan* (or Summons to Prayer).—3d. Forms of Prayer.

SECT 1. *Wuzoo and Tyammoom, or Ablutions before Prayer.*

Previous to engaging in prayer, if any of the before-mentioned four *gosool* (or legal washings, p. 53) are required, it is the divine command that those preliminary purifications should be performed antecedent to prayer. Should they not be found necessary, it is indispensably requisite that before each season of prayer the person perform *wuzoo* (or the washing of the face, hands, and feet, after a certain manner): for thus has God commanded.

The manner of performing *wuzoo* is as follows. First, the teeth are to be thoroughly cleaned with *munjun* (dentifrice), or by means of a *miswak;* then having washed both hands as far up as the wrists three times, and gargled three times, water is to be snuffed up each nostril thrice, and each time, by the introduction of the little finger of the left hand into them, the cavities are to be emptied of their contents. Then, having taken up water with both hands, the face is to be well washed three times, from the upper part of the forehead to the chin, including the beard, and from ear to ear. After that, the arms are to be washed, from the end of the fingers up to the elbows; first the right, then the left. Then a little water is to be poured into the palms of the hands, and caused to flow along the fore-arms three times. It is to be borne in mind that every little operation in *wuzoo* is to be repeated three times, whereas in what is called *musah* only once. The latter is then performed thus: the right hand, slightly wetted in water, is drawn over a quarter, half, or the whole of the head; then, if a man have a long beard and whiskers, he takes a little water separately, wets and combs them with the fingers of his right hand, moving them in the case of the beard with the palm facing forwards, from the inferior and posterior to the superior and anterior part of it; then, putting the tips of the fore-fingers into each ear, twists the fingers round, when the thumbs are behind the ears, rubs them along the back part of the cartilages of the ear from below upwards, bringing them around the top. Then with the back of the fingers of both hands touching the neck, draws them from behind forwards; after that, the inside of the left hand and fingers are drawn along the outside of the right arm from the tips of the fingers to the elbows, and the same operation is gone through on the other arm with the hands reversed. Then the hands are clasped together, the palms necessarily touching each other. These constitute the rite of *musah*.

After that, the feet and ankles are washed, first the right

and then the left; and this concludes *wuzoo*.* Lastly, the water that remains is drunk with the face turned towards the *Qibla*, which is considered a meritorious act. These different ablutions are accompanied with a number of supplications detailed in the sacred *Mishqat*; but, owing to their prolixity, they have been here omitted.

The observance of *wuzoo* is of great efficacy; for the Prophet has declared, that the countenance, hands, and feet of him that purifies himself for prayer by these ablutions, will at the day of judgment be recognised among the crowd by their shining in all the bright effulgence of the full moon.

It is not requisite to perform *wuzoo* each time that one goes to prayer, but merely when his body becomes defiled by the occurrence of any one of the following circumstances; *viz.* obeying a call of nature, expelling wind, having a discharge of matter or blood in any part of the body; vomiting, sleeping, fainting, laughing loudly and immoderately during prayers, or bringing the genital organs of the sexes into contact. Any of these is sufficient to contaminate a person, and *wuzoo* is rendered indispensable; until the performance of which, it is not lawful for him to engage in prayer.

Should any one be unavoidably prevented by indisposition (fearing lest the application of water to his face and hands would, by increasing the malady, incapacitate him for prayers) from attending to the rite *wuzoo* or *gosool*, it is the divine command that he should perform *tyammoom*; also, if water be at a distance, or if in a well and there be no means of getting at it, or if in attempting to procure it

* Though the detail of these ceremonies is tediously long, the performance of them does not occupy above a very few minutes.

one's life is exposed to jeopardy, or if there be but very little water and either himself or a neighbour be dying of thirst, and he, instead of drinking or offering it to the other, perform *wuzoo*, his soul is in danger (*i. e.* of the divine wrath). All the circumstances above stated, which make a repetition of *wuzoo* necessary, are equally applicable to *tyammoom;* and the virtue of the latter ceases at the sight of water.

The mode of performing *tyammoon* is as follows: The individual, at the commencement of the operation, vows by an Arabic sentence, the purport of which is this: "I vow "that by this act of *tyammoom*, which I substitute for "*gosool* (or *wuzoo*, as the case may be), I purify myself "for prayer, by cleansing my body from all filth and cor-"ruption." Having repeated this, he performs the lustrations by clapping his open hands on fine sand or dust, shaking off the sand, drawing his hands over his face, then by a second clapping of his hands on the sand, drawing the left hand over the right up to the elbow, and then in like manner the right over the left.

SECT. 2. *Azân, or Summons to Prayer.*

It is commanded by the Prophet at the five periods of prayer to proclaim the *azân;* the object of which warning is to caution the people of the arrival of the period of prayer, thereby reminding them of the will of God, and exhorting them to flee for salvation. The sound of the *azân* is to be listened to with the utmost reverence; *e. g.* if a person be walking at the time, he should stand still; if reclining, sit up; and to the words of the *Mowazun*, (or crier) as directed in the sacred *Huddees*, he must reply in some appropriate ejaculation, such as *lub-bek duwut ool huq*, (*i. e.* Here I am, awaiting God's invitation).

The origin of *azân* is as follows. On one occasion, as

the Prophet (the blessing,) &c. was sitting in company with his companions, (may God reward them!) he observed to them, that it would be advisable to adopt some sign by which the congregation could be assembled for prayers; and they consulted together on the subject. One moved that it should be done by the beating of a drum, which the Prophet did not approve of, on account of its being too warlike a sound. Another proposed the ringing of a *naqoos** (or bell); that was objected to by the Prophet, because it was a Jewish custom: while some said, "let a "fire be lighted," to which the Prophet remarked, "that "would indicate us to be worshippers of fire." While the Prophet was thus engaged, starting objections to every proposal advanced, as he was about to rise, (for thus it is related in the *Shurra-e-kurkhee*), a youth named Abdoollah, son of Zeid Ansaree, approached the Prophet and thus addressed him: "Oh, thou messenger of God, I dreamed, "and behold I saw in my dream a man dressed in green "apparel ascending a wall, who stood on it, and with his "face towards the *Qibla*, proclaimed aloud, *Allah-ho-akbur*," &c. (as it is in the *azan*, page 77). The Prophet being highly delighted with this, directed Abdoollah, the son of Zeid, to teach it to Billal, who possessed a powerful voice. At the same time Ameer-ool-momeeneen-Oomur (may God reward him!) was present, who got up and said, "O Pro-"phet of God, I likewise saw the very same thing in my "dream, and was about to come and tell your holiness of

* Or rather "a thin oblong piece of wood suspended by two strings, "used by the Eastern Christians to summon the congregation to "divine service."—*Shakespear's Dict.* The Moosulmans of Hindoostan consider *naqoos* to be (and call it so) the *sunk'h* (or *conch-shell*), blown by Hindoos at divine worship, and which they believe the Jews use.

" it, when I found that Abdoollah-ibn-e-Zeid had already " done so."

The manner of proclaiming the *azan* is as follows. At the proper season of prayer, any one of the congregation who comes first to the *Musjid* (or mosque), or a man called a *Mowazun* (or crier), who is entertained for the purpose with a fixed monthly salary, standing on a *chubootra*,* *mayzuna*,† or *mimbur*,‡ with his face towards the *Qibla* (or Mecca), with the points of his forefingers introduced into his ears, and his hands clapped over them, calls out four times successively, *Allah-ho-akbur* (God is great); twice, *Ush-hud-do-un La-il-la-ha Illul-la-ho* (I bear witness there is no other god but God); twice, *Wo-ush-hud-do-un Mohummudoor Russool-oollahe* (and I bear witness, that Mohummud is indeed the Prophet of God). Then turning to the right hand, he repeats twice, *Hy-ul'-us-sulwat* (come enliven your prayers); then to the left, twice, *Hy-ul'-ul-fullah* (come for refuge to the asylum). Then turning towards the *Qibla*, again adds, in the morning prayer only, this sentence, twice, *Us-sul-la-to Kheyr-roon-min-nun-nowm* (prayer is preferable to sleep). Then finishes by repeating twice, *Allah-ho-akbur* (God is great); and lastly, once, *La-illa-ha Illul-la-ho* (there is no God but the true God). Then having read some supplication, he draws his hands over his face and concludes.

There are four descriptions of people for whom it is unlawful to sound the *azan*, viz. an unclean person, a drunkard, a woman, and a madman.

---

* Or an elevated seat, or platform, in front of the mosque, on which the crier stands and summons people to prayer.

† Do. but higher, with steps to mount up.

‡ Or the minarets of a mosque.

SECT. 3. *The Forms of Prayer.*

There are established *rukats** for all the five seasons or periods of prayer, which are these:

The *fujur kee numaz* (or morning prayer) consists of four *rukats* (or forms), *viz.* two *soonnut* and two *furz*.

The *zohur kee numaz* (or meridian prayer) comprises twelve *rukats*, viz. four *soonnut*, four *furz*, two *soonnut*, and two *nufil*.

The *ussur kee numaz* (or afternoon prayer) contains eight *rukats*, viz. four *soonnut gyr mowukkeda*, which are read by few, the generality only reading the four *furz*.

The *mugrib kee numaz* (evening prayer or vespers) embraces seven *rukats*, viz. three *furz*, two *soonnut*, and two *nufil*.

The *aysha kee numaz* (or night prayer) includes no less than seventeen *rukats*, viz. four *soonnut gyr mowukkeda*, omitted by most people, the generality repeating four *furz*, two *soonnut*, two *nufil*, three *wajib-ool-wittur*, and two *tush-fee-ool-wittur*.

The method of performing prayers is as follows. Having spread a *moosulla* or *jae-numaz*, the individual stands on it with his face directed towards the *Qibla*; and having repeated the *istugfar* (deprecation, or asking forgiveness), and repeated two morning *soonnut rukat* prayers, he makes a *neeut* (or vow) in Arabic† to this effect: "I desire to offer "up unto God this morning (or mid-day, &c. as the period of devotion may be), with my face *Qibla*-wards, two (or four, as it may happen) *rukat* prayers." Having repeated the words *Allah-ho-akbur*, with his thumbs touching the lobules of his ears, he places his right hand upon the left below his

* *Rukat;* vide note, p. 79.

† Those unacquainted with Arabic, vow in their mother tongue.

navel. This being done, he is not to look about, but directing his eyes to the spot which he is to touch with his head, in the posture of *sijdah*, he is to stand with the most profound reverence and the utmost self-abasement, as if in the presence of a mighty monarch. After that, he repeats the *suna*, *tuooz*, and *tusmeeah;* then the *soora-e-alhumd* (or the first chapter of the *Qoran*), followed by any other, without repeating *bismilla;* he then comes to the position of *rookoo*, repeats three (four) or five times the following *rookoo-kee-tusbeeh*, viz. "*soobhánu rubbee ool azeem*," (praised be the great God our preserver). Reassuming the erect posture, he repeats "*sum'má alla'ho lay'mun hum'mayda rub'buna lúkulhumd*," (Thou, Almighty God, art the hearer of my praises; Thou art my support). Then he comes to the position of *sijdah* (or prostration), and in that situation repeats three or five times "*soobhánu rub'bee ool alláh*" (O thou holy and blessed preserver); sits up and rests himself for a few seconds, again performs *sijdah*, and repeats its *tusbeeh* as before. This constitutes the first *rukat** prayer.

It is to be remembered that the assumption of every new posture is to commence with the word *allah-ho-akbur*.

From the *sijdah* (or prostrate position) he assumes that of the *qeeam* (or standing attitude); reads the first chapter of the *Qoran* with the *bismilla*, and then another without *bismilla;* makes *rookoo;* stands up again, and makes *sijdah* twice as before; then sitting, repeats the whole of the *attuhyat* (or the concluding part of their prayers), finishing it with its accompanying part, the *durood* (or blessing): then turning his face first to the right and next to the left, he

---

* The combined performance of these different ceremonies and prayers constitutes what is denominated a *rukat*, and not simply "bending the body in prayer," as Shakspear has defined the term in his dictionary.

repeats each time the *sulam* (or salutation thus, *asullâ moon alykoom ruhmut-oollahe* (or the peace and mercy of God be with you all).* Then joining the two hands from the wrists, both hands spread open and held up in a line with the shoulders, he asks *moonajat* (or supplication†), and drawing his hands over his face, concludes. Here ends the second *rukat* prayer.

Should the performance of four *rukats* have been vowed, it is observed with the following trifling deviation. The two first are gone through as just described, with this difference, that only half of the *attuhyat* is read in the second *rukat*, and after pausing awhile, instead of repeating after it the blessing and salutation, the worshipper begins the third *rukat* by rehearsing the first, but beginning with the *tusmeeah* (omitting the *suna* and *tuooz*, &c. which is done in every *rukat* except the first). The third and fourth are repeated like the two first, but the whole *attuhyat* is this time read. The above four *rukats* comprehend what are called *soonnut rukats*.

In the three *furz rukats* the two first are performed as those preceding, except that the chapter after the *alhumd* is omitted, and the whole of the *attuhyat* read in the third *rukat*, and they conclude with the *sulam*.

---

* The Mohummudans do not, after the conclusion of prayers, repeat *Ameen* (Amen), but they invariably do so after reading the first chapter of the *Qoran*: and after *moonajat* (or supplication), the congregation say *Ameen*.

† The manner of supplicating is as follows. Having raised the extended hands meeting at the wrist to a level with the shoulder (or rather the middle of the arm), with eyes half open, the individual is to confess his sins, ask pardon for them, hoping for mercy. He must dread the miseries of hell, and pray for protection from the crafts and subtleties of the devil; and by making use of an appropriate sentence or verse of the *Kulam-oollah* (or word of God), or by some established prayer suitable to his case, or in his own words, in any language he pleases, he is to make known his requests.

In the four *furz rukats* there is this difference, that in the first and second *rukats* after the first chapter of the *Qoran* another is necessarily read, as in the preceding forms; but not so in the third and fourth, where the latter chapter is omitted. And again, previous to the vow at the commencement, the *tukbeer* (which differs very little from the *azan*) is to be repeated, *viz.* four times successively, *Allah ho akbur;* twice, *Ush-hud-do-un La-il-la-ha Il-lul-la-ho;* twice, *Wo-ush-hud-do-un Mohummud-oor Rus-sool-ool-lahay;* twice, *Hy al'us sulwat;* twice, *Hyal-ul-fullah;* twice, *Qud qamut sulwat* (or stand up to prayers); twice, *Allah-ho-akbur;*. and once, *La-il-la-ha Illul-la-ho.* (Vide *Tukbeer, Glossary.*)

In the *ay-sha* (or night) prayer, in the third *rukat* of *wajib ool wittur*, after having read the *alhumd*, and another chapter, on assuming the *rookoo* posture, the person is to call out, touching the lobes of his ears with the points of the thumbs, *allah-ho-akbur:* then placing his hands on his navel, he is to repeat a prayer termed the *doa-e-qoonoot* (or prayer of adoration); then resuming the position of *rookoo*, and proceeding with the *sijdahs, attuhyat,* &c. he is to finish as before.

It is the divine command, that after an individual, male or female, has attained to the age of discretion and reached maturity, he is to observe the five appointed seasons of prayer; and the moment it is prayer-time, to spread the *ja-e-numaz* on a clean spot to the west of him, and engage in devotion. Should a street happen to be before him, or a large concourse of people passing and re-passing present an obstacle, he is to place a *suttra* (or mark of defence), such as a stick two feet long, or a sword, or any thing else stuck into the ground, or placed in front of the carpet. Prayer should, on no account, be neglected. If a sick person cannot stand up to say his prayers, he must do it sitting; if he cannot sit up, he must repeat them lying down; and if so unwell as not to be able to say them aloud, he must pray in his mind. However, it is only the pious and devout that observe these rules. Where do we find every one possessed with the ability to do it!

If a person be pressed for want of time, such as when required to obey the imperious orders of a commander, the prayer may be deferred until a more convenient season; but it is never to be wholly omitted.

A traveller may likewise curtail the four *rukat furz* (but not the four *soonnut*) by reading only two; but a two or three *rukat* prayer is in no wise to be diminished; and he alone is deemed a traveller who has been on his journey three days and three nights.

After the *moonajat* (or supplication), some read the *tusbeeh*, which is *moostuhub* (or desirable); *i. e.* the observance of it is beneficial, though the neglect of it is not a sin.

To read with the use of a *tusbeeh* (or rosary) is meritorious; but it is an innovation, since it was not enjoined by the Prophet (the blessing, &c.) or his companions, but established by certain *Mushaekhs* (or divines).

They use the chaplet in repeating the *kulma* (confession of faith) or *durood* (blessing), one, two, or more hundred times.

CHAPTER XIV.

Concerning Marriage, which comprises eleven Sections.

Section 1. *Concerning the looking out for a suitable Partner; the ascertaining by the Science of Astrology whether the match will prove a propitious one; and the offering of proposals, and arranging matters for the ceremonies.*

1. When a man is desirous of entering upon the happy state of matrimony,* he sends for three or four female go-betweens by (profession called *Mudawutneean*), to whom he declares his intentions, requesting them to endeavour to ascertain whether any one has a daughter marriageable, who is beautiful, eligible, clever, accomplished, rich, and whose manners, pedigree, and religion are good; and in the event of their meeting with such a one, they are speedily to bring him word. He does not despatch them, however, without giving them ample assurances (which, alas! too frequently turn out to be but empty promises) of a very handsome reward awaiting them, in case success should attend their zealous efforts. In a few instances, however, and among honourable men, the engagement is strictly

* "The first marriage is usually solemnized when the youth is "eighteen, and the young lady thirteen or fourteen at the most. "Many are married at an earlier age, when, in the opinion of the "parents, an eligible match is to be secured. And in some cases, "where the parents on both sides have the union of their children at "heart, they contract them at six or seven years old, which marriage "they solemnly bind themselves to fulfil when the children have "reached a proper age. Under these circumstances, the children are "allowed to live in the same house, and often form an attachment for "each other, which renders their union a life of real happiness."—Mrs. M. H. Ali's "Observations on Mussulmans of India," vol. i. p. 346.

adhered to; and either during some part of the nuptial ceremony, or on the completion of the marriage, they offer the reward agreeably to promise.

The female go-betweens* being in the constant habit of going about, selling articles of female dress, ornaments, &c. at the different houses, sitting and gossiping there, become acquainted with every thing relating to their families, connexions, opulence, or poverty; and should circumstances turn out favourably, they settle matters in some degree, and convey the joyful intelligence to the intended bridegroom and his friends. Should they approve of the choice, the match is made up, otherwise the internuncios are desired to look out in some other quarter. Should the girl be at the house of a friend or acquaintance, the parents, or maternal grandmother, &c. go themselves, without requiring the assistance of go-betweens, and concert with the girl's parents respecting the marriage; there being no need of internuncios among friends.

2. When the family connexions, pedigree, religion, and customs of both families are found to correspond, and the two parties consent to the union, *seers* are consulted to ascertain the future destinies, good or bad, that await the new couple; for which purpose a few persons, in company with astrologers and *moollas* (or men of understanding in the times), assemble, cast their horoscope, and prognosticate their future destiny. For example, if a person's name begin with any of the following seven letters of the Arabic alphabet, the element of his temperament will be

1st. Earth: *viz. bay, waoo, yay, swad, tay, zwad, noon.*—2d. Water: if *zal, hy, lam, ain, ray, khay, gaeen.*—3d. Air: if *jeem, zay, kaf, sheen, qaf, say, zoee.*—4th. Fire: if *alif, hay, toee, meem, seen, dal.*

---

* Or "Mrs Gad-abouts," as Mrs. Meer Hassan Ali calls them, are well described by her in vol. i. p. 351.

Other astrologers again refer to a table, of which the following is a sketch, to ascertain by the initial of the individual's name his constitutional elements :

SIGNS OF THE ZODIAC.			The Planets.	Genders.	The twenty-eight Letters of the Arabic Alphabet.	The Four Elements.
In Arabic.	In Hindoostanee.	In Teloogoo.				
Humul, or Ram.	Bukra.	Mayshum.	Mirreekh, or Mars.	Male.	Alif, lam, aeen, yay.	Fire.
Sowr, or Bull.	Gaee.	Wroosh-abhum.	Zohura, or Venus.	Female.	Bay, Waoo.	Earth.
Jowza, or Twins.	Do-Soorut.	Meed-hoo-num.	Oootarid, or Mercury.	Male.	Qaf, Kaf.	Air.
Surtân, or Crab.	Kay*n*-kra.	Kurkat-kum.	Qumur, or the Moon.	Female.	Hy, Hay.	Water.
Assud, or Lion.	Shér.	Seem-whum.	Shums, or the Sun.	Male.	Meem.	Fire.
Soom-boola, or Virgin.	Khoosh-e-Gool.	Kunneea.	Ootarid, or Mercury.	Female.	*G*aeen.	Earth.
Meezan, or Scales.	Turazoo.	Toola.	Zohura, or Venus.	Male.	Ray, Tay, Toee.	Air.
Aq-rub, or Scorpion.	Bich-chhoo.	Writch-cheekum.	Mirreekh, or Mars.	Female.	Zal, zoee, noon, zay, zwad.	Water.
Qows, or Archer.	Kumân.	Dhunu-soo.	Mooshtu-ree, or Jupiter.	Male.	Fay.	Fire.
Juddee, or He-Goat.	Mugur.	Muku-rum.	Zohul, or Saturn.	Female.	Khy, Jeem.	Earth.
Dullow, or Waterpot.	Dól.	Koon-bhum.	Zohul, or Saturn.	Male.	Swad, say, seen, sheen.	Air.
Hoot, or Fish.	Much'h-lee.	Meenum.	Mooshtu-ree, or Jupiter.	Female.	Dâl.	Water.

In order to find out the future fate of the new couple, the following plan is adopted; in the first place it is to be discovered, by reference to the preceding scheme, to which of the elements of fire, air, earth, and water, the initials of the parties belong; and, if their constitutional elements correspond, it is to be concluded that they will harmonize: *e.g.* If the man's name be Jaffur, his initial being a J. and his temperament earth; and the woman's name be Bano Beebee, her initial being B. and the temperament also earth, these agreeing, it is held that they will live most happily together.*

---

* Should the connexion be found desirable, there is sometimes an omen consulted by the father before negociations are commenced. It is related by Mrs. Meer in these words: "Several slips of paper "are cut up; on half the number is written *to be*, on the other half "*not to be*. These papers are mixed together and placed under the "prayer-carpet. When the good Mussulmaun is preparing for his "evening *numaz*, he fails not in his devotions, to ask for help and "guidance in an affair of so much importance to the father as the "happiness and well-being of his son. At the portion of the service "when he bows down his head to God, he beseeches with much "humility, calling on the great power and goodness of God to in-"struct and guide him for the best interest of his child; and then he "repeats a short prayer expressive of his reliance on the wisdom of "God, and his perfect submission to whatever may be His wise "decree in this important business. The prayer concluded, he seats "himself with solemn gravity on the prayer-carpet, again and again "imploring Divine guidance, without which he is sure nothing good "can accrue. He then draws one slip from under his carpet; if *to be* "is produced, he places it by his left side;—a second slip is drawn "out: should that also bear the words *to be*, the business is so far "decided. He then offers thanks and praises to God, congratulates "his wife on the successful issue of the omen, and discusses those "plans which appear most likely to further the prospects of their "dearly loved son. But, should the second and third papers say "*not to be*, he is assured in his heart it was so decided by 'that wisdom "which cannot err;' to whom he gives praise and glory for all "mercies received at His hands; after this no overture or negociation "would be listened to by the pious father, from the same quarter."—Vol. i. p. 352.

Here follows a more particular description of the system:

If the temperament of both be Earth,—they will for the most part agree, though not always.

If it be Water,—they will agree for a time; but their affections will soon decline.

If it be Air,—they will be ready to quarrel with each other; but as ready to make up the matter.

If it be Fire,—though brawlings and bickerings will occur between them, these will not prove of long duration; for a mutual reconciliation will soon take place.

If the temperament of the Man be Earth, and of the Woman, Water,—they will agree remarkably well together, and maintain a reputable character; the woman being subject to her lord and master.

If the man's be Water, and the Woman's Earth,—they will agree as above; but the wife will wear the breeches.

If the man's be Earth, and the Woman's Air,—they will constantly be quarrelling, and as frequently be settling their differences; but the woman will be under subjection to her husband.

If the Man's be Air, and the Woman's Earth,—love as well as discord will exist between them: the wife will rule the husband.

If the Man's be Earth, and the Woman's Fire,—they will cherish but little affection towards each other, and in nothing will they agree, or please one another. The wife will govern the husband.

If the man's be Fire, and the woman's Earth,—the same as the preceding; with this difference, that the husband will rule the wife.

If the man's be Water, and the Woman's Air,—in general they will not be affectionate; however should they be so, their happiness will be very great. The husband will be under petticoat government.

If the Man's be Air, and the Woman's Water,—the same as the preceding; except that the husband will govern the wife.

If the Man's be Water, and the Woman's Fire,—they will find it a very difficult matter to agree together. The husband will rule the wife.

If the Man's be Fire, and the Woman's Water,—the same as the last; but the wife will rule the husband.

If the Man's be Air, and the Woman's Fire,—their affection for each other will increase gradually; the man will submit to his wife's control.

If the man's be Fire, and the Woman's Air,—the utmost degree of love and happiness will reign betwixt them: the woman will submit to her husband, who will treat her with great kindness and affection.

1. When their future destinies have thus been calculated, and they bid fair to agree together, a few of the bridegroom's female relations repair to the bride's house, and among various pleasantries facetiously observe, that they are come from such a one's house to partake of some *meetha polaoo* (or sweet *polaoo*), or *shukur bhat* (sugar and rice). The opposite party good-humouredly return the jokes or not, as they feel favourably or unfavouraby disposed towards the match.

The women do not arrange the business at this first interview, but after the interchange of a few visits matters are adjusted: that is, the day is fixed upon by the bride's relatives for the ceremony of *k'hurray-pan*, *shookrana*, or *mangnee*. These three customs are not all observed together, but any one of them is chosen according to the pleasure of the parties. In some families the one is usually practised; in others, either of the rest. The first is most common, and being least expensive, is preferred by the lower classes of people: the second is general among the middling ranks of society. The last being the most expensive, as the giving of valuable presents is an indispensable accompaniment to it, is only adopted by those who can afford it.

The object of these ceremonies is, that should any necessity exist for postponing the celebration, whether for some days or for years, the parties by this stipulation solemnly bind themselves to marry no other person in the interim, and this engagement is considered inviolable.

It is customary not to offer in either house any thing in the way of food or drink, such as betel-leaves, tobacco, &c. or even water, to persons of the opposite party, until they have tasted something sweet in the house, which they do on the *shookrana* day, or afterwards, at an entertainment given on purpose.

SECT. 2. *Concerning Betrothment, viz.*

1. *K'hurray pan bantna*, or the distributing of betel-leaves standing. 2. *Shookrana* (properly *Shukur-ana*, or the bringing of sugar). 3. *Mangnee*, or asking in marriage. 4. *Pooreean*, or a kind of patties or cakes. 5. *Dhayleez k'hoondlana*, or treading the threshold. 6. *Numuck chushee*, or tasting the salt.

1. *K'hurraypan bantna* is a ceremony as follows. Four or five men and as many women on the bridegroom's side, go with some *pan-sooparee* to the house of the bride, and distribute a *pankabeera* (or *betel*-leaf parcel) to each of her relatives, they all receiving also one in return from them, the females observing the same among themselves. This mutual interchange of *betel*-leaves by the two parties con-

stitutes the sum total of the ceremony. On the occasion of this rite, no *churawa*, that is, jewels and dresses, are necessary. From the circumstance of women always denominating this custom *pan oothana* (or the taking up of *betel*-leaf), and *khurray pan bantna*, men have employed the same terms.

By the way, an extraordinary coincidence just occurs to my recollection; *viz.* If, on any account, a person be required to be sworn in, he is desired to take up a *betel*-leaf parcel, which is considered equivalent to swearing by the *Qoran*. This custom is held most sacred by the vulgar among the Moosulmans, who use it in every case where it is requisite to render a contract binding. For instance, a *pan-ka-beera* is given to the person, and he is desired to say, "From "such or such a thing, I shall on no account ever retract "as long as I live." But this mode of taking an oath is neither prescribed by any divine nor human law; it is an innovation introduced by the *Moosulmans* of Hindoostan. However, they consider it of such importance, that should a person, after so consenting to a marriage, swerve from his word, much brawling and bickering is the consequence. Agreeably to the Mohummudan law, after the performance of any of the three ceremonies above mentioned, should any thing objectionable be discovered in the pedigree or character of either of the couple, the *Qazee* (judge), or any man of repute may pronounce such oath as that of the *betel*-leaf to be null and void: that is, in the event of some gross misconduct being proved against one or other of the parties.

The common people are usually made to swear in this way; and the same form is not unfrequently employed in the field in swearing *seepahees* (Indian soldiers), who after thus taking up the *betel*-leaf, never swerve from the word or action to which they become pledged.

2. *Shookrana* is the name given to the undermentioned ceremony:

From the bridegroom's house are sent to the bride the following articles, *viz.* some jewels; a pair of *ungooshtan* (alias, *huddeearoo*), or rings of gold or silver; a green or red *cholee* of *tafta* (a kind of silk); a set of *chooreean* or green *bungreean*; abundance of *pansooparee*; sugar, *k'hopra*, flowers, odoriferous oils, red thread for the *choontee*, a comb and *sundul*. These are carried on two or three platters, accompanied with *baja bujuntur* (or music), and attended by a retinue of people, including the relations and friends (with the exception of the bridegroom), and conveyed to the bride's. The ladies repair thither in *doolees*, either before or after the procession, and on their arrival withdraw to the female assembly.

To the relative of the bride who first makes his appearance in the male assembly, whether a brother or any other near connexion, they hand the *qowl-beera* (or contract-parcel), which consisting of seven or nine *betel*-leaves, and as many *areca*-nuts tied up in a small red handkerchief, folded in the form of a *betel*-leaf parcel, they make him promise, saying, "Mirza Boolund Bukht, the son of Mirza nujum ood "Deen, is betrothed to Khoorsheid Bee,* the daughter of "Anwur Beg: Declare, in the presence of this assembly, "whether you do or do not consent to their marriage." His answer is, "I do." After having put the question at full length three times, and received the same reply, they offer *neeut kheyr ka fateeha*, that is, they read the *soora-e alhumd* (or first chapter of the *Qoran*) once, and the *Soora e Eezâjâ* (or 110th chapter of the *Qoran*) once.

These ceremonies of the *fateeha* and the giving the *qowl*

---

* *Bee*, an abbreviation for the surname *Beebee*.

beera are performed by a *Qazee, Khuteeb, Naeb-e-qazèe, Mushaekh, Mowluwee, Moonshee, Moolla*, or any learned man; in short, by any intelligent and respectable individual present.

In some countries the ceremony of the *qowl-beera* is dispensed with; the person who offers *fateeha*, naming the couple, says, "I hereby betroth them," and performs the *fateeha*.

On the conclusion of the *fateeha*, having distributed among the men some of the sugar and *pan-sooparee* (which among the great they give in charge to their servants, but the poor themselves tie up in their handerchiefs), the bride's company carries all the articles sent by the bridegroom to his intended. When the flowers, *sundul*, jewels, &c. together with the remainder of the sugar and *pan-sooparee*, have been brought to the female assembly, one of the bride's female relatives brings her to them on her lap, where she sits modestly, with her head bent towards the ground, eyes closed, and face covered. Then the women from the bridegroom's side, having made the bride sit before them, anoint her head with the sweet-scented oil, tie up her hair with the red twist, put on her the *cholee, bungree*, and flowers, apply *sundul* to her neck, and adorn her with the jewels they have brought. Then some old woman on the bride's side, placing one hand at the back of her neck and the other under her chin, holds up her face to the view of the party. Then each of the ladies of the bridegroom's suite, taking a peep at the bride's face, offer her a present of a ring or some ready cash (two or four rupees or a *gold mohur*), and take, the *bullaeean** as they call it, (literally, evils) from her face.

* *Bullaeean lena*, or taking all another's evils on one's-self, is a certain form of blessing. This ceremony is performed by drawing the

Independently of the bridegroom's mother and sister, the father, brothers, near relatives, &c. likewise, on beholding the bride's countenance, make her a present of some jewels or money, and pronounce a blessing on her.

This ceremony of *shookrana* is also called *shukur khoree* (or eating of sugar), *nisbut* or *mangnee* (or the asking) *shurbut khoree* (or the drinking *shurbut*), and *hurree bayl* (or the green creeper); but in some parts of the country they have restricted the term *mangnee* to the same when performed with great splendour and magnificence, and where the giving of valuable *churawa* (presents) to the bride, &c. are necessary accompaniments.

3. *Mangnee* is as follows. Should the bridegroom be present in the town, he goes to the house of the bride on horseback, accompanied with *bâjâ-bujuntur*, *kunchneeân kay nâch*, *tâsâ-murfa*, *thuptee*, *toortooree;* if at night, along with fireworks and flambeaux (if not, without the latter); and with him are carried the following articles and fruits, in large covered trays, *viz*. One or two kinds of jewels, *uttur*, odoriferous oil, a *cholee*, a pair of *bungreean*, a comb, a pair of *ungooshtan*, a red twist, a *damnee* or *eezar* or a *saloo* in trays; and in earthen pots, dried dates, almonds, raisins, poppy-seeds, dried cocoa-nuts, sweetmeats, soft sugar, sugar-candy, *goor* (treacle), sugar-cane, *pan-sooparee*, flowers, &c. according to his means. He is accompanied by his father, brother, and their relatives, friends, and attendants. The procession generally starts in the afternoon, and halting at every ten or twelve paces, discontinue the music and cause the dancing-girls to dance and sing, to whom the

---

the hands over the head of the person blessed, and cracking her fingers on her own temples, in token of taking all the other's misfortunes upon herself: only practised by women.

attendants on this occasion make some present. Passing in this way throughout the *bazar*, they reach the bride's house about eight o'clock in the evening. While they move along, the bands of music continue playing. If poor, they arrive at the bride's before dusk, the women proceeding to the assembly of females either a little before or after the rest. Should the bridegroom not be in town, the articles above-mentioned are despatched without him, with the same pomp and state.

When the men have assembled and sat for a while, the custom of *qowl beera* (if it be the one fixed upon by the party) is then performed; and *neeut kheyr kay fateeha* having been offered over the above-mentioned articles, after a public exhibition of them to the bride's friends, they are sent into her room. The trays being all removed, the relatives as well as the friends present are entertained by the bride's people with a dinner, consisting of sweet *polaoo*, or rice and sugar, as their means will allow. In some parts of India they give them on this occasion *shurbut* to drink; hence the name *shurbut-khoree* (the drinking of *shurbut*) is also given to this ceremony. Some, while drinking it, are in the habit of putting into the salver one or two gold mohurs, rupees, an eight or four anna-piece, according to their means. On dismissing the company, they are offered *uttur*, *pan-sooparee* and flowers, the usual signal to retire. If they be poor, *betel*-leaf alone serves the purpose of giving the hint.

Should the bridegroom himself be at the feast, it is customary for him to receive from the bride's side a pair of shoes, a shawl, or a *doputta*, a red cotton,* or *tafta*-(silk) hankerchief, or rings of gold or silver. Should he be absent,

---

* Yellow, red, and green, are the only colours used on marriage ceremonies; black is emblematic of mourning, white of grave clothes.

these are handed over to his parents, in order that they may be despatched to him wherever he may be.

The women are likewise sumptuously and ceremoniously entertained.*

4. *Pooreean*, *i. e.* ten or fifteen days after *mangnee*, the bride's people prepare various kinds of *pooreean*, and having filled the trays and earthen pots (in which were brought from the bridegroom's house the *mangnee* articles) with them, they despatch them in pomp and state, attended with music, to the bridegroom; whose company again convey part of them, accompanied with music, to their several relatives and friends in the town.

5. *D'hayleez k'hoondlana* (or treading the threshhold), is a ceremony observed as follows. If after *mangnee* it should appear requisite to postpone the marriage for six months or a year, or longer, they perform the ceremony of *dhayleez k'hoondlana*, prepare *meetha polaoo*, *khara polaoo*, a variety of *salnay* (or curries), and having invited the bridegroom, their relations, friends, &c., despatch dancing-girls and music to escort them, to the house.

On this day the bridegroom likewise receives *sulamee;* that is, on his making a *sulam* (salutation) to his *saas* (mother-in-law), she presents him with a handkerchief, a gold ring, and some money on a tray. The reason of this ceremony is this: It is not customary for the bridegroom either to go to the house of the bride, or eat any of her victuals, until the marriage is consummated; but after this

* While our author cursorily passes over all that occurs in the female apartments on this occasion, Mrs. Meer furnishes us with a minute account of what took place when she herself performed the part of "officiating friend;" She decorated the young lady with the sweet-jessamine ornaments and the gold tissue dress, and fed her with seven pieces (the lucky number) of sugar-candy with her own hand, &c.—Vol. 1. p. 362.

ceremony is performed, he may go there and eat of any dish seasoned with salt, at any feast or occasion whatsoever.

5. *Numuck-chushee.* In some places, a day or two after the ceremony of *mangnee* or *nisbut,* the bridegroom's people send in trays *polaoo, birreeanee, zurda, moozafur,* together with *feernee, nan,* &c. more or less, according to their means, as also a *pandan* (the *betel*-box) to the bride's people, who eat and distribute them among their relatives and friends. A day or two afterwards, the bride's people send victuals, in like manner, to the bridegroom's. This ceremony is termed *numuck chushee;* after which, dispensing with the rule of partaking only of sweet things at the bride's house, as heretofore, he may eat of food that is seasoned with salt or acid.

The bridegroom, on repairing to the house of his intended, carries along with him sweetmeats, flowers, and *betel*-leaves on trays, and his relatives also take something nice and acceptable to the bride's people. After *mangnee,* if their means will allow of it, the bridegroom sends to the bride, and *vice versâ,* at every feast *eedee* (or holyday gift). For instance, at the *Mohurrum* festival, *anteean abeer,* a handkerchief, a small purse filled with *betel*-nuts, coffee, *sook'hmook'h, cardamoms,* &c. and some money; at the *Akhree-char-shoomba* feast, *pooreean, goolgoolay,* &c.; at the *Shaban,* various kinds of eatables and fireworks; at the *Rumzan* festival, *sayweean,* sugar, *k'hopra,* dry dates, almonds, *ghee,* &c. and money. At the *Eed-e-qoorbunee,* a sheep, some cash, &c. At the *Rumzan* feast, they are usually conveyed attended with music. Independently of these, the food over which *fateeha* is offered in the name of saints, dressed on the occasion of fulfilling vows, is also sent.

SECT. 3. *Concerning the application of Huldee (or Turmeric) to the Bridegroom and Bride, alias Munja bithana (or sitting in state), and Puttee, Juhaz, and Mudar ka ch'handa.*

A day or two, or even a week, before the application of *huldee* to the bridegroom, they fill the bride's lap with *muelleda* and *pan-sooparee*, and apply *huldee* to her. This preliminary ceremony, which they term *chor** *huldee*, is performed solely by the ladies of the house, and is a mere excuse for having her body perfumed by rubbing it with *chiksa*, which they do morning and evening.

After the bridegroom has had *huldee* applied to him, either on the evening of the same day, or the next, they apply what is called *saoo*† *huldee* to the bride. On that day they entertain their female relatives, friends, and neighbours in the morning with a meal, consisting of *dal* and rice, or *khichree*, and in the evening with a dinner composed of *meetha polaoo* or *khura polaoo*. After that, having put some *mulleeda* and *pan-sooparee* into the laps of the ladies, and seated the bride on a chair with a red cloth canopy held over her, they spread a red handkerchief‡ before her on a red carpet, and singing, at the same time, perform *chowk bhurna* thereon, *i. e.* they place a quantity of unboiled rice on it in the form of a hollow square, forming various devices with the rice within it. They

* *Chor* (lit. a thief) here signifies clandestinely, from the circumstance of its being done quietly, without inviting any one, or having a dinner, &c.

† *Saoo* means revealed, in contradistinction to *chor* (private), because it is done in a public manner.

‡ Dyed red with safflower, not white, because that resembles grave-clothes; not black, because that is a mourning-dress, and bears some analogy to the devil; not green, because that is the dress of *fuqeers* (or devotees).

place a log of *sandal*-wood, wound round with red thread, near the stool for the bride or bridegroom to place their feet on, as it is considered unpropitious to tread on the *chowk* (or square). The bride's younger sister, standing behind her, with a red *daoonee*, takes hold of her ears. They take two *k'hopray*, fill them with dry dates and poppy seed, roll them up in red cloth along with a log of sandal wood. The bundle so formed, which is called *gode* (lap) they place in the bride's lap. Then each of the *sohagin* (or married) ladies, applies a little *huldee* to the bride's face, body, or apparel. While this operation is going on, *baja* and *domneea*n (musical instruments and musicians) continue playing and singing; they likewise do so at the time of applying *huldee* every morning and evening from that day till the day of *joolwa*, both in the house of the bride and of the bridegroom.

From that day, should Providence have blessed them with the means, they invite their relatives daily, morning and evening, to dinner, and entertain them with the performances of dancing-girls, while outside the door, *baja*, *tasa*, or *nowbut* (musical instruments) continue playing.

After having applied the *huldee* to the bride, they make her sit in a separate apartment, and do not allow her to engage, as usual, in any sort of employment whatever; and as food, she is permitted to have nothing save *khichree*, *rotee*, *ood*,* and sugar. The frankincense is administered to impart a sweet smell to the body, and the ladies of the house rub her body with *chiksa* (*vide* Glossary) every morning and evening until the *joolwa* day, repeating the operation without washing off the preceding application,

* *Ood*, or benjamin. In this case, it is prepared by putting a quantity of it between two wheaten cakes, closed all round and fried in *ghee*.

with the view of improving the lustre of her skin, and perfuming her body.

The ceremonies attending the application of *huldee* to the bridegroom are, in every respect, similar to those of the bride, except that the *chiksa* is rubbed over him by the barber, if he be present, every morning and evening.

Besides, it is customary with some to observe *puttee*, *juhaz*, and *mudar ka ch'handa*, either one, two, or all three of them.

With many, it is the custom to float *puttee*; that is, the evening before that of *huldee*, they take a branch of the pomegranate tree, and having decked it out in a piece of red cloth, and having bent it, or made it to bend after the modest manner of the bride, they ornament it with garlands of flowers, putting on sometimes even a silver *hunslee* (or neck-ring), they stick it up into one and a quarter *seer* of unboiled rice, put into an earthern pot, having a wide mouth like a washhand-basin, and place around it for the night *k'hara polaoo*, *meetha polaoo*, and various kinds of fruits; and *arbanees*, or *duff* and *surod*-players, sit up all night in presence of this *puttee*, and playing and singing, recount the history of Salar Musuood *Gazee*, even to the very conclusion of his battle and martyrdom. Some have suspended against the wall a curtain on which are painted representations of his martyrdom, battles, &c. Next morning the *puttee* is carried in the basin on the shoulder of the bridegroom, accompanied by the above musical *fuqeers*; and burning frankincense as they go along, they proceed to the water edge, where, having offered *fateeha* in the name of Salar Musuood, they set it adrift on the water.

In the evening of that day, about eight or nine o'clock, having launched the *juhaz* (or ship), the ladies apply *huldee* to the bridegroom after the same manner as was done to the bride. The *juhaz* is a wooden frame-work in the shape of a stool, to the four legs of which are fastened as many earthern pots or pumkins; or it is made of straw and bamboos in the shape of a boat, so as to prevent its sinking, and it is variously ornamented. To it are suspended flowers and fruits, such as lemons, oranges, plantains, guavas, (*vide* Glossary) pomegranates, *nariel, khopra,* (cocoa-nuts and its dried kernels), &c. and having placed on it *hulwa pooreean,* sugar, and betel leaves, and covered it over with a red *koossoom* (safflower) coloured cloth, and lighted a lamp made of wheat flour with *ghee* in it, they cause it to be carried on the bridegroom's, or some other person's head, and along with it *malleeda sheer-birrinj,* alias *k'heer,** milk, *dulleea, meethee rote,*† &c. accompanied by *baja tasa,* and with torch-lights, they proceed to the banks of the river, sea, or tank, and having there offered *fateeha* in the name of Khoaja Khizur‡ (the peace of God be on him!) over the eatables, the shipwright takes them off and distributes some among the assembled throng of poor who have come to witness the fun, as well as among those who attended the procession, then replacing the lamp on it, they set it adrift on the water.

Should any one by special invitation have been asked to

---

* There are three varieties of dishes, of rice and milk, with sugar, distinguished by their consistence: 1. *dulleea,* thinnest; 2. *kheer,* somewhat thicker; and 3. *fitnee,* of a still firmer consistence.

† Sweetened, flat round cakes.

‡ The name of a Prophet, who, according to Oriental tradition, was prime minister and general to an ancient king of Persia, called Alexander, or to Caicobad (not Alexander of Macedon). They say that he discovered and drank of, the Fountain of Life, and that in consequence he will not die till the last trumpet. He is by some confounded with the Prophet Elias. For further particulars of *Khoaja Khizur* (Neptune?) vide chap. xxvii.

accompany the ship, they are taken home, treated to *sheer-birrinj*, *polaoo*, &c. and dismissed with *pan-sooparee*. All this being done, they apply the *huldee*.

Mudar ka ch'handa,* alias *bhundara*, i. e. They take a cow and some wheat flour, and desire some of the *fuqeers* of the *Mudar* tribe to prepare *chukoleean* (alias *sootreean*), and to dress it with the meat. Then having offered *fateeha* in the name of Zinda Shah Mudar, they scramble for it. The history of Shah Mudar will be more particularly noticed hereafter in the feast held in the month *Jummadee-ool-awul*, (*Vide* chap. xix.)

Those whose means will allow, have the bridegroom on this occasion decked out in a pink *pugree* and *jama* (the poor in yellow ones), a yellow *shâl*, a gold *mala* (necklace), a *pudduck* and *chundunhar*.

The bridegroom does not, as usual, go about shopping, but his friends go in his stead; if he be poor, however, he is, of course, obliged to go himself.

From the day that the *huldee* has been applied to the bridegroom, until the day of *shubgusht*, breakfast is daily sent, by such as can afford it, from the bride's house, for the bridegroom, consisting of *choba*, *shurbut*, *meetha polaoo*, or *khichree* milk, *muleeda*, with a *tumbaloo*, having a red thread tied round its neck, and being bespattered all over with *sundul*, containing *shurbut*, or plain (lit. sweet) water, wherewith to rinse the mouth, and a thin twig of a branch of the pomegranate tree, with red thread wound round it for making a *miswak* or tooth brush (Gloss.) and *pan-sooparee*, cloves, *cardamoms*, with, or without gold or silver leaf pasted over them, with the breakfast, accompanied with music.

* *Ch'handa* means a share.

The first day, however, whether rich or poor, they necessarily send *meetha* (sweet) *polaoo*, in order that after having partaken of this sweet dish, the bride and bridegroom may live lovingly together, and enjoy the sweets of life.

The women who accompany the breakfast from the bride's party, see the bridegroom wash his face in their presence, take his breakfast, and chew *pan-sooparee*, before they take their departure. Sometimes they only deliver them and go away.

SECT. 4. *Concerning the carrying of Huldee and Maynh-dee from the Bridegroom's to the Bride, and vice versâ.*

Among the rich they construct a frame-work, somewhat in the shape of a *taboot*, with red, green, yellow, or white paper, ornamented with mica and tinsel, and this they term *maynh-dee;** within this they place a couple of plates, one containing *huldee*† to apply to the body. The other *maynh-dee*‡ for the hands and feet, and accompanied by a large concourse of people, relatives, and *sumdeean* (or the fathers and mother-in-law) as attendants, they proceed with music, such as *baja*, *tasa* (instruments of music), and *kunch-neean kay nach* (or the dance of dancing-girls), and with lighted torches, and fireworks, to the house of the bride. They also convey along with the above, on separate trays, *mulleeda* flowers, betel leaves, *sundul*, and two or four § phials of a red dye, made of *shuhab* (or safflower) to sprinkle

---

* It is esteemed a highly unpropitious circumstance, if any call this fabric by the name of *taboot*, which in fact it is, since that term is solely applicable to a bier.

† *i. e. Huldee* (turmeric), triturated with water.

‡ *Maynh-dee, i.e.* the leaves of the *Maynh-dee*-tree (Lawsonia spinosa, Lin. or Eastern privet), together with a little catechu, areca-nut and the stalks of betel-leaves: triturated with rice gruel, or water.

§ Not three, as that is an unpropitious number.

on the body, and over these they hold a red *mundup* (or canopy), that is, a square piece of cloth fastened by its corners to four poles carried by men. Should they have a *shahmeeana* (or canopy) of velvet, broad-cloth, or chintz, they carry the phials, &c. under them. On their arrival at the bride's, the women proceed, as they are wont, to the female assembly, while the men remain in company with the men.

Among female, as well as male *sumdeeans*, a number of tricks are frequently played at dinner; such as, for instance, a dish full of bones, with a little *polaoo* over them, is set before a person, who unthinkingly dips his fingers into what he conceives to be *polaoo;* when, behold, he finds it to be a plate of bones; upon which the bride's party facetiously observe to him, "Why, what a glutton you "must be, to have finished already, and to have filled "your plate with bones, while the rest of the company "have scarcely begun."

Previous to sitting down to dinner, the men and women have some *choba* and *shurbut*, served up to them. The *choba** is a dish of *meetha polaoo*, with the dried kernel of the cocoa-nut, dates, and almonds cut into thin slices, mixed together, and covering it over: it is brought on a plate and handed round; and after giving the guests a draught of *shurbut*, they taste a little of the *choba*. On this occasion, one of the bride's relations also winds a long piece of thread round the point of his fore-finger, and dipping it into the *choba*, begs of one of the *sumdeeans* to allow him to feed him. On swallowing the morsel, the end of the thread goes along with it, when the feeder withdrawing his finger, and displaying to the company the ridiculous

* The term *choba*, in this case, is applied to the mixture, but is properly the name of any of the three fruits cut into thin slices.

sight as of a fish hooked, calls out, "Look here, gentle-"men, this man's intestines are all coming out!" which, of course, excites a vast deal of laughter among them; and in this way they play off many such jokes, merely for the sake of amusement.

After dinner the men retire to their houses, while the women call the bride to them, and with their own hands apply the *maynh-dee* to her hands and feet (*i. e.* to the inside of the hands and nails of the fingers, and to the soles of the feet and nails of the toes), and the *huldee* to her body. Sometimes they rub her body also with *chiksa* (Glossary). The ingredients are pounded, mixed with a little water, and rubbed in the same manner as Moosulmans are wont to rub themselves in bathing. On every occasion where *chiksa* is used, it is employed in the above way. There are women who go about vending *chiksa*, ready pounded and prepared, folded up in paper; while druggists, or shopkeepers, have the different articles for it in their natural state for sale.

If the people be poor, they carry the *mulleeda* flowers, betel, &c. in trays, the two phials of red dye, and the saucers containing the *huldee*, and *maynh-dee*, with a canopy held over them, without the *maynh-dee* (or *taboot*), accompanied, as above-mentioned, with men and women, music, dancing-girls, lighted torches, &c.

The next day, in the same manner as the *huldee* and *maynh-dee* came from the bridegroom's to the bride's, it is carried from her house to his When the bride's-women come to apply *maynh-dee* to the bridegroom, the bridegroom's *salee* (sister-in-law), or, in her absence, any near relative, comes with them. If a younger sister-in-law, she stands before the bridegroom without the intervention of a skreen, and makes all sorts of fun with him. If an elder sister-in-law, she stands before him with a curtain held between them, and having applied the *maynh-dee* she catches hold of his finger; then the bridegroom's mother, sister, &c., by putting into the *salee's* lap a *nuqday ka jora*, a *cholee*, or *daoonee*, get her to liberate his finger. It is necessary on that day to give to the *salee* a suit of clothes conformable to the means of the parties.

SECT. 5. *Concerning Paoon Minut or Paoon Mayz, or the measuring for the Bride and Bridegroom's Wedding Dresses.*

The wedding garments of the bride are provided by the bridegroom's parents, and his by her's, each according to their means.

For the purpose of taking the measure for them, they send from the house of the one to that of the other, a tailor accompanied by an old woman, a red thread, some *pan-soo-paree* and sugar carried in trays, attended with music. While the tailor stands without, the old dame goes in, and with the red thread measures the bride for a *cholee*, *koorta*, *peshwaz* (alias *tilluck*), *soorwal*, a pair of shoes, &c. and having given the measure to the tailor, they both return with the music to the bridegroom's house. The tailor himself takes the measure of the clothes for the bridegroom, consisting of a *jama*, *neema*, *paee jama*, &c. In some countries the tailor does not go to the bride's house, but women go and bring the measure to him.

At the time of taking the measure they apply *sundul* to the tailor's neck, throw garlands of flowers over his head, and give him (independently of the established hire, which he receives afterwards) one seer and a quarter of unboiled rice, some *dal* (a kind of pulse) and *goor* (or *jaggree*), together with a few (lit. two or four) *pice*; in order that he may bless them for their liberality, and being pleased, be induced to execute his commission to the entire satisfaction of the parties.

The bridegroom's clothes are sewed at the bride's house, and *vice versâ*. The clothes at the bridegroom's house, when ready, are despatched with the *burree** to the bride; and those at that of the bride's, with the *jayhez*† to the bridegroom.

SECT. 6. *Concerning the Ceremonies observed on the Shub-gusht Day, viz.* 1. *The custom of depositing the Kulus kay Mat (water-pot) under the shed.*—2. *The method of painting the Tail ghurray (oil-pots).*—3. *The fashion of making the Mundway kay Beebeean (ladies of the shed).* 4. *The forms attending the conveyance of the bridegroom's Burree (wedding gifts) to the bride.*—5. *The mode of carrying the bride's Jayhez (bridal paraphernalia) to the bridegroom's house.*—6. *The ceremony of Jhol phorana (breaking open the pots).*—7. *The manner of beating the Putkay chawul (virgin rice).*—8. *The observance of the rite Tail churhana (raising the oil-pots).* 9. *The Shub-gusht (nocturnal perambulation).*

1. *Kulus kay mât.* Previous to the commencement of the marriage ceremonies, a *mundwa* (or *pandaul*, alias a shed) is erected in the houses of both the bride and bridegroom; under which, on the *burree*-day, it is customary, about six or seven o'clock in the morning, to place a couple of red *kulus kay mât* or water-pots.‡ These are filled with water, besmeared with *sundul*, and placed on the sand in the shed, at the right-hand side of the house. They also

* Vide p. 109. † Vide p. 116.

‡ And are removed, Vide, chap. xiv. sect. 9.

scatter on the sand four or five kinds of grain, in order that these may germinate, as emblematic of their good wishes that the newly-married couple may in like manner be flourishing and productive. The *kulus kay mât* is in some countries called *jhol kay ghurray;* into these, instead of water, is put *duhee* (curdled milk) and large *sohaleean* (cakes), and having covered their mouths with red cloth, they reserve them for future use.

2. The custom of painting the *tail ghurray* (oil-pots). Previous to the *fateeha* of the *mundway kay beebeean*, at about eight or nine o'clock in the forenoon, five *sohaginan* women commence besmearing small red *tail ghurray* (or oil-pots), seven in the bridegroom's and nine in the bride's house, with *sundul*. This being done, they tie a red thread round the necks of the vessels, put into each of them some *chiksa* powder and some *burra* (cakes) and close their mouths with *sohaleean* (thin wheaten cakes) fastened on by means of red thread. These pots are also placed with the rest of the things to be used at the oblation to take place at the ensuing ceremony.

3. It is the custom to make, both at the houses of the bride and bridegroom, what they call *mundway* kay beebeean* (lit. ladies of the *pandaul* or shed). The particulars of the ceremony are as follow. On the *burree*-day, about ten o'clock in the forenoon, they take some *dal*, boiled rice, *duhee*, *ghee*, *poorean*, *mât kee bhajee*, sugar, and *shurbut* (among the poor, together with the wedding dresses and ornaments intended for the opposite party), and having offered *fateeha* over these, in the name, first, of his highness and all the other prophets, then of their deceased ancestors,

* So named because the ceremony is observed under the *mundway* (or shed).

and those married women of the house who are defunct and their husbands left widowers, they distribute them among the men. Some of this food is dispatched from the house of the bridegroom to the bride, and *vice versâ*, accompanied with music, and is termed *jun-bhat*, *mundway kay beebeean kay khana*, and *sheesh kay basun*.

They further take five or seven plates of the above food, and having separately offered *fateeha* over them, in the name of Beebee-Fateematooz-Zohura (Fatima the beautiful, the daughter of the prophet Mohummud Moostaffa) distribute it among women of high rank and noble birth; honourable women, who have been faithful to their husbands; and these are called *Beebee ka basun* (or *Sanuk*) *khanay walay* (i. e. partakers of the lady's, *Beebee Fateema's*, dish). It is on no account allowed to be indiscriminately dispensed among women: others being supplied with the food which remains, without *fateeha* having been offered over it.

Moreover, it is customary among some women to place along with the other *fateeha* things, a red earthen cup containing some slaked lime. All these are arranged on one or two new mats edged with red tape. The *fateeha* being concluded, the above-mentioned ladies, who have fasted all that day, each one having first dipped either once or twice the tip of the fore-finger of her right hand into the lime and licked it, proceeds to partake of the other eatables. On the day of making the *mundway kay beebeean*, either before or after *fateeha* is offered, they spread a red cloth on the carpet, and having tied red thread round the neck and handle of a *chukkee* (a handmill), and marked it with *sundul* all round, they place it on the carpet, and seven *sohagin* women in the bridegroom's, and nine in the bride's *mundwa*, sing *chukkee-namu* (*i. e.* some song which they are in the habit of singing at weddings, when grinding with the hand-mill) and pound *chiksa*. When ready, they tie up some of the *chiksa* in a corner of the *daoonee*, of each *sohagin* woman, put a little of it into the *tail ghurray*, and apply it to the bride and bridegroom The bride's party put some of it into boxes or paper parcels, and keep it in their *singardan*, which is given with the *jayhez* paraphernalia. The ceremony is termed *chukkee nowree*.*

4. The *burree*† apparatus, in addition to the wedding-dress (already alluded to), together with some jewels (more or less,‡ according as the husband or his parents can afford them), consists of the undermentioned eatables placed on brass dishes or wooden platters, *viz.* sugar-candy, soft-sugar, almonds, dates, pistachio-nuts, filberts, walnuts, raisins, poppy-seed, *nariel*, *khopra*, plenty of *pan-sooparee*, sweetmeats, sugar-cane, and *sohagpoora* (*i. e.* a piece of red paper folded up containing a bit of nutmeg, mace, a clove or two, some catechu and poppyseed and a rupee, having externally a piece of mica conforming to the size of the parcel fastened on to it with red thread); also *lutkun muhbun*, or a silk twist with two or four silk tassels suspended to it for the bride's *choontee* (head-ornament), likewise flowers, and a flower *chonda* (for the hair braided on the top of the head); and lastly a *kunggun* (bracelet). At about four or five in the afternoon they carry these, accompanied by a number of people, including all the relatives

---

* Women esteem these customs most sacred; nay, even more so than the *Qoran* and *Huddees*. It is owing to the ignorance and foolishness of these people, that they have been established in Hindoostan; in Arabia, Persia and other countries, they are entirely unknown, According to the *Qoran* and *Huddees*, they are innovations and consequently unlawful.

† The *Burree* ceremony, seems in some part of the country, to be denominated *Sachuq*. Vide Mrs. Meer, vol. i. p. 371.

‡ Any selected from among those contained in the list of them. Vide Appendix.

and friends (except the bridegroom and his parents) as marriage attendants, with bands of music consisting of *baja bajuntur*, *tasa murfa*, (musical instruments), &c. playing, halting every now and then to look at the performance of the dancing-girls, and thus they proceed to the bride's house, the women in carriages, *meeanas* (a kind of palankeen), either preceding or following the procession.

If the people are wealthy, the above fruits &c. (except the sugar-cane,) instead of being carried on trays, are put into innumerable earthen pots fancifully painted with various devices on them in different colours (by Moochee-men), and are called *sachuq kay mutkee*an.* Nay, some have them conveyed on elephants, camels, bullocks, or carts.

On the arrival of the different articles, they are, in the first place, exhibited one after the other to some of the bride's relatives, and then delivered over.

After that a very grand and sumptuous entertainment is given to all the people; *i. e.* according to their means. Some dismiss the marriage attendants by merely offering them *shurbut*, *pan*, and flowers.

Some people performing *burree*, *jayhez*, and *shub-gusht* all in one day, give only one entertainment in the evening, called the *shub-gusht*-dinner; and the same evening they also perform on both bride and bridegroom, the ceremonies of *tail churhana* and also that of *put ke chawul ch'hurana*.

The description of a Moosulman dinner party, whether among the rich or poor, is as follows:

Having spread in the *dewan-khana*† or in the house a carpet more or less rich, or simply a cloth, on the floor, the company take off their shoes outside of the door, and

---

* Or, the *Maynhdee* pots, so called because the latter accompany the former.

† A public room detached from the house.

as they enter, call out *Us-sulam-oon-ally-koom* or ("peace be unto you.") It is not customary, and it is even disrespectful, to go in with their shoes; and moreover it is a sin to eat with shoes on. The landlord, or any other present, replies, *wo ally koom-oos sulam* ("and unto you be peace"); and if they be particular friends or men of rank, enquires after their welfare: they then take their seat* next the wall, close to one another. After this, two servants in attendance, one with a basin in his hand, the other with an ewer of water, serve the guests with it to wash their hands;† commencing with the seniors, they all wash either one or both hands as they please. This office concluded, the servants proceed to lay a *dusterkhwan* of white cloth or chintz, in front of the guests, on the carpet; leaving the latter uncovered in its centre; after which they arrange the dinner on it; *viz.* plates containing *polaoo*, *feernee*, and *roteean* (unleavened bread), cups with curries, saucers with *chutnee* and *kubab*, placing each one's share (or *tora*, as it is termed) before him. This being done, the landlord, or the senior present, calls out *bismilla* (as much as to say, "commence"); "eat," for Moosulmans never partake of a morsel without first uttering the word *bismilla* (lit. in the name of God), meaning to say, "I commence in the name of God." After this they commence eating, and that with the right hand, without the use of spoons or knives and forks. They loath eating with the left hand, as that hand is employed by them for ablution after visiting the temple of Cloacina. During the repast,

---

* Of course on the ground, with their legs crossed; as is customary for natives to sit.

† An act of cleanliness indispensable, where the hands are used instead of spoons or knives and forks. In eating, men of rank have a servant standing on each side of them to wipe their hands each time that they take a mouthful.

two or three of the relatives act as *surburans* (or stewards), and supply what is wanted, while some are in waiting with *gugglets** (goblets) and cups† to help any one that chooses to water. These stand in the centre of the dining room. Dinner being finished, and the plates removed,‡ the basin and ewer are again brought, and the guests wash their hands as before; but, using *baysun*,§ instead of soap, which is an excellent substance for removing the grease from the hands; if this cannot be got, they wash in pure water. But previous to washing the hands, it is the command of the prophet to lick the fingers: however, very few adhere to this precept. The nobility generally have two *dewan-khanas;* (one in which the company is received), the other in which the dinner is laid out; and when ready, the landlord respectfully says to the company, "let us withdraw" (*i. e.* to the dinner room). If there be a numerous party, first, part of them wash their hands and sit down to dinner; when these have done, the others follow the same practice. When dinner is over, they who please retire to the *dewan-khana*, where they first assembled. Here they spend the time in conversation, reciting pieces of Hindoostanee or Persian poetry, puzzling each other with riddles, composing acrostics, &c.

Of the latter I shall present a few specimens.

* Vulgo gogglets.

† Several drink out of the same cup, which is washed out a little, after every time that one has drunk.

‡ They repeat aloud, or whisper or say silently in their hearts, the words *Alkumd-o-lillah*, "Praise be to God," or *Shookr-e-khoda*, "thanks" or "gratitude to God," or some other prayer, by way of grace after meat.

§ *Baysun*, powder of *chunna* (or Bengal horse-gram), of *moong ke dal* (green gram, phaseolus radiatus, Lin.) of *toowur kee dal* (pigeon-bean, citysus cajan, Lin.) or of *maash* (black ulandoo, phaseolus max willd).

RIDDLES.

1

A well that won't admit a hair,
And yet all animals drink there:
Not those, indeed, that fly in air,
But elephant, camel, man, and mare.

Answer. "The nipple."

2.

What is it that's round and runs about,
With two living names though life without;
He's an ass (*khur*) who does not find it out,
Nay, even a goat (*booz**) his wit would scout.

Answer. "A musk-melon (*khur-booz.*)"

3.

A pair of pigeons, black and white,
Asunder always in their flight;
And though they range around the sky,
Yet from their cage they never fly.

Answer. "Day and Night."

4.

There is a place I know full well,
Where lifeless persons only dwell,
In war 'tis peopled ev'ry rood,
In peace a desert solitude.

Answer. "A Chess-board, with its men, elephants, camels," &c.

5.

I saw two husbands with one wife
'Twixt whom was no discord or strife!
But both the men from her were sprung,
'Tis therefore fit they should be one.

Answer. "A Quilt, consisting of two folds of cotton cloth stitched together, with raw cotton betwixt them; the two first being formed of the same material as the latter, they are therefore all of one caste."

ACROSTIC.

W ise king, thy gracious countenance I claim,
I ASK OF THEE MY PURE BUT SECRET AIM.
N ow, if you take a letter from each line,
E re long, my heart's desire you will divine.

Answer. "Wine."

---

* In Persian *khur* means an ass, and *booz* a goat, which together make *khur-booz*, a musk-melon.

DOUBLE ENTENDRES.

1.

What is it? It is abundant in creation,
And I've seen it. An elephant mounted on a horse.
Answer. " A Rubber for a horse, termed *Hathee.**"

2.

Paper which is straight, they term *Tao;* (crooked).
To a poor singer who sings well, they say *Gao* (a cow).
The moon is single, yet they call it *Chund* (many).
To a boat which is coming, they call out *Nu Ao* (don't come).†

3.

That they cook a fowl (*jhar pur*‡) on a tree, is known to all in the town;
Tell me friend, what is it that has two legs upon its head? (*Sir pur do pa'on?*)§

ENIGMA.

The teeth of the mountains were set on edge by the eating of betel,
Which caused the sea to smile on the beard of the firmament.||

Dancing girls are also frequently in attendance to entertain the guests with their performances, while the *hooqqa* (Indian pipe), and *cheroots* (segars) are presented to regale them;

---

* *Hathee* means both an elephant and a hair-cloth glove, used in rubbing down a horse.

† *Tao,* also signifies " a sheet (of paper)." *Gao,* is the Persian for " a cow;" but in Hindoostanee means " sing." In Hindoostanee, *chand* signifies " the moon," and in Persian, *chund* " many."

‡ *Jhar* signifies " having plucked," as well as " a tree," and *pur,* means " the feathers" as well as " *on.*"

§ *Sir,* a head; *pur,* feathers; and *do paon,* two legs.

|| The *lal* (or redness) (*a*) of a sweetheart's teeth was so bright, that when compared to the *lal* (or ruby) produced on mountains, the latter looked dim. The sea smiled on the beard (that is, the rays) of the sun, and observed to him, that its " water" produced a brighter red (*b*) than his " heat." (*c*)

(*a*) Occasioned by the chewing of *pan,* or betel-leaves.
(*b*) Alluding to the betel-leaf being nourished by water.
(*c*) Which they conceive to be the cause of the production of rubies.

and in the mean time *pan-sooparee*, tobacco, flowers, and *uttur* are handed round, and rose-water sprinkled over them. After sitting for an hour or two (lit. two or four *ghurrees*), they go home. On retiring, the senior guest, addressing the host, says, "Be pleased to (or will you) "give us leave, (or permission to depart)?" adding, "may "God bless and prosper you! I have made a hearty "meal, or dined heartily (orig. eaten a bellyful)." To which the other replies: "It is the will of God and Mohummud," (*i. e.* not mine;)" or, "very well:" "certainly." Then the whole company rise, calling out, "*Us sulamoon ally koom!*" (Peace be unto you) and take their departure.

Should any one, through indisposition, or unavoidable accident, be obliged to leave the party, he gets up, makes his apology to the host, takes leave as above, and withdraws.

As the men are entertained in the male assembly, so the women, who come from the bridegroom, are treated, in like manner, in the female party; with this exception, that there are no dancing-girls, and no smoking, or use of tobacco takes place.

When the female guests, whether of the bride's or bridegroom's party, enter, and leave the house, a lady stands at the door of the room, and puts into the mouth of each, as she passes her, a bit of sugar-candy, and applies a little *sundul* to her neck, while two others hold a red cloth as a canopy over her head, a white or red *chandnee* (cloth) being previously spread on the ground for her to walk on, extending from the door of the house to the place where they sit. This is likewise sometimes done, though very rarely, among men.

At the time of washing the hands of the near relatives of the bride and bridegroom, male or female, the servants supply them with *shurbut*, instead of pure water; and while washing, they drop a *rupee*, an eight or four *anna piece*, or a ring into the basin, for the attendants.

Women of the lower class, on entering the female assembly, must not say, "*sulam*;" if the hostess be a lady of rank, they perform *quḍumbosee* (the ceremony of kissing the feet *) to her, and merely make *sulam* to the rest. When going away, they request permission in the same way as the men, and then take their departure. The men of the better ranks of society, however, when coming in and going away, say, "*sulam bundugee, tusleemat*,† according to the rank of the lady of the house. I may remark here, that the *sulâm* made by females, is not like that of the males, touching the forehead with the right hand, but it consists in touching the *puttee* (or hair above the right temple).

In the evening of the *burree*-day, abundance of provision, consisting of *polaoo*, curries, &c., accompanied with music, is sent from the bride's people for the bridegroom, and the food is termed *rungburree ka k'hana*.

5. The next day they carry the *jayhez*‡ (or bridal paraphernalia), from the bride's house to that of the bridegroom.

If the carrying of the *jayhez* take place on the day

---

* Or rather, touch her feet with the right hand, and then kiss the latter or, more generally, make sulam with it; while her ladyship, scarce allowing it to be done, out of politeness and condescension withdraws her foot, and, taking hold of her hands, says, "nay, don't do that;" or, "enough;" "long may you live;" "come, be seated." Or, if she be married, "may God render your *sohag* durable" (*i. e.* may God preserve your husband). If he be dead, "may God cause your end to be happy."

† *i. e.* My "blessing" "service" or "salutation to you."

‡ *Maynhdee* would seem to be the term applied in some parts of Hindoostan, to the *jayhez* paraphernalia. Vide Mrs. Meer's Obs. vol. i. 377.

following that of the *burree*, it is on the *jayhez*-day that, in the bride's house, they perform the ceremonies of placing the water-pots, painting the oil-pots, and making the *mundway* ladies, as before described; and some of the food of the *mundway* ladies, accompanied with music, is also sent to the bridegroom for his dinner. On the *jayhez*-day, her *qoran* (if she have one), is first forwarded, accompanied with music; then, about four o'clock in the afternoon, the following bridal paraphernalia, *viz.*

A *sayhra* of *moqeish*,* and one of flowers,† or only one of flowers, (*i.e.* a garland tied round the head, and hanging down to the knees).

The bridegroom's wedding dress; consisting of a red *pugree*, or turban; a red *mundeel*, a cord of silk and gold, or only of gold thread, rolled over the turban; a red *jama*, a very loose garment worn over the *neema;* a red *neema*, or a garment, half as loose as the *jama;* a red *shal*, or shawl; a red *doputta*, (lit. two breadths). It is like the next article, but of double the breadth, and is thrown over the shoulder; a red *putka*, a cloth worn round the waist; a red *romal*, or handkerchief; a red *eezar*, or long drawers, with its *nara* or band; a red *jootee ka jora*, or pair of shoes; a red *kunggun*, an ornament consisting of a red thread tied round the wrists of the bride and bridegroom; a red *p'hoolsoongnee*, any sweet-scented flower enclosed in a piece of cloth for the bride to smell; and two red (or *koossoom*, safflower coloured) *romal*, or handkerchiefs to wave over the bridegroom.

A quantity of the bride's clothes which have been worn.

---

* *Moqeish*, (gold or silver thread).

† If the *jayhez* and *shubgusht* take place on different days, both *sayhras* are sent on the latter day, as otherwise the flowers would fade.

A *Sohagpoora.* (*vide* Glossary).

Jewels; if among the rich, a considerable number; if among the poor, in value according to their means. For the nose, a *nuth*, a large ring worn on the left nostril, of gold; and a *boolaq*, a ring worn on the centre cartilage of the nose, of gold. For the neck, a *luchcha*, a necklace worn tight round the neck, of gold and glass beads, and a *neembolee* (alias *hullah*), one ditto hanging down. For the wrists, a *bungreean ka jora*, a set of bracelets of coloured glass. For the fingers, an *unggothee*, or ring, of gold or silver. For the thumb, an *ungooshtan* (thumb-ring) of the same metal. For the toes, an *anwut*, a ring furnished with little bells, worn on the great toe, of silver, and a *bichhway*, one without bells for the other toes, of silver.

A *Singardan* (reticule or toilet-bag, if I may so call it) of chintz, velvet, &c. containing, a *pandan*, a box of gold, silver, copper, or brass, for holding betel and its appendages; a *chow-ghurray*, a small box of gold or silver, with four partitions for holding spices, *viz.* cloves, cardamoms, nutmegs, mace, &c.; an *aeena*, or looking-glass; a *kunggy*, or comb of wood; a *meesee-dan*, a box of gold, silver, copper, or brass, for holding *meesee* (or powder made of vitriol); a *soorma-dan*, a similar box for holding *soorma*,* generally considered to be antimony, but what is used in India is an ore of lead; a *kajuldan* (alias *kujlotee*), a box for holding *kajul* (or lampblack), of gold or silver, with its *sulaee* (or probe) of gold or silver; an *utturdan*, a vial for containing *uttur* (or *otto* of roses), lit. uttur-box, a receptacle for uttur; a *golabpash*, a bottle of glass, gold, or silver, out of which rose-water is

* *i. e.* Collyrium for staining the eye, to give it a brilliant appearance.—(*vide* Glossary).

sprinkled; a *jeeb ch'hilnee*, or tongue-scraper, of gold or silver.

An *Asmangeeree*, of *tafta*, *chheet*, or *k'harwa*; or a *chandnee* of white cloth (a canopy or cloth fastened to the ceiling); a *deewargeeree*, tapestry or cloth to adorn a wall; a *purda*, or curtain; a *jae-numaz*, a cloth, &c. on which they perform their devotions; a *shutrunjee* (alias *jamkhana* or a large carpet); a *dusturkhwan*, a substitute for a tablecloth, which is spread on the ground; a *khwan-posh* (or *tora-posh*), a cloth for covering a tray, a tray-lid, a cloth covering for dishes; a *sur-posh*, a lid for any vessel, as a cup, dish, &c.; a *boqcha*, a cloth for wrapping others in.

Furnitures, *viz.* a *Pullung*, bedstead or cot, with its appendages, *viz.* a *toshuk*, or mattress; a *tukeea*, or pillow; a *girday* (alias *gul tukeea*), a small round pillow laid under the cheek; a *pullung-posh* (corrup. *palampore*), a coverlet, a counterpane; a *ruzaee*, a quilt; a *sayjbund*, silk cords, with gold or silver tassels to them, for fastening the mattress to the bedstead; a *galeecha*, a small carpet spread near the bed; a *gadee*, a thin mattress, or any thing stuffed, spread on the *galeecha*, to sit or lie on; a *chowkee*, or stool; a *sundooq*, a chest or trunk of wood; a *sundooqcha*, a box of the same; a *paytara*, a large rattan close basket; a *paytaree*, a small one; a *jamdanee*, a sort of leathern portmanteau; a *baylun*, a rolling-pin; a *putra*, board on which dough is kneaded and moulded; a *sundul ka k'hor*, a piece of the heart (core) of sandal-wood; a *sundlasa*,* a flat circular stone on which the sandal-wood is triturated or ground down; a *sayweean ka tukhta*, a board for making *sayweean* (or vermicelli) on.

* The stone being too insignificant an article, is not sent with the rest; but furnished afterwards.

Utensils, *viz.* a *Dayg*, a copper caldron; a *daygcha*, a small one of the same metal; a *kufgeer*, an iron skimmer perforated with holes, like a colander; a *tambukhs*, a large copper spoon, to serve out rice with; a *sheen*, a copper cover for pots; a *lunggree*, a large shallow pan, used for kneading dough, and at meals for serving rice, &c.; a *luggun*, a large flat, hollow, copper utensil, in the form of a basin; a *thalay*, a small flat copper dish; a *tubuq*, a large brass one; *raykabeean*, copper saucers; a *badeea*, copper bowls; *salun kay kutoray*, copper curry-cups; *tushtureean*, small copper-plates; a *chumcha*, a copper spoon; a *tumbaloo* (alias *lota*), a copper or brass pot for holding water; a *chillumchee* (alias *sylabchee*) a copper or brass wash-hand basin; an *aftaba*, or ewer of the same metal; a *sorahee*, or goblet (*gugglet* or *goglet*) of *kala-just* (blende); a *panee ka kutora*, or drinking-cup, of copper or *kala just;* a *k'hopra ch'hilnay kee chowkee* or an instrument of iron for rasping the kernel of the cocoa-nut; a *pooreean kay choôntee*, or a pair of pincers for ornamenting *pooreeans* (a kind of cakes); a *peekdan* or *oogaldan*, a spittoon of gold, silver, copper, brass, or *vidry;* a *shuma*, or a lamp of brass or *kussund;* an *ood buttee ka ek-a*, a receptacle for pastils, of brass or *kussund;* a *palkee*, or palankeen; a *bandee*, or female slave; a *golam*, or male slave; a horse, cow, buffalo, goat, sheep, &c.

They tie a red thread to each of the above articles, with the exception of the animals, and mark it with *sundul*, putting into each utensil a *pan ka beera* (or mouthful of *betel*), prepared for mastication.

Each person gives a greater or smaller number of the articles contained in the above list, as his means will allow.

As was done with respect to the *burree* apparatus, so

these articles are in like manner carried with a similar train, accompanied with music, &c., and attended by all the relatives (save the bride herself and her parents), and friends, (as marriage attendants) are taken to and delivered at the bridegroom's house, where both men and women are sumptuously entertained, as has been minutely detailed on the *burree* occasion.

As on the *burree* evening, *polaoo*, &c. were sent from the bride's house to the bridegroom's, so likewise on the *jayhez* evening, *polaoo* and curries, &c. are despatched from the bridegroom to the bride. The latter, as well as the former, is termed *rungburree ka k'hana.*

The *jayhez* (or the above paraphernalia), remains the bride's property as long as she lives. In the event of her dying childless, her nearest of kin may claim it. But if she have children, it becomes their property.

6. *Jholphorna, i. e.* about three o'clock in the afternoon of the *shubgusht*-day, having decked out the bridegroom's sister in a new suit of clothes, they get her to perform *jhol phorana;* which consists in her forcibly pressing on the cloth tied over the mouth of the *jhol kay ghurray* (or pots) before-mentioned (*vide* p. 107.), which being rent, and her hand getting into the contents of the pot, she tastes a little of the *duhee* (curdled milk), herself, and then distributes the rest amongst the people. The same ceremony is performed by the bride's sister in the bride's house. The pots are left where they were unwashed.

The *shubgusht* invitations being issued, and the guests assembled at the bridegroom's house, the men are entertained with *k'hara polaoo* from three in the afternoon till dusk; and the women in the female apartment in the evening. After dinner, the latter go to the bride's house, and perform on her the ceremony of

7. *Put kay chawul chhurana* (or winnowing the rice of chastity, or virgin-rice).

They put a *seer* and a quarter of unboiled rice into a red handkerchief, and with a *moosul* (or long heavy wooden pestle, in use in clearing rice from the husk), to which a betel-leaf parcel, tied with a red thread, *nara** is attached, all the women, together with the bride, go through the sham operation of beating it; at the same time singing some song usually sung on such occasions.

8. Afterwards, the ceremony of *tail churhana* is performed: that is, they put the seven empty *tail ghurray* (oil-pots) painted by the ladies, together with an arrow having a *pan kee beeree* and a *sohalee* fastened to it with red thread, into a basket; also a small piece of sugar-candy wrapped up in a betel leaf, and a little *meesee* tied up in paper, and some sweet oil, or scented oil, in cups. But previous to transporting these to the bride's place, the ladies rub a little *meesee* on the bridegroom's teeth, and give him the sugar-candy mentioned above, to hold between his teeth for a few minutes, apply a little of the oil to his forehead, and then placing the cups on trays with the above *meesee* and sugar-candy, carry them, accompanied by music, to the bride's house. On their arrival there, having brought the bride out under the shed, and seated her on a stool, they hold a red handkerchief over her head in the form of a canopy; and first of all any old *sohagin*-woman takes up, with the tip of her fore-finger, two or three times, some of the *meesee*, and applies it to the bride's teeth, and then makes her rinse her mouth: the reason of which is, that the

---

* By Mrs. Meer's account, it appears that it is the office of the elder of the house to tie the *nara* (which is a cord of many threads, dyed red and yellow) to the *moosul* on this occasion. (Vol. i. p. 391.) The custom, Mrs. M. remarks, is altogether of Hindoo origin.

bride may become as old a *sohagin*-woman as herself: and all the other women in rotation take hold of the arrow with both hands, dip the end of it into the oil, and then apply it three times to her knees, shoulders, *puttee* (or hair over the temple), and forehead. They then place the oil-pots, four on the right side, and three on the left of the bride. A woman, standing on the right side, hands the four pots over the bride's head to a woman on the left; and the latter, in like manner, hànds over the three on the left side to the former. This operation is repeated three times.

During the performance of all this, there are certain songs current among women which they sing. The bride holds between her teeth, during the ceremony of *tail churhana*, the piece of sugar-candy which the bridegroom had in his mouth (page 122); and after the ceremony is over she gives it to any child present.

This rite being concluded, the bridegrooom's female friends go home, and the bride's proceed in the same manner to the bridegroom's, with the nine oil-pots painted by the *sohagin*-women at her house, together with the *meesee*, some of which they had applied to her teeth, and a bit of sugar-candy which she had held in her mouth, lift the oil-pots (as just described) apply the *meesee*, and make him hold the bride's sugar-candy in his mouth. In short, they perform the same ceremonies to him as they did to the bride.

It is a general custom not to use *meesee* until a person, male or female, is married; it is therefore thought very improper to do so. Men, however, on being circumcised, necessarily apply it once (p. 44), on the day that they are adorned with flowers; but females never use it before their wedding-day: and it is by the black mark in the crevices between the teeth, occasioned by the application of the *meesee*, that people generally distinguish whether a woman be married or not; which circumstance as to men is not so easily discovered, since they never apply *meesee* to their teeth, except at their marriages;* (and at circumcision).

At the houses of both the bride and bridegroom, the empty oil-pots, after one or two of the Fridays of the honeymoon, are given away to the aforesaid *sohagin*-women who painted them.

In some countries, in order to perform the above ceremonies with the oil-pots, the latter are conveyed with the *burree* and *jayhez* respectively.

Among women of some of the castes, the two above customs of *put kay chawul ch'hurana* and *tail churhana* are considered of such consequence, that no marriage is thought to have been properly celebrated, and no woman is esteemed fit to move in genteel society, at whose wedding either of them has been omitted.

Should the *shubgusht* take place on a different day from that of *burree* and *jayhez*, after the ceremony of *tail churhana*, the flower and *moqeish sayhra*, mentioned in the *jayhez*, and a flower *pak'hur*† for the horse, are despatched with music to the bridegroom.

9. The bridegroom's *shubgusht*, alias *shuhurgusht* alias *suhurgusht* (i.e. nocturnal, city, or dawn-of-day, perambulation):—

---

* Consequently their teeth are always clean. It is only by enquiry that the circumstance can be ascertained. Women conceiving *meesee* to be a sign of being a *sohag* invariably use it, and a few men do the same. At the time of the ceremony of *tail churhana*, at the bride's and bridegroom's, they also perform *chowk bhurna*, as described under the head of *huldee* (p. 97). They never observe the former rite without the latter.

† *Pak'hur*, literally an iron armour for the defence of a horse or elephant; but here alluding to an ornamental one made of flowers and thrown over the body of the bridegroom's horse.

The night on which this takes place, justly deserves to be esteemed a grand one; since the principal part of the nuptial ceremony then takes place.

After the *tail churhana*, the bridegroom has himself shaved and bathes; and if he wear long hair on his head, he has it fumigated with the smoke of *ood* (*benjamin*). After this, in tying on the turban, should any venerable old man of the family, whose wife is still living, be present, he makes two or three turnings with the end of it on his own head,* then removes and places it on that of the bridegroom, who finishes the winding of it on. Having then decked himself out with the rest of the wedding dress provided by the bride's friends, and having applied *soorma* to his eyes, *meesee* to his teeth, chewed betel, pasted *afshan*† on his cheeks, put garlands of flowers round the neck, tied the golden and flower *sayhra* on the head, and thrown over the whole the *muqna*‡ (or veil), he is mounted on a horse, or seated in an *ambaree*,§ and commences his tour after midnight, accompanied by a numerous throng of spectators, relatives, and friends. These carrying with him various descriptions of artificial trees, made of different kinds of coloured paper, *bhend*‖ and wax,

* With this idea, that since he and his wife have lived for many years happily together, the new-married couple may do the same.

† Shreds of *moqeish* or cloth woven with gold or silver thread, chipped very fine, or slips of gold or silver leaf pasted on with gum. This is properly a female ornament in use among the lower orders, but men are sometimes foolish enough to adopt it.

‡ Among the great, one woven with golden thread; among the poor, of red coarse muslin.

§ *Ambaree*, a seat with a canopy placed on an elephant, in which they ride.

‖ *Bhend* or *Shola*, netty shrub or pith (aeschynomene paludosa, Roxb.) the light, spungy, white, corky-looking wood of a handsome shrub, used in making artificial birds, flowers, toys, hats, turbans, &c., and to float nets.

and ornamented with mica and *zurwuruq* (gold-leaf or tinsel), letting off fireworks of all sorts at intervals, proceed with flambeaux and lights placed in earthen cups fixed on ladders,* attended by dancing-girls, some on foot, others dancing in *tukht-e-rowan* (travelling thrones erected on platforms carried on men's shoulders), *tasa murfa*, *baja bujuntur*, *nuqara nowbut* (bands of music of different descriptions), innumerable flags, sepoys, a great retinue with much pomp and state, like the splendid procession of a monarch, halting every now and then to witness the performance of the dancing-girls. He thus proceeds to the *musjid* (mosque), whence, having performed two *rukat* prayers and *shookreea*, he repairs to the bride's house, while a flower or paper umbrella, beautifully constructed, painted, and ornamented with mica, is whirled round over his head.

On arriving at the bride's house, a general scramble for the *araish* (artificial trees, &c.) takes place among the persons who have accompanied him. Sometimes the person to whom they belong, prevents this frolic, and on the *kunggun*-day carries them along with the bridegroom; but on that day, they must be given up to be scrambled for; unless they be borrowed, in which case, of course, this does not happen. During the scramble, there is much bustle and confusion, shoving and pushing: some have their clothes torn, and others are thrown down as I myself have witnessed. After that, the bridegroom's *sala*, or some one of the bride's party if *he* be not present, holds a bamboo across the gate, for the purpose of obtaining the *d'hingana* (vulgo *dheegana* or forfeit), and with the assistance of others, stands to oppose his entrance. In general they take with them a small earthen *mutkee*, either fancifully

* Carried horizontally.

painted or plain, (to receive the expected present) and demand the *d'hingana ;* on which the bridegroom's party call out, " Pray who are you that dare thus obstruct the " king's cavalcade ?" To which the others reply, " Why, " at night so many thieves rove about, that it is very pos- " sible you are some of them." In short, in this way they hold a long jocular conversation together. Nay, at times, out of *frolic*, there is such pushing and shoving, that frequently many a one falls down and is hurt. At last they give them ten or twenty *rupees* (or two or four, in short something or other), according to their means, either dropping them into the above *d'hingana budhnee*, or putting them into their hands, and thus gain admittance. In entering the compound, one of the bridegroom's people takes him off his horse, and carries him in on his back. The slaves of both sexes of the bride's party again demanding a present, obstruct his passage in the area, and make a great deal of sport with the burden-carrier, to his no small annoyance. The bridegroom, out of pity toward the unfortunate fellow who bears him, consents to give something, and proceeds in.

On entering the house, the bridegroom alone is borne by the man, who carries him to the door of the dwelling, or to the court-yard around it, where he stops. The women then holding up a curtain between, and one of them having brought the bride in her arms* to the other side of it, they put into her hands flowers, sugars, and unboiled rice, and direct her to throw them three times over the skreen, on the head of the bridegroom, who does the same to her. This ceremony being concluded, the bridegroom withdraws to the male *dewankhana*.

* Or rather, the bride is seated astride on the woman's hip, with the arms of the latter around her waist, as is the general manner of nursing amongst all classes of the natives of India.

SECT. 7. *Concerning* 1. *Neekah,* or the solemnization of Matrimony.* 2. *Joolwa, or the first Interview of the new-married Couple.*

1. *Neekah.*† Should the hour at which the bridegroom reaches the bride's house, after the preceding perambulation, be a propitious one, the *neekah* is immediately performed; otherwise it is deferred to the fourth, or any other auspicious hour afterwards. In the latter case, the people all retire to their own homes, and are summoned at the appointed time. At this juncture, should any thing in the bride appear objectionable to the bridegroom, the match may be dissolved.

The *qazee*, or his deputy, is generally present on these occasions; if not, they send for either of them. Previous to commencing the reading of the *neekah*, the bride's people send a *palkee* (palanquin) accompanied by *baja bujuntur* (musicians), for the bridegroom's mother; or, in her absence, for his elder sister, maternal aunt, &c. and until their arrival the solemnization of *neekah* does not take place. They then commence the business of *neekah*, discontinuing the music, dancing, &c.

The *qazee* appoints two bearded individuals as witnesses on the side of the bridegroom, and desires them to go to the bride's party, and request them to issue orders regarding

---

* *Neekah* and *Shadee* are often used synonymously; though in Bengal the former is only applied to a secondary kind of marriage, called half-marriage. By the ignorant, it is esteemed unlawful and disreputable, equivalent to keeping a mistress. Whereas, in reality, it is the foundation of matrimony, *shadee* signifying, and being merely the "rejoicings" on the occasion.

† This ceremony of *neekah* would appear, by Mrs. Meer's statement, to be called, in that part of the country where she resided, *burat* (assignment). Because on that night the dowry is fixed, and generally the bridegroom takes his wife to his own home. Vol. i. p. 383.

the *neekah*, and to state the nature of the marriage portion. When these have carried the message, an absolute *wukeel* (agent) appointed on the side of the bride, accompanies them back, to arrange the matter. On their return from the bride with the *wukeel*, her people dismiss them with a *pankabeera* (mouthful of betel); but, for the sake of diversion, they inclose the leaves of some tree or other in a betel-leaf, and fold it up in the form of a betel-parcel, and give it to them. Occasionally, at the time of so doing, the husband's brother-in-law with a leathern strap gives the witnesses two or three gentle stripes, observing to them that this is the punishment they deserve for giving false evidence. The *qazee* then repeats the same thing over to the *wukeel*, who, either of his own accord, or as it is suggested to him by some clever old dame at the bride's house, says many witty things: *e.g.* that "the child's dowry is something "so considerable, that it is beyond the power of the bride-"groom to bestow it. But first deliver to me, as earnest-"money, the following articles, *viz.* twelve ships laden with "silk, ten camel-loads of needles, a couple of vessels freighted "with garlic and onion husks, fifty white elephants, and ten "lak'hs of gold mohurs: I shall then acquaint you with the "extent of the marriage-portion." The *qazee*, on hearing this, enquires of the witnesses whether the statement of the *wukeel* be correct, or whether he has been bribed to speak thus in the bride's favour. The witnesses, though present at the conference, carry on the joke by saying, "He went "in behind the skreen, and had a private consultation; so "that we cannot say but he may have been bribed." The *qazee* also, in return, sends back a jocular reply: such as, "Had I previously been aware of the circumstance, I "should have forwarded these articles with the *burree* "apparatus; but since you have only now taken a fancy "to them, I shall forthwith dispatch paper dolls to procure "them, and the instant they arrive they shall be duly "weighed in a balance, having heaven and earth for its "scales and the wind for its weights, and safely delivered "over. In the mean time, however, it is necessary that "you inform us what the settlement is to be."

After contesting the point in this way for awhile, a marriage-portion similar to that which the bride's mother or her father's sister may have had, being fixed upon, the *qazee* states the same to the bridegroom, and inquires whether he be satisfied with it; to which he replies, "Perfectly so." Some settle a larger, some a smaller dowry than this, just as the bridegroom may stipulate. Then the *qazee*, having taken the *muqna* and *sayhra* (veils) off the face of the bridegroom, and thrown them over his head, before which period they were not allowed to be removed, makes him gargle his throat three times with water, and seating him with his face turned towards the *qibla*, requests him to repeat after him in Arabic: 1st. the *ustugfar* (deprecation); 2d. the four *qools* (chapters of the *Qoran* commencing with the word *qool*, i. e. "say," *viz.* the 109th, 112th, 113th, and 114th chapters); 3d. the five *kulmay* (creeds); 4th. the *sift-e-eeman* (articles of belief), *viz.* belief, 1. in God; 2. in his angels; 3. in his scriptures; 4. in his prophets; 5. in the resurrection and day of judgment; and 6. in his absolute decree and predestination of good and evil. 5th. The *doa-e-qoonoot* (prayer of praise); and if he be illiterate, explains to him the meaning of these in Hindoostanee.

Then, having made him repeat the *neekah ka seegah** (also in Arabic, and illustrated its signification), he desires the *wukeel* and bridegroom to join hands together, and

* *Neekah ka seegah*, or the marriage contract.

directs the former to say to the latter, "Such a one's "daughter, such a one, by the agency of the *wukeel* and "the testimony of two witnesses, has, in your marriage with "her, had such a jointure settled upon her: do you con- "sent to it?" The bridegroom replies, "With my whole "heart and soul, to my marriage with this lady, as well as "to the above-mentioned settlement made upon her, do I "consent, consent, consent!!!"

During the performance of the above ceremony of *neekah*, a tray is placed before the *Qazee*, containing some sugar-candy, dried dates, almonds, and betel-leaves. In some places a *seer* or a *seer* and a quarter of unboiled rice, some *sundul* in a cup, with a *pote ka luchchha* (necklace of two strings of black glass beads) in it, and in the tray also the *Qazee's* gifts (alias fee), *viz.* two and a quarter rupees, together with such other presents as they may choose to give him, consisting usually of a suit of clothes together with a shawl, according to their means.

It may here be remarked, however, that the *Qazee* has no right to expect a fee; for when a Moosulman wishes to enter into so lawful an engagement, sanctioned by the precepts of Mohummud, it is not only highly improper and unbecoming, but unlawful, in a *Qazee* to take a fine from him in this way; and, for this reason, that *Qazees* have had grants of land in *eenam* (gift) or *jageer*,* or daily pay, or monthly salaries bestowed on them by former kings, which the Honourable East-India Company (may its good fortune be perpetual!) has continued to them, solely for the following purposes, *viz.*: To bury and inter the helpless poor when they die; to solemnize their *neekah* (marriage);

* *Jageer;* land given by government as a reward for services, or as a fee; a pension in land.

to impart spiritual knowledge to their offspring; to act as *eemam* (priest), and read prayers daily at the five seasons in the mosque; to appoint a *mootuwulee* or superintendent of the mosque; a *khuteeb* (preacher) to deliver the *khootba* (sermon) on feast days and Fridays (their sabbaths); a *mowazun* (crier) for sounding the *azan* (summons to prayer), and a *khidmuttee*, to sweep the mosque and bring water wherewith the congregation may perform their ablutions, all of whom he pays out of his own purse.

If these neglect their duties in the least degree, the ruler may very justly remove and dismiss the *Qazee* from his situation, and appoint another in his stead; for the object of it is to afford ease to God's servants, which is completely frustrated when a poor *seepahee* (soldier) who wishes to get married is obliged to pay two and a quarter rupees for nothing. But, in most places, the servants of mosques, above enumerated, are appointed by kings and rulers, and receive pay from them, and are not in the *Qazee's* employ, therefore the latter (the *Qazee*) will not perform the *neekah* unless he receive the usual fee.

Governors have appointed *Qazees* solely for the advantage of the ignorant and uneducated; men of science, who can exercise their own judgment, have no occasion for them. Being masters in their own families, they can solemnize matrimony and perform the funeral obsequies, &c. themselves, against which there is no prohibition, either by God or the Prophet.

After *neekah* the *Qazee* offers up a supplication to heaven on their behalf, saying, " O great God! grant that " mutual love may reign between this couple, as it existed " between Adum (Adam) and Huwa (Eve), Ibraheem " (Abraham) and Sara (Sarah), and affection as was between " Yoosoof (Joseph) and Zuleekha (Potiphar's wife), Moosa

"(Moses) and Sufoora (Moses's wife Zipporah), his highness "Mohummud Moostuffa and A-aysha, his highness Ally-ool "Moortooza and Fateemat-ooz-Zohura." Then having helped himself to the contents of the tray, and blown (*i. e.* the supplication) on the sugar-candy, he inserts a small bit of the latter into the bridegroom's mouth, and delivers the *pote* (or glass beads) and a little sugar-candy to the bride-groom's mother, or any other near relative, and desires him to convey them to the bride; and tells her, that from this day she must consider herself married to such a person, the son of such a one, and that such is the jointure settled upon her; that she is to wear the necklace as emblematic of it, and chew the sugar-candy.* On hearing this the bride weeps; or rather, as many do, pretends to weep.

In the assembly of the men the bridegroom falls on their necks (embraces) and kisses their hands, and is loaded with congratulations from all quarters. Were the bridegroom even a slave, he would, on an occasion of this kind, be allowed to embrace all the gentlemen present.

Should dancing-girls be present, as a token of participation in the bridegroom's joy, they continue dancing to the sound of the music; in the meantime, the bridegroom's party are entertained with a dinner of *meetha polaoo*.

Along with the bridegroom two or four of his near relatives go as *sumdeeans* (near relatives), to whom the opposite party offer *sundul hat'h;* that is, a red cloth is spread on the floor near the carpet to walk on, while a red cloth canopy is held over their heads, and as they enter, they have *sundul* applied to their *hat'h* (hands). In so doing, many out of frolic besmear also their mouths with some of it, and enjoy a hearty laugh at their expense. Having

---

* As emblematic of the sweets of matrimony.

handed them a *pankabeera*, they take and seat them on the carpet. By placing under the carpet leather or fragments of earthern vessels, they contrive to play them a number of tricks; after which they bring the washhand-basin and ewer, and holding a red cloth over them and a red curtain all round, first pour a little *shurbut* on their hands and then give them water to wash. They put *pan kay beeray* on a tray and *shurbut* into a bowl or bottle, and with a small cup help each of them to some of it, and hand them a *pankabeera*. On partaking of the beverage, each *sumdee* drops a *rupee* or a *fanam* into the cup; some, also, into the washhand-basin while they are washing. They frequently, out of fun, substitute a decoction of horsegram for *shurbut*. The instant any one has drunk the *shurbut*, a wag, who is a near relative, in jest, rubs his mouth so excessively hard with a well-starched towel, handkerchief, or brocade, as sometimes to make his lips bleed.

After that, they hand a *pankabeera* to each of the guests, spread the *dusturkhwan* and serve up *choba*. Having mixed plenty of *ghee* with the *meetha polaoo*, and put it on the plates, they cover it over with the *bund* (or slices, *viz.* the *choba*), and set it before the *sumdeeans*. The bridegroom also joins the *sumdeeans* at dinner, when his hands are washed by his brother-in-law, who puts four or five handfuls of the above food into his mouth. At every mouthful he makes some witty remark, in the manner detailed under the head of *huldee maynhdee* (page 117), after which the bridegroom eats with his own *hand*.* If the brother-in-law be not present, any one else feeds him. The money that is dropped into the cup or washhand-basin

* No spoons, knives, or forks, are at any time used by natives; the fingers serve as a substitute.

in the act of drinking *shurbut* and washing hands, becomes the perquisite of the servants; but, in some places, the landlord takes it himself.

This being concluded, betel-leaf, flowers, *uttur*, &c. are handed round; after which, the marriage attendants retire, while the bridegroom's nearer relatives remain in company with him.

Neekah, agreeably to the sacred *Qoran* and the *Huddees-i-Nubuwee* (prophetical traditions), depends on three things: 1st. The consent of the man and woman; 2dly. The evidence of two witnesses; 3dly. The settling a marriage portion on the wife. Should any one of these be wanting, the marriage is unlawful.

Men of property usually pay the whole, or sometimes a third of the dowry at the time of the marriage, while the poor pay it by instalments. It being the divine command to give it, they must, partly by jewels, partly by valuable dresses, or in short somehow or other, satisfy the women to a certain extent, and get the bride to remit the remainder. Should the husband not have obtained an immunity or cancelled the debt, his guilt becomes great. On his death, his father or his son is obliged to discharge it. Should the wife die, it becomes her parents' due; and if not paid, they can demand it by force of law. In this there are certain provisos; that is to say, if the woman of her own accord leave her husband, she forfeits the dowry; if the husband turn her out of doors, he is first obliged to pay her the marriage portion.

2. The mode of performing *joolwa* (the first meeting of the bride and bridegroom in presence of the relations) is as follows:

Previous to the bridegroom withdrawing from the male

to the female assembly, the women, having bathed the bride, prepare her for his reception, by decking her out in all sorts of finery, with ornaments, &c., adorning her agreeably to the wonted fashion on these occasions.

After the *neekah* is over, the bride's *sayhra*, accompanied with music, arrives from the bridegroom's. The women are entertained with *meetha polaoo*, in the same way as the men.

At the time of *joolwa*, the bridegroom's mother, sister, and other relatives, &c. are all present at the bride's house.

About five or six o'clock in the afternoon of the *neekah*-day, the *mooshata* (female jester) having fastened the *sayhra* on the bride's head, brings her on her lap and seats her on the cot. Then, having seated the bridegroom opposite to her, with their faces turned towards each other and having a piece of red cloth held up as a curtain between them, she, holding one end of a long piece of red thread, puts the latter, along with some unboiled rice, into the bride's hand, and taking hold of it makes her throw it over the curtain on the bridegroom's head. The sister of the latter, tying a gold or silver ring to the extremity of the thread, and also putting some unboiled rice along with it into the hand of her brother, takes hold of it, and makes him throw them to the bride. When they have thus thrown it (the ring) backwards and forwards three times, all the while singing some current epithalamium (called *hujooloha*), the *mooshata* desires the bridegroom to remove the curtain. After placing the bride and bridegroom on the bed, the female jester exercises her ingenuity in saying many witty things. On the bridegroom's mother or his sister requesting her to show the bride's face to the bridegroom, she observes, "The bride "eclipses the moon in beauty; and were I to indulge him "with a single glance, the poor fellow would go mad and "become distracted."

After two or three (lit. four) *ghurrees* passed in this way, she places a bit of sugar-candy on the bride's head, and desires the bridegroom to pick it up with his mouth. That being done, she puts the same on her shoulders, knees, and feet; but, instead of removing it in the latter case with his mouth, he offers to do it with his left hand (a thing totally inadmissible among them), which, of course, the *mooshata* does not sanction; and at this juncture amuses the bridegroom's mother and sister not a little by insisting upon the performance, observing that it is but right, since he has taken up the rest with his mouth, that he should do so in this case. After a few minutes, he is allowed to take it up with his right hand.

Then the *mooshata*, singing, takes hold of the bride's head, moves it backwards and forwards two or three (lit. four) times, and does the same to the bridegroom; after which, holding a looking-glass between them, she directs them to look at each other in it. The bridegroom takes a peep, and obtains a faint glimpse of his fair one (immediately after which the *Qoran* is exhibited to his view), while the modest virgin does not so much as venture to open her eyes.*

They then give the bridegroom some milk in a cup to drink, and touch the bride's mouth with his leavings (hoping thereby to create a mutual affection between them).

Having assembled all the bridegroom's female relatives, and such of the near male ones as are privileged to see her,

* All this is pretended modesty; since, before the match was concerted, the couple have repeatedly been in each other's company, and become sufficiently well acquainted with one another.

and displayed her to them, the latter, on being gratified with a sight of the Beauty [not unfrequently she is ugly enough], put a ring, a rupee, or some jewel, into her hands, and pronounce a blessing upon her, saying, "Long may "you live and prosper."

The bride's and bridegroom's mothers, fathers, sisters, brothers, and other relatives, being assembled, the bride's mother takes hold of her right hand, and placing it into that of the bridegroom's father, says, "Hitherto has this "girl's modesty, honour, reputation, and character been in "our hands, and we now resign them over to you." The opposite party, on the other hand, by numerous consolatory assurances, give her to understand that she need labour under no apprehensions on that subject, that her daughter will be well taken care of.

After that the bridegroom stands up to make his *sulamee* (obeisance), and addressing each individual male and female relative of the bride by name, makes his *tusleem* (salutation) to them. The ladies in return, offer him a present of a handkerchief, ring, rupee, half-rupee, *doputta*, or shawl; and if any one of his brothers be present, they also offer a handkerchief or a ring.

After that, in the same style as the bridegroom came the preceding night to the bride's house, he now proceeds home on horseback, and she along with him in a *meeana* (a palankeen) with doors shut, attended by music, dancing-girls, and accompanied by all the relatives, &c. On reaching his house, the attendants, musicians, &c. are dismissed with betel.

Then the bridegroom, on taking the bride out of the palankeen, and carrying her in his arms into the house, meets with a little opposition from his sister, who insists upon his promising to let her have his first daughter; to which he facetiously replies. "You shall most undoubtedly have the first daughter of my bond-maid, or of my cat." After a little sham altercation, he promises his daughter, and takes in the bride.

After this a fowl or sheep is sacrificed in the name of the couple, and distributed in charity. Then having placed the bride's and bridegroom's arms round each other's neck, with their faces turned towards the *Qibla* (temple of Mecca), they cause them to make two *sijdahs* (prostrations). After which the bride first washes the bridegroom's feet in a mixture of *sundul* and water, and then he her's.

That being done, the couple retire to their bed-room to enjoy themselves as they think proper, disburdening themselves of all the fatigues of the preceding night; but that is among the better ranks of society. The lower orders consider the ceremony of the *kunggun* of such moment, that they never think of consummating the rites of wedlock, until this be performed; for which see the following section.

SECT. 8. *Concerning Kunggun k'holna, or untying the Kunggun (Wedding Bracelets) from the wrists of the Bride and Bridegroom.*

On the third or fourth day after *shubgusht* it is customary to untie the *kunggun*. If the ceremony take place on the former day, it is termed *bhoora;* if on the latter, *chowthee*.

The *kunggun* consists of a few pearls, some grains of unboiled rice, one or two flowers, and a quarter rupee piece tied up in a bit of red cloth in the form of a bundle, and fastened on by means of red thread to the right wrist of the bride and bridegroom on the *shubgusht* night.

On the *kunggun* day, in order to fetch the bride and

bridegroom, the bride's parents despatch a horse, a *doolee*, some *k'heer* and *k'hichree* for their breakfast, and *chicksa* to rub on their bodies, accompanied with music, dancing-girls, &c. On this occasion, the bridegroom's *sala* (brother-in-law) is mounted on horseback, and the bride's *salee* (sister-in-law) rides in a *palkee*, in coming to call on the bride and bridegroom. On the arrival of the *sala* at the door of the house, the bridegroom's people having gone out to meet him, offer him a *doputta*, or a printed handkerchief, and assist him in dismounting from his horse. In the same manner the females go and welcome the *salee*, offer her a *daoonee*, *cholee*, and *bunggree*, or merely a *cholee*, or a pair of *bunggrees*. Until these are given they never quit their conveyances; for it is indispensable on this day to give them these presents.

About three o'clock in the afternoon, the bride and bridegroom proceed with the same splendour and pomp as at the *shubgusht*, without flambeaux, accompanied by all the marriage attendants, to the bride's house. The females of the bridegroom's house go thither in carriages or *doolees*.

Among some classes of people, they drink *taree*, *sayndhee*, &c., and women as well as men continue intoxicated with delight, mirth, and jollity.

All that day the people of both houses, men as well as women, remain soaked in red and yellow dye,* with which, taking it out of a pitcher, they bespatter one another, by squirting it through syringes, or pelting one another with eggshells or balls made of sealing wax, formed very thin,

* The yellow-dye is made by infusing in water *pulas ka p'hool* (butea frondosa, kœnig.), the tree on which the *lac*-insect feeds, adding turmeric to it and boiling. Red-dye is made of safflower. Vide *koossoom* in the Glossary.

filled with it, or merely throwing it with the hands. This is called *rung-k'helna* (or the playing with colours).

In the evening, at the bride's house, an entertainment with *k'hara polaoo* is given to all.

After dinner, the men having retired home, the bride and bridegroom are seated on a carpet under the shed. Into a large *seen* (alias *thalee* or brass dish) they put some water, greens, *sundul*, *betel*-leaves and lemons. The *Mooshata* then taking the *kunggun* off their wrists, and throwing them into the dish placed between them, calls out, "Let us see which of you will be the first to take "them out." The bride modestly sitting with her eyes shut, and head hanging down, the *mooshata*, or some one of her relatives, or one of the ladies near her, takes hold of her hands, and dipping them into the dish takes them out.

Should the bridegroom be the first to seize them, he is in a trice attacked from all quarters. The bride's sister and near relatives, such as are adroit in sporting and playing tricks, strike him with flower *ch'hureeuns* (wands), pelt him with sweetmeats, such as mangoes, figs, *butashu* and *luddoo*, and with *guavas*, *pooreean*, garlic, or onions; and one of the bride's sisters, with others, rubs the poor fellow's cheeks and ears well. In short, they have a great deal of fun and merriment on the occasion.

When the bridegroom gets the *kungguns*, he makes the bride beg for them in the most humiliating manner, saying, "I am your wife and slave." She, in return, causes him to do the same, should she succeed in obtaining them. Having thus taken the *kungguns* out three times, they resign them to the dish.

After that they braid the bride's *meehree* (side-locks) and plait her cue behind; and then make the bridegroom unravel one of the side-locks with one hand. The instant he calls in the aid of the other, he is assailed by the bride's sister, and handled in the same rough manner as at the untying of the *kunggun* just mentioned.

Subsequent to this ceremony from the bride's, according to their means, presents of *khilauts* or suits of clothes are offered to the bridegroom's mother, father, sister, brother, &c. It is not customary to offer money on this occasion, nor would it be accepted, if it were so.

Then taking their departure thence, all accompany the bride and bridegroom home. In fact, it is that night only that the husband experiences the delights of *ziffaf* (or "leading a wife home").

SECT. 9. 1. *Hât'h burtana, or the resumption of the use of the Hands; 2. Joomagee, or the giving of Entertainments on five successive Fridays (the Mohummudan Sabbath) during the honey-moon; 3. Kulus kay mat'h oot'hana, or removing the before-mentioned Water-pots.*

1. *Hât'h burtana* (or the resumption of the use of the hands) takes place three or four days after the taking off of the *kunggun*; nay, sometimes it is deferred till the last *joomagee* (or the fifth Friday of the honey-moon); and until the ceremony is observed, the newly-married pair are not permitted to engage in any sort of employment whatever.

On the day appointed, the new-married pair and all relatives, friends, &c. are invited by the sending of *cardamoms*, and in other forms, to an entertainment at the bridegroom's house.

The bride's mother, sister, &c. on coming to the party, bring with them a large quantity of wheat flour, sugar, *ghee*, almonds, dates, raisins, betel-leaves, flowers, a handkerchief, and a ring. Then, for form's sake, they get the bride and bridegroom to make and fry two or three *pooreean* (cakes), and afterwards make them perform some other light work; such as lifting a pot of water, swinging a *chheenka** (sling), stirring about the *polaoo* with the skimmer, dipping the hand into the vessel containing gram, picking vegetables, or causing the bridegroom to unlock a trunk and therein put ten or twelve (lit. ten or fifteen) rupees, and getting the bride to lock it again. But before making them fry *pooreean*, they cause them to sit down in one place, and get them to break *kanchee*, that is, they fill a plate with wheat *thoollee*, place on the latter ten or twelve (fifteen) *kungooray* (or small triangular lumps made of *thoollee*), a little apart from one another, and deposit a piece of thread in a particular winding direction around them, with the two ends of it so artfully concealed that it is almost impossible to discover them, and place one or two of these before the bridegroom, whom they desire to find out the extremities of the thread and disentangle them. Should the bridegroom be a shrewd lad he is not long of unravelling it; if the reverse, he continues a good while groping about. In the latter case, the *sala* or *salee* pelts him, as has been detailed under the head of *kunggun* (p. 141). Ultimately the bridegroom's mother or sister shows it to him. After that, they get the bride and bridegroom to break the *kungooray*, and make them eat a little of it out of each other's hands, and distribute some to all the ladies. This ceremony is denominated *kanchee*.

Having entertained the men and women, and the bridegroom's party having made presents of suits of clothes or

---

* A network made of strings or cords, to place any thing on; the cords of a bangy.

*khilauts** to the bride's father, mother, and sister, the party break up.

2. There are five *joomagee*, or successive Fridays of the honey-moon, on which entertainments are given: on the first, at the bride's house; on the three following, either at the same place, or at the house of any one of the near relatives; and on the fifth at that of the bridegroom. On these occasions, musicians, &c. are despatched to escort the bride and bridegroom, together with their relatives, to the feast. In the forenoon they are entertained with a dinner, consisting principally of *k'heer* and *k'hichree;* and, in the evening, of *polaoo*. Then having offered the bridegroom a present of a ring and a handkerchief, and bestowed on him their blessing, they dismiss them.

It is necessary that both the bride and bridegroom be bathed on that day.

3. On the fifth *joomagee* (or last Friday) the water-pots, called *kulus kay mât'h*, are removed, and thus conclude the ceremonies of marriage.

SECT. 10. *Concerning* 1*st. the number of Wives authorized;* 2*d, Relatives whom it is unlawful to marry; and* 3*d, the subject of Divorce.*

1. Agreeably to the precept of the Prophet (the peace, &c.) Moosulmans are allowed, both by the *Qoran* and *Shurra*, to have *four* wives. The generality, however, have only one; a few, two or three; scarcely any four: though some, contrary to the *Shurra*, have them without number:

* *Khilaut* signifies nothing more or less than a suit of clothes, the same as *libas* or *jora;* the former being the court language, the latter used by the common people, independently of the value in either case.

such as, for instance, Tippoo Sooltan (now in Paradise), who actually married no less than nine hundred women.*

2. It is unlawful for a man to unite himself in wedlock with the following fourteen of his relations, *viz.* 1. His *ma*, mother; 2. *my dur ma*, step-mother; 3. *baytee*, daughter; 4. *rubeeba baytee*, step-daughter; 5. *buhun*, sister; 6. *p'hoop-hee*, paternal aunt; 7. *khala*, maternal aunt; 8. *bhuteejee*, brother's daughter; 9. *bhanjee*, sister's daughter: nieces; 10. *daee doodh-pillaee*, or *doodh ma*, wet nurse, or foster-mother; 11. *doodh buhun*, foster sister; 12. *saas* or *khoosh-damun*, wife's mother (mother-in-law); 13. *buhoo*, daughter-in-law; 14. *salee*, sister-in-law, which last he may marry, however, after his wife's death.

On this head there is a certain limitation in the case of foster children.

If a child, previous to his completing the age of two years and a half, drink the milk of another mother, her suckling becomes as his brother or sister, and the mother stands in the same relation to him as to her own child; and the same relations whom one is prohibited marrying of his own, he is also prohibited marrying of his foster-brother's. After the age of two years and a half, if he suck another mother's breasts it is of no consequence.

3. There are three forms of *tulaq* or repudiation: 1st. *Tulaq-ĕ-byn*, which consists in the husband only once saying to his wife, "I have divorced you." 2d. *Tulaq-e-rujaee*, in repeating the same twice. 3d. *Tulaq-e-mootuluqqa*, in three similar repetitions.

If a man divorce his wife by the *tulaq-e-byn*, he may

* These, according to Mrs. Meer, are called *doolee* wives; of whom she has likewise heard of some sovereign princes in Hindoostan possessing seven or eight hundred.

within three menstrual periods take her back, but not afterwards.

If he have given her the *tulaq-e-rujaee*, he may, if both agree, either maintain her within-doors, or giving her the dowry send her away. In the former case, should the woman be unwilling to remain, she may, by resigning half or a quarter of the dowry, depart with the rest. Such a woman it is unlawful for him to take back, unless he marry her over again.

With a woman divorced by the *Tulaq-e-mootuluqqa*, it is unlawful for the husband to cohabit until she has married another man and been divorced by him.

If a woman wish for a divorce, and the husband be disposed to grant it, he has recourse to the stratagem of expressing to her his disinclination; adding, that if she insists upon it, he will indulge her, but then she must consent to give up her claim to the marriage portion. The woman having no alternative, resigns her dowry and accedes to the divorce. Had he not adopted the above scheme, he would have been obliged to have given her the dowry before repudiating her.

With a slave girl, it is unlawful for her master to cohabit after the *Tulaq-e-rujaee* (as in the case of a free woman after the third divorce), and she need wait only two menstrual periods, instead of three, before she marry again.

In repudiating a wife, the husband is to wait till postmensem, and then, without touching her, divorce her. Should she be with child, he is to wait until she be delivered; and then, taking possession of the child, dismiss her; and, if he please, the mother is obliged to suckle the infant two years.

After once settling the dowry (that is after *neekah*), but previous to consummating the hymeneal rites, if a man wish to divorce his wife, he is obliged to give her half the dowry; if he give the whole, it is so much the more commendable.

It is directed in the sacred *Qoran*, that a woman may, four months and ten days after her husband's demise, marry again. But in Hindoostan, some women conceiving it more honourable not to marry after the death of one husband, never do so; and when it is done, only *neekah* is performed, not *shadee* (rejoicings), the woman being a widow and no virgin.

SECT. 11. *Concerning postponing and expediting the performance of the matrimonial rites.*

Most princes and nobles at their nuptials continue the *huldee* for six months, during which period they have music and entertainments daily; and performing the other ceremonies every fortnight, month, or so, complete the marriage in the course of a year.

Such as can afford it occupy two or three months in performing the various matrimonial rites.

Among the respectable and middling classes of society marriage is usually finished in eleven days, or less: *e. g.*

The first three days, *huldee* (or sitting in state); on the fourth, the sending of *maynhdee* from the bridegroom to the bride, and on the fifth, vice versa; on the sixth, the bride's *paoon minut* (measuring for her wedding dress); and on the seventh, the bridegroom's; on the eighth, the ceremonies of *kuluskaymat'h*, *tail-ghurray*, *beebeean* and *burree*; on the ninth, *jayhez*; on the tenth, *jholp'horna*, *put kay chanwul*, *tail churhana*, and *shubgusht*; on the eleventh, *neekah* and *joolwa*. After two or four days is performed *kungun k'holna* and *hat'h burtana* any time within the honeymoon, usually on the fifth *Joomagee* or Friday.

Among the poor of the lower classes of people, all the above ceremonies are performed in three days. The first day, the ceremonies of *huldee maynhdee* and *paoon minut;* the second, *burree, &c. jayhez,* and *shubgusht;* the third *neekah* and *joolwa.*

If they be much pressed for time, all these take place in one day; a ceremony every hour or so.

CHAPTER XV.

Concerning the *Mohurrum*, or first month. It comprises three subjects, *viz.* 1st. The *Mohurrum kee eed*, or feast.—2d. The cause of the martyrdom of their highnesses Eemâm Hussun and Hosein (may God reward them!).—3d. The ceremonies observed during the *Ashoora*, or first ten days of the month *Mohurrum*.

SECT. 1. *The Mohurrum kee Eed, or Feast.*

The *Mohurrum* feast was in existence in the days of his highness Mohummud Moostuffa (God bless him!), it having been observed as such by prophets before his time; but the prophet Mohummud, the messenger of God, enjoined on his followers the observance of ten additional customs during the *Ashoora*, *viz.* 1. Bathing; 2. Wearing finer apparel than usual; 3. Applying *soorma* to the eyes; 4. Fasting; 5. Prayers; 6. Cooking more victuals than usual; 7. Making peace with one's enemies, or establishing it among others; 8. Associating with pious and learned divines; 9. Taking compassion on orphans and giving them alms; and 10. Bestowing alms in charity.

Nay, in certain traditional and historical works it is stated, that it was on the tenth day of the month *Mohurrum* that the following events took place: 1st. The first fall of rain; 2d. Adam and Eve's descent on earth, and the establishment of the propagation of the species; 3d. Divine mission granted to the souls of ten thousand prophets. 4th. The creation of *Ursh*, the ninth heaven, or the empyrean throne of the divine glory and majesty; 5th. Of *Koorsee*, the eighth, or crystalline heaven, supposed to be the judgment seat of God; 6th. *Bihisht*,* or the seven heavens; 7th. *Dozukh*,† or hell; 8th. *Lowh*, or the tablet on which the decrees of the Deity are inscribed; 9th. *Qulum*, the pen wherewith they are written; 10th. *Tuqdeer*, fate, or destiny; 11th. *Hyat*, or life; and 12th. *Mumat*, or death.

These did the Almighty in his infinite wisdom create.

---

* The Mohummudans, exclusive of the eighth and ninth, which they do not term *bihisht*, reckon seven heavens, *viz*. 1st. *Dar-ool-jullal* (meaning the mansion of glory), composed of pearls.—2d. *Dar oos sulam*, (the mansion of rest), of ruby and garnet.—3d. *Junnut ool mawa* (the garden of mirrors), of yellow pewter.—4th. *Junnut ool khoold* (the garden of eternity), of yellow coral.—5th. *Junnut oon Nueem* (the garden of delights), of white diamond.—6th. *Junnut-ool Firdoos* (the garden of paradise), of red gold.—7th. *Dar ool qurar* (everlasting abode), of pure musk.—8th. *Junnut-ool-udun* (the garden of Eden),(*a*) of red pearls.

† Of hell, also seven, *viz*.—1st. *Juhunnum* (meaning a deep pit), destined for such of the worshippers of the true God, as are guilty.—2d. *Luzza* (a blazing flame), for the Christians.—3d. *Huttuma* (an intense fire), for the Jews.—4th. *Sueer* (a flaming fire), for the Sabians. 5th. *Suqur* (a scorching heat), for the Magi or *G*uburs (or fire worshippers).—6th. *Juheem* (a huge hot fire), for the Pagans and idolators.—7th. *Haweea* (a dark bottomless pit), for the hypocrites.

I may add here, that the Mohummudans also consider the earth and sky to be each divided into seven parts, *viz*. The 1st. earth is composed of ashes; 2d. of crystal; 3d. of gold; 4th. of pewter; 5th. of emerald; 6th. of iron; 7th. of pearl.—1st. Firmament (Adam's residence), composed of pure virgin silver; 2d. (Enoch's and John the Baptist's), of gold; 3d. (Joseph's), of pearls; 4th. (Jesus's), of pure white gold; 5th. (Aaron's), of pure silver; 6th. (Moses's), of ruby and garnet; 7th. (Abraham's), of crystal.

(*a*) This is the name of the terrestrial paradise, and probably refers to it, leaving seven heavens, as before noticed.

SECT. 2.—*The cause of the Martyrdom of their highnesses Eemâm Hussun and Hosein (may God reward them!).*

There are various versions of the history of the death of their highnesses Eemâm Hussun and Hosein (may God, &c.); but all concur in one circumstance, *viz.* that it was occasioned by the instigation of Ayzeed, who, wretched from all eternity, was the ring-leader. It was pre-ordained that he alone should be the author of their martyrdom: how is it otherwise possible for one to be deprived of life by the mere enmity, tyranny, or command of another? But thus it is, that whatever the eternal *Moonshee* (or Registrar) has recorded as a man's destiny, must unquestionably come to pass; as a proverb justly observes, "diversified are the modes of dying, and equally so are the means of living:" that is, though the hand of the Almighty does not appear visible in either, yet he is the author of both.

His highness Oosman (the peace! &c.), during his reign granted the government of Syria to his relative Maweea, and to his son, as successor.

Now it so happened, that when Ayzeed, the son of Maweea, succeeded to the monarchy of Syria, his highness Eemâm Hussun was on the throne at the illustrious *Mudeena* (Medina), having succeeded the four companions* to the *kheelafut* (or sovereignty) of Arabia.

Ayzeed's subjects excited enmity between him and his highness Hussun, by representing the latter to him as a mere boy, the son of a *fuqeer* (religious mendicant), a poor miserable wretch and without any military force; express-

* Aboo Bukur, Oomur, Oosman, and Ally.

ing their surprise that he, who was a mighty monarch, had an inexhaustible treasury at his disposal, and a numerous army at command, could for a moment submit to be ruled by a Medinite.

Ayzeed (*e-pulleed*,* or the polluted), thus worked upon, became highly elated with pride and demanded homage from Hussun. He wrote to him thus: "Come and be "subject to my sway, and I will, of my own accord, not "only make you king over Medina and Mecca, but will "bestow on you great possessions and wealth."

Hussun replied, "This is passing strange! Pray, whose "duty is it to pay homage? Whence did the constitution of "this subjection and sovereignty originate? Take a retro-"spective view of it for a moment, and consider the sub-"ject with impartiality. Do not pique yourself thus on "worldly wealth and possessions: to-morrow you may "have to answer for it unto God." Ayzeed, on hearing this, became still more jealous.

After this, another affair took place. Ayzeed was led to understand that Abdoollah Zoobayr, an inhabitant of Medina in his service, had a most beautiful wife; and being himself a debauched and dissipated character, contemplated, by some means or other, gaining possession of her.

On one occasion he addressed Zoobayr, saying, "you "are a Medinite, and I have amongst my relatives a virgin "sister, a quick, sensible, and interesting damsel: if you "choose, I will give her to you in marriage." Poor Zoobayr, unaware of his stratagem, answered, "O king of the "whole earth! I do with all my heart and soul consent." He then took Zoobayr to the palace and requested him to

* This particular nickname they gave him on account of its rhyming with his name, a common practice in the East.

be seated. After the expiration of an hour he came out to him and said: "The girl observes, that you are already "a married man, and unless you divorce your present wife "she will not agree to be yours." The moment he heard this he gave his wife the *tulaq e mootuluqqa* (p. 145-6). Ayzeed again retired, and after several hours had elapsed, returned, and said, "The girl has certainly consented to "have you, but requests that the amount of the marriage "portion may be first paid, for until it be delivered into "her hands she will on no account consent to the union." Zoobayr said, "I am a poor man, and probably the dowry "is something considerable; in which case, whence can I "procure it?" Then Ayzeed satisfied him by granting him the government of a distant province, and sent him thither. In the meantime he wrote off to his predecessor, apprising him of Zoobayr's appointment to succeed him, and directing him, by some means or other, to put him to death; which was accordingly done.

Then Ayzeed despatched Moosa Ushuree as his ambassador to Zoobayr's wife, with this message: "Behold, your "husband has, without the least cause or reason whatever, "through sheer worldly covetousness, divorced you; and, "you see, God has consequently not prospered him: and "now, if you will consent to be mine, you may be the wife "of a king."

On the arrival of the ambassador at Medina, his highness Hussun observing him, enquired whence he came and whither he was going. The ambassador replied, "I am "sent by the Syrian monarch to this city to Zoobayr's "wife, whose husband is dead, with a message, offering "marriage." Hussun, on hearing this, said: "O Moosa "Ushuree, should she not consent to Ayzeed's proposals, "deliver you the same message in my name also."

When the ambassador had related to Zoobayr's wife all that Ayzeed had commissioned him to do, and eulogized his wealth and grandeur, she said, "Well! what next?" He continued, "Eemâm Hussun, the *khuleefa* of this town, "the son of Allee and of the daughter of Mohummud "(the blessing! &c.), has also offered you proposals." She inquired, "Any thing else?" "Why," says he, "if you "look after manliness or beauty, here am I present."

Then she taking a peep at him from behind the screen, and discovering him to be an old and infirm man, said: "O Ushuree, you are old enough to be my father; and as "to your beauty, it certainly cannot exceed mine. Re-"specting Ayzeed, who can place any confidence in his "wealth and possessions? which are only of two days' "duration, and may be compared to the noontide shade, "which inclines to one side or the other, and never remains "stationary. It is preferable, therefore, to accept of "Hussun, whose wealth will last to the day of judgment, "and whose grandeur and dignity are in the very presence "of the Deity."

The ambassador informed Hussun of her having decided in his favour, adding, that he might now marry her, and bring her home.* Then Ushuree, accompanying Hussun to her house, performed the ceremony, and Hussun brought her home.

After that, Ushuree went and related minutely all the circumstances which had occurred to Ayzeed; who finding all his well-concerted schemes entirely frustrated, was highly indignant at Ushuree, and from that time became the mortal enemy of Hussun.

* Among Moosulmans the marriage rites are always solemnized at the house of the bride, even though her rank be much inferior to that of the bridegroom.

To lengthen out this narrative will avail nothing; suffice it to say, that through Ayzeed's contrivance Hussun was made to drink poisoned water, and became a martyr. Previous to this, it is said that poisons, &c. were administered to him in various ways at different times; but these accounts are so contradictory that I have omitted them. However, this one circumstance is undoubtedly true, that Hussun was ordered to be poisoned by having poisoned water given him to drink.

Hussun, as I have observed above, now became Ayzeed's most inveterate enemy, both in a religious and moral point of view. Ayzeed used to write to him hundreds of letters in the form of royal mandates. He likewise addressed deceitful letters to the inhabitants of Koofee (Cufa), urging them to contrive some means to entice Hussun into their town and slay him, promising the situation of *wuzeer* (or minister) to the man who should kill him.

The Koofeeans were in the habit of continually writing to Hussun, setting forth bitter complaints and accusations against Ayzeed's bad conduct toward them, and stating their utter dislike to him and their having renounced his sway; adding, that if his highness should come amongst them, they were prepared to join him in battle against Ayzeed. Hussun placing confidence in the friendly disposition expressed in their letters, took his departure for Koofee. When he did this, Ayzeed despatched his minister Murwan to Medina. On the road, about two or three marches from Koofee, his highness Hussun, finding the climate of a town called Mousul highly salubrious, took up his abode there, and resided in the house of another. The landlord of the house gave him poison along with his food; but it had no effect. He gave it a second time, mixed up with something else and Hussun became very ill.

He then wrote off to Ayzeed, apprising him of his having twice administered poison to him, and that although not dead, he was seriously indisposed in consequence. Ayzeed wrote again, requesting him to endeavour somehow or other to put an end to Hussun's life, and that he would reward him with a *wuzeer*-ship. This letter, by some means, fell into Hussun's hand; who, on its perusal, maintained a profound silence, and said nothing about it; since it is unbecoming for one while living in another man's house to hurt his feelings; but it appeared evident to Hussun that his residence there was no longer advisable.

One day an inhabitant of that town, pretending to be blind, and supporting himself by a spear inverted, the point of which he had previously poisoned, came to pay his respects to Hussun, and addressed him thus: "I am a "blind man, and am desirous of rubbing my eyes on your "august feet; peradventure, by so doing, they may become whole." So saying, he gradually approached Hussun, supported by the spear, and struck his thigh with it. Hussun began to experience excruciating pain and torture, and the wound bled profusely. The people were about to slay the man, when Hussun observed, "Why so? From the "beginning it was ordained *blood for blood;* but, you see, "I am still alive; therefore why kill the man without cause? "God himself will punish him, by making his pretended "blindness real." In short, they applied ointments and pledgets to the wound, and it healed; but not for a considerable time, in consequence of its being a poisoned one.

Then his highness Hussun, disgusted with the place, returned to Medina; where at that time was residing Murwan, Ayzeed's minister, to whom Ayzeed wrote, saying, "If "you will any how procure the death of Hussun, you shall "be exalted to high dignity."

Murwan sent for a woman named Joada, and, handing her some virulent poison folded up in a piece of paper, said, "If you can throw this into Hussun's gugglet, he, on "drinking a mouthful or two of the water, will instantly "bring up his liver piecemeal;" at the same time loading her with a variety of presents, and further tempting her by fair promises of receiving greater afterwards.

That wretch of obscenity, through his contrivance and her love of gold, repaired in the dead of the night to Hussun's chamber, and there found a gugglet standing near the head of his bedstead, having its mouth covered with a piece of white muslin: through this she sifted the poison which she had brought with her. Hussun being unwell, asked his sister Koolsoom for a draught of water during the night, and she handed to him the gugglet. The instant he swallowed a little of it he began to eject pieces of his liver (or rather stomach), and continued from time to time vomiting blood: he became extremely restless, and was affected with violent cramps in the liver* and a difficulty of breathing. Having then called his younger brother to him, he gave him numerous precepts and admonitions, and delivered his son Qasim into his charge. The families and relatives of the Hoosnein† made a doleful wailing at the sad catastrophe of his highness Hussun (the peace and mercy of God be on him!) resigning his soul to God. Alas! alas! what language can express, what tongue utter, the sum of their lamentations? (Couplet)

Pen ink and paper! vain the writer's art,
To tell a tale so piercing to the heart!‡

---

* Properly stomach.

† The word Hoosnein includes both Hussun and Hosein.

‡ Subjoined is a literal translation of the author's own words. After adverting

Murwan, on hearing this joyful intelligence, was highly delighted; and giving Joada a *khillaut*, and various other presents, sent her off to Syria. (A verse).

At hearing this sad tale of Hussun's fate
His friends roll'd in the dust and prostrate lay;
While his malignant foes, in guilt elate,
To Syria exulting took their way.

His highness Hussun was buried in the burying ground at Medina, called *Junnut-ool-Buqqeea*.

Then Hosein being left alone, became very pensive; and said, "O thou protector! all are become the enemies of "my house; whither shall I flee, or from whom seek pro- "tection but from thee?"

Again the Koofeeans apologized to Hosein for their conduct, and earnestly besought forgiveness by writing to him various letters containing declarations of their future fidelity, saying: "We, the undersigned, swear by God, that "if you come amongst us this time, we shall all join, and "fight to our last breath for our religion with you against "Ayzeed." Hosein placing confidence in their loyalty and goodwill, despatched his uncle's son, his highness Mooslim, to Koofee. Mooslim, on his departure, took his two motherless children along with him. On his highness Mooslim's arrival at Koofee, thirty thousand men came and paid him homage, and were day and night subject and obedient to him. His highness Mooslim, delighted with the behaviour of the Koofeeans, wrote off to Hosein,

---

adverting to the incapacity of man's ability to describe the acuteness of grief exhibited by the spectators, he breaks forth thus to himself. "Destroy the pen, burn the paper, throw away the ink, and be "silent; for how is it possible, O Lalla! for paper to contain so melan- "choly a narrative!"

informing him that the Koofeeans were at present all of one mind, and were in his favour, and that, if he came there now, they might revenge themselves on the polluted Ayzeed. Hosein, with all his own and his brother's household, set off for Koofee.

Ayzeed wrote off to the Koofeeans, saying, "Behold, "beware! If I find it true that any of you have paid "homage to Mooslim, as it is reported some of you have, "I shall dismiss you and all your household from my "service, and not permit you to reside at Koofee."

When his highness Mooslim ascertained from the Koofeeans the purport of this epistle, he inquired of them what their intentions were? They replied, "My Lord, we "are poor defenceless creatures, and he is a mighty prince "who thus commands and threatens us. Besides, he has "despatched both horse and foot from Syria, urging his "people somehow or other, by intimidating us with his "vengeance, to alienate our affections from you towards "himself, and desiring them to make a martyr of you at "some fit opportunity." The Koofeeans further said to him, in a friendly way, that his residence among them was no longer advisable, because, should they publicly profess their attachment to him, the despicable Ayzeed would be highly enraged at them; and to see him dishonoured would, agreeably to their religion, be their ruin;* since every Moosulman is obliged to fight in the defence of his religion.

His highness Mooslim concealed himself in the house of an honest inhabitant of the town, named Hanee. The

* That is, they would be obliged to defend his (the just) cause, and would all lose their lives.

governor, Abdoollah, on his arrival from Syria, hearing of the circumstance, said to Hanee, "I have been positively "informed that Mooslim is concealed under your roof: "therefore deliver him up immediately, or I shall cause "you to be beheaded, and your house, and all your pro-"perty to be burnt." Hanee replied, "As long as I live "will I not betray him." Then Abdoollah, the governor, burning with rage, at the head of the assembly directed Hanee to be instantly whipped to death, and he forthwith attained the rank of a martyr.

Immediately after, his highness Mooslim was likewise translated by martyrdom.

The two orphans, six and seven years of age, were taken and confined in prison. The gaoler was a good man and a descendant of the prophet, and liberating the boys, advised them to make their escape. They went and hid themselves in the house of a *Qazee* named Shurra.

Abdoollah issued a proclamation through the town, directing the man who might have concealed Mooslim's sons to deliver them up speedily, otherwise when he should get accurate information respecting the person thus guilty, he would make him suffer. The *Qazee*, Shurra, becoming alarmed, in the morning before daybreak said to his son, take these lads and let them join the *karwan* (caravan) bound for Medina, which is encamped in the vicinity. Then the *Qazee's* son, agreeably to his father's desire, said to the children, "Look, yonder goes the *qafeela* (or body of tra-"vellers), run and accompany them." The two boys, partly with goodwill, and partly with reluctance, ran crying. It being still somewhat dark they lost the road, and seeing a date forest went into it. (Couplet).

While anxious here I meditate,
There on me smiles impending fate.

The boys went and hid themselves in the hollow of a date-tree, which was situated near a well, into which their shadows fell. Haris's bondwoman, in the act of drawing water, discovering them by the reflection of their image in the water, inquired who they were? They, through fear, began to cry. She asked, "Are ye Mooslim's sons?" They, on the bare mention of their father's name, cried still louder. The slave-girl brought them home, and said to her mistress, "I have brought Mooslim's sons with me." That excellent lady acted towards them as if she had been their own mother. Embracing them, she wept bitterly; and having washed their hands and feet, and given them food to eat, she put them to sleep. Oh! how wonderful are the ways of Providence! While this good woman's husband, Haris, is from morning till night in search of the lads to apprehend them, here is she at home nourishing them. In short, in the evening Haris came home quite fatigued, and called out to his wife, "Bring dinner quickly; for both I "and my horse are completely exhausted to-day by a "fruitless search after Mooslim's two sons, whom, if I "could but apprehend, I might, by delivering them to "Abdoollah, obtain a handsome reward from Ayzeed." The wife said, "What, art thou deranged? What cause "have we to harbour any malice against the Prophet's and "Allee's offspring and descendants? What sort of a Moos-"sulman art thou, and how readest thou thy creed in their "maternal grandfather's (Mohummud's) name! Be ashamed "of thyself." Thou seemest to take such pains in ob-"taining worldly riches; what will it profit thee after "all?" That wretch, after loading his wife with curses and reproaches partook of his meal without the least relish and went to bed.

The two lads sleeping in the next room dreamed that his

highness the Prophet (the peace, &c.) inquired of Mooslim how it was that he came and had left his two sons amongst his enemies? To which he replied, "They will doubtless "be here to-morrow." As the boys' own father had appeared to them in their dream, they were naturally crying while relating this to one another. Haris awoke at the noise, and inquired what children these were crying in the house? So saying, he went to them, and discovering them to be Mooslim's sons, exclaimed, "Well done, you! "—While I have been fatiguing myself in searching after "you all over the *jungles* (or forests), here you are snugly "asleep!" Having tied the side-locks of the two boys together, he set off with them early in the morning. His bond-man, bond-woman, son and wife, all interceded in behalf of the lads as he started with them; but he, after wounding some, and killing others, proceeded on his journey.

On his way meeting with a river, he made martyrs of both; and throwing their bodies into the water, carried their heads, and laying them before Abdoollah, said, "Through your goodness and bounty I am in expectation "of the promised reward." The members of the assembly, on seeing the heads of the poor orphans, all wept bitterly at their having been put to death at so early an age. Even Abdoollah could not help being grieved, and in a violent rage asked Haris how he dared murder these children without orders? For his command was, that whoever apprehended the youths should, on bringing them to him, receive a reward. He further demanded of him where he had slain them? On being told, in reply, "Near the bank of such "a river," he desired this tyrant and oppressor to be forthwith carried thither and beheaded; and directed the heads of the children to be thrown into the same river. Accordingly they took Haris there, and despatched him to hell with great torture and pain. In the *Rowzut-oos Shohuda*, it is stated, that after the heads had been thrown into the river, the two headless corpses rose from the bottom to the surface, and having united with their respective heads, sunk again.

Meanwhile Eemam Hosein arrived at Koofee; and on hearing of the martyrdom of Mooslim and his sons, was extremely dejected. A few days after, two of the villainous Ayzeed's *wuzeers* (ministers) arrived from Syria to meet Hosein, to wage war with him, and wrote to him to the following effect: "Hosein, if your life be dear to you, come "and pay homage to king Ayzeed; otherwise, you shall "not depart hence alive." His highness Hosein felt greatly incensed at this, and replied: "Ye, of our race, accom-"plices of Ayzeed, have ye no wisdom or discernment? "Do ye call yourselves Moosulmans and pious men! "Pray, whose, in truth, is the *Khilafut* (successorship of "Mohummud)? In whose family did it orignate? Whose "father or grandfather established the religion of Islam? "Whether is it just that I should pay obeisance to Ayzeed, "or he to me? Notwithstanding this, Ayzeed has, with-"out cause, butchered my nearest relatives, my innocent "brothers. If ye desire to make *juhad fee-subeel-illah* "(or holy war) with me, I am ready to offer up my head "in the service of my God."

Having transmitted Hosein's letter to Syria, they obtained the order for battle; which was to this effect: that they should cut off Hosein by any means in their power. In short, they ultimately fixed on the expediency of going to war. Ayzeed's army encamped near the banks of the river Foorat (Euphrates), and Hosein's on the other side of an intervening jungle (or plain) called Mareea. It is the same that is also denominated Dusht-bulla Kurb-bulla (vulgo Kurbula).

On Hosein's arrival at the jungle he addressed his people, saying, "Ye Islamites! as ye must now stand up to fight, "if there be any among you who cherish regard for their "wives and familes, I do with my whole heart and soul "grant them leave to return; for I see plainly, that this is "the spot destined for my martyrdom. And why should "you unnecessarily suffer trouble and distress?" On hearing this, some took their departure for Medina, others for Mecca or Cufa.

On that day Hosein's forces, including himself, consisted of seventy-two men. Afterwards, however, a few of Ayzeed's people under Oomur and Abdoollah, came over to him: the first of whom was Hoor (e-Shuheed, or the martyr). He joined his highness Eeman Hosein, and fought most bravely against the Ayzeed-eeans, killing many hundreds of them. The enemy's forces amounted to thirty thousand men, while on the other side were only seventy-two.

A more minute detail of the circumstances of the war may be found in a Persian work entitled *Rowzut-oosh Shohuda*,* of which there is both an enlarged and an abridged edition, in prose, by Moolla Hosein Kashufee, the author of the *Tufseer-e-Hoseinee*. In Hindee, the *Rowzut-ool-Athar* and the *Rowzut-oosh-Shohuda*, in verse, are well known.

Among the martyrs the following are those who suffered and distinguished themselves most; *viz*. 1. Hoor (e-Shuheed, or the martyr); 2. Abdoollah; 3. Aown; 4.

* Book (praises, &c.) of the martyrs.

Huntulla; 5. Haylâl; 6. Abbas (e-Ullumdar, or the standard-bearer); 7. Akbur; 8. Qasim.

When each one's turn for attaining the dignity of martyr had arrived, save that of Hosein, his highness Zein-ool-Abaydeen, who was confined by a severe fever, and much afflicted at seeing his father the sole survivor, expressed his wish to join the fight and encounter martyrdom. Hosein comforting and consoling him, said, "Long "may you live and prosper, light of mine eyes! By you "will the Almighty continue my progeny; you shall not be "killed; therefore do not, without cause, go and harass "yourself. Come, and I will impart to you many hidden "mysteries of godliness, as they have been revealed to me "by my father, paternal grandfather, and brother, word "for word,* in order that the right of succession may be "known in all the earth, even to the end of the world."

Having therefore, according to the established custom among *Peers* and *Mooreeds*, given Zein-ool-Abaydeen such admonition and advice, praise and blessing, as he thought proper, he mounted his steed Zool-junna,† repaired to the field of battle, and thus addressed the enemy: "O ye tribe "of the followers of the Faith! Be it known unto you that "I am the grandson of the Prophet, and the son of Allee, "he, whose grandfather's creed (There is no God but the "one true God, and Mohummud is his messenger!) ye "repeat night and day. Behold, consider who it is of "whom Mohummud is the friend.‡ If ye have any fear "of God or his messenger before your eyes, or expect the

---

* In the original, "hand in hand, from ear to ear;" an expression in use, from the circumstance of the two persons holding each other's hands, while the secret is whispered into the ear.

† Meaning a winged wolf.

‡ They call Mohummud the friend of God.

"intercession of my grandfather at the day of judgment, "then fear and tremble. Ye have already exalted many "of my relatives, friends, and companions to the dignity "of martyrs! Be it so. I have only one request to make; "and that is, allow me and my household to quit Arabia "and proceed to Ujjum* (Persia). If not, for God's sake "give us a little water to drink. Your cattle, elephants, "horses, and camels have plenty to drink, but my family "is exceedingly distressed and crying out for water. "Among what tribe do ye find it thus? The children's "throats are parched with thirst, and for want of water "the milk is dried up in the mother's breast."

Many, on hearing Hosein's sweet voice and sound argument, were confounded and withdrew from his presence. Immediately the *tubbul* (or drum) of peace sounded.

Hosein, from concomitant circumstances, was led to conceive the probability of the Almighty having softened the hearts of his enemies; and wishing to see the result, whether it would prove a message of peace or otherwise, returned to his tent. Here, amongst his family, nothing was to be heard but lamentable calls of "Thirst! thirst!"

The author would observe, that however great the discrepancy in the details of the events here narrated, one thing is certain, that they suffered dreadful distress from the want of water, even to such a degree as none of Adam born ever before endured.

The next day the *tubbul* (or alarm) of war beat again. Hosein then strictly enjoined his family, on no account to make any noise or clamour after his martyrdom, by beating upon their breasts, or crying and bewailing with dishevelled hair; observing, that such customs and usages only became

* *i.e.* Any country not Arabian.

the ignorant; but to be sorrowful and bear it with quietness and patience: for that such was the conduct that God and his messenger delighted in.

After giving them further admonition, his highness Hosein displayed great intrepidity and bravery, driving the enemy twice back as far as the Euphrates. On one of these occasions he was prevented from quenching his thirst through the artifices of the enemy; on the other he avoided it, by bringing to his recollection the deplorable situation of his family.* His highness Hosein being faint from the loss of blood, dismounted and let his charger loose "on the road to God."† Then Oomur and Abdoollah Zeead said to their horsemen and footmen, "Now is the time, while "Hosein is sitting exhausted: whoever brings his head "shall be handsomely rewarded by Ayzeed."

It is stated in the *Kunz ool gurraeb*, by Abil Hoonnooq, that the moment his highness Hosein dismounted from his horse, a man appeared to him having a human countenance, but the arms, legs, and body of a horse. The figure, after making its obeisance, thus addressed Hosein: "If you will "allow me, I shall instantly vanquish all your foes." Hosein inquired, "Who art thou, that at this season of "distress hast in pity come to my succour?" He replied, "I am Jaffur the son of Tyar, king of the Fairies. I am "under infinite obligations to you; for your father ren-"dered mine an essential service at the battle of Beer-ool-"ullum. When the whole race of Genii were overruled "and made Moosulmans, he appointed my father king "over them." Hosein observed, "Thou wilt be invisible "to them, though they be visible to thee: such treacherous

* Meaning, why should he indulge himself with a draught of water when his poor family were dying of thirst?

† That is, in pity, that the poor animal might not also be slain.

"warfare is not pleasing unto God, nor will I sanction it." Jaffur entreated him a second time, saying, "I beseech "you, Hosein, for your own sake, to allow me for a couple "of *ghurrees** to assume a human form and stand up in "thy defence." Hosein again replied with his blessed tongue, "What use is there now in fighting? I am only "a momentary sojourner in this transitory world (lit. a "guest of one breath): my relatives and companions are "all gone, and what will it profit me to remain behind? "I long for nothing now, save my martyrdom; therefore "depart thou, and may the Lord recompense and bless "thee." Jaffur then departed, much grieved, and weeping.

As each of Ayzeed's party approached Hosein to cut off his head, they shrunk back at the very sight of him; for who would, without cause, willingly bring upon his head† the blood of Hosein?

At last came Seenan the son of Arwa, together with Shoomur-Zil-Jowshun, who had previously offered a stipulation to Oomur and Abdoollah, that they would bring them Hosein's head, provided these would promise to recommend that each should receive a *jageer* as his reward. The point rested with them; they both consented. Seenan stood behind Hosein, while Shoomur with a veil over his face stood before him. Hosein addressed the latter, saying, "What is thy name? Take off thy veil." When he uncovered his face, behold, he had a couple of boar's tusks, and on his chest was a black mark. This, however, is not a well-attested fact, both signs being doubtful. Hosein said to him, "Wait a moment: this is Friday (the Mohum-"mudan sabbath), the tenth day of the month *Mohurrum*,

---

* Two and a-half *ghurrees* are equal to about one hour.

† Lit. "Upon his neck."

"and it is the season for the *zohur* (or afternoon) prayer; "grant me a reprieve while I offer up two *furz-rukat* "prayers." Shoomur stept to one side, and after the first *sijda* (prostration), as he was in the act of making the second, Shoomur severed his blessed head from his body. Alas! alas! and woe 's me a hundred times! for it was an awful catastrophe which no man can describe.

After Hosein's martyrdom, Oomur and Abdoollah had all their own dead collected; and having had the *numaz-e-junaza* (or funeral service) read over them, caused them to be buried.

On the third day, having mounted Hosein's family on camels, and distributed all the heads of the martyrs, including that of Hosein (the mercy and peace, &c.) among part of the soldiery, horse and foot, to each a few enclosed in boxes, and delivered Hosein's to the particular charge of an officer named Khoolee, a relation of Shoomur, he directed them to be conveyed to Ayzeed in Syria. On passing through each town the head of Hosein was displayed on the point of a lance. (Vide p. 180).

As Hosein's holy family were about to proceed to Syria, the soldiers conducted them along the road over the field of blood where the headless bodies of their relatives still lay. Shuhur-bano, the wife of his highness Eemam Hosein, and Zynub and Koolsoom his two sisters, perceiving the corpses of the martyrs, began to shriek and bewail, beating their breasts, and crying, "Oh grandfather! oh Ahmud!* Yon-"der lies Hosein, thy daughter's son, whose neck † was "the spot where thou was wont to kiss; and lo, now it "bears the mark of the bloody weapon (the dagger); and

---

* A name of Mohummud.

† Literally, "whose throat was thy *bosu-gah;*" perhaps meaning, on whose neck he used to hang in kissing (him).

"these are of thy family and household, now without house "or home, deserted and forlorn." Thus distressed and lamenting, they were led captive to Syria. In witnessing how deeply Zynub and Koolsoom were affected and agitated, not only their friends, but even their enemies shed tears.

At every stage on the road some miracle or other used to be manifested from Hosein's head. It is stated by Eemam Ismaeel, on the authority of Abil Hoonnooq, that on the arrival of the heads in the city of Mousel, they were all, including Hosein's, deposited in a temple, and locked up during the night. One of the mounted sentinels, in the dead of the night observed, through an orifice in one of the doors, the figure of a man with a white beard and of immense stature, who took Hosein's head out of the box, and kissed and wept over it. By and by a whole assembly of ancestors arrived, and in like manner kissed and wept over it. Conceiving that these people might probably walk off with the head, he instantly unlocked the door and went in; when some one gave him a violent slap on the face, and interrupted him by saying, "The prophets are come hither on "a morning visit to the head of the deceased. Whither art "thou venturing thus disrespectfully?" The slap left a black mark on his cheek. In the morning he related the circumstance to the commanding officer, and showed him his cheek.

On the heads being brought to Ayzeed, they first brought Hosein's, and displaying it to the grandees, observed, "Behold, ye nobles of Syria, the head of him whose object "was the destruction of the race of Abee Soofeean and "Oomeea,* and whose ambition was to become the *khuleefa*

* Oomeea begat Abee-soofeean, Abee-soofeean begat Maweea, Maweea begat Ayzeed.

"(caliph) of Arabia and Ujjum (Persia). God has punished him according to his deserts, without permitting him to execute his project." This speech was considered highly improper by Zein ool Abaydeen, who said, "Ye Ayzeedeeans, avaricious noblemen, residents of Syria! Do ye read the creed of Abee Soofeean, or of my grandfather Hosein? Keep the fear of God before your eyes." Ayzeed, in a rage, ordered the boy to be beheaded; observing, that he was extremely impertinent. Many petitioned and interceded on his behalf, saying, "He is yet a lad, and the death of his father is still fresh in his memory; and, besides, he is an orphan." Ayzeed then desired Zein ool Abaydeen to state without reserve what his wishes were? he replied, "Three things, *viz.* 1st. Deliver up to me my father's executioner; 2dly. Despatch me, giving me the heads and families, to Medina; 3dly. To-morrow being Friday, let me read the *khootba* (sermon or service)."

Ayzeed consented to his requests, but privately desired his own Syrian *khuteeb* (priest) to read the *khootba*, and to offer up praises and eulogiums in the names of the descendants of Abee Soofeean and Oomeea. Accordingly, on Friday the Syrian *khuteeb* read the *khootba*, and praised the race of Abee Soofeean and Oomeea, and spoke with contempt of the descendants of the Prophet, the offspring of Allee, and of the paternal grandfather and grandmother of both the *Eemams*.* Zein ool Abaydeen was much hurt at this; and observed, "If thou be a monarch, act not contrary to thy promise. Didst thou not assure me that I should read the *khootba*?"

All present petitioned the king, saying, "He is a Me-

* *i. e.* Hussun and Hosein.

"dinite, and one who is in the habit of performing the "pilgrimage;* we also are particularly desirous of putting "the skill and eloquence of this boy to the test, and ascer- "taining their extent." Then Zein ool Abaydeen read the *khootba;* and, after praising and eulogizing the descendants of the Prophet and of Allee, the Almighty put words with such effect into his mouth, that the devout Syrians on hearing them wept; which Ayzeed observing, quickly directed the Mowazun to read the *qamut*,† lest symptoms of war should appear, for the hearts of the congregation had melted away.

After prayers, all the heads, with expenses for the road, clothes, &c. having been given to Zein ool Abaydeen, they were sent off to Medina. Some say that the executioner was also delivered up to him, while others contradict it. At all events, they were despatched; forty days after, they brought them back to Kurbulla, and buried the heads separately, each with its own body, and departed to Medina. Here they wept over the tombs of Mohummud Moostuffa (the peace, &c.) and Hussun; and all Medina become subject to Zein ool Abaydeen.

Hosein's martyrdom happened in the forty-sixth year of the *Hijree*, now 1202 years ago; since which, the rejoicings at the *eed* (or festival), have been abolished, and mournings and lamentations established in lieu thereof.

* These are generally very eloquent.

† *Qamut* (or creed); meaning, to proceed with the service.

SECT. 3. *The Ceremonies observed during the Ashoora, or first ten days of the Month Mohurrum.*

The *Mohurrum** or Mohurrum festival, commences on the evening the new moon becomes visible, which is called the first *k'hun*, or day of the moon; but the first day of the month *Mohurrum* is dated from the morning† following.

The *Mohurrum*, including the *Zeearut*,‡ may be said to last till the twelfth of the month (*i. e.* the thirteenth *K'hun*); but the feast itself continues during the first ten days of the month, which period is called *Ashoora*.

Houses are appropriated for the purpose, in which they set up *ullums*, *taboots*, *shah-nusheens*, *booraqs*, &c.; and sometimes, for the sake of ornament, they set up *tutteeans* (screens, *vide* page 185.) around them, made of *mica*, &c. These places are called *Ashoor-khana* (ten-day-house); *Tazeea-khana* (the house of mourning); and *Astana* (a threshold, or *fuqeer's* residence). Strangers are not permitted to go near them, as the threshold is required to be kept pure and undefiled for the purposes of reading the *fateeha* and *durood*.

Five or six days previous to the *Mohurrum*, they prepare the *Ashoor-khana*, by plastering, white-washing, erecting a shed in front, &c., and wait in expectation of the new

* This feast is in commemoration of the martyrdom of Hussun and Hosein: the latter of whom was killed on the tenth day of the month after a desperate battle of twenty days; the former was poisoned a short time before, as has been related in the preceding section.

† The Mohummudans calculate their days from 6 A.M. to 6 P.M., and night *vice-versa*; and consider the night preceding the day, as the one belonging to it.

‡ Or visiting; the relatives of the deceased visiting the grave on the third day of one's demise. Vide Chap. xxxix.

moon. The moment that they see the *Mohurrum* new moon, they perform *kodalee marna.* That is, after having offered *fateeha* over some sugar in the name of the *Hoosnein*, attended by music, at the spot where they intend digging the *allawa*, they strike the *kodalee* (spade) two or three times into the earth, and two or three days afterwards dig the hole.

In front of each *ashoor-khana* is dug a circular pit, from one cubit and a half to eight cubits in diameter, and the same in depth; occasionally, with a small wall round it. This is called an *allawa* (bonfire). These are dug annually on the same spot. Commencing from that day inclusive, they kindle fires in these pits every evening during the festival; and the ignorant, old as well as young, amuse themselves in fencing across them with sticks or swords; or only in running and playing round them, calling out, *Ya Allee! Ya Allee!* (Oh Allee! Oh Allee!); *Shah Hussun! Shah Hussun!* (noble Hussun! noble Hussun!); *Shah Hosein! Shah Hosein!* (noble Hosein! noble Hosein!); *Doolha! doolha!* (bridegroom! bridegroom!); *Haee dost! haee dost!* (alas, friend! alas, friend!); *Ruheeo! ruheeo!* (stay! stay!) Every two of these words are repeated probably a hundred times over, as loud as they can bawl out.

Of those who have vowed, some leap into the still-burning embers, and out again; others, leap through the flame, and some scatter about handfuls of fire.

Women likewise, without an *ashoor-khana*, dig an *allawa*, and repeating *murseea** beat upon their breasts.

In general it is customary to play round the *allawa* at night; seldom in the day.

---

* A funeral eulogium, particularly one sung during the *mohurrum* in commemoration of the descendants of Allee.

Women, in addition to the above-mentioned exclamations, call out aloud, while violently beating their breasts,* hundreds of times over, the following words: *Haee! haee!* (alas! alas!); *Shah juwan! Shah juwan!* (excellent youths! excellent youths!); *Teeno! teeno!* (all three! all three!); *Luhoomen! Luhoomen!* (in blood! in blood!); *Doobay! doobay!* (drowned! drowned!); *Giray! giray!* (fallen! fallen!); *Muray! muray!* (dead! dead!); *Puray! puray!* (prostrate! prostrate!); *Ya Allee!* (Oh Allee!)

Having called out *Ya Allee*, (pronouncing it only once and very long,) as a sign of conclusion, and taking breath awhile, should they know any *murseea* (dirge), or recollect a line or couplet of one, they repeat it, with mournful lamentations; and beating upon their breasts, again reiterate the exclamations above mentioned.

Some women substitute in the place of an *allawa*, a lamp placed on a wooden mortar, or an inverted earthen pot, over which they make their lamentations.

On the first, third, or fourth *k'hun*, they deck out the *ashoor-khana*† with carpets, ceilings, tapestry, transpa-

---

* Women who thus beat upon their breasts are called *Seena-zunnee* (breast-beaters), and are all of the *Sheeah* persuasion; *Soonnees* consider it unlawful to do so.

† "The opulent people of Mussulman society (particularly in "upper Hindoostan), have, instead of an *ashoorkana*, what they call "an *emambara*, which is a sacred place erected for the express pur-"pose of commemorating Mohurrum. The founder not unfrequently "intends this also as the mausoleum for himself and family. It is a "square building, generally erected with a cupola top, the dimensions "guided by the circumstances of the founder. The floor is matted "with date-leaf mats, in common use in India, on which is a *shut-"runjee* (cotton carpet), and over this a clean white calico covering, "on which the assembled party are seated, during the several periods "of collecting together to remember their leaders. These meetings "are termed *mujlis*.

"The

rencies, hanging-lamps, lustres, *chundoo*, floor-lamps, wax-candles, benzoin-pastile stands, fishes formed of paper or tinsel, ostrich eggs, artificial flowers of paper, fountains, &c.

" The *tazeea* is placed against the wall on the side facing Mecca " under a canopy of rich embroidery. A reading-desk or pulpit " (*mimbur*) is placed in a convenient situation for the reader to face " Mecca, and his voice to be heard by the whole assembly of people; " it is constructed of silver, ivory, ebony, &c. to correspond with the " *tazeea*, if possible: the steps are covered sometimes with gold cloth, " or broadcloth of black or green if a *Syed's* property, being the " colour worn by that race for mourning. The shape of a *mimbur* " is a flight of steps with a flat top, without any railing or enclosed " place; the reader, in his recitings, occasionally sitting on the steps " or standing, as may be most convenient to himself.

" On the walls of the *emambara*, mirrors and looking-glasses are " fixed, in suitable situations, to give effect to the brilliant display of " light from the magnificent chandeliers suspended from the cupola " and cornices. The nobles and the wealthy are excited with a desire " to emulate each other in the splendour of their display on these " occasions. All the mirrors, glass lustres, chandeliers, &c. are " brought together to this place from their several stations in the " mansion; and it is due to them, to admit the effect to be often im-" posingly grand, and the blaze of light splendid.

" On each side the *tazeea*, the whole length of the wall, banners " are arranged, in great variety of colour and fabric; some of them " are costly and splendid. I have seen many constructed of the richest " embroidery, on silk grounds, of gold and silver, with massy gold " fringes, cords, and tassels; the staff is cased with gold or silver, " worked into figures of birds and other animals in every variety; the " the top of which has a crest, in some a spread hand, in others a sort " of plume, and not unfrequently a crest resembling a grenade, " formed of the precious metals, and set with stones of great value.

" On the base of the *tazeea*, the several articles are placed con-" ceived likely to have been used by Hosein at Kurbulla: a turban of " gold or silver tissue, a splendid sword and belt, the handle and hilt " set with precious stones, a shield, the Arabian bow and arrow. " Wax-lights, red and green, are also placed in great numbers about " its base, in silver or gold candlesticks; and censers of gold and " silver, burning incense perpetually during *mohurrum*. Many " other minor tributes to the *emams* are discovered near the *tazeea*, " as choice fruits and garlands of sweet-scented flowers, the offerings " of ladies of the family to their relative's *tazeea*."—Mrs. M. H. Ali's Obs. on Mussulman's of India, vol. i. p. 33

The *ullums* are also called *shudday*, *punjay*, *eemam-zaday*, *peeran*, *sahiban*, and *eemamein*; and all such as come out previous to the tenth *k'hun*, are further termed *suwaree* (mounted) *ullums*, and distinguished by having two or three lemons suspended to them.

An *ullum* is a representation of a standard. Among all royal forces* there are standards called *mahee* and *mooratib*. *Mahee* (fish) derives its name from the circumstance of the figure of the head of a fish, made of silver or gold, being fixed on the top of a long pole, which is decorated with a *tash* or *moqeish doputta* from top to bottom; and *mooratib* is any one of the *ullums* (crests) similarly fastened to a bamboo, and decorated with *tash* and *badla*, *moqeish* and *zurbuft*, shawl, *tafta*, or white cloth. These, mounted on elephants, are carried at the head of the regiment, and are meant for colours.

In like manner, at the *Mohurrum* they form *ullums* intended to be fac-similes of Hosein's banner, and to these the people of Hindoostan have given the names of particular martyrs. Thus they have the *punja-e-Hydur*, alias *Hyduree punja* (Hydur's† palm *i. e.* of the hand); *punja-e-moortooza Allee* (the palm, or fist, of Allee the chosen†); *punja-sher-e-khoda* (the palm of the lion of God†); *punja-e-muzhurool ajaeb* (the palm of the displayer of wonders†); *punja-e-mooshkil koosha* (the palm of the disperser of difficulties†); *Beebee ka ullum*, or *ullum-e-Beebee Fateema* (Lady Fatima's standard); *Hoseinee ullum*, or *Hoseinee surwur* (the Hoseinee standard or leader); *ullum-e-Abbas*, or *Abbas-e-ullumdar* (Abbas, the standard-bearer); *ullum-e-qasim*, *ullum-e-Allee-akbur*, and *ullum-e-usgur* (these are likewise called *Eemam-zaday*, priest-born); *ullum-e-doazda*

* *i. e.* Of Indian princes. † Different names of Allee.

Eemam, (the twelve *Eemams*, or chief-priests); *ullum-e-Eemam zamin; d'hal sahib; burzukhee* or *qoodruttee ullum; zoolfuqqar* (or double-bladed sword of Allee, originally *Mohummud's*); *nal sahib.*

These *ullums* are generally made of copper, brass, or steel, occasionally of gold or silver, and even set with precious stones; and *nal sahib*, besides, of paper or wood.

Those made of metal, whether new ones, or old ones given to be cleaned and burnished, are brought in pomp and state on trays, accompanied with music, from the goldsmith's house to the *ashoor-khanas*, in each of which, four, five, six, or seven are set up. They are fixed on sticks or staffs, which are occasionally of silver, though generally of wood, and decked out in clothes;* and on the first, fourth, or fifth evening of the moon, stuck up in holes made in the floor, or are fastened on stools, and in front of them are placed lights, *moorch'huls*,† *oodsoz*,‡ toys, &c.; and sometimes on one side is a representation of the foot of the Messenger, called *Qudum-e-russool* (*vide* page 234.). At the time of setting up the *ullums*, while burning incense, they offer *fateeha* in the name of the martyrs, over sugar or *shurbut*, and then distribute them to both rich and poor. In like manner, every evening they make *fateeha* and *khutum-e-qorân*.§ and adorn the *punjay* with flowers. *Fu-*

* "These are in the shape of a long scarf of usually white muslin, "but sometimes of rich silk of bright florid colours, forming an agreeable variety, some being blue, purple, green, yellow, &c. embroidered "very deep at the ends, which are furnished with gold and silver "bullion fringes. It is caught together near the middle and tied "with rich gold and silver cords and tassels to the top of the staff, "just under the head or crest."—Mrs. Meer H. Ali. These dresses of the *Ullums* are called *dhuttees*.

† Fans for driving away flies.

‡ Utensils for burning *ood*, as a perfume.

§ *Khutum*, a reading through of the entire *Qoran*. For the method of doing it, vide chap. xxxix.

qeers of various descriptions are in attendance. In the morning they only read the *Qoran*, and sit up all night reading the *Rowzut oosh Shohuda* (Book of Martyrs), or reciting *murseea nowh* (mournful dirges), and make lamentations, beating their breasts. Should Providence have blessed them with the means, then either in the morning or in the evening, or at both periods, they have *k'hichree* cooked without meat, and *shurbut* prepared; and having offered *fateeha* over these in the name of Eemam Hoosnein, they partake of these themselves, as well as distribute them among the poor.

Every night *murseea khwanee* (the recitation of funeral eulogiums) takes place in the *ashoor-khana* of some one or other. They train up for the purpose, boys possessing musical voices, invite their friends, *fuqeers*, and numerous spectators to hear them; and hold *shub-baydaree* (nocturnal vigils). The day is spent at each *ashoor-khana* in reading the *Qoran*. From the first to the seventh *k'hun*, with the exception of the above-mentioned *fateeha, durood, khutum-e-Qoran, Murseea*, preparing victuals, *shurbut*, &c. nothing takes place.*

On the seventh *k'hun* (and by the ignorant on the seventh day of the month), the *ullum-e-qasim-e-shuheed*, distinguished by having a little silver or gold umbrella fixed on

---

* By Mrs. M. H. Ali's account, (vol. i. p. 57.) it would appear that at Lucknow the banners are taken out of the *ashoorkhanas* or *emambaras* on the fifth day, and conveyed in solemn procession to a particular *durgah* situated in the suburbs of that city, for the purpose of being consecrated, which is done by touching with them the original crest of Hosein's banner, deposited there. The order of procession of one of the *Ullums*, and that of a rich man, she describes with great minuteness and accuracy; justly adding, that some are more splendid than others, and that the very poor people parade their banners with perhaps no other accompaniment than a single drum and fife, and the owner supporting his own banner.

his head, makes his debut out of doors in the afternoon.* He is borne by a man on horseback, accompanied with music, &c.; but instead of the dancing-girls who are present, singing songs, they repeat *murseea nowh* (funeral eulogiums); and making lamentations, beating upon their breasts, proceed to the places desired. If they cannot afford a horse for the *ullum*, a man on foot carries it, running every now and then, reeling to and fro like a drunken man, pretending to be distracted with grief; while many run after him like so many madmen, all exclaiming aloud *doolha! doolha!* (*i. e.* bridegroom! bridegroom!), on account of Qasim's recent marriage before martyrdom.

When the *ullum-e-qasim* meets with any *allawas* on the road, he goes to their *ashoor-khanas*, and having made his obeisance to the *ullums* there, and offered *fateeha* over the smoke of Benjamin, takes his leave.

After having thus gone round his visiting excursion, with a *moorch'hul* waving over him and frankincense burning, he is conveyed home to his own *ashoor-khana*, where they lay him down on a stool. Considering him just to have suffered martyrdom, they cover him up with any description of cloth, and treat him as a real corpse; and as, on the death of any one, they are wont to strike their heads and beat their breasts, so, in like manner, they weep sometimes for the deceased and lament his loss. After having offered *fateeha* over two or three earthen pots of *shurbut*, termed *run ka shurbut* (the war-lemonade), they

* "This night is called the night of *Maynhdee* in some parts of the "country, where they have a public display, intending to represent "the marriage ceremony, so called, for *Qasim*, who was married to "the favourite daughter of Hosein on the morning of the celebrated "battle. On this night they have the same showy parade which dis-"tinguishes the *Maynhdee* procession of a real wedding ceremony." Mrs. M. H. Ali, vol. i. p. 74.

distribute it among such attendants and spectators as partake of Moosulman food and drink. They then go away, and the landlord sets up the *ullum* again in its place.

On the seventh *k'hun*, in the forenoon or afternoon, they also take out the *neeza* (spear) on its peregrination. The *neeza* is a lance or spear, which they dress up with clothes, leaving two *shumlay** waving in the air, and fix a lime on the top of it, emblematic of Hosein's head, which was thus carried by Ayzeed's order through different cities on the point of a javelin (vide p. 168). Some substitute a thin bamboo for the spear, on which they wind a turban-cloth, and near the top of it, below the lime, fasten a split bamboo bow across, to the two extremities of which they sometimes suspend a couple of swords; and above the bow they generally wind, for the sake of ornament, red and white, or black and white cloth, in a spiral form. Accompanied with music, *fuqeers*, &c. they walk about with it from house to house, begging. The people of the house first throw one or two pots of water on the *neeza*-bearer's feet, and then make him a present of a rupee, fanam, or pice, or a little grain. The *moojawir* (attendant of the *ashoor-khana*) with his own hands takes some *eebodee*, or the ashes of the *ood-dan*, and gives it to him: he receives it with great devotion, and applies it to his own eyes as well as to those of his children; and sometimes even eats a little, and makes them eat of it. After that they bring it home and stick it up in front of the *ashoor-khana;* and when the *taboots* and *ullums* are taken out, the *neeza* is carried in front of them. There is one of these at each *ashoor-khana*.

---

* *Shumlay*, the worked or embroidered end of a turban or *kummurbund*, sometimes tucked into the folds and sometimes left flying loose.

In the evening of that day they take out the *Beebee ka ullum*, *Hoseinee ullum*, *nal-sahib*, and *zoolfuqqar*, accompanied with flambeaux, as before, repeating *murseea-nowh*, making lamentations after the same fashion as has been detailed in the case of *ullum-e-qasim*, but without the horse.

Nal-sahib (vulgo *nalsab*; literally Mr. Horse-shoe) is made of gold, silver, steel, copper, brass, or other metals; or, what is more common, of wood or paper besmeared with *sundul*, of a somewhat larger size* than a common horse-shoe. With this (as an emblem of Hosein's swift horse), they run most furiously, frequently upsetting infirm men, women, and children, to the infinite diversion of the by-standers, who quiz them (the sufferers) into the bargain. Some, through ignorance, construct with cloth something of a human shape, and substitute the shoe for its head. Many people take a long thin bamboo, like a fishing-rod, wind round it any two kinds of paper, pasting them over its whole length, and on the upper end of it fix an *aftab-geeree* (parasol), consisting of a fan in the shape of a *peepul*-leaf, to ward off the rays of the sun. The fan is made of coloured paper, tinsel, or mica, with a fringe all round, prettily constructed with one or three *moorch'huls* tied to the point of it; and they fasten a rope or two which reaches to the ground close to the *aftab-geeree*. Resting the lower end of the bamboo on the *kummurbund*, they support it with one hand while they balance it by means of the rope with the other, and thus run with *Nal-sahib's* cavalcade. When it is too heavy for one, other two men assist him in balancing it, by means of two ropes acting like the stay of a ship's mast. Whenever he halts, they lower the *aftab-geerees* and shake them over his head; and in their eagerness to do so, they very

* Sometimes a foot long.

often strike them against one another, by which they are broken. Many do this, after their wishes have been accomplished, to fulfil vows (vide *Nuzur-o-nyaz*, chap. xxvii.) which they may have made.

Sometimes a woman makes a vow to *Nal-sahib*, saying, "Should I, through your favour, be blessed with offspring, "I shall make it run with your equipage." Should it so happen that she afterwards brings forth a child, she accordingly puts an *aftab-geeree* into its hand when it attains the seventh or eighth year of its age, and causes it to run along with the cavalcade. The rich make their children run only a short distance, and then let servants run for them; whereas the poor are wont to run themselves; and some with swords and shields, or only with sticks, run round and round the procession. A greater crowd accompanies it than any other.

In short, in this way, on the evening of the eighth *k'hun*, they take out the *burzukhee*, alias *qoodruttee ullum*; and on the following night (the ninth) the *Abbas ka ullum* and *Hoseinee ullum*.

The day for taking out the various *ullums* differs in a trifling degree in different countries. If two *ullums* on their mounted excursions meet one another on the road, they mutually embrace (or rather the men cause them to touch), and having offered *fateeha*, after burning incense they pass on.

On the tenth *k'hun* all the *ullums* and *taboots* (except the *ullum-e-qasim*) carried on men's shoulders, attended by *fuqeers* of every description, perform *shubgusht* (nocturnal perambulation) in great pomp and state; the lower orders in the evening, and the higher at midnight. On that night the streets are illuminated, and every kind of sport takes place. Among others is an exhibition of the phantasmagoria or magic-lantern kind, in which the shadows of the figures fall on a white cloth skreen, representing battles, &c., which attracts crowds of people to the spot. In short, the whole town is awake that night, and presents one general scene of noise, bustle, tumult, and confusion.

The *taboot* alias *tazeea* (or bier) is a frame-work of bamboo in the shape of a mausoleum, (intended to represent the one at the plain of Kurbulla erected over the remains of Hosein,) made with a sort of net-work of paper nicely clipped (sometimes with plates of mica on the back,) and pasted to it. It is further ornamented with different kinds of coloured paper, formed into various devices, tinsel fringes, &c., with a dome, which is sometimes so contrived as to move round at the slightest breath of air. When the whole is lighted up within and without, it has a beautiful appearance. It is a square edifice, its sides varying from two to fourteen cubits, and the proportion of its height is half as much again as that of one of its sides (vide Plate I. fig. 1). Within it are placed *ullums*, or a couple of little artificial tombs, intended to represent those of Hussun and Hosein. Some, instead of the net-work paper about the *taboot*, construct it by tying *bunggreean* to one another, and over the places where they touch, fasten various kinds of flowers made of white paper; and behind the *bunggrees* they tie red (*koossoom*-coloured) cloth, or paste red paper. When lighted up, it has a very pretty appearance. This is termed *bunggreeun-ka-taboot*.

Others again, instead of using the paper net-work, make it of flowers and leaves formed of wax of various colours, so admirably executed as to resemble natural roses and tuberoses;* which the people view with astonishment.

* Polyanthus tuberosa.—*Lin.*

When it is carried about on the *shub-gusht* night, they squirt water on it by means of syringes, to prevent its melting by the heat of the torches and blue-lights. With the beautiful effect produced by the reflection of the torches and blue-lights, it is not unlike a *chumum* (parterre) with flowery shrubs in full bloom. This is called *mom ka taboot* (or wax *taboot*).

Some construct a *tazeea*, consisting of a representation of the *Mudeena nuqsha* (Medina picture), which is a fac-simile of the Prophet's mausoleum there. This they ornament variously with gilding and enamelling, and so beautifully, that by candle-light it has a very splendid appearance. It is so elegantly formed that the spectators never tire of viewing it.

The generality of people conceiving it to be an exact resemblance of the Prophet's tomb, proceed eagerly to the spot to obtain a glimpse of it. Instead of the net-work on the *taboots*, some people substitute cloth, and by dabbing it over with earth get *surson* (mustard-seed) to vegetate on it, which makes the *taboot* look by candle-light as if it were entirely formed of emerald. In the same way, they sometimes construct and erect a camel, *punjay*, and *ullums* with *surson*, and some make an artificial *chumbaylee kay mundwa*, uncommonly well executed, in imitation of the *chumbaylee* (jasmine) creeper on a *mundwa* (shed); and as they carry this about on the *shuhadut*-day, people throw *gujray* on it as it passes along the streets.*

* In short, the *tazeea* is formed, as Mrs. Meer observes, "of every "variety of materials, from the purest silver down to bamboo and "paper. Some have them of ivory, ebony, sandal-wood, cedar, &c." and she has seen some beautifully wrought in silver filigree. The handsomest, to her taste, is in the possession of his Majesty the king of Oude, composed of green glass with brass mouldings, manufactured in England.

Some, instead of a *taboot*, erect a *shah-nusheen* (royal seat), alias *dad-muhal* (palace of justice). This, like the *taboot*, is constructed of bamboos, paper, tinsel, &c., and in shape somewhat resembling a palace. It is placed against the wall, and *ullums* are set up therein. It has sometimes in each corner a transparency in the form of a table-shade, whirled round with the least breath of air, and hence its name, *churkhee fanoos* (revolving-shade).* These shades are at times made apart and placed in front of the *shah-nusheen*. Some also construct around the *taboots* and *ullums*, or set up separately in the *ashoor-khanas*, what they call *tutteean*,† made of *ubruk* (mica) and mercury, which glitter and shine with great splendour by the reflection of the light. When blue-lights are burnt before them they present such an elegant appearance that it baffles description: it can only be credited on ocular demonstration. Many hundreds of thousands of rupees are annually expended in the construction of these *tuttees*: in the city of Hydrabad they are particularly in vogue. Some erect in the *ashoor-khanas* artificial *mango*, pine-apple, custard-apple, and other trees, so beautifully formed that they appear like real trees laden with blossoms and fruits; and on these they have likewise representations of different species of birds and squirrels, in the act of eating the fruits. Crowds of people assemble to see them, and view them with astonishment; for they resemble real trees, birds, and animals. Sometimes they set up human figures of different kinds, of various colours and shapes. Some, for instance, are

* Also termed *fanoos-e-kheeal;* a lantern which revolves by the smoke of the candle within, and has on the sides of it figures of various animals, &c. For these see Plate I. fig. 2 and 2.

† *Tutteean.* Frameworks containing square pieces of *mica* made into looking glasses.

represented as in the act of praying, or of going through the different forms of sitting, standing, and prostration; one, in the character of a *sepoy*, appears as sentinel, with his musket on his shoulder, walking up and down, keeping watch; one sitting, moves his head backwards and forwards;* another saluting (*i. e.* making *sulam*). Near to these, again, they also place artificial birds and animals; such as *buglay* (paddy-birds), *myna* (martins), parroquets; also snakes, ducks, cats, dogs, &c.; and, by some ingenious contrivance, an artificial dove comes every now and then out of its cage, and after cooing awhile like a real dove, he walks into it again. In some *allawas*,† on a raised *chubootra*, they set up a large doll or female figure, made of cloth or wood, dressed up as a female, and place a *chukkee* (hand-mill) before her: she taking hold of the handle of it with one hand, and putting wheat or rice into it with the other, goes through the operation of grinding. As the flour accumulates round the mill the proprietor removes it.

Sometimes they take a cucumber, a water-melon, or a green plantain, and having pierced it through near its centre with a couple of sharp knives, with their cutting edges inclined from one another, pointing upwards and downwards, they suspend the one by its two ends to a beam or rafter, whilst they attach a stone weighing ten or twelve *seers* (twenty or twenty-four pounds) to the other; and strange as it may seem, the knives do not divide this very succulent vegetable.

On the night of the 7th of the month *Mohurrum*, the *boorâq*, made of wood, about two or three feet high, beautifully painted and decorated, with such neck, arm, nose,

---

* As Moosulmans are wont to do in the act of reading.

† *Ashoor-khanas*, in common conversation, are called *allawas;* because the latter are in front of them.

and ear-jewels and head ornaments as are usually worn by Moosulmans, is brought from the painter's house, accompanied by lighted torches, *murseea-nowh*-reciters, &c. to the *ashoor-khana*, where it is placed before the *ullums* facing forwards. This is intended to be a fac-simile of the *boorâq*, or horse,* which the Almighty sent from heaven by the angel Jibreel (Gabriel), to convey to him his highness Mohummud Moostuffa (the peace, &c.) on a visit. The description of this animal is as follows:—He had the head and face of a man; ears long; forehead broad, and shining like the moon; eyes black, like those of a deer, and brilliant as the stars; neck and breast of a swan; loins of a lion; tail and two wings of a peacock; stature of a *sooreea-gaee* or of a mule; speed of *burq* (lightning): hence the derivation of its name, *booraq*.

Many of the Hindoos have such faith in these *taboots*, *ullums*, *booraqs*, &c. that they even erect them and likewise become *fuqeers*. And if any fighting and bloodshed take place between the two *castes*† during the *Mohurrum*, the Hindoos who have turned Mohummudan *fuqeers* take the part of the Moosulmans and fight against the people of their own caste; nor do they, during that period, partake of any animal food that has not been regularly made *zubuh*, or sacrificed according to the Moosulman rites (vide *zubuh*, Glossary).

---

* Or an ass, according to some authorities. Plate I. fig. 1.

† As was the case at Cuddapah in 1821; when owing to the greatest feast of each of the two castes, *viz.* the *Mohurrum* of the Mohummudans, and the *Dusserah* or *Churruck Pooja* of the Hindoos, occurring on the same day, neither would give way and many were killed. It may here be remarked, that agreeably to Moosulman custom, their feast can *not* be deferred; whereas that of the Hindoos may, and they may be bribed to postpone their's to a more convenient season.

During the thirteen days of the *Mohurrum* festival, Moosulmans keep their dwellings and garments remarkably neat and clean, and their bodies pure and undefiled. They even refrain from conjugal embraces; and what is also extraordinary, some from the first, others from the fourth, fifth, sixth, or seventh day of the moon till the ninth, prohibit themselves even the use of meat and fish, *betel*-leaf, and sleeping on a bed. Should they sleep on a cot, it is turned topsy turvy; and for this reason, that it would be disrespectful in them to sleep on an elevation, when their *Eemams* (priests) are standing on the ground. On the tenth some partake of these enjoyments; but others abstain from the tenth to the thirteenth day.

From the fifth *k'hun*, at every *ashoor-khana*, the nobility in front of their *dewan-khanas*, merchants at their gates, and shopkeepers before their shops, have *abdar-khanas* (places where water is kept for drinking), nicely decorated with a cloth ceiling, and other ornamental contrivances. There they dispense milk, *shurbut*, water cooled and scented, to all the people; and at night have illuminations, &c. at these places.

On the fifth *k'hun*, almost all people, men and women, old and young, put on a *sylee** or *gujra*, especially unmarried people, who are particularly fond of it: the married seldom wear them. Married women are not allowed to show their faces to their husbands during the ten days of the first *Mohurrum* after marriage, at which time they are

---

* *Sylee* is emblematic of the dress of the real *Banwa-fuqeers* who are said to have turned *fuqeers* through grief for Hussun and Hosein. They have it made of hair; whereas, on this occasion, it is made of thread, green or red, the former to represent the green colour of Hussun's body, rendered so, soon after his death, by the effects of the poison; the latter the blood with which Hosein's body was imbued when slain in the field of battle.

kept apart from one another. They observe the same custom during the *tayra tayzee* (first thirteen days of the month *Sufur*) as also during the days of the *bara wufat*, from the first until the *oors**-day (in the month *Rubbee-oos-sanee*); for these days are esteemed evil, and no pleasure or enjoyment should take place during them. The learned consider such things unlawful and never wear them.

It is undoubtedly unlawful and contrary to the Mohummudan law; but so it is, that in Hindoostan they attend more to these customs than to the (*furz*) divine commands. I mean, such as applying *ubeer* to the faces of children, putting on them green dresses, such as *jamas*, *ungurkhas*, or *koortas*, and wearing these themselves. The nobility, as well as the respectable among the middling classes of people, content themselves with merely tying a *sylee* or *gujra* round their wrists.

Description of the Mohurrum Fuqeers.

Of these there are many varieties, most of whom attire themselves in their new garb on the fifth *k'hun*; a few on the second; and still fewer on the sixth or seventh. These I shall separately notice; and

1st. The *Sylee wala* (vulgo *Suhaylee wala*), or those who wear a *sylee* (a necklace of coloured† thread worn by *fuqeers*).

Attaran (perfumers) and *putway* (makers of fringe and tape) manufacture for the occasion red and green *sylee*, alias *anteo* (a necklace of a skein of thread), as well as bracelets, termed *soomurun* and *gujra*, beautifully ornamented with gold and silver thread, which are purchased; but

---

* Vide *Oors*, Glossary.

† *Sylees* of flowers are worn on other occasions.

previous to putting them on, they place together with them on a tray, some sweetmeat, and *maywa* (*viz. choorway*, sugar, and *phootanay*), and a *churagee;* and having offered *fateeha* over them, they first put a small *antee* around the *shudday's* neck, and then, either there or after going home, wear them round their necks and wrists. If the *gujra* be worn only on one hand, it is invariably on the right; the *soomurun* is always on the right only. Their dress is the usual one. The *moojawir* after the *fateeha* helps himself to the *churagee* and some of the fruits, and returns the rest.

In addition to the above, some old and young people tie a piece of green cloth on both the upper arms.

Some of these *fuqeers* apply *ubeer* to their faces; and holding an *ood buttee* (benjamin pastile) lighted in their hands, go out abegging.

2. *Banuwa* (prop. *bay nuwa*, *i. e.* indigent,) *fuqeeran*. They are distinguished by the following dress. They wear on the head a *topee* (*fuqeer's taj* or cap), a *sylee*, a shawl, or a gold *mundeel;* on the neck, a *kufnee* or an *alfa*, red, green, or white, and a *sylee*, *tusbeeh* (see Glossary), and *kuntha;* on the wrists, a *soomurun* or *gujra;* round the waist, a *loong*, *dhotee*, or *lunggote;* and round the right ankle, a *dal* or a silver *tora*, or nothing at all. They apply *ubeer* to the face, and carry in the hand a fan or *ch'hurree* (a switch), a sword, or *sang* (a javelin wholly composed of iron).

The *fuqeers* of this class have a distinct *guroh* (band) among themselves, with different ranks and denominations, thus: 1. a *moorshud* or *sur-guroh* (chief of the troop), whom they all agree to obey. Under him there is, 2. a *khuleefa*, who stands in the same relation to him as a minister to a king; 3. a *b'hundaree shah*, a house-steward who has charge of the storehouse, or distributer; 4. an *iznee shah*, to call and assemble the people and convey orders (an aide-de-camp?); 5. an *adalut shah*, to direct the order of movements; 6. a *kotwal*, to keep order and discipline; 7. a *dost*, the friend; 8. an *al hookm-e-lillah* (literally, God is the judge); 9. an *al-umr-e-lillah*, commander; 10. a *nuqeeb-ool-foqra*, whose business it is to proceed in front of the troop, and proclaim the praises and attributes of the Deity, as an injunction to the other *fuqeers*.

On arriving at an *ashoor-khana*, the troop of *fuqeers*, drawing themselves up in two or three lines in front of it, the *dost* calls out his own name "*dost*;" the *kotwal* answers "*hur-chay-ruza-ay-ost*."* Then the *al-hookm-e-lillah*† from the right flank calls out his own name twice, and from the left *al-umr-e-lillah* re-echoes his name twice. After, the *adalut shah* repeats the *fateeha kay durja*‡ alone with a loud voice, and at the conclusion calls out the word "*fateeha*;" when all the *fuqeers* repeat the *soora-e-alhumd*§ once, and the *qool-hoo-allah*|| three times, and read the *durood*, and finish by drawing their hands over their faces. Then the *adalut shah* (lawgiver) repeats sentences or couplets which have reference to the excellence of his own profession—the law,—and then bawls out the following exclamations: "*Ek-nara-e-hyduree*;" ¶ when the rest resound "*Ya-hoo!*"** Again, the former calls out "*ek nara-e-punjutun!*"†† they all exclaim "*ya hoo!*" "*ek nara-e-char-yar-e-basuffa!*"‡‡

* "What pleases Him," *i.e.* the Almighty.

† Which, like *Al-umr-e-lillah*, signifies, "the command is from God."

‡ Or introductory part of the *fateeha*.

§ Chap. i. *Qoran*.

|| Chap. cxii. *Qoran*.

¶ An exclamation to Hydur.

** *O He!* (*i.e.* God).

†† A call to the five, *i.e.* Mohummud, Allee, Fateema, Hussun, and Hosein.

‡‡ A call to the four virtuous friends, *viz.* Aboo Bukur, Oomur, Oosman, and Allee.

the rest call out "*ya hoo!*" "*ek nara-e-shuheedan-dusht-e-kurbulla!*"* they reply "*ya hoo!*" After that the *adalut shah*, having repeated the following hemistich, remains silent, viz. "*ya hoo ya mun hoo la-il-la-ha il-lul-la-ho:*"† the band of *fuqeers* reply, "*wuh do-hoo la shureeku lú hoo o ush-hud-do-un'na Mohum'mudoon ubdu-hoo oomdu-hoo' o russool-lu-hoo.*"‡ Then the *adalut shah* repeats this line, "*arzoo darum kay khákayan qudum.*"§ The band answer, "*foo-tee-â-ay, chusm-e-sázum, dum-bu-dum.*"||

As they proceed, the *nuqeeb ool foqra* calls out "*hosh bur-dum; nuzur bur qudum; suffur dur wutun; khilwut dur anjomun. Bu-fuzul-e punjutun. Ya allee mudud.*"¶

If this band of *fuqeers* sit at any *ashoor-khana*, the proprietor of it treats them with a *hooqqa*, *tumbakoo* (tobacco), *shurbut*, cloves, and cardamoms; and if he can afford it, entertains them with *k'hichree*.

Those *dus-masee*, or ten-month-*fuqeers* (so called because for ten *days*) speak and converse in the same style as the real *fuqeers* or devotees, who are termed *bara-masee*, or twelve-month-*fuqeers*, because they continue so from one

* An exclamation to the martyrs of the plain of Kurbulla.

† "O God, thou art the only true God, and there is none else."

‡ "He is One and there is not another with him, and I give true "witness that the man Mohummud is his faithful servant sent by him."

§ Grant me the dust, beneath that foot which lies,

|| As a collyrium to adorn mine eyes.

¶ Literally "guard your breath;" *i. e.* have always God's name on your lips. "Keep your eyes on your feet;" *i. e.* whilst walking, constantly repeat the *kulma.* (*a*) "Travel sitting at home;" *i. e.* let your mind contemplate God and his works. "In assemblies converse with your beloved;" *i. e.* in all places, even in a crowd, have sweet communion with God. "By the grace of the Punjutun. O Allee! Assist."

(*a*) This consists in four words which the pious invariably repeat over and over when walking, and revolve in their minds one word at every step they take. The words are, 1st. *Lah*, 2d. *Il-lah-hah*, 3d. *Il-lay*, 4th. *Lah*.

end of the year to the other. Among themselves they call one another by the name of "*eea hadee allah*;" "*eea moorshud allah*," "*eea hosein*," "*eea eemum*;" and if they call one, or address him, they say, "*bawa!*" or "*data!*" or "*dooneea-dar!*" "What! will you not give the *fuqeers* some *kowra-kowree** (money) to purchase *soombool* (arsenic—their food)?" *Fuqeers* technically denominate rupees *kowra-kowree*. If any one does not give them something, they repeat the following couplet:

Data thay so mur gy-ay, ruh-gy-ay mukk'hee choos;
Dayna-layna kooch nu-heen, lurnay ko mowjood.

The gen'rous all are dead and gone,
And niggard churls remain alone;
Of charity we hear no more,
But struggling each to swell his store.†

When they are about to depart from any place, the *nuqeeb-ool-foqra* repeats the following couplet:

Ugur gaytee, sur-a-sur, bad geerud,
Churag-e-Mooqbillan hurgiz numeerud.

Were this vast universe one blast of rushing air,
The lamp of God's elect would burn undying there.‡

and after, calls out "*shakir ko shukur, moonkir ko* "*tukkur*."§ Then the band reply, "*rah e-mowla deen-e-pygumbur*."‖

---

* *Kowra* literally means a large shell; *kowree* a small one.

† Literally,
"The generous are all dead, misers are only left;
"There is no giving or taking, but they are e'er ready to fight."

‡ Lit. "Were the whole universe filled with wind, it could not "possibly extinguish the light (*i. e.* the offspring) of the Elect."

§ Literally, "sugar to the believing (*i.e.* grateful worshipper), and a "thump to the unbelieving;" *i. e.* may the benevolent be rewarded, and those who deny us be punished; or, blessings be to the charitable and curses to those who refuse us.

‖ "We are on the road to heaven, and our religion is that of the "Prophet."

These *fuqeers* go about repeating and acting as above described.

3. *Mujnoon*.* The dress is as follows: on the head, a fool's-cap, or a long sugar-loaf paper cap, having a queu behind, made of slips of paper, trailing along the ground, beautifully ornamented with gold-leaf, &c. Sometimes the cap is made with panes of glass all round, in the form of a lantern, having suspended on the outside of it shreds of *baygur* (tinfoil) or tinsel, or white and red net-worked paper. They put a lighted wax-candle inside of it, and wearing it at night, walk about: it has a pretty appearance. Instead of a cap they sometimes wear a shawl or red *doputta*, or any other cloth; others again have ripe lemons threaded dangling all round the head. Round the neck, a red, yellow, black, or white *doputta* is twisted, and worn in the form of a *budd'hee* or *heemael*, or a shawl or handkerchief passed through rings. The body is besmeared with *sundul* or *k'hurree* (pipe-clay). On each arm two or three handkerchiefs are tied, with their ends dangling, and sometimes a *bazoo-bund* over one of them. Round the waist is a *goorgee* (breeches) or *loonggee*. In their hands they carry a *korla* (prop. *kora*) cat-o-one (thick) tail, a *kut'har* or dagger, a sword, a *bich'hwa* (sort of dagger), a *maroo*, or two antelope-horns joined at their base, a *sang* (a javelin all of iron), a *qumchee* (whip), or a *ch'hurree* (switch). On the legs is a *g'hoongroo* or *g'hântee*. Some also having fixed limes to the points of a couple of *bich'hway*, fasten one on each arm.

Thus equipped, they proceed to each *ashoor-khana* and dance in a circle (which dance is termed *ghoomna*, or whirling), and keep step to the music of the *duff*. (Append. Mus.

* Literally, "Frantic," the name of a famous lover, whose mistress was Lyla (p. 195): the Abelard and Heloise of the East.

Instr.) The figure of the dance consists in four motions, to which they keep time by repeating the following words protracted in the utterance "*allee! allee! allee! b'hum!*"*

4. *Lyla*, the wife of (the preceding) *Mujnoon*. Among the *Mujnoon* set of *fuqeers* there is one to represent Lyla, whose dress is as follows: He has the whole surface of his body, from head to foot, glued over with cotton; even the cloth which he wears in the form of a *lunggote* around his waist (the only dress he has) undergoes the same operation. In his hands he holds a cup, sometimes full of *sundul* or *shurbut*, or a man's skull-cup, a cocoa-nut shell, or a turtle *chippa* (calipash) and a fan or paper nosegay. On the head he wears a three-cornered paper cap.

5. *B'hurrung*. This man's whole body is besmeared with *lal gayroo* (red ochre) mixed with water. He ties a shawl, handkerchief, or any coloured cloth on the head with a small flag fixed on the top; and like the *mujnoons* he wears *heemaels* (shoulder-belts) of *doputtas*. On his loins or legs are *g'hoong-roo*, *ghanteean*, or *zung* and *goorgee* (breeches). He girds his loins well, and in dancing, kicks his posteriors with his heels, calling out "*Allee! Allee!* "*Allee! zung!*"

6. *Mullung*. Their head-dress consists of a knob or knot on one side made with the hair or cloth, passed through a *chukkur*,† around which they twist red thread, *kinnaree*,‡ or *got'ha*.§ On each wrist are two or four *kurray*

* *B'hum*, or *Bhoom*, a corruption of *g'hoom* (*i. e.* go round).

† *Chukkur*, a weapon (resembling a quoit in size and shape), used principally by the *seeks* (sikhs) consisting of an iron ring, which they throw with great dexterity. They carry it about them on the head placed on the top of their turbans.

‡ *Kinnaree*, broad gold or silver lace.

§ *Got'ha*, narrow gold or silver lace.

(metallic bracelets*). The edge of a handkerchief (*gooloo-bund*) is passed under one arm and the two upper ends fastened over the opposite shoulder, and a *sylee, kunt'ha, mala*, and *tusbeeh* are put round the neck. A *kummur-bund* of any kind of cloth encircles the waist; a *lungota* is passed round the loins, and on the right ankle is a *dal* or *tora*.

These men likewise roam about, visit the *ashoor-khana*, and moving their hands, rattle the *kurray*; and so doing call out "*Kurk shah mudar!*"† or "*Kurk hoo!*"‡ Then one of the *mullungs* repeats the following couplet:

> *Hurchu daree, surfkoon dur rah-e hoo,*
> *Lun tunaloo'l buru huta tunfuqoo;*
>
> Let all your wealth to pious works be given,
> What's sown in charity is reaped in Heaven.§

then all the rest sing out in reply, "*Kurk deen!*" ||

7. *Anggayt'hee shah* (or king Chafing-dish). His garb is as follows, *viz.*: the head bare, or a *sylee* wound round it; a *lunggotee* round the loins, and an iron chain for a waist-belt. The body is rubbed over with *k'hurree* (pipe-clay) or *bhubhoot* (cow-dung ashes); and he carries in one hand a *dust-punna* (or pair of tongs).

He walks about with an *anggaythee* or chafing-dish; *i. e.* a fragment of an earthen vessel held on the palm of his hand, kindling and blazing a fire, in which he heats one end of an iron chain, while the other end, with a rope fastened to it, hangs outside. Thus he visits the *ashoor-khanas*; and there holding up the chain by the rope with

---

* Of iron, brass, or copper.

† A call to our saint, Shah Mudar!

‡ A call to Him!

§ Lit. Whatever you have, spend it on the road of Him (in the service of God): they will never obtain any good until they bestow it.

|| A call to religion!

one hand, dips the other into oil, and draws it along the red-hot part; when instantly an immense and sudden blaze is produced, to the great consternation and surprise of the bystanders, who are equally astonished that his hand does not burn by carrying in it so much fire on a thin earthen vessel. The latter, however, he contrives to do, by filling the bottom of the chafing-dish with a mixture of the pulp of aloes and cow-dung, and placing over it ashes, which remain moist under a kindled fire twenty-four hours, and prevent the vessel getting hot.

8. *Siddee* (prop. *syedee*), or African. Ten or twelve men blacken their bodies with lamp-black and oil, to resemble so many negroes. Their dress is as follows. For the head, an ill-shaped cap, made of sheep or goatskin, with the wool or hair on, or of blanket or mat. Round the waist, over a small *lunggotee*, they wear deer or sheepskins with the hair or wool on, blankets, sackcloth, or mats. In the left hand they carry a bow made of bamboo, and in the right a small stick fastened to a cocoanut-shell, containing some gravel covered with white cloth, and sometimes having *ghoongroos* (small bells) also attached to it.

Thus equipped they visit the *ashoor-khanas*, and dance to the rattling of their cocoanut-shells, with the handle of which they strike their bows.

In place of the bow and cocoanut-shell, they sometimes have a *moosul* in the left hand, on which they strike with a stick in the right.

By contorting their mouths, they mimic the talk of negroes, to which the imitation bears a strong resemblance, and they appear to people like real Africans.

Sometimes among their troops one assumes the character of the gentler sex. Her complexion and head-dress is the same as that of the men, but she has a blanket wrapped round her waist, hanging down to the feet, and wears a *cholee* (bodice), and is more particularly distinguished by having an artificial breast dangling down to her knees. She is employed in beating the ground with a *moosul* (or long wooden pestle), while the men, dancing round her, laugh and joke with her.

9. *Bu-go-lay* or *bug-lay* (paddy birds). Ten or twelve men, all of one height, rub the whole of their bodies over with cow-dung ashes, and wear on their heads white paper caps, all of one pattern, and a *lunggota* round the loins.

They go about, holding one another by the waist, imitating the sound of paddy-birds. One of them assumes the character of a *bhyree shah* (king hawk), and every now and then suddenly darts upon the paddy-birds; who instantly crouch or disperse, and conceal themselves behind the people. If they surround any one out of fun, they keep whirling round him and do not allow him to escape. In short they sport like real falcons and herons.

10. *Kuwway shah* (king crow). They besmear their whole bodies with pipe-clay, wear a *jama* made of a blanket and *sylees* on their heads and around their necks; and saying a variety of ludicrous things, walk about each with a cage in his hand, containing a crow, (sometimes also a frog) or carrying a branch of a tree, with a crow fastened to it by the legs.

11. *Hat'h kutoray-walay* (carriers of jugs in their hands). They wear a shawl, *sylee*, or *doputta* on the head, and a *gooloobund* and *kufnee*, or *heemael*, all red, green, or yellow, round the neck. The body or face is besmeared with *sundul*, and they have *gujray* on their wrists; handkerchiefs on their arms; a *loong* round their loins, and a silver *toray* or *dal* round the right ankle.

With a cup in the hand, they go about recounting the

sorrows of the *Mohurrum* before-mentioned, narrating celebrated battles, or reciting eulogiums on individuals. The people, on being pleased with these, drop some money into the cup. These go about in pairs, and moving their cups from side to side, sometimes sing to the following effect:

Pysa day na ray Baboo;
Pysa day na ree Maee:
Pysa day na ray Allah;
Hât'h kutora doodhka.

O God! grant some money;
Good master! some money;
Sweet mistress! some money;
For the milk-jug, my honey!*

or,

Durreea men juhazan chulana;
Deen ka bowta churhana;
Baygee Bungala layna;
Syr kurro Room o Sham ka.

Our ships must sail across the ocean,
Our sacred flag be put in motion.
To seize Bengala's plains combine,
Then march through Rome and Palestine.†

Concluding with the chorus "*Hâth-kutora doodh ka,*" (or the milk hand-jug).

12. *Jullaleean* or *khakeean*. These have no particular dress, but wear fanciful caps of every description, and immense turbans of straw, leather, or mat. On the neck they have rosaries and necklaces made of all sorts of fruits. Some have their faces half blackened. Their bodies are covered all over with pipe-clay; they wear thousands of kinds of garlands around their necks; and sometimes have dried pumpkins hanging suspended from all parts of them.

One of the band carries in his hand a female doll of a

---

* Lit. I say, master, give pice! I say, mistress, give pice! O God, grant some pice! To the carrier of the milk-jug.

† Or rather through Syria and Turkey or the Eastern empire.

hideous form, with which he taunts people by telling them that it is their grandmother; while each of the rest has some leather rolled up in the form of a club, with which they strike every poor man or woman on the head that comes in their way. Thus they go about sporting.

13. *Nuqsha-bundee* (a particular class of *fuqeers* so called). Very few assume this character. Their dress is similar to that of the *Banuwa fuqeers* before mentioned, with two things additional, a *koorta* and an *alfa;* but their characteristic mark is a lamp burning in the hand, and their making their appearance only at night. The lamp is formed into two compartments, the upper one (in the centre) contains the oil; the other is empty, to receive the pice or cowries, or such presents as the charitable are disposed to give. They walk about the lanes and *bazars*, repeating excellent verses in praise of the Deity, and on the anguish of the grave: also rehearsing the innumerable advantages of a light; thus:

Lâkh'ân kuror khurch ka,
Bând'hay uggur muhul,
Khâlee purra ruhayga
Dumree ka nuheen churag.

If on one palace millions you expend,
Without a lamp of half a farthing's cost,
Your edifice is void from end to end,
Its colours blank, its gorgeous beauties lost.

He is generally accompanied by a great number of spectators, men, women, and children. When any one brings a child to him, he applies a little of the burnt wick of his lamp to its forehead or cheek, in order that the child may not cry much and be obstinate.

14. *Hajee Ahmuq and Hajee Bay-wuqoof* (Pilgrim Fool and Pilgrim Idiot). They wear uncommonly long caps on the head; *alfa*, or a large *joobba* and *mala*

round the neck; and each one carries in the hand an enormous sized rosary, a wooden platter, large or small, and an immense long walking-stick. They have a beard reaching down to the navel, mustachios, the hair of the head formed of flax, and enormous artificial paunches; which, visiting the *ashoor-khanas*, they strike against one another; and standing back to back, say their prayers, and stooping, also strike their posteriors together. They hold such comical conversations, and have such ogling with one another, that a person who has not smiled for a dozen years, or is absorbed in religious reverie, will at the very sight of these buffoons, and on hearing their arguments, scarcely be able to refrain from laughing.

15. *Booddha, Booddhee* (an old man and an old woman). A couple of men representing these, sit on a high scaffolding. The old man exhibiting a male countenance painted on cloth fastened to his face, with a long white beard, and a wooden sword in his hand, threatens the spectators below, if any one utter aught against the old woman, his wife. He sits in a state of taciturnity shaking his head; the two every now and then kissing each other. The old woman, also wearing a female mask painted on cloth with a large *nuth* (or ring) suspended to her nose, and imitating the shrill voice of an old woman, keeps chattering a number of such ridiculous things as no one ever heard before. As to the volubility of *Hajee Ahmuq*, &c. they may be said to be children or infants compared to this old woman whose gift of the gab exceeds anything of the kind to be met with among old women in real life, and can only be conceived by hearing her.

16. *Bâgh* (or tiger). They make an artificial figure of a tiger with split bamboos and cover it with cloth painted like its skin, arming his nails with sharp iron claws like

those of that animal. The man entering his cell runs crawling on all fours, playing about in the *bazar*. Or they paint their own bodies in imitation of a tiger, wear a *cholna* and *kach'ha* about the waist, and a chain or rope tied to the loins, with a long bamboo tail supported by two or three men; and walking and running about with a piece of flesh in their mouths, frighten the people. The children run away at the sight of them. If, to witness sport, any person gives one of them a sheep, he throws it down on the ground, and like a real tiger, catches it by the throat with his teeth and sucks its blood; and tearing open its abdomen, he takes out its entrails and even eats a little of its flesh: the people who attend him walking off with the rest. Some make a hollow tiger's head with wood, and insert the head into it, and wear a *shurraee* and *angurk'ha* painted over like the skin of a tiger.

17. *Mutkee Shah.* Four or five of the *jullalee fuqeers* carry each a *mutkee* (small earthen pot) in their hands, containing *chunnay* (Bengal horse-gram), rattling them as they go along. Every now and then they take a handful of the gram and offer it to the people; but the moment any one stretches out his hand to receive it, they put it into their own mouth and point to the heavens.

First one of them repeats some ludicrous verse or other by himself; then the rest join him and repeat the same in chorus.

18. *Chutnee Shah.* His dress is like that of the *jallalee*, but he has a small mortar tied to his loins and a pestle in his hand. Having put into the mortar a little green ginger, garlic, tamarind, *chillies*, sweetmeats, *majoon*, *bhung*, in short any thing eatable, he pounds them, singing, "I am "making *qazee's chutnee!*" "I am making *kotwal's* "*chutnee!*" "I am making *soobuhdar's chutnee!*" "Most

"delicious *chutnee!*" "Bravo, *chutnee!*" and as he sometimes distributes some of it among children, there is generally a great number surrounding him. Occasionally both men and women among the spectators beg some of it and eat it; for being composed of a variety of eatables, it has at the time a very agreeable taste; but when *majoon* or *bhung* is mixed with it, the young and old people, not accustomed to the use of inebriating substances, are so much affected by it, that some lie insensible for hours, while others become incoherent in their speech.

19. *Hukeem* (or physician). His dress is like that of the *banuwa.* He assumes the character of an old sage, and having procured a lean miserable looking *tattoo*,* places on his back upwards of two hundred little bags, with all sorts of seeds, leaves, fruits, flowers, &c. and either takes his seat on the animal or walks alongside of him. Wherever he rests he takes the drugs off the horse; and repeating their names, jocularly descants on the peculiar and excellent virtues of each. For example, holding up a parcel to the spectators, he observes: "This contains an excellent powder "which is a capital laxative; if given to one whose bowels "are regular and who does not require it, it gently opens "them, procuring certainly not more than a hundred "evacuations, and each motion reducing the patient to his "last extremity. By the use of it, not the slightest vestige "of impurity or corruption will remain; nay, the very "intestines themselves will be purged out: but, that is a "matter of not the least consequence. To remedy the "looseness, I shall administer such a bolus, that the dis-"charge will continue even after death." Again: "I "have a pill of such virtue in my possession, given to me

* A very inferior species of horse, bred in the country, value from seven to twenty rupees, *i. e.* from about fourteen to forty shillings.

"by my father on his death-bed, called *jummal akhta*, that "if it be exhibited to a *ba-wuqoof* (sensible man), he will in "a very few minutes be transformed into a *fakhta*, alias "a *bay-wuqoof* (or fool)." And "Here is an *unjun* made of a "seed which his highness my preceptor, *Zad oolla hoo* "*Oomuruhoo*, first of all taught me, named *jummâl gota*:* "a capital application, and an excellent remedy for diseases "of the eye. If you apply the *jummâl gota* to one eye, "instantly both become *lota* (blind). In short, I have "such excellent remedies, that whoever makes use of them "dies even before his appointed time."

In this way he talks ironically, merely for the sake of being listened to. He adds: "The Almighty has endowed "me, to such a wonderful degree, with the knowledge and "skill of the healing art, that into whatsoever house I "enter, *my footsteps* seem to it like the welcome approach "of the angel of death." Should any one say to him, "Doctor Sahib, feel my pulse;" or should the doctor himself offer to do so, he applies some of the down found on the pod of the cowitch† to the end of his fingers, and rubs it on the wrist while in the act of feeling the pulse. The instant it touches the patient's skin, it occasions such an intolerable degree of itching, that by unavoidable scratching swellings are produced. The patient, in distress, inquires of his physician what he has done to him. To which the other replies, "Nothing at all, my child; Almighty God "has blessed me with such powers of working miracles and "cures, that the mere touch of my finger has developed "your malady. Do not be alarmed. I am now about to "apply such a capital embrocation to it, that it will make

* Croton nut. Croton tiglium, Willd.

† Cow-itch or cow-age. Stizolobium pruriens, P. S.

"the artery burst, and cause the blood to flow so freely, "that the moment life becomes extinct the itching will "cease." So saying, he is about to apply something, when the patient alarmed and in a great rage, loads him with abuse and walks off.

20. *Moosafir Shah* (or his majesty the traveller). His dress, &c. is like that of the *bunuwa fuqeers.* He carries a large bag, with a great number of smaller ones in it, containing eatable materials and cooking utensils, together with a mortar and pestle, sieve, furnace, &c. on his back, in imitation of a traveller, visits every *ashoor-khana*, and there makes a display of them. He is so well provided with all the requisites of a traveller that he does not require to go elsewhere for anything. Sometimes going to one of the principal *ashoor-khanas*, i.e. where there is a *surguroh*, he puts down his load, lights a fire and prepares *rotee* or *salun*, and takes and deposits it in presence of the *surguroh*, eating a little of it himself, and distributing some by small portions among the other *fuqeers;* for it is a technical phrase among them

Where'er their bed, there is their seat,
And where they sleep, they cook and eat.

21. *Mogol* (Mogul). His dress is like that of *Hajee Ahmuq*, but he carries in his hand only a rosary and a stick. He has four or five attendants about him, dressed like himself. The names of all of them terminate in *beg:* thus, Gajur Beg,* Shulgum Beg,† Mirchee Beg,‡ Bygun Beg,§ with whom he jocundly converses in a jargon of Persian and Hindee.

22. *Bayaj-khora* (usurer). Their dress is like that of the *jullalee;* only that some have their faces half blackened,

* Lord Carrot. † Lord Turnip. ‡ Lord Chilly, (kyan pepper).
§ Lord Brinzal, or egg plant; solanum melongena, Lin.

others wholly so; and they observe, "I am such a fair "beauty, that I shall be the first individual whom the "Almighty will summon at the day of resurrection; for I "shall be speedily recognized by every one, who will "observe, 'Ah! this is one of God's elect.' As to the "profession of gaining my livelihood by usury, it has "descended to me from my forefathers, and therefore, "should even my own father owe me interest, were it "merely a *cowree*,* I would not permit his corpse to be "buried until the said interest was paid; and if any one "wishes to borrow money from me, let him first pay me the "interest of the same for the period he is desirous of having "the loan of it, and when that time is expired as much "interest again; for God has enjoined in the *Qoran*, that "the face of every man who receives usury shall be turned "black at the day of resurrection,—mine excepted."

He moreover carries a paper in his hand, and looking into it says to every one he meets, "I have a small account "to adjust with you. Look here: on such a day you "borrowed money from me, and have not discharged the "debt; I may remit the principal, but I shall, on no "account, give up the interest."

23. *Moorda furosh* (carriers of the dead). Ten or twelve *jullaleeans* lay an artificial human figure, shrouded, on a country (Indian) cot, with a shoe and a slipper under the head for a pillow; and waving over him a broom for a *moorchhul*, they put some fire on a large piece of a broken *chatty* (earthen pot), or on a plate, and instead of burning incense they burn dried cow or horse-dung, near its head. Weeping and saying many amusing things, they walk about

---

* A *cowree*, from eighty to one hundred of which go to a pice (or halfpenny).

with it through the *bazars*, calling out, "This individual "died without any owner; pray bestow something for its "burial." The people of every house to which they go, anxious to get rid of so disagreeable and inauspicious a sight, instantly give them something as an inducement to depart. Should they not give any thing, but begin to dispute the point, they throw red *chillies*, hair, and all sorts of offensive materials, into the fire on the plate, and placing it before them observe, "This is scent which will refresh "your spirits: smell it well; for it is the odour destined "for you after death." They get vexed at this, and in order to get rid of such an additional annoyance, they hasten to give them a trifle; and these, on the other hand, never depart until they get something.

24. *J'har shah* (king tree). His dress is that of the *jullalee*. He takes a small tree, suspends various kinds of fruits on its branches, ties a crow to it by the legs, and carries it about, calling out, "Take care! crouch down! "for a black owl has made its appearance and devoured "the prince of fruits!" concluding with "*Hât, hât bhu-"goray!*"*

25. *Jogeean* (Hindoo mendicants). Four or five men having rigged themselves out in the garb of Hindoo *jogees* (mendicants), go and remain at the *ashoor-khanas;* and playing upon *seetar, duff, dholkee*, and *khunjeeree*, sing songs, elegies, mournful ditties, and funeral poems, in a beautiful manner.

26. *Buqqal* (a Hindoo shop-keeper). He is dressed like one of that caste, *viz.* on his head a turban; on his forehead streaks of cow-dung ashes, with a spot in the centre, made with a mixture of turmeric and quicklime, or *sundul* and

* An exclamation for driving away birds, &c.

turmeric; to his ears, *pogool* (alias *koondul*) or large Hindoo ear-rings; suspended from his neck, a *zoonar* (Brahminical thread); on his wrists, *kurray* (bangles); on his fingers, gold or silver rings; round his waist, a *kurdora*, and round his loins, a white *punchee*. He carries in his hand an iron style and a bundle of palmyra leaves whereon to write his accounts.

One accompanies him in the uniform of a sepoy, who, ever and anon, beats and threatens him, saying, "Look "here, you fool, you have considerably overcharged me." He, on the other hand, not understanding a word the sepoy says, returns him, in joke, plenty of abuse in his own peculiar phraseology.

27. *Showbala* (or boy). They select an uncommonly pretty boy, deck him out in female apparel of gold or silver tissue, and adorn him with a superfluity of ornaments and jewels, and seat him on a small eminence. While he assumes a very sedate countenance, jesters and buffoons stand below, and say a variety of obscene and ludicrous things, endeavouring to make him laugh, but in vain. Should he, however, betray the slightest symptom of a smile, they instantly drop a curtain to prevent its being perceived by the spectators, and a few minutes afterwards raise it again.

28. *Sur-e-bay-tun, tun-e-bay-sur* (head bodiless; body headless). In some *ashoor-khanas*, one man, by some contrivance, conceals his head under ground or under a country-*cot*, and only displays his body; while another buries his body, and makes his head appear above ground, to represent a decapitated corpse. Between these they place a bloody sword, and sprinkle the spot with a red dye to imitate blood. Sometimes two persons, resembling robbers, are seen there; and a man, acting in the character of a

woman, sits crying and saying, "Robbers have murdered "my brother (or husband); bestow something that I may "go and bury him."

29. *Nuqlee shah* (king Story-teller). His dress is that of the *jullalee*. He keeps about him a dog, a cat, a rat, a crow, and an ass, and relates a number of most amusing anecdotes. A large concourse of people always surround him.

30. *Kummul shah* (king Blanket). Two or three people take each a country-blanket, and having made a hole in it, put their heads through. Advancing forwards, and stepping backwards, they repeat verses replete with ludicrous allusions, such as

Upon my wedding day a good fat cock was slain,
And with two pounds of rice we fed ten thousand men.
A penny was provided for a treat so grand,
And when the bills were paid three farthings left in hand.*
Chorus. Say, how how how? Say how how how? Say how how how?
Why! so so so! why! so so so! why! so so so!

Again:

My doating mother reared me with tenderness in stores;
She decked me in a blanket, and turned me out of doors.

31. *Khogeer shah* (king Saddle). One in the dress of a *jullalee* wears a *khogeer* (a native saddle) round his neck and a red *sylee* wound round his head; and promising a horse to a parcel of boys, calls out, "I am going to get a horse given "you! I am going to get a horse given you!" Six or seven lads, dressed in blankets, or like *jullalees*, call out, following him, "Now he has proved himself a liar! Now he has "proved himself a confounded liar!" He only answers as

* *Lit.* At my marriage was slaughtered one cock:
Half a seer of rice distributed to lak'hs!
At my wedding was said to be expended one pice!
But on settling accounts remained three quarters.

he goes along, "Han! han! (yes, yes), I am going to get a "horse given you!"

Sometimes he repeats verses somewhat to this effect:

In every lane, in every street,
The heaps of sweetmeats rise;
Nose-jewell'd damsels, not less sweet,
View them with longing eyes.*

32. *Shurabee* (a drunkard). He is dressed as a *jullalee* or *banuwa*, having a black *alif* (or letter A thus ا,) marked on his forehead, with a grog-bottle filled with *shurbut* or water in his hand, repeating verses and sentences of the *Qoran* in praise of wine, and imbibing it at the same time in liberal potations. Many of the *Mohurrum* fuqeers sit with him for two or four days together in the same spot, contending and disputing on the subject with much argument and controversy; as in the *Qoran* God has pronounced both drinking wine and eating pork to be unlawful; yet he, declaiming eloquently on the lawfulness of his beverage, helps himself to it. He sometimes wears a leathern *zoonnar* (or Brahminical thread) around his neck.

33. *Qazee*†*-e-Lueen* and *Qazee-e-Bay deen* (the cursed priest and the irreligious priest—that is, the devil's chaplains). They wear a large *alfa*, a leathern cap, and flaxen beard and mustachios, and counting chaplets which they carry in their hands, they disseminate their religious principles and doctrines among the people; but all ironically. Thus: "He that prays, fasts, or gives alms, will be exalted to the seventh hell; he that gets drunk, gambles,

---

* In every lane I traversed, I beheld heaps of *goolgooleean*
And a *nut'h-*(or *Boolaq-*) lady casting at them longing looks.

† *Qazee* signifies a judge or magistrate, civil or ecclesiastical; here the latter only, or rather a priest.

"commits adultery, accepts of usury or bribe, will be "doomed to the seventh heaven."

34. *Nuwwab* (nabob). This man has his whole body wound round with straw, wears an enormous cap or turban of the same material, long flaxen beard and mustachios.

He is mounted on horseback, and has four or five people attached to his train, one of whom carries a chair, another a *hooqqa* (consisting of an earthen vessel with a bamboo fixed to it), and like other great folks, he talks big, and in a peremptory tone delivers his commands to his dependents, while in mounting his horse he frequently tumbles over on the opposite side.

35. *Maykh Shah* (king Tent-peg). He is dressed like one of the *jallalee*, but has a few cords tied round his waist, to the end of one of which a parcel of tent-pins are fastened, trailing along the ground. He carries a tent-peg in one hand and a mallet in the other, and says to every one whom he meets: "If you dare speak, I'll hammer you;—if you "dare stir,—if you dare say 'yes,'—if you dare say "'humph!',—if you dare look at me,—if you dare remain "silent,—I'll hammer you."

36. *K'hodon-garon* (dig and bury). He wears on his head a straw cap or turban encircled with ropes; on his body, a mat with a hole in the middle through which the head is thrust; his waist is entwined with ropes; he carries on his shoulder a spade, and on his back a *tuttee* (or frame).

Thus attired he goes about, saying, "whomsoever I "please, I take hold of, throw down (*k'hodon-garon*), dig "and bury (or *k'hoda gara*), have dug and buried; and "should he speak, I throw a few additional *tuttees* (or "frames) of earth over him. For digging a small grave I "charge a hundred rupees, for a large one, five rupees."

At times he stands still, eulogizing the beauty of his suit

of clothes, saying: "I am decked out in a turban, a *mun-* "*deel*, a *jama* and a *shâl*, and armed with a pickaxe;" as well as a variety of other pleasantries; and through mischief, when he sees a villager, he quickly digs a small hole, and catching hold of him lays him down in it, and throws a few spadefuls of earth on him. Then one observes to him, "Arise, thou dead, and eat some *k'heer*;" and he, nearly suffocated, gets up as quickly as he can, and runs off; while the others enjoy a hearty laugh at his expence.

37. *Hoonnoor Hosein kay fuqeeran* (*fuqeers* of St. Hoonnoor Hosein). One or two, dressed like the *banuwa*, save that their *alfa* is dyed with red ochre, and that they have over their ears ringlets of natural or artificial hair, carry in one hand a small tray, or a *sooplee*, with a couple of cakes of dried cow-dung on it, covered with ten or twelve beautiful gold and silver-tissue handkerchiefs, and adorned with flowers; in the other a *moorch'hul* waving over it, declaiming in praise of it thus: "The remains of "a personage of no small consequence are concealed here: "he performed wonderful miracles. Whoever will undertake "a visit to his tomb and make the circuit (*tuwaf*) of it, shall "never experience the torments of hell-fire; therefore pe- "tition him, and make your requests known unto him."

When any express great anxiety to see the gentleman, he removes the handkerchiefs one by one, with great dilatoriness, and at last displays the contents of the tray; on beholding which, those who asked him for a sight of it, feel quite ashamed.

38. *Nanuk shah*, alias *Nanuk punthee* (a follower of *Nanuk*). Four or five men assume this character. They wind round their heads two or three coloured *sylees*, or wear white caps; in the centre of their foreheads is a *teeka* (or spot) of lamp-black; their faces are besmeared with *sundul*; on their necks are a *gooloobund*, *heemaeel*, and a

necklace of white beads;* round their waists two coloured *doputtas* are twisted; and they carry in their hands a couple of clubs.

They visit every *ashoor-khana*, and to the music of their clubs struck together, they sing verses in honour of Hosein.

39. *G'huggree walay.*† Their dress is either white or red. Their faces and bodies are rubbed over with cowdung ashes; they wear on their heads a *doputta* with a *sylee*, or a quantity of fringe, tape, thread, or either broad or narrow gold or silver lace wound over it, or only *sylee*, with gold or silver tassels dangling from it; on their ears they have gold or silver *toorra* (or feather cockades); round each arm three handkerchiefs are tied *à la Mujnooan*, and round the upper arm *bazoo-bunds* or *bhooj-bunds* (armlets); a *lungotee* or *loong* round their loins, and on their right ankles a *torray*.

One of them precedes the rest with a lamp in his hand, and two standard-bearers carry the colours, which are white, green, or red. All of them, with the exception of the *adalut shah*, wear on the right thumb a couple of *g'huggrees;* and while repeating the versified narrative and eulogies of Hosein, they keep time by rattling them.

In front of the band of *fuqeers*, a couple of boys, or *rumnay walay*, each having a painted earthen-pot with some gravel in it, or with a *chown-ur*‡ in their hands, dance or rather move their legs backwards and forwards; and at the conclusion of each verse, by stooping or sitting, and getting up quickly, they mark time.

---

* Such as *Rajpoots* wear, made of *sunk'h*, or a species of large shell.

† From *g'huggree*, which are hollow brass rings worn on the thumb, containing a few brass shots which tingle on being shaken.

‡ *Chown-ur*, or *chownree*, an instrument for driving away flies.

Two or four *adalut shahs* (p. 191.) stand on each flank, or walk up and down in front, with drawn swords in their hands; and two men act as *sang burdar* (spearsmen), *i. e.* they carry a spear, or a long thin bamboo in the shape of a spear, rolled over with two or three kinds of coloured paper, in their hands, and go before the *guroh*. When the latter halts any where, they tie the *sangs* in the middle like a pair of scissars, and stand with them in front at a short distance, to prevent other *gurohs* approaching them, and continue reciting verses in praise of their *javelins*.

These have likewise a *sur guroh* (chief of the troop), and in many respects resemble the *banuwas*.

40. *Ga-rro-ree shah*. His dress is like that of the *jullalee*, but he wears a *toorra* or feather on his turban, and carries a *poonggee** in his hand. Ten or twelve form this band, and perform at every place many jugglers' tricks.

41. *Chindurr shah* (or king Ragamuffin). A man encircles his head with a quantity of rags, which he also suspends all round his neck, hanging down to his feet, and thus he quietly walks about the lanes and *bazars*, without uttering a single word to any one.

42. *K'hind-ur shah* (Tatterdemalion, or king Clout). Eight or ten men wear rags on their heads, or only *k'hindrray*† round their necks, and *cholnay*; have *k'hind-ray* handkerchiefs in their hands, and going in front of each *ashoor-khana*, first flog one another with them, and then come to kicks and blows, and falling down roll and tumble themselves about on the ground.

43. *Guleez shah* (king Filth). He is marked with a black *teeka* or spot on the forehead, and wears a raw leather

* *Poonggee:* Vide list of musical instruments, Appendix.

† Several folds of old cloth, chintz, rags, &c. sewed together in the form of a thick quilt.

gooloobund and a *lunggotee*. He has his whole body anointed with honey, to attract flies, and walks about, singing satirical and ludicrous verses; and invariably makes it a rule to go into the midst of a crowd.

44. *Reech'h shah* (king Bear). A man dresses himself out in a black goat's skin with the hair upon it, and two or three fellows dressed in blankets run after him, all imitating the growling of the bear. They go about in every lane and *bazar* frightening women and children.

45. *Boorr-boo-rrook shah* (king Double-drum). Two or four men representing this character, of a class of Hindoo devotees of that name, wear their garb. They wear an enormous turban, made up of two or three different colours, a *jama* and *eezar*, with a *doputta* tied round the waist, and carry in their hands a *boorboorka*.*

Whenever he sees a person approaching him, he says, "I "saw a good omen to-day: you will become a very wealthy "man, and receive a *palkee*, an elephant, and a horse, in a "present." Thus saying, he goes about sounding his *boorboorka*, and blessing people.

46. *Marwaree*. Their dress is like that of the *Marwaree*.† They stick a long pen in one of their ears with a book of accounts in the hand, and one or two bags full of small broken pieces of earthen-ware, the mouths tied up and sealed, placed on the shoulders of one or two men; they have them carried along with them to represent bags of rupees or gold-mohurs; and walking about, they say in the Marwaree tongue, to every one they meet, "So long we "have had dealings with one another, let us now settle our "accounts; for I am about to proceed to my native country.

---

* A small double-drum.

† *Marwaree*, the inhabitants of Marwar, a division of the Ajmeer province, to the west of *Jye-Nuggur*.

"My wife, after an absence of twelve years, has written to "me that she has been brought to bed." When any enquire, saying, "Mr. Merchant, why you have been here "for the last twelve years, how could your wife bear you "a child? It is probably some other person's:" he replies, "No, sir; I had a meeting with her in my dream, and she "conceived; and such is the case with women of our caste, "that they bring forth children without the union of the "sexes, and on the birth of the child send word* to the "husband wherever he may happen to be, and he on hearing of it becomes so delighted, that he prepares *luddoos* "and distributes them." Those of the Marwaree caste, on hearing this, feel very much ashamed and angry; while the spectators enjoy a laugh at their expence. This *fuqeer* says so many ludicrous things, that people eagerly crowd round him to listen.

47. *Oont shah* (his majesty king Camel). They construct a small camel with bamboos, cover it over with paper or cloth, and paint it over with a colour resembling that of the camel. A hole is left from the back to the belly of the figure, and the man entering it stands on the ground, with his head and chest above the camel's back, to represent a man mounted on it, while his body and legs down to the calf, are concealed within its body. The camel is fastened, with its legs above ground, to the waist of the man, who, thus equipped, goes dancing with it round every *allawa*. It is so well formed, that were it not for the legs of the man being visible and its low stature, it would with difficulty be distinguished from a real one.

* The natives are likewise in the habit of transmitting money to their relatives and friends at a distance by the hands generally of friends, sometimes of a mere acquaintance; and it is surprising that they are not oftener robbed of such remittances.

Lunggur Neekalna (or the taking out the anchor), is as follows:

Men as well as women sometimes make vows, that if a son or daughter be born to them, they will take out a *lunggur* (anchor) annually, for three years, or for twelve, or as long as the child lives. In the event of the death of the parents, the individual for whom the vow was made fulfils it himself, by carrying out his own *lunggur*.

Those who have thus vowed, perform the ceremony in general on the fifth *k'hun* (*i. e.* the fourth day of the month *Mohurrum*); sometimes not until the sixth. In short, it may be done on any day between the fourth and tenth.

They fasten to the waist of the boy or girl a string of flowers, or of the leaves of *subzay*, with or without an iron chain,* both long enough to trail along the ground. They put into one hand of the child an *ood buttee kay jhar* (benjamin-pastile tree); into the other, a silver *ullum* of two or four annas' worth, or a golden one of ten or fifteen rupees'; and holding a canopy over him, he is accompanied on both sides by a crowd of boys, each carrying, for shew, a cocoa-nut leaf, or a little flag. In ten or twelve red earthen jars they put *shurbut*, and covering them with earthen saucers, place a small pot on the top of each. To the necks of the jars they fasten garlands of flowers and *subzay*-leaves with red thread, coat them outside with *sundul*, and carry them in *bhungeean* (*bangies*) or on Coolies' heads; in trays they have sugar or *goor*; in a couple of dishes *polaoo* or *k'hichree*, some ready money, benjamin, flowers, a bundle of wood, accompanied with music, *fuqeers* of the *banuwa*, *g'huggree*, &c. kind. If it be at night, they are accompanied with flambeaux and fire-works; and loudly vociferating

---

* This is intended to represent the anchor.

"*Shah Hosein!*" "*Eea Eemam!*" "*Eea Allee!*" and burning benjamin they proceed to the *ashoor-khana*. On reaching it, having walked round the *allawa* three times, and thrown the bundle of wood into it, and offered *fateeha* in presence of the *ullums*, the *moojawir* (or proprietor) puts the flowers which were brought, on the *punjay;* takes the *lunggur* from off the loins of the child, and gives the benjamin tree back to the party; keeps the plate of *k'hichree* or *polaoo* and a couple of jars of *shurbut*, together with the ready-money offered to the *ullum*. Then having, after *fateeha*, poured one or two *g'hurray* of *shurbut* into the *allawa*, and with the retinue returned home in the same manner as they went, the attendants are entertained with *k'hichree*, *shurbut*, *duhee*, *chutneean*, *salnay*, *turkareean*, without animal food or fish.

In some countries the poor and indigent, Hindoos as well as Moosulmans, make a vow for the child, or merely as an offering, that in the event of success attending their wishes, they will take or send to the *shudday*, one or two small silver *ullums*, and three or four pots of *goor-shurbut*, together with some *k'hichree*, one and a quarter or one and a half *pice* as a *churagee*, and some benjamin and flowers for the *ullums*.

The nobility and the wealthy also take out *lunggur*, whether it be to fulfil a vow or not. This they do in great pomp and state, *e.g.* First proceed the standards carried on elephants; then follow *rocket-men*, drummers, &c. succeeded by a line of infantry; in the rear of them *nuqarchee* in *howdas*, playing; then again come the *khasburdars* (matchlock-men), a number of respectable people, some on elephants, others on foot; men firing off muskets (or matchlocks), horses richly caparisoned, musicians followed by porters, carrying branches of lime and orange-trees, and abundance of cocoanut-leaves. After that a *shameeana* (canopy) embroidered, or of plain white cloth, under which goes the individual in whose name the vow was made, with the wreath of flowers, and a silver chain fastened on to his loins, holding in his hands ten or twelve small silver *ullums*, and four, five, or six benzoin-pastile trees. Sometimes dancing-girls accompany them, repeating *murseea;* and all round about him call out, "*Eea Allee! Eea Allee! Eea Hussun! Eea Hussun! Eea Hosein! Eea Hosein! Doolha! Doolha!*"

When they send the *lunggur* merely for the sake of their own welfare, or as an offering (and not to fulfil a vow), it is carried by a servant under a *shameeana*, accompanied by two or three caldrons of *k'hichree*, one or two *puk'hals*, and hundreds of earthern pots of *shurbut* prepared with sugar-candy, soft sugar, &c. having cloths tied over their mouths; and one or two bundles of wood, also covered with red cloth. If the person vowed for pleases, he rides in an *ambaree** or *howda*†. Last of all come the *nuqaray*, beating, on an elephant or camel; and thus they proceed to the particular *ullum* to which they had vowed to go.

I shall now describe some of the *Mohurrum Nuzur-o-Nyaz* (or *Mohurrum* vows and oblations) as practised by women.

They vow thus: "If such or such a thing which I wish "come to pass, I shall, fasting, sweep the ground around "such an *ashoor-khana's allawa* with my wet locks." Or, "I shall bathe my head in fire." In which latter case she sits, having her head covered with a sheet, and the *moojawir* (or proprietor) throws some fire on her head, with a *kufgeer*

* *Ambaree*, a *howda* with a canopy or cover.

† *Howda*, an open litter fastened on an elephant, and used in the east, in which the nobility travel.

(skimmer), three times, and as readily brushes it off again with a *moorch'hul*.* Or, "I shall break fast with no other "food than what is procured by begging." Or "at such "an *ashoor-khana* I shall burn a *ghee* lamp and have "*fateeha* offered over sugar." Or, "I shall suspend to "(lit. mount on) such an *ullum* a flower *gend guhwara* or "a silver *rote*." Or, "I shall go and tie on to such an "*ullum* an unripe or a silver lime, over which I have had "*fateeha* offered."

When their particular desires are accomplished they fulfil their vows most rigorously. Or they go and beg at ten or twelve houses, and to what they may collect add some money of their own; and having had a gold *door* or *baoolee* (ear-rings) made on the *Shuhadut ka roz* (lit. day of martyrdom; *i. e.* the tenth of the month *Mohurrum*), they have it inserted into the ears of their boys by the goldsmith, under the *taboot* borne on men's shoulders. If the offspring be a girl, a *boolaq* is put into her nose. The goldsmith at the same time receives a present of some *dal*, *chawul*, *goor*, and a few *pice*; or merely a few *pice*.

On the night of the tenth *k'hun* takes place the *Mohurrum kay Shub-gusht* (or the *Mohurrum* nocturnal perambulations).

On that night an innumerable throng of men and women, *Hindoos* and Moosulmans, in short the people of the neighbouring villages from the distance of eight or ten miles, assemble, and the shopkeepers also decorate their shops on the occasion.

All the *ullums*, (large and small), *taboots*, *booraqs*, &c.

---

* *Moorch'hul*, a fan for driving away flies, especially made of peacock's feathers, held over great men as a token of royalty, &c. Also used at ceremonies with the same view; such as over *ullums*, &c., at the *mohurrum*, and on other occasions.

after *fateeha* has been offered over *sheerbirrinj*, *polaoo*, *shurbut*, *k'hichree*, &c. in the name of the Hoosnein, are taken out; by the lower classes of people during the first watch of the night, and by the great at about midnight, accompanied with flambeaux, fireworks, *baja bujuntur*, *tasa murfa*, the various troops of *fuqeers* (called *mayla*), and dancing girls reciting *murseea*; or sometimes without any music, &c. Having performed with them the circuit of their respective *allawas* thrice, they traverse every *bazar* and lane, burning incense and Benjamin-pastiles, making lamentations, and repeating *murseea nowh*. Having done this with great noise and bustle, they return home with the *ullums*, *taboots*, &c. to their respective *ashoor-khanas* at daybreak, or somewhat earlier, next morning; and having laid the *ullums* down to sleep, betake themselves also to rest.

Some people, after offering the above-mentioned *fateeha*, instead of taking the *ullums*, &c. on their peregrinations, merely perform the circuit of their *allawas* three times, bring them in, and lay them aside (*thunda kurtay;* lit. cool them).

The next day (tenth of *Mohurrum* or eleventh *k'hun*) is the *Shuhadut-ka-roz* (day of martyrdom).

On it, from nine A.M. to three P.M., generally about nine or ten o'clock in the forenoon, all the *ullums*, &c. from every *ashoor-khana* are carried with the same pomp and state as on the preceding night, save without lights, to the *Kurbulla ka mydan* (or plain of *Kurbulla*), *i.e.* a plain near the sea or any river or tank, whither they are annually in the habit of carrying them.

On taking out the *ullums*, &c. from the different *ashoor-khanas*, they first kindle the fire in their respective *allawas*, go round them three times, and with the *ullums* facing the *Qibla* perform *fateeha*. After that they put into a little earthern pot a half or a whole pice, with some milk and *shurbut*, and having adapted a cover to it, place it at the bottom of the *allawa*, and fill it up with earth, forming a little mound over it, and having stuck up a branch of the pomegranate tree on it proceed to the plain of Kurbulla.* The following year, when the same spot is dug, the pot formerly buried is found; and the women, by giving something to the *moojawir* (proprietor) of the *ashoor-khana*, obtain the *pice* which was put into it. Having bored a hole or attached a ring to it, they suspend one of these coins to the necks of each of their children, with the view of warding off evil spirits.

Some people, after the *allawa* is closed, pour a pot of *shurbut* over it, and place on it the vessel which contained it, inverted.

Some burn a light on it every night, for three or for forty days.†

Some, chiefly shopkeepers, to fulfil vows which they have made, throw at the *ullums*, &c., as they pass their shops, or on the plain of Kurbulla, handfuls of *nuqol*, *rayooreean*, or *cowries*; and women, esteeming such *cowries* or shells sacred, eagerly pick them up, and threading each one separately, suspend one round the necks of their children, in order that they may be preserved from the attacks of the devil.

In the progress of the *ullums*, &c. towards the plain, whenever they meet with an *ashoor-khana*, they offer *fateeha* at it, and proceed.

---

* For further particulars of this imposing spectacle, vide Mrs. M. H. Ali's description, vol. i. p. 81.

† In imitation of visiting the grave of the deceased on those days after death. Vide chapter 39 and 40.

Some vow that should they recover from any particular disease with which they may be afflicted, they will, in front of the *ullum* or *taboot*, go rolling on the ground, all (or part of) the way to the plain of Kurbulla. Should such wishes be accomplished, they tie on a *loong* which covers the pelvis, the rest of the body being naked, and roll themselves on the ground. Women perceiving them thus rolling,* throw water on them to cool them; while their friends precede, clearing the way through the crowd, and removing any stone, bone, thorn, or other obstacle on the road, to prevent their sustaining any injury.

At the plain of Kurbulla an immense concourse of people assemble; rich and poor, great and small, of all classes and denominations. The crowd is so great, that it is difficult to pass through it. In some parts, shopkeepers of every description erect booths; and turn which way you will, you see nothing but shops full of fruits, sweatmeats, *pan-sooparee*, coffee, *sook'hmook'h*, all sorts of play-things, *majoon*, *bhung*, &c.; and here and there are to be seen tumblers, jugglers, wrestlers, bear and monkey-dancers, &c., whirligigs and swings (in which their owners allow people to swing, on paying some *pice*); and spectators sitting under awnings, or in tents and *raootees*, enjoy the sight. There are also *abdar-khanas*, where water and *shurbut* are dispensed; and water-carriers going about with leathern bags full of water, ringing their cups; and either by taking a few *cowries* or gratis (in which case they call out *sibbel, sibbel*, i.e. gratis, gratis) they give the people water to drink.

Having placed the *taboots*, *ullums*, &c. near the water-edge, and given *fateeha* in the name of the Hoosnein and

* Probably in the middle of a sultry day, under a burning sun, on a heated, dusty, or sandy road!

the martyrs over *rote,** *shurbut,*† *choonggay,*‡ *boottee,* *k'hichree,*|| *polaoo* sweetmeats, they distribute part of it on the spot and bring the rest home as a sacred thing. Those who can procure even the smallest morsel of this food, consider themselves very fortunate; and partake of it with great satisfaction.

After the *fateeha*, having taken off all the tinsel about the *taboot* and removed the *ullums* out from the interior, they take the two models of the tombs that were in it, and dip them in the water. Some bring home the *taboot* uninjured, while others throw them into the water. In which latter case, should one express a wish to have any part of the paper net-work, &c. no objection is made. ¶

The *taboots* that are brought home unmutilated are set up as they were before, for the three days** following. After that, having offered *fateeha*, they take off the network paper, &c. and keep it for future use.

From the *ullums* they also take off the *dhuttee*, flowers, ornaments, &c., which they put into *puttaras*, dip them naked in the water two or three times, and wash them. Men and boys, Hindoos as well as Moosulmans, eagerly run

---

* *Rote*, sweetened wheaten cakes besmeared with *sundul*.

† *Shurbut*, made of *goor* (raw sugar) and water, and prepared in a new red pot.

‡ *Choonggay*, or fried cakes made of wheat flour, sugar (or *goor*) and *ghee*.

§ *Boottee*, or a mixture of *tyar* (curdled milk) and rice.

|| *K'hichree*, that variety prepared with meat.

¶ During the first ten days, it is supposed to be alive (or to contain the real bodies of the martyrs); when no European is allowed to touch it; but now the corpses being removed and this bier of no further use, may be kicked about and any thing done with it.

** Mohummudans reckon part of a day for the whole; thus, what they mean by three days, is, the day on which it is brought home and the two following; *i. e.* the eleventh, twelfth, and thirteenth *k'hun*.

into the water after them, and catch the drops of water as they fall; and conceiving it good (possessed of peculiar virtue), drink it, and apply it to their eyes. After washing them, they lay them in *puttaray*, (i.e. rattan boxes), or on trays; and having covered them up and offered *fateeha** over some of the before-mentioned food, distribute it, carrying a small portion home.

The *booraqs* and *nal-sahibs* do not undergo the operation of ducking. They are taken home and laid aside; the former is painted afresh, and the latter annually besmeared with *sundul*.

Waving *moorch'huls* on all, burning incense, repeating *murseea* and *alweeda*, they return to their respective *ashoor-khanas*; and there having set them down and made lamentations over them, they offer *fateeha*, eat, and distribute the victuals brought home. After which the different people retire to their own houses.

The *booraqs* and *taboots* have only a thin cloth curtain thrown over them, and are brought home as the *ullums* to their *ashoor-khanas*, and placed near the latter.

The *ullums*, &c. which were not taken to the plain of Kurbulla are this forenoon taken out, and made to perform the circuit of their *allawas* three times, bathed, *fateeha* offered, and the food distributed.

Those who have become *fuqeers*, either at the plain of Kurbulla, or having come home, bathe themselves, and lay aside their mendicant's garb, &c.; and those who had worn *sylee* and *gujra*, either throw them away into the water, or wet them and bring them home. And every band of *fuqeers*, previous to taking off their *fuqeer's* dress, have

* The *fateeha* is offered either before or after the bathing of the *ullums*.

fateeha offered in the name of the Hoosnein over sweetmeats, send some of it to each *sur-guroh*, and distribute the rest among themselves. Sometimes all the *fuqeers* sit in the market-place at the plain of Kurbulla, conversing together for a short while, and reciting funeral eulogiums. Some do not change their *fuqeer's* habit till after the third-day-*zeearut*.

On that day (the *shuhudut-ka-roz*), in every house they must cook *palaoo* or *k'hichree*, *curries*, meat, &c. and having uttered *fateeha* over them in the name of Mowla Allee and the Hoosnein, they eat, distribute among their friends, and give them away in charity.

From that day (the 11th *k'hun*), the generality of people commence eating meat, though some not until the twelfth or thirteenth.

Some people on the *shuhadut-ka-roz*, in the afternoon, take out what is called *run ka taboot*, or *run ka dola*,* which consists in little square frame-works made of thin pieces of bamboo, somewhat in the shape of *taboots*, and covered with white cloth. These are carried, with the same pomp and state as the *taboots* were, to the plain of Kurbulla; and on returning thence they run with them, calling out, "*Deen! Deen!*", and every now and then halting and repeating *murseea*, beat vehemently on their breasts; and having brought them home, set them up as they were before, till the third day after, when they are taken to pieces, and reserved for future use.

The *zeearut* † of the *ullums*, or the third-day *teeja*,† fol-

* They are intended to represent the boxes in which the heads of the seventy-two martyrs were carried (vide page 168), and sometimes are composed of that number, as in Bengal.

† *Zeearut* (or the visiting); that is, of the grave of deceased persons on the third day after their demise; which is also called *Teeja*, meaning

lows. On the 12th *k'hun*, they again sit up all night reciting *murseea*, reading the *Qoran* and *Mudh-e-Hosein*.* Early next morning (the 13th *k'hun*), they prepare *polaoo* or *k'hichree*, with meat, or *k'hichra*, and *shurbut*, &c., and having offered *fateeha* in the name of the Hoosnein, they eat and distribute them in charity. That night they place near the *ullums* all kinds of fruits, flowers, *urgujja*, *uttur*, betel-leaves, &c.; and after the *fateeha*, distribute these likewise.

They take down the sheds that were erected in front of the *ashoor-khanas*, and lay by the *ullums* in boxes.

Should they have borrowed the *dhuttee* clothes from any one, they go and return the same to them; but if they be *tukhtee* (*i. e.* covered with gold and silver-leaf ornaments), bought in the *bazar*, they reserve them for future use. If any one at that time desire to have part of them, they grant it, receiving something by way of a *nuzur* in return; or give those away, which people had brought and mounted on them, to fulfil vows. Women generally take these and tie them round the necks, or upper arms of their children, to prevent the shadows (evil influence) of Genii and Fairies from falling upon them.

Some likewise observe the tenth, twelfth, and fortieth† day of mourning, &c., nay, some even the intermediate days, when they cook various kinds of food, have *fateeha* offered over them, and eat and distribute them.

---

meaning "the third day," when oblations are offered. For further particulars, vide chap. xxxix.

* *Mudh-e-Hosein*, or eulogiums on Hosein.

† Chiefly on the fortieth day, which happens on the twentieth of the following month *Sufur*, and in some part of the country is held as a festival called *sur o tun*, or head and body, in commemoration of the junction of the head and body of Hosein.

Some perform the fortieth day *teeja* (*vide* note p. 227 and chap. xl.), and on that day assemble a great crowd to repeat *murseea;* and if they please, invite the assembly by letter. Whether the crowd meet during the day or night, they come in parties in succession, sit in the assembly for a short time, and recite *murseea.* The auditors, on hearing the melancholy narrative, make grievous bewailings.

The *dungul-kurnay-wala, i. e.* assembler of the crowd, offers to the *murseea*-reciters coffee, betel-nuts, *sook'hmook'h,* or sweetmeats; and those who can afford it entertain them with dinner.

From that day till the following year there is an end of the *mohurrum* mourning.

During the thirteen festival days Moosulmans never do any work, perform no conjugal duty, and neither drink intoxicating liquors, nor marry, &c. Should any one happen to die, they are, of course, obliged to perform the funeral rites; but, with this exception, they do no work of any description whatever.

CHAPTER XVI.

Concerning the *Tayra tayzee*, or the first thirteen evil days; and the *Akhree Char Shoomba kae Eed*, or feast, held on the last Wednesday of the second month, *Suffur*.

The *Tayra tayzee* (or the first thirteen days) of the auspicious* month *Suffur* are considered extremely unlucky, on account of the Prophet's (the blessing! &c.) having been seriously indisposed during those days, and it was on the thirteenth day that some change for the better showed itself in his malady.

Should a marriage take place about this time, the bride and bridegroom are on no account allowed to see one another, nor is any good work undertaken on those days.

On the 13th *tayzee*† (i.e. the 12th day of the month), and some on the 13th day of the month, all bathe. They take some *maash*, unboiled rice, wheat, and *til*, mix them together, and put them on a tray, and deposit a small cup containing oil, in the centre of the dish of corn: sometimes, in addition, eggs and a pice or two. They then look at their faces in the oil three different times, and each time taking up a few grains of corn drop them into it. After this, these articles

---

* Several, not all of the months, have some such honorary title affixed to them; thus, 1st. *Mohurrum ool Huram*, or the sacred month *Mohurrum*; 2d. *Suffur ool Moozufir*, or the victorious month *Suffur*; 7th. *Rujub ool-Moorujib*, or the honoured month *Rujub*; 8th. *Shaban ool-Moajin*, or the revered month *Shaban*; 9th. *Rumzan ool-Moobarik*, or the blessed month *Rumzan*; 10th. *Shuwal ool-Mookurrum*, or the noble month *Shuwal*.

† Calculated from the evening, on which the moon becomes visible; whence called *Tayzee* (the day of the moon), similar to what *k'hun* was in the month *Mohurrum*. The first day of *Suffur* not beginning till six A.M. the day following.

are given away in alms to beggars and *hulalkhors*.* Instead of the above, some prepare thirteen small *rotes* and dispense them in charity.

On this day they prepare and eat *k'hichree*, sheep's *kulleejee* and head, and despatch some to their relatives and friends.

Others make a decoction of *chunna* and wheat, and add to it sugar, sliced *k'hopra*, and poppy-seed; and having offered *fateeha* in the name of the Prophet (the blessing! &c.), they throw a small quantity on the top of the house, and eat and distribute the rest.

There is no proper reason for observing the bathing, &c. on this day: it is entirely a new custom, introduced by the female sex.

The last Wednesday of this month is termed *akhree char shoomba*, i.e. the last Wednesday. It was on this day that the Prophet, experiencing some degree of mitigation in the violence of his distemper, bathed, but never after; having, on the 12th day of the following month (vide p. 233), resigned his soul to God. It is on this account customary with every Moosulman, early on the morning of that day, to write, or cause to be written, the seven *sulams*, with saffron-water, ink, or rose-water, on a mango, *peepul*, or plantain leaf, or on a piece of paper, *viz.* 1st. *Sulamoon qowlun min ribbir ruheem;* Peace shall be the word spoken unto the righteous by a merciful Lord (*Qoran*, chap. xxxvi. Sale,† p. 306). 2d. *Sulamoon alla Noohin fil alumeen;* Peace be on Noah among all creatures (chap. xxxvii. p. 312). 3d. *Sulamoon alla Ibraheem;* Peace be on Abraham (ib.

* Outcasts, or at least the lowest caste of people, generally sweepers or employed in the meanest or dirtiest employments; so called, because by them all sorts of food are considered lawful.

† Sale's *Koran*, edition of 1825.

p. 314). 4th. *Sulamoon alla Moosa wo Haroon;* Peace be on Moses and Aaron (ib.). 5th. *Sulamoon alla Eeleeaseen;* Peace be on Elias (ib.). 6th. *Sulamoon allykoom tibtoom fu'udkhoolooha khalideen;* Peace be on you! ye have been good; wherefore, enter ye into Paradise; remain therein for ever (chap. xxxix. p. 333). 7th. *Sulamoon heea hutta mutla il fujr;* It is peace—until the rising of the morn (chap. xcvii. p. 497). They then wash off the writing with water,* and drink the liquid that they may be preserved from afflictions and enjoy peace and happiness.

---

* This would at first sight seem strange, that the writing could be so easily effaced; but Mrs. Ali has the following remark (vol. ii. p. 69). "The ink of the natives is not durable; with a wet spunge may be "erased the labour of a man's life." And again: "out of reverence "for God's holy name," (always expressed in their letters and every other species of writing by a character at the top of the first page, which is an *A*, or | for *Allah*, an abreviation for *Bu Ism Allah;* contr. *Bismilla*, *i. e.* in the name of God), "written paper to be "destroyed is first torn, and then washed in water before the whole "is scattered abroad. They would think it a sinful act to burn a piece "of paper on which that holy name has been inscribed."

As even Mrs. Meer confesses her ignorance of the composition of Indian ink, by observing that she has that "yet to learn," I hope I shall be excused for inserting here an excellent receipt for preparing the same:—Take of lamp-black twelve pice weight (six ounces); gum arabic five pice weight (two and a-half ounces); *Heera kushish* (green vitriol), and *Mahphul* (gallnuts), of each a half pice weight (two drams); and *Bol-e-chinia* (socotorine aloes), a-third of a pice weight (eighty grains). Boil a handful of *Neem*-leaves (Melia azadirachta, Lin.) in any quantity (say, one seer) of water. When boiling, throw into it the lamp-black (*kajul*) tied up in a bit of cloth. After a little while, the oil which the lamp-black may have contained will be found floating on the surface; then take it out and throw away the water. Pound and sift well the other four ingredients, put them into a copper vessel or cup, with the lamp-black, and with a pestle made of the wood of the *Neem*-tree, mounted at the end to about an inch with copper, mix them all together. Make an infusion of *Boojaysur* (Dukh.), and *Ekseekurra* or Soween-kurra (Tel.) four pice weight (two ounces). Infuse for two days in boiling water, two pounds. Triturate the powders with a sufficient quantity of the infusion every day for forty days; (or

The writing of such amulets is the province of *Mowlu-weean* and preceptors, who from regard to God write them gratis.

On the above account, it is highly proper on this day to bathe, wear new clothes, use *uttur*, prepare *goolgoolay*, offer *fateeha* over them in the name of the Prophet, eat and distribute them, to enjoy walks in gardens, and say prayers. Some of the lower orders of the people have, for their pleasure and amusement, either in gardens or their own houses, dancing-girls to dance and sing to them, and a numerous throng regale themselves on such occasions with *saynd'hee* and other intoxicating beverages.

On this day, also, tutors grant *eedees* (p. 49) to the scholars; *i. e.* they write a verse on illuminated or coloured paper, and insert at the bottom of it the name of the pupil; and giving it to the child, desire the latter to take and read the same to its parents. The child accordingly does so, not only to the parents but other relatives, who on hearing it give the scholar a rupee or two, according to their means, to carry to the schoolmaster.

(or five or six days; the longer however, the better;) till all is dissolved. Then form lozenges, dry them in the sun, and preserve for use.

A more common process and simpler method for preparing it, is thus detailed in Ainslie's "Materia Medica of Hindoostan:"—"Take "of lamp-black and gum-arabic, equal quantities, and pound them "together into a very fine powder. Moisten it with the juice of the "pulp of the *kuttalay* (small aloe), and rub well at intervals for two "days together; after which, form it into little cakes, put them on "plantain-leaves and dry in the sun." When required for use, dissolve in water.

A late publication gives another receipt for what it states to be the Persian mode of making ink, and that "the finest and most durable "in the world." It is as follows:—"Take of lamp-black and (green) "vitriol, equal parts: the weight of both of fine galls; the weight of "all three of pure gum-arabic: pulverise and triturate them on a "marble slab for five or six minutes, mixing water till it be of a "proper consistency to write with."

CHAPTER XVII.

Concerning *Bara Wufat*, or the Death of the Prophet on the twelfth day of the third month *Rubbee-ool-awul*.

The *Rubbee-ool-awul* month is likewise denominated *bara-wufât*,* because on the twelfth day of the month his high excellency the Prophet, Mohummud Moostuffa (on whom be ! &c.) departed this life.

On this account, on that day, the following *fateeha* is observed by all Moosulmans in every country, whether Arabian or foreign. It is a duty incumbent on all of them to perform, for its virtues are superior to that of the *mohurrum* and all other *fateehas*. It is therefore but right that *sipahees* should have leave on this occasion for a couple of days, to enable them to celebrate the *sundul* on the 11th, and the *oors* on the 12th.

Where there are learned and scientific men, they, either in *musjids* or in their own houses, constantly rehearse, during the first twelve days of the month, the praises, eulogies, and excellencies of Mohummud Moostuffa (the peace ! &c.) as contained in the sacred *Huddees*, in Arabic or Persian, and explain it in Hindee to the vulgar.

Some assemble daily in the morning or evening, either at their own houses or in the mosques, and read the sacred *Qoran*; and having cooked *polaoo* or *k'hichree*, with *nan* and *quleea* or *sheerbirrinj*, and arranged every one's portion separately on the *dusturkhwan*, burning benjamin, they offer *fateeha* before and after dinner in the name

* From *bara*, twelve; and *wufat*, death.

of the Prophet (the peace! &c.), and transfer the beneficial influences of the sacred *Qoran* to their souls.*

Some people keep a *qudum-e-russool*† (Footstep of the Prophet), or the impression of a foot on stone in their houses, placed in a box and covered with a *mahtabee* or *tugtee* covering; and this, they say, is the impression of the foot of the Prophet (the peace! &c.).

On this day such places are elegantly decorated. Having covered the chest with *moqeish* and *zurbaft*, they place the *qudum-e-moobarik* (blessed foot) on it, or deposit it in a *taboot*, and place all round it beautiful *moorch'huls* or *chown-urs;* and as at the *Mohurrum* festival, so now, they illuminate the house, have music, burn frankinsense, wave *moorch'huls* over it. Five or six persons, in the manner of a song or *murseea*, repeat the *mowlood*, *durood*, *Qoran*, his *mowjeezay* (or miracles), and *wufat nama* (or the history of his death); the latter in Hindoostanee, in order that the populace may comprehend it, and feel for him sympathy and sorrow.

---

* Moosulmans conceive men to have three souls or spirits; one the *Rooh-e-Siflee* (lower) alias *Rooh-e-Jaree* (the travelling spirit), whose seat during life and death is the brain or head; 2d. *Rooh-e-moqeen* (the resident spirit), which inhabits the grave after death; and 3d. *Rooh-e-oolwee* (the lofty spirit), which dwells aloft in the heavens.

† The history of the blessed foot is said to be as follows. As the Prophet (the peace! &c.) after the battle of Ohud (one of the forty or fifty battles in which the Prophet had been personally engaged) was one day ascending a hill, in a rage, by the heat of his passion the mountain softened into the consistence of wax, and retained, some say eighteen, others forty impressions of his feet. When the angel Gabriel (peace be unto him!) brought the divine revelation that it did not become him to get angry, the Prophet (the peace! &c.) inquired what was the cause of this rebuke? Gabriel replied, "Look behind "you for a moment and behold." His excellency, when he perceived the impressions of his feet on the stones, became greatly astonished, and his wrath immediately ceased. Some people have these very impressions, while others make artificial ones to imitate them. —*Note of the Author.*

In short, on the eleventh and twelfth, splendid processions take place, similar to the *Mohurrum shubgusht* (*vide* p. 220).

On the eleventh, in the evening, some people a little before sun-set, perform the Prophet's (the peace! &c.) *sundul; i. e.* they place one or more cups containing *urgujja* (Gloss.) on one or two *boorâqs*, or on a tray, or in a *taboot*, called *maynhdee* or *musjid* (p. 102), and cover it with a *p'hool kay chuddur* (or flower-sheet). Along with this they carry ten or twelve trays of *mulleeda* with a canopy held over them, accompanied by *bâjâ*, *tâsâ*, &c. fireworks, flambeaux, repeating *durood* and *mowlood* in Hindoostanee or Persian, and burning frankincense proceed from some celebrated place to the house where the *qudum* is. On their arrival there, having offered *fateeha*, each one dips his finger into the *sundul* or *urgujja*, and applies a little of it to the foot: they then spread the flower-sheet on the *qudum* and distribute the *mulleeda* amongst all present.

The reason why they carry the *sundul* on a *booraq* is, that it was the Prophet's steed. The *booraq* should not be taken out at the *Mohurrum* as is usually done; it would be more proper to take him out on this occasion, that the common people may know that it was on such an animal Mohummud Moostuffa (the peace! &c.) ascended into heaven; but agreeably to the *Shurra*, doing such things, and keeping such models, as well as keeping other pictures in the house, are unlawful. The *booraq* is left near the *qudum* until the morning of the thirteenth. In general, the landlord of the *qudum* likewise makes a *booraq* and carries out *sundul* on it, and all vowers also have them made and bring them as offerings to the *qudum*.

On the twelfth, or day of *Oors*, they have grand illuminations, and sit up all night reading *mowlood, durood, Huddees, Qoran khwanee*; and having prepared *polaoo*, &c. distribute them to all.

The women, each agreeably to her means, carry some *ghee*, sugar, *goor*, sweetmeats, *ood*, and a *churragee* to the *qudum*, and burning frankincense, have *fateeha* offered there, give a little of the sweets to the landlord, pour the *ghee* into the lamp,* and bring the rest home.

At the place where the foot is, they burn benjamin and benjamin-pastiles daily, for the first twelve days of the month.

For the Prophet's (the peace! &c.) *fateeha* they usually prepare *sheerbirrinj*, as he was particularly fond of that dish, and at times called it *syed-ool-taam* (the prince of foods).

Some people, during the first twelve days or any day in the month, fill two or more *koondon* (large earthern pots) with *sheerbirrinj* and *pooreean*, which ceremony is called *poor* (full).

Some keep by them an *asar-e-shurreef* (*i. e.* the sacred emblem), alias *asar-e-moobarik* (the blessed token), which they say is a hair either of the Prophet's beard or mustachios. This is preserved in a silver tube, imbedded in *ubeer*, and its dignity is supposed to be even greater than that of the sacred foot.

At the place where the hair is they likewise offer *fateeha*, repeat *durood*, have illuminations, music, &c. Most of these hairs, however, are impositions and counterfeits.

---

* Which is a large one; and when full, after the donors have taken their departure, it is in a great measure emptied into a vessel, for the reception of a fresh supply, and the decanted *ghee* is reserved for culinary purposes.

CHAPTER XVIII.

Concerning his excellency, Peer e Dustugeer Sahib's *Geearween*,* on the eleventh day of the fourth month *Rubbee-oos-Sanee*, and the putting on of the *Bayree*, *Towq*, or *Buddhee*.

His high excellency Peer-e-Dustugeer (may God sanctify his beloved sepulchre!) has no less than ninety-nine names; but the principal, and those best known, are the following: *Peeran-e-Peer; Gows-ool-Azum; Gows-oos-Sumdanee; Muhboob-e-Soobhanee; Meeran Mo-hy-ood-Deen; Syed abd-ool-qadir-Jeelanee Hussunee-ool-Hoseinee.*

He is esteemed the chief among *wullees*, and is a great performer of miracles. The disciples and followers of his household are very numerous. To them at various times he appears whilst they are asleep, and gives lessons. The author speaks from personal experience; for to him at times of need, when he was oppressed in mind concerning things which he desired, he used constantly to repeat his ninety-nine names, and vow before the Holy God, imploring his assistance by the soul of Peer-e-Dustugeer; and through the mercy of the Almighty, his excellency Gows-ool-Azum presented himself to him in his sleep, relieved him of the perplexities which distressed him, and vouchsafed his behests. Let those of my persuasion not conceive these assertions absurd or false, or that I affirm them with a view to raise the dignity of my *peer*, or to aggrandize myself; for should it prove true, may God's curses descend upon those who disbelieve it, and may their religion and livelihood be annihilated!

* *Geearween*, or the eleventh.

The *soonnees* consider Peer-e-Dustugeer, a great personage, and in their hearts believe in him; whereas some of the *sheehas*, through ignorance, slander him, by asserting, that in the days of king Haroon-oor-Rusheed, this *peer*, Mahboob-e-Soobhanee (may God! &c.) occasioned the death of his excellency Eemam Jaffur Sadiq (may God! &c.) by causing him to swallow melted lead. This proceeds from pure malice, and is impossible; for the space of time which had elapsed between the days of his excellency Eemam Jaffur Sadiq and that of his excellency Muhboob-e-Soobhanee, was no less a period than two hundred and fifty years.

The sacred tomb of Peeran-e-Peer (the saint of saints) is at Bagdad.

On the tenth of this month they perform his *sundul*, on the eleventh his *churagan* (lamps) alias *oors* (oblations). That is, on the evening of the tenth, they carry out a large green flag, having impressions of the hand made on it with *sundul*, and with it they carry *sundul*, *muleeda*, sugar, flowers, benjamin, accompanied with numerous flambeaux and music, and having perambulated the town in great pomp and state, proceed to the place appointed, and there set it up. Then, having offered *fateeha* in the name of Peer-e-Dustugeer, they apply the flowers and *sundul* to the flag, and distribute the *muleeda*, &c. to the people.

On the eleventh day they cook *polaoo*, &c., read *Mowlood*, *Durood*, and *Khutum-e-Qoran*,* offer *fateeha*, and distribute the victuals, and sit up all night, having illumination, and reading the *Mowlood*, *Durood*, *Qoran*, and repeating the ninety-nine names of his excellency Peer-e-Dustugeer.

When the cholera or any plague is raging, they take out

* *Khutum-e-Qoran*, or the finishing the reading of the whole *Qoran*. It is done in two ways. Vide chap. xxxix.

in the above-mentioned manner, in the name of his holiness Peeran-e-Peer, a *j'hunda* (flag) and walk about with it through every street and lane, halting every now and then, when the *azan* is proclaimed. At this time Hindoos as well as Moosulmans, according to their means, make them presents of something or other, which they deposit on the *ood-dan*. Sometimes they also offer *fateeha* over sweetmeats or sugar. After perambulating the city they bring it back and set it up in its original place. In this way they walk about with it, either one, or three, or five successive Thursdays in the month. Many make small *j'hundas* in the name of his holiness, and having offered *fateeha* over them in his name, set them up in their houses or over the doors of their houses, and that with the view of obtaining security from misfortunes. In general, by having recourse to this means, through the blessing of his holiness, the virulence of such plague is arrested.

Some people vow to this saint, that should they be blessed with a son or daughter, they will make him or her his slave; and should their wishes be accomplished, on the tenth or the eleventh of this month they take a large silver *hulqa* (ring), alias *Bayree* (lit. a fetter, but here meant for a ring worn round the ankle), on which they annually pass a small ring. They dress some *mulleeda*, place on it eleven small lamps made of flour-paste, and light them with *ghee* and red cotton wicks; and burning wood-aloes or benjamin, offer *fateeha* and put them on; if a *bayree*, on the right ankle; if a *towq* (collar), around the neck of the child. Some, instead of these, have a silver or leathern *Buddhee* (belt) made, and put on. The generality only prepare a small quantity of *polaoo* merely for the *fateeha*; while a few have abundance of *polaoo* cooked, invite their relatives and friends, and entertain them (as also feed *fuqeers*) with it.

The *fateeha* is termed *gearween* (or the 11th) on account of its being the day that Gows-ool-Azum departed this life. Some, however, say that he died (lit. marched, *i.e.* to the other world) on the 17th of that month. But as for eleven days in every month, he was himself in the habit of offering *fateeha* in the name of the Prophet (the peace! &c.), and usually abstained from eleven things, the former day has been preferred as the one on which to offer *fateeha* in his name.

Some people on any day during the month, others on the 11th of every month, have *fateëha* offered in the name of his excellency Peeran-e-Peer over *polaoo*, or merely over some (more or less) sweets.

Some have a *maynhdee* in the shape of a *taboot* (vide p. 102), made with green paper, or of wood painted green, with some silver about it; and on the *oors*-day, or on any day of that month, suspend to it flowers, *sayhras*, and fruits moist and dry, light lamps, and set it up.

Many have the *maynhdee* carried about in pomp and state, accompanied with music, &c., and after having perambulated the town, bring it home again and set it up. Some people collect, in the name of Peeran-e-Peer, what is called *gulla;** that is, they take a *tumbaloo* or *mutkee*, besmear it outside with *sundul*, tie up its mouth with a piece of cloth, in the centre of which they make a small rent, place it in some clean spot, and deposit into it, through the opening in the cloth, a pice or two daily, or a handful of cowries or pice daily, or four or eight annas, or one or two rupees, every week, fortnight, or month, according to their means; and that from one end of the year to the other. And on the *oors*-day, or on any day in that month, they take out

* Literally, grain or corn, but here signifying money.

all the *gulla* and sum up the amount, and with it perform his holiness's *geearween*. Some, adding more money to what has been collected, give sumptuous entertainments.

His excellency's *bhanja* (sister's son) was Syed Ahmud Kubeer Rufaee; from whom has descended the class of religious mendicants called *fuqeer-e-rufaee* or *goorzmar*: for an account of whom vide Chap. xxviii, which treats of the different classes of *fuqeers*.

CHAPTER XIX.

Concerning *Zinda Shah Mudar's Churagan*, and *Buddhee; Dhummul koodana*, and *Gaee lootana*, observed on the seventeenth day of the fifth month, *Jummadee-ool-Awul.*

His excellency Shah Buddee-ood-Deen, alias Zinda Shah Mudar of Syria (may the holy God sanctify his sepulchre!) was a great *wullee* (saint) and a performer of miracles. He lived to a great age; nay, some consider him ever alive, though apparently dead, wherefore he is called *Zinda* (i.e. the living) *Shah Mudar*. He was partial to black clothes, and neither married nor ever had sexual intercourse. He travelled through various countries; and on reaching Hindoostan admired the situation of Muk-k'hunpoor,* and took up his abode there, where his blessed tomb now is.†

* A town about forty miles from Cawnpore.

† His shrine is visited annually by nearly a million of people, men, women, and children. A *mayla* (fair) is the consequence of this annual pilgrimage, which continues seventeen days in succession, and brings together, from many miles distant, the men of business, the weak-minded, and the faithful devotees of every class in the upper provinces. "Women can never, with safety to themselves, enter the

As in the preceding case of Peer-e-Dustugeer, so in this, they vow; and making flower or leathern gold and silver *buddhees*, put them round the necks of their children.

It was on the 17th of this month that he died. Some on that day, others on the 16th, prepare *sootreean*, *polaoo*, or *mulleeda*, and having placed thereon seventeen lamps, offer *fateeha* over them, and put the *buddhee* on the child.

Some perform *d'hummul koodana;* that is, they kindle a large heap of charcoal, and having sent for the *tubqatee* or *Shah Mudar fuqeers* (ch. xxviii. sec. 2.), offer them a present. The latter perform *fateeha*, sprinkle *sundul* on the fire, and the chief of the band first jumps into it, calling out "*dum Mudar;*"* when the rest of them follow him, and calling out "*dum Mudar! dum Mudar!*" tread out the fire. After that, they have the feet of these *fuqeers* washed with milk and *sundul*, and on the examination of the (probable) injury find that not a hair has been singed, and that they are all as they were at first. They then throw garlands of flowers around their necks, offer them *shurbut* to drink, and having given to each some *polaoo* or *sootreean* alias *chukoleean* and *muleeda*, with some ready money, a handkerchief or *loong*, grant them their leave, *i.e.* to depart.

Gaee lootana. Some having vowed a black cow, a few on the 17th, either at their own houses or at any of the *astanas* (p. 172), make a *zooba* (sacrifice) of it in the name

---

"mausoleum containing his ashes; they are immediately seized with "violent pains, as if their whole body was immersed in flames of fire." Vide Mrs. Meer's Observations, vol. ii. p. 321.

* *Dum Mudar*, or "by the breath of Mudar," having the same superstitious faith in this charm as the Persians, who believe it to secure them against the bite of snakes, and the sting of scorpions; and the courage with which those who are supposed to possess it encounter those reptiles, is remarkable.

of Shah Buddee-ood-Deen, and distribute it in charity among *fuqeers*.

In some places they set up an *ullum* in the name of Zinda Shah Mudar, and the place is called *Mudar ka astana*. Here they generally erect a black flag (*j'hunda*), and on the 17th perform his *oors*; on the 16th (the day preceding, agreeably to custom) his *sundul*; and in a similar manner they carry this flag, with the same pomp and state as they did that of Peer-e-Dustugeer. Both nights they sit up reading and recounting his *mudah* (eulogiums), *moonaqib* (virtues), celebrate his praises. At the *oors*, as at all *oorses*, they have splendid illuminations and perform nocturnal vigils. The above *ullum* is left all the year round in its original situation, and never removed as those of the *mohurrum* are.

CHAPTER XX.

Concerning *Qadir Wullee Sahib's Oors*, observed on the 11th day of the sixth month *Jummadee-ool-Akhir* (or *Akhir Muheena*).

The sacred shrine of Qadir Wullee Sahib* is at Nagoor near Nagputun (Negapatam); the Mohummudan inhabitants of which place are chiefly of the *shafaee*† sect, such

* It would seem by an account given by Monsieur Garcin de Tassy on the authority of Jawan, in his work entitled "*Bara Masa*," that this saint is likewise named Khwaja Moyeen ood deen Chishtee; and hence the month itself is sometimes called by that name. "*Memoires sur des particularités de la religion Musulmane dans l'Inde*," p. 63.

† There are four principal *qowm* (sects) of the Mohummudan faith, called after their respective founders; *viz.*

1. *Hunufee*

as *lubbays,** *mapullays* (Moplays†) &c.; and thèse people highly revere this great personage.

At that place is held on the ninth, his *sundul;* and on the tenth his *oors;* both, in the manner above described (p. 238). Such as preparing *maleeda*, cooking *polaoo*, reading *mowlood*, &c., sitting up all night, making illuminations; and that in a splendid style. Probably upwards of ten thousand rupees are expended on this occasion.

On the eleventh they break the *k'heer kee hundee* (the rice-and-milk pot); that is, on seeing the new moon, or on the second or fourth day of it, a *sir-gurroh* of any of the *silsillas*, or else a *fuqeer*, generally one of the *Mullung* tribe, sits on a bedding‡ spread on the ground in a closet; and, without either eating, drinking, sleeping, or obeying the calls of nature, he engages himself the whole time in the contemplation of the Deity. He does not go out of it, nor speak to any one, until the 11th, when the *moojawirs* cook *k'heer* in a large pot, and placing it on the head of one among them, convey it in great pomp and state, attended

---

1. *Hunufee* حنفي or *Hanifites*, from their founder, Aboo Huneefa, chiefly found in Turkey and Usbec Tartary; but comprising persons from among all the four sects, Syed, Sheikh, Mogol, and Putthan.

2. *Shafaee* شافعي or *Shafeites*, from their founder, Aboo Abdoollah Shafeeut, met with principally at Nagore (Coromandel Coast); comprising the Nuwa-aytays and Lubbays (both Sheikhs).

3. *Malukee* مالكي or *Malekites*, from their founder, Malek Ebn Ans, most prevalent in Barbary and other parts of Africa.

4. *Humbulee* حنبلي or Hanbalites, from their founder Ebn Hanbal, chiefly found at Bagdad, in Arabia; generally very devout.

Of the two last of these, none are to be met with in Hindoostan; but they are numerous in Arabia.

* A class of people who go about selling beads, precious stones, &c.

† This class of people are chiefly to be met with on the Malabar coast.

‡ *i.e.* A mattrass or quilt.

by *Baja Bujuntur*, to the above-mentioned *fuqeer*. The latter offers *fateeha* over it and tastes a little of it; then getting up, leaves his closet and goes and joins his own class of *fuqeers;* while the *moojawirs* take the *k'heer*-pot, with the same pomp and state as before to the sea-beach, the spot where they are annually wont to carry it, and there dash it to pieces. Then all the people, falling one upon another, scramble for some of the *k'heer:* nay, many regard even a piece of the broken pot, as well as the sand of the spot, sacred relics. In the act of scrambling they take up so much sand, as to leave an excavation of a cubit or a cubit and a-half in depth; but, strange as it may appear, amidst all this bustle and confusion not an individual is ever hurt.

A few days previous to the *oors*, various tribes of *fuqeers* from a distance as well as from the vicinity, resort to the place and sit in assembly together (*chowk byt'h-tay**), but the different bands apart from one another. In each there is a *sir-gurroh* or leader. If any one of the *fuqeers* have been guilty of an improper act unworthy of his calling, he is punished on this occasion agreeably to the decision of the *sir-gurroh*, by being loaded with numerous beddings procured from all the *fuqeers* present, or in some other way; he is further made to express contrition for his fault, to beg for mercy, and to give a written bond to that effect. He is then restored to his former tribe; or, in presence of the *jumma-oollah*, his *tusma* is cut into two, and he is excommunicated from their *gurroh*. In the latter case, he is considered unworthy thereafter to sit in the assembly of *fuqeers*.

They act also in this way at other noted *oorses;* such as

---

* *Chowk byt'h-na* is the technical term applied to the assembly of *fuqeers*, and it signifies sitting together in a circle, though the term *chowk* literally means a square.

that of *Tubur-e-Alum*, *Bawa-boodun* (alias *Hyat-Qulundur*) and *Bawa-Fuqur-ood-Deen*, &c.

When a *fuqeer*, or one of their *peers* has never been to an *oors*, he is esteemed imperfect.

At some *oorses*, *fuqeers* accept of money from *moojawirs* by way of present (*nuzzurs*), and, distributing it amongst them, take their departure home.

Moosulman ship-captains and sailors are in the habit of making vows and oblations in the name of his excellency Qadir Wullee Sahib; e. g. when they meet with any misfortune at sea, they vow, that should the vessel reach the desired haven in peace and safety with their property and cargo, they will spend a certain sum of money in offering *fateeha* to him.

On first beholding the new moon of that month, they erect a flag (or *gom**, as it is called) in his name, about five or six cubits long.

In other parts of the country also, as at Nagore, those Moosulmans who venerate this saint set up a *gom*, and annually offer *fateeha* in his name; or some (each according to his means,) merely offer *fateeha* in his name over a little *maleeda*.

As to his miracles, they are innumerable; suffice it to relate two or three noted ones as specimens.

1st. A certain person's ship sprang a-leak at sea, and the vessel was nigh sinking, when the *nakhoda*† (captain) vowed with a sincere heart, that should Qadir Wullee Sahib vouchsafe to stop the leak, he would offer up, in his excellency's name, the profits of the cargo, and likewise a couple

* *Gom* or centipeded flag, because made somewhat in the shape of a centipede.

† *Nakhoda*, from *nao*, vessel, and *khoda*, god; the lord or master of the vessel.

of small models of vessels formed of gold and silver. At that moment the saint was engaged with the barber, in the operation of shaving, and instantly became acquainted with the predicament in which the captain stood. Out of kindness he threw away the looking-glass he held in his hand,* which by some wise dispensation of Providence flew off to the vessel, and adhering to the aperture of the ship stopped the leak. On the vessel's reaching its destination in safety, the commander, agreeably to promise, brought his offering of gold and two little vessels, one of gold, the other of silver, and presented them to him. The saint directed the captain to restore to the barber his looking-glass; on which the skipper, in astonishment, inquired what looking-glass he meant; and received in answer, that it was the one adhering to the aperture at the bottom of his ship where the water had entered. On inspection, it was found firmly attached to the vessel; and was accordingly removed and produced.

2d. On one occasion, as he was washing his face near the edge of a tank, having at the time a small boil on one of his hands, he observed a woman with unusually large breasts. He imagined they were large boils (or abscesses†); and feeling compassion for her, said to himself, if the pain that I experience from so small a boil be so intolerable, what excruciating agony must that poor woman not endure! He supplicated heaven, saying: "Grant, O God! "that this woman's boils may be far removed from her;" and, it is said, her breasts instantly withered away. The

* It is customary with natives, while the barber shaves, for the individual who undergoes the operation to look at himself in a small looking-glass which he holds before him.

† This saint is said to have passed his life in deserts, and never seen a woman before; whereas, at Nagore, the women go about with the upper half of their bodies completely exposed.

woman, in consequence, became sadly grieved, and related to her neighbours that a *fuqeer* had seen her, and by mumbling something to himself had caused her breasts to dry up. They repaired to his holiness, and stated, that at his desire the woman's breasts had disappeared; to which he replied, that he had supposed them to be immense boils, and hoped that since they were breasts, the Almighty would restore them to their original condition. On his saying this, her breasts re-appeared.

3d. Near the sacred tomb of this saint is a grove of cocoanut-trees. The custom-house officer observed to the owner, that the revenue which it yielded was considerable, and that therefore it was but just that he should pay a tax for it. The proprietor replied, that the garden belonged to a great *wullee* and had never been taxed before, and why should it now? The other said, it did not signify to whom it belonged; the duty must be paid: adding, that cocoanuts had no horns that he should be afraid of them. No sooner had he uttered these words, than horns sprouted out of a couple of them! From this circumstance the duty on these trees has been dispensed with. To this day are the two-horned cocoanuts suspended near the head of his blessed shrine.

God knows whether these things be true or not. I have only stated what I have heard. The lie be on the neck (head) of the inventor of it!

CHAPTER XXI.

Concerning 1. *Rujub Sálárs Kundoree;* 2. *Syed Jullál-ood-Deen's* (of Bokhara) *Koondon*; 3. His holiness *Mohummud Moostuffa's* (the peace! &c.) *Miraj* (or Ascension), observed in the seventh month *Rujub.*

SECT. 1.—*Rujub Salar's Kundoree.*

This takes place on any Thursday or Friday in the month *Rujub*, agreeably to a vow previously made, in the name of Rujub-Salar, alias Salar-Musuood Gazee, whose miracles are well known, and whom people esteem a great *wullee.* His sepulchre is at Bhuranch.*

The ceremony of *kundoree* is performed as follows. First of all a hole which was dug at the first *kundoree*, either within doors or out, for the purpose of washing the hands over it, and of throwing therein any refuse, such as bones, rinds and stones of fruits, the parts of vegetables not eaten, &c., and that has been covered up, is opened after offering the *kundoree ka fateeha;* and the vow being concluded, it is closed, after this *fateeha* has been again offered. This hole is termed an *allawa:*—which many people dispense with altogether. It is the superstitious part of the female sex alone, who, supposing it inauspicious for the sky to behold any part of this food, dig *allawas*, and bury the refuse in them.

With the exception of fish and eggs, they prepare all sorts of rice, bread, curries, vegetables, also wheat-flour horses boiled in syrup, and take fruits, radishes, onions, leeks, mint, *chutnee*, cheese, vinegar, &c., and arrange them on plates and in cups on the *dusturkhwan*, each one's

* A town about thirty miles north-east of Lucknow

portion separately by itself. Then burning incense, they offer *fateeha*, eat, and distribute them.

Some make little horses of wheat-flour and boil them in syrup made of soft sugar or *goor* (*jaggree*), sometimes adding milk, and a plate or two of *chunnay kay dal*, soaked in syrup of *goor*, as if intended for the horses; and having offered *fateeha*, eat and distribute them within doors; the generality of people partaking first of a little of the *chunna*, and then of the other victuals.

Some occasionally prepare what they call *k'hoolay-g'horay* (loose horses), so called because the eating of them is not confined within doors as the former; but *fateeha* having been offered, they are distributed and sent abroad.

The reason for observing this *fateeha* is as follows. Sick people, especially those affected with disorders of the legs, vow that should they, through the favour of his excellency *Salar Musuood Gazee*, recover, they will prepare *k'hoolay-g'horay*, have *fateeha* offered in his name, and distribute them.

SECT. 2.—*Syed Jullal-ood-Deen's Koondon*.

Some people, on any Thursday or Friday of that month, place either in conjunction with the above-mentioned *kundoree*, or separately, two or four (or more) large or small *koondon*,* containing *meetha-polaoo*, or *k'hara-polaoo*, or *sheerbirrinj*, almonds, dates, &c. The generality of people fill them brimful, nay, as high as possible, with *duhee*, sugar, and boiled rice; and having offered *fateeha* in the name of *Syed Jullal-ood-Deen* (of Bokhara), some eat them out of the *koondon*,† while others serve them up in plates, eat, and distribute them.

---

* *Koondon*, or earthen pots used for kneading dough in.

† Eight or ten dipping their hands in at the same time.

Some people, especially *sheeahs*, perform *koondon* in the name of *Mowla Allee*.

The observance of such rites is not enjoined in books; they are only current in Hindoostan.*

SECT. 3.—*Mohummud's Miraj* (*or Ascension*).

On the 15th or 16th (most of the learned say on the 27th) of *Rujub*, the angel Gabriel conveyed his holiness the Prophet Mohummud Moostuffa (the peace! &c.) mounted on the *booraq* (*vide* p. 186) to the Almighty. People regarding that as an important night, commemorate it by sitting up all night, reading the numerous narratives written concerning it, and next day (the 27th) keep fast. I may, however, remark, that the custom is peculiar to the learned, pious, and devout; the vulgar neither observe nor know any thing about it.

The account of it is contained in the *huddees* (or traditions regarding Mohummud). The particulars may be learnt by consulting a work entitled *Marijin-nubooa*, as well as others well known.

CHAPTER XXII.

Concerning the *Shaban* feast; *viz.* *Shuh-e-Burat*, held on the 14th; and its *arfa*, on the 13th day of the eighth month, *Shaban*.

The word *burut*, agreeably to the interpretation in the *Qoran* and dictionaries, signifies a register. It is the book of record, in which are registered annually all the actions of

---

* The above ceremony would appear to be also called *Hazaree*, according to professor Garcin de Tassy, on the authority of the Bara Masa, by Jawan, page 59.

men, which they are to perform during the ensuing year; and it is said to be on the fifteenth night of this month, that the true and holy God annually records them in the book. Owing to this circumstance, the feast in commemoration of the event has obtained the name of *Shub-e-Burat*, or the night of the record.

In the *Khuzana-Juwahir-Jullaleea*, by Mowlana Fuzzul-Oollah, son of Zeea-ool-Abasee, the *burat* is thus noticed, *viz.* That Almighty God has in the *Qoran* given four names to this night. He has called it—1st. *Burat*, or the night of record; 2d. *Lylut-ool-moobarik*, or the blessed night; 3d. *Ruhmut*, or the night of mercy; 4th. *Farayqa*, or the night of discernment.

The ceremony of its *arfa** is observed by some, and is as follows. On the 13th of the month, either during the day, or in the evening,† they prepare in the name of deceased ancestors‡ and relatives, *polaoo*, and curries, or *hulwa* and bread, or only some *meetha polaoo*; and putting some of it on separate plates in each one's name, they offer *fateeha*, first in the name of the Prophet over one dish, then over the others in the names of the respective individuals. That being done, they put the rice, &c. on a large platter, and having offered *fateeha* over it in the name of all those collectively to whom they are under obligations, or from whom they hope for favours, they dispatch a portion of the food to the houses of all their relatives and friends.

---

* The *arfa* of feasts are always observed on the day previous to the feast itself. The following two only have them, *viz.* the *Shaban* feast, alias *Shub-e-Burat*, and the *Buqr-Eed*.

† Which is the evening of the 14th of the month according to the Mohummudans.

‡ *i. e.* of as many as they can remember; for they keep no written register of them.

The 14th is the feast day. Those who have not observed the *arfa* prepare, either during the day or at night,* certain delicious viands, and offer *fateeha* over them in the name of the Prophet (the peace! &c.) and their deceased ancestors, and amuse themselves in letting off fire-works.

Boys generally, for two or three days previous to the feast, go about playing on small *tumkeean* and *tasay*.

Those who have performed *arfa* prepare on this day *sheer-birrinj* or *meetha polaoo*, and offer *fateeha* over it in the name of his holiness Mohummud Moostuffa (the peace! &c.).†

Some, in the name of their children, when they have a family, make, if they be boys, elephants, if girls, *paootees*,‡ of clay, ornamented or plain, either large or small, and light lamps on them. In front of these on trays they place *choorway*, *k'hopray*, dates, almonds sliced, and sugar, with all kinds of fruits, and offer *fateeha* over them in the name of the Prophet (the peace! &c.).

Some also offer *fateeha* over the elephants in the name of Moortooza Allee, and over the *paootees* in the name of Beebee Fateema. This last is also a species of vow.

In front of the elephants and *paootees* they erect a scaffolding with sugar-cane or wood, and make illuminations by lighting lamps on them: they have also fire-works, such as blue-lights, matches, and flower-pots, &c.

The female relatives, after the conclusion of the *fateeha*, drop into the lamp a rupee or half-rupee piece. The following morning the *choorway*, fruits, &c. are sent from the person who performed the vow, by the hands of the boys and girls, to the near relatives; who, on receiving them,

---

* *i. e.* the night of the 15th of the Mohummudan month.

† Learned men never offer *fateeha* over food; probably because the Prophet never did.

‡ *Paootee*, a kind of lamp.

put into their hands a rupee, a half, or a quarter rupee piece, as a present. With this money, as well as with that put into the lamps the preceding night, they prepare *chukoleean* (alias *sootreean*), and distribute them among their friends; after which they place the elephants and *paootees* over the doors of their houses or on the walls of their compound.

The sitting up all that night, repeating one hundred *rukat* prayers, reading the sacred *Qoran* and *durood*, fasting next day, are all commands of the Prophet. The *arfa* is *bidaut-e-hoosna*;* but all the other ceremonies are innovations, and are superfluous and extravagant.

On the night of the 15th many spend large sums of money in all kinds of fire-works,† and frequently have sham battles, by standing opposed to each other, and letting off fire-works one upon another. This sport generally terminates seriously; for the clothes of many catch fire, some even lose their lives on these occasions, and numbers are wounded.

At this feast, likewise, schoolmasters, by distributing *eedeean* (p. 49) among their scholars, exact presents of money from the childrens' parents, in the manner described under the head of *akhree char shoomba* (p. 232).

---

* That is, it may either be observed or not. Its observance is not meritorious, and *vice versâ*.

† There are more fire-works let off at this feast than at any other, and presents to one another on this day invariably consist of fire-works. *Vide* p. 37.

CHAPTER XXIII.

Concerning 1st. The *Rumzan ka Roza* (or Fast); 2d. The *Turaweeh* Prayers; 3d. *Ay-tay-kaf* byt'hna; 4th. *Lylut-ool-qudur's Shub-bay-daree*, observed in the ninth month, *Rumzan*.

SECT. 1.—*The Rumzan Fast.**

The appointed time for breaking fast (*suhur* or *suhur-gahee*, as this meal is termed during the Mohummudan Lent) is from 2 to 4 A. M., beginning with the morning that succeeds the evening when the *Rumzan* new moon becomes visible. From the above period until sun-set it is unlawful to eat, drink, or have connubial intercourse.†

In this manner they fast every day during this month, and continue day and night engaged in the contemplation of the Deity.‡

The blessings attendant on the observance of this fast, with further particulars respecting it, will be found in Chap. xii. sect. 3. p. 56.

* It was in the sacred month, *Rumzan*, that the sacred *Qoran* descended from heaven. It is the divine command, that both the commencing and the breaking of fast daily should be preceded by the performance of *neeut*, or vowing to that effect.

† In the evening, before the *Mugrib* (page 55) prayer season they breakfast; this meal is termed *Iftar*.

‡ "There are some few who are exempt from the actual necessity "of fasting during *Rumzan*; the sick, the aged, women giving nou-"rishment to infants, and those in expectation of adding to the mem-"bers of the family, and very young children: these are all com-"manded not to fast. There is a latitude granted to travellers also; "but many a weary pilgrim, whose heart is bent heavenward, will be "found taking his rank among the *Rozadars* of the time, without "deeming he has any merit in refraining from the privileges his code "has conferred upon him. Such men will fast whilst their strength "permits them to pursue their way."—Mrs. Meer's Observations, vol. i. page 190.

SECT. 2.—*The Turaweeh Prayers.*

These consist of twenty *rukat* prayers, which it is the Prophet's command (to his followers) to read aloud in the company of others, with the *eemam*, after the time of the *aysha* (p. 55) prayer, and when three *rukats* of the *wajib-ool-wittur* prayers (p. 78) are still unrepeated. After the former being concluded, the latter are to be read.

For the purpose of reading the *turaweeh* prayers it is necessary to employ an *eeman* or *hafiz*, as they finish them in a few days. When the whole *Qoran* has been read through, the *turaweeh* prayers are discontinued. The *hafiz*, or he who has officiated in reading the *turaweeh*, is, after the conclusion of the *Qoran*, rewarded with money or clothes, as may have been previously settled.

Some, after the *Qoran* has been once read through, continue repeating the *turaweeh* prayers and reading the chapters of the *Qoran*, commencing from the one entitled *Alum-e-turkyf* or *Feel* (Elephant, *i. e.* chap. 105.), or from any succeeding chapter to the end of the book, over and over, until the day before the last of the month.

If there be no *hafiz*, it is necessary to repeat the *turaweeh* for thirty days. At the end of every fourth *rukat*, the *eemam* with uplifted hands offers supplications to heaven, and all the congregation respond *Amen!* and *Amen!*

The *sheeas* do not read these prayers, nor even enter the mosque; and for this reason: that after every four *rukats* the congregation, as well as the priest, repeat eulogiums in the name of the four companions, which they cannot bear to hear.

Every Friday* the congregation assemble in the mosque,

* The Mohummudan sabbath.

and the *qazee*, *khuteeb*, or even the *mowazun*, stands in front of them. When the *mowazun* is present, he first of all sounds the *azan* (or summons to prayer, p. 75) they then repeat any thing that they may remember or are in the habit of doing; after which, the *khuteeb* (priest) reads the *khootba* (sermon), which contains praises and eulogiums, admonition, and advice; but on the last Friday of the month, they give such a solemn and pathetic discourse on the *Rumzan* separation called *ulweeda*, and on the excellencies of the night, first in Arabic, and then expound it in Hindee or Persian, that many of the respectable and learned are seriously affected by it, even to tears.

The generality of *Sheeas* observe the night of his excellency Allee; (may God reward him!), and that in a grand style, either on the 21st or 20th of this month. They form a *zureeh* (tomb) in the shape of a *taboot*, and take it out. Beating upon their breasts, they perambulate the streets and bring it home; and having cooked various kinds of food, they offer *fateeha* in the name of his excellency Allee, and eat and distribute them. The reason for observing it on these particular days is, that his excellency Allee departed this life on one of them (which is uncertain).

The *Soonnees* likewise, without taking out the *zureeh*, according to their means, cook victuals and offer *fateeha* over them.

SECT. 3.—*Ay-tay-kaf byt'hna* (*or to be engaged in constant prayer in the mosque*).

Most people during the whole month, some for fifteen days, while others merely on the last day or during three days and three nights, remain in a corner of the mosque enclosed by a curtain or skreen, never go out except to obey the calls of nature, or for the legal purifications *wuzoo* and *gosool*. They never converse with any one on worldly matters, and never cease reading the *Qoran* or praising the Almighty. It is highly meritorious to read it in a loud and audible voice. By such actions many have become men of excellence and penetration, and whose words are powerful as a sharp sword.* In the case of those professional men whose pressing avocations afford no leisure, the observance of *Ay-tay-kaf* for a day and a night is sufficient.

The rite of *ay-tay-kaf byt'hna* is *furz-keefaeeu*, by which term, in fact, many denominate it; that is, if one individual of a town perform it for the whole population, or a single person out of an assembly, this is equivalent to all having observed it. In the same way as at *rumzan*, when one man out of a town sits *gosha nusheen* (*i. e.* in a corner or retired place, engaged in the contemplation of the Deity), it is the same as if all the inhabitants did so; *e. g.* if, when one makes a *sulam* to an assembly, any member of the company rise and return it, every one's "neck" is thereby equally relieved from the obligation.

SECT. 4.—*The Lylut-ool-qudur* (*night of power*).

This has been decided by learned men, both in Arabia and *Ujjum*, to be, agreeably to the *Qoran*, the twenty-seventh night of the month *Rumzan*.

On this date they sit up all night, burning frankincense-pastiles, repeating *nuflen*,† reciting the praises of the Almighty, reading the *Qoran*, and proclaiming the *azan*‡ (*vide* p. 77).

On those who remain awake all that night, the angels

* Whose blessings or curses take effect.

† Pl. of *nufil*—particular prayers. Vide p. 78, and Glossary.

‡ They proclaim the *azan* (or summons to prayer), every now and then during the night.

from heaven continue showering down every hour the peace and blessing of God, even until sunrise next morning. The excellencies of that night are innumerable.*

Among the people of the faith (Moosulmans) there are two things, which are not known to any but prophets; *viz.* 1st. *Lylut-ool-qudur*, a night on which the whole vegetable creation bow in humble adoration to the Almighty, and the waters of the ocean become sweet; and that, all in an instant of time. 2d. *Ism-e-azum* (the great attribute). It is an attribute possessed of such virtues, that a person endowed with a knowledge of it can effect whatever he pleases. He can kill the living and raise the dead to life; and he can instantly transport himself wherever he pleases.

The G*yr Muhdee* (p. 14) erect, each in his own district of the town, a *Jummaut-khana* (meeting-house), where on the night of *Lylut-ool-qudur* they assemble, read *dogana* (two *rukat*) prayers in the name of *Muhdee*, after which they call out three times these words: "*Allah-illah-unna Mohummud Nubeena al Qoran wul Muhdee amunna wo sidqunna*;" *i. e.* "God is almighty, Mohummud is our prophet, and the *Qoran* and *Muhdee* are just and true;" and conclude by saying, "*Eemâm Muhdee* has come and is gone; whoever disbelieves this is an infidel." On hearing which the *soonnees* become so enraged, that they first get boys to pelt them with stones as if in sport, and then attack them with swords. The adversaries, on the other hand, considering it martyrdom to die on such a night, stand up in self-defence at the risk of their lives. For the above

* What is included in this section under the head of *Lylut-ool qudur's Shub-baydaree*, would seem to have been confounded by Mrs. Meer with *Shub-e-Burat*, treated of in the preceding chapter, and observed in the preceding month.—Vide Mrs. M. H. Ali's Obs. vol. i. p. 303.

reason this inveterate hatred continues to exist between these two classes of people to this very day, and numbers of lives are in consequence annually sacrificed. The author has himself been present at two or three of these bloody battles, but has never seen the *Gyr Muhdees* come off conquerors. He has also remarked, in confirmation of a common report, that their dead invariably fall on their faces. When people bring this circumstance to their notice, saying, that their falling in that position arises from their unbelief, they reply, "Not so: our corpses are in the act "of *sijdah* (or prostration in devotion)." The real origin of their enmity is this: The *Soonnees* and *Sheeas* expect the coming of Eemam Muhdee,* while the *Gyr Muhdees* consider Syed Mohummud of Jeo*on*pooree (Jeypoor?) to have been Muhdee, and assert that he has been on earth, and is departed, and will never return; and they venerate Muhdee as highly as they do the Prophet (the peace! &c.), and say, whoever denies him is undoubtedly destined for hell. On that account they are called by others *Gyr Muhdee* (without *Muhdee*), while they name themselves real *Muhdee-walay*, or *Daeeray-walay*;† and denominate others by the appellations *kafir* (infidel) or *Dustugeer-walay*: by the latter, because they themselves place no faith in Peer-e-Dustugeer (p 237). The generality of *Gyr Muhdees* (Note, p. 14), are of the *Putt'han* tribe; but their number is so small in comparison to the *Soonees* and *Sheeas*, that this adage is quite applicable to them: "as salt in wheat flour."‡

* Eemam Muhdee, the twelfth and last *Eemam*, Mohummud surnamed Muhdee; *i. e.* the director and leader, whom the Persians believe to be still alive, and who, according to their belief, will appear again with Elias the prophet on the second coming of Jesus Christ.

† The name of the circular wall which they erect on this occasion.

‡ Alluding to the small quantity of salt which is mixed with a large proportion

CHAPTER XXIV.

Concerning *Eed-ool-fitr*, or *Rumzan kee Eed*, held on the 1st day of the tenth month, *Shuwal.*

The *Eed-ool-fitr* (or feasts of alms), called also the feast of *Rumzan*, is observed on the first day of the month *Shuwal.** This month is likewise termed *Doodh-ka-Muheena*, *Khalee Muheena*, and *Eed-kay-Muheena*, or the feast month. It is called *Doodh-ka-Muheena* (the milk month) by the lower orders, from the circumstance of their preparing *sayweean* (vermicelli) boiled in milk on this occasion; and *Khalee Muheena* (or the vacant month) for this reason, that it is the only month in which no feast takes place.†

On this day, before the feast-prayers, all Moosulmans, of both sexes and all ages, bathe, apply *soorma* to their eyes, wear new clothes, and perfume themselves. But previous to going to the *eed-gah*‡ to prayers, it is first necessary to distribute the *sudqa*§ alias *fitr* (p. 57) in alms amongst *fuqeers* or the poor. It consists of two seers and a half of wheat, dates, grapes, or any grain commonly used for food

---

proportion of flour in preparing the wheaten cakes, which constitutes the chief food of the *Putt'hans.*

* This feast forms the conclusion of the fast kept during the preceding month.

† The one just detailed being considered as belonging to the preceding month *Rumzan*, hence denominated the *Rumzan kee eed* or the *Rumzan* feast, it being the breaking up of the Mohummudan Lent, and consequently attached to it.

‡ *Eed-gah*, a place of feast; or *Numaz gah*, a place of prayer; from *Eed*, feast; *numaz*, prayer; and *gah*, a place.

§ *Sudqa*, alms, propitiatory offerings. Vide Glossary.

in the country, or the value in coin: they may then go to prayers.

In general the people conduct the *qazee* from his house to the *numaz-gah*, and bring him back again in great pomp and state, accompanied by *baja bujuntur;* and the people of every quarter of the town also assemble and proceed thither, and return home in the same manner. On their return, their mothers, sisters, &c. take some water coloured red or yellow, and while still outside of the door wave it over their heads and throw it away; in order that, should any malignant eye have fallen upon them, or should they have trampled upon any thing unpropitious, the effect may be averted. This ceremony, however, many dispense with. While proceeding from their houses to the *eed-gah*, they repeat, or should repeat, softly all the way the *tukbeer* (or creed) viz. *allah-ho-akbur, allah-ho-akbur, la-illah-ha Illaylah, allah-ho-akbur, allah-ho-akbur, wul lillahhoo ul humd;* (p. 81) *i. e.* "God is great, God is great, there is "no other God save the one true God; God is great, God "is great, and praise be to God."

Should those who keep the fast neglect to give the *fittra*, their fast, *turaweeh*, *ay-tay-kaf*, and prayers, will be kept suspended in the air midway between earth and heaven.

The *khuteeb* (priest), after repeating two *rukat* prayers, alias *shookreea*, ascends to the second or middle step* of the

---

* The *Soonnees* have three, the *Sheeas* four steps to their *mimbur* or pulpit, in the centre of the wall which constitutes the *Eed-gah*, or a place of assembly. It is said, that the Prophet used to stand on the uppermost step; his successor, Aba Bukur, on the second; and Oomr, his successor, on the third or lowermost; but Oosman his successor, remarking that at this rate they would reach the bottom of the earth, discontinued the practice of descending one step at each succession, and fixed upon the second, or middle step, as the established one for standing upon, in reading the *khootba* or sermon.

mimbur, and the congregation being seated, he reads the *khootba; i.e.* offers glory to God, praises the Prophets, and passes eulogiums on his companions. He then descends to the lowermost step, recounts the many virtues of the king, and offers up supplications on behalf of him. The king is he whose coin is current in the realm, and in whose name prayers are offered up after the *khootba* is read at the mosques and at feasts.*

Should a *nuw-wab* (nabob), as the king's representative, be present, he makes the *khuteeb*, at the time of reading the *khootba*, a present of a *khilaut;* or some opulent native of the town, or the liberal-minded among *soobah-dars*† and *jumadars*‡ spread a piece of muslin over him as a present. Some throw gold and silver flowers over the *qazee's* head, and which his servants or relatives pick up for him.

After that, the *khuteeb* again ascends to the middle step and offers *moonajat; i.e.* supplicates heaven for the prosperity of their religion and for the remission of the sins of all Moosulmans, for the safety of pilgrims and travellers, for the recovery of the sick, for increase of rain, for abundance of corn, for preservation from misfortunes, for freedom from debt. He then descends from the pulpit, sits on a *jae-numaz* (p. 78, 119), and offers up supplications in behalf of all people; the congregation at the end of each sentence (or prayer) say *ameen* (amen). On the conclusion of the *moonajat*, the whole congregation rising up, call out the word "*deen*" (religion), and fire off guns and muskets.

* At present (1832) it is in the name of the king of Dehli; but in the author's opinion erroneously, as it should be in the name of the Honourable East-India Company.

† *Soobah-dar* (holder of provinces;) but now applied to the first rank in the native army of the Honourable East-India Company.

‡ *Jumadar* (properly *Zumeendar* or land-holder), to the second rank.

Then friends mutually embracing, and strangers shaking hands, congratulate one another by wishing each other "good health" on the occasion of the feast; and, repeating the *durood* (or blessing), they perform *dustbosee*, or shake (lit. kiss) hands with the *qazee*.

At such times there is a large concourse of *fuqeers* and beggars assembled, who crave charity; when, those who can afford it, dispense among them *cowries*, *pice*, or quarter, half, or rupee pieces. Should people at that time not have had an opportunity of meeting with any of their relatives or friends, or with any men of rank, they proceed to their houses, to pay them visits, when the latter offer the visitors *pan-sooparee*, and sometimes also apply *sundul* to their necks and *uttur* to their clothes, and even entertain them with something in the way of food.

The same ceremonies are observed at the *buqr-eed* (vide p. 266).

The above prayers are to be read between 7 or 8 A. M. and noon, and not to be deferred till after that time.

On this day, previous to going to hear the *khootba* read, they prepare *sayweean*, and cook it with *ghee*, milk, sugar, almonds, dates, dried cocoa-nuts sliced, poppy-seed, *cheerownjee* and *moonuqa;* and having offered *fateeha* over it in the name of the Prophet (the peace! &c.), they, either then, or after their return from hearing the *khootba*, send off a portion of it to all their friends, distribute some among the poor, and partake of it themselves.

Some people send to their relatives and friends more or less, according to their means, of the different ingredients of which it is composed, uncooked.

At this feast, also, schoolmasters (as related before, p. 49) distribute *eedeean* (holiday gifts) among their scholars on the day preceding, and receive presents.

CHAPTER XXV.

Concerning *Bunda Nuwaz*'s *Churagan* (or lamps, *i. e.* illuminations), observed on the 16th day of the eleventh month, *Zeeqaeda;* also called *Bunda-nuwaz*'s month.

His holiness Bunda Nuwaz, surnamed *Gaysoo duraz*, or "the long-ringletted," (may God sanctify his sepulchre!) was a great *wullee*. He observed in one of his religious reveries, that in the event of people being unable, for substantial reasons, to undertake the pilgrimage to Mecca, their visiting *his* mausoleum, once in their lives, would be attended with the same benefit as performing the pilgrimage. His blessed shrine is at Gool-burgah* (Calburgah). There, on the 16th of the month, in the day-time, they perform his *sundul*, and on the night following the 17th day (*i.e.* the 18th night of the Mohummudans), they observe his *oors* with the same splendour and state as that of his excellency Qadir Wullee is observed at Nagore-Nagputtun (p. 243); nay, if any thing, with greater splendour.

In other countries, however, it is on the 15th and 16th that they have illuminations in his name, cook *maleeda* or *polaoo*, offer *fateeha* over them, send some to their relatives, partake themselves of it, and distribute to others.

On the night of the 16th, (*i. e.* the 17th night of the Moosulmans,) some people pour *ghee* into sixteen lamps previously prepared of silver or paste, and having therein lighted wicks, place them on *maleeda* and offer *fateeha* over them, as described at p. 238.

---

* *Gool-burgah*, or a place of roses; from *goolburg*, rose-petals, and *gah*, a place.

CHAPTER XXVI.

Concerning the *Buqr-eed* (*qoorbanee*, or sacrifice); alias *Eed-ool-zoha*; its *Arfa* and *Eed* (or feast), held on the 9th day of the twelfth month, *Buqr-eed*.

On the day or evening of the 9th of the month *Zil-hujja* or *Buqr-eed*, they cook *polaoo*, *hulwa*, and *chupateean*, and perform *arfa*, in the same way as the *shaban*, alias *shub-e-burat arfa*, was observed and described at p. 252; such as offering *fateeha* in the names of deceased ancestors; and on that day some even keeping fast; a fast called *nuhur*, which continues for one and a quarter watch (*i. e.* till within a quarter of ten A.M.).

On the morning of the 10th they proceed to the *eed-gah* to prayers, repeating the *tukbeer* aloud all the way from their houses to the *eed-gah*, in the same manner as they did at the *Eed-e-Rumzan* (or *Eed-ool-fitr*, p. 261).*

Among the opulent, each person, after prayers, sacrifices a sheep† (carried thither on purpose) in the name of God; or seven individuals, men women and children conjointly, sacrifice a cow or a camel,‡ (p. 67) for those who offer such sacrifices will be carried by these animals as quickly as

---

* Kings, princes, or *Nuw-wabs* proceed to the *Eedgah* in great pomp and state. A very interesting and accurate account of processions on these occasions is given by Mrs. M. H. Ali, vol. i. p. 263.

† This feast is held in commemoration of Abraham's intending to sacrifice his son Ismaeel, agreeably to the Mohummudans, and not Is-haq (Isaac).

‡ The reason for sacrificing the camel, &c. (according to Mrs. Meer), is that such animals will be in readiness to assist those who offer them, on their passage over the *Poolsirat*, to eternity. Vol. i. p. 140.

a horse goes, or as lightning, over the *Pool-sirat.** This does not include poor people, because they are not *Sahib-e-nissab* (p. 58).

Other particulars relative to the sacrifice, having already been detailed under the head of *Pilgrimage* (p. 60), *Turweea* (p. 65), and *Qoorbanee* (p. 67), I have here treated the subject concisely.

Moreover, after every *furz* prayer, from the morning of *Arfa* (the 9th) until the season of the *ussur* (or afternoon-prayer, p. 55) on the 13th of the month, they are to repeat once the *tukbeer*†*-e-tushreek* (p. 69).

After prayers they prepare *kubab* of the meat sacrificed as above, and *rotee*; and each one at his own house having had *fateeha* offered over them, in the name of his holiness Ibraheem and Ismaeel, and having distributed them to people, they breakfast.

Some fast till after the *khootba*, when having prepared *seekh-rotee*,‡ they offer *fateeha* over it, and eat.

Many cook various delicious dainties on the occasion and distribute them.

Some, who possess the means, send to each relative or friend, according to their rank, one, two, or more sheep; while others again send one or two fore or hind quarters, or distribute only some portions of it.

The flesh of the animal so sacrificed is divided into three portions; one is for the use of the sacrificer himself; a second is given in alms to the poor and indigent; the third is bestowed among relatives and friends (p. 67).

As at the *Eed-e-Rumzan* (p. 264), so at this, school-

---

* *Pool-sirat*, the bridge over the eternal fire, across which the Moosulmans believe they must pass into paradise. † Page 262.

‡ *Seekh* properly means a skewer; but here signifies meat trussed on skewers broiled, and served up with *rotee* or bread.

masters distribute *eedeean* (p. 49) among their scholars, and procure in return *eedeeana* (holiday presents).

Among Moosulmans, the *eed-ool-fitr* and *eed-ool-Zoha* (or *Buqr-eed*) are two grand *eeds* (festivals). On these occasions, both the learned and illiterate resort to the *eed-gah*, considering them real feasts. Independently of these, however, there are others; such as the *Ashoora*, *Akhree-char-shoomba*, *Shub-e-burat*, &c. which properly are not feasts, but are observed as such; consequently, with the exception of the two former, all that has been related, as occurring in the other months of the year, are nothing more than *fateeha* offered in the names of eminent saints, and cannot be comprehended under the denomination of *eeds* or feasts.

In many towns and villages there are the shrines (*chillas* or *astanas*, as they are called) of celebrated saints; where the inhabitants of the place, annually, in different months of the year, perform, according to their convenience, *sundul*, *oors*, and *fateeha*, in their names. For example, at Hydrabad, in the name of his holiness Mowla Allee, they perform his *sundul* on the 16th, and his *churagan* (or *oors*) on the 17th of the month *Rujub*, and that on a hill named after him, about five miles to the north-east of the cantonment of Secunderabad and about three or four coss (six or eight miles) from the city of Hydrabad. The noise and bustle, which take place there on that occasion, can only be conceived by an eye-witness. It continues during the above two days in all its grandeur, but people are busily occupied about it,* a day or two before and after. Nay, there is

* Erecting booths where all sorts of things, eatables, drinkables, &c. are sold, decorating houses (some of the latter with European articles of furniture), from the terraces, windows, and verandahs of which, a fine view is obtained on the festival days, of the scene below, where

more fun and sport going on at this than even at the *ashoora*.*

On the 18th day of this month another feast is celebrated, and that solely by the *Sheeahs* or *Emameins*, called Gudeer غدير (alluded to at p. 10). It is described in the *Bara Masa* as being a great solemnity, which the soul rejoices to reflect upon, the happy mention of which, is listened to with delight. All use but one language (the author observes) in extolling the excellencies of this feast, which is in commemoration of the express declaration, made on that day by Mohummud, agreeably to the command of God, that Allee, the commander of the faithful and the king of saints, was to be his successor. This message was delivered at a place called *Gudeer Khoom*, a halting station for *karwans* (caravans), where there are a number of constantly running streams, situated half-way between Mecca and Medina. It is from the name of this place, that the feast has derived its appellation. It is moreover said, that whoever observes this feast will be entitled to place his foot in the kingdom of heaven.

CHAPTER XXVII.

Concerning *Nuzur-o-Nyaz*, or Vows and Oblations.

There are various kinds and descriptions of vows and oblations, or dedications.

Men and women, *Sheeahs* and *Soonnees*, to the extent

---

where an innumerable crowd of men, women, children, elephants beautifully caparisoned, horses, &c. passing and repassing, present a motley appearance.

* *i. e. Mohurrum*, q. v. p. 172.

of each one's belief in these things, vow, that when what they desire shall come to pass, they will, in the name of God, the Prophet, his companions, or some *wullee*, present offerings and oblations. For instance, if any should recover from sickness, or find a lost sheep, or obtain employment (service), or be blessed with offspring, or if his foe be ruined or killed, or if his master be pleased with him, or if he obtain promotion, then in the name of each of these, there are certain forms observed, and particular victuals cooked. Of this I shall select a few examples.

Nuzur-Oollah (an offering unto God). This consists in preparing *polaoo*, *qoorma*, and *rotee*, and distributing them among friends and the poor, and giving any sort of grain, a sacrificed sheep, clothes, or ready-money in alms to the indigent.

Some women prepare *dood'h-payray*, or *pindeean*, with sugar, milk, and rice, or wheat flour; others also *mulleeda* and *goolgoollay*, offer *fateeha* over them, and distribute them to all.

It is not essentially necessary that *fateeha* should be offered in the name of God; it is sufficient to say, at the time of making the vow, that the oblation is in the name of God. It is merely the vulgar who have such faith in it, that they never dispense with the custom, or eat the food, without first having offered *fateeha* over it. The above *pindeean* are called *oollah-ruhum kay pindeean*, or only *ruhum*.*

Some fry flour in *ghee*, add to it sugar, fruits, *k'hopra*, dates, sliced almonds, and *chironjee*,† and offer *fateeha* over them. This is called *asan* (easy).

---

* *i. e.* The merciful God's *Pindeean*; or "the merciful."

† Nut of the chironjia sapida, Roxb. also called *Pyal*.

Many women prepare *ruhum* (*vide* above) *goolgoollay*, *mulleeda*, and observe *rutjugga* (nocturnal vigils), sitting up all night, playing on the *d'hol* and singing.

Some women, at weddings, or at any other time, after their wishes have been realized, prepare *pindeean*, in the name of Peer Shittab. The manner of doing this is as follows. A *sohagin* (married) woman, or a widow, is bathed, dressed neatly, and supplied with red twisted thread, on which are formed nine, eleven, or nineteen knots. She is then dispatched to all their relatives and friends for the purpose of begging. On her arrival at the doors of the different houses, she calls out, "I am come to untie the "knots of Peer Shittab." Then the people of the house throw into her lap half a *seer* or a *seer* of unboiled rice; whereupon she unravels one of the knots. When all the knots have been thus undone, and she has begged at the several houses corresponding to the number of knots, and returned home, the mistress of the house, with the rice thus obtained, prepares *pindeean*, and transmits one to every house where the woman had begged.

Or, in the name of Peer-millaoo, they prepare *rotee* of wheat, or dress *maat-kay-bhajee*,* and place along with them *goor*, sugar, *ghee*, or *til* (gingilie) oil,† offer *fateeha* over them, eat, and distribute them within doors, but never carry them abroad. Some dig an *allawa* (p. 173), in a corner of the room, over which they wash their hands;‡ and having thrown the food, together with the remnants of the meal, into it, they fill it up with earth.

* Amaranthus tristis, Lin.

† Ol. Sesam. orientale, Lin.

‡ The Indian mode of washing hands differs from the European: they do not dip their hands into the water, but, while an attendant pours water out of an ewer, wash the hands over the basin.

Or, they fill Peer Deedar's *koonday*,* with *duhee* and boiled rice.

Or, in the name of *Kat Bawa Sahib*, they prepare a curry of a cock and *rotee*, offer *fateeha* over them, and distribute.

Some women preserve *choontees* † (p. 32), from one to five in number, on their children's heads, and consecrate them in the name of some celebrated *wullee*, saying, "I "dedicate this to so and so; and when the child has at- "tained such an age (specifying it), I shall prepare *polaoo*, "&c., offer *fateeha*, and have the *choontees* shaved by the "barber."

Again, some in the Dukk'hin (or south, erroneously written Deccan), after their wishes have been fulfilled, float *juhaz* (mimic ships), as has already been described under the head of *huldee*, in the third section of the chapter treating on "Marriage."

Or, they merely take one, two, or three lamps made of paste or earth, light them with thread-wicks in *ghee*, put them on an earthen or brass plate, with *cowries* in them, more or less according to their means, and carry them to the sea-beach, or to the margin of any river, spring, or well, offer *fateeha* over them, and leave them there. In carrying them thither, shopkeepers as well as travellers put *cowries* and *pice* into them. After the *fateeha*, children scramble for the *cowries* and *pice*; but the brazen dish is brought home by the owner.

There are some people who, every Thursday in the year, put a few flowers and some sugar in a *dona*,‡ and launch it

---

* An earthen vessel, somewhat in the shape of a flower-pot.

† *Choontee*, the plait or tie of hair behind the head.

‡ *Dona*, a leaf folded up so as to hold a parcel of *betel*-leaves, flowers, food, or any other thing.

on the water, in the name of Khoaja-khizur, and at times throw a number of *kowries* into the water.

I understand that, in Bengal, it is usual, on any Thursday (but among the rich generally on the last one) of the Bengalee month *Bhadon*, for both men and women to fast all day in the name of Khoaja-khizur; and that having made one or two *juhaz*, alias *bayra*, or *mohur-punk'hee*, or *luchka*, of split bamboo frame-work, covered with coloured paper, ornamented with tinsel, beautifully formed, and elegantly lighted up with *kuwn-wul** and decorated with flowers, they burn incense, and carry *sheerbirrinj* or *duleea*, and *roteean*, or fowl-curries with *roteean*, or sweetmeats, sometimes to the amount of twenty rupees' worth; and playing on *tasa-murfa*, *baja-bujuntur*, *nuqaray*, letting off fire-works in great pomp and state, accompanied by friends and relatives, convey them on men's shoulders, as they do *taboots* (p. 182), to the brink of the river, where they fix them on floating rafts, made by trussing the trunks of plantain-trees on bamboo skewers. They also take a couple of plates, one containing the food of oblation, the other the paste or silver lamps, lit up with *ghee* and thread (as a wick), and having had *fateeha* offered over them by the *moolla* in the name of Khoaja-khizur, they give to the *moolla* his fee of a rupee or two for performing the *fateeha;* and having put the above two plates, with some cash, as an offering, into it they set it adrift on the water. Afterwards, grown-up persons as well as boys jump into the water, swim for, and plunder it.

Some take the *bayras* to the middle of the river, and

* *Kuwn-wul*, lit. the *lotus*, but here referring to a sort of a shade made with mica and coloured paper, intended to represent the *lotus*, within which they burn wax candles.

there set them adrift; but, previously to so doing, set afloat on the stream hundreds of earthen-plates, one after another, containing lamps. A few of the more wealthy construct the above rafts on a scale sufficiently large to allow hundreds of people to stand on one of them; and fixing numbers of *mohur-punk'hees*, &c. on it, with a great deal of illumination, letting off fire-works, burning blue-lights, and firing off matchlocks, they float down with the tide in the middle of the river. The whole presents a fine spectacle, and the crowd of spectators enjoy its splendour in a most agreeable manner from the shores. After which, the vowers bring the food home, entertain their friends and relatives with it, and distribute some of it among the people of the house.

The poor place on two earthen plates, two *goochee** *betel*-leaves, with five *sooparee*† in each, a little *peetalee sheernee*‡ folded up in plantain§ leaves, and two lamps with *ghee*, together with five, nine, or twenty-one *kowries*, or as many *gundas*‖ of them, and take along with these an empty *lota*, and proceed in the evening to the banks of the river; and there, having lighted up the lamps, they get the *fateeha* offered in the name of Khoaja-khizur by the *moolla* (to whom they give the *kowries*), and float the plates on the water, which the children immediately plunder. People behold the fun, enjoy a laugh, and are delighted. At last the person who has made the vow fills the *lota* with water and brings it home, and with a mouthful of that water breaks fast, takes his meal, and goes to sleep.

After the same fashion they perform other vows: such as,

---

* A *goochee* is a bundle, of a hundred betel-leaves.

† *Sooparee*, areca-nuts, or betel-nuts.

‡ *Peetalee sheernee*, cakes of *jaggree* or raw sugar.

§ Musa paradisiaca, Lin

‖ Four of any thing is a *gunda*.

Lunggur, detailed under the head of *Mohurrum*, p. 217
Gendguhwara 220
Door, Baoolee, Bolaq .... do.
Bayree 239
Budd'hee 242
Kundoree 249
G'*horay* 250
Koonday .... do.

And in the same manner, in the name of renowned individuals, they put on their children *nut'h-nees*, *hunslees*, *towqs*, *zunjeers*, and *torras*.

It is a general custom that when about to undertake a journey, or when a misfortune befalls a person, they tie up a *pice*, a quarter, half or one *rupee* piece, or a *ch'hulla*,* in a bit of cloth dyed yellow with turmeric, in the name of Emam Zamin, and wear it tied on to the left upper arm. On reaching their destination in safety, or in getting rid of their affliction, they take it off; and with its value, or adding something to it, they purchase *sheernee*, or prepare *maleeda* or some sort of *polaoo*, and offer *fateeha* in the name of his holiness.†

Learned men, exclusive of the *nuzur-oollah*, *nyaz-e-russool*, *fateeha e huzrut-shah*‡ and *peer-e-dustugeer*, perform

* *Ch'hulla*, a thin wiry metallic ring.

† "When any one is going on a journey, the friends send bands of "silk or riband, in the folds of which are secured silver or gold coins. "These are to be tied on the arm of the person projecting the journey, "and such offerings are called *Emam zaminee*, or the *Emam's* pro- "tection. Should the traveller be distressed on his journey, he may, "without blame, make use of any such deposits tied on his arm, but "only in emergencies. None such occurring, he is expected, when "his journey is accomplished in safety, to divide all these offerings of "his friends amongst righteous people. The *Syeds* may accept these "gifts, such being considered holy, (*paak*)."—Mrs. Meer, vol. i. p. 253.

‡ *Huzrut Shah*, a name of Mowla Allee.

two or four other vows and oblations; such as *tosha*,* in the name of Shah-Ahmud-Abd-ool-Huq of Rad'holee. They prepare *hulwa* with equal weights of *ghee*, sugar, and flour; the more devout preparing and eating it themselves, on no account ever giving any of it to smokers or to women.

In the name of Su-munnee, alias Shah Shurf Boo Allee Qulundur, and Shah Shurf ood Deen Yeh-eea Moonayree, and Ahmud Khan, and Moobariz Khan, they prepare a dish of food, of one *maund*† of *qoorma* made of meat, one *maund* of *duhee*, one *maund* of wheaten *munday* or *rooteea*n (*i. e.* leavened or unleavened bread), offer *fateeha* over them, and distribute them among men and women.

They also perform the *tosha* of the *ashab-e-kuhuf*;‡ dressing meat or *roteea*n with *duhee*. Seven brothers, called Aleekha, Muksulimta, Tub-yu-nus, Kushfootut, Udurqut, Yunus, and Yuânus, were very cordial friends together, and the most virtuous among the children of Israel; and they had also an affectionate dog, named *Qutmeera*. In the name of these seven, they take out seven plates full of the above food, offer *fateeha* over, then eat, and distribute them. They have likewise a separate dish for the dog, which is not placed with the others, but given to some dog to eat.

The *Sheeahs* prepare *hazree* (breakfast) in the name of his holiness 'Abbas Allee Ullum-burdar, Hosein's step-bro-

* *Tosha*, provision, particularly, of a traveller, or that which is carried with the funeral of a deceased person, to support him during his journey to the other world. *Viaticum*.

† A *mun* or *maund*, equal to forty seers or eighty lbs.

‡ *Ashab-e kuhuf*, or the companions of the cave; *i.e.* the seven sleepers. This is founded on a legend of seven young Christians of Ephesus, who fled, as they say, from the persecution of the emperor Decius, and slept in a cave, accompanied only by their dog, for three hundred and nine years. Mohummud has adopted this story in the eighteenth chapter of the *Qoran*.

ther; *i. e.* they cook *polaoo, rotee*, curries, &c. and distribute them; but among none save *Sheeahs*. In fact, after the *fateeha*, they even revile the companions before they partake of the food.

The generality of their women vow and make *poorun* in the name of Eemam Jaffur Sadiq (may God be pleased with him!). That is, they dress *pooreean*, offer *fateeha*, eat, and distribute it to all.

Some women make the *kundoree* of her ladyship, Beebee Fateemat-ooz Zohura. That is, they prepare various kinds of food in a private* place, of which respectable and virtuous ladies are alone entitled to partake: no one else is allowed a share. Men are not even permitted to look at it, and the *fateeha* is offered over it, under cover of a curtain.

Sometimes they prepare *beebee ka sanuk*, alias *beebee ka basun*, (p. 108).

Some women prepare, in the name of Shah Dawul, *roteean* with *juwar*,† *bajray*,‡ or any other kind of grain, *maleeda*, *maat kay bhajee*, and place *goor* along with them, and offer *fateeha*. Some prepare them with their own money, with more or less grain procured by begging. The man or woman who is sent to beg, goes to the houses either of their relatives or of strangers, and calls out *shah-dawul*. The landlord, on hearing the sound, gives him a *seer* or half a *seer* of any kind of grain. Some sacrifice a sheep in his name, cook *polaoo* and *quleea*, eat and distribute.

Some, when any difficulty or misfortune befalls them, set out on their travels with their wives and families, all dressed in blue; and subsist (lit. fill their bellies) by begging.

---

* In secret, because being her ladyship's food, it is not proper that every one, especially men, should see it.

† *Juwar*, or great millet (Holcus saccharatus, Lin.).

‡ *Bajray*, (Holcus spicatius, Lin. Panicum spinatum, Roxb.).

When their difficulties have been removed they return home, and make vows according to their means.

Some irreligious women prepare *kurrahee** (or *goolgoollay*), in the name of Sheikh Suddoo, and by artifice, (for if known that it is *Sheikh Suddoo's fateeha,* no one would perform it) contrive to get the person who offers *fateehas* to do it over this food. This ceremony is denominated *meean kee* (or *Sheikh Suddoo*† *kee*) *kurrahee.*

Moreover, some impious women fix upon a day, and dressing themselves in men's clothes, have a meeting at night, which is called *bythuk.* In this assembly they have flowers, *pan, uttur, sundul,* and *sheernee. Domneeans* or other women play on the *puk'hawuj* or *d'holuk,* and sing. Then this wicked woman, on whose head *Sheikh Suddoo* is, becoming as if intoxicated, continues whirling her head round; and foolish women who wish any particular thing to happen, apply to her, to direct them how to succeed in accomplishing it. For instance, a woman says " Meean, I go *sudqee*‡ (or I offer my life for you;) that I " may have a child." Then the revolving woman, if she pleases, gives her a *beera,*§ some of her own *oogal,*|| or some *sheernee,* which she, with profound faith, actually eats. However, God is Lord of all, and it depends upon his will and pleasure whether the woman shall be with child or not. But if perchance she should bring forth a child, the belief of these unfortunate creatures in these things is wonderfully confirmed, and they turn real infidels. Should she not have a child, she concludes Meean is angry with her, and re-

* *Kurrahee,* or frying-pan. † Vide Plate.

‡ *Sudqee jana,* to become a sacrifice for the welfare, &c. of another.

§ *Beera.* Vide Glossary, *pan ka beera.*

|| *Oogal,* that which is spit out after chewing *betel*-leaf.

peats the ceremony with redoubled credulity. The case is similar in other affairs.

Sensible and learned people have no faith in *Sheikh Suddoo*, but consider him in the light of a devil. His tomb, or rather the spot marked out where he disappeared, is at Amrohee, where there is always a great deal of noise and bustle.*

Besides these there are other objects of superstition; such as malignant spirits, fairies, *Nurseea*,† *Mata*,† &c. in which many believe. May God blacken the faces‡ of such people.

Some, to obtain the accomplishment of their wishes, petition his majesty Seekundur (Alexander the Great), vowing that should their desire be gratified they will offer up horses in his name. Accordingly, when their wishes are realized, they cause small burnt earthen-horses with riders on them to be made, and having had *fateeha* offered in his highness's name, they convey them in great pomp and state to the spot fixed on for his *astana*, and place them there; and at such places hundreds of such horses lie in heaps.

Some, after making small horses, place them in front of their houses, or set them up over their doors.

Many, among Hindoos as well as Moosulmans, have

---

* "The ignorant part of the population of Hindoostan," Mrs. M. H. Ali observes, "hold a superstitious belief in the occasional visi-"tations of the spirit of Sheikh Suddoo. It is very common to hear "the vulgar people say, if any one of their friends is afflicted with "melancholy, hypochondria, &c.: 'Ay, it is the spirit of Sheikh "Suddoo has possessed him.' In such cases the spirit is dislodged "from the afflicted person by sweetmeats, to be distributed among "the poor; to which is added, if possible, the sacrifice of a black "goat." For further particulars of the history of Sheikh Suddoo, vide Mrs. M. H. Ali's "Observations on the Mussulmans of India," vol. ii. p. 324.

† Hindoo deities.

‡ That is, send them to hell; for the moment they get there, their faces are supposed to get black by being scorched in the fire.

great veneration for the above celebrated character; and I have observed, in some places, Hindoos offer horses in the above way in the name of some of their deities; consequently it cannot be discovered without enquiry whether such places are *astanas* or idol temples.

Independently of these, there are innumerable other saints, at whose shrines oblations are offered; and that usually at their *oorses*; at many of them by Hindoos as well as Moosulmans. I shall name a few of those most generally known, *e.g.*

Sooltan Sarwar, at Baloutch, four coss from Moultan.

Shah Shums-ood-Deen-Dariai, at Depaldal in Lahore.

Qoottoob Sahib, or Qoottoob-ood-Deen, near Dehli.

Sheikh Buha-ood-Deen, Zakaria (or Zukhmee; *vide* Mooltan Ham. Gaz.) at Cotcaror in Moultan.

Furreed-ood-Deen (surnamed Shukurgunj), at Ghanawal near Moultan.

Shah Nizzam-ood-Deen Owleea, at Dehli.

Kubeer punthee, or Nanuk punthee, at Ruttunpore in Oude.

Baba Lal, at Dhianpoor in Lahore.

Shah Dola, at Sealkote in Lahore.

Syed Shah Zouhour, at Allahabad.

Sheikh Mohummud Ali Hazin Gillanee, at Benares in Allahabad.

Hosein Abdaul, or Baba Wullee, in a valley called Hosein Abdaul, in Lahore.

Peer Julal, near Lucknow, in Oude.

Syed Zein ool Abay Deen, at Rowza, in Aurangabad.

Shah Arzanee, at Patna, in Bahar.

Shah Lohaunee, at Monghir, in Bahar.

Nekmundun, at Bhowanipoor, in Bengal.

Asoph-ood-Dowlah, at Lucknow, in Oude.

Shah Selim Chishtee, at Futtipoor Sikra, in Agra.

Hafiz, at Shiraz, in Persia.

Mowluwee Meer Askaree, at Juanpoor.

Kureem-ood-Deen.

Zain Shah, &c.

In the Duk'hun:

Huzrut Baba Fuqr-ood-Deen Gunj-ool-Israr, at Pilgoonda, in Mysore.

Chundur Buddun, and Mohy Yeear, at Cuddry Caticul, in Canara.

Tubur-e-Allum, or Nuthur Wullee, at Trichinopoly.

Syed Abd-ool-Qadir, at Oodgeer.

Hajee Ruhmut Oollah, at Rumtabad.

Baba Boodun, or Hyat-ool-Buhur, on Baba Boodun's Mountains, (S.E. of Nuggur or Bednore), in Beejapoor.

Malik Ryhan Sahib, at (Burra) Serah, in Mysore.

Sheikh Furreed, at Gooty in the ceded districts.

Seekundur Padshah, at Madura, in S. Carnatic.

Karwa Owleea at Tripetty in the Carnatic.

Hydur Wullee, at Muroodga.

Tippoo Padshah, at Arcot, in the Carnatic, &c. &c.

CHAPTER XXVIII.

Concerning *Tureequt*, or the Path (*i. e.* to Heaven). It comprises three sections; *viz.* 1st. The becoming a *Mooreed* (disciple); 2d. The manner of making a *Fuqeer* (devotee), and the investiture of the *Kheelafut* (deputyship); 3d. The austerities requisite to be practised in order to become a *Wullee* (saint).

SECT. 1. *The becoming a Mooreed, or Disciple.*

The custom of making *Mooreeds* had its origin with our ancestors. The becoming one is also termed *Tulqeen* or *Byat*. For this purpose, there are sages or *Mushaekhs*, who are great votaries, virtuous, sensible and learned, and whose office it is to do it.

When a man or woman wishes to become a *Mooreed*, he goes to one of the sages belonging to the household of the particular *peer* (saint), in whose *silsilla* (family descent) he himself has established his belief, or invites him and other friends and relations to his own house, and there, should Providence have blessed him with the means, he entertains them with *polaoo*, &c.

Either before or after dinner, in the presence of the assembly, or in a closet, the *Moorshud*, after performing *wuzoo*, with his face turned towards the East, seats the candidate for the *mooreedship* before him, with his face towards him,* or, as with some, facing any way. Then he takes hold of the right hand of the *Mooreed* with his (their thumbs touching one another, somewhat after the manner of shaking hands), and keeps them together. If it be a female, and one in the habit of going about openly, she takes hold of one extremity of a handkerchief or *putka*, and he the other, while he is making her a *moreed;* but if she be one who is veiled from public observation, she sits concealed behind a skreen or curtain (and that because the *peer* is one of the excluded, that is not a relative, although he be a *Moorshud*), and she thus lays hold of the handkerchief or *putka* as above, and becomes a disciple. They deposit near them, for the *Moorshud*, according to their means, a suit of clothes, a *khilaut*, some ready-money, *d'han-kay k'heeleean*, *butasha*, *sheernee*, *sundul*, ornaments or garlands made of flowers, and lighted benjamin-pastiles.

First of all he directs the disciple to repeat the *Ustugfar* (or deprecation), and the five *kulmay* (or creeds), besides

---

* So that the disciple may look towards the West or the *qibla*.

some other supplications; after which the *Mooreed* says to his *peer*, "Whatever sins I have intentionally, or unin-"tentionally committed, I do now, this instant, repent of, "and I promise sincerely, before my *peer*, and in the "presence of God and his Messenger, never to commit "them again." Then the *Moorshud* sums up to him the names of all his *peers* contained in the *Shujra*,* which goes back as far as the time of the Prophet (the peace! &c.); and enquires, "Do you consent to acknowledge these "*peers*?"

Some *peers*, naming merely their own *Moorshud*, ask, "As I have accepted him, do you accept me as your "*moorshud*?" The disciple replies, in either case, "I "do." When he has repeated all their names, he lets go the disciple's hand, takes a cup of *shurbut*, offers certain supplications over it, and, having blown upon it, and taken two or three mouthfuls of it himself, hands it to his disciple, who instantly rises from his seat, and drinks the whole off with the utmost reverence. Some *Moorshuds* make them also read two *rukat* prayers of *Shookreea* (thanksgiving). After this, such money, &c. as was intended for the *Moorshud* is presented to him. The candidate, after having been made a *Mooreed*, makes *qudum-bosee*† to the *Moorshud* and *sulam* to all present, who return the *sulam*, adding, "Be thou blessed."

Next day or the day after, the *Moorshud* furnishes his disciple with a copy of the *Shujra*, in order that he may remember them.

Some foolish and ignorant people consider these *Shujras* as most sacred, and even venerate them more than the *Qoran*:

---

* *Shujra* (vulgo. *Shijra*). A list of saints or holy predecessors, in the form of a genealogical tree given to disciples.

† Vide *Sulam*, Gloss.

nay, they make amulets of them, and wear them round their arms and necks; and when they die are buried with these placed on their breasts.

The *Moorshud* then reveals to the disciple, in a whisper, (lit. breast to breast, hand in hand, and ear to ear), all the secret mysteries of godliness.

They esteem *moorshuds* as their own fathers, and people in the world are said to have four fathers: as stated before, when treating of the *Qoran kee Huddeea*, p. 48.

SECT. 2. *The manner of making a Fuqeer (Devotee); the consideration of the four Peers (Saints,) and fourteen khan-waday (Households), from which Fuqeers in general have descended; together with other varieties of Fuqeers, as also of Mushaekhs; and the investiture with the Kheelafut (Deputyship).*

When a *moorshud* is about to make any one a *fuqeer*, either in his own *silsilla* (race) or in any other in which he has the authority so to do, the candidate, according to his means, prepares *polaoo*, *birreeanee*, or *quleea*, and *nân*, and gives a *mayla*.* On this occasion about forty or fifty *fuqeers*, more or less, of various tribes, together with their friends and beggars, are assembled by invitation, and the *fuqeer* whose office it is to bear the messages of invitation is named *Iznee*. At the time of making one a *fuqeer* they have flowers, *sundul*, *sheernee*, *ganja*, *bhung*, *sook'ha*, *goorakoo*, all present. The *moorshud* first of all gets the candidate's four *abroos*, *viz.* the hair of his beard, of his mustachios, of his eyebrows, and of the rest of the body, removed; or instead of shaving these, they clip a few (lit.

---

* *Mayla*, literally signifies a fair, but is a term also applied to entertainments given to *fuqeers*.

five or seven) hairs off each part with a pair of scissors. During the operation of shaving off the hair and paring the nails, &c. there are certain sentences of the *Qoran*, or supplications in Arabic which the *moorshud* repeats. Then, after having had the *fuqeer* bathed, he makes him stand or sit before him, and repeat the five*Kulma y-e-Shureeut; viz.* 1st. *Kulma-e-ty-ub*; 2d *Kulma-e-shuhadut*; 3d. *Kulma-e-tumjeed*; 4th. *Kulma-e-tow-heed*; 5th. *Kulma-e-rud-e-koofoor*; and the common *ustugfar*, as well as ten other *kulmay* (creeds) current among *fuqeers*.

Having then imparted to him such admonition and advice as he deems necessary, he repeats again the names of all his *moorshuds* to him; and asks, "Have you consented to "acknowledge me and all these?" The other replies, "I "have." When he has made him repeat this three times, he, either with his own hands places a *taj* (cap) on his head, or gets another to do it; he then ties a small cloth turban of eight or ten cubits' length around it, puts a *kufnee* or *alfa*, *tusbeeh-an*, *kuntha*, and *sylee* round his neck, a leather *tusma*, a *lungote*, or *loong*, and *kummurbund* about his waist, suspends a small circular piece of white mother-of-pearl called *dal* to his foot, and hands to him a *ch'hurree-romal** and a *kuch-kole*, alias *kishtee*,† &c. He then gives him some of his own *jhoot'ha* (contaminated) shurbut to drink. On putting on each article, he repeats certain sentences of the *Qoran* or some Arabic supplications. When the *fuqeer* is completely decked out in his new garb, the *peer* gives him a new name; such as Bismilla-shah, Umr-

* *Ch'hurree-romal*, i.e a *ch'hurree* or twig of a tree, (p. 295) with a *romal* or handkerchief wound round the upper end of it.

† A beggar's wallet, which consists generally of the shell of the double sea cocoa-nut, (cocos maldivica, Willd; Lodoicea sechellarum, Lab.)

oollah-shah, Hussun-oollah-shah, Lutteef-shah, or Goolzar-shah, &c. In short, in every instance they have the word *shah* (king) affixed to their names; as much as to signify, that he is lord over his own will and has renounced the world. Then all the *fuqeers* call out, "he is made! he is "made!" and the man ever after goes under his new name. Then the *moorshud* makes him direct his face towards the *qibla* and perform *sijdah* (prostration) to God. After which, instead of uttering the usual salutation *ussulam-oon-aly-koom*, he, adopting the *fuqeers*' technical mode of expression, says to the *moorshud* and all the members of the assembly, "*Eshq-Allah, wo Moorshud-Allah*,"* or, "*Eshq-Allah jumma fooqra Allah*;"† to which the *moorshud* and others, instead of replying "*wo-ally-koomoos-sulam*," as other people would do, answer, "*sudara eshq, jummal Allah*."‡ These various ceremonies observed by *fuqeers*, such as reading certain sentences of the *Qoran*, wearing *alfa*, *kuntha*, &c., are not consonant either to the *shurra*, the word of God, or the traditional sayings of the Prophet. They have notwithstanding gained ground, like many other customs which have been corrupted, in Hindoostan.

At the conclusion of this the *moorshud* gives to the *fuqeer* the following precepts; *viz*. 1st. what stands, do not touch; what lies down, do not move; (meaning, do not steal). 2d. Let your tongue observe truth; (or, do not lie). 3d. Keep your *lunggotee* on tight; (*i.e.* commit no adultery). 4th. Treasure these up in your mind, child. Beware. Exert yourself; gain your livelihood by begging or working, it matters not which; but eat things lawful.

---

* To the elect of God, and the spiritual guide to God.

† To the favourites of God, to all the *fuqeers* of God.

‡ Be always beloved, thou beauty of God.

Then they distribute food among the *fuqeers*, giving each such share as he is entitled to.*

When all this is done, the above individual is constituted a real *fuqeer*; and no one reproaches him thereafter, for associating with *fuqeers*.

It is a rule with *fuqeers*, whether they do or do not perform prayers at the appointed seasons, that they must repeat something or other on their beds, and make *sijdah* to the deity. This, in their phraseology, is called *bisturray kay ashnan ruh-na* (*i. e.* being friends with one's bed). When they have occasion to *sulam* to any one, they say, "*Allah* "*Allah hy burray, baboo! khoosh ru-ho*;"† or "*saeea* "*Allee wo nubbee ka ruhay.*"‡ In like manner, when people of the world salute a *fuqeer*, they say, "*bundugee* "*hy shah sahib*," or "*sulam hy shah sahib*," (*i. e.* I salute you master sire!); because, in becoming *fuqeers*, they rise in dignity.

All *fuqeers* have originated from *char peer* (or four spiritual guides); and *chowda khan-waday* (or fourteen households); and the following is the connexion. The 1st. *peer* was Huzrut Moortooza Allee; he invested with the *kheelafut* (deputyship) the 2d. *peer* Khoaja Hussun Busree; he constituted his deputies, the 3d. *peer* Khoaja Hubeeb Ajmee, and the 4th. *peer* Abd-ool-Wahid bin Zyd Koofee.

From the third *peer* have descended nine households, *viz.* 1st. Hubeebeean, from Hubeeb Ajmee; 2d. Tyfooreean, from Baeezeed Bostamee, surnamed Tyfoor; 3d. Kur-

---

* Alluding to the custom among them of giving a double portion to *moorshuds*, *khuleefas* and *Mukandar* (or who are resident; *i. e.* not, as most are, travelling) *fuqeers*; and to all the rest, one.

† Or "God, God is great, squire. Be happy."

‡ May the favour (lit. the shadow) of Allee and of the Prophet be upon you.

kheea*n*, from Sheikh Maroof Kurkhee; 4th. Joneideea*n*, from Joneid Bugdadee. To these the *Tubqatee fuqeers* trace their origin.—5th. Suqteea*n*, from Sirree Suqtee; 6th. Gazrooneea*n*, from Abo-oollah-Huqeeqee, alias Huneef Gazroonee; 7th. Turtooseea*n*, from Abdool furrah Turtoosee. The *Qadiree fuqeers* descend from these. 8th. Firdoseea*n*, from Nujum-ood-Deen Kubree Firdosee; 9th. Sohurwurdeea*n*, from Sheikh Zeea-ood-Deen Aboo Nujeeb Sohurwurdee. From these have sprung the *Sohurwurdee fuqeers.*

From the fourth *peer* have sprung five lineages, *viz.* 10th. Zydeea*n*, from Abd-ool-Wahid bin Zyd; 11th. Aeeazeea*n*, from Foozyl bin Aeeaz; 12th. Adhumeea*n*, from Eebraheem Adhum Bulkhee; 13th. Hoobyreea*n*, from Ameen-ood-Deen Hoobyrut-ool-Busree; 14th. Chishteea*n*, from Sheikh Aboo Is'haq Chishtee. From these have descended the *Chishteea*n *fuqeers.*

Besides these there are a few other families among *fuqeers*; but these fourteen are the principal ones, from which the rest have branched off.

The origin of most of them may be traced to his holiness Allee-ool-Moortooza, and of one or two to Aboo Bukur Siddeeq, and from them to his holiness Mohummud Moostuffa (the peace! &c.)

The following are a few of the *fuqeers*, descendants of the above, whom we meet with in this country (Hindoostan).

1st. *Qadireea*, alias *Banuwa*, sprung from Syed Abd-ool-Qadir Jillanee, surnamed Peer-e-Dustugeer (p. 237), and his disciples assuming his name call themselves *Qadireea.* Their dress is white, green, or coloured with red ochre.

2d. *Chishteea*, followers of Khoaja Bunda Nuwaz (the

long-ringletted, p. 265). These *fuqeers* are extremely partial to vocal music, as was their *peer*, Khoaja, who in one of his fits of religious reverie observed, that singing was the food and support of the soul, it is therefore proper that we should both sing and listen to singing. They dress as they please.

Sheeahs generally become *fuqeers* of this description. They tie the *d'huttee* (clothes, p. 177, 227) which had been fastened to the *eemamein* (*ullums*) to their necks, upper arms, or *ch'huttee* (p. 295) with great faith, and preserve *kakools* on their heads; *i. e.* shave half the head and leave long hair on the other half; and they constantly repeat Allee's name, and esteem him equal to God and the Prophet.

3d. *Shootareea*, descendants of Shah Abd-oollah Shootar-e-Nak; their garb is similar to that of the *Qadireea.*

The *Qadiree*, *Chishtee*, and *Shootaree fuqeers* are also called *Bay-nuwa*. Moreover, those who have had their four *abroos* (*vide* p. 284) shaved, are denominated *Moolhid-nooma* (resembling infidels*); while those who do not shave them, except over the right temple, from which the *moorshud* at the time of making the *fuqeer* has clipped a few hairs, are termed *Russool-nooma* (displaying the Messenger, *i. e.* the Prophet).

4th. *Tubqateea* or *Mudareea.*† These are followers of *Zindu Shah Mudar* (p. 241). They generally wear a *pugree*, *jama*, *doputta*, all black; also a *loong*, and a black neckcloth; and having fastened one end of a chain to one

---

* The term is not used as one of reproach, but merely from the circumstance of its not being conformable to the precepts of the *Shurra*. Consequently, they who act contrary to it are considered in the light of infidels.

† This class of wandering *fuqeers*, according to Mrs. M. H. Ali, are also called *duffalees*, from the small hand-drum they carry with them.

of their ankles, they stand in front of the shops, and continue throwing out and drawing towards them the other end. Or they go about the *bazars* quarrelling and fighting with the shopkeepers for alms; and if their demands be not complied with, they abuse people most obscenely, until they prevail on them to grant something.

Some among them rear tigers, bears, or monkeys, and contrive by some means or other to tame them, and to teach the two latter species of animals to dance and perform all sorts of antics; tying strings to their necks, they walk about the *bazars* and houses with them, displaying their tricks to the people, who on seeing them reward the owners according to their means.

Some among them are also jugglers. For instance, they cut a figure of a man or an animal out of a piece of paper, and make it dance without any visible mechanical means. Again, placing an earthern chaffing dish, without a bottom to it, on the head, they kindle a fire in it, and, placing an iron *kurrahee* on it, cook *pooreea*n; and that without their hair being at all singed by the fire. Thus they perform various juggling tricks of legerdemain, to the no small astonishment of the spectators.

5th. *Mullung fuqeers* are descendants of his highness Jummun Juttee, a follower of Zindu Shah Mudar (p. 241). Their dress is the same as that of the *Mohurrum Mullung fuqeers* (p. 195), except that they wear the hair of the head very full, or it is matted and formed into a knot behind. Sometimes they wind some sort of cloth round the knob. Some of them tie round their waists a chain or thick rope as a substitute for a *kordulla*,* and wear a *lunggotee* so

---

* *Kordulla*, a string tied round the waist, into which a piece of cloth is tucked in before and behind, constituting a dress called a *lunggotee*.

slender that it conceals but a small portion of what it is intended to cover. They resemble much the *gosaeen*,* and usually wander in deserts and on mountains, and visit the shrines of all reputed saints. Wherever they happen to sit down they burn *d'honee*,† and sometimes rub its ashes over their bodies.

6th. *Rufaee* or *Goorz-mar*. They originate from Syed Ahmud Kubeer, whose *fuqeers* strike the point of the *goorz* against their breasts, or into their eyes, level blows at their backs with the sword, thrust a spit through their sides, or into their eyes both of which they take out and put in again; or cut out their tongues, which on being replaced in the mouth, re-unite. Nay, they even sever the head from the body, and glue them together again with saliva, and the body becomes re-animated, and stands up, and what is strange, no hemorrage attends all this cutting and slicing; or should there be any it is very trifling; and in that case, the operator is considered inexpert. The wound is healed by the application of a little spittle; for at the time of becoming *fuqeers*, the *moorshud* takes a small quantity of his own spittle, and applying it to their tongues, says, "Wield without apprehension the *goorz* "upon yourself; and if cut, apply a little of your spittle "to the wound and it will quickly heal, by the influence "of Syed Ahmud Kubeer." They obey the injunction accordingly.

Sometimes they sear their tongues with a red-hot iron, put a living scorpion into their mouths, make a chain red-

* A particular class of Hindoo mendicants, who go about almost stark naked.

† A fire lighted by *fuqeers*, over which they sit inhaling the smoke, either by way of penance or for the purpose of extorting compliance with their demands.

hot, and pouring oil over it they draw their hands along it, when a sudden blaze is produced. I have heard it said, that they even cut a living human being into two, and unite the parts by means of spittle. They also eat arsenic, glass, and poisons, and stand rattling the *goorz* at the shopkeepers' doors. Should the latter not give something corresponding to their means, or make any delay in bestowing it, they begin to brandish the *goorz*. Sometimes these *fuqeers* even throw away the *pice* they thus receive, it being unlawful to take money by extortion.*

---

* This order of devotees are called by Mrs. Meer (vol. ii. 315.) *chillubdars*. She observes, that "the presumed powers of their "founder are said to have been chiefly instrumental in curing the "sick, or in removing temporal afflictions; but his effectual prayers "in behalf of people in difficulty, they say, surpassed those of any "other of the whole tribes of devotees that have at any age existed.

"They all practise one plan, whenever called upon to remove the "difficulties of any person who places sufficient confidence in their "ability. On such occasions, a young heifer, two years old, is sup-"plied by the person having a request to make, after which a fire of "charcoal is made in an open space of ground, and the animal sacri-"ficed according to Mussulman form. The tender pieces of meat are "selected, spitted, and roasted over the fire, of which, when cooked, "all present are requested to partake. Whilst the meat is roasting, "the *chillubdars* beat time with a small tambourine to a song or "dirge expressive of their love and respect to the memory of the "departed saint, their founder and patron, and a hymn of praise to "the Creator.

"The feast concluded, while the fire of charcoal retains a lively "heat, these devotees commence dancing, still beating their tam-"bourines and calling out with an audible voice, 'There is but one "God! Mahumud is the Prophet of God!' Then they sing in praise "of Ali, the descendants of the Prophet, and lastly, of Syaad Ahmud "Kaabeer, their beloved saint. Each then puts his naked foot into "the fire: some even throw themselves upon it, their associates "taking care to catch them before they are well down; others jump "into the fire and out again instantly; lastly, the whole assembly "trample and kick the remaining embers about, whilst a spark "remains to be quenched by this means. These efforts, it is pre-"tended, are sufficient to remove the difficulties of the persons sup-"plying the heifer and the charcoal.

"These

7th. *Jullaleea, i.e.* followers of Syed Jullal-ood-Deen Bokharee (p. 250). Their dress generally consists of a *sylee* of (*pushmee,* or) wool, or of thread of various colours, on the head; a *gooloobund, loong,* or *lunggotee;* in the hand they carry a *sonta* (club); on the right upper arm they have a sear made by the application of actual cautery; for it is customary among the household of this tribe, at the time of making them *fuqeers,* to form a match of cloth, light it, and mark them on the arm with it. These *fuqeers* likewise go about the *bazars* begging, and if their demands are not speedily complied with, some cauterize themselves with a cloth-match; others, dispensing with that, raise a noise and uproar.

8th. *Sohageea,* descended from Moosa Sohag, whose name they bear. They are distinguished by being dressed like women, but generally wear a cap, together with *chooreea*n and other female ornaments on the wrists; and they accept of money from *kunchneea*n (dancing girls) and *bungurharo*n (*bungree*-makers), as *nuzurs.* When any refuse them alms, they break their *bungreans* (glass bracelets) to pieces, masticate, and swallow them.

These *fuqeers* generally play upon the *tumboora, seetar, sarung, been,* &c. sing and even dance, in presence of their *moorshud* and *jumma allah.** Moreover, should other

---

" These religious mendicants live on public favour and contri-
" bution; they wear clothes, are deemed harmless, never ask alms,
" but are always willing to accept them; and have no laws of celibacy,
" as is the case with some wandering beggars in India, who are naked
" except the wrapper. Sometimes they settle, making fresh con-
" verts; but many wander from city to city, always finding people
" disposed to administer to their necessities. They are distinguished
" from other sects, by each individual carrying a small tambourine,
" and wearing clothing of a deep buff colour."

* In all assemblies of *fuqeers* there is one *moorshud,* and the rest are all called *Jumma Allah* (God's assembly).

people wish to hear them sing, they perform before them; and they sometimes sit singing of their own accord. These *fuqeers* are generally great musicians. Nay, they say, that their music hath such charms, as to cause the rain to fall out of season, to soften rocks into the consistence of wax; nay more, the very wild beasts in *jungles* become so enamoured of their music, that they come, surround them, and listen.*

9th. *Nuqsh-bundeea* are followers of Khoaja Buha-ood, Deen Nuqsh-bund. They are characterized by carrying each a lighted *shuma* (lamp) in their hands, and going about at night, singing verses containing expressions of honour to their *moorshuds*, glory to God, and eulogiums on the Prophet. Shopkeepers, &c. drop *pice* or *cowries* into their lamps.

Fuqeers of this household are generally eminent practitioners in the science of *dawut*, *reeazut*, *wird*, *wuzaet*, and *zikkir*; and it is a highly respectable tribe.

People in general who are desirous of having their wishes accomplished unite themselves to this *silsilla*, as they obtain their object more successfully in this than in any other.

10th. *Bawa peearay kay fuqeeran.* Their garb consists of a white *tahbund* or *loonggee*. The body dress is a quilt made of *bhugwee* (cloth died with red-ochre), on which are sewed, at the distance of three or four fingers from each other, triangular or square pieces of white cloth: it reaches down to the feet in the form of a *joobba*. On their heads

* From this it will be seen that the natives of India, though according to our ideas so utterly deficient in musical science and taste, are not at all behind in extravagant admiration of its effects. The above passage will remind the reader of the fable respecting the strains of Orpheus, and the famous lines of Shakespear.

Music hath charms to sooth the savage breast,
To soften rocks and rend the knotted oak.

they wear a long *taj*, and over it a *p'hayta* (small turban). They carry two thin sticks as clubs in their hands. When they go begging, they first call out "*Allah-ho-gunnee*;"* then offer up some supplication, and crave alms. They are generally found in parties of two and three. Sometimes they first offer people some fruit, and then receive a present.

In this country, with the exception of the above varieties of *fuqeers*, we meet with few.

Fuqeers never carry about with them any other instruments save some of the following; *viz.* a *ch'huttee*, alias *ch'hurree*,† (a switch, wand, or delicate twig of the branch of any tree,) sometimes painted; a *sonta*, or *asa* (club of wood); a *zufur-tukeea*,‡ called a *byraga*,§ of iron; a *posht-khar*, that is, a little artificial hand with a handle to it, made of copper, brass, gold, or silver, with which to scratch the body; a *heemacha*, or bag made of the skin of a lamb; a *kuchkole* or *kishtee* (vide p. 285); a *mirwaha*, alias *badkush*, termed *punk'ha*, or fan; a *goruk dhunda*,|| of iron. Some carry in their hands a *burch'hee* (spear or lance, with a wooden stock); a *sang* (spear or javelin all of iron); a *tulwar* (sword); a *paysh-qubz* (a particular kind of dagger); a *kutar* (dirk or dagger); a *ch'hooree* (knife); and a *maroo* (a couple of antelope's horns joined at their bases, which overlap each other in contrary directions).

When they go to visit any one, they carry one or two

* *Allah ho gunnee*, "God is independent."

† *Ch'hurree romal*; vide note, p. 285.

‡ Lit. the pillow of victory.

§ A small crooked stick or piece of iron, which the *byragee* (devotee) places under his armpit to lean upon as he sits.

|| Resembling a Chinese puzzle, consisting of a number of pins put through holes in a board, the pins having knobs at one end, and at the other, rings, through which a long compressed ring is passed.

fruits of some kind or other, or some sweet-scented flower or leaf, and offering them recite the following hemistich:

"The green leaf is the *dervis's* delight."

Fuqeers are of two classes: one termed *bay-shurra** (without law); the other class *ba-shurra*† (with law).

The generality of them are *bay-shurra*, and great debauchees. They indulge in the use of *ganja*,‡ *bhung*,‡ *afeeoon* (or opium), *shurab* (or wine), *boza*,‡ *mudud*,‡ *churs*,‡ *sayndhee*,§ *taree*,|| *nariellee*,¶ &c. all intoxicating, and conceive them lawful. They do not fast, pray, or govern their passions, agreeably to the precepts of Mohummud.

The other, or *ba-shurra*, pray and fast; in short observe all the precepts inculcated in the *Shurra* of Mohummud.

Among the above-mentioned *Fuqeers* or *Durwayshes*** (for these terms are synonymous), there are certain varieties. For instance, the

1st. class of *Durwayshes* is denominated *Salik*.††

---

* *i. e.* They do not act up to the *shurra*, or precepts of Mohummud, but are a kind of latitudinarians.

† The reverse of the former, acting according to the *shurra*, or disciplinarians.

‡ For these inebriating substances, vide Glossary.

§ The juice (or *toddy*) of the wild date tree. Elate Sylvestris.—*Lin.*

|| The juice of the *tar*, or palmyra tree. Borassus flabelliformis.—*Lin.*

¶ The juice of the *nariel*, or cocoa-nut tree. Cocos nucifera.—*Lin.*

** Whom Mrs. M. H. Ali denominates *soofees* (or mystics of the east); and observes, "that there are two classes of the professed de-" vout *soofees*, viz. the *saalik*, and the *majoob*," vol. ii. p. 248. In another part (p. 272), she remarks, "*soofeism*, it appears, is a mys-" tery; the secret of which can only be imparted by the professor to " such persons as have been prepared for its reception by a course of " religious instruction." And again, at p. 273, she says, "Many " are devout *durweishes*, who are, nevertheless, unacquainted with the " mystery of *soofeism*; to use their own words (by which the natives " distinguish them), every real *soofee* is undoubtedly a *durweish*, " but all *durweishes* are not *soofees*."

†† *Salik*, literally, a traveller or pilgrim, but here signifying a *devotee*.

They are *Ba-shurra;* have their wives and families, employ themselves in horticultural, agricultural, or commercial pursuits, or live by begging.

2d. set of *Durwayshes* are called *Mujzoob.** They are *Bay-shurra*, and have no wives, families, or possessions: in fact, *bazars* and lanes are their homes. Their dress consists solely of a *lunggotee*, and their hair is dishevelled. If any offer them food, they accept of and eat it; if not, they fast. They rarely beg. Sometimes they speak, at other times remain mute. They are so totally absorbed in religious reverie, that they do not discern between things lawful and unlawful, and regard no sect or religion. Sometimes they go about in a state of nudity, and lie down wherever it may chance to be, regardless of every kind of dirt and filth.

Some among these become such powerful workers of miracles, that, whenever they choose, they can instantly effect what they please; and what is strange, though some of them lie in one spot for months and years together, and there obey every call of nature, there is not the least offensive smell about them. They are, moreover, neither afraid of fire or of water; for when they please, they stand on hot embers, or sit in a large frying-pan, or a boiling *caldron*, for hours together: and they dive and remain under water for two or three hours.

3d. *Azad.*†—These are likewise *Bay-shurra*. They shave their beards, whiskers, mustachios, eyebrows, and eyelashes, in short, the hair in every part of the body, and lead lives of celibacy. They have no inclination for reading prayers daily. If they get any thing to eat or drink, be it good or

---

* *Mujzoob*, signifies "abstracted."

† *Azad*, solitary, lonely.

bad, they partake of it. They have no fixed place of abode; the generality of them travel and subsist on alms.

4th. *Qulundur.* Among these, some have wives, others not; some are *Ba-shurra*, others *Bay-shurra.* They erect solitary straw huts out of towns, or select a suitable (retired) spot within the city, where they beguile their days in solitude, trusting to Providence; people of the world providing such with food and drink. Such residencies of *Fuqeers* are termed (not houses, but) *tukeea.**

5th. *Russool Shahee.* These shave their mustachios, beards, and eyebrows, wear *topees* and *lunggotees* to conceal their nakedness, and a sheet to cover them in cold, wet, or hot weather. They sacrifice liberally to Bacchus, do not marry, and gain their livelihood by begging.

6th. *Eemam Shahee.* They shave their mustachios, beards, and eyebrows, and wear *alfas, tahbunds,* and *sylees;* but their distinguishing mark is a black narrow perpendicular line, extending from the tip of the nose to the top of the forehead. These, likewise, lead lives of celibacy, and maintain themselves by what they obtain in charity.

Nay, among them, some possess the power of working miracles; it is, therefore, advisable to court their blessing and avoid their curse. *Apropos,* a very pert couplet has just come to my remembrance, *viz.*

> "View not with scorn the humble sons of earth,†
> Beneath the clod a flower may have birth."

In short, to understand all regarding *Durwayshes,* to acquire a knowledge of their *zikkirs* (reminiscences), and

---

* *Tukeea,* lit. signifies a pillow, but is the technical term for a *fuqeer's* stand; for not having a house, wherever he lays his head, that constitutes his pillow or home.

† Alluding to the bodies of *fuqeers* being besmeared with cow-dung ashes.

to learn how to obtain the accomplishment of one's wishes, are things which can only be attained by unwearied perseverance, by associating with holy men, and by the study of the science of *tusuwwoof.**

Of *Mushaekhs*, alias *Peers*, or *Moorshuds*. They are of two kinds; the one, *Juddee*, the other, *Khoolfaee*.

1st. The *Juddee Mushaekhs* are those in whose families the custom of *byat* (p. 281), or that of *peers* making *mooreeds*, has continued current, either from their grandfather's or grandmother's side; or it must have descended from two or three generations back.

2d. The *Khoolfaee Mushaekhs* are those whose fathers and grandfathers were of different trades and professions from themselves, or were sages, and in whose families such relationship had no existence; but some *Moorshud-e-juddee* or *Khoolfaee*, first established the custom among them.

The dress of both these classes of *Mushaekhs* consists in a *taj*, *ammama*, *pyruhun* or *qumees*, *koorta*, *doputta*, *shal*, *doshala*, *romal*, *Eezar*, *loong*, &c., out of which they select which they please. Some wear around their necks a *tusbeeh*, or *sylee;* around their waists, *tusma;* on their wrists, *soomurun;* and carry in their hands a *ch'hurree*, or any of the weapons mentioned under the head *Fuqeers* (p. 295). They are *Ba-shurra* and family-people. They subsist upon the services† (as it is called) of their *mooreeds*, or on what

* Theology of the *soofees*, or mystics of the east.

† The technical phrase among these people for alms in charity, is "service." Thus a *moorshud* advises his *mooreeds* to "do service to *moorshuds;*" observing, "it is a virtue so to do." They never ask for money. The *mooreed* (disciple) according to his means, once, or oftener, in the year, proceeds to the house of his *peer*, and offers him some present; sometimes depositing it, during conversation, under the mat or bed on which he happens to sit, without saying a word about it; at others, while handing it to him, begs his acceptance of the trifle, apologizing for not having the means of offering more.

other people choose to give them as an offering to God, or the *Zukat* which a *Sahib-e-Nissab* (p. 58) pleases to offer to them, being resigned to the will of God: or, they receive from kings, nobles, or nuwwabs, a daily, monthly, or annual allowance, in the way of a *jageer*, or *eenam*, to live upon.

Some of them, independently of making *mooreeds*, gain additional subsistence by fortune-telling, composing amulets and charms, practising medicine, pronouncing blessings, or exercising incantations.

Sometimes, after the lapse of a year or two, they proceed on their circuits to their *mooreeds*, by way of going on a pleasure or shooting excursion; and should they be offered any money by their disciples, they accept of it. Should they meet with any new candidates for the *mooreed*-ship, they appoint them.

The method of investing one with the kheelafut (deputyship) is as follows:

The *peer* seats the individual who is to be invested with the *kheelafut* before him, as they do in the case of making one a *mooreed* (p. 282); and having repeated certain supplications, he grants to the new candidate such *shujray*, *sunnud*, and *zikkirs* belonging to this subject, as have descended to him from his *moorshuds*; and says, "I have now constituted thee my *khuleefa* (deputy or successor, by Europeans vulgarly written *caliph*), and given thee authority in such and such a *silsilla*; in which thou mayest hereafter make *mooreeds*, *fuqeers*, or *khuleefas*, as thou pleasest." He then, with his own hands, dresses him out in his own *joobba*, *dustar*, *loong*, and *doputta*, either a suit which he has worn before or a new one, and reads to him the *shujra-e-khuleefut*.

Peers grant *khuleefuts* "for the sake of God" (*i. e.* gratis);

but should *khuleefas*, conceiving it a meritorious act, offer them presents of money or clothes, there can be no objection to their accepting of them.

Should the *khuleefa* be a man of property, he, on the occasion of this installation with the *kheelafut*, invites several *mushaekhs*, *fuqeers*, all his relations, &c. in the town, and having had *fateeha* offered over *sheernee* or *polaoo*, distributes it among them, and in their presence gets himself installed. After which the newly-created *khuleefa* may, in like manner, invest others with the same privileges.

Fuqeers who are *mushaekhs* have necessarily, at the commencement, or in the middle of their names, the word *shah ;* and at the termination of them, the words *qadiree*, *chishtee*, *tubqatee*, or *shootaree :* thus, Shah Abd-oollah qadir qadiree, Hummeed Oollah Shah Chishtee. Tubqatee and Shootaree occur but rarely.

SECT. 3. *Penances requisite to endure, in order to become a wullee (or saint).*

Next to the dignity of a prophet is that of a *wullee*, for it will continue till the day of judgment. Though prophecy has ceased the office of *wullees* continues.

In order to attain the rank of a *wullee* the grace of God is indispensable. Verily, as the eternal registrar has decreed, so it must happen in this world. In short, there are certain acts and austerities current among *mushaekhs*, which it is necessary to know and practise. To publish in books the manner of performing them, or to reveal it to every body, is forbidden by *moorshuds*. It is to be disclosed only to those *mooreeds* who become *talibs* (enquirers), and who are of the Moosulman persuasion, and mean to make it their study.

Suffice it at present merely to name them ; and should

any wish to study them, *i. e.* the *shuguls, zikkirs, kussubs,* &c. they must apply to *mushaekhs* or *moorshuds*, for a knowledge of the *reeazuts* (penances), *aoorads* (repetitions), *deeds* (viewings or beholdings), and *zikkirs* (reminiscences). The two principal precepts to be particularly observed are, to eat things lawful, and always to speak the truth.

Some *mushaekhs* and *durwayshes* have likewise enjoined the imprisonment within one's self, of the following five *mowzeea*n (or noxious things, alias vices):

The 1st *mowzee* is the snake (technically, the ears), who on hearing anything, without sufficient investigation, immediately takes revenge. The 2d *mowzee* is the kite (eagle? a technical term for the eye), who covets whatever he sees. The 3d *mowzee* is the *bhown-ra* (or a large black bee), whose habitation is the nostrils, and who envies every thing that smells sweet. The 4th *mowzee* is the dog, whose seat is the tongue, who delights in nice and savoury articles. The 5th *mowzee* is the scorpion, concealed in the penis, and necessarily inclined to sting in the unlawful spot (*viz.* the vulva). These it is necessary to restrain.

In order to derive benefit from these *zikkirs*, it is requisite zealously to practise such as are good; to remove from one's heart envy and covetousness; to keep the mind pure and undefiled; to depend on, reflect on, and think of, God alone; to be every instant immersed in his contemplation; to cherish no love for relatives or the world, but consider all (comprehended in) HIM; to take no delight in troubling and annoying people, but to perform, with zeal and perseverance, such occupation as his *moorshud* has desired to be attended to; and then will the Almighty elevate the performer to the rank and dignity of a *wullee*.

There are many things which require to be repeated aloud and to be said: and it is easy enough to do so with the mouth; but to endure the hardships attending the performance of them is a most difficult task.

CHAPTER XXIX.

Concerning the science of *dawut*, or exorcism.

Recourse is had to this science for the following purposes, *viz.* 1st. To command the presence of genii and demons, who, when it is required of them, cause any thing to take place. 2d. To establish friendship or enmity between two persons. 3d. To cause the death of one's enemy. 4th. To cause the increase of one's subsistence or salary. 5th. To obtain victory in the field of battle. 6th. To call for and obtain an income gratuitously or mysteriously. 7th. To secure the accomplishment of one's wishes, both temporal and spiritual.

We shall divide the subject into four sections, and consider,

1st. The rules necessary to be observed, and the articles required by the exorcist.

2d. The giving of *nissab*, *zukāt*, &c. of the *Isms*, and the manner of reading the *dawut*.

3d. The commanding the presence of genii and demons.

4th. The casting out of devils.

SECT. 1. *Rules necessary to be observed, and the articles required by the Exorcist.*

The exorcist is first of all to acquire a thorough knowledge of the science of exorcism from some learned *moorshud* (guide to salvation). He only is considered an erudite *moorshud,* who is acquainted with the different *usma-e-oozzam* (great *isms**) of the Deity, and to whom demons have imparted information concerning things great and small, and in whose bosom is treasured up a knowledge of all truths. A man of this description, however, should never cherish a haughty spirit on account of his being endowed with revelation, and possessing the power of performing miracles; nor should he be over-anxious to make a display of his abilities before the world. When an individual is found possessing the above qualifications, he may well be honoured with the title of a perfect *moorshud.*

Some *mushaekhs* (divines), without possessing a practical knowledge of the science, pretend to teach it to others; but, in such cases, the tutor having been experimentally unacquainted with its beneficial influences, no real advantage can be expected to accrue from the practice of it to the student. Verily, it is unprofitable to learn or teach the science in such wise. Moreover, he exposes his life to danger; for by such reading many have injured themselves, and becoming mad, have mixed up human offal and rubbed themselves with it, and wandered about in deserts and upon mountains: whereas, when the tutor is learned, there is no danger of apprehending such consequences. If, however, through any defect on the part of the reader, any of the above circumstances should occur, it is in the power of an erudite teacher immediately to remedy it, as if nothing had

* *Ism,* literally signifies a name. It is in this sense also used in this chapter, and applied to the attributes of the Deity: but the great *isms* are short supplications made use of in this science. Accordingly they are of two kinds; the former is termed *usma-e-oozzam* (or the mighty attributes); the latter *usma-e-hoosna* (or the glorious attributes). These *isms* are of two kinds; 1. *Jullalee isms,* (*i. e.* fiery), or the terrible attributes; 2. *Jumalee isms,* (*i. e.* watery, airy and earthy); or the amiable attributes.

happened. Without recourse to such means, madness or death will be inevitable.

This teacher-of-the-alphabet* has for a long time cherished the greatest curiosity to dive into this mysterious science, and has, consequently, associated much with divines and devotees, exorcists and travellers from Arabia and Ujjum,† by which he has acquired some knowledge of it; but all the advantage he has derived therefrom may be summed up in a well-known proverb, "*Koh kundun; moosh girruftun.*"

"To dig a mountain up, and find a mouse!"‡

Should any wish for further information than what I am about to give on this subject, there is not a better or more valuable work that I can refer him to, than the *Juwahir-e-khumsa;* in which the author, his excellency Mohummud Gows Gow-layree (the mercy of God be on him!) has treated on it most minutely.

When one enters upon the study of this science, the first thing he does is to pay the utmost regard to cleanliness. No dog, cat, or stranger is allowed admittance into his closet; and, it is usual to burn sweet-scented perfumes, such as wood-aloes, benjamin-pastiles, &c. When he has occasion to obey the calls of nature, he wears, on his exit out of doors, a separate *taj* and *loong* (garments appropriated to the express purpose), leaving the other suit behind, and on his return assumes his former habit, depositing the contaminated clothes on an *algunee*;§ or merely performs *wuzoo* (or ablution) and re-enters his closet. The object of using a couple of suits is, that no flies may be attracted towards

* *i. e.* "The author of this work," an epithet of humility.
† Every country in the world, save Arabia.
‡ "Montes parturiunt; nascitur ridiculus mus."
§ *Algunnee* is a line or rope for hanging clothes on.

it, and by alighting on it cause the body of the exorcist to be defiled. Moreover, should he experience a nocturnal pollution, whether it be in the day or night, he bathes instantly, and on no account for a moment delays it.

As long as he endures *chilla* (*i. e.* for forty days) he sleeps on a mat, &c. spread on the ground, not on a cot. Some keep a fast during those days, and bathe once or twice daily. They converse but little and scarcely sleep; nay, some even go so far as to remain within doors, and have the entrances to their apartments built up for the time.

Generally, in order to endure *chilla*, they repair to some house or other out of town; or to a mountain, cavern, or well, or any place where water is near at hand; for the noise and bustle of cities are apt to distract the attention from the object, and render the reading defective; for it is necessary in this affair to engage one's mind with such energy as to be entirely absorbed in it; since, when the train of thought is diverted into a different channel, his wishes are less effectually accomplished. On the contrary, out of town there is no fear of such hindrances, and the object is more easily attained.

Their diet depends upon the kind of *isms* they are to read; *e. g.* If it be the *jullalee* ones, they refrain from the use of meat, fish, eggs, honey, musk, *choona* (quicklime), and oysters, and from sexual intercourse. If the *jumalee* ones, from *ghee*, curds, vinegar, salt, and ambergrise.

With readers of both kinds of *isms*, the following are accounted abominations, *viz.* garlic, onions, and assafœtida, as well as blood-letting and killing lice.

If one fail to adhere to the observance of any of the above-mentioned conditions, he exposes his life to imminent hazard.

Besides these there are two other general rules to be

observed, and those the most important of all, *viz.*, to eat things lawful, and always to speak the truth.

If the exorcist has to read the *jullalee isms*, or if their number predominate, he is to commence on the first day of the week (Saturday); if the *jumalee*, on a Monday; if both together, *i. e.* if an equal number of each, on a Sunday.

If these be read to establish friendship, or undertaken for any good work, he is to begin them after the new moon; if for enmity or for any evil purpose, after the full moon.* In both cases his face is to be turned towards the residence of the individual who is the object of the undertaking.

In every case he is to fast the three preceding days, and commence upon the reading of the *isms* on the morning of the fourth.

If his victuals are cooked by a servant, he also must observe the same system of abstinence as his master. Should he be unable to submit to such privations, the master must dress his own food.

Previously to commencing the reading of *isms* in the name of a particular person, it is requisite to ascertain the initials of his or her name; and that, in the *hooroof-e-tuhujee* (or Arabic alphabet),† which consists of twenty-eight letters; and these are considered by exorcists to be connected with the twelve *booroojan* (signs of the Zodiac), the seven

* This rule is likewise observed in effecting other good or bad undertakings.

† As there are seven letters in other (eastern) languages which have no corresponding ones in the Arabic, an equal number of the latter are substituted in their place; thus,

Not Arabic.	P-ay.	T-ay.	Ch-eem.	D-al.	Rr-ay.	Zh-ay.	G-af.
	پ	ٹ	چ	ڈ	ڑ	ژ	گ
Arabic.	B-ay.	T-ay.	J-eem.	D-al.	R-ay.	Z-ay.	K-af.
	ب	ت	ج	د	ر	ز	ک

seetaray (planets), and the four *ansurs* (elements). The relation of these towards each other will be better comprehended by a reference to the annexed table; in which, for convenience, I have inserted, in a column additional to what is usually met with, each planet's *bookhoor* (or perfume) which is directed to be burnt. To render the sketch still more perfect, I have likewise included the qualities of the planets, together with the numbers which the twenty-eight letters of the Arabic alphabet represent.*

THE FOUR ELEMENTS.				The Planets, with their influences.	The Planets' Perfumes.
Water.	Air.	Earth.	Fire.		
Dal 4	Jeem 3	Bay 2	Alif 1	Saturn, evil.	Benzoin and Coriander Seed.
Hy 8	Zay 7	Waoo 6	Hay 5	Jupiter, good.	Benzoin and Sugar,
Lam 30	Kaf 20	Ee-ay 10	To-ee 9	Mars, evil.	Benzoin and Wood Aloes.
Aeen 70	Seen 60	Noon 50	Meem 40	Sun, middling.	Benzoin and Cinnamon.
Ray 200	Qaf 100	Swad 90	Fay 80	Venus, good.	Benzoin and White Sandal-wood.
Khy 600	Say 500	Tay 400	Sheen 300	Mercury, good.	Benzoin and Red Sandal-wood, *i. e.* Logwood.
Ghein 1000	Zoee 900	Zwad 800	Zal 700	Moon, middling.	Benzoin and Camphor.
Crab, Scorpion, Fish.	Twins, Scales, Watering-pot.	Bull, Virgin, She-Goat.	Ram, Lion, Archer.	} SIGNS OF THE ZODIAC.	

* These form eight words; *viz.* 1. *Abjud*, 2. *Huwuz*, 3. *Hoottee*, 4. *Kulaymun*, 5. *Suafus*, 6. *Qurushut*, 7. *Sukhiz*, 8. *Zuzig*; and the Arabian mode of calculating by these is denominated the reckoning by *Abjud*. Vide *Abjud*, Gloss.

By way of further illustration of the above table, we shall give an example. For instance, a man named *Ahmud* has in view the establishment of an intimacy with a woman of the name of *Rabaya*, which he must accomplish by the reading of some of the *dawut-isms*, as presently to be detailed; but, in the first place, it is requisite to know whether their elements, planets, and zodiacal signs be amicably or inimically disposed towards each other, and this is done by reference to the above table. Should amity exist between all these, then, doubtless, affection will reign between the couple; should any one of them differ in the least, there will be some degree of friendship and some of enmity between the two; but should no friendship exist at all among the three elements, &c. no love will or can take place between the couple.

For example, the initial

of *Ahmud* is Alif (or A)...	of *Rabaya*, is Ray (or R.)
his element is Fire	her element Water;
— planet is Saturn;	— planet Venus;
— sign of Zodiac { Ram, Lion, Archer.	— sign of Zodiac { Crab, Scorpion, Fish.

From this we learn, first, that their elements are very contrary and opposed to one another; for water is by no means friendly to fire. Secondly, astrologists have determined the relative dispositions of the planets to be as follows:

Venus and Saturn	Venus and Moon	Jupiter and Venus	Jupiter and Sun	Sun and Moon	Jupiter and Moon.	Sun and Venus	} FRIENDSHIP.
Moon and Mercury	Saturn and Mercury	Jupiter and Mercury	Mars and Mercury	Venus and Mercury	Mars and Venus	Sun and Mercury	} INDIFFERENT, (or mixed).
Saturn and Sun	Saturn and Moon	Mars and Moon	Mars and Sun	Saturn and Mars	Jupiter and Mars	Jupiter and Saturn	} ENMITY.

Consequently, *Ahmud* having Saturn for his planet, and *Rabaya* Venus, and these entertaining friendship towards one another, it would appear by this criterion that they would live happy together.

Thirdly, with regard to the signs of the zodiac, they stand as follows:

Males.	Females.	Hermaphrodites.
Ram.	Bull.	Twins.
Lion.	Scales.	Virgin.
Scorpion.	Crab.	He-Goat.
Fish.		Watering-pot.
Archer.		

Between males and females exists friendship; between males and hermaphrodites, sometimes friendship, sometimes enmity; between females and hermaphrodites, the most inveterate enmity.

In this instance, part of one corresponding with the other, it is so far favourable.

From these several considerations it is to be concluded that some degree of harmony and some of discord may be expected to be the natural result of the union.

SECT. 2. *The giving of Nissab, Zukat, &c. to each ism; and the manner of reading the Dawut.*

There are what are called *nissab, zukat, ushur, qoofool, dowr* and *mooduwir, buzul, khutum,* and *surreeool-eejabut,* appointed for each *ism.*

In the *juwahir-e-khumsa* there are in all forty-one *isms;**

* *i. e.* Of the first variety, termed *usma-e-oozzam,* or the mighty attributes (p. 304).

the first of which runs thus: *soobhanuka, la illaha illa-unta, eea rubba koollu shyn o warusuhoo, o razuquhoo, o rahaymuhoo;* i.e. "Glory be to Thee! There is no "God save Thee, the Lord of all, the Preserver, the Sup-"porter, the Merciful!"

By way of example, we shall offer the *nissab,** &c. of the above *ism*.

---

* To find out the *nissab*, &c. of this *ism*, the number of letters composing the *ism*, which is 45, as noted below,† is to be considered as so many hundreds; which makes

1. Its

---

† 1. S-een (p. 308) stands for	60
2. B-ay	2
3. H-y	8
4. A-lif	1
5. N-oon	50
6. K-af	20
7. L-am	30
8. A-lif	1
9. A-lif	1
10. L-am	30
11. H-ay	5
12. A-lif	1
13. L-am } as a *tushdeed* doubles the letter;	30
14. L-am	30
15. A-lif	1
16. A-lif	1
17. N-oon	50
18. T-ay	400
Ee-ay 10, A-lif 1 } omitted (*a*)	
19. R-ay	200
20. B-ay } doubled with *tushdeed*	2
21. B-ay	2
22. K-af	20
23. L-am } Do.	30
24. L-am	30
25. Sh-een	300
26. Ee-ay	10
over it add	
27. Humza, which stands for an Alif	1
28. W-aoo	6
29. W-aoo	6
30. A-lif	1
31. R-ay	200
32. S-ay	500
33. Hay	5
34. W-aoo	6
35. R-ay	200
36. A-lif	1
37. Z-ay	7
38. Q-af	100
39. H-ay	5
40. W-aoo	6
41. R-ay	200
42. A-lif	1
43. H-y	8
44. M-eem	40
45. H-ay	5
	2613

(*a*) In all other *isms* the *eeays* are to be left out, and *tushdeeds* and *humzas* added.

Its *Nissab* (or alms) consists in the repeating of it	4,500 times.
Zukat (the prescribed offerings)	6,750
Ushur (or tithes)	7,875
Qoofool (literally "lock," *i.e.* for resolving mysteries)	563
Dowr and *Mooduwir* (or circle implying repetition)	16,876
Buzul (gift or present to avert calamities)	7,000
Khutum (the seal, or conclusion)	1,200
Surreeool-Eejabut (a speedy answer)	12,000
Total	56,764

The giving of *nissab*, *zukat*, &c. to *isms*, is considered in no other light than as alms or charitable offerings, essentially requisite to be given for the purpose of ensuring the success of the individual's undertaking, and that his labours may not return unto him void.

The above-mentioned chief *ism* has for its demons *Hoomraeel* and *Humwakeel*, and for its genius *Shutkheesa*.

---

1. Its *nissab* 4,500

Half of that number (*viz.* 2,250) added to it, gives

2. Its *zukat* 6,750

Half of the above half (1,125) added to its *zukat*, forms

3. Its *ushur* 7,875

Half of the above half (1,125)

4. Its *qoofool* 563

Add its *qoofool*	563
to its *ushur*	7,875
will give	8,438
double that	8,438
will give	16,876, which is

5. Its *dowr* and *mooduwir* 16,876

There is no rule required for the following, they being always the same for every *ism*; *viz.*

6. Its *buzul* 7,000
7. Its *khutum* 1,200
8. Its *surreeool-eejabut* 12,000

In commencing the reading of the *isms*, their demons are addressed first by prefixing to their names the word *eea* (O!) and to that of genii the words *buhuq*, *nidda*, *mudud* or *koomuk* (meaning "by the aid of"). As a specimen, I shall state how these are used, by adding them to the above-named *ism*, viz. *Eea Hoomraeel, eea Humwakeel, buhuq-e-Shutkheesa, Soobhanuka la illaha*, &c. (p. 311).

Thus, whether it be this *ism* or any one of the forty-one alluded to above, or any other which a person may have received in the form of a *sunud* (grant) from his tutor (for there are innumerable others current), it is necessary that its *nissab*, &c. be given, in order to command the presence of genii. Previous to reading the *ism*, he is each time to address its demon and genius by name. Should the *ism* have no genius, the demon alone is to be invoked; and after that the *ism* read: *e.g.* if an *ism* is to be repeated a hundred times, he is to name the demon and genius as often.

Amongst the forty-one great *isms*, some have two demons and one genius, and *vice versâ*. Each *ism* has a separate genius; but the same demons are common to several *isms* (*vide* p. 315).

After having given the *nissab*, *zukat*, &c., the exorcist, in order to familiarize himself to it, or to cause the presence of the genius, is, within the space of forty days, to repeat the *ism* 137,613* times (having previously divided the

---

* The total number of letters forming the above *ism*, is 45 (p. 311).

This number is to be considered as so many thousands	45,000
which sum is to be multiplied by........................	3
and will give	135,000
add to this the combined number which the letters of the *ism* stand for (vide p. 311.) *viz.*	2,613
and we have	137,613

This sum is called in Persian *dawut*, and in Hindee *sojna*.

number as nearly in equal parts as possible for each day's reading); for by this rehearsal of it, his mind will become enlightened, and he will at times become quite transported, and fancy himself, whether awake or asleep, carried and accompanied by demons and genii to distant realms, to the highest heavens, or down into the bowels of the earth. There, they not only reveal to him all hidden mysteries, and render the whole human race subject and obedient to his will, but cause all his desires, temporal as well as spiritual, to be accomplished.

Most exorcists have, by experience, proved the validity of these *isms;* and whoever has strictly followed the rules laid down has invariably obtained his soul's desire.

The uses and beneficial effects of this *ism* alone, are numerous; but as they are to be noticed hereafter in the third Section, we shall at present pass them over.

I shall now describe the second variety of *ism*, termed *Usma-e-Hoosna* (or the glorious attributes of the Deity, p. 304), as connected with the twenty-eight letters of the Arabic alphabet (the knowledge of which my late Father bestowed on me as a sacred relic); and shall exhibit them, together with the demons attached to each, in the form of a table.

A-LIF.	B-AY.	J-EEM.	D-AL.
Eea Allah-o.	Eea Ruhman-o.	Eea Ruheem-o.	Eea Malik-o.
O God!	*O thou Merciful!*	*O thou Compassionate!*	*O thou Lord!*
Kulkaeel-o.	Umwakeel-o.	Rooeeaeel-o.	Roodaeel-o.
H-AY.	W-AOO.	Z-AY.	H-Y.
Eea Qooddoos-o.	Eea Sulam-o.	Eea Momeen-o.	Eea Mohimmin-o.
O thou Holy One!	*O thou giver of Health!*	*O thou Protector!*	*O thou Defender!*
Ittraeel-o.	Humwakeel-o.	Rooeeaeel-o.	Sumkaeel-o.
T-OEE.	EE-AY.	K-AF.	L-AM.
Eea Azeez-o.	Eea Buseer-o.	Eea Jubbar-o.	Eea Mootukubbir-o
O thou Beloved!	*O thou All-seeing!*	*O thou Great One!*	*O thou Lofty One!*
Loomaeel-o.	Jurjaeel-o.	Kumlaeel-o.	Looqaeel-o.
M-EEM.	N-OON.	S-EEN.	A-EEN.
Eea Khaliq-o.	Eea Baree-o.	Eea Moosuwwir-o	Eea Guffar-o.
O thou Creator!	*O thou glorious One!*	*O thou who fashioned us!*	*O thou Forgiver of Sins!*
Ittraeel-o.	Jibbraeel-o.	Shumsaeel-o.	Surkusaeel-o.
F-AY.	S-WAD.	Q-AF.	R-AY.
Eea Quhhar-o.	Eea Wuhab-o.	Eea Ruzzaq-o.	Eea Futtah-o.
O thou Avenger!	*O thou Bestower of Benefits!*	*O thou Sustainer!*	*O thou Conqueror!*
Ruftamaeel-o.	Israfeel-o.	Kulkaeel-o.	Surhumakeel-o.
SH-EEN.	T-AY.	S-AY.	KH-Y.
Eea Aleem-o.	Eea Qabiz-o.	Eea Basit-o.	Eea Hafiz-o.
O thou Omniscient!	*O thou Seizer (of Souls)!*	*O thou Providence!*	*O Guardian!*
Meekaeel-o.	Jibbraeel-o.	Humwakeel-o.	Tunkaeel-o.
Z-AL.	Z-WAD.	Z-OEE.	G-AEEN.
Eea Rufeeu-o.	Eea Mowz-o.	Eea Moozzil-o.	Eea Summeeu-o.
O thou who exaltest!	*O thou who honourest!*	*O thou who abasest!*	*O thou that hearest!*
Ittraeel o.	Rooqaeel o.	Looqaeel-o	Israfeel-o

If a man wish the accomplishment of his desires, he may either read one of the above-mentioned *usma-e-oozzam* (p. 304.) or one of the *usma-e-hoosna*, both which will equally answer the purpose; but the beneficial effects of the former are greater, though they are seldom had recourse to, owing to the trouble and inconvenience attending the reading of them.

The manner of reading the *dawut* is as follows. For instance, a *talib* (*i. e.* a seeker), is desirous of making another subject and obedient to his will. In this case, suppose the *mutloob* (the object or thing wished) to be a man named *Boorhan*, which name is composed of five letters, *viz.* B R H A and N. After the exorcist has ascertained, by reference to the above table, the different attributes of the Deity attached to each letter, together with the names of their corresponding demons, by first repeating the names of the demons and then those of the Deity, as detailed before in the case of the first of the *isms* contained in the *Juwahir-e-khumsa*, a certain number of times (as will presently be more particularly stated), the object will become subject and obedient to his will.

Whether the wisher reads them himself or employs another to do so for him, it is necessary that the substance of the following, in any language, be read daily four times; *i. e.* twice at the commencement of the *Durood*,* and twice at the end of each day's task, *viz.* "O Lord, grant that "the object, Sheikh Boorhan, may so deeply be distracted "in love with such a one (the seeker), as to be day and "night entirely forgetful of his natural wants."

* The *durood* is as follows: "*Allahoomma Sullay-allah Mohummudin, wa-Allah Allay Mohummudin wo barik wo sullim.*" *i e.* "O "God! grant blessing, prosperity, and peace to Mohummud and his "posterity."

I may here premise what is essential to be known in order to be able to read the *ism*, that the reckoning by Abjud is divided into four parts, *viz.* units, tens, hundreds, thousands. If the numeral representing the letters fall on the Units, it is to be considered as so many hundreds;

Tens .... thousands;
Hundreds .... tens of thousands;
Thousands .... hundreds of thousands.

By this rule the following are the letters of Boorhan, *viz.*

B-ay, in the Table (p. 308.)...	2	is equal to	200
R-ay	200	...	20,000
H-ay	5	...	500
A-lif	1	...	100
N-oon	50	...	5,000
		Total.........	25,800

The exorcist having previously divided the sum-total into any number of equal parts, and fixed upon the number of days in which to finish the reading of it, such as a week or two, he must conclude it within the appointed time; or, his labour will be vain. Burning benjamin, or any other sweet perfume, with his face turned towards the house of, or directly at the object, he is to read it thus:

Umwakeel-o—Eea Ruhman-o!
Surhumakeel-o—Eea Futtah-o!
Ittraeel-o—Eea Qooddoos-o!
Kulkaeel-o—Eea Allah-o!
Jibbraeel-o—Eea Baree-o!

Previously to repeating these five *isms* 25,800 times in the way I have exhibited here once, it is necessary to give their *nissab*, *zukat*, &c.; but in reading this species of *ism*, instead of repeating it for the *nissab*, &c., the number of times as laid down for the other *isms* (p. 312), if it be repeated in the above way one thousand times for each *ism* with its demon, it is enough; and equivalent to its *nissab*, &c., even to the end of *khutum;* there being no occasion to read its *Surree-ool-eejabut.*

SECT. 3. *Of commanding the presence of Genii and Demons.*

When an exorcist has once commanded the presence of genii and demons, he may, through their means, cause whatever he pleases to be effected. He can obtain things mysteriously, such as his daily food, or ready cash equal to his real expenses, by demanding it of them; and I have generally heard it said that they never ask for more than what they absolutely require.*

Previous to commanding the presence of genii and demons, it is requisite to confine one's-self in a closet, and the apartment is to be besmeared with red ochre; and, having spread a *moosulla* (which if also red, so much the better), he is to sit on it, and observing the utmost cleanliness, is to discharge its *nissab*, &c. in the course of a week. The sooner the better.

After that, in order to cause the presence of these beings, he is again to shut himself up for forty days, and repeat the *ism* 137,613 times, having previously divided the number into forty parts, a part being read each day.

For such *chilla* (or a forty days' abstinence), the place most congenial is a secluded spot; somewhere in the vicinity of the sea, in a rocky cavern, in a garden, or out of town, where no noise or bustle is likely to disturb the mind of the exorcist.

---

* For a very good reason! because it would not be granted by those aerial spirits.

After he has commenced the reading of the *ism*, every night, or week, or every now and then, some new and fresh phenomena will present themselves; and on the last week the demons and genii, attended by all their legions, will appear before him; and two or three from among the latter, or one of the demons or genii himself, will advance, and respectfully addressing him, say, "Well, Mr. Exorcist, "wherefore hast thou demanded our presence? Here we "are, with our assembled forces." At this critical juncture it behoves the exorcist to muster up his courage, and not to speak to them all at once, but by a motion of the finger or hand beckon to them to be seated. Having concluded his daily task, he is to inquire after their names, demand of them a sign or token, and ascertain how often it will be necessary for him to repeat the *ism* to cause their presence. They will then inform him on these points, and he is strictly to attend to their injunctions. Should he speak to them before concluding his daily task, they will cause some misfortune to befall him; nay, he will be in danger of his life; or they will all disappear of a sudden, and render the pains he has taken of no avail.

Then having adjured the genii and demons by a solemn oath, in the name of Almighty God, and of Solomon the son of David, (peace be! &c.) he is to dismiss them. He is, on no account, to say a word about the interview to any one.

He is never to command their presence when his body is at all filthy or unclean, and he is never to delay bathing himself after coition or nocturnal pollution. During his whole life he must abstain from adultery: in short, he is to do nothing but what is lawful.

It is advisable for the tyro in the art not to undertake it for the first two or three times, unless his tutor be present;

for otherwise he may forfeit his life. Many, from want of due regard to this, have grown and daily do grow mad and insane. Much rather abstain from it altogether.

For the information of Europeans (may their wealth ever increase!) I shall now relate some of the well-known and celebrated virtues of the first *ism* recorded in the *Juwahir-e-khumsa.*

1st. When any one wishes to go into the presence of a monarch, a noble, or a grandee, or that of his gracious master, without requiring to give the *nissab, zukat,* &c. and *dawut* (*i.e.* the familiarizing one's self with it, vide p. 313), if he merely repeat the chief *ism* seventeen times with open hands upheld to heaven, and having blown on them draws them over his face once, the instant the person beholds him he will become so fond of and attached to him, that however great his anger might have previously been against him, he will now be pleased with him.

2d. Should any one repeat the above-mentioned *ism* after every morning and evening prayer, as they are in the habit of repeating other things, forty or seventy times, his mind will become vivid and enlightened, and he will cherish in his bosom nothing but supreme love to God. No worldly concern will he allow to disturb his peace of mind; events about to come to pass will be revealed to him in dreams.

3d. When a person wishes any particular circumstance, temporal or spiritual, to happen, if he repeat the *ism* twenty-four times on a Sunday morning, before sun-rise, through the grace and blessing of God, that very same day, his wishes shall no doubt, be realized.

4th. If a person be anxious to make another subject and obedient to his will, he is on a Wednesday, after bathing, to put on clean clothes; and burning sweet-scented odours, repeat the *ism* a hundred and twenty-one times, over some food or drink, and having blown on it, cause the person acted upon to partake of it, and he or she will immediately become his or her *talib* (wisher).

5th. If an individual has a number of enemies, who profess friendship towards him outwardly, but in their bosoms harbour enmity, who slander him behind his back and by their haughty looks keep him at a distance, he is, after the usual devotions have been performed, to read that greatest of all *isms* forty-one times, morning or evening, for forty days successively; and by so doing, all his ill-wishers will become his intimate friends.

6th. Should any one desire to make princes or grandees subject and obedient to his will, he must have a silver ring made with a small square silver tablet fixed upon it, on which is to be engraved the number that the letters composing the *ism* represent; which, in this case, is 2,613 (p. 311). This number by itself, or added to that of its two demons, 286 and 112, and its genius, 1,811, amounting in all to 4,822,* (agreeably to the rules laid down in the

---

* The number of the *ism* (p. 311) is 2,613

First Demon, Hoomraeel.	*Hay* (p. 308)	5	
	Meem	40	
	Ray	200	
	Alif	1	
	Eeay	10	
	Lam	30	
			286
Second Demon, Humwakeel.	*Hay*	5	
	Meem	40	
	Waoo	6	
	Alif	1	
	Kaf	20	
	Eeay	10	
	Lam	30	
			112
	Carried forward		3,011

32d chapter, which treats on the subject of the science of *tukseer*,) formed into a magic square of the *solasee* or *robaee* kind, and engraved. When the ring is thus finished, he is for a week to place it before him, and daily, in the morning or evening, to repeat the *ism* five thousand times, and blow on it. When the whole is concluded, he is to wear the ring on the little-finger (lit. ear-finger*) of his right hand.

In short, it is no easy matter to command the presence of genii and demons ; and, in the present day, should these race of beings be near any one, so as to obey his calls, such a one would, no doubt, instantly be set down as a *wullee* (saint), or one endowed with the gift of miracles.

The author of the present sheets (lit. this teacher of the alphabet) has endeavoured to prove the effects of the reading of two or three of these *isms ;* but he found it a most difficult task to finish them ; for he met with such strange sights and frightful objects as completely deterred him from concluding any one of them. Moreover, conceiving it labour lost, he relinquished the design altogether.

Independently of these mighty *isms*, there are a great number of the attributes of the Deity, and verses of the *Qoran*, which one may read without much trouble, and

	Brought forward......		3,011
Genius Shutkheesa.	*Sheen*	300	
	Tay	400	
	Khay..............	600	
	Eeay	10	
	Say	500	
	Alif	1	
			1,811
			4,822

* So called, because made use of to clean the ear.

their effects are well established; but a knowledge of them can only be obtained by the most humble supplications to the great, or adepts in the art: and these folks again, communicate them privately (lit. breast to breast, hand in hand, ear to ear).

If they do describe them in books, it is never with sufficient minuteness for comprehension.

To this teacher of the A, B, C, through the grace of God and the favour and kindness of his tutors, a great variety of powerful *isms* and select sentences of the *Qoran* have descended; but as they have been imparted to him as profound secrets, it would be improper for him to disclose them.

However one verse is so well known, that I may as well mention it; and that is, the *Aet-e-footooh*, which literally signifies a verse for receiving an income gratuitously; such as, obtaining one's daily subsistence by some means or other, or getting service somewhere, or having one's income abundantly increased. If a person make constant use of that verse, for a time, God will undoubtedly, within forty days, grant his behests and prosper him. The ancients have repeatedly tried the effects of it by experiment. The *Aet-e-footooh*, which is to be repeated forty times after the five appointed seasons of prayer, is as follows:

"With Him are the keys of the secret things, none "knoweth them besides himself. He knows that which is "on the dry land and in the sea: there falleth no leaf "but He knoweth it; neither is there a single grain in the "dark parts of the earth, neither a green thing nor a dry "thing, but it is written in the perspicuous book." (Sale's *Qoran*, chap. vi. p. 150, new edit. 1825.)

For the purpose of obtaining an increase to one's subsistence or wealth, a person should, after the morning and evening prayers, repeat one thousand times the following two attributes of the Deity. Should he derive any benefit from its repetition within two or three months, he may continue the rehearsal one thousand or five hundred times, for as long a period as he chooses to benefit by it.

Eea gunnee! (O thou independent!)

Eea mo-gunnee! (O thou causer of independence!)

SECT. 4. *Concerning the casting out of Devils.*

In the *Shurra-e-Bokharee*, Aboo Hoorayree* (may God! &c.) observes, that the Prophet Mohummud Moostuffa (the blessing! &c.) has stated, that Adam was created of *teen* (clay), that is, of two of the elements, water and earth; and genii of *marij* (or flame without smoke), *i. e.* of air and fire.

Genii are spirits, and constantly reside in the lowest or first firmament.† They possess the power of rendering themselves visible to human beings in any form they please. Some sages assert that genii have bodies; but from the circumstance of their being invisible to us, the term *jin* (or internal, that which is not seen) has been applied to them. The extent of their knowledge is likewise hid from us; on which account a madman is frequently nicknamed in Arabic *Mujin-oo* and *Jin-noonee* (derived from *jin*), because the condition of his intellectual functions is concealed from others.

As Adam and Eve were the parents of mankind, so Jan and Marija were the parents of the race of genii.

Genii differ from man in three particulars; *viz.* in their spirits, their form, and their speech.

---

* This last word signifies "the father of cats." He was so nicknamed by the prophet, on account of his partiality to those animals, of which he had always a great number about him as pets.

† Mohummudans reckon seven firmaments. Vide p. 149.

Those among them who perform good actions have the appellation *Jin* (or Genius) given them; those who perpetrate evil deeds, *Shytan* (Satan or Devil). When the former do perform bad actions, such as causing the death of any one, or affecting a separation between two persons, it is not that it is according to their nature so to do, but they execute it through the means used by the exorcist, and by the influence of the *isms* of the Deity.

The food of such of them as are poor and indigent consists chiefly of bones and air.

The name of the genius who was most beloved of God was Hoorras.

In the *Tufseer-e-byzawee* (Commentary on the *Qoran*), and the *Tuwareekh-e-rowzut-oos-suffa*, it is observed, that Satan was originally an offspring of genii, and that God, of his infinite mercy, honoured him with the title of *Azazeel* (a fallen angel), their names having all a similar termination, such as Jibbraeel, Meekaeel, Israfeel, Izraeel, &c. Eeman-zahid has recorded, that it was owing to his disobedience he received the title of *Ib-lees* (or one who despairs of God's mercy), because he refused to prostrate himself before Adam; and when, through obstinacy and malignity, he tempted Adam and Eve to eat wheat, and caused their separation,* the name of *Shytan* (Satan) was given him; and, by so doing, he not only ruined himself, but also all Adam's race. He was the son of Hooleeanoos, who was the son of Tarnoos, who was the son of Soomas, who was the son of Jan.

Satan has four *khuleefay* (caliphs or deputies); *viz.* 1. Muleeqa, the son of Aleeqa; 2. Hamoos, the son of

---

* Adam, they say, was driven from Paradise to Ceylon, where a mountain exists at which they go to worship, and Eve to some country near Mecca.

Janoos; 3. Mubloot, the son of Bullabut; 4. Yoosuf, the son of Yasif.

As, among the offspring of Adam, Cain was the vilest character; so, among the race of genii, was he, who is called Satan.

As the name of the wife of Adam (the peace of God! &c.) was Hu-wa (Eve), so Satan's wife name was Aw-wa.

As Adam's surname was Abool-bushur, so Satan's was Abool-Murra.

As Adam had three sons, *viz.* Habeel (Abel), Kabeel (Cain), and Shees (Seth); so Satan had nine, *viz.* 1. Zulbaysoon, who with his host inhabits bazars; and all the wickedness committed therein is accordingly attributed to his agency. 2. Wuseen, the ruler over grief and anxiety. 3. Awan, the companion of kings. 4. Huffan, the patron of wine-bibbers. 5. Murra, the superintendent of music and dancing. 6. Laqees, the lord of the worshippers of fire. 7. Musboot, the master of news, who directs people to circulate malicious and false reports. 8. Dasim, lord of mansions. When people come home from journies, he prevents their calling upon God to return thanks for their safe return, and frustrates their good designs by causing wars and contentions to take place. Some say he is lord of the *dustur-khwan* (table-cloth), and does not allow people to say *bismilla* (grace) on sitting down to meals; and after it is over, he causes them to forget to return *shookoor* or *ehsan* (thanks) for it. (Vide p. 111, 112.) 9. Dulhan, he whose abode is places appropriated to devotional ablutions and prayers, where he defeats the objects of the pious, by throwing difficulties into the way of their performance of their duties.

These nine sons of the undaunted, the infernal Satan, are the mortal enemies of Adam's race. They never allow them to do a good action, but exert all their influence in causing them to sin. He has nine children added to his family for every one born among men.

In the *Shurra e-bokharee*, Jabir, son of Abd-oollah Ansaree (may God! &c.) observes, that God Almighty formed all created beings into four gradations or ranks: 1st. angels; 2d. devils; 3d. genii; and 4th. mankind.

But Abbee-durda, a companion of the Prophet (may God! &c.) has differently construed these divisions, assigning to the 1st rank snakes and scorpions; to the 2d, insects; to the 3d, spirits; to the 4th, Adam's progeny, and all quadrupeds, birds, &c.

Mulik *G*utshan is king of all the genii, and inhabits Mount Qaf.* To the eastward he possesses 300,000 domestics. To the westward reigns Abd-ool-Ruhman, his son-in-law, who has 33,000 dependants. To both of them his holiness Mohummud Moostuffa himself (the peace! &c.) during his life-time gave the above Moosulman names.

Kings of Moosulman-genii have their names terminating in *noos;* as Tarnoos, Hooleeanoos, Dukheeanoos, &c. Kings of Tursa (worshippers of fire) genii, in *doos;* as Seedoos, &c. Kings of Jewish genii, in *nas;* as Juttoonas, &c. Kings of Hindoo genii, in *tus;* as Nuqtus, &c.

The last-mentioned genius (Nuqtus), when he entered the service of his excellency the Prophet Shees (peace be unto him!), was converted to the Mohummudan faith.

Among Moosulman-genii there is a sect of *eemams:* (leaders or priests). Such were Aboo-furda, Musoor, Durbag, Qulees, and Aboo-malik.

In the *Tufseer-e-kubeer* it is stated that genii are of four

* *Qaf*, a fabulous mountain. Vide Glossary.

kinds, *viz.* 1st. the *Fulkeeu*, or those who inhabit the firmament; 2d. the *Qootbeeu*, who reside about the North Pole; 3d. the *Wuhmeeu*, who haunt the human imagination; and 4th. the *Firdooseeu*, who dwell in Paradise.

In the *Tufseer-e-neeabeeu* it is said that genii are divided into twelve bands or troops: six inhabiting the countries of Room (the Turkish empire), Furhung (Europe), Yoonan (Greece), Roos (Russia), Babel (Babylon), and Suhbutan; the other six, the regions of Gog (country of the Calmucs), Magog (country of the Esclavonians), Nowba (Nubia), Zungubar (Ethiopia), Hindh (Hindoostan), Sindh (Sind or Western India). Among these, three legions are Islamites or Moosulmans, and their king is Bukhtanoos.

As to the real nature of genii, they are nine-tenths spirits and one-tenth flesh.

In short, we have now considered the origin, birth, and nature of genii and devils. Although this narrative should have had a place in the second section of this chapter, yet, as it was in a great measure connected with our present subject, I have preferred inserting it here.

I have long been desirous of describing the manner in which the devil is cast out, and have therefore been more particular in mentioning his family connexions, names, pedigree, &c. This I have done in as concise a form as the extent of my poor abilities would permit.

I have always been accustomed, (having from my youth up had a great taste for it), to practise the reading of the *dawut* (exorcism), write amulets and charms, and by consulting horoscopes, prognosticate future events.

Many a time have persons possessed of the devil applied to this teacher of the A, B, C, for assistance, and whether owing to my reading *doa* (supplications), tying on an amulet, or burning a charm, or, to the force of their belief, or to some wise contrivance of my own, which I put in practice, they have been cured.

I used to entertain great doubt and suspicion in my own mind as to the effects produced; and frequently said to myself, "O God! What relation or connexion can possibly exist between genii and man, that the former should possess such powerful influence over the latter, or that by our merely reading incantations they should be cast out?" With these doubts in my mind, I was constantly employed in the search and investigation of the subject, by consulting very learned men and divines, and reading noted works on the subject, such as the *Tufseer* (commentary on the *Qoran*), *Huddees* (traditional sayings of the Prophet), and others, in order that I might acquire some knowledge concerning these matters. Whatever I have seen, heard, and read, I have related.

When individuals labour under demoniacal possessions, the symptoms are as follows. Some are struck dumb; others shake their heads; others grow mad and walk about naked; they feel no inclination to pursue their usual avocations, but lie down and are inactive. In such cases, if it be required to make the demoniac speak, or to cast the devil out, there are a variety of contrivances resorted to, and which I shall now endeavour to describe.

Magic circles, squares, and figures, are sketched on the ground, or on a plank, with various coloured powders, *bhubhoot* (cowdung ashes), charcoal, or *sundul*; and the demoniac being seated in the centre of it, the *afsoon* (incantation) is read. Around these diagrams are placed various kinds of fruits, flowers, *pan-sooparee*, *sheernee*, sometimes *sayndhee*, *taree*, *nariellee*,* *daroo*,† &c. Some sacrifice a

---

* Intoxicating liquors; vide Glossary.

† Ardent spirits.

sheep in front of the circle, &c. sprinkle the blood round it, set up the head in front, placing a lamp upon it, lighted up with a *puleeta* (charm-wick); or they merely slay a fowl, and sprinkle its blood around. Some give a rupee or two, according to their means, into the hands of the person possessed by the devil, to deposit therein. These things are denominated the apparatus of worship (*vide plates*).*

The following Arabic incantation (*vide* p. 331) is to be read over some *bhubhoot* (cowdung ashes), or over a few (lit. five) different kinds of grain, seven times, and each time the exorcist is to blow† upon the object, and throw it at the head and shoulders of the demoniac; or he is to breathe on flowers and throw them at him; and burning some *ubeer*, *ood*, *dhunneea*, *uggur*, or *sundul*, near the demoniac, he is, during the process, to read the spell over them twenty-one times, desiring the patient to sit with his eyes shut and smell well the fumes exhaled, while he repeats the supplication. During the reading of the incantation, should any motion of the body be perceptible, the exorcist is to say, "If thou be a male devil, bow thine head to the right; if a female, to the left; and if a hermaphrodite, forward." Some demons shake the head and body of the demoniac most violently. When the reading of the supplication has been concluded, the exorcist is to inquire of his patient whether he feels any degree of intoxication or lassitude, or sense of weight in the head, or whether he experience the emotion of fear in his mind; or whether he be aware of a sensation like that of some one behind him shaking his head? If any of these symptoms be felt, the

* The object of the following diagrams being to inspire terror, they cannot be made too frightful.

† The word used in the original (*p'hoonkna*) means "to blow with "the breath," therefore the verb "to blow" does not exactly express it.

A Magic Circle.

No. 1. (to face Page 330)

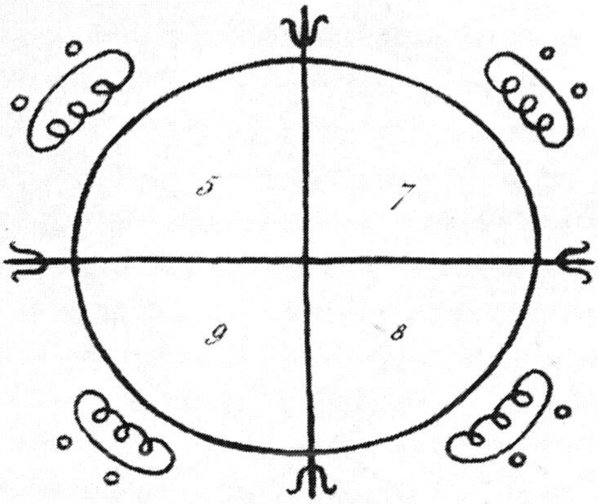

A Magic Square.

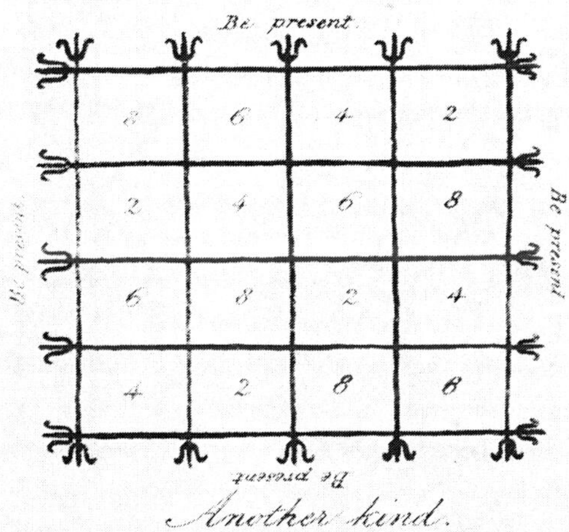

Another kind.

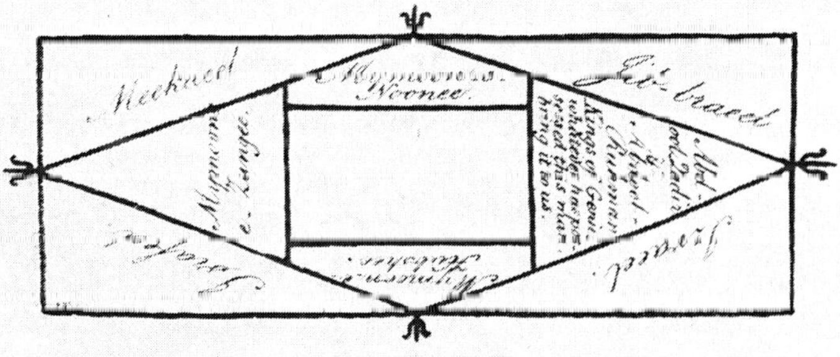

A Magic Figure.

No. 2. (To face Page 330.)

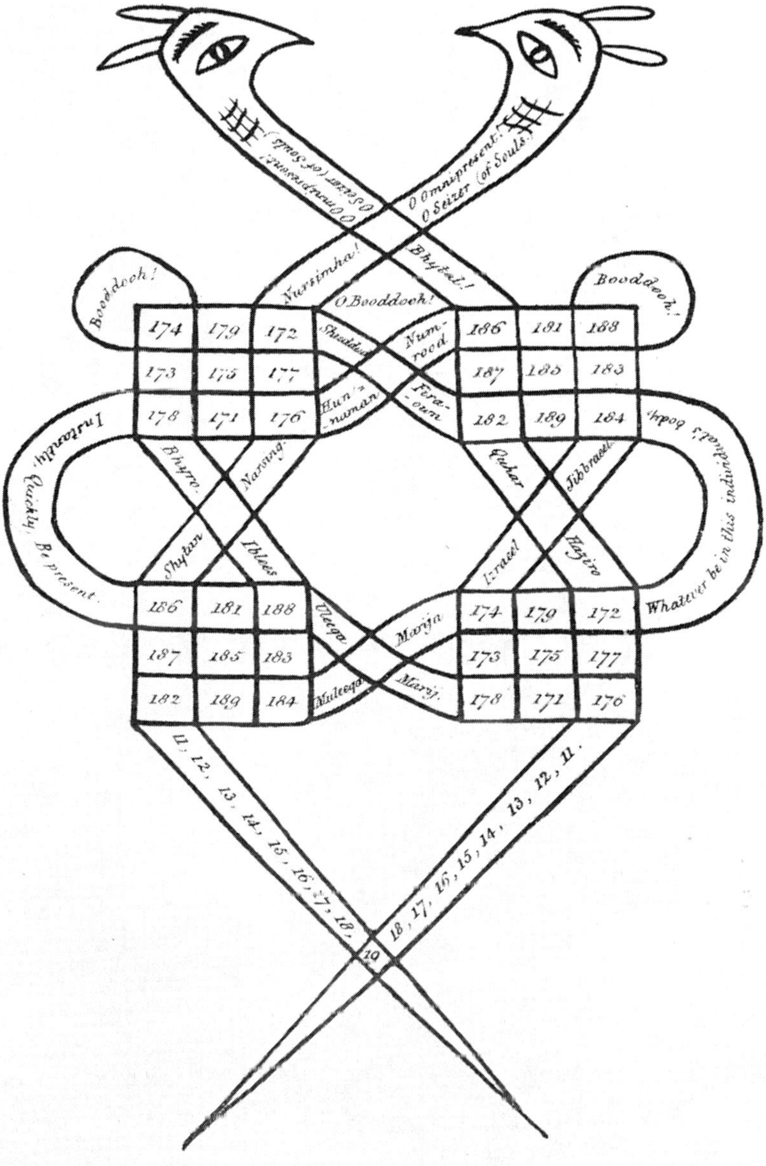

Other Species.

No. 3. (to face Page 350.)

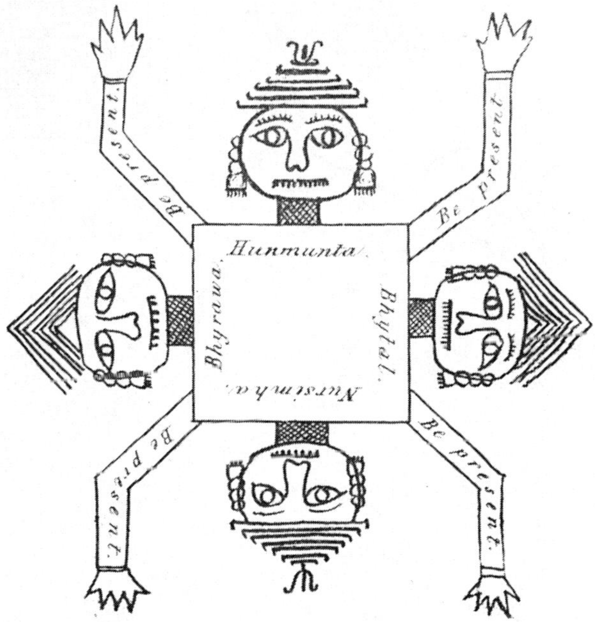

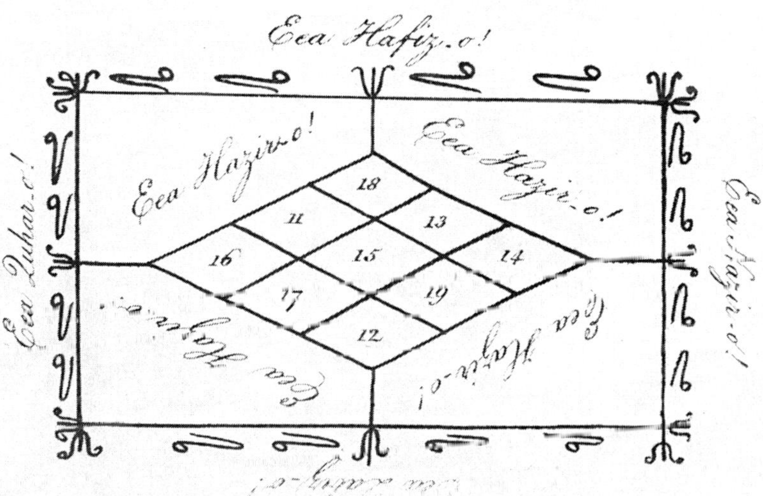

Different Varieties.

No. 4. (to face Page 330)

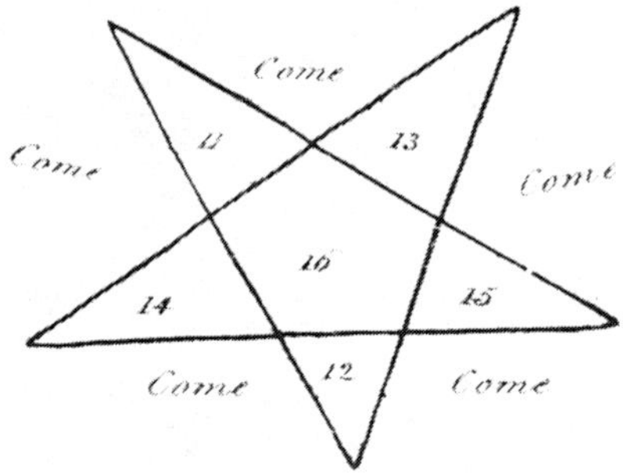

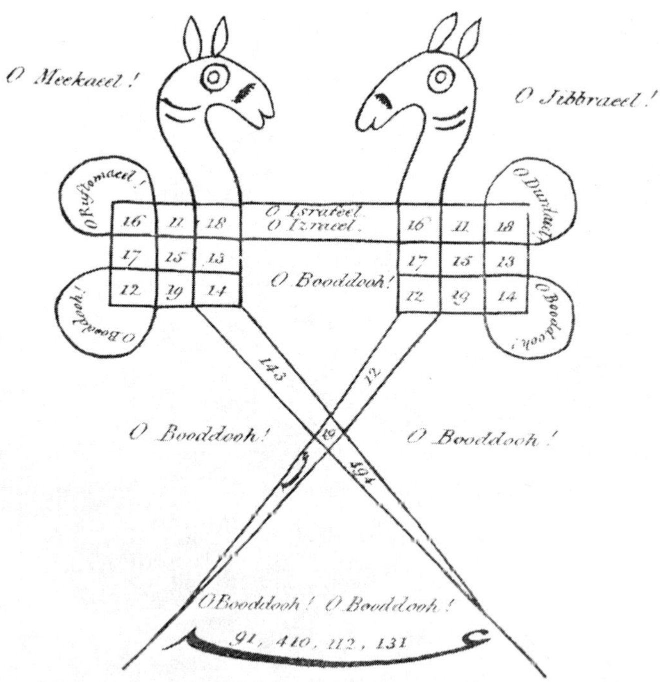

A Magic Figure.

No. 5. (to face Page 330.)

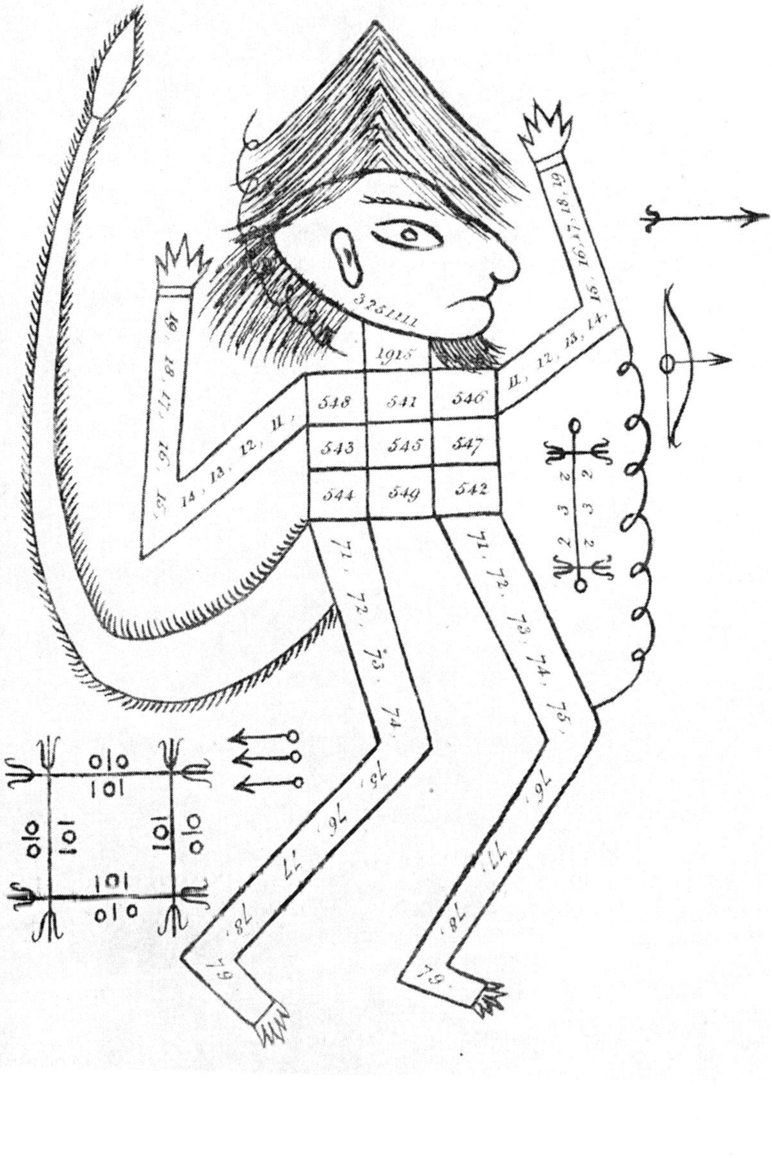

case may be considered as that of a demoniac; otherwise not. The circumstance of the devil catching a person, is in reality, nothing; its seat is merely in the fancy and imagination of the vulgar.

The Arabic *afsoon* (incantation), above alluded to, is as follows:—" *Azumto Alykoom, Futhoonu Futhoonu, Hubbeebayka Hubbeebayka, Almeen Almeen, Suqqeeka Suqqeeka, Akaysun Akaysun, Bulleesun Bulleesun, Tuleesun Tuleesun, Soorudun Soorudun, Kuhulun Kuhulun, Muhulun Muhulun, Sukheeun Sukheeun, Sudeedun Sudeedun, Nubeeun Nubeeun, Bayhuq-e-Khateemay Soolayman bin-Daood (Ally him-moos-Sulam) Ohzayroo, min Janaybil Musharayqay wul Mugaraybay wo min janaybil, i-munnay wul I-sur-ray.*"* Having read this, the exorcist is to add, " Whatever it be that has " taken possession of the body of such a one, come out of " him! come out of him!"

Incantations for causing the devil to enter a person's body, in Arabic, Persian and Hindoostanee, are very numerous; but, owing to their prolixity, I have omitted them. Should any one, however, wish to acquire a knowledge of them, he may easily do so by applying to those who practise the art.

Some devils, when they seize a person, do not let him go for two or four weeks together; nay, for as many months; and the demoniac then never speaks, and though the devil be present in him, he does not move nor walk.

To prevent certain devils from escaping, they tie a knot in the hair of the demoniac, after having read the following verse of the *Qoran* in Arabic three times, and blown upon it, *viz.*—"*Innuma amruhoo, eeza aradu shyin un eeuqoollu*

* *i. e.* I adjure you Futhoonu, &c. (various names of demons, ending with "Nubeeun") by the seal of Solomon, the son of David, come from the East and from the West, from the right and from the left.

"*luhoo koonfu-ee ay-koona fu soobhanulluzee bay eud-*
"*dayhil mullukooto koollu shyin wu illyhay toorjaoona.*"
i. e. "His command, when he willeth a thing, is only "that he saith unto it, 'Be,' and it is: wherefore praise be "unto him, in whose hand is the kingdom of all things, "and unto whom ye shall return at the last day." (Sale's *Qoran*, chap. xxxvi., p. 308., edit. 1825.)

Some read the following verse eleven times over any kind of odoriferous oil and blow it into the ear* of the demoniac:—*Wuluqud futtunna soolaymana wu ulkyna Alla Koorsee ye-ay-hoo jussudun soomma annab.* "We have "tried Solomon, and placed on his throne a counterfeit "body. Afterwards he turned unto God."—Sale's *Qoran*, chap. xxxviii., p. 321., edit. 1825.)

Sometimes they repeat the following invocation of the Most High God nine times, and blow it into one or both ears:

يا سَمِيعُ تَسَمَّعْتَ بالسَّمْعِ والسَّمْعُ فِي سَمْعِ سَمْعِكَ يا سَمِيعُ

Eea summee-o tussummata bis summay, wus summay fee summay sumuka eea summee-o. "O Hearer! thou hearest "with ears; thine ears are within hearing, O Hearer!"

After the demoniac is well filled with the devil, he sometimes screeching takes a *kakra* (large wick), continues lighting and extinguishing it by putting the lighted end into his mouth; (some, biting the neck of a fowl, suck its blood); and when he begins to speak somewhat rationally, the exorcist inquires after the demon's name; his sign; whence he came, and whither he is bound; when he intends taking his departure; and what he was doing and causing to be done, while in the body of the demoniac? If

---

* A common technical expression, meaning that after reading the verse, they blow upon it and thereby transfer it (*i. e.* the virtues of the sentence) to the patient.

he reply to these queries, well and good; if not, the exorcist reads some incantation or other over a rattan, and flogs the demoniac well, which has the effect of making him relate every thing. For some devils are so wicked that they will not reveal their names, nor state when they mean to depart. What is strange, all this flagellation leaves no marks on the body of the demoniac. After this, the exorcist asks what his desire is at present, and what articles or eatables he would wish to have? Whatever he names he is to be supplied with; such as any of the following articles: a *seer* or half a *seer* of *juwar* or *d'han kay k'heeleea*n (fried great-millet or paddy) or *moot'koolay*,* curdled-milk, boiled rice, curries of flesh, fish, or fowl, eggs, a sheep, *sayndhee taree*, *shurab*, *sheernee*, various kinds of fruits and flowers, *ghee*-lamps made of flour, two images, male and female, made of flour, and besides these, many others which the devil may ask for. These are arranged on a large piece of a broken earthen pot, or on a winnowing or common basket, which the exorcist waves three times from the head to the feet of the demoniac, first in front, then behind. He afterwards distributes its contents among beggars, or places the whole under a tree or on the bank of a river. The day of his departure is the one on which these are to be given him.

At the period of his going away, the exorcist is to inquire of him the particular place at which he means to throw down the patient when making his exit, and what he intends taking away with him. To which he replies, "on this "very spot;" or, "out of doors;" or, "under such a tree:" and "I shall take with me meat, *kuleejee*, &c.;" or, "nothing at all."

Should this not meet with the approbation of the exor-

* Balls of paste boiled (dumplings).

cist, he is to say to him, "Nay; but thou must throw him "down here, or in the area, and take up a shoe or a sandal "with thy mouth, or bear a *sil** on thy head." When he accordingly does so, he runs with such speed, and makes such a noise, that the people all, through fear, flee before him. The demoniac frequently runs away with stones so large that two or three persons could scarcely lift them. Sometimes, he merely runs without carrying away any thing. The operator is then to continue holding on by his hair, either at the back or on one side of the head, and wherever he may fall down, there he must let him lie; and having read the incantation, or the *aet-ool-koorsee*,† over an iron nail or wooden peg, he is to strike it into the ground. The moment the demoniac falls down, the exorcist instantly plucks out one or two hairs from among those which he holds in his hand, and reading some established spell over them, puts them into a bottle and corks it up; whereupon the patient's devil is supposed to be imprisoned therein. Then he either buries the bottle under-ground or burns it; after which the devil never returns.

Some *Seeanas* (p. 372) make a small wax doll, fasten one extremity of a hair to the crown of its head, and the other to the bottom of a cork, fill the bottle with smoke, put the doll into it, and cork it up. They put in smoke to prevent people's distinguishing the doll, which remains suspended in the middle of the bottle. The *Seeana*, the moment the demoniac falls on the ground, pulls out a hair or two as above-stated, and contrives to insert them into the bottle; which, holding up to public view, he exclaims, "Behold! I have cast the devil out of the demoniac and

---

* *Sil*, a stone on which spices, &c. are ground.

† Vide Sale's Qoran, chap. ii. p. 44., from "God! there is no God," &c. to "they shall remain therein for ever," p. 45, ed. 1825.

"confined him in this bottle. There he is, standing in the "middle of it, longing to come out. Now, if you give me "so much money, well and good; if not, I will let him "loose again." Those foolish people, on beholding the doll in the bottle, actually believe it to be the devil himself, and out of fear give him any sum of money he asks, and get it buried or burnt.

The instant the devil leaves the demoniac he regains the use of his faculties, and in utter amazement, staring round, inquires, "Where am I? who brought me here? and why "has all this crowd assembled around me?"

After that, the following supplication is to be read over a handful of water and dashed at the face of the patient; a form which is repeated three times, viz. *Atmukh Atmukh, Tummakh Tummakh, Turmeehim, kul qussussay kanuhoo jummal-latin, suffrin oh'riq oh'riq.* And afterwards this supplication: *Lahowl wo laqoow-wuta illa billa hil Allee ool azeem* (or, There is no refuge or power but in God the high and mighty), is to be read over water, which is then breathed upon, and the patient is made to drink it.

Having brought him home from the place where he fell, they wash his face, hands, and feet; and either on that day or the following, a *taweez* (amulet) of a particular kind which is used for the purpose is fastened to his neck or arm, in order that the devil may not seize upon him again.

When a person has for a considerable time been afflicted with any particular distemper and does not recover, in order to ascertain whether it be the devil or enchantment that has attacked him, they mark out the following sketch on the ground or on a plank. Some flowers being put into the hands of the sick person, he is to be desired to grasp them firmly in his hands and place his fists near the diagram. While he does so, the exorcist is to take some more flowers, and having read the undermentioned incantation over each flower and blown upon it, he is to dash it against his patient's hands. In a few minutes the hands will begin to move into one of the squares.

Here follows the sketch, with the incantation after it:

Demons.	Fairies.
Diseases.	Enchanters
Genii.	

" *Innuhoo Minnus Soolayman, o Innuhoo Bismilla*
" *Hirruhma Nirruheem unta taloo Ala atoonee Mooslay-*
" *meena.**—*Ribtun ribtun Buhuq-e-Kaf, Hay, Eeay,*
" *Aeen, Swad, wo Hy, Meem, Aeen, Seen, Qaf.*†—*Jullee-*
" *ooshin Murbooshin Hyoosin tuffa-ay-lin murqoodushin*
" *sulmooshin murtooshin Myloomashin Duddumun, zur-*
" *bun, qooroo eeun Aheeoon,*‡ *bay burkut-e-Soolayman bin*
" *Daood.*—*Akhbirnee Akhbirnee, o eeumshay, o izhubba*
" *eeudanay, bay ummur Illahay ta-ala, illu soo in nuq-*
" *shay.*"§

And he is to continue saying every now and then, " In " these five compartments are inserted the names of the " five afflictions. God grant that the hands of the patient

* As far as this, to be found in the *Qoran; viz.* " It is from Solo- " mon, and this is the tenor thereof. In the name of the most merciful " God, rise not up against me, but come and surrender yourselves unto " me." (Sale's Qoran, chap. xxvii. p. 231. edit. 1825.)

† " Binding him, binding him by the aid of the letters K, H, E, A, S, (Vide Sale's Qoran, chap xix. at the beginning); and by H, M, A, S, Q, (ditto chap. xlii)."

‡ This sentence of the incantation has no meaning.

§ " By the blessing of Solomon the son of David warn me, warn " me. May both his hands go, and by the command of God Almighty " reach this diagram."

"may enter the square containing the name of the malady "he is affected with."

Some devils generally attack people in their sleep, and harass them not a little.

Some do not enter the body so soon as their presence is required. In this case, the demoniac is to be made to sleep, and continue sitting night and day in one of the circles, &c. before described (p. 330) etched on the ground, and at night, either for the purpose of commanding the presence of, or for casting out the demons, a *puleeta** is to be lighted in three kinds of oil or one of balsam, for three, five, or seven nights successively. Within these periods, should a *puleeta* have been employed to command his presence, he makes his appearance; if for his departure, he makes his exit.

The modes of lighting *puleetas* are various; however, I shall give one only as an example.

Take a red or black earthen pot, fill it with all kinds of fruits, some cash, such as a rupee or half a rupee, as the operator's fee, and adapt a cover to it of the same colour, the exterior surface of both being marked with *sun-dul.* Having besmeared the place where the patient sleeps with cowdung or red earth, stroke the demoniac from head to foot with a piece of blank paper, and write the *puleeta* on it; roll it up obliquely, round, or flat, to make it burn well, and to prevent its unfolding itself wind a piece of thin muslin, or a flock of cotton, or thread round it; then light it with three kinds of oil, *i. e. ghee*, gingilie oil, and either castor oil, *kurrunj kay tail*,† or linseed oil, in the cover of

* *Puleeta*, a wick composed of paper, inscribed with mystic characters; by inhaling the smoke of which, demons are said to be expelled from those possessed.

† Oil of the *kurrunj*-tree, or tree dalbergia; dalbergia arborea, Willd.

the earthen pot. On lighting the lamp in the evening, perfumes are to be burnt, and the patient is to be desired to sit near the lamp and stare at it. After he falls asleep the lamp is to be continued burning.

On lighting the *puleeta* (charm-wick) two or three distinct flames of various hues, such as black, green, or yellow, will become visible both to the patient and to bystanders. Some demoniacs cannot bear to sleep in a light of this description; they either get up and walk about, or do not feel at all sleepy: while others, though they do not disrelish looking at it, seem evidently excited. At all events, by the burning of this *puleeta* the devil is cast out. Should he be present, they converse with him as above detailed (p. 332), and cause him to depart, which by the influence of the charm he no doubt will do; and should the patient be labouring under any corporeal affection, it will be removed. (Vide Plates.)

If devils throw stones, and occasion annoyance in any one's house, from among the stones thus thrown the operator takes one, paints it over with *turmeric* and quicklime, reads some spell over it, and throws it in the direction whence the stones came. If it be really the devil, he returns the self-same painted stone; by which means they know, to a certainty, that it is he; otherwise, they conclude that it is an enemy who has done it, and have recourse to other means for remedying the evil.

Sometimes *seeanas* (conjurors, p. 373) have recourse to various tricks to obtain money. Thus, when they find out a rich man who is subject to fear, they either themselves throw an immense number of stones or bones on his house, or cause them to be thrown, either during the night or day, in such a way as not to be discovered. The land-

A Puleeta (or Lamp-Charm,) for Casting out Devils.

No. 6. (to face Page 338.)

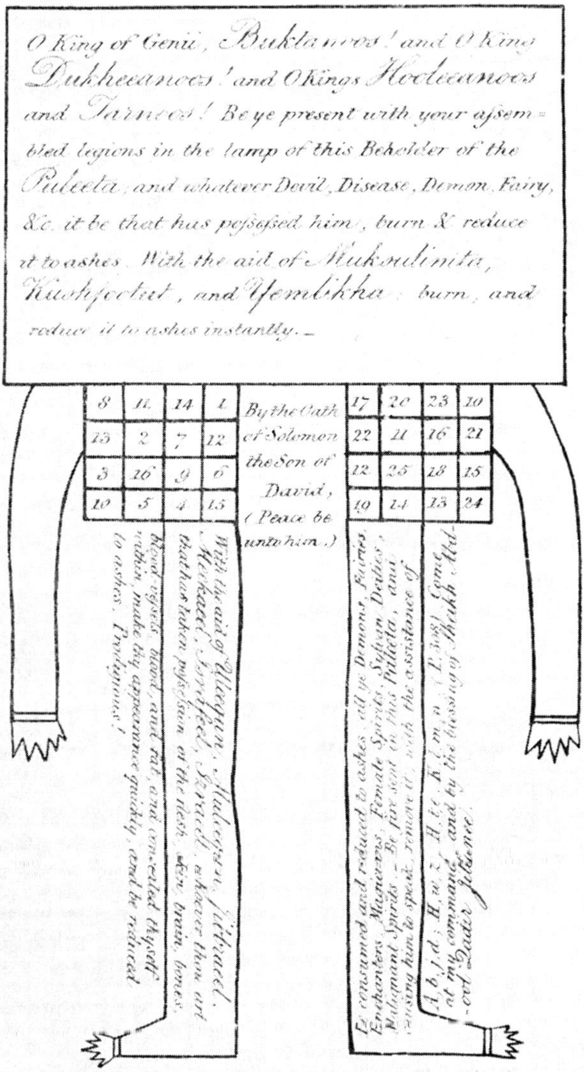

A Puleeta, (or Lamp Charm.)
for commanding the Devil's presence.

No. 7. (to face Page 338)

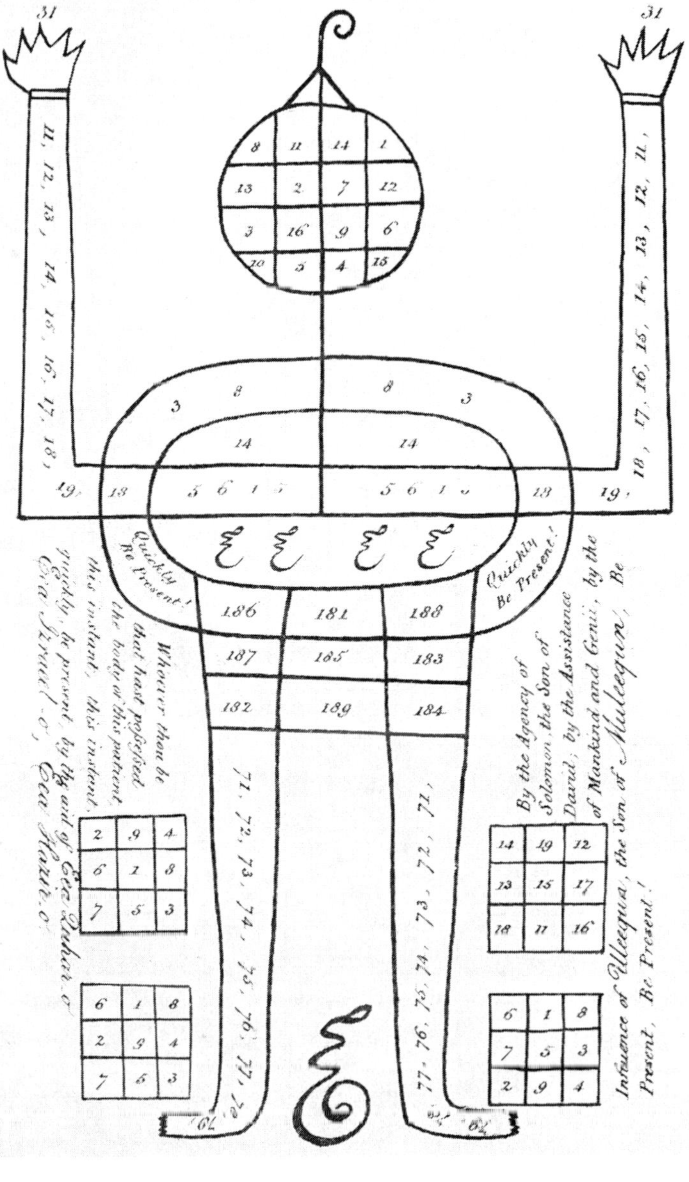

A Puleeta, (or Lamp-Charm:) for Casting out Devils.

No. 8. (to face Page 338.)

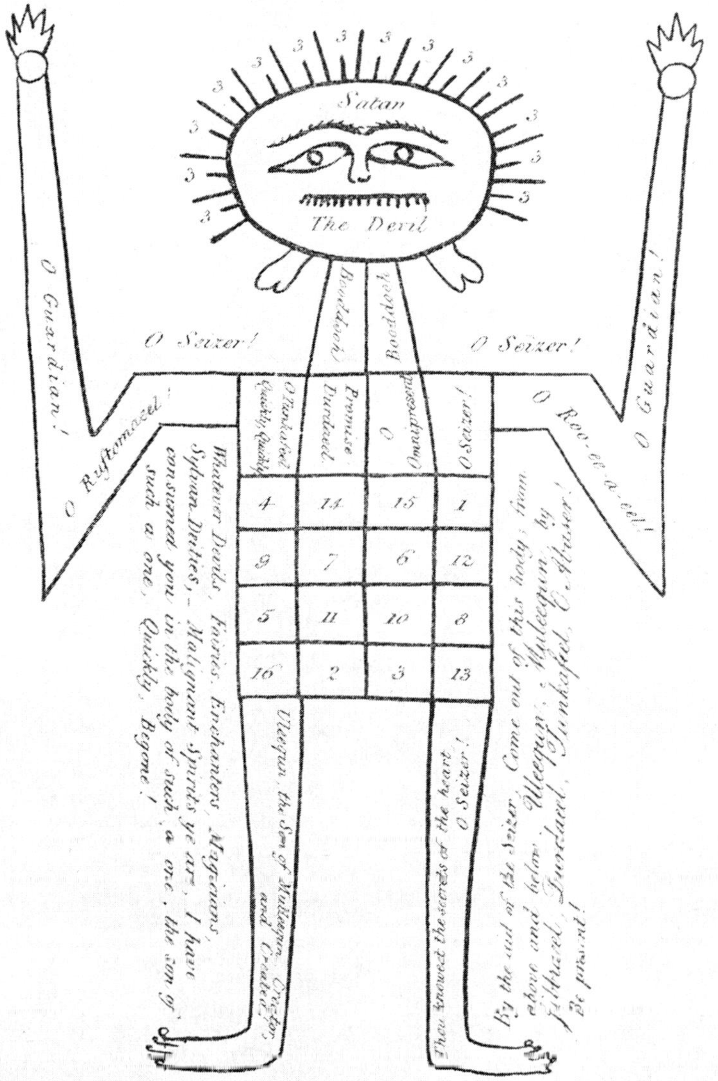

A Lamp-Charm,
for Causing the Devil's presence.

No. 9. (to face Page 338.)

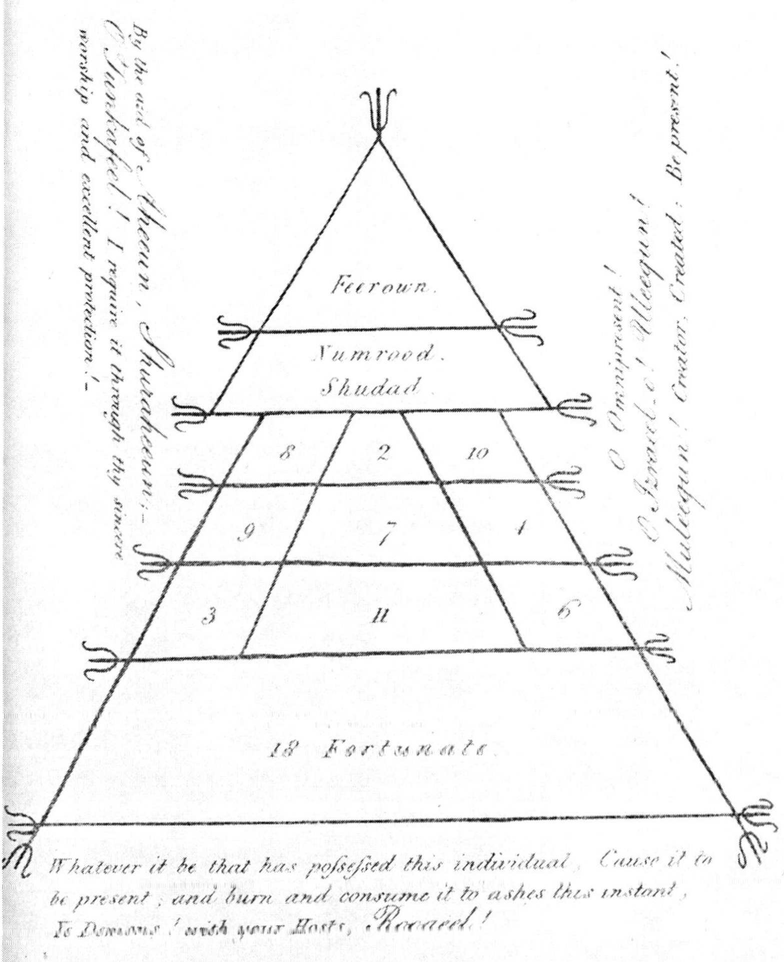

A Puleeta (or Lamp Charm,)
to cast out the Devil.

No. 10 (to face Page 338.)

8	11	14	1
13	2	7	12
3	16	9	6
10	5	4	15

Whoever ye are, Demons, Fairies, Genii, Malignant Spirits, Devils, Nursoo,* Chooraeel,† Sheikh Suddo,‡ (by the aid of Uheeun, Shuraheeun,) that have taken possession of the flesh, skin, brain, bone, blood-vessels, blood! Be present instantly, this very hour, in this body, and be burnt and reduced to ashes; — Uleequn, the Son of Muleequn, Numrood, Murdood, Shuddad, Haman, Feeraown, Qaroon, Aheeun, Shuraheeun, O Quhar-o, O Izraeel-o. Moosuhur Mumee Allah See Meġ-Meġ, Yemmay, Yemmay.

* Nursoo (alias Narsinga;) 4th Aŏŏ-tar of Vishnoo.

† Chooraeel, the Ghost of a woman who died while pregnant.

‡ Sheikh Suddo, (P. 278.) a Moosulman, who became a Demon.

A Puleeta, (or Lamp-Charm,) for Casting out the Devil.

No. II. (to face Page 338.)

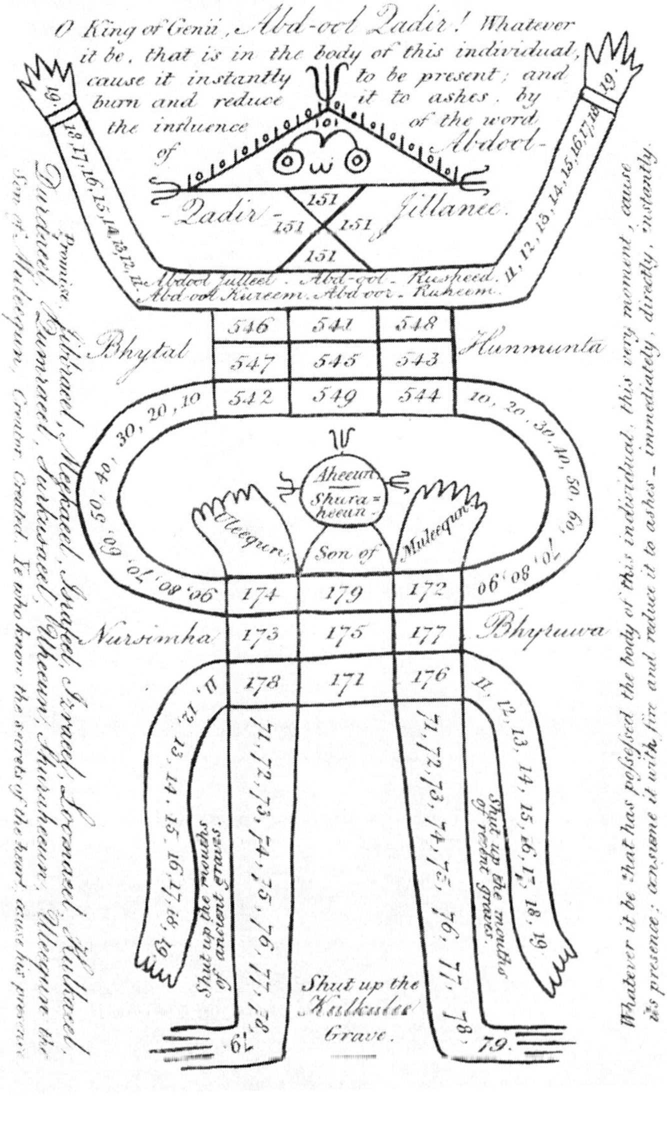

lord, wishing to ascertain the cause, and becoming alarmed, sends for one of the *seeanas*, and desires him to cast his horoscope. The latter frightens him still further, by assuring him it is the devil, describing him as a most hideous monster who inhabits the atmosphere, residing between heaven and earth, having four heads; one, of an elephant; a second, of a male buffaloe; a third, of a hog; a fourth, of a horse; and adding that he is desirous of devouring his *kuleeja*,* which is the reason of his pelting stones at him from the sky, and that he will no doubt kill him unawares by strangling him. So saying, he shews him a sketch of the monster. On hearing and seeing all this, he gets alarmed to such a degree, that his very *kuleeja*† melts away into water. Meantime the other continues, that he will verify his assertion. So saying, he takes up a stone or bone, paints it as above stated, and pelts it. The stone (as he takes care that it shall be) is thrown back. This frightens his dupe still more, and he offers the *seeana* as much money as he wants, in order to get rid of so unwelcome a guest. The *seeana* performs some spell or other and walks away with his booty. This is a thing of which I myself have been an eye-witness.

Should genii reside in any one's house, and decamp with eatables and frighten people, so that the inhabitants of the dwelling are constantly disturbed and troubled, and scarcely ever exempt from sickness, nay, find life burdensome, the undermentioned verse is to be read for three days twenty-one times, mornings and evenings, over some fresh water; which, having been blown upon, is then to be sprinkled over the floor. Or the verse having been read twenty-one times

* Lit. "his liver," but here his whole inside, or perhaps pluck, (vide Johnson).

† Here doubtless refers to the heart.

over four iron nails or wooden pegs, and blown upon, the latter are to be struck into the four corners of the house, by which means the devils or genii will be removed. The verse is as follows:

انهم يكيدون كيدا و اكيد كيدا فمهل الكافرين امهلهم رويدا

" *Innuhoom ekkeedona kydun o akeedo kyda fummu-*
" *haylil kafayreena umhilhoom, roowayda.*"

" Verily, the infidels are laying a plot to frustrate my
" designs; but I will lay a plot for their ruin. Wherefore,
" O Prophet, bear with the unbelievers: let them alone
" awhile."—(Sale's *Qoran*, chap. lxxxvi. last verse.)

Some write the names of the seven A*shab-e-kuhuf* (vide p. 276), together with that of their dog, as stated below, on paper, and paste them on the walls of their houses. Their names are Aleekha, Muksulimta, Tub-yunus, Kush-footut, Udurqut, Yunus, Yuanus; and that of their dog, Qutmeera.

The following three are smoke-charms, and are employed in removing tertian fevers, demons, fairies, fears, and false imaginations. They are thrown into the fire, and the patient being covered with a sheet, is fumigated with the smoke arising from them. These are in much more general use than the preceding larger ones. (*See Plate.*)

Besides these, there is a great variety of other spells and charms for raising devils and for expelling and burning them: but on account of the length of the description, I have abridged and limited it at this point.

Smoke-Charms.

No. 12. (to face Page 540.)

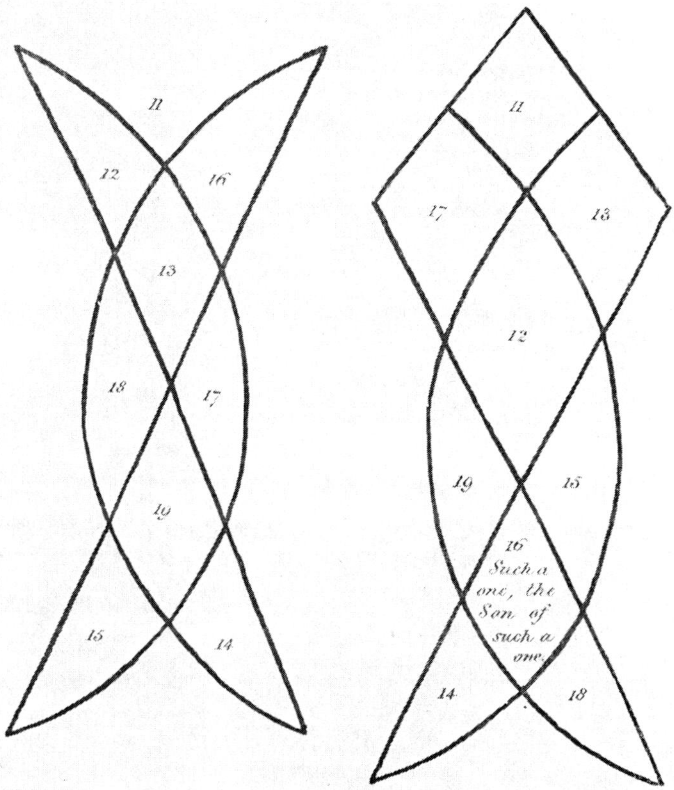

Numrood, Shuddad, Hamaa, Lood, Qaroon, Iblees, Aboojuhil, Firaoun

Depart, Depart. Be consumed. Be consumed, Be consumed out of the body of such a one the Son of such a one.

CHAPTER XXX.

Concerning the method of establishing Friendship between two persons, and of captivating the hearts of the members of assemblies.

It is customary with Moosulman women, when their husbands or paramours are tyrannical, brutal, or jealous, or take a fancy to other women and neglect them, to procure something eatable or drinkable, or some embrocation or other, from a practitioner who is skilful and learned in the art; and having had some supplication read over it, cause them to swallow it, or apply it to their bodies. By such contrivances, Almighty God, who is able to turn the hearts of men, does certainly cause their husbands or lovers to be enamoured of them.

Some debased females, and prostitutes, in order to render men (strangers) obedient to their will, and thereby possess themselves of their wealth and property, as well as with a desire to rule them, have recourse to the most filthy means, as will presently be hinted at. God Almighty grant that none of Adam born may ever hear of, eat, or practise them.

By way of specimens, I shall select a few of the substances used for this purpose; but, for God's sake, don't in disgust, conceive my assertions false.

Ex. gr. Panniculus fluore menstruo fœdatus, et in cineres, siccatus, redigitur: hi autem cineres, calce vivâ (quæ vulgò cum foliis piper betle, Lin. [Vernac. *betel-leaf,*] aliâve escâ comeditur) mixti, viro comedendi præbentur; aut quocunque modo insidiosé efficiunt, ut partem quandam ex sanguine suo menstruo, in viri caput perfricent. Aliquando quidem, propriam urinam cum caryophyllo, cardamomo, nuce moschatâ, et macide, miscent; vel, in eadem, Areca

Catechu, Lin. [Anglice, *betel-nut*,] macerant, et fœtore quocunque modo expulso, efficiunt ut vir ex ea aliquid comedat.

For the above reason, when a man is cordially submissive to any woman and overlooks her bad conduct, the common saying among the vulgar is, that "the woman must have "fed him with betel-nuts."

Many women of bad caste make the men eat the flesh of the chameleon, and various kinds of wild roots and herbs. Many, by the use of these, not unfrequently get sick, and even die.

They likewise procure some of the ashes of the dead from the place where the Hindoos are wont to burn theirs; and having read some incantation over it, sprinkle it at night on his bed, or on himself, when asleep. Or they apply to their own foreheads or eyebrows a well-known kind of philter, termed *mohnee ka kajul*,* and thus come into the presence of their husbands, in order, that by beholding them they may fall in love with and be kind to them.

Sometimes they apply a small quantity, about the size of a mustard-seed, of the above lamp-black to the hair or soles of the feet of the man.

It is a very common custom with unchaste women, courtezans, and dancing-girls, with the view of causing men to be submissive and obedient to their will, to practise these things and cause them to be practised. It therefore behoves every man of sense, to be on his guard against the craftiness and subtlety of these people.

To the writer of these pages it would appear that if a married woman, to prevent her husband acting improperly or committing adultery and fornication, instead of having

---

* Lit. the philter lamp-black.

recourse to such vile practices has the same object effected by the reading of something out of the sacred *Qoran*, it is highly proper, for no harm is done on either side; because, writing on, or reading a supplication from the *Qoran* over any thing, and afterwards drinking or eating it, is peculiarly meritorious; besides, the not permitting her husband to act improperly is greatly to her advantage.

Many people, when they wish a man or woman to be subject to, or in love with them, effect it by repeating some of the verses of the *Qoran*, as detailed before under the head of *Dawut* (p. 307), which it is therefore unnecessary for me to recapitulate.

If a man meet with a beautiful woman and cannot obtain possession of her, or if she be opulent and disregard him, and he wishes her to become enamoured of him and be subject to his will, in such cases it is with men as with women, they have recourse to the basest means. *Ex. gr.* Quibusdam insidiis efficiunt ut sordes inter scrotum et femora, necnon in axilla acervatas, et pilos quosdam ex pubere, etiamque aliquid seminis, et unguinum præsegmina cum urina triturata, et in pilulas facta, fæminæ conglutiant. Præterea, cum generis asinini mas et fæmina coeunt, siquid seminis externé decidat, idem summâ cum curâ colligunt ex eodemque parte quâdam cum proprio semine mixtâ, et his, quodam cum cibo commixtis, efficiunt ut fæminæ hac ex mixtura aliquid comedant: whereupon they become enamoured of their admirer, and are rendered obedient to his will.

To captivate the Hearts of Members of Assemblies.

There is a variety of means; but I shall content myself with alluding to a few, by way of example.

Some have a tablet, with a particular *taweez* (magic

square) or *ism* (attribute of the Deity), which is employed for the purpose, engraved on it, set in a ring or *kurra*, and wear it on the finger, wrist, or upper arm.

Others have amulets engraved on plates of copper, silver, or gold; or writing them on paper, fold them up in any of the above metals; or enclose them in a bit of *kumkhwab*, *mushroo*, &c. sew them up, and wear them either on the hair of the head, or on the turban, arm, wrist, or neck.

Again, some use for this purpose various kinds of roots, leaves, creepers, &c., the gathering of which is performed with great ceremony. For instance, on the day before, they go and invite the tree, saying, "We intend to come "to-morrow morning or evening, or at such or such a time, "and take you away for such and such a purpose." These roots, leaves, creepers, &c. are only known to a few, who, when they go to fetch them, take with them such things as fruits, &c. fowls, and liquor, and depositing them near the tree, apply some of the blood of the fowl to the tree and bring away what they require, and give the things gathered to the *talibs* (agents), in order that they, for the purpose of establishing friendship and subjection, may administer and apply them to their objects. It is by reading supplications, or by some such contrivances as these, which may be learnt from practitioners in the art and from *sunneeasees*, that they effect their purpose.

CHAPTER XXXI.

Concerning the causing of Enmity between two individuals, and the effecting the death of one's enemy.

When a person is desirous of causing enmity between two people, the *Soora-e-ullum-turkyf* is a well-tried chapter, which one bareheaded is to read at noon, or at any other period, forty-one times over some earth taken out of a grave, and throw it on them, or on their road, or house.

Or, if taking forty corns of black pepper, he, for a week, morning and evening, read the above-mentioned chapter once on each pepper-corn in the name of the two individuals, or if for forty days, each time using forty pepper-corns, he read the chapter once on each, and then burn them, enmity will be established between the persons.

Or he is to repeat the undermentioned verse of the *Qoran* or the *ism* bareheaded, in the burying-ground or mosque, with his face turned towards the enemy's dwelling at noon, forty-one times, for forty-one days, and enmity will take place between them; *viz.*

وَالقيسا بينهم العداوت والبغضا الي يوم القيامة - يا قهار يا جبار
يا عزريل

" *Wul-qy-sa, by-na-hoo-mool, adawutta, wul bugza-a illa eeowmil, qya-mutay.*" *i. e.* " We have raised up enmity and hatred among them till the day of resurrection."

(Sale's *Qoran*, ch. v. p. 120, ed. 1825.)

The *ism* is, *Eea Quhar-o, Eea Jubbar-o, Eea Izra-eel-o.*

" O Avenger! O Great One! O Izraeel!"

To cause the death of an enemy.

If a person have an enemy on whom he has not the power

to be revenged, though he is constantly distressed and harassed by him, the following is what people, in the habit of doing these things, perform, either for themselves or for others, for a reward. However, it is not every one that succeeds in performing these; and practitioners only undertake them for those actually in need of relief: and the Almighty again, on his part, will only hear the supplications of those who are really distressed.

He is to read the *tubut-maqoos*,* or the *chayhul qaf* (lit. forty Q.) morning and evening daily, for twenty-one days, at each period forty-one times.

Or, with some earth taken out of a grave, or the earth of the Hindoo *musan*,† he is to make a doll about a span long, more or less; and repeating the *soora-e-ullum-turkyf*, with the name of its accompanying demon, or the *tubut* reversed, or the *chayhul qaf* over twenty-one small thin wooden pegs, and repeating it three times over each peg, he is to strike them into different parts of the body of the image; such as one into the crown of the head, one into the forehead, two into the two eyes, two into the two upper arms, two into the two arm-pits, two into the two palms of the hands, two into the two nipples, two into the two sides of the body, one into the navel, two into the two thighs, two into the two knees, and two into the two soles of the feet. The image is then to be shrouded in the manner of a human corpse, conveyed to the cemetery, and buried in the name of the enemy, who (it is believed) will positively die after it.

What the *tubut-makoos* and the *chayhul qaf* are, may be ascertained by inquiring of adepts in the art

* Or, the chapter *tubut* read *makoos* (backwards); *i.e.* every word spelt backwards.

† The place where Hindoos burn their dead.

A different method.

A human figure is to be sketched on the ground, or on an unburnt brick, or an image formed with earth; and having read over it the undermentioned incantation five hundred times daily, at noon, for a week, he is to give it a cut with a sword, or strike it with an arrow from a bow.

The following is a well-established spell or incantation:

يَا قَاهِرُ ذَالْبَطْشِ الشَّدِيدْ اَنْتَ الَّذِي لَا يُطَاقُ اِنْتِقَامُهُ

"*Eea qahir-o, zulbut ish shudeed-e-untoolluzee, la-*
"*e-taq-o, inteqamuhoo.*"

i. e. O Punisher! full of wrath, thou art terrible; whose vengeance no one can endure.

CHAPTER XXXII.

Concerning the science of *tukseer* (or numbers); comprising the art of constructing *taweez* (amulets); and *puleeta* (charms); the uses to which they are applied; and in the name of the sick to consult horoscopes and predict future events.

Amulets are of various descriptions; and the magic squares extend to a hundred houses in a line: but, I shall explain the subject by delineating them as far as a ten-house square. The science resembles arithmetic; and in whichever way the numbers are added together, the sums total invariably correspond.

These magic squares embrace the following varieties; *viz.* 1. *dopaee*, 2. *solasee*, 3. *robaee*, 4. *moorubba*, 5. *khomasee*, 6. *moosuddus*, 7. *moosubba*, 8. *moosummum*, 9. *moostussa*, and 10. *moashur*, *i. e.* two-footed, ternary, quaternary, &c.

1. In filling up a *Dopaee* (or two-legged) magic square,

nothing is to be subtracted; but the number is to be divided by 12, and with the quotient the squares are to be filled up, increasing one in every square as you proceed; in manner following:

3	8	1
2	4	6
7		5

Should any thing remain, it is to be added to the number in the sixth or *kussur kay ghur* (fractional house). For example, the numerical quantity of the word *bismilla*, 786, divided by 12 gives 65; and 6 over. With this fill up, adding 65 in each house and 6 more in the 6th compartment;

195	526	65
130	260	396
461		325

2. The mode of forming a *Solasee* magic square, is this. From a given number subtract 12; and with one-third of the remainder, fill up the divisions of the square as follows:

4	9	2
3	5	7
8	1	6

The above is the magic square of Huwa (Eve), whose number is 15. Deduct 12, there remain 3, a third of which being one, with this unit fill up the square, adding one in each division, until the whole be filled up; and whatever way the numbers are added together, they will form the same amount.

In thus subtracting and dividing, should 1 remain over and above, it is to be added (in addition to the other number), in the 7th house, if 2, in the 4th square; and then, the sums will correspond.

In forming *solasee* magic-squares, the house with which to commence is likewise varied, according to their elements, whether it be earth, water, air, or fire; thus—

AIR.

2	7	6
9	5	1
4	3	8

FIRE.

4	9	2
3	5	7
8	1	6

EARTH.

6	7	2
1	5	9
8	3	4

WATER.

6	1	8
7	5	3
2	9	4

3. To form a *Robaee* magic-square, deduct 30 from the given number; divide the remainder by 4; and with a quarter fill up 16 squares; thus,

8	11	14	1
13	2	7	12
3	16	9	6
10	5	4	15

This magic-square is that of the word *ujjul* (death); its number 34. Deduct 30, remain 4; divide by 4, remains 1; with the latter fill up.

Should 1 remain over, add 1 to the 13th square; if 2, add 1 to the 9th; if 3, 1 to the 5th.

Besides this mode, there is another, by which *robaee* squares are formed; *viz.* subtract 21 from a given number, begin the remainder from the 13th house, and fill up to the 16th square; having previously filled up from 1 to 12 as above directed, fill up the other four: *e. g. Mureeum's* (Mary's) name is 290; deduct 21, remain 269; with it fill up thus:

8	11	270	1
269	2	7	12
3	272	9	6
10	5	4	271

4. *Moorubba* magic-squares are also, like the *solasee*, of 4 kinds; depending upon their elements; thus:

EARTH.

8	11	14	1
13	2	7	12
3	16	9	6
10	5	4	15

WATER.

14	4	1	15
7	9	12	6
11	5	8	10
2	16	13	3

AIR.

15	1	4	14
10	8	5	11
6	12	9	7
3	13	16	2

FIRE.

1	14	15	4
8	11	10	5
12	7	6	9
13	2	3	16

5. *Khomasee* magic-squares are formed by subtracting 60 from any given number, dividing the remainder by 5, and with one-fifth filling up 25 squares, by increasing one in each house; thus:

7	13	19	25	1
20	21	2	8	14
3	9	15	16	22
11	17	23	4	10
24	5	6	12	18

If, in making the division for forming this square,

1 remain, one is to be added in the 21st square;
2 .... 16th do.
3 .... 11th do.
4 .... 6th do.

6. To form a *Moosuddus* magic-square, deduct 105 from any given number, divide by 6, and with one-sixth fill it up; thus,

36	18	30	19	7	1
13	26	2	34	24	12
5	9	22	29	15	31
25	6	14	8	35	23
21	32	10	17	3	28
11	20	33	4	27	16

In forming the above square, should

1 remain, add one in the 31st compartment.
2 .... 25th. do.
3 .... 19th. do.
4 .... 13th. do.
5 .... 7th. do.

7. To make a *Moosubba* magic square, you must deduct 160, divide by 7, and with one seventh fill up, as follows:

40	23	13	45	35	18	1
32	15	5	37	27	10	49
24	14	46	29	19	2	41
16	6	38	28	11	43	33
8	47	30	20	3	42	25
7	39	22	12	44	34	17
48	31	21	4	36	26	9

In forming the above, if from 1 to 6 remain, add one in the 43d house.

8. To make a *Moosummun* magic-square, subtract 252, divide by 8, and with the quotient fill up the square, thus:

36	43	35	32	27	60	26	1
41	4	49	59	21	17	45	24
37	15	11	10	58	51	50	28
23	47	57	52	12	9	18	42
3	46	8	13	53	56	19	62
25	63	54	55	7	14	2	40
31	20	16	6	44	48	61	34
64	22	30	33	38	5	39	29

In forming this square, if from 1 to 7 remain, add one to the number in the 75th house.

9. If a *Moostussa* magic-square be required to be made, subtract 360 from the given number, divide by 9; and with one-ninth fill up as follows:

70	59	27	16	76	55	43	22	1
50	39	28	6	66	54	33	12	81
40	18	7	67	56	34	13	73	61
60	29	17	77	46	44	23	2	71
20	19	78	57	45	24	3	72	51
30	8	68	47	25	14	74	62	41
9	79	58	37	35	4	64	52	31
10	69	48	36	15	75	53	42	21
80	49	38	26	5	65	63	32	11

If in this from 1 to 8 remain, add one in the 73d square.

10. *Moashur* magic-squares are formed by subtracting 495 from any given number, dividing the remainder by 10, and with one-tenth filling it up thus:

28	60	42	61	39	70	98	72	34	1
33	4	26	74	76	95	84	24	21	68
69	83	13	92	10	90	86	12	18	32
2	79	14	50	53	56	43	87	22	99
71	96	85	55	44	49	54	16	5	30
66	19	8	45	58	51	48	93	82	35
36	20	94	52	47	46	57	7	81	65
37	23	89	9	91	11	15	88	78	64
63	80	75	27	25	6	17	77	97	38
100	41	59	40	62	31	3	29	67	73

In this, if from 1 to 9 remain, add one in the 91st house.

Such magic-squares are used for establishing friendship and creating enmity, to shut one's mouth in regard to another; to prevent dreaming, to cast out devils, &c. &c.

For cementing friendship they are written about the new moon,* and the days best adapted for the purpose are Fridays, Mondays, Wednesdays, and Thursdays; and the hours most propitious on those days are those of Jupiter, Mercury, and Venus (vide p. 20). In this way exorcists have likewise fixed the hours and days for causing enmity, &c., particulars of which may be learnt by studying the science of *tukseer* (p. 347).

* That is, from the 1st to the 15th of the month.

These magic-squares are, for all purposes, written on a white porcelain plate, or on paper, the inscription is then washed off with water and the latter drank; or they are worn about the person; or they are burnt, and the individual is smoked with their fumes; or they are kept suspended in the air; or having been made into charms by being enveloped in cotton, they are dipped in odoriferous oils and burnt in a lamp; or they are engraved on rings and worn on the fingers. Some persons write the *taweez* or *ism* on *bhooj-putur*,* or have it engraved on a thin plate of silver, gold, &c., roll it up or fold and form it into a *taweez* or *puleeta*, cover it with wax, and sew some superior kind of cloth or brocade over it; or they insert it into a square hollow case or tube of gold or silver, seal it hermetically, and wear it suspended to the neck, or tie it to their upper arms or loins, or stick it into their turbans, or tie it up in a corner of their handkerchiefs and carry it about their person. People very generally have empty *taweezes* made, and suspend them to the necks of their children, together with a *nadulee*† in the centre, as well as some *baghnuk* (tigers' nails) set in silver, &c.; and when they obtain a *taweez* from any renowned *mushaekh* or *moolla*, or can procure a little of any sacred relic offered on shrines, such as flowers, *sundul*, &c., they put these into them.

Some by witchcraft familiarize themselves with, and bring under their command various species of creepers and roots of trees,‡ part of which they dig up, and putting them into tubes of iron or brass, &c., wear them on their upper arms;

* The epidermis of the betula bhojpatra.—*Wall.*

† A stone, having generally a verse of the *Qoran* engraved on it.

‡ Or rather they bring under subjection the devils or genii who are supposed to preside over these, so that by the use of them they obtain their wishes.

or twist some white or two or three-coloured thread round them, and wear them in the form of a *taweez*.

Some few kill a double-headed snake on an *amows** Sunday, or on any Sunday or *amows*-day; and having read some incantation over it, put it into an earthen pot and bury it under ground. After its flesh has undergone the process of putrefaction, they take the bones, thread them, and wear them around the neck as a cure for *scrofula*. Sometimes they also suspend them to the necks of their children.

Independently of these *taweezes*, &c., they tie on the feathers, hairs, bones, &c. of various kinds of birds and quadrupeds, for the purpose of warding off apparitions, genii or devils, misfortunes, &c.

At the time of forming these *taweezes*, the face of the *talib* (seeker) is to be directed towards the house of the object.

In constructing *taweezes* or *puleetas* with the sentences of the *Qoran* or other supplications, the numerical value of the letters (p. 308) are added together, and with the sum total the squares are filled up.

Some people make magic-squares with the number of any one of the ninety-nine names of the Most High God.

In the sacred *Huddees* the Prophet (the blessing! &c.) has said, that if any one keep in mind the ninety-nine names of God the Most Glorious, and constantly repeat them, God will preserve him from the torments of hell and the anguish of the grave.

The ninety-nine names or attributes of the Deity, with the numerical value of their letters, are as follow:

* *Amows*, the day on which the conjunction of the sun and moon takes place.

1 *Allah-o!*......... 66. God, or worthy and fit to be worshipped. *Use*. For all purposes.

2. *Ruhman-o!* ... 298. The Bestower (the clement, the beneficent). *Use*. For the enlightening of one's mind.

3. *Ruheem-o!*...... 258. The Merciful, and the giver of daily food of various kinds. *Use*. for increase of rank.

4. *Malik-o!* ...... 91. The Lord, entitled to govern the whole universe. *Use*. For obtaining wealth.

5. *Qooddoos-o!* ... 170. The Holy, and pure from all blemish. *Use*. For fear.

6. *Sulam-o!* ...... 131. The Securer from all evils (Saviour). *Use*. For health.

7. *Momin-o!* ...... 136. The giver of security at the day of judgment. *Use*. For security against enemies.

8. *Mohymin-o!* ... 145. The acquainted with men's actions, secret or revealed. *Use*. For one's protection and defence.

9. *Azeez-o!* ...... 94. The excellent and incomparable (august). *Use*. For increase of honour and dignity.

10. *Jubbar-o!* ...... 206. The Almighty supreme. *Use*. For being independent of princes.

11. *Mootukubbir-o!* 662. The lofty doer. *Use*. For increase of wealth and dignity.

12. *Khalik-o!* ...... 731. The creator. *Use*. For obtaining an easy labour.

13. *Moosuwwir-o!* 336. The sculptor or fashioner. *Use*. For the cancelling of debts.

14. *Guffar-o!* ......1,281. The pardoner of sins. *Use.* For pardon of sins.

15. *Quhar-o!* ...... 306. The ruiner of the arrogant. *Use.* *Use.* For preservation from tyranny.

16. *Wuhab-o!* ...... 14. The discoverer. *Use.* For finding things lost.

17. *Ruzaq-o!* ...... 308. The giver of daily food to mankind. *Use.* For increase of subsistence.

18. *Futtah-o!* ...... 459. The accomplisher of affairs. *Use.* For victory.

19. *Aleem-o!*......... 150. The omniscient. *Use.* For acquiring science.

20. *Qabiz-o!* ...... 903. The punisher of tyrants, (the hard grasper). *Use.* For ruining enemies.

21. *Basit-o!* .... 72. The maker abundant of daily bread, of whose he will. *Use.* For the increase of one's daily bread.

22. *Khafiz-o!* ... 1,481. The subduer of whom he wills. *Use.* To cause the distress of one's enemies.

23. *Rafay-o!* ...... 351. The exalter of whom he wills. *Use.* For the raising of one's dignity.

24. *Moiz-o!* ...... 117. The giver of greatness in the world to whom he wills. *Use.* For honour.

25. *Mozil-o!* ...... 770. The ruiner of whom he wills. *Use.* For the ruining of one's enemies.

26. *Sumeeu-o!* ... 180. The hearer without ears. *Use.* For ear-ache and deafness.

27. *Busseer-o!*...... 302. The see-er without eyes. *Use.* For knowing the secrets of the heart.

28. *Hukum-o!* ...... 68. The commander. *Use.* For sovereignty.

29. *Adul-o!* .... 104. The just. *Use.* For justice and happiness.

30. *Luteef-o!* ...... 129. The conferrer of favours upon mankind. *Use.* For obtaining good fortune.

31. *Khubeer-o!* ... 812. The communicator of information. *Use.* For ascertaining mysteries.

32. *Huleem-o!* ...... 88. The long-suffering towards sinners. *Use.* For the relief of pains and afflictions.

33. *Azeem-o!* ... 1,020. The great. *Use.* For greatness.

34. G*uffoor-o!* ... 1,286. The pardoner of sins. *Use.* For the pardon of sins.

35. *Shookoor-o!* ... 526. The rewarder of true worshippers. *Use.* For the removal of sorrow.

36. *Alee-o!* .... 110. The Most High. *Use.* For greatness.

37. *Kubeer-o!* ...... 232. The lord of greatness. *Use.* For having one's wishes granted.

38. *Hufeez-o!* ...... 998 The guardian. *Use.* For fear.

39. *Moqeet-o!* ...... 550. The giver of strength. *Use.* For establishing an affair firmly.

40. *Huseeb-o!* ...... 80. The taker of accounts of his servants on the day of resurrec-

tion. *Use.* For liberty from confinement.

41. *Juleel-o!* .... 73. The glorious. *Use.* For generating fear in the mind of an enemy.

42. *Kureem-o!* ...... 270. The munificent. *Use.* For the accomplishment of one's affairs, spiritual as well as temporal.

43. *Ruqeeb-o!* ...... 312. The guardian of mankind. *Use.* For liberation.

44. *Moojeeb-o!* ...... 55. The answerer of prayer. *Use.* For one's prayers being heard.

45. *Wasay-o!* ...... 137. The He whose gifts are various. *Use.* For the opening (*i. e.* the prosperity) of one's shop.

46. *Hukeem-o!* ...... 78. The performer of, not by art alone. *Use.* For a knowledge of God.

47. *Wudood-o!* ...... 20. The friend of the devout. *Use.* For affection.

48. *Mujeed-o!* ...... 57. The lord of glory. *Use.* For recovery from serious indisposition.

49. *Baees-o!* ...... 573. The raiser of the dead from their graves. *Use.* For the anguish of the grave.

50. *Shuheed-o!* ... 319. The knower of things, visible and invisible. *Use.* For the removal of disobedience in children.

51. *Huq-o!* .... 108. He whose nature is unchangeable. *Use.* For the acquisition of art.

52. *Wukeel-o!* ...... 66. The protector of human affairs. *Use.* For protection from lightning and fire.

53. *Quwee-o!* ...... 116. The giver of strength. *Use.* For overcoming an enemy.

54. *Muteen-o!*...... 500. He whose strength is all powerful. *Use.* For the increase of woman's milk and of water.

55. *Wulee-o!* .... 46. The bestower of friendship. *Use.* For making one's master subservient to his will.

56. *Humeed-o!* ...... 62. The praised. *Use.* For the removal of the habit of evil speaking.

57. *Mohsee-o!* ...... 148. The wise. *Use.* For curing forgetfulness.

58. *Moobdee-o!* ... 56. The creator (without materials) of mankind. *Use.* Employed by women for facilitating labour.

59. *Moeed-o!* ...... 124. The raiser of mankind after death. *Use.* For the knowledge of hidden things.

60. *Mohee-o!* ...... 58. The burner of corpses. *Use.* To ward off devils and fairies.

61. *Moomeet-o!* ... 490. The destroyer of the living. *Use.* For the death of an enemy.

62. *Hyee-o!*......... 18. The living one who never dies. *Use.* For the riddance of insects that infest fruit on trees.

63. *Qyeeoom-o!* ... 156. He who exists from everlasting to everlasting. *Use.* For long life.

64. *Wajid-o!* ...... 14. The finder out, whose rank is exalted. *Use.* For finding things lost.

65. *Majid-o!* ...... 48. He, whose dignity is high and lofty. *Use.* For the attainment of wealth.

66. *Wahid-o!* ...... 19. The one, who has no equal in nature and attribute. *Use.* For liberation.

67. *Sumad-o!* ...... 134. The independent. *Use.* For preventing indigence.

68. *Qadir-o!* ...... 305. The Lord of power. *Use.* For removing distress and distraction.

69. *Mooqtudir-o!*... 744. The all-powerful. *Use.* For obtaining dignity and wealth.

70. *Moquddim-o!* 184. The bringing forward good and bad. *Use.* For warding off distress.

71. *Mowukhir-o!*... 846. He who puts whomever he wills last. *Use.* For the fulfilment of one's desires.

72. *Uwwul-o!* ...... 37. The first, or from eternity. *Use.* For conquering one's enemy in battle.

73. *Akhir-o!* ...... 801. The last or to eternity. *Use.* For preservation from fear of every kind.

74. *Zahir-o!* ......1,106. He whose existence is clear. *Use.* For preservation from blindness.

75. *Batin-o!* ...... 62. He whose secrets are hidden. *Use.* For becoming the friend of mankind.

76. *Walee-o!* ...... 47. The king from beginning to end. *Use.* For preservation from all domestic misfortunes.

77. *Moota-Alee-o!* 551. The most sublime. *Use.* For obtaining the accomplishment of one's wishes.

78. *Bur-o!* .... 202. The doer of good. *Use.* For removing evil.

79. *Tuwab-o!* ...... 409. The hearer of those who repent. *Use.* For the pardon of sins and admission into the presence of the deity.

80. *Moontuqeem-o!* 630. The taker of revenge on sinners. *Use.* For the enlightenment of the grave.

81. *Afw-w-o!* ...... 156. The eraser of sins. *Use.* For the pardon of sins.

82. *Ruoof-o!* ...... 286. The merciful. *Use.* For causing the liberation of the oppressed from the hands of the oppressor.

83. *Malik-ool-Moolk-o!*... ... 212. The distributor (in the world), or Providence. *Use.* For wealth.

84. *Zool-jullal-wul-ikram-o!* 1,100. The lord of greatness and glory. *Use.* For the answering of prayer.

85. *Moqsit-o!* ...... 209. The just or equitable. *Use.* For keeping off evil imagination.

86. *Jamay-o!* ...... 114. The assembler of mankind on the day of judgment. *Use.* For uniting with those from whom one has separated.

87. Gunnee-o! ... 1,060. The opulent. *Use.* for wealth.

88. *Mogunnee-o!* 1,100. The maker of independence.

Use. For becoming independent of mankind.

89. *Mooatee-o!* ... 129. The giver to whom he wills. *Use.* For preservation from ignominy.

90. *Manay-o!* ...... 161. The protector from misfortunes. *Use.* For preservation from an enemy's power.

91. *Zarr-o!* ...... 1,001. The spoiler of whom he wills. *Use.* For warding off the devil.

92. *Nafay-o!* ...... 201. The bestower of gain. *Use.* For profits in agriculture and trade.

93. *Noor-o!* .... 256. The giver of light. *Use.* For the illumination of one's mind.

94. *Hadee-e!* ...... 20. The director or guide. *Use.* For the accumulation of possessions.

95. *Budee-o!* ...... 86. The creator of new things. *Use.* For the comprehension of things abstruse.

96. *Baqee-o!* ...... 113. The Eternal Exister. *Use.* For the approval of one's actions.

97. *Waris-o!* ...... 707. The He who will remain when creation is no more. *Use.* For tranquillity.

98. *Rusheed-o!* ... 514. The all-wise director. *Use.* For one's important desires to be fulfilled.

99. *Suboor-o!* ...... 298. The most patient or long-suffering towards sinners. *Use.* For the silencing of an enemy.*

---

* The above ninety-nine names, as given by different authors, vary in some trifling degree. Our author has inserted them in this work according to that which he considered the most correct.

Besides the preceding, there are other descriptions of amulets, charms, &c., used for various purposes, a few of which I shall offer as examples; for instance,

If a person void urine involuntarily in his sleep, the following amulet is to be written and suspended to his neck.

مرمسلح ١١١ Mur-Moosullah 111.	٥ مسلح ٥١١١ 5. Moosullah 5111.	١١ س ٣٠ 11. S. 30.
د ه ح ح ح D. h. H. H. H.	١١١ ع ا ند d. n. A. a. 111. Rijal-ool-*gyb*.	يم مر ١١٥ Yem-mur. 115.

By keeping the following talisman near one, demons, fairies, and enchanters will not attack them.

8	1490	1493	1
1492	2	7	1491
3	1495	1488	6
1489	5	4	1494

If one be afflicted with *naf-tulna* (lit. shifting of the navel),* a few of the following talismans are to be written, the writing washed off with water, and the latter drank;

* Or the umbilical vein; (perhaps the aorta or cœliac artery, as it is said to pulsate:) which is supposed by the Indian physicians to be occasionally shifting from its place, and thus to occasion various morbid symptoms.

and one of them is to be tied on with thread over the navel.*

Wulakin *but*	**Amreehee** *his purposes*	**Ala** *over*	**Gálaybo** *is Lord*	**Wo Allah-o** *for God*
Aksur *the generality*	**Wulakin** *but*	**Amreehee** *his purposes*	**Ala** *over*	**Gálaybo** *is Lord*
Unnas *of men*	**Aksur** *the generality*	**Wulakin** *but*	**Amreehee** *his purposes*	**Ala** *over*
La *do not*	**Unnas** *of men*	**Aksur** *the generality*	**Wulakin** *but*	**Amreehee** *his purposes*
Eealumoon *understand*	**La** *do not*	**Unnas** *of men*	**Aksur** *the generality*	**Wulakin** *but*

The following is a cure for the *itch*. Two or three such are to be written; and every now and then, one is to be washed in water, and the fluid drank.

* The charm is to be read from right to left, horizontally, and then downwards, or *vice versâ;* when it will run thus: "for God is Lord "over his purposes; but the generality of men do not understand."—(*Sale's Qoran* 1825, chap. xii. page 60.)

15	35	92	6
بہ	و ر ٢ w. r. 2	و ر w. r.	و د ع w. d. a.
ا ع A a	18	23	5
2	88	23	ا La-a
ه ع 5 a.	39	9	2

The following *ism* is to be repeated over water; and then having blown your breath upon it, the patient is to drink it off, and the *piles* will be cured.

"Departest thou? Depart! depart! Running water, "dry up! Such is the speech of *Juhaneea Sahib*, the "Lord of mortals, who has travelled all round the world. "Quickly, begone!"

This *robaee* magic-square, if written and tied on to the neck, will render an attack of the *small pox* mild; *viz.*

8888	12221	15554	1111
14443	2222	7777	13332
3333	17776	9999	6666
11110	5555	4444	16665

The under-written *dopaee*-magic-square, formed out of the number of the sacred volume, (*i.e.* the *Qoran*), answers for all purposes.

2,911,536,642	7,764,097,710	970,512,213
1,941,024,426	3,882,048,855	5,823,073,284
6,793,585,497		4,852,561,068

When a house is haunted by genii and devils, the following amulet is to be written and put up over the door, and they will vanish.

§§§§§§§ § §§§§§§§

O Mohummud!

§§§§§§§§§§§§§§

§§§§§§§§ O GOD! §§§§§§§§

MEEKAEEL! JIBBREEL!

il Momeneen *the Faithful*	Unnuzur-o-fee *he regards*	Hil Momeneen *to the faithful*	Nusseroon-Min Allah *Succour is from God*
Fa Innuka *verily*	Fa Innuka *verily*	Wo Futtah *victory*	Unnuzur-o-fee *he regards*
Khyr-ool Nasayreen *The best of Helpers*	Qureeb *elect*	Lee Usluh *the best for us*	Fa innuka *verily*
Wul Bushur-o *towards men*	Asbureen *the most patient.*	OonNasayreen *of helpers*	Khyr *The best*

O ALLEE! O ALLEE!

IZRAEEL! ISRAFEEL!

The following diagram is to be written and put up against a wall facing the individual beset with the devil, in order that the patient's sight may daily fall upon it. By so doing the devil will be removed.

JIBBREEL OR ABOO BUKUR.

MEEKAEEL OR OOMUR. (left) — IZRAEEL OR ALLEE. (right)

Innuhoo Verily it is	*min* from	*Soolaymân* Solomon	*Wo Innuhoo* and verily it is	*Bismilla* in the name of	*Hir-ruhman* the Merciful	*Nir-ruheem* the Compassionate,
min from	*Soolaymân* Solomon	*Wo Innuhoo* and verily it is	*Bismilla* in the name of	*Hir-ruhman* the Merciful,	*Nir-ruheem* the Compassionate,	*in* do
Soolaymân Soloman	*Wo Innuhoo* and verily it is	*Bismilla* in the name of	*Hir-ruhman* the Merciful,	*Nir-ruheem* the Compassionate.	*in* do	*la* not
Wo Innuhoo and verily it is	*Bismilla* in the name of	*Hir-ruhman* the Merciful	*Nir-ruheem* the Compassionate,	*in* do	*la* not	*ta-al-oo* rise
Bismilla in the name of	*Hir-ruhman* the Merciful	*Nir-ruheem* the compassionate,	*in* do	*la* not	*ta-al-oo.* rise	*ala* against me
Hir-ruhman the Merciful,	*Nir-ruheem* the Compassionate,	*in* do	*la* not	*ta-al-oo* rise	*ala* against me	*wa atoonee* but come and surrender
Nir-ruheem the Compassionate,	*in* do	*la* not	*ta-al-co* rise	*ala* against me	*wa atoonee* but come and surrender	*Moosleemeen* tc Moosulmans

ISRAFEEL OR OOSMAN.

To consult horoscopes in the name of the sick.

The manner is as follows. Having learnt the name of the patient and that of his mother, the numerical value of them are to be ascertained by means of the *abjud kay hissab* (vide Glossary); the numbers added together and divided by 12. Should 1 remain, the patient's destiny is considered to be in the sign of the zodiac *Hummul*, or the Ram; if 2, *Sowr*, or the Bull; if 3, *Jowza*, or the Twins; if 4, *Surtan*, or the Crab; if 5, *Ussud*, or the Lion; if 6, *Soomboolla*, or the Virgin; if 7, *Meezan*, or the Scales; if 8, *Aqrub*, or the Scorpion; if 9, *Qows*, or the Archer; if 10, *Juddee*, or the He-goat; if 11, *Dullo*, or the Watering-pot; and if 12, *Hoot*, or the Fishes.

When his sign of the zodiac has been thus ascertained by reference to the table at p. 85, we ascertain what his planet is; and by further consulting the dispositions of planets at p. 20, we are informed of what *his* qualities are. But our present object is solely to state the years in which he or she (man or woman) stands in danger of forfeiting their lives; which fatal period if they can survive, they will attain the full period of life, *viz.* one hundred and twenty years. The same has been exhibited collectively in the annexed table, where the particular years in question, of males and females are set down under their respective signs of the zodiac. The cure is to be effected (*i.e.* death warded off) by having recourse to amulets, charms, &c.

SIGNS OF THE ZODIAC.	Hummul or Ram.	Sowr or Bull.	Jowza or Twins.	Surtan or Crab.	Ussud or Lion.	Soomboolla or Virgin.	Meezan or Scales.	Aqrub or Scorpion.	Qows or Archer.	Juddee or He-Goat.	Dullo or Watering-pot.	Hoot or Fishes.
Man.	7 13 20	12 30	4 12 20 30 40 50	7 19 30	8 16 20 40 50	2	18	30 39	2	7 15	30	7
Woman.	1 9 20 50	5 30	2 4 10 15	4 19 30 40	5	16 20 40	17	4 12 3	2	3	1	2 56 30 40

In the name of the sick, to predict future events.

When a person requires the future destiny of a sick person to be foretold, it is necessary to ascertain, first, the time when the individual was taken ill. Having ascertained the day, by consulting the statement given below for every day in the week, his lot is to be foretold. Should the day have been forgotten, the number of the name of the patient and that of his mother are to be added together and divided by 7. Should 1 remain, he must have been taken ill on a Saturday; should 2 remain, on a Sunday; should 3 remain, on a Monday; should 4 remain, on a Tuesday; should 5 remain, on a Wednesday; should 6 remain, on a Thursday; and should 7 (*i. e.* 0) remain, on a Friday.

Having thus determined the day, the event is to be prognosticated as follows:

Saturday is Saturn's day. If one be taken ill on that day, the *cause* may be attributed to grief, or heat of blood, or to a malignant eye. The *symptoms* are, headache, palpitation of the heart, urgent thirst, restlessness, want of sleep, bleeding from the nose or bowels. *Prognosis.* His disease will be of seven days' duration, but will remain at its height one day and three hours, and he will ultimately recover. *Cure.* For such a patient they must give *sudqa*;* and have recourse to such remedies as amulets, charms, &c.

* *Sudqa*, alms or propitiary offerings. That is, rupees, pice, any animal, clothes, grain, eatables, &c. are waved over the patient, or only shewn to him, or solely in his name given away in alms to *fuqeers*: or they are merely placed near the foot of a tree, or near some water-edge, or on the spot where four roads meet, &c. *Moollas* and *seeanas*, however, establish *sudqas* of various kinds. The following is a specimen of one of them. They form an image of *mash*-flower, about a span and a half or two spans long, in the shape of a man, or that of *hunnomán* (the Hindoo-monkey-god). They place a stick about a span long, having rags wound round its two ends, into the

Sunday is the sun's day, on which if any one be taken ill, the case is as follows:—*Cause.* The disease is occasioned by the malignant eye of a green-complexioned woman, in whose presence he has partaken of some rich and savoury dish. *Symptoms.* First, the patient complains of lassitude, succeeded by universal rigours, followed by heat, headache, soreness in all the bones of the body, eyes suffused with blood, countenance yellow, no rest or ease all night. *Prognosis.* The disease will be of fourteen days' duration, when it will cease. *Treatment.* The usual remedies for such symptoms are to be employed.

Monday is the moon's day, on which, if one be taken ill, the *cause* is, catching cold after bathing or over exertion. *Symptoms.* Pain in the loins and calves of the legs, palpitation in the liver, retching, giddiness, great drowsiness. *Prognosis.* The disease will continue forty days, after which the patient will be restored to health. *Treatment.* The exhibition of the usual remedies.

---

the doll's mouth, and light the two ends, as well as the lamps formed of paste on the head and hands of the image; and on its forehead they form *namum* (the mark which *Hindoos* make on their foreheads). Nay, they even pierce its body all over with nails, and thus set it up in a large *koonday* (or *theekray*, a broken piece of an earthen pot). In front of it they place balls formed of boiled rice, coloured black, yellow, and red, eggs also of those colours, and a *kuleeja*, which they pierce or not, with the thorns of the *kara*-tree (*webera tetrandra*, Willd.; the thorny caray), sheep's blood, two or three undressed fishes, and scatter flowers, *bhajee* (greens), &c. all round it. They then light a *jotee* (or large lamp made of flour paste), having four wicks, formed of clothes which had been worn by the patient, in four or five kinds of oil, and place the *jotee* on the blood. When all the lamps are thus lighted, the doll presents so hideous a figure, as to resemble the devil himself. Having waved the *theekray* over the patient, they deposit it in some place or other, as above stated; after which, they wash the patient's face and hands, and tie on to his neck such *taweez* or *gunda*, as may be required.

Tuesday is Mars' day, on which if one be taken ill, the *cause* is, the patient is attacked by demons and fairies. *Symptoms.* Pain in the chest, abdomen, and especially around the navel; shiverings, want of sleep and appetite, great thirst, incoherence of speech, eyes bloody. *Prognosis.* The disease will continue seven days, after which the patient will recover. *Treatment.* The administration of the usual remedies.

Wednesday is Mercury's day, on which if one be taken ill, the *cause* is, the having made a vow for the dead and not fulfilled it; or, being over sorrowful for any thing lost, or labouring under dread of an enemy. *Symptoms.* Pain in the head, neck, wrists, or feet. *Prognosis.* The disease will last nine days; but at its acme, a day and a watch (15 hours): ultimately the patient will recover. *Treatment.* The usual one.

Thursday is Jupiter's day, on which if one be taken ill, the *cause* is being beset with the shadow of a fairy. *Symptoms.* Pain about the neck and umbilicus, startings in sleep, disrelish for food and drink, laying quiet with eyes shut. *Prognosis.* The disease will continue ten days, after which the patient will experience a recovery. *Treatment.* The usual remedies are to be had recourse to.

Friday is Venus' day, on which if one be taken ill, the *cause* is, some corporeal affection. *Symptoms.* Great drowsiness and lassitude. *Prognosis.* The malady will continue twelve days, and the height of the exacerbation two days, after which the patient will recover. *Treatment.* As usual.

CHAPTER XXXIII.

Concerning 1st the ascertaining of unknown things by the viewing of *Unjun*, or lamp-black, *alias* the Magic Mirror. 2d. Viewing of *Hazirat*, or the flame of a charm-wick. 3d. The giving of the *Purree kay Tubuq*, or Fairy-Tray; and the performing of *Nahown*, or the Fairy-Bath.

SECT. 1. *Viewing of Unjun (lamp-black), or the Magic Mirror.*

For the purpose of ascertaining where stolen goods are concealed, or the condition of the sick who are possessed by the devil, or where treasure has been buried, they apply *unjun* to the palms of the hand of a child or an adult, and desire him to stare well at it.

I have generally heard it said, that *Jogees* and *Sunneeasees* are accustomed to practise these arts, and that they have often in this manner made themselves masters of treasure hid in the earth.

Some of the ignorant and foolish among the vulgar say, that treasure concealed, lies scattered about at night like sparks of fire, and sometimes rolls about like a ball of fire at the place where it is deposited; and that it is either by this circumstance, or by the application of *unjuns*, that its situation is ascertained.

The person to the palm of whose hand the *unjun* is applied occasionally mutters a great deal of ridiculous nonsense. For example, that "at such and such a place there is a *lota*, *degcha*, or *kurrahee*, full of *rupees*, *pagodas*, or *gold mohurs* buried." Or if it be to learn something regarding the condition of the sick, that "the malady is a corporeal one, or that it is produced by conjuration, or that the demon of such and such a place wishes for certain eatables." Thus he continues talking and describing all the particulars relative to these things.

Unjuns are of five kinds, *viz.*—1st. *Urth unjun*, used for discovering stolen property. —2d. *Bhoot unjun*, for ascertaining what regards devils, evil spirits, and the condition of the sick.—3d. *Dhunna unjun*, for finding out where treasure is concealed.—4th. *Surwa unjun*, applicable to all purposes.—5th. *Alope unjun*, which, if applied to the eyes or forehead of a person, renders him, wherever he be, invisible to others while they may remain visible to him.

I myself place no faith in such *unjuns* and *hazirats*. Although born in this very country (Hindoostan), bred and educated among this (the Moosulman) race of people, through the blessing of God and the friendship of the great, by the studying of good books and the hearing of good counsel, the credibility of the existence of any such thing has been entirely effaced from my breast. Let no one imagine I assert this to flatter Europeans (may their good fortune ever continue !) God preserve me from any false assertion.

1st and 2d. *Urth* and *B'hoot unjun.*—For both these they take *agara kee jur** and *suffeid goomchee kee jur*,† or merely *suffeid bis-k'hopray kee jur*,‡ triturate it well with water, rub it on the inside of a piece of a new earthen pot, and place it inverted over a lamp lighted with castor-oil and collect the lamp-black. The latter is then mixed with oil and applied to the hand of a footling child, who particularly details every thing regarding it : such as concern-

* Root of the achyranthes aspera, Lin. The rough achyranthes.

† Root of the white abrus precatorius, Lin Jamaica wild-liquorice.

‡ Root of the trianthema decandra, Willd., the trailing trianthema.

ing property stolen, the condition of the sick, whether the patient has only a corporeal affection or is beset with the devil, &c.

3d. *D'hun unjun.*—They take a piece of white cloth, and soak it in the blood of any of the following animals, *viz.*, a cat, *kolsa* (king-Crow), *ghooghoo* (owl), or a *chogod* (a particular large species of owl), and having rolled up their eyes, liver, and gall-bladder in it, use it as a wick in a castor-oil lamp. The lamp-black procured from it being mixed with castor-oil and applied to the hand, the treasure, &c. will become visible.

4th. *Surwa unjun.*—A handful of *bullayr kay dana,** is burnt in a new earthen *lota*, so as to prevent its smoke escaping, is reduced to charcoal, pounded, and well lavigated with castor-oil. This is applied to the palm of the hand of any one, and he is desired to stare well at it. After two or three *g'hurrees* he will say something to this effect: "First, I observed the *Furash*† coming; he swept "the ground and departed. Then came the water-carrier, "sprinkled water on the floor and went away. The *Furash* "re-appeared and spread the carpet. Next came a whole "army of genii, demons, fairies, &c.; to whom succeeded "their commander, who was seated on a throne." Thus he relates the different circumstances as they present themselves to his view. Then, whatever the affair may be for which they have caused the officer's presence, it is stated to him, and he never fails to grant what is required of him.

Surwa unjun is one which any person by applying to the hand may behold; whereas the other kinds of *unjun* require to be viewed by a child, whether boy or girl, born

---

* Seed of the dolichos lablab. Var.

† *Furash.* A man whose business it is to sweep the ground and spread carpets.

foot-foremost (or a footling case), with cats'-(*i. e.* grey) eyes, and a first-born; one that has not been bitten by a dog, or that has no large scar of a burn on him. To such a one the *unjun* and *hazirat* will certainly appear; to others, most probably not.

5th. *Alope unjun.*—For its use, *vide* p. 377.

SECT. 2. *The viewing of Hazirat, or Charm-wick.*

There are certain well-known and established *puleetas* which are solely used for this purpose. When they wish to light one of the *hazirat-puleetas*, they take, at the place appointed for the *hazirat*, a new earthen pot and an earthen cover, wash them well with water, apply a few patches of *sundul* on the pot, tie some wreaths of flowers around its neck, and deposit near it all sorts of fruits and sweetmeats, and burn benjamin-pastiles. Then placing the cover on the pot, they put some odoriferous or sweet-oil into the lid, and having lighted the *puleeta* which constitutes the wick, read some established spell over it in Arabic. The boy or girl having been bathed, decked out in clean clothes, and adorned with flowers, is desired to stare at the flame, and to relate what he observes in it; and, as detailed under the head of *unjun*, he will describe every thing respecting property stolen, diseases, &c.

Some people write the following *taweez:*

			9	
12	0 Allseeing!	3	0 Omnipresent!	
	4	11	5	
		6		10
	13			

and paste it on the back of a looking-glass, and desire the child to look into the glass.

Some write the following magic square

4	9	2
3	5	7
8	1	6

on a porcelain or copper plate, fill it with water, and desire the child to look into it.

Some people, while performing any of the preceding three things, write the undermentioned on the child's forehead, *viz. Fu-kushufna unka gitta-aka, fu-busurokul ee-ow-ma juddeed uhzur-ool-ginnay jaffur bin tyar*; i. e. "We "have removed the veil from off thee, and thy sight is "become new this day. Come, Genius, Jaffier son of "Tyar."

Other *Hazirat*-magic squares are as follows, which are to be written, together with the intention for which they are used, on the *puleeta*.

9	3	7	1
6	2	8	4
3	9	1	7
2	6	4	8

11	14	1	8
4	5	10	15
6	3	16	9
13	12	7	2

The following is a specimen of an Arabic incantation: *Bismilla hir-ruhman nir-ruheem.—Ushteetun, Shuteetun, Kubooshin, Shaleesha, Sheesin, Qoorbutashin, Murmoonin, Mymoonin.**

SECT. 3. *The giving of the Purree kay Tubuq* (or *Fairy Trays*), *and the performing of Nahown*† (or *Fairy Bath*).

It is had recourse to by both men and women under the following circumstances: *viz.* When a person is subject to constant sickness, or has the misfortune not to succeed in obtaining a wife; or, if married, have no progeny for three or four years; or if a girl at the age of thirteen or fourteen, not having been unwell, become pregnant, or being possessed with fairies, devils, enchantments, &c. be, in a few

* After the commencement, which is, "In the name of God, the "merciful and compassionate," it comprises merely the names of genii.

† *Nahown*, (lit. bathing) signifies in its more extended sense, and as usually made use of to express, the bathing a person with water, accompanied by the reading of something, and the observance of certain forms and ceremonies.

days or months, seized with uterine hemorrhage followed by abortion, or if a child be born, and die either immediately or in a few days after birth, or remain puny and weak; or if man and wife do not agree; or a man cannot obtain employment; or, if in service, it prove unprofitable to him. When such misfortune befals any one (male or female), it becomes necessary for him or her to have the ceremony of *Nahown* performed, or to give the fairy *tubuq*, with a view of causing such circumstances to take a favourable turn.

The viewing of *Unjun* and *Hazirat* are used to ascertain things unknown; whereas *Nahown* is employed for removing known evils, such as devils, &c.

Nahown is practised by *Seeanas*, (conjurors), alias *Moollas** and *Purree-walees* (fairy-women).

The method of performing it by the former is as follows:

They take water from seven or nine different places, such as wells, rivers, seas, &c. put it into a new earthen pot, together with a few of the leaves of seven or nine of the following different trees and plants, *viz.* of the pomegranate, guava,† lime, orange, *moogra*,‡ *chumbaylee*,§ *subza*,‖ *maynhdee*,¶ *downa*,** *murwa*,†† *goolcheenee*,‡‡ *gaynd*,§§ read once over it, if intended for the removal of the devil,

---

* Lit. a learned man, a doctor.

† Psidium pyriferum, Lin.

‡ Jasminum undulatum, Lin.; the wavy-leafed jessamine.

§ Vitex trifolia, vel vitex negundo, Lin.; the three leafed or five leafed chaste tree.

‖ Ocimum basilicum, Lin.; the basilic basil.

¶ Lawsonia spinosa, Lin.; the prickly lawsonia, Ivenie, Eastern privet, or Henna.

** Artemisia austriaca, Lin.; Southernwood, Old man, or Lad's love.

†† Origanum marjorana, Lin.; sweet marjoram.

‡‡ Chrysanthemum indicum, Lin.; Christmas flower.

§§ Tagetes erecta, Lin.; Indian or African marigold.

enchantment, &c. the *Soora-e-Eeaseen* (chap. xxxvi.), or the *Mozummil* (chap. lxxiii.); and if for *bukht k'holna* (changing one's bad luck), the *Soora-e-Innafut-huna* (chap. xlviii.) blow upon the water, and set it aside. They then place in front of the patient a human figure (vide note, p. 373), or that of Hunnoman,* in length between a span and a cubit, made of *maash kay ata*;† tie to its neck one end of a cord formed of three kinds of coloured thread, and the other to the patient's waist or neck, before whom they deposit the *kuleeja* of a sheep, cocoa-nuts, two or three kinds of flowers, some *k'heeleean*, *bungreean*, a piece of yellow cloth, a sheep, or a fowl; and taking nine limes, they repeat the *aet-ool-koorsee* over each, and divide them into two, placed on the head, shoulders, loins, back, knees, and feet of the patient, respectively; then bathe him with the above-mentioned pot of water. In bathing, they necessarily dig the place a little, to allow of the water being absorbed into the earth; for should any other person happen to put his foot on the water, the same misfortune would befal him as did the patient: for this reason, they usually perform the ceremony near the water-edge or in a garden.

Nahown is performed on the three first Saturdays, Sundays, Mondays, Tuesdays, or Thursdays in the month. On the last of which they pour three new *lota*-fuls of water on the patient; one on his head, the second on his right shoulder, the third on his left, and dash the *lota* to pieces on the ground in front of him.

Immediately after the bath, they tie to the neck, upper arm, or waist of the patient, the particular magic-square for

---

* One of the Hindoo deities, having the form of a man but the head of a monkey.

† Flour of maash, Phaseolus max, Lin. or black-gram.

casting out the devil, or removing the misfortune which besets him.

The *purree* (fairy) *nahown* is well known among women, and is performed by *purree-walee* (fairy-women),* who are few in number.

The *ak'hara* (fairy assembly)† of each of them usually meets on Thursdays or Fridays; either during the day, or at night. It takes place as follows:

They suspend a *chandnee* (canopy) to the ceiling of the apartment, and spread a beautiful *fursh* (carpet) on the floor. The *purree-walee*-woman puts on a clean suit of some superb dress, red or white, applies *sundul* to her neck, and *maynhdee* to her hands, (which latter is washed off after her hands have become red), adorns herself with flowers, and applies *uttur* to her clothes, *kajul* or *soorma* to her eyes, and *meesee* to her lips and teeth. The necessitous, and those women possessed of demons, &c., and spectators (females), having bathed and dressed themselves in good clothes, assemble at her house; while *domneeans* playing sing fairy-songs. Then the fairy woman causes the *asayb-walee* (or possessed) woman to be seated in front of her on either kind of *tubuq*.

Purree kay tubuq (or fairy-trays), I may observe, are of two kinds: the one called *p'hool ka tubuq* (or the flower-tray), consisting of a square white cloth spread on the ground, on which are arranged in a circle, flowers, *sundul*, *ood*, *abeer*, *pan-sooparee*, and fruits of all kinds; in the centre of which the fairy woman sits: the other, *mayway ka tubuq* (or the fruit-tray), hereafter to be described. p. 387.

---

* *i. e.* Women who have fairies under their control.

† They believe that, on this occasion, all the hosts of fairies are present, though invisible.

After she has sat there awhile the fairies descend upon her. She then becomes distracted, and on hearing the sound and harmony of music, becoming intoxicated with delight, she dishevels her hair, and sitting on her knees or cross-legged,* moves and whirls her head round and round; and taking hold of her own long locks, brushes the patient with it two or three times. The latter then becomes affected with the contagion, and revolves her head in a similar manner. At this juncture, either she or the fairy-woman† appoints the number of *nahowns* or *tubuqs* that the patient requires, the places where, the day of the month when, and whether in the day or evening, morning or midnight, they are to take place; and accordingly the same takes place at the hour so fixed. After which they either sit mute, or lay themselves down for a short time and then get up again. This they continue to do, singing and playing for two or three watches of, or all the night. The moment a fairy besets the fairy-woman, she commences whirling her head round; and when it leaves her, she rests herself a little by laying down.

There are altogether fourteen *purreean kay ak'haray* (fairy assemblies); and the fairy-woman acts according to the particular kind of fairy that has possessed her. For instance, if the shadow of a fairy belonging to Rajah Indra's Ak'hara falls upon her, she ties *g'hoongroos* to her ankles and begins dancing; if that of Gend Badshah, or Seekundur Badshah or others, she puts on a suit of men's clothes, such as a *puggree*, a *jama*, or an *ungurk'ha*, a *doputta*, &c. which were previously deposited on the *tubuq*, and taking a

* Literally, sitting on two or four knees; as *do-zanoo*, is kneeling on two knees and sitting upon the feet behind; *char-zanoo*, or sitting on four knees, signifies, sitting cross-legged.

† Or rather, as they conceive, the fairies inhabiting her body.

kutar (dagger) in her hand, she, as if stroking and twisting her whiskers, pretends to be angry, and with a loud voice addresses the woman after the manner following: "I say, "thou fool of a woman, thou coquette, hast thou forgotten "me and created another?" To which the other replies, in a humiliating tone: "*Meean*," (or, my friend) "I am your "self-same devoted old slave; and have repeatedly made "known my situation to your wife, probably she has forgot-"ten to mention it to you." She then says: "No one has "informed me of it; but, since such is the case as you state, "I forgive you." Then laughing heartily, she pelts the woman with some kind of flower, fruit, or her *oogal*, which the latter with great faith takes up, and either eats or retains by her. Thus they continue whirling round their heads and burning incense; and during the ceremony, those who desire any thing, state their wishes: such as, inquire whether their friends at such or such a place are in good health or not, and when they intend returning; or, whether they are unwell; and if so, whether their disease is that of the shadow of a demon having fallen upon them, or is a corporeal affection. According to the advice of the fairy-woman, the inquirers employ the remedies prescribed, with a firm belief in their efficacy. Some of the females who venerate these fairy-women, at the time of their whirling their heads wave a *moorch'hul* or a handkerchief over them, or cool them by fanning. Sometimes the fairy-women being gratified, give a little of the refuse, &c. to their believers to eat; who, on partaking of it, likewise perchance become intoxicated, and commence swinging their heads for a while and lay themselves down; after a few minutes, they awake and sit up. The object of the fairy-women in moving their heads about, is merely to exhibit before other females, their powers of working miracles, in order to strengthen their faith in them. They never perform it in presence of men.

Sensible and respectable women not only do not sanction such ceremonies being performed, but consider it improper even to witness them.

Sometimes, women who desire something, or those possessed of devils, instead of going to the fairy-woman's *ak'hara*, send for her to their own houses, and give her the flower-tray (*vide* p. 384), when she sits on it and whirls herself, as well as causes the woman beset with the demon to whirl, as before described, and replies to the questions put to her by those who desire to know any thing, and make arrangements regarding the *mayway kay tubuqs* or *nahowns*.

The *mayway ka tubuq* (fruit-tray) is as follows. They place on a *fursh* all kinds of fruits fresh and dried, sixteen dishes of *meetha polaoo*, sixteen small earthen jugs of *goor-shurbut*, seventeen earthen plates of *k'heer*, seventeen earthen pots of milk, *shurbut*, *pooreean*, two large platters of *til* and *rice* soaked in syrup made of *goor* (or coarse sugar), into which they put *k'hopra*, almonds and dates sliced, and poppy-seed, flowers, *sundul*, *pan-sooparee*; a *mushroo*, or *soosee eezar*, or a *luhnga*, and a red *damnee*, a *cholee*, a *nuqday ka jora*, or green *bungreeans*, and a pair of shoes, together with some rupees, and sit up all night singing and playing, the fairy-woman moving her head as before detailed, p. 386.

Early on the morning following, the fairy-woman, after repeating the names of all the fairies,* performs *sijdah*

* By way of specimens of the names of fairies, and to exhibit the foolishness of these women, this teacher of A. B. C. will here insert the names of a few of them; *e.g.* red fairy, green fairy, yellow fairy, earthy fairy, fiery fairy, tiger fairy, hoor (a virgin of Paradise) fairy, emerald fairy, diamond fairy, and so forth.

(prostration), and takes a few of the above fruits, and a little of all the other articles, with all the green *bungreeans*, puts them on a large platter, covers them over with a *koos-soom* (red or saffron-coloured) handkerchief, and takes them to the bank of some river or tank, &c.; and there deposits them as the share of the fairies. After which she distributes, by way of a sacred relic, a little of every thing to all present, and walks off home with the remainder, together with the suit of clothes.

The fairy-woman's *nahown* is as follows. They take seven new earthen pots, fill them with the water of seven or nine wells, put into them a few of the leaves of seven or nine species of trees, and having spread a red (*koossoom*) coloured handkerchief over each, set them aside. They then seat the woman beset with the fairy on a stool, and while four women hold a *koossoom*-coloured handkerchief by way of a canopy over the patient's head, the fairy-woman with her own hands pours the water contained in the pots through the canopy on her; she also divides the limes as before described, p. 383.

That done, she takes her to the brink of some tank, river, &c., and there bathes her. During the performance of this ceremony some one of the fairies descends on the fairy-woman, who, becoming in consequence beset by her, commences swinging in a standing position; and, while women, in rapid succession fill smaller earthen pots with water out of the larger ones and hand to her, she pouring it on the affected individual, calls out to herself, "Catch "hold of the polluted shadow that is upon her, bind it, "and banish it to Mount Qaf*, and imprison it there and "burn it to ashes." At such a critical juncture, should

* Mount Qaf. A fabulous mountain. Vide *Glossary*.

the women be tardy in handing her the water, she stares them in the face, and in a peremptory tone remarks, "O "ye unfortunates,* (or wretches), what evils have come "upon you? I shall entirely annihilate you. Give water "quickly. I shall beat immediately with shoes the pol-"luted wretch that is upon her, and exterminate it" At such language these women become dreadfully terrified, and hand to her the water as fast as they can; when she, having poured water sufficiently, according to her wishes, repeats the names of some of the demons, fairies, &c., blows upon her, and putting a dry suit of clothes on her, waves a black cock or hen, &c. over her, and gives it away as a sacrifice for her welfare. The fairy-woman then takes three different coloured silk or cotton thread, either plain or twisted, and forms *gunda*, that is, she forms twenty-one or twenty-two knots on it. The Moollas or Seeanas in making each knot, read some incantation or other over it, and blow upon it; and when finished, it is fastened to the neck or upper arm of the patient; but these fairy-women are an illiterate class of people; many of them do not so much as know the name of God. Having merely made the knots on the thread, they tie them on, and depart with the money, &c.

During the performance of the various ceremonies above-mentioned, the fairy-woman holds a cane in her hand; either one that is ornamented by having slips of silver-leaf, &c. wound round it, or plain. On the *tubuq*-day she places it before her, and every now and then fumigates it with the smoke of benjamin, occasionally observing to the bystanders that the cane appertains to the fairies.

Of late years, young men have also commenced this prac-

* A term used reproachfully.

tice, pretending that fairies beset them likewise, and whirling their heads as above-mentioned, contrive to make money. Nay, I have heard, that they even, by various stratagems under this assumed practice, defile other men's wives. They are a disreputable set.

CHAPTER XXXIV.

Concerning the art of detecting thieves.

There are a few excellent contrivances for this purpose, by having recourse to which thieves are induced through fear to deliver up stolen property.

When a person's property is stolen he sends for a thief-catcher; and should he suspect any particular individual, he assembles together a few of his neighbours along with that person. Then the thief-catcher having besmeared the floor of an apartment with yellow or red ochre or cow-dung, and sketched thereon a hideous figure of prodigious size, selecting any one from among those employed in the casting out of devils (p. 329), giving it four frightful faces (p. 330, pl. no. 3), he places a handmill in the centre of it, having previously rubbed some assafœtida about the centre betwixt the two stones. The upper stone of the mill is placed obliquely, resting on the pin in the centre of the lower one, or some cloth or flax is wound round the pin, about the distance of a finger or two from the top, and on this the upper stone rests, so that it appears as if suspended in the air and not resting on any thing. He places near the mill a few fruits, &c. burns frankincense, and places thereon a lighted lamp, made by burning oil in a human skull-cap.

He then desires the men and women to go one by one into the room, touch the centre of the mill, and return to him; adding, that should none among them be the thief, they need not hesitate in so doing; observing, "Behold, by the "power of my science the stone is suspended. Whoever is "the thief, his hand will be caught between the stones, and "it will be no easy matter for him to extricate it. Nay, "the chances are, the upper stone will fall and crush his "hand to atoms." While they do this, the thief-catcher sits in a place by himself; and as each individual comes to him, he smells his hand, to ascertain whether it have the odour of assafœtida, and then sends him away to a separate apartment, that they may have no communication with each other. He who is the guilty person, through fear of being detected, will not on any account touch it; consequently his hand will not smell of assafœtida, and he must be set down for the thief. The operator then takes him aside, and tells him privately, "I swear that I will not "expose you, provided you deliver up the article to me, "and your honour will remain wholly unimpeached." In consequence of which, should it be a reputable man, he will immediately confess it and deliver up the stolen goods; if the reverse, he will deny having taken it and not give it up.

A second contrivance is as follows: The thief-catcher having besmeared an apartment as above stated, places therein a couple of human skulls, one filled with milk, the other with *shurbut*, makes an image with flour paste and places a lamp upon its head, and deposits a few species of fruits and flowers in front of it, and thrusts as many small sticks as there are persons present into the body of the doll; then calling the people into the room, he sits moving his lips as if in the act of profound devotion; and asking each his name, hands to him a stick pulled out of the body, saying, "Whoever is the thief, his stick will "undoubtedly grow in length." He then directs them to go out and stand apart from one another, and after a little while to return to him. On their return he measures each one's stick with one of the standard length in his own possession, and finds that the person who is the thief, through fear of its increasing in length, has broken off a piece of his, in which case he may unquestionably be considered the culprit.

But the most effectual way of catching theives is as follows: In the two left hand squares of the subjoined magic-square write the name of the persons present, with those of their fathers; thus:

Such a one,	43	43
the son of such a one.	43	43

each one's on a separate piece of paper; fold them up and enclose them in bolusses made of wheat flour. Put fresh water into a *lota*, and throw all the boluses at once into it. The ticket of the thief will come up and float on the surface of the water.

Or, if the following diagram be sketched on an egg and buried in a grave, the abdomen of the individual who has stolen will swell, and remain so, until the egg is taken out of the earth. In the square is to be written, "May the "belly of him who is the thief, through the influence of this "diagram, swell."

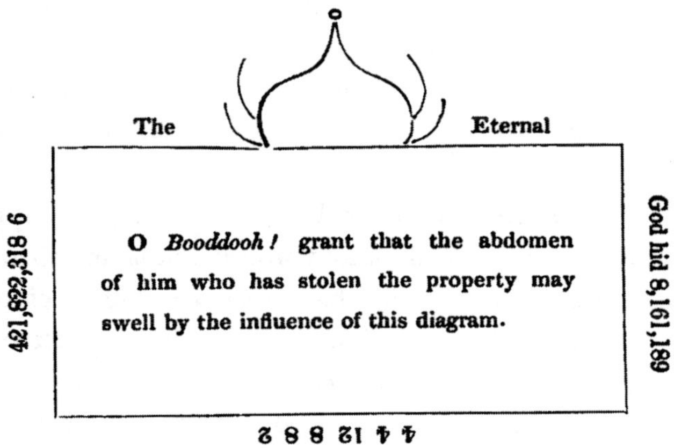

The following verse of the *Qoran*, if written on a green lime and burnt in the fire or buried in the earth, will cause the ruin of the thief. Rather than that he should meet with so great a calamity, he will deliver up the stolen property. The verse translated, signifies, "Afterwards he "causeth him to die, and layeth him in the grave; here-"after, when it shall please him, he shall raise him to "life. Assuredly. He hath not hitherto fully performed "what God hath commanded him. Let man consider his "food, in what manner it is provided. We pour down "water by showers; afterwards we cleave the earth in "clefts, and we cause corn to spring forth therein."—Sale's *Qoran*, Edit. 1825, chap. lxxx. vol. ii. p. 476.

Again, if the same verse, on his delivering up the property, be read over some water, the latter breathed upon and given to the thief to drink, all his affliction and misery will vanish.

Or, two persons are to support a goglet, by the points of their right fore-fingers applied to the projecting ring at the bottom of its neck, on which is to be previously written the names of the persons one by one, and the *Soora-e-Eeaseen* read once over it, from the commencement to the part where it saith, "and he said, that my people knew how merciful "God hath been unto me, for he hath highly honoured "me."—(*Sale's Qoran*, chap. xxxvi. p. 302 to bottom of p. 304. Ed. 1825.)

When the name of the individual who is the thief happens to be on it, it will undoubtedly vibrate from side to side.

A certain method, which I have seen with my own eyes, is this. They apply some of any kind of lamp-black to the bottom of a *kusund ka kutora*;* and having assembled a parcel of boys, direct them to place their hands, one by one, upon it. Whatever boy it may be, on the placing of whose hands the cup begins to move, the thief-catcher keeps his hands upon those of the boy, and says, "May the cup "move towards him who is the thief; or, may it go to the "place where the property is concealed;" and there is no doubt, but it will happen as he wishes.

To try the experiment, this teacher of the alphabet had it performed at his own house, when a girl had taken his sister's *nuth'*, hid it in a *jam* (drinking cup), and covered it with a *khwancha* (a small tray). On his sister's mentioning to him the circumstance of her *nuth'* having been stolen, and requesting him to endeavour to find out the thief, he assembled a few boys, and having applied a little lamp-black to the bottom of a cup, he got them to place their hands on it. On one of them so doing the cup began to move, when he desired it to go in the direction of the thief, and immediately it proceeded to the water-closet, where they found the girl hid. He then desired it to proceed to the spot where the *nuth'* was concealed, and it went straight to the cup in which the *nuth'* was hidden, and there remained

* A bell-metal cup; from *kusund*, bell-metal, and *kutora*, a cup.

stationary. Many will doubtless not credit this; but the author can only say, that he has stated just what he had performed at his own house and been an eye-witness to. People may either believe it or not, as they please.

CHAPTER XXXV.

Concerning travelling.*

They say, that on the day of starting on a journey, the *Rijal-ool-gyb*† should not be in front of the traveller, nor on his right, but either behind or to his left. In the former case the traveller will meet with much distress, have to endure many hardships and privations, and have his property stolen.

Rijal-ool-gyb is also named *Murdan-ool-gyb*. These are a class of people who are mounted on clouds, and remain together each day in a different part of the hemisphere.

Some astrologers say, that there is a planet named *Skookoor-e-Yildooz*, which is a very bad one, and that if a traveller has him either in front or to the right of him, he will suffer distress, as above stated.

The *Rijal-ool-gyb* takes up his abode in different places on different days of the month; to ascertain which, tables, couplets, and hemistiches are made use of. From among these I have selected and described below three tables, a couplet, and a hemistich, that it may the more readily be comprehended. The first table is the one in most general use.

---

* Note. *Vide* page 275.

† *Rijal-ool-gyb*, is an invisible being which moves in a circular orbit round the world. On different days his station is in different places. His influence on each day is especially exerted during nine *ghurrees* (or three hours and thirty-six minutes), at the close of that *tith*, or lunar day; and, in that interval, it is unfortunate to begin a journey.—*Shak. Hindust. Dict.*

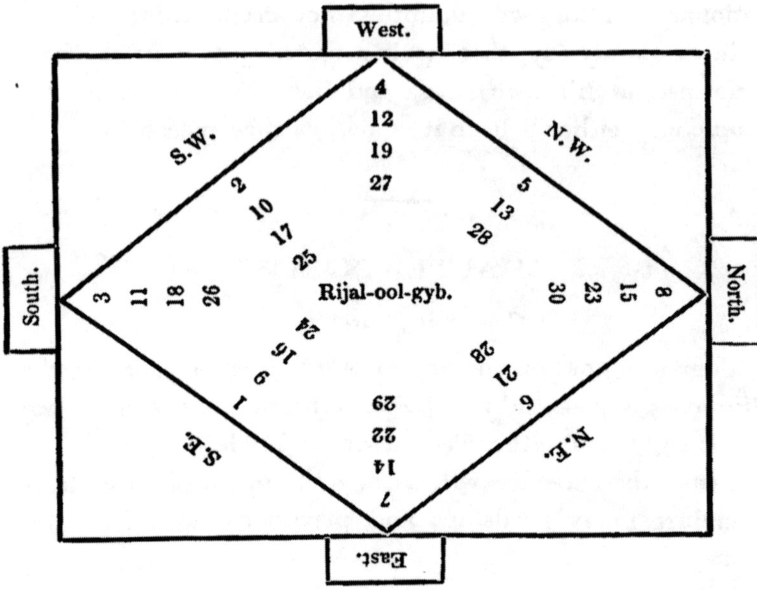

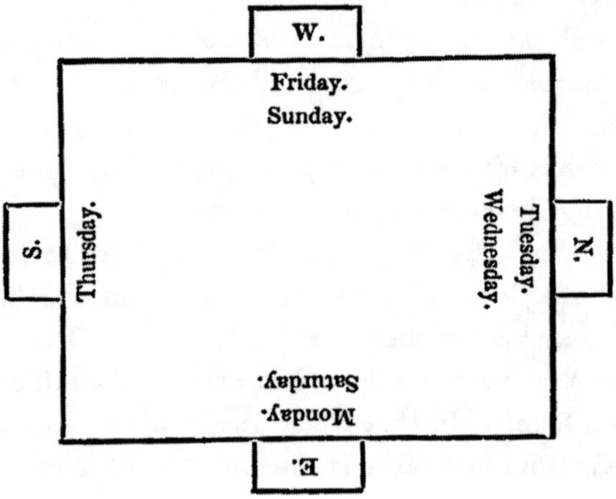

There is also a couplet made use of to retain the above in one's recollection, *viz.*

East, on Saturday and Monday; on Friday and Sunday, West;
On Tuesday and Wednesday, North; on Thursday, South addrest.

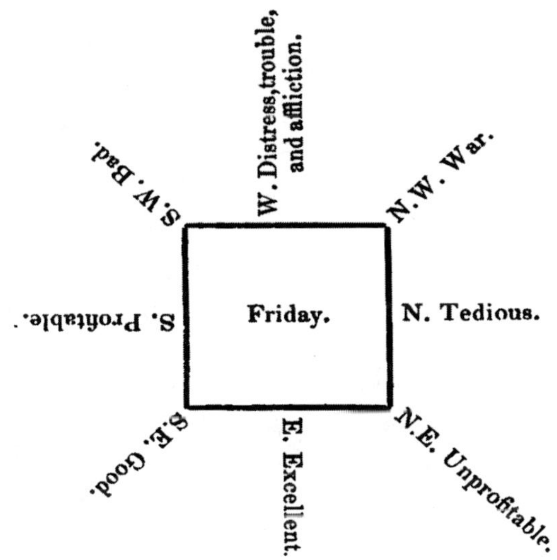
W. Distress, trouble, and affliction.
N.W. War.
N. Tedious.
N.E. Unprofitable.
E. Excellent.
S.E. Good.
S. Profitable.
S.W. Bad.
Friday.

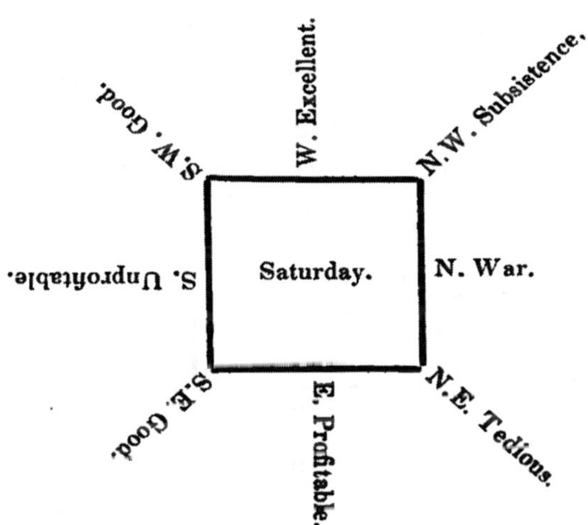
W. Excellent.
N.W. Subsistence.
N. War.
N.E. Tedious.
E. Profitable.
S.E. Good.
S. Unprofitable.
S.W. Good.
Saturday.

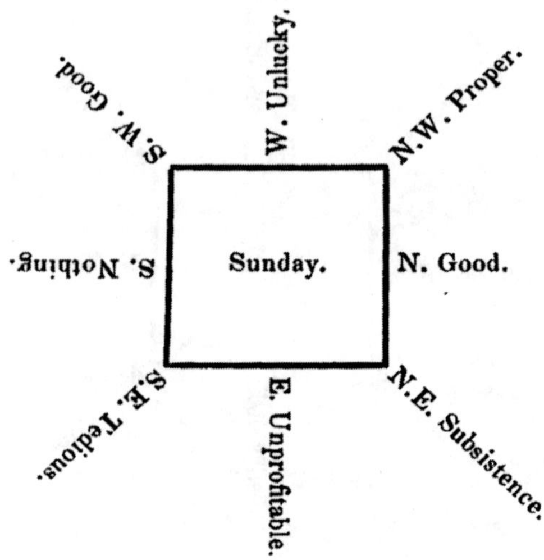
W. Unlucky.
N.W. Proper.
S.W. Good.
Sunday.
N. Good.
S. Nothing.
N.E. Subsistence.
E. Unprofitable.
S.E. Tedious.

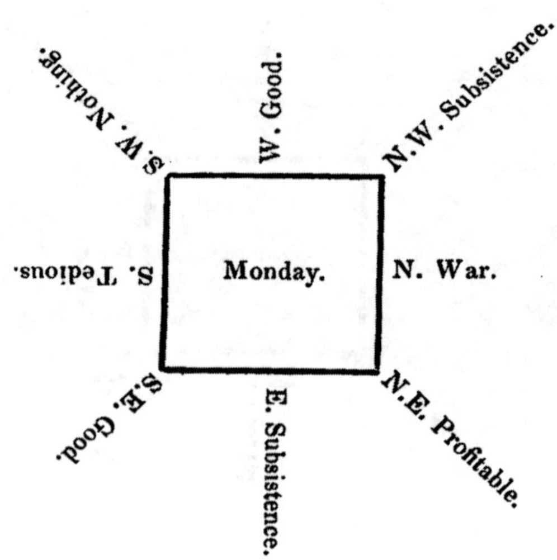
W. Good.
N.W. Subsistence.
S.W. Nothing.
Monday.
N. War.
S. Tedious.
N.E. Profitable.
E. Subsistence.
S.E. Good.

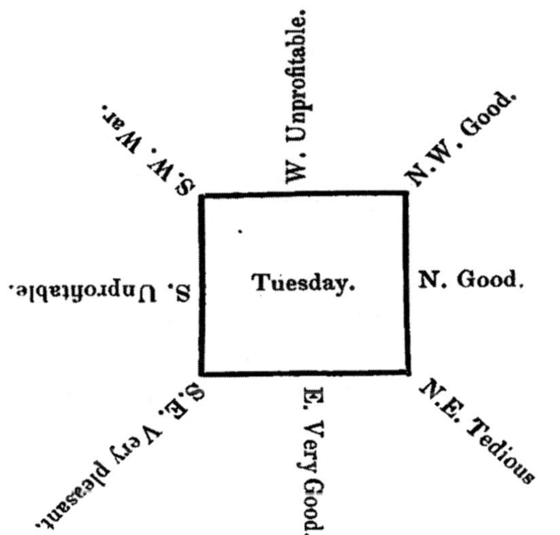
Tuesday.
W. Unprofitable.
N.W. Good.
N. Good.
N.E. Tedious
E. Very Good.
S.E. Very pleasant.
S. Unprofitable.
S.W. War.

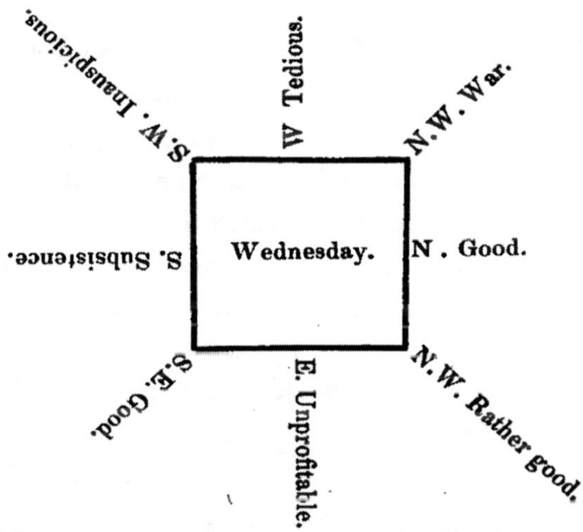
Wednesday.
W Tedious.
N.W. War.
N . Good.
N.W. Rather good.
E. Unprofitable.
S.E. Good.
S. Subsistence.
S.W. Inauspicious.

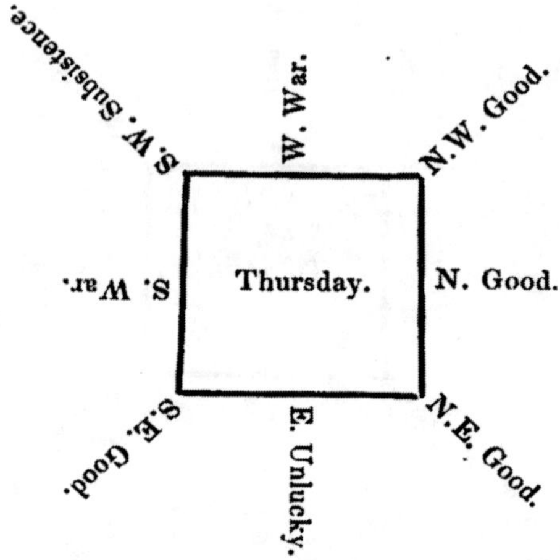

To ascertain the station of the *Rijal-ool-gyb*, some have recourse to a *misra* (hemistich). The letters which compose it, stand for the different quarters of the globe. They are, K N J G B A M sh, K N J G B M sh, repeated twice, so as to form words which are pronounced

Kunujgin bamshin, kunujgin bimush,
Kunujgin bamshin, kunujgin bimush.

The 1st letter K stands for .... S.E.
2d ...... N .... S.W.
3d ...... J .... South.
4th ...... G .... West.
5th ...... B .... N.W.
6th ...... A .... N.E.
7th ...... M .... East.
8th ...... sh .... North.
9th ...... K .... S.E.
10th ...... N .... S.W.

The 11th letter	J	stands for	South.
12th	G		West.
13th	B		N.W.
14th	M		N.E.
15th	sh		East.
16th	K		North.
17th	N		S.E.
18th	J		S.W.
19th	G		South.
20th	B		West.
21st	A		N.W.
22d	M		N.E.
23d	sh		East.
24th	K		North.
25th	N		S.E.
26th	J		S.W.
27th	G		South.
28th	B		West.
29th	M		N.W.
30th	sh		N.E.

If a person wish to proceed on a journey on a Saturday, he is to eat fish previous to starting; for his wishes in that case will soon be accomplished. If on a Sunday, should he eat betel-leaf before his departure, all his undertakings will prosper. If on a Monday, should he look into a mirror, he will speedily obtain wealth. If on a Tuesday, should he eat coriander seed, every thing will happen agreeably to his wishes. If on a Wednesday, should he eat *duhee* (curdled milk), he will return home in good health and with a large fortune. If on a Thursday, should he eat *goor* (*jaggree*, or raw sugar), he will return with plenty of goods and chattels. If on a Friday, should he eat dressed meat, he will return with abundance of pearls and precious stones.

CHAPTER XXXVI.

The hour and day of the month most propitious for the undertaking of any particular business.

In every month there are seven evil days, on which no good work is on any consideration to be commenced.

In every Month there are Seven Evil Days, on which no good work is to be undertaken.

3d	5th	13th
16th	21st	24th
	25th	

Others say that in every month in the year there are two evil days. Vide the annexed table.

Mohurrum.	Sufur.	Rubee-ool-awul.	Rubee-ool-Akhir.	Jummadee-ool-Awul.	Jummadee-ool-Akhir.	Rujub.	Shâbân.	Rumzân.	Shuwâl.	Zeeqyda.	Zeehujja.
4	1	10	1	10	10	11	4	3	8	2	6
10	8	20	11	11	4	13	6	20	20	3	25

Some, dispensing with the above tables, count the days of the month on their fingers, beginning with the little finger, considering it as 1, the ring finger 2, the middle 3, the fore-finger 4, the thumb 5; the little, again, as 6, and so forth. The dates that happen to fall on the middle finger are considered evil. There are altogether six which fall on it, *viz.*

3d	8th	13th
18th	23d	28th

Of the days of the week, Monday, Wednesday, Thursday, and Friday, are esteemed good and auspicious; the others evil.

As to the qualities of the hours of the day and night, they have already been detailed in a table contained in the chapter treating of the birth and naming of children. (p. 18. and 20.)

CHAPTER XXXVII.

Concerning the measuring for, and wearing of new clothes; the keeping of the beard, mustachios, hair of the head, &c.; the custom of bathing and shaving; and of eating and drinking, &c.

If a person have his measure taken for new clothes on a Sunday, he will be sorrowful and crying. If on a Monday, he will have ample food and provisions. If on a Tuesday, his clothes will be burnt. If on a Wednesday, he will enjoy happiness and tranquillity. If on a Thursday, it will be good and propitious. If on a Friday, it will be well. If on a Saturday, he will experience numerous troubles and misfortunes.

If one put on a suit of new clothes on a Sunday, he will experience happiness and ease. If on a Monday, his clothes will tear. If on a Tuesday, even if he stand in water his clothes will catch fire. If on a Wednesday, he will readily obtain a new suit. If on a Thursday, his dress will appear neat and elegant. If on a Friday, as long as the suit remains new he will remain happy and delighted. If on a Saturday, he will be taken ill.

If a person put on a suit of new clothes in the morning, he will become wealthy and fortunate. If at noon, it will appear elegant. If at about sunset, he will become wretched. If in the evening, he will continue ill.

The *eezar* should not extend in length below the ankle-joint. The *jama* should reach down to a little above the bottom of the *eezar*. The *pugree* should be tied, and the two *shumlas*, (or ends), left waving behind. Some, however, have the latter dangling on the right or left side. The beard should be preserved at least to the extent of a fist in length. The mustachios should either be cropped or shaved off clean.

In the *huddees* it is stated that, should a person not preserve his beard, he will rise at the day of judgment with a black face like that of a hog; and if a person keep mustachios of such length that in the act of drinking he wet them, the water of the *howz-e-kowsur** will be denied him, and the hairs of them will on the last day become like so many spits; so that, if he attempt to make *sijdah*, they

* *Howz-e-Kowsur*, a fountain in Paradise.

will prevent him; and should he, notwithstanding, bend his head, his forehead will not reach the ground. It is advisable, therefore, to prune the hair over the lips. To remove the hair in the armpits and under the navel, to circumcise, and to pare the nails, are five things enjoined by Ibraheem (may God reward him!), but which our Prophet has not insisted upon. To preserve the hair over the whole body is *soonnut;* but to do so on a quarter or half the head is improper.

Of Gosool, *or Bathing;* i. e. *simply Washing; not including the four* Gosools *(Baths or Purifications,* p. 53.) *which are of divine command.*

If a person bathe on a Sunday, he will experience affliction. If on a Monday, his property will increase. If on a Tuesday, he will labour under anxiety of mind. If on a Wednesday, he will increase in beauty. If on a Thursday, his property will increase. If on a Friday, all his sins will be forgiven him. If on a Saturday, all his ailments will be removed.

For *Shaving,* four days of the week are preferable to the rest, *viz.* Mondays, Wednesdays, Thursdays, and Fridays; the other three are evil and inauspicious.

The *flesh* of certain animals is lawful, whilst that of others unlawful for *food.*

In the *Kunz-ool-duqaeq* and *Shurra way-qaeea* it is written, that among Quadrupeds: 1. The flesh of those that are cloven-footed, that chew the cud and are not beasts of prey, is lawful food; such as the flesh of the sheep, goat, deer, antelope, hare, rabbit, cow, bull, female or male buffalo, &c. 2. Those which are neither cloven-footed nor chew the cud are unlawful; for example, the jackass, &c. 3. Others, which though cloven-footed do not chew the cud, having canine teeth (or tusks), or those which merely have canine teeth, are unlawful; for instance, the hog, wolf, jackal, tiger, bear, hyæna, and the like.

Although Eemam-Azum (lit. the great *Eemam* or priest), named Aboo Huneefa* of Coofee, has pronounced the flesh of the horse unlawful, his disciples have decided it to be the reverse; therefore some, conceiving it *mukroo*,† partake of it; while the generality of people esteeming it unlawful, do not eat it.

Of Birds, all those that seize their prey with the claws, or wound them with their bills, are unlawful: *e.g.* the *shikra* (hawk); *bhyree* (a species of hawk); *baz* (falcon); the kite, crow, vulture, bat, king-crow, owl, &c. Such as do not seize their prey with the claws, but pick up their food with the bill, are lawful; such as, the *bugla* (paddy-bird), duck, peacock, partridge, quail, goose, snipe, dove, pigeon, &c. Locusts are proper for eating.

With respect to creeping things, all are unlawful; as scorpions, snakes, earth-worms, &c.

Of those that live in water, all are unlawful, with the following exceptions; *viz.* fish that have scales, and a few without scales (such as *bam*, *tumboo, kutt'hurna*, &c. which are *mukroo*), and which do not weigh less than a *dirrum*, nor more than a *mun* ‡ and a-half. The rest (not answering these conditions) are unlawful; such as alligators, turtles, frogs, crabs, &c. Shrimps however are only *mukroo*, and may be eaten.

Fish found dead in the water is unlawful; but, if it be

---

* The founder of the principal of the four sects of Moosulmans called the *Hunefites*. Vide page 244.

† *Mukroo*, lit. abominable; but it refers here to anything which the Prophet abstained from himself, yet did not interdict to others.

‡ The *mun* or *maund* here alluded to is equal to forty seers or eighty pounds.

taken out alive and die afterwards, the act of taking it out is equivalent to its *zoobuh*. (Vide Gloss.)

DRINK. To drink *shurab* (wine), *ganja*, *bhung*, *taree*, *afeem* (opium), *mudud*, *churs*, *boza* (or fermented liquors), *majoon*,* and many other such intoxicating liquors, is unlawful.

If hog's-lard, however, or any other of the prohibited articles be used as medicine in diseases, and prescribed by a physician, when in his opinion the patient cannot survive without them, it is then lawful to have recourse to them; but not otherwise.

Water should not be drank in a standing position, except in three cases: *viz.* the water of *zum-zum* (p. 61.), *sibbel*-† water (p. 223.), and the water used for *wuzoo*. (p. 74.)

CHAPTER XXXVIII.

Concerning the affording consolation to the sick on his death-bed, and the shrouding and burial of the dead.

Four or five days previous to a sick man's approaching his dissolution, he makes out a *wuseeqa* (*i.e.* a bond or written agreement), or a *wuseeut-nāma* (or will), in favour of his son or any other person, in presence of two or more witnesses, and either delivers it to others or retains it by him. In it he likewise appoints his executor.‡

When about to expire, any learned reader of the *Qoran*

---

* *Vide* Glossary for the particulars of these.

† Water offered at any time, gratis (p. 223) to any person, dispensed "in the name of God."

‡ Moosulmans only require one executor.

is to be sent for, and requested to repeat with a loud voice the *Soora-e-yaseen*, in order that the spirit of the man, by the hearing of its sound, may experience an easy concentration.* It is said, that when the spirit was commanded to enter the body of his holiness Adam (the peace of God be with him!), the soul having looked into it once, observed, "this is a bad and dark place and unworthy of me; it is "impossible I can inhabit it." Then the just and most holy God illuminated the body of Adam with "lamps of "light," and commanded the spirit to re-enter. It went in a second time, beheld the light, and saw the whole dwelling; and said: "There is no pleasing sound here for me to listen "to." It is generally understood from the best works of the mystics of the East, that it was owing to this circumstance that the Almighty created music. The holy spirit on hearing the sound of this music became so delighted, that it entered Adam's body. Commentators on the *Qoran*, expositors of the *Huddees*, and divines have written, that that sound resembled that produced by the repeating of the *Soora-e-yaseen*; it is therefore advisable to read at the hour of death the *Soora-e-yaseen*, for the purpose of tranquillizing the soul.

The *Kulma-e-tyeeb*, as well as the *Kulma-e-shuhadut*, are also read with an audible voice by those present. They do not require the patient to read them himself, as at such a time he is in a distressing situation, and not in a fit state of mind to repeat the *kulma*. Most people lie insensible and cannot even speak, but the pious retain their mental faculties and converse till the very last.

The following is a most serious religious rule (lit. deci-

---

* Or death; for they conceive that the living principles of the whole system become concentrated and shut up in the head; when death is the consequence.

sion), amongst us; *viz.* that if a person desire the patient to repeat the *kulma*, and the sick man expire without being able to do so, his faith is considered dubious; whilst the man who directed him so to do, thereby incurs guilt. It is therefore best, that the sitters-by read it, in anticipation of the hope that the sick man, by hearing the sound of it, may bring it to his recollection, and repeat it either aloud or in his own mind.

In general, when a person is on the point of death, they pour *shurbut* made of sugar, &c. down his throat, to facilitate the exit of the vital spark; and some among the great substitute, though rarely, the water of the *zumzum* (vide note p. 61).

The moment the spirit has fled the mouth is closed; because, if left open, it would present a disagreeable spectacle. The two great toes are brought in contact and fastened together with a thin slip of cloth, to prevent the legs remaining apart. They burn *ood* or *ood-buttee* near the corpse. Should the individual have died in the evening, the shrouding and burial takes place before midnight: if he die at a later hour, or should the articles required not be procurable at that late hour, he is buried early on the following morning. The sooner the sepulchral rites are performed the better; for it is not proper to keep a corpse long in the house, and for this reason, that if he was a good man, the sooner he is buried the more quickly will he reach heaven; if a bad man, he should be speedily buried, in order that his unhappy lot may not fall upon others in the house; as also that the relatives of the deceased may not, by beholding the corpse, weep too much or go without food.

There are male and female *gussalan* or *moorda-sho*,*

* Lit. Bathers, or corpse-washers.

whose province it is to wash and shroud the corpse for payment. Sometimes, however, the relatives do it themselves.

In undertaking the operation of washing, they dig a hole in the earth to receive the water used in the process, and prevent its spreading over a large surface, as some men and women consider it bad to tread on such water. Then they place the corpse on a bed, country-cot, plank, or straw. Some women, who are particular in these matters, are afraid even to venture near the place where the body has been washed. Having stripped the corpse and laid it on its back, with its head to the East and feet to the West,* they cover it with a cloth reaching, if it be a man, from the navel to the calves of the legs; if a woman, extending from the chest to the feet; and wash it with warm or with cold water. They raise the body gently and rub the abdomen four or five times, then pour plenty of water and wash off all the dirt and filth with soap, *seekaykaee*, or *reet'ha*, by means of flocks of cotton or cloth; after which, laying the body on the sides, they wash them; then the back, and the rest of the body; but *gently*, because life having but just departed, the body is still warm and not insensible to pain. After this they wash and clean it well, so that no offensive smell may remain. They never throw water into the nostrils or mouth, but clean them with wet wicks of cloth or cotton. After that they perform *wuzoo* (p. 72.) for him; *i. e.* they wash his mouth, the two upper extremities up to the elbows, make *musah* (p. 73.) on his head and throw water on his feet; these latter constituting the four parts of the *wuzoo* ceremony ordered by God. They then put some camphor and *bayr-kay pât*,† with water into a new large earthen

* Towards the *Kaaba*.

† Leaves of the *bayr*, or Indian plum tree. (Zizyphus jujuba, *Lin.*)

pot, and with a new earthen *budhnee* they take out water and pour it three times, first from the head to the feet, then from the right shoulder to the feet, lastly from the left shoulder to the feet. Every time that a *budhna* of water is poured, the *kulma-e-shuhadut* is repeated, either by the person washing or by another. The *Kulma-e-shuhadut* is as follows; *Ush-hud-do-unna la il-laha illaylaha wuhduhoo la shureequ-luhoo wo ush-huddo-unna Mohummudun abduhoo wo russoolluhoo:* that is, "I bear witness that there is no God save God, who is the One and has no co-equal; and I bear witness that Mohummud is his servant, and is sent from him."

These ceremonies conjoined are called *gosool* or bathing.* Having bathed the body and wiped it dry with a new piece of cloth, they put on the shroud. The *kuffun*, or shroud, consists of three pieces of cloth if for a man, and five if for a woman. Those for men comprise 1st. a *loong* or *eezar*,†

* It is thus described by Mrs. M. H. Ali, vol. i. p. 130. "The dead body of a Mussulman, in about six hours after life is extinct, is placed in a coffin and conveyed to the place of burial, with parade suited to the rank he held in life. A tent or *kaanaut* (screen) is pitched in a convenient place where water is available near the tomb, for the purpose of washing and preparing the dead body for interment. They take the body out of the coffin and thoroughly bathe it. When dry, they rub pounded camphor on the hands, feet, knees, and forehead, these parts having, in the method of prostrating at prayer, daily touched the ground. The body is then wrapped neatly in a winding-sheet of neat calico, on which has been written particular chapters of the *Khoraun*. The religious man generally prepares his own winding-sheet, keeping it always ready, and occasionally taking out the monitor to add another verse or chapter, as the train of thought may have urged at the time."

† A piece of cloth extending from the navel to the ankles, and which is torn in the middle up to the extent of two-thirds. The two divisions cover the legs and are tucked under them on each side; the upper part left entire, covers the forepart of the pelvis. The sides are tucked under on each side, and the corners tied behind.

reaching from the navel down to the knees or ankle-joints. 2d. Called a *qumees*, *koorta*, *alfa*, or *pyruhun*;* its length is from the neck to the knees or ankles. 3d. A *luffafa*, or sheet, from above the head to below the feet. Women have two additional pieces of cloth; one a *seena-bund* (lit. breast-band), extending from the arm-pits to above the ankle-joints; the other a *damnee*, which encircles the head once and has its two ends dangling on each side.

The manner of shrouding is as follows: Having placed the shrouds on a new mat and fumigated them with the smoke of *benjamin*, and applied to them *abeer*, *uttur*, or *gool-ab* (rose-water), the *luffafa* is spread first on the mat, over it the *loong* or *eezar*, and above that the *qumees*; and on the latter the *seena-bund*. If it be a woman, the *damnee* is kept separate and tied on afterwards. The corpse must be carefully brought by itself from the place where it was bathed, and laid on the shrouds. *Soorma* is to be applied to the eyes with a tent made of paper rolled up, with a *ch'hulla* (ring), or with a *pice*, and camphor, to seven places; *viz.* on the forehead including the nose, on the palms of the hands, on the knees and great toes; after which the different shrouds are to be properly put on one after another as they lay. The colour of the shroud is to be white; no other is admissible. It is of no consequence, however, if a coloured cloth is spread over the bier or *sun-dooq*† (*i. e.* coffin; lit. trunk), for that, after the funeral, or after the fortieth *fateeha*, is given away to the *fuqeer*

* It consists of a piece of cloth with a slit made in the middle, through which the head is passed, and drawn down before and behind.

† It is a square box, of the length of the corpse and a yard in breadth. This is not buried with the corpse. The latter is taken out and buried, and the box brought home.

who resides in the burying-ground, or to any other person, in charity.

Previous to shrouding the body, they tear shreds from the cloths for the purpose of tying them on; and after shrouding the body, they tie one band above the head, a second below the feet, and a third about the chest; leaving about six or seven fingers' breadth of cloth above the head and below the feet, to admit of the ends being fastened. Should the relict of the deceased be present, they undo the cloth of the head and shew her his face, and get her, in presence of two witnesses, to remit the dowry which he had settled upon her; but it is preferable that she remit it while he is still alive. Should the wife, owing to journeying, be at a distance from him, she is to remit it on receiving the intelligence of his demise. Should his mother be present, she likewise says, "the milk with which I suckled "thee I freely bestow on thee:"* but this is merely a custom in this country; it is neither enjoined in books nor by the *Shurra.* Then they place on the corpse a *p'hool-kay chuddur* (flower-sheet), or merely wreaths of flowers and some *abeer*, and offer *fateeha;* after which they read the *Soora-e-fateeha* once, and the *Qool-hoo-Allah* three times, with the view of bestowing on the corpse the rewards attached to them. That done, they take up the body along with the mat, and place it on a bed or country-cot, and covering it with split bamboos, form it somewhat into the shape of a *dola* (bier); and if they can afford it, put it into a box. Four from among the near relations, every now and then relieved by an equal number, carry it on their shoulders, some touching it with the hands, and all

* A person who has sucked a woman's milk is considered to be under great obligations to her, as without it he could not have lived; which debt she now remits.

repeating the *Kulma ty-eeb*, *i. e. La illahah illay lah Mohummudoor russool oollah*; or the *Kulma shuhadut* (p. 411), or the *Durood, Mowlood.* They proceed to the *musjid* (mosque) burying-ground, or an open plain, where the owner of the corpse, or if he be not present or is unlearned, any other person, at the request of the relatives, reads the funeral service. The *qazee* (priest) or his *naeb* (deputy) are people appointed to read the funeral service for such of the poor as are friendless. The form of the service is as follows: First, any person calls out, as they do in summoning to daily prayers, three times *Ussulat-e-junaza*, *i. e.* Here begins the prayers of the funeral service. On hearing the sound of this, many within hearing repair to the spot. Then they all stand up in three rows, and the *eemam* in front of them, opposite the head if the body be that of a male, and in a line with the abdomen if of a female. The funeral service contains four *tukbeers* (creeds), and the *doa* (blessing); all which, owing to their prolixity, are here omitted. I shall merely describe the forms observed in the reading of them. The first *tukbeer*. The *eemam* having made the *neeut* (p. 78) for the funeral service, applies his thumbs to the lobes of his ears (p. 78), and calls out *Allah-ho-akbur!* then places the right hand over the left a little below the navel (as in the act of "standing at ease"), and the congregation do the same. Then, again, the *eemam* having read the *doa*, which is always read without removing his hands, reads the second *tukbeer*, and in like manner the third and fourth; after which he calls out again the words *Allah-ho-akbur*, the last time adding *Ussulam-o-allykoom-wo ruhmut oollahay;* and turning his face over the right shoulder, sufficiently round for the congregation to see his face or mouth, and then over the left shoulder in the same manner, repeats the same words and concludes. The congregation repeat the *tukbeer* and *sulam* along with the *eemam*. After that the owner of the corpse calls out *Rookhsut-e-am*, "permission to all" (*i. e.* to depart); meaning, those who are inclined to remain to see the body put under ground may do so, the others may go away. Again, having offered *fateeha* in the name of the deceased, they take the bier near the grave, and one or two persons, relatives or others, descend into the grave to lay the body down; while two others take the sheet that covered the body, twist it round, and lifting up the body put it under the waist; then standing one on each side of the grave hold on by the two ends, and by the assistance of two or three at the head, with as many at the feet, hand the body to the men who had descended into the grave. They then lay the body on its back, with the head to the north and feet to the south, turning its face towards the *Qibla* (or Mecca, *i. e.* west); and after reading some sentence in Arabic, each person takes up a little earth or a clod, and having repeated over it, either in his own mind or in a whisper, the whole of the *soora* entitled *Qool-hoo-Allah* (*Qoran*, chap. cxii), or this *aet* (verse) *Minha khu-luknakoom wufeeha noo-eedokoom o minha nookhray-jokoom tarutun ohkhra*; *i. e.* "We created you of earth and "we return you to earth, and we shall raise you out of the "earth on the day of resurrection," puts the earth gently into the grave, or hands it to one of the persons who had descended into it to deposit it round the body. After that, having previously to burial had a small brick or mud wall built on each side within the grave, about a cubit and a half high, leaving room sufficient for laying the body, they place planks, or slabs of stone or wood, or large earthern pots resting on the wall within the grave, cover them with earth, and smooth the surface over with water, forming it into the shape of a tomb. Some, after the body has been deposited in the grave, place wood obliquely over it, one end resting on the east edge of the grave, the other at the bottom of the west side; on them they put mats, &c. to prevent the earth from falling on the body, and putting earth over it form it into a tomb. Some, to prevent the pressure of the earth upon the corpse, form what they call a *bug-lee* (or hollow, lit. arm-pit) grave, which consists in a sort of a cave or hollow of the length of the body, made on the east side on a level with the bottom of the grave, into which they deposit the remains, and placing mats or wood at the mouth of it, fill the grave up with earth.

Some among the opulent, during their lives, select a suitable spot somewhere or other, and have a grave dug lined with brick and mortar; others have a *moqbirra* (mausoleum) built over it, or merely a square wall all round it, and fill the grave up with sand or some kind of grain, generally wheat or paddy. In the latter case, they annually distribute the old grain in charity and supply its place with new. When the owner dies they bury him in it, and form a *taweez* with square stones over it. Poor people, who cannot afford the above materials, throw the earth on the body and smooth it over with clay. The object of placing wood, &c. over the corpse, is to prevent the pressure of the earth upon it; and great men have established this custom, to prevent the friends of the deceased from fancying, which they are apt to do, that the pressure of the earth was uncomfortable to the body.

In Hindoostan they make the tombs of earth, broad at one end and narrow at the other, in the shape of a cow's tail or the back of a fish; and pour water on it with a *budhna* in three longitudinal lines, so that it leaves an impression something in this form:

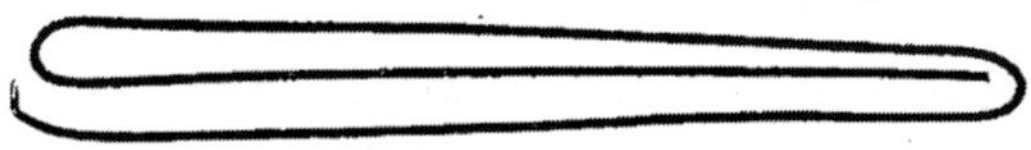

In pouring the water they begin at the feet and terminate at the head, where they place the vessel inverted, and stick a twig of the *subza*, or pomegranate-tree, near it into the earth. In Arabia and other countries it is not customary to pour water on the grave; but if it blow a hurricane, or should there be much wind, they sprinkle some water on it to prevent the dust from blowing about.

After the burial they offer *fateeha* in the name of the defunct. Then, as they return home, when about forty paces from the grave, they offer *fateeha* in the name of all the dead in the burying-ground conjointly, which is called *daeeray kee fateeha* (or the cemetery *fateeha*). At this juncture, it is said, two angels, *viz.* Moonkir and Nukeer, examine the dead. Making him sit up, they inquire of him who his God and prophet are, and what his religion is. If he has been a good man, he replies to these queries; if a bad one, he becomes bewildered and sits mute, or mumbles out something or other. In the latter case, the angels severely torment him, and harass him by means of the *goorz*. (p. 291.)

After that, every one according to his means, distributes wheat, rice, *mussoor*,* salt, *roteean*, *pice*, or *cowries*, in charity to beggars and *fuqeers* (religious mendicants), in the name of the dead.

The people that have remained, accompany the friends of the deceased home, where they offer *neeut kheyr kee fateeha* in the name, and for the welfare of the family, and console the master of the house, recommending to him patience and comfort, and then take their departure. Or, they are offered

* A kind of pulse, Ervum lens, *Lin.*

some liquid food, such as *duhee, ch'haach,* or any other food or drink in common use in the country, before they go home. Or some of the relations, &c. send them the above-mentioned eatables from their houses, or bring them themselves for those persons to partake of.

The rule for digging a grave is, that if it be for a woman, the depth should be to the height of a man's chest; if for a man, to the height of the waist. In general, the grave-diggers dig the grave without measuring the length of the corpse, allowing four or four cubits and a-half for its length and one cubit and a-half for its breadth. If it be intended for a particularly tall person, or for children, they then measure the body. If they afterwards, when laying the body into it, discover that the grave is a little too short in length or breadth, the illiterate consider the deceased to have been a great sinner, and esteem the circumstance very unlucky. They give the grave-digger from eight annas to five rupees, according to their means; and the wealthy, by way of a present, a great deal more. It is customary for the grave-digger, without receiving any additional remuneration, to plaster and smooth the surface of the mound properly over the grave, which he does the day previous to the third-day-*zeearut*. The burying-ground-man,* (with the exception of those corpses that have no owner), never allows a grave to be dug without taking money, *viz.* from one rupee to a hundred and more, from and according to the means, of the parties: nay, he obtains his livelihood by this means. The cloth which was spread on the bier becomes his perquisite, This, however, he spreads on the grave on every *zeearut*-day until the fortieth, when he keeps it to himself. Some persons, independently of the above cloth, have coloured cloths constantly spread on the grave.

* *i. e.* the *fuqeer* who resides there, of whom there is one at each cemetery.

Poor people pay the *gussalans* (or those who wash the corpse) the sum of four annas, while the opulent pay as far as from fifty to a hundred rupees. The clothes which are upon the body of the deceased when he dies, are also taken by the *gussalans*; and I have even seen them obtain, in this way, a pair of shawls, brocades, &c. It is frequently the ardent desire of these people, that some great nobleman of wealth and fortune may die, that they may receive plenty of money and clothes. Most of the ignorant among the wealthy have a very great horror of a corpse, and do not relish even touching the clothes and furniture which had been used by the deceased before his death, and therefore give them away, by way of charity, to the *gussalans* or *fuqeers*, who are in the habit of disposing of them in the *bazars*.

The generality of people have tombs made of mud and stone, or brick and mortar, or only of a single stone hewn out in the shape of a tomb, forming first three square *taweezes* or platforms, one or one and a-half cubits in height, or somewhat less. Above that, if for a man, they form a *taweez* about a cubit (more or less) in height, and a yard or somewhat less in length, resembling the hump on a camel's back or the back of a fish, in breadth one span or one and a-half. If for a woman, its length and breadth are the same as those of men, but in height it is less, being from four fingers breadth to a span, and flat in shape. The *taweez* of a boy is of the same description as that of a man, and that of a girl like that of a woman, only smaller in size. Some people make various kinds of *churagdan* (niches for lamps) near the head of the grave.

The *Sheeas* make their tombs for men of the same shape as the *Soonnees* make those for females; and for women like those of the *Soonnees* for men, but with a hollow or basin in the centre of the upper part.

Some cause a stone to be inscribed with the name of the deceased, either alone or in conjunction with that of his father, together with the year, day of the month and week on which he died, and set it up at the north side on the grave. Besides this, some have the same written in prose or verse on all the four walls.

A few have the name, &c. of the deceased engraved on a square stone tablet, and have it fixed into the wall over the outside of the entrance-door of the mausoleum, or they write it with ink over the door.

It is highly meritorious to accompany a bier; and that *on foot*, following behind it: for this reason, that there are five *furz kufaeea** incumbent on Moosulmans to observe. 1st. To return a salutation. 2d. To visit the sick and inquire after their welfare. 3d. To follow a bier, on foot, to the grave. 4th. To accept of an invitation. 5th. To reply to a sneeze; *e. g.* if a person sneeze, and say instantly after *Alhumd-o-Lillah* (God be praised), the answer must be *Yur-humuk-Allah* (God have mercy upon you).

In the *Mishkat-ool-Mussubeeh* it is stated, that when a bier passes an individual, whether it be that of a Moosulman, Jew, or any other sect, the person is to stand up, and accompany it at least forty paces. No one is to walk in front of the corpse, as that space is to be left free for the Angels, who on such occasions are said to proceed before.

To build tombs with mortar, stones, or burnt bricks, to sit upon them or touch them with the feet, to write a verse of the *Qoran*, or God's name on them, and the like, are all forbidden. But so it is, that the generality of people do not attend to these rules.

---

* *Kufaeea*, or sufficient; *i. e.* if among eight or ten persons standing or living together, one observe the *furz* (command or religious duty) it is sufficient; it is equivalent to all having performed it.

CHAPTER XXXIX.

Concerning the *teeja*, alias *zeearut*, or *p'hool-churhana* of the dead; or the visiting the grave on the third day after burial.

On the third day after the burial of the dead they perform what is called *teeja*, *zeearut*, or *p'hool-churhana:* That is, they take all sorts of fruits, *choorway*, and *pan-sooparee* with its accompaniments, some *nan*, *hulwa*, others merely *nuqol* and *pan-sooparee*, together with a sheet made of flowers, *urgujja*, *ood*, and *ood-butteean*, and place them, the day previous to the *zeearut*, on the spot where the individual died. On the *zeearut*-morning, at dawn of day, the male relatives alone of the deceased, and *moollas*, &c. accompany the above articles to the grave, and there make *Khutum-e-Qoran*;* *i. e.* have the whole of the *Qoran* read over by the *moollas*, once, twice, or oftener. This is done by distributing four or five *jooz* (sections, of which there are thirty) to each of the readers, who get through them very rapidly. Among the rich fifty or one hundred *moollas* sit down, and reading it through bestow its benefits on the deceased. Some have the greater part read the night before, and get it only concluded at the grave on the morning following. This done, they spread on the tomb a white, red, or any other coloured cover, lay over it the *p'hool-kee-chuddur* (sheet formed of flowers), and burning benjamin or aloes wood pastiles, they offer *fateeha*, and each one throws a few flowers into the *urgujja*, and offering supplications for the remission of his sins, applies some of the above *urgujja* together with the flowers to the grave, nearly over the posi-

* Or the transferring the benefits of the reading of the *Qoran* to the person deceased.

tion of the head or chest. *Fateeha* being offered, they distribute the eatables among the *hafizans*, *moollas*, poor, *fuqeers*, &c. and to all others. Or men merely take the above articles to the grave, offer *fateeha*, and distribute them there; and as at the funeral, so now, they give away in charity wheat, rice, salt, and *pice* (coppers), or only a few *pice*. Then having offered the *daeera kee fateeha*, they depart.

These ceremonies are not agreeably to the laws of Mohummud; but merely customs current in Hindoostan.

CHAPTER XL.

Concerning the *fateeha*, or offerings to the dead, on the tenth, twentieth, thirtieth, and fortieth day after the demise; and the quarterly, half-yearly, nine-monthly, and annual *fateeha*.

The tenth-day zeearut. For nine days after the death of a person, most people neither go to eat or drink any thing in the house of the family of the deceased, nor invite any of its members to any entertainment at their's. Moreover, none of the family eat flesh or fish for nine days; nay, they refrain from all food which is seasoned. This is likewise not agreeably to books, but merely a custom in Hindh (India).

On the ninth, at noon, they prepare *nan* and *hulwa*, or *hulwa* and *chupateean*, and having delivered *fateeha* over them in the name of the deceased, all the members of the household partake of them and distribute a little to the neighbours around.

In the evening they dress *polaoo* and curries; and having invited their relatives, friends, and neighbours, beggars and *fuqeers*, to partake of them, they eat and distribute, and send to the burying-ground-*fuqeer* his portion. It is however customary among the vulgar, never to eat any food cooked at their own houses after having partaken of the above tenth-day food, and when they receive such shares of the food, they never allow it to be brought within doors; but go and eat it outside in the area in front of the house. Some foolish people conceiving the tenth-day food bad, do not partake of it at all; believing, that by so doing they would be deprived of the very useful faculty of speech. All this is nothing but mere fancy and imagination.

On the morning of the tenth they perform the *zeearut*, as detailed for the third day in the preceding chapter.

On the nineteenth they prepare *nan*, *chupateean*, and *hulwa*; offer *fateeha* over them in the name of the deceased, and distribute them. At the time of the *fateeha*, such flower-sheet, *sundul*, &c. as were deposited near the food, they convey to the grave, and spread the former on, and apply the latter to it. But there is no *zeearut* on the morning of the twentieth day.

A few also dress some food on the thirtieth, offer *fateeha*, eat and distribute.

On the thirty-ninth, during the day, they cook *polaoo*, as on the tenth, but at night they prepare plenty of curries, *tulun* (or fried food), *polaoo*, &c. (*i. e.* such dishes as the deceased was in the habit of eating during his life), arrange them on plates, together with *urgujja*, *soorma*, *kajul*, *ubeer*, *pan-sooparee*, some of the clothes and jewels of the deceased, which they deposit on the spot where the individual gave up the ghost, and over them suspend to the ceiling a flower-garland. This ceremony is denominated *luhud bhurna*, or filling the grave.

Some foolish women believe that on the fortieth day the soul of the dead leaves the house, if it has not done so previously; and if it has, it returns to it on that day, takes a survey of the above articles, partakes of such as he takes a fancy to, swings by the flower-wreath, takes a smell of the *sundul*, and departs. These nonsensical sayings and doings, however, are all innovations, and consequently unlawful.

They sit up all that night, and if there be any *Qoran* or *mowlood*-reciters present, they continue repeating them.

The following is another custom; *viz.* that for forty days they place daily, on the spot where the man departed this life, a new *ab-khora* (earthen tumbler) filled with water, with or without a *rotee* (wheaten cake). The water is left there all night, and next morning poured on any green tree, and the bread and *ab-khora* are given away to some *fuqeer* or other.

They generally light a lamp on the spot where the person died, where the body was washed, and some also on the tomb for three, ten, or forty nights, and until the fortieth day. They send every evening to the *musjid* a new *ab-khora* of water, a *rotee* with *ghee* spread on it, or without *ghee* but sugared, or *duhee*, boiled rice, &c. And any one there offers *fateeha* over them in the name of the defunct, and eats them.

On the morning of the fortieth they perform *zeearut*, as before detailed.

On the third, sixth, ninth, and twelfth month after the death of a person (women generally observing these ceremonies a few days before the expiration of the above periods) they in like manner prepare *polaoo*, &c. and having had *fateeha* offered over them, eat, and distribute.

They whom God has blessed with the means, give away in charity on the above-mentioned days, for the sake of the deceased, clothes and money; and on the evening of the above *fateeha* day, they spread a *p'hool-kee-chuddur* (flower-sheet) on the grave.

Many women go without fail to the grave on the fortieth

day and annual *zeearuts*. On the other days they are prohibited from repairing thither, and it is moreover not customary for them to do so.

It is meritorious for men to go and offer *fateeha* on the grave every Friday; but the generality of people do it on Thursday.

After the first year the deceased is numbered with deceased ancestors, and *fateeha* offered in their names conjointly, by some at the *fateeha* of *Shub-é-Burât* (p. 252), and by others at the *arfa* of the *buqr-eed*-feast (p. 266).

Those who can afford it dress victuals, of some kind or other, more or less, on the anniversary day of the individual's death, and have *fateeha* offered in his name.

In conclusion, I may here insert the number of days required for the performance of different ceremonies, and the celebration of the various festivals, &c. detailed in this work, and for which leave is generally granted to *Seepahees*.

For the rites of *ch'huttee, chilla, uqeeqa, moondun, salgeera, bismilla, khutna, Qorân ka huddeea, balig hona, juhaz kee nuzur, mooreed hona,* or for any other like ceremony, more than one day and a-half is not required.

Shadee (or marriage;) ten days. If pressed for time, five or seven is sufficient; but vide p. 147.

Joomagee, one day.

On the death of a relative, three days; *i. e.* until the third day-*zeearut*.

Mohurrum, thirteen days; if pressed for time ten days.

Akhree char-shoomba, one day and a-half.

Bara-wufat, one day and a-half.

Dustugeer kay Geearween, one day.

Zinda Shah Mudar kay oors, one day and a-half.

Qadir kay oors, one day and a-half; but only one day to

those at a distance from his shrine, who merely perform *churagan* in his name.

MowlaAllee kay oors, one day and a-half.

Shaban kay eed, two days and a-half.

Rumzan-fast requires no leave.

Rumzan kay eed, (in *shuwal*) one day.

Bunda Nuwaz kee churagan, one day.

Buqr-eed, two days.

By the grace and blessing of God, the *Qânoon-e-Islam* has been completed, with great diligence and perseverance, and at the particular request of a just appreciator of the merits of the worthy, a man of rank, of great liberality and munificence, Dr. Herklots (may his good fortune, age, and wealth ever increase, Amen and Amen !) for the benefit of the honourable English gentlemen (may their empire be exalted !)

Nothing relative to the customs of Moosulmans in Hindoostan will be found to have been concealed.

The only thing I have now to hope for from my readers is, that they will wish the author and translator well, for which they will receive blessings from God and thanks from mankind.

This is my hope from ev'ry liberal mind,
That all my faults indulgence meet may find:
Those who through spite or envy criticise,
Are witless wights, and the reverse of wise.

FINISHED AT ELLORE.

ADDENDA.

There are three feasts mentioned by Mrs. Meer Hassan Ali in her very accurate "Observations on the Mussulmauns of India," which seem to have been overlooked by our author. Probably they are more particularly observed in Bengal and the upper provinces, where the authoress resided, than in the Deccan (the birth-place of the writer of this work), I shall therefore take the liberty of quoting the lady's own words.

1. "*Now-roz* نوروز (new year's day) is a festival or *eed* of no mean importance in the estimation of Mussulman society. The exact period of commencing the Mussulman new year, is the very moment of the sun's entering the sign Aries. This is calculated by those practical astronomers who are in the service of most great men in native cities. I should tell you, they have not the benefit of published almanacks as in England; and according to the hour of the day or night when the sun passes into that particular sign, so are they directed in the choice of a colour to be worn in their garments on this *eed.* If at midnight, the colour would be dark puce, almost a black; if at mid-day, the colour would be the brightest crimson. Thus to the intermediate hours are given a shade of either colour, applicable to the time of the night or the day when the sun enters the sign Aries; and whatever be the colour to suit the hour of *now-roz*, all classes wear the same livery, from the king to the meanest subject in the city. The king on his throne sits in state to receive congratulations and *nuzzurs* from his nobles, courtiers and dependents. '*Moobarik Now-roz*

(may the new year be fortunate!)' are the terms of salutation exchanged by all classes of society, the king himself setting the example. The day is devoted to amusements, a public breakfast at the palace, sending presents, exchanging visits, &c.

"The trays of presents prepared by the ladies for their friends are tastefully set out, and the work of many days' previous arrangement. Eggs are boiled hard, some of these are stained in colours resembling our mottled papers; others are neatly painted in figures and devices; many are ornamented with gilding; every lady evincing her own peculiar taste in the prepared eggs for *now-roz*. All kinds of dried fruits and nuts, confectionary and cakes, are numbered amongst the necessary articles for this day's offering. They are set out in small earthen plates, lacquered over to resemble silver, on which is placed coloured paper, cut out in curious devices (an excellent substitute for vine-leaves), laid on the plate to receive the several articles forming *now-roz* presents.

"Amongst the young people these trays are looked forward to with child-like anxiety. The ladies rival each other in their display of novelty and good taste, both in the eatables and the manner of setting them off with effect.

"The religious community have prayers read in their family, and by them it is considered both a necessary duty and a propitious commencement to bring in the new year by 'prayer and praises.'

"When it is known that the *now-roz* will occur by daylight, the ladies have a custom of watching for the moment the year shall commence by a fresh rose, which being plucked from the stalk is thrown into a basin of water, the eye downwards. They say, this rose turns over of itself towards the sun at the very moment of that luminary passing into the sign Aries. I have often found them thus engaged, but I never could say I witnessed the actual accomplishment of their prediction.

"The *now-roz* teems with friendly tokens between the two families of a bride and bridegroom elect, whose interchange of presents are also strictly observed. The children receive gifts from their elders; their nurses reap a harvest from the day; the tutor writes an ode in praise of his pupil, and receives gifts from the child's parents; the servants and slaves are regaled with dainties and with presents from the superiors of the establishment; the poor are remembered with clothes, money, and food; the ladies make and receive visits; and the *domnees* attend to play and sing in the *zunana*. In short, the whole day is passed in cheerful amusements, suited to the retirement of a *zunana* and the habits of the people."—Mrs. Meer, vol. i. p. 283—287.

This day is likewise celebrated, by the liberation of prisoners, &c.

---

2. "There is a festival observed at Lucknow, called *bussunt* بسنت (spring). I should remark here, that almost all the trees of India have perpetual foliage. As the season approaches for the new leaves to sprout, the young buds force off the old leaves, and when the trees are thus clothed in their first delicate foliage, there is a yellow tinge in the colour, which is denominated *bussunt*. A day is appointed to be kept under this title, and then every one wears the *bussunt* colour: no one would be admitted at court without this badge of the day. The elephants, horses, and camels of the king, or of his nobles, are all ornamented with the same colour on their trappings.

"The king holds a court, gives a public breakfast, and

exhibits sports with ferocious animals.—The amusements of this day are chiefly confined to the court. I have not observed much notice taken of it in private life."—Mrs. Meer, vol. i. p. 287.

---

3. " The last month of the periodical rains is called *Shaban*. There is a custom observed by the Mussulman population, the origin of which has never been clearly explained to me. Some say, it is in remembrance of the prophet Elisha or Elijah, and commences the first Friday of *Shaban*, and is followed up every succeeding Friday through this concluding month of the rainy season.*

" The learned men call it a *zunana*, or children's custom; but it is common to see children of all ages amongst the males partake of and enjoy the festival with as much glee as the females, or their juniors.

" A bamboo frame is formed to the shape of a Chinese boat; this frame-work is hidden by a covering of gold and

---

* I presume Mrs. Meer must allude to a custom adopted by Moosulmans in fulfilling vows, particularly noticed under the head of "vows and oblations" in this work (p. 273). About Lucknow, it may probably be observed on the different Fridays of the month, but in Bengal it is performed on the Thursdays, and that in the Bengalee month *Bhadoon* (perhaps in the last month of the periodical rains). It could not invariably fall in the month *Shaban*, as the Moosulman months are lunar, and therefore moveable as regards the seasons of the year. At all events, being merely the accomplishment of a vow, the observance of it on Fridays in one part of the country, and on Thursday in another, may easily be accounted for.

Shakespear in his Dictionary, in explanation of *khwaja khizur*, has the following words: The name of a prophet skilled in divination, and who is said to have discovered the water of life; hence he is considered the saint of waters. The Muhammadans offer oblations to him of lamps, flowers, &c. placed on little rafts and launched on the river, particularly on Thursday evening in the month of *Bhadon;* and it is in his honour that the feast of *bera* is held.

silver tissue, silk, or coloured muslin, bordered and neatly ornamented with silver paper. In this light bark many lamps are secreted, of common earthenware. A procession is formed to convey the tribute called "*Elias ke kishtee*," to the river. The servants of the family, soldiers, and a band of native music attend in due order of march. The crowd attracted by this childish play is immense, increasing as they advance through the several streets on the way to the river, by all the idlers of the place.

"The *kishtee* (boat) is launched amidst a flourish of trumpets and drums, and the shouts of the populace; the small vessel, being first well lighted by means of the secreted lamps, moves down gently with the stream. When at a little distance, on a broad river, in the stillness of evening, any one who did not previously know how these little moving bodies of light were produced, might fancy such fairy scenes as are to be met with in the well-told fables of children's books in happy England.

"This custom, though strongly partaking of the superstitious, is not so blameable as that which I have known practised by some men of esteemed good understanding, who having a particular object in view, which they cannot attain by any human stratagem or contrivance, write petitions to the *Emam Muhdee* on Fridays, and by their own hands commit the paper to the river, with as much reverence as if they thought him present in the water to receive it. The petition is always written in the same respectful terms as inferiors here well know how to address their superiors; and every succeeding Friday the petition is repeated until the object is accomplished, or the petitioner has no further inducement to offer one."—Mrs. Meer, vol. i. p. 288.

In like manner, Professor Garcin de Tassy (on the authority of the *Baramasa*, p. 64, the only book in which he finds it made mention of), furnishes us with an additional feast, called

Goga or Zahir Peer ;

after the name of the saint; to whom Mussulmans are greatly attached, devoting themselves to him with all their heart and soul and undergoing various acts of humility and penance. In celebrating this festival, which happens in the Bengalee month *Bhadon*, they go about the streets armed with lances, playing on different musical instruments, chaunting his praises. These processions continue a whole month. At the end of which period they assemble and fix their lances in one spot, where a fair is held noted for all kinds of amusements and curious spectacles. I understand that the shrine of this saint is in the Dooab, and that this feast is observed every where.

MOOSULMAN SAINTS OF INDIA.

Abd-ool-qadir,

surnamed Gows-ool-Azum (p. 237), the great contemplative, born at Jal, near Bagdad, A.H. 471 (A.D. 1078-79). He was endowed with great virtue and with the gift of miracles, had many disciples, and is still much revered. He is called Sheikh, but was a *Syed, i. e.* of the race of Hosein, and died in A.H. 571 (A.D. 1175), aged ninety-seven years. Where he died or was buried does not appear.

Sooltan Surwur,

at Balooch, four coss from Mooltan. He was distinguished for piety and purity of manners, and died as a martyr with his brother, fighting against a troop of idolators, and was buried with his wife (who died of grief) and his son, in the same tomb. Several miracles are related as having happened at his tomb. A camel's leg, when broken, was forthwith made whole; the blind, the leprous, the impotent were cured. (Araesh-e-Muhfil.)

SHAH SHUMS OOD DEEN DARIAI,

at Depaldal in Lahore. He is stated to have had even a pious Hindoo among his disciples. The latter having expressed a wish to go and bathe in the Ganges, the saint directed him to shut his eyes, when lo! the Hindoo found himself among his relations and friends on that sacred stream, in which (as he supposed) he bathed with them. On opening his eyes again, he straightway found himself beside his spiritual guide in Lahore. His tomb is guarded by Hindoos, who will not resign their posts to the Moosulmans. It is also related that some carpenters having proceeded to cut down a tree which grew near his tomb, split it into many pieces for use. Suddenly a dreadful voice was heard; the earth shook, and the trunk of the tree arose of itself; the workmen fled terrified, and the tree did not fail to resume its flourishing condition.

QOOTOOB SAHIB, OR QOOTTOOB OOD DEEN,

near Dehli. He lies buried at Qootoob, a town near Dehli named after him, in which the late Shah Alum and many members of the royal family of Dehli are buried. His tomb is much frequented by pilgrims, he being one of the most renowned and venerated of the Moosulman saints.

SHEIKH BUHA OOD DEEN ZAKARIA,

Born at Cotcaror in Mooltan. He was a great traveller, having it is said, overrun Persia and Turkey, and a disciple for some time of Shihab ood Deen Sohurwurdee at Bagdad. He died on the 7th *Sufur*, A.H. 665 (7th Sept. A.D. 1266), and was buried at Mooltan.

FURREED-OOD-DEEN,

Born at Ghanawal near Mooltan. He was so holy, that by his look clods of earth were converted into lumps of sugar. He was therefore surnamed Shukur-gunj, which means in Persian the treasury of sugar.

SHEIKH SHUREEF BOO ALI QULUNDUR,

Born at Panniput, a town thirty coss north-west of Dehli, to which capital he came at forty years of age, and became a disciple of Qoottoob ood Deen. He devoted himself for twenty years to external sciences; after which he threw all his books into the Jumna, and began to travel for religious instruction. In Asia Minor he profited greatly by the society of Shums Tubreez and Mowluwee Room. He then returned home, lived retired and worked miracles, and is said to have died A.H. 724 (A.D. 1323-24).

SHAH NIZZAM OOD DEEN OWLEEA,

By some supposed to have been born at Gazna, A.H. 630 (A.D. 1622-3), and by others in A.H. 634 (A.D. 1236) at Badaam, a town in the province of Delhi where he lived. He died A.H. 725 (A.D. 1325), and was buried near Delhi, hard by the tomb of Qoottoob ood Deen. Through his great piety he was considered one of the most eminent saints of Hindoostan.

Kubeer.

A celebrated Hindoo Unitarian, equally revered by Hindoos and Moosulmans, founder of the sect called Kubeer Punthee or Nanuk Punthee, from which Nanuk, founder of the Sikhs, borrowed the religious notions which he propagated with the greatest success.

Baba Lal.

A Durwaysh (and likewise a Hindoo), who dwelt at Dhianpoor in the province of Lahore, the founder of a sect called Baba Lalees. He held frequent conversations on the subject of religion with Dara Shifroh, eldest son of Shah Juhan, and brother of Aurungzebe, which have been published in a Persian work by Chundurbhan Shah Juhanee.

Shah Dola,

Died in the seventeenth year of the reign of Alumgeer, at first a slave of Kumayandar Sialkoti in Lahore. But he seems afterwards to have attained great affluence as well as fame; for having settled at Ch'hotee Goojrat (little Guzerat), he built tanks, dug wells, founded mosques, and bridges, and embellished the city. And no wonder; for though his contemporaries came to visit him from far and near, and made him presents of gold, money, and other objects, he returned to each three or four-fold more than he received. His generosity was such, that had he been contemporary with Hatim Tai, no one would have mentioned the name of that hero.

Syed Shah Zoohoor,

Distinguished by his wisdom, piety, and austerity of life. He built a small monastery of earth at Allahabad, which still remains. He was celebrated for his miracles, and by his prayers the most frightful chronic complaints were immediately removed, of which an instance is given in respect to the case of the governor of Allahabad, Nuwwab Oomdut ool Moolk Ameer Khan. This saint (Zoohoor) boasted of having lived three hundred years.

Sheikh Mohummud Ali Hazin Gillanee.

His tomb is at Buxar, where he died in A.H. 1180 (A.D. 1766-7), distinguished for his science, learning, and literary talents. He wrote in both prose and verse with equal skill.

APPENDIX.

I. RELATIONSHIP.

As the Mohummudans have a great variety of terms whereby to express the different degrees of affinity, it may I hope not be deemed altogether irrelevant to offer them here in a tabular form.

Owlad اولاد, or Paternal Offspring.

A man's

Father,	باپ			
Father's brother (elder)	تايا	his	wife,	تاي
			son,	تايرا بهاي
			daughter,	تايري بهن
Father's brother (younger)	چچا	his	wife,	چچاني
			son,	چچيرا بهاي
			daughter,	چچيري بهن
Father's sister,	پهوپهي	her	husband,	پهوپها - پهوپهو
			son,	پهپهيرا بهاي
			daughter,	پهپهيري بهن
Father's father,	داده			
Father's mother,	دادي			
Father's father's father,	پرداده			
Father's father's mother,	پردادي			

Āl آل, or Maternal Progeny.

A man's

Mother,	ما - مان			
Mother's brother,	مامو	his	wife,	مماني
			son,	مولیرا بهاي
			daughter,	مولیري بهن

b

Mother's sister, خالا - خالہ her { husband, خالو - خالاي
son, خليرا بهاي
daughter, خليري بهن }

Mother's father, نانا
Mother's mother, ناني
Mother's father's father, پرنانا
Mother's father's mother, پرناني

A man's

Brother, بهاي his { wife, بهاوج
son, بهتيجا
daughter, بهتيجي }

Sister, بهن her { husband, بهوناي
son, بهانجا
daughter, بهانجي }

Son, بيتا his { wife, بهو
son, پوترا - پوتا
daughter, پوتري - پوتي }

Daughter, بيتي her { husband, داماد - جوائي
son, نواسا
daughter, نواسي - نتني - ناتي }

Grandson, } Vide above, Son's son and daughter, and
Granddaughter, } daughter's son and daughter.
Great grandson, پرپوتا - پرپوترا
Great granddaughter, پرپوتي - پرپوتري

A man's

Wife, جورو her {
father, سسرا or سسر
mother, خوشدامن or ساس
brother, سالا his { wife, بهاوج
son, بهتيجا
daughter, بهتيجي }
sister, سالي her { husband, سارو
son, بهانجا
daughter, بهانجي } }

A woman's Husband, خصم } his { father, سسر or سسرا
mother, ساس or خوشدامن
brother, elder, جيٹهه his wife, جيٹهاني
brother, younger, ديور / ديوڑا - ديوڑها } his wife, ديوراني
sister, ناند her husband.*

For the easy reference of Europeans, it may not be amiss to arrange the preceding here alphabetically.

Bāp باپ father.

Baytā بيٹا son.

Baytee بيٹي daughter.

Bhaee بهاي brother.

Bhānjā بهانجا sister's son (or wife's sister's son).

Bhānjee بهانجي sister's daughter (or wife's sister's daughter).

Bhāwuj بهاوج brother's wife (or wife's brother's wife).

Bhow-naee بهونائي sister's husband.

Bhuteeja بهتيجا brother's son (or wife's brother's son).

Bhuteejee بهتيجي brother's daughter (or wife's brother's daughter).

Buhoo بهو son's wife.

Buhun بهن sister.

Chu-cha چچا father's younger brother.

Chu-chānee چچاني father's younger brother's wife.

Chuchayra bhaee چچيرابهاي father's younger brother's son.

Chuchayree buhun چچيري بهن father's younger brother's daughter.

Dāda داده paternal grandfather.

Dādee دادي paternal grandmother.

Dāmād or *Juwānee* داماد يا جواني mother's daughter's husband.

---

* For this and other degrees of affinity not enumerated above, no peculiar epithets are known.

Daywur دیور *Daywura* دیوڑا or *Daywurha* دیوڑھا husband's younger brother.

Daywurānee دیوراني husband's younger brother's wife.

Jayth' جیٹھہ husband's elder brother.

Jay'thānee جیٹھاني husband's elder brother's wife.

Joroo جورو wife.

Juwanee جواني or *Damad* داماد daughter's husband.

Khāla خالا mother's sister.

Khāloo خالو or *Khulaee* خلائي mother's sister's husband.

Khooshdāmun خوشدامن wife's or husband's mother.

Khulayra bhaee خلیرا بهاي mother's sister's son.

Khulayree buhun خلیري بهن mother's sister's daughter.

Mā ما or *Mān* مان mother.

Māmoo مامو mother's brother.

Momānee مماني mother's brother's wife.

Mowlayra bhaee مولیرا بهاي mother's brother's son.

Mowlayree buhun مولیري بهن mother's brother's daughter.

Nānā نانا maternal grandfather.

Nānee ناني maternal grandmother.

*Nānud*نانِد husband's sister.

Nātee ناتي or *Nutnee* نتني daughter's daughter.

Nuwāsa نواسا daughter's son.

Nuwāsee نواسي daughter's daughter.

P'hoopa or *P'hoop'ha* پهوپا - پهوپها or *P'hoopoo* or *P'hoop'hoo* پهوپو - پهوپهو father's sister's husband (or uncle).

P'hoopee or *P'hoop'hee* پهوپي - پهوپهي father's sister.

P'hoopayra bhaee پهوپیرا بهاي father's sister's son.

P'hoopayree buhun پهوپیري بهن father's sister's daughter.

Pota پوتا or *Pōtrā* پوترا son's son.

Potee پوتي or *Potree* پوتري son's daughter.

Pur dāda پرداده paternal great grandfather.
Pur dādee پردادي paternal great grandmother.
Pur nāna پرنانا maternal great grandfather.
Pur nānee پرناني maternal great grandmother.
Pur pota پرپوتا or } great grandson.
Pur potra پر پوترا }
Pur potee پر پوتي or } great granddaughter.
Pur potree پر پوتري }
Sās ساس wife's (or husband's) mother.
Sāla سالا wife's brother.
Sālee سالي wife's sister.
Sāroo سارو wife's sister's husband.
Soosur سسر or } wife's or husband's father.
Soosra سُسرا }
Tāee تائي father's elder brother's wife.
Tāeea تايا father's elder brother.
Tāeera bhaee تايرابهاي father's elder brother's son.
Tāeeree buhun تايري بهن father's elder brother's daughter.

II. WEIGHTS. (Apothecary's.)

From the *Ulfaz-Udwiyeh* الفاظ ادويه.

N. B. (a) signifies Arabic, (p) Persian, (h) Hindoostanee.

حب	*Hubba* (a) equal to 1 *jow* جو or com. barleycorn.		
تسو	*Tussoo* (a) - - - - - - -	2	do.
قيراط	*Qeerat* (a) or *Carat* - - -	4	do.
گهونگهچي	*Ghoonghchee* (h) }		
سرخ	*Soorkh* (h) or } - - -	8	do.
رتي	*Rutty* (h) }		
ماشه	*Māshā* (h) - - - - -	8	*Rutties.*
تولہ	*Tolā* (h) - - - - -	12	*Mashas.*
تانگ	*Tāng* (h) - - - - - - -	4	do.
دانگ	*Dāng* (h) or }		
دانق	*Dānuq* (h) } - - - - -	$4\frac{1}{6}$	*Rutties.*

درم *Dirrum* (p) or درهم *Dirhum* (a)	- - - - - -	4 *Masha* and 1 *Rutty*.
مشقال *Mishqāl* (a)	- - - - - -	4 *Mashas* and 3½ *Rutties*.
استار *Istar* (a) or سرشاهي *Seer shāhee* (h) or Royal Seer	- - - - - -	1½ *Tolas* and 2 *Mashas*.
أوقيه *Owqeea* (a) or وقيه *Wuqeea* (a)	- - - - -	7½ *Mishqals*.
من طبي *Mun-e-tibbee* (a)	- - - -	40 *Istars*.

From the *Mujmooaee Akburree*; selected from the "*Huddees, Secha-o-Sittah, Logut-i-Kamoos*, and *Logut-e-Jukheeray*."

حبه 1 *Hubba*	- - - -	= 1	barleycorn.
تسو 1 *Tussoo*	- - - -	= 2	do.
قيراط 1 *Qeerāt*	- - - -	= 4	do.
دانگ 1 *Dāng*	- - - -	= 8	do.
درهم 1 *Dirhum*	- - - -	= 48	do.
مشقال 1 *Mishqāl*	- -	= 68	do.
استار 1 *Astār* or technically *Assār*		= 4½	*Mishqals*.
أوقيه 1 *Owqeea*	- - - -	= 7½	do. and 9 *Ruttuls*.
رطل 1 *Ruttul*	- - - -	= 2	*Muds*.
مد 1 *Mud*	- - - -	= 6	*Owqeeas*.
رطل بغدادي 1 *Ruttul-e-Bugdadee*		= 90	*Mishqals*.
رطل مکه يا مدينه 1 do. *Mecca* or *Medina*		=	somewhat more.
من طبي 1 *Mun-e-tibbee*	-	= 2	*Ruttuls*.
درهم 1 *Dirhum*	- - -	= 6	*Dangs*.

دانگ 1 *Dāng* - - -	=	2	*Hubbas.*
حب 1 *Hubba* or barley-corn - -	=	6	Mustard seeds.

AVOIRDUPOIS WEIGHT according to the *Shurra* (or Law of Muhummud).

1	*Dirhum* - - -	=	10	*Dirrums* = 7 *Mishqals.*
1	*Mishqāl* - - -	=	$1\frac{3}{4}$	do.
200	*Dirrums* - - -	=	180	*Mishqāls.*
1	*Mishqal* as at present in use	=	2	*Dirrums.*
1	*Sāah* - - -	=	314	*Mishqāls.*
1	do. as at present in use	=	40	*Dams* = $1\frac{1}{4}$ *Seer.*

MEASURES.

1 *Kile* (an Arabian measure).

1 *Mukkook* = 3 *Kiles* = 2 *Sāahs.*

1 *Sā ah* = 4 *Muds* = 2 *Rutluls* = 1 *Mun.*

APOTHECARY'S WEIGHT, from a respectable Moosulman Practitioner.

					oz.	dr.	gr.
1	*Massa* or *Māsha*	=	8	*Ghoonghchee* - -	0	0	15
1	*Tola* - - -	=	12	*Mashas* - - -	0	3	0
1	*Tānk* - - -	=	4	do. - - -	0	1	0
1	*Wāsikh* - -	=	4	*Goomchee* (*Dukh.*)	0	0	$7\frac{1}{2}$
1	*Dirum* or *Dirhum*	=	$3\frac{1}{2}$	*Mashas* - - -	0	0	$52\frac{1}{2}$
1	*Mishqāl* - -	=	$4\frac{1}{2}$	do. - - -	0	0	67
1	*Astār-o-dam* -	=	18	do. - - -	0	4	30
1	*Udkeeuh Owqeea* (?) -	=	7	*Mishqals* - - -	0	7	52

				oz.	dr.	gr.
1 *Ruttul-e-tibbee* or *Mukkee*	=	19	*Dirhums* - - - -	2	0	$37\frac{1}{2}$
1 *Ruttul Bugdādee*	=	30	do. - - - -	3	2	15
1 *Mun-e-tibbee* -	=	40	*Dams* - - - - -	5	0	0
1 *Zurra* - -	=	1	Mustard-seed.			
1 *Karush'ma* -	=	3	*Zurras.*			
1 *Khirdul* - -	=	4	*Karushmas.*			
1 *Surshuf* - -	=	2	*Khirduls.*			
1 *Gundooms* -	=	8	do.			
1 *Soorkh* - -	=	2	*Gundooms.*			
1 *Dām* - - - -	=	4	*Mashas* - - -	0	1	0
1 *Dāng* - - - -	=	6	*Rutties* - - -	0	0	$11\frac{1}{4}$
1 *Māsha* - -	=	8	*Ruttees* or *Goomchees* -	0	0	15
1 *Tola* - - - -	=	30	*Chinnas* - - -	0	3	0
1 *Chinna* - - - -	=	4	*Soorkhs* - - -	0	0	6
1 *Soorkh* - -	=	4	*Dhan kay dana* (or Paddy corn) or 8 grs. of rice -	0	0	$1\frac{1}{2}$
or 1 *Soorkh* - -	=	$3\frac{1}{2}$	*Jow* or barleycorn: generally considered as = 2 grs.	0	0	$1\frac{85\frac{1}{2}}{100}$
1 *Rāee ka dana* Mustard seed, or *Khirdul* -	=	12	*Fuls.*			
1 *Ful* - - -	=	6	*Futteelas.*			
1 *Futteela* - -	=	6	*Nuqeers.*			
1 *Nuqeer* - -	=	8	*Qetmeers.*			
1 *Qetmeer* - -	=	12	*Zurras.*			
1 *Zurra* - - - -	=	6	*Hubba*			
1 *Hubba* - -	=	5	*Wahh.*			

III. A LIST *of* DRESSES *worn by Moosulman Men and Women.*

I. Male Dresses.

1. Head Dress.

Taj or *Topee* تاج - ٹوپي—a cap, generally conical.

Gōshbund or *Gōsh-romāl* گوش بند - گوش رومال—a handkerchief tied over the lower edge of the *Taj*, which covers the ears also; hence its name.

Pugree (Dukh.) or *Dustār* (Pers.) پگڑي - دستار—the common people conceive these names different; but they are synonymous terms for a turban, which consists of a piece of cloth of from forty to seventy cubits long, and from twelve to eighteen inches broad. The following are varieties of them, viz. 1. *Khirkeedār*, such as are used among *Chowkeedars* (watchmen), and *Chobdars* (macebearers); 2. *Nustāleekh*, by kings, nobles, &c. 3. *Arabee*, by Arabs; 4. *Putnāoo*, as used in Bengal; 5. *Jooraydār*, a turban tied on, as women tie their hair behind in a knot; 6. *Chukkreedār*, i. e. circular; 7. *Goondee*, globular; 8. *Teenkonee*, three-cornered, as Tippoo Sultan used to wear; 9. *Moottheedār*; 10. *Lutputtee*, irregular, or twisted, as worn by *Rachaywārs* (a warlike race inhabiting *Bobilee*, &c. in the Northern Circars); 11. *Qudum e Russool, Allum e Russool, Cheera*, or *Phaynta*, worn by kings, princes, &c.; 12. *Seepayree Allee*, very broad, like a shield; 13. *Bānkee*, crooked; 14. *Mushāckhee*, as worn by *Mushāekhs*; 15. *Luttoodār*; 16. *Ek-paycha*; 17. *Murg-paycha.*

Ammāma عمامہ—ten to twenty-five cubits long, worn on the head like a turban.

Mundeel منديل—a band ten or twelve cubits long, woven either partly with thread or silk and partly with gold, or wholly with gold thread, and applied over the turban; worn by all classes of people that can afford it.

Surpaych سرپیچ—a band two or two and a half cubits long, which only encircles the turban two or three times. It consists of square pieces of gold plates, threaded together, each plate being set with precious stones; chiefly worn by kings, princes, the nobility, &c.

Gōsh-paych or *Gōsh-wara* گوش‌پیچ یا گوشواره—a band of silk, two or two and a half cubits long and four fingers broad, worn over the turban.

Zeega or *Jeega* زیغه یا جیگا—a band about six inches long and two broad, consisting of a piece of velvet beautifully embroidered, and a gold plate set with precious stones sewed on it. It is worn obliquely in front of the head on the turban, and tied behind by means of silk thread, which is fastened to each end of the band. Only worn by kings, princes, and nobles.

Kulgee کلغي—a *hoomma* or phœnix-feather (Gloss.) fixed into the turban, having generally a pearl fastened to the end of it. Worn only by kings and the great.

Toorru طره—worn as the preceding, and made of gold, or gold and precious stones.

2. Dress worn round the Neck.

Gooloobund گلوبند—or neckcloth, is a kerchief worn round the neck.

3. Body Dresses.

Mirzāee مرزائي—a cotton or muslin jacket (or *banian*) with long loose sleeves and open cuffs; worn under the *quba*.

Kufcha کفچہ—as the preceding, but sleeves tight.

Dugla ڈگلہ—a quilted *mirzaee*.

Koorta or *Koortunee* کرتہ یا کرتني—a kind of shirt. It is called in Arabic *Qumees;* whence the Hindoostanee term *kumees* for our shirts. It is long, reaching down to the ankles, and is put on by being thrown over the head. Instead of always having the slit or opening in the centre of the front, it has it not unfrequently on one side of the chest. It has no strings, but a button at its upper end, which in Bengal is on the right side, in the Deccan on the left.

Joobba جبہ—as *mirzaee*, but reaching down to the ankles, without plaits, having two triangular pieces or flaps on each side the skirt; body and sleeves very loose.

Quba قبہ—a long gown with flaps in the skirt; the skirt and breast open, and sometimes slits in the armpits.

Aba عبا—a cloak or habit, very loose, and open in front all the way down the centre, not unlike a boat-cloak.

Chupkun or *Bulabur* چپکن یا بلابر—as the *quba*, but breast covered.

Anga or *Angurk'hā* انگ یا انگرکھا—as the *quba*, without open flaps; breast and armpits covered. (Also termed *choga*, *mogolaee*, *buhadooree*, *bundy*, or *kulleedar*.) In the Deccan, the *angurk'hās* have plaits on each side.

Pyruhun or *Alkhāliq* پیرھن یا الخالق—as the *quba*, but having buttons instead of strings, and that in three places; at the neck, navel, and between the two.

Jāma جامہ—a long gown, as the preceding, but having an immense quantity of cloth (from eleven to thirty breadths) in the skirt, which at the upper part is folded into innumerable plaits; the body part is tied in two places on each side, being double-breasted. The upper one of the right side is generally made into a knob with a number of strings. The Mohummudans tie their *jāmas* on the right side; the Hindoos on the left.

Neema نیمہ—as the preceding, but with only from five to seven breadths of cloth forming the skirt.

Neema Āsteen نیمہ آستین—a sort of a *banian*, worn over either of the two preceding, and never by itself. It reaches to below the knee, is single-breasted, and fastened above by one button in the centre of the chest; has short sleeves. It is a very expensive dress.

Kumurbund or *Putka* کمربند یا پٹکا—a girdle. A long piece of cloth, girt round the loins.

Doputta دوپٹہ—*lit.* two-breadths. A cloth thrown loosely over the shoulders. It should properly have a seam in the centre, to indicate its being formed of two breadths, whence its name; but vulgarly the name is applied to any cloth thus worn.

Doshāla دوشالہ—or a pair of shawls, worn as the preceding. A single shawl is never worn; the wearer would be laughed at if he did.

Sayla سیلہ—a piece of muslin worn as a *doputta.*

Doo-lāee دولائی or *Ek-lāee* اکلائی—generally made of silk (scarcely ever of cloth), edged with a border of silk or *tash* (*i. e.* silver or gold woven with silk) of a different colour. When it consists of one breadth, it is called *ek-laee*; of two, *doo-laee.* It may be worn in different ways. If the individual choose to indulge his fancy by twisting it round his head, it forms a turban; if thrown over the shoulders, it may be called a *doputta*; if worn round the loins, a *kumurbund.*

Chuddur or *Chādur* چدر - چادر or *Dohur* دہر—a large piece of cloth or sheet, of one and a half or two breadths, thrown over the head, so as to cover the whole body. Men usually sleep rolled up in it.

Loong or *Loonggee* لنگ یا لنگی *Tahbund* or *Tuhmut* تہبند یا تہمت—a piece of cloth, which should, according to Moosulman rule, be merely wrapped round the body, or rather pelvis, and its ends tucked in, after the custom of the *Moplays ;* and not, as is generally done, in imitation of the Hindoo mode of wearing it, by passing the end between the thighs and tucking it in behind. *Loonggee* is the name given to coloured cloth worn thus. *Dhootee*, a similar cloth with a coloured border, is seldom worn by Moosulmans, because a Hindoo dress.

Tusma تسمه or *Duwalee* دوالي—the former a leathern strap, the latter of thread or string, tied round the loins, to which the following (*lunggotee*) is fastened fore and aft. Worn only by *fuqeers*.

Lunggotee لنگوٹي—a bit of cloth about two feet long and six or eight inches broad, passed between the legs, and the ends tucked in before and behind to the preceding *tusma* or *duwalee*.

4. Hands.

Romal رومال—or handkerchief.

Dustāna دستانہ—or gloves of leather, cloth, &c. Among the nobility sometimes of shawl. These are of the form used in England for children, having a receptacle for the thumb, but the fingers are all contained in the same bag or cyst.

5. Leg Dresses.

Pāee-jama پائي جامه or *Tumbān* تنبان—long drawers, or loose trowsers, remarkably wide in the legs, *i. e.* from one to three cubits in circumference.

Shurāee شراعي or *Shilwār* شلوار *Soorwal* سروال or *Eezār* ازار—long drawers, as the preceding, but not so wide; not being wider than a foot, if so much.

Goorgee گُرگي—Breeches or short drawers. They reach below the knees, and fit tight.

Chōlna چولنا or *Churna* چرنا or *Jangeea* جانگيا — still shorter breeches than the preceding, reaching only half way down the thighs.

Chuddee چڈي—shorter still than *cholna*, having scarcely any legs at all.

Moond مونڈ—a cloth three cubits long, wound round the pelvis, worn by *Moplays*.

Pāeetāba پاي تابه—stockings or a short kind of socks, worn by the opulent during the cold season, called *Joorāb* جراب , made of cotton or silk, or both intermixed, and of various colours. Those which are remarkably thick rarely reach above the ankles. Persons of the first rank have their *joorābs*, as also their *dustānas* or gloves, made of shawl.

6. Foot Dresses.

Jootee جوتي—or shoes, which are of different forms; such as 1. *Nowkdār* نوك دار , the toe part is terminated by a long pointed strip, usually of leather lined with cloth, that curls inwards over the toes; without this the shoes would be considered both unfinished and vulgar; 2. *Āppashāec* آپاشاي ; 3. *Chānddoree* چاندوري ; 4. *Chuppul* چپل ; 5. *Zayrpāee* زيرپاي ; 6. *Kufsh* كفش ; 7. *Ghetlee* گهيتلي ; 8. *Payshawuree* پشاوري ; 9. *Nalyn* نعلين ; 10. *Churhuwān* چڑهوان . Some of these shoes are made of a very thick and rich stuff, embroidered in a splendid manner with silver and gold, and beset with spangles.

Moza موزه—or boots, made of different sorts of coloured leather.

II. Female Dresses.

1. Head Dresses.

Taj تاج—the same as that worn by men.

Assa عصه or *Kussāwa* كساوا—a handkerchief tied round the head on going to bed.

Muqna مقنع or *Ghoongut* گهونگٹ—a handkerchief of fine muslin thrown over the head, which covers the face after the manner of a veil.

Moobāf مباف—a slip of red cloth, a skein of thread, or a fillet of brocade tied to the end of the *choontee*, to prevent its unravelling.

2. Body Dresses.

Būzoo بازو *Koortunee* كرتني *Koorta* كرتہ or *Koortee* كرتي— a kind of short shirt, reaching down to the hips, with very short (if any) sleeves; sometimes open at the upper part of the chest in front.

Cholee چولي—a sort of a bodice or spencer, which fits close, and only extends downwards to cover the breasts, but completely shows their form. It has tight sleeves, which reach half way (or less) down between the shoulder to the elbow;* and a narrow border of embroidery, or silk, &c. of a different colour sewed on round all its edges. It is put on as a spencer, and the two ends tied together in front.

Ungeea انگيا or *Muhrum* محرم—in regard to the sleeves and length of bodice as the preceding, but instead of being tied in front and only at the bottom, it is put on as a straight jacket, and fastened behind above and below, leaving about four fingers breadth of the back bare.

Pishwūz پشواز or *Tilluk* تلك—not unlike the male *jama*, but only reaching to below the knees, and is of coloured muslin; it is double-breasted, and the two flaps fastened in two places on each side.

3. Leg Dresses.

Shurrūee شرعي or *Shilwūr* شلوار—long drawers, the same as that of the men, except that women generally wear them tighter.

L'hunga لهنگا or *Tobund* توبند—a kind of petticoat, or a mere skirt, which is tied round the loins, and extends to the feet or ground.

Sūree ساري—a dress consisting of an entire piece of cloth (white or coloured), wrapped several times round the

---

* Never longer, as that would approximate too much to the Hindoo manner of having it entirely down to the elbows. The latter avoid shorter ones, for a contrary reason.

loins; and falling down over the legs to the ankle, serves as a petticoat. The other end is passed over the head, and hangs down on one side.

Orhnee اوڑھني *Dāmnee* دامني or *Dāoonee* داوني—a wide piece of muslin, generally coloured and of superior quality, thrown over the left shoulder, which passing under the right arm is crossed under the middle, and being tucked into the *l'hunga*, hangs down to the feet. One end of it is sometimes spread over the head, and serves for a veil.

Kuppur-p'hool کپڑ پهول—a silk cloth, worked with gold and silver flowers, worn as a *sāree*.

G'hānsee گهانسي—a piece of gauze, worn as an *orhnee* over a *l'hunga*.

Chudur چدر corrupt. of *Chādur* چادر—a sheet, thrown over the head, which covers the whole body, and reaches down to the ground. Women generally wrap themselves in it on going out into the streets, taking especial care to conceal with it their faces; which, if they be old and ugly, they are more particular in doing. They also sleep wrapped up in it.

Boorqa بُرقع—a white sheet thrown over the head, which conceals the whole body. It has a net-worked space opposite the eyes through which they see, while the face is effectually hid from view. This is used by modest women, who cannot afford to go in *doolees* or palankeens, but are obliged to walk. It is not unusual to see such a figure mounted on a bullock, which to a stranger and at a distance does not look unlike a ghost.

4. Foot Dresses.

Jootee جوتي—or shoes, or rather slippers (which, as soon as they return home from walking to their seat on the carpet are thrown aside); named according to their form, *kowsh* کوش, without heels, the back part being flattened down under the foot. *Chinauls* چنال , without any back piece, the quarters terminating under the ankles on each side, with raised heels perhaps an inch high.* *Payshawuree* پشاوري , *Ghaytlee* گهيتلي , or *Chāndoree* چاندوڙي .

N. B. Children, in addition to wearing any of the preceding clothes, wear in their infancy what is called a *shulooka* شلوکا , which consists of a couple of pinafores, one worn on the breast, the other on the back, and fastened above and below the shoulders.

IV. A LIST *of* JEWELS *or* ORNAMENTS (زيور يعني گهنا) *worn by Moosulman Women.*†

Ornaments worn on the Head.

Soorij سورج or *Sisp'hool* سس پهول—a large circular beautifully embossed golden ornament, worn on the back part (nearly on the crown) of the head.

Rāktee راکتي—(usually worn by Hindoo women) the same as the preceding. When worn by Moosulman women it

---

* Men usually wear only embroidered shoes; but women have an abundance of various coloured foils, principally purple or green, or the wings of green beetles, fastened down to the body of the vamp (which is of some bright coloured broad-cloth), and serving by the manner in which they are disposed to fill up the pattern of the embroidery. This is either of gold or silver thread, or very small bugles, not dissimilar to seed pearls. Those who cannot afford such decorations, are content with silken ornaments.

† All ornaments worn on the head, ears, nostrils, neck, arms, wrists, and hands, by the respectable classes of people are made of gold; by the lower classes of people, the ear ornament called *dundeean*, and the neck ring called *hunslee*, together with all worn on the arms, wrists, and fingers, are of silver. Butchers (be they ever so rich, and able to afford to have them of gold), durst not make them but of silver. The other ornaments, *viz.* of the loins, ankles, feet, and toes, are by the lower and middling classes of people of silver; but among the nobility of gold. It is inconceivable what some women undergo for the sake of displaying their riches in this way.

is made a quarter of the size, and worn between the preceding and the following one.

Chānd چاند—a semi-lunar golden ornament worn under two others on the head.

Choontee چونٹي—false hair braided together, having a large golden knob or cup above and several smaller ones below, this is plaited with the natural hair of the head. The *choontee* sometimes consists of silk or cotton thread, with which the hair is tied.

Mirza-bay-purwa مرزا بي پروا—three small delicate golden chains, worn as the *teeka*, fixed to the hair by small hooks; the lower hanging ends being either set or not with precious stones.

Māng مانگ or *Māngputtee* مانگ پٹي —a golden ornament worn over the line on the top of the head where the hair is parted, reaching to the back part of the head.

Teeka ٹيکا or *Māng-teeka* مانگ ٹيکا—any golden ornament worn on the forehead, whether it be a single round one set with precious stones fixed on or glued to the centre of the forehead, or one hanging from the parting of the hair to the spot between the eyes. This frontal ornament has usually a star or radiated centre, of about two inches in diameter, set in gold, and richly ornamented with small pearls, of which various chains are attached, aiding to support it in its position on the centre of the forehead. A triple or quadruple row of pearls passes up the centre of the *māng*, or the part where the hair is parted; the hair being divided and kept down very flat. The centre piece (and occasionally each end piece also) is composed of precious stones, such as topaz, emerald, ruby, amethyst, &c. Sometimes the centre is of one colour and all the rays of some other; or the latter are alternate. Thus the *māng-teeka* is not a very light ornament, but it is extremely splendid, and being generally set in gold often very valuable. One of a very ordinary description will cost full twelve or fifteen guineas, though composed of coloured glass or crystal, or foils. When made of precious stones, the price may reach to any extent.

Surra-surree سراسري—(a Hindoo ornament). An elegant and delicate golden ornament, which forms two semi-circles, bordering the edge of the hair parted in a similar manner to each side.

1. Ornaments worn on the Ears.

European ladies are content with one appendage at each ear, while the females of Hindoostan think it impossible to have too many.

Kurrunp'hool كرن پهول—a gold ornament, having a star or radiated centre of about an inch and a half in diameter, sometimes richly ornamented with precious stones. It is fixed into the lobe of the ear both by the usual mode of piercing, and by a chain (*sunkulee*) of gold passing over the ear, so as to bear the weight of the *kurrun-p'hool* and *jhoomka*, which would else cause the lobe to be greatly extended downwards. It is however to be remarked, that most of the inferior women have large holes in that part of the ear, wide enough to pass a finger through (and the *Arwee* [Malabar] women on the Coromandel coast, especially at Madras, large enough to pass a ring an inch and a half in diameter). Even the higher orders consider an aperture, such as would admit a pea, rather honourable than otherwise, from its indicating the great weight and consequent value of their jewels.

Jhoomka جهمكا—is always of solid gold, and consists of a hollow hemisphere or bell, curiously fillagreed, and about an inch in diameter. The edges suspend small rods or pendants of gold, each furnished with one or more small pearls, garnets, &c., sometimes a dozen or two pendants being attached to the circumference of each *jhoomka*, sometimes suspending a hundred pearls. In the upper part is a small perforated stud, sometimes ornamented, through which a ring about the thickness of a fine knitting needle, and not less than half an inch in diameter, is inserted, it previously passing through the ear in the part usually pierced. This ring, like every other fastening made to pass through the ears or nose, is of the purest gold. It is so pliant, that the little hook made at one end, by bending the wire to fix it into a minute loop or eye formed at the other end by twisting it, may be straightened at pleasure by means of the nail only. In general however the *jhoomka* is fixed to the lower edge of the *kurrunp'hool.*

Sunkulee سنکلي—or gold chains (sometimes ornamented with pearls) which support the ears and its appendages.

Kullus کلس.

Boogray بُگڑي—(a Hindoo ornament).

Pātan پاتان—lit. leaves, because resembling them, worn in any part of the ear except in the lobe and the little ear.

B'hādooreean بهادريان or *Dundeean* ڈنڈيان—these which comprehend a number of small rings of pure gold, or in case of poverty of silver, or even of tin, are affixed, all along the border of the ear, which is pierced for that purpose. The number worn is from four to eleven, generally the latter: that is to say in one ear, the left having invariaby one less.

Moorkeean مرکيان—or a small *jhoomka*, worn in the little ear.

Morneean مورنيان—the same as *baysur* (nose orn.) worn on the top of the ear.

Alloluq الولق.

Ooddrāj اُدراج—stone ear-rings.

Hulqa حلقہ or *Door* دُر—a ring worn on the little ear.
Kān Bāoolee کان باولي .
Long لونگ .
Punk'hā پنکھا .
Much-ch'hee مچھی .

2. Ornaments worn on the Nose.

The nose has its share in the decoration of the Hindoostanee ladies, and bears several ornaments.

Nut'h نتھ—an ornament passed through the left nostril, consists of a piece of gold wire as thick as a small knitting needle, with the usual hook and eye, and furnished at the centre, or nearly so, with several garnets, pearls, &c., perhaps to the number of seven or more, separated by a thin plate of gold, having generally serrated or scolloped edges, and being fixed transversely upon the wire, which passes through their centres, as well as through the garnets, pearls, &c. The common diameter of the circle of a *nut'h* is from one inch and a half to two and a half. On the coast of Coromandel a somewhat similar ornament is worn in each ear by men of respectability (called *pogool*. Vide Index).

Boolāq بلاق—of these there are two varieties, viz. *boolāq* and *chānd kay boolāq*. The *boolāq* is a nasal trinket, flat, in form not unlike that article of furniture called a footman, and has at its narrowest part a couple of eyes. It is appended to the middle septum or centre cartilage of the nose, by means of a gold screw passed through an orifice in it. The ornament lays flat upon the upper lip, having its broad end furnished with pendants of pearls, and its surface set with precious stones.

Baysur بيسر or *Mōrnee* موريني—worn on the right nostril. Those who wear this ornament and the next are nick-named *baysur-wālee* and *p'hoollee-wālee*.

P'hoollee پھلي—this ornament, like the *baysur*, is invariably worn on the right wing of the nose.

Nut'hnee نتهني—a small ring worn on the left nostril by children.

3. Ornaments worn round the Neck.

The neck is not forgotten among those lavish decorations, of which the native ladies are so fond. It is furnished with various kinds of necklaces.

Luch-ch'hā * لچها—a necklace worn tight round the neck, formed of gold beads (called *munka* منكا), and *pote* پوت (or glass beads).

Hulla هلا or *Neembolee* نيمبولي—the same as the preceding, but longer and hanging down.

Chowkree چوكري—an ornament worn tight round the neck, formed of stars of gold, strung on three black silk or wire threads, with *kalee-pote* † or black glass beads filling up the interstices.

Jignee جگني—a small semilunar ornament worn in the centre of a string of beads, &c.

Pudduck پدك.

Jow-un Mālā جون مالا.

Chundun-hār چندن هار or *Nowsur-hār* نوسرهار.

Mohun-mālā موهن مالا.

Gulsayree گلسري.

Chowsayree چوسري—not unlike the *bāzoo-bund*, but worn tight round the neck and hooked behind.

Chumpā-kullee چنپا كلي—this is made of separate rays, each intended to represent the unblown flowers of the chumpa (Michelia champaca, *Lin.*), to the number of from forty to eighty or more, strung together. This orna-

---

* The *luch-ch'ha*, *gulsayree*, *nut'h*, and *bunggree*, are four ornaments quite essential to matrimony. Even the poorest cannot enter the connubial state without having them.

† *Pote* or glass beads. Of these three varieties are in use, viz. *kālee-pote* or black glass beads, most generally used; *hurree pote* or green glass beads; and *lal pote* or *lal deeān* red glass beads; the former cast into a round shape, the latter cut.

ment is usually worn rather loose, that it may reach half way down the bosom. The mounting is gold or silver, according to the means of the wearer, and the rays or flower-buds are in imitation of the *māng-teeka;* either crystals set in foils, chiefly white, or precious stones of one colour, throughout the ornament; or, it is wholly composed of gold.

Dooluree دلڑي—lit. two strings. Two rows of small round gold beads (*munkay*) threaded on silk. When the ornament consists of three rows, it is called *tee-luree;* of four, *chāoo-luree;* of five, *puch-luree* or *pānch-luree.*

Toolsee تلسي—nearly the same as the *doo-luree*, except that instead of the gold beads being round they are of an octagonal shape.

Poorneeā kay Gulsayree پرنيا كي گلسري.

Towq توق *Hans* هانس or *Huns-lee* هنسلي—is a solid collar of gold or silver, weighing from four ounces to nearly a pound. The latter must be highly oppressive to the wearer, especially as they are only used on high days and holidays; the general standard may be computed at about six or seven ounces. Being made of pure metal, they are easily bent, so as to be put on and off. They are commonly square in front under the chin for several inches, and taper off gradually to not more than half their greatest diameter, terminating at each end with a small knob, cut into a polygonal form. This ornament is sometimes carved in the oriental style, either through the whole length, or only on the front.

Munkeeān ka hār منكيان كا هار or *Har* هار—or necklace, of pearls, large gold beads (*munkay*), corals, garnets, &c.

Puttā پتا— .

Tāweez تاويز—most of the Hindoostanee women wear round their necks, strung upon black silk thread, *tāweezes*, which are silver cases enclosing either quotations from the *Qoran*, some mystical writings, or some animal or vegetable substance. Whatever may be the contents, great reliance is placed on their efficacy in repelling disease and averting the influence of witchcraft (*jădoo*), of which the people of India, of every sect, entertain the greatest apprehension. Hence it is not uncommon to see half a dozen or more of these charms strung upon the same thread; sometimes with the addition of *bughna* بگهنا, or the teeth and nails of a tiger, which are hung round the neck of a child. Vide p. 356.

4. Ornaments worn on the Upper Arm, or Armlets.

Bhooj-bund بهج بند or *Băzoo-bund* بازوبند—a trinket adorned with semicircular ornaments made hollow, but filled up with melted rosin. The ends are furnished with loops of the same metal, generally silver, and secured by silken skeins.

D*holnay* ڈهولني.

Băoota باوٹي—on ornamented gold ring.

5. Ornaments worn round the Wrist, or Bracelets.

The wrists are always profusely decorated.

Kurră کڑا—a ring worn on the wrist, ankle, &c. a massive ring of solid silver, weighing from three to four ounces. These rings are commonly hexagonal or octagonal, of an equal thickness throughout, and terminated by a knob at each end, the same as in the *hunslee*. This ornament being of pure metal, may be opened sufficiently to be put on or off at pleasure; the ends being brought together by an easy pressure of the other hand.

Kunggun کنگن—*Ek-hara*, K. and *Do-hara*, K.

Powncheeăn پهنچیان—*Ăg kay p'hool kay P.* and *Luhsun kay phănk kay P.*; a bracelet formed of small pointed prisms of solid silver, or hollow of gold filled with melted rosin, each about the size of a very large barley corn, and having a ring soldered to its bottom. These prisms are strung upon black silk as close as their pointed or perhaps rounded ends will admit, in three or four parallel rows, and then fastened.

Puttree پتري—gilt brass rings, a quarter of an inch broad: from one to four are worn on each wrist. Should they wear *bunggrees*, only a couple of these are worn, one on each side of the *bunggrees*.

Choor چوڑ—an ornament consisting of several *puttrees* joined together.

Mungguttee منگتي.

Ale ايل.

To-rray توڑي

Bunggreeān بنگريان—they consist of thin rings made of different coloured glass, and worn on the wrists. They are universally worn by the women in the Deccan, and their fitting closely to the wrist is considered as a mark of delicacy and beauty; for they must of course be passed over the hand. In doing this the fingers are cracked and the hand well squeezed, to soften and mould it into a smaller compass; and a girl seldom escapes without drawing blood and rubbing part of the skin from her hand. Every well dressed woman has a number of these rings on each arm. The usual number is from ten to sixteen. If they wear other golden ornaments along with them they are fewer, if not, a greater number, agreeably to fancy; but invariably one more on one wrist than the other.

Chooreeān چوڑيان—*bangles* or rings made of sealing-wax (*lac*), and ornamented with various coloured tinsel. Also called *Nuqday ka jora*.

Himbalay—worn along with *bunggrees*, singly, and next to the body.

Astur—worn singly, and next to the hand.

6. Ornaments worn on the Fingers, or Rings.

Unggothee انگوٹهي or *Ch'hāp* چهاپ—rings of various sorts

and sizes worn on any finger, generally of gold, those of silver being considered mean.

Ārsee آرسي or *Āeena* آينه—or looking-glass. The thumb of each hand has a ring which fits close, having a small mirror about the size of a halfpenny fixed upon it by the centre, so as to accord with the back of the thumb. The *āeena* should be of gold; but on account of the quantity of gold required wherein to set the glass, many content themselves with silver mounting. That a small looking-glass may at times be commodiously situated at the back of the thumb, will not be disputed; but what shall be said of that preposterous custom which Europeans have witnessed, of wearing a similar ornament on each great toe.

Unggooshtān انگشتان or *Huddeeāroo* هديارو—a particular kind of ring, an inch broad, worn on the thumbs, only during the wedding days, or for six or twelve months after, when it is melted down and converted into any thing else.

Ch'hullay چهلي *Kungnee ke Ch'hullay*, *Kunkree ke beej ke Ch'hullay*, *Sāday Ch'hullay*—usually about the fifth of an inch broad, very thin, and for the most part with bended edges.

7. Ornaments worn round the Waist or Loins.

Kummur-puttā كمرپتا or *Sāda-puttee* ساده پٿي—i. e. plain, or a simple flat ring, one inch and a half broad, which encircles the waist, being carved at the ends where they are hooked.

Kummur-sāl كمرسال or *Koorsān ka puttee*—consisting of small square tablets two inches broad, which are carved and fixed by hinges, worn as the preceding.

Zur-kummur زركمر.

8. Ornaments worn round the Ankles (Anklets) and Feet.

Lool لول.

To-rray توڑي—an ornament like a chain.

Pyn-jun پينجن—little bells fastened round the feet of children.

Pāel پايل.

Pāezēb پاي زيب—consists of heavy rings of silver resembling a horse's cub chain, set with a fringe of small spherical bells, all of which tinkle at every motion of the limb.

Maynhdee مينهدي.

Ghoonggroo گهنگرو—are of two kinds, viz. 1. *Ammeeneeān* امنيان; 2. *Ch'huglee Ghoonggroo* چهگلي گهنگرو.

Ku-rrā کڑا—rings of silver, made very substantial, not weighing less than half a pound each.

9. Ornaments worn on the Toes.

Anwut انوٹ—a ring furnished with little bells, and worn on the great toe.

Bich'hway بچهوي or *Kooireeān* کويڑيان—rings worn round the toes, and attached along each side of the foot to the *pāee-zeb*.

Chitkeeān چٹکيان.

Ch'hullay چهلي—is like the one of the same name worn on the thumb. This is worn on the great toe.

Muttay مٹي—a Hindoo ornament.

Besides the preceding, there is an ornament which covers the pudendum in young girls, made generally in the shape of a vine leaf, and suspended to a string tied round the waist.

V. MOOSULMAN COOKERY,

(including the various Dishes alluded to in this Work).

1. Polaoos پلاو.

Polaoo Yekhnee, vulgo, *Ak'hnee Pillaoo* يخني پلاو or *K'hara Polaoo*—the common kind is prepared with rice, meat, ghee, *duhee* (or curdled milk), and spices; such as *shah zeeree* (a variety of the cummin seed), cardamomums, cloves, cinnamon, *dhunneea* (or coriander seed), and *kōtmeer* (or the leaves of the coriander plant), black pepper, green ginger, onions, garlic, and salt. A good receipt for it is as follows: Take half a *seer* of mutton, four or five onions (whole), one piece of green ginger, two dried cassia leaves (*tayj-pat*), eight corns of black pepper, six *seers* (or twelve pounds) of water; boil these together in an earthen vessel, until one and a half or two seers of fluid remain; take the pot off the fire, mash the meat, &c. with the liquor, and strain it through a towel. Set aside this *yekhnee* (or broth). Take rice one *poa* (eight ounces), wash it well and dry it by squeezing it firmly in a towel. Put one *poa ghee* (or butter) into a saucepan or tinned copper vessel and melt it; fry in it a handful of onions sliced longitudinally, and when they have acquired a red colour, take them out and lay them aside. In the *ghee* which remains, fry slightly a fowl which has previously been boiled in a half or one *seer* of water, then take out the fowl, and in the same *ghee* add the dried rice, and fry it a little. As the *ghee* evaporates add the above broth to it, and boil the rice in it. Then put into it ten or twelve cloves, ten or twelve peppercorns, four pieces of mace, ten or twelve lesser cardamoms, all whole; one dessert spoonful of salt, one piece of green ginger cut into fanciful slices, and two *tayjpat* or dried cassia leaves. When the rice is sufficiently boiled, remove all, except a very little fire from underneath and place it on the top of the brass cover. If the rice be at all hard, add a very little water to it and stir it about, and put the fowl also now in to imbibe a flavour. On serving it up, place the fowl on a dish and cover it over with the rice, garnishing the latter with two or four hard boiled eggs cut into two; and the fried onions.

Qoorma Polaoo قورما پلاؤ—as the preceding, except that the meat is cut into very thin slices.

Meetha Polaoo ميٹھا پلاؤ—made of rice, sugar, *ghee*, aromatics; and instead of ginger, aniseed.

Moozāfur Polaoo مزعفر پلاؤ or *Shushrunga Polaoo* ششرنگا پلاؤ—as *Moozāfur Shola*, but not so watery.

Tāree Polaoo تاڑي پلاؤ—rice, meat, turmeric, and *ghee*.

Sooee Polaoo سوئي پلاؤ—prepared with the addition of *sooee* or dill seed.

Much-ch'hee or *Māhee Polaoo* مچهي يا ماهي پلاؤ—same as *yekhnee*, but substituting fish for the meat.

Umlee Polaoo املي پلاؤ—as *yekhnee*, with the addition of tamarind.

Dumpokht Polaoo دم پخت پلاؤ—as *yekhnee*, but when nearly ready adding the *ghee* and giving *dum*, (*i. e.* leaving it closed up with hot embers put both below and above it, till the moisture be evaporated).

Zurda Polaoo زرده پلاؤ—as the preceding, with the addition of saffron.

Kookoo Polaoo كوكو پلاؤ .

Moala Polaoo معلي پلاؤ .

Dogosha Polaoo دوگوشه پلاؤ—rice, meat, *ghee*, and spices; making it excessively hot with the spices.

Polaoo-e-Mugzeeat پلاؤ مغزيات—to *meetha polaoo* add kernels of fruits (such as almonds, pistachio nuts, &c.).

Moozāfurshola مزعفرشوله—made with rice, saffron, milk, rose-water, and sugar, of a thin consistence: it is very cooling.

Birreeānee برياني—as *qoorma polaoo*, with marrow and plenty of spices, and the addition of limes, cream, and milk; or take raw meat one *seer* (two pounds), cover it with *duhee*, ginger, garlic, and salt, and set it aside for three hours in a covered vessel. Fry four *pice* weight (two ounces) of onions sliced, in one and a half *pow* (twelve ounces) of *ghee* in an earthen pot; take out the fried onions and three quarters of the *ghee*, fry half the meat in the *ghee*, and take it off the fire; boil one *seer* (two pounds) of rice in water. On the fried meat scatter half the boiled rice, sprinkle some spices and onions over, and pour a little of the *ghee* into it; repeat the layers of meat, rice, spices, onions, and *ghee* as before. Afterwards pour a little milk over the whole, sufficient to soften the rice; make the earthen pot air-tight with flour,* and cook it on a charcoal fire.

Mootunjun Polaoo متنجن پلاؤ—rice, meat, sugar, *ghee*. Sometimes adding pine-apples or nuts.

Kush or *Huleem Polaoo* كش يا حليم پلاؤ *Boont Polaoo* بونت پلاؤ—or *Chunnay kay Dal* (or Bengal horse gram) *kay Polaoo*, made of wheat, meat, and spices.

Lubnee Polaoo لبني پلاؤ—prepared in a silver dish; cream, kernels, sugarcandy, *ghee*, rice, spices, particularly aniseed.

Jāmun Polaoo جامن پلاؤ .

Teetur Polaoo تيتر پلاؤ—as *yekhnee*, but with the meat of the partridge, (Tetrao cinerea, *Lin.*)

Butayr Polaoo بٹير پلاؤ—as the preceding, but with quails, (Tetrao coturnis. *Buch.*)

Kofta Polaoo كوفتہ پلاؤ .

K'hāree Thoollee كهاري تهولي—meat with *sooiee* or *moong dal.*

K'hāree Chukoleean كهاري چكوليان—meat, vermicelli, and green (*kuchcha*) *dal.*

2. K'HICHREE كهچڑي—commonly made thus: Take one *poa* (four ounces) *sona* or *hurree moong kay dāl*, (Phaseolus aureus, *Roxb.* Phaseolus radiatus, *Lin.*) green gram or rayed kidney-bean; fry it a little with a small quantity of *ghee* or butter in an earthen vessel to impart a nice smell to it, this is called *bug'harna*, or to season; then moisten it, by sprinkling a little water on it

* The flour best adapted for this purpose is *māsh ka ātā.* Phaseolus max, *Willd.* or black gram.

while on the fire; after, boil it in one and a half *pow* (twelve ounces) of water in a tinned copper vessel. When pretty soft (though not quite so), take it off the fire. Put two *ch'huttacks* (four ounces) of *ghee* or butter into another tinned copper vessel, and when melted, throw into it a handful of onions peeled and sliced lengthways; continue frying them until they acquire a fine red colour: then take them out and lay aside. To the remaining *ghee* put one *poa* (eight ounces) of rice properly washed and fry it a little; then add the *dāl* with the water in which it was boiled, and two pieces of green ginger cut into slices. When the water has nearly evaporated, remove part of the fire from below and place it on the brass cover taking the pot occasionally off the fire and shaking it, which is called *dum dayna:* but before so doing add to the rice ten or twelve cloves, one or two large pieces of mace, ten or twelve pepper corns, two dried cassia leaves, a dessert spoonful of salt, and cover it up. This is what is termed *suffeid,* or white *k'hichree.* When required of a fine yellow colour, add a little pounded turmeric about the quantity of the size of a pea to it, at the time that the *dāl* is added. When served up, ornament it with four hard boiled eggs, and the above fried onions, as in the case of the *polaoo.*

Oobālee K'hichree ابالي كهچڙي—rice and *dāl*, *gurrum*, and all *thunda mussāla*, Gloss. (except *chillies*, or kyan-pepper) and salt.

Kush K'hichree كش كهچڙي—as the preceding, with the addition of meat.

Bhoonee K'hichree بهوني كهچڙي—as the following, but with more *ghee.*

Bughāree K'hichree بگهاري كهچڙي or *Quboolee K'hichree* قبولي كهچڙي—as *Oobālā K.* but with *ghee.*

K'hichrā كهچڙا—rice, wheat, and as many kinds of *dāl* as are procurable; such as *toowur*, *chunnay*, *moong*, *lobay*, *buller*, *mussoor*, &c.

Shola شولہ—*k'hichree* with meat.

Shoortāwā شرتاوا—*k'hichree* without meat, but made thin.

3. CHAWUL چاول or RICE (RAW).

Khooshka خشکہ or *Bhāt* بہات—boiled rice.

Oobālay Chāwul ابالي چاول—i. e. paddy (or rice in the husk) parboiled and dried in the sun, afterwards winnowed and boiled for use. It is much used by the natives, who prefer it to the other kinds, as it has a richer flavour.

Toorānā ترانا (*Panto-bhat*, Beng.) or *Bāsee K'hānā* باسي کہانا—boiled rice kept in cold water over night, and used next morning, when it will have acquired an acid taste. Much in use among the poorer classes.

Chulāoo or *Bughārā Khooshka* چلاؤ یا بگہارا خشکہ.

Gooluhtee گلہتی—or rice boiled to a pap, with the addition of *ghee;* recommended to patients labouring under bowel complaints, being considered easy of digestion.

Jāwā جاوا *Owgrā* اوغرا or *Gunjee* گنجي—rice gruel; commonly called by Europeans *conjee*.

4. ROTEE روٹي OR BREADS.

a. Leavened:

Nān نان or *Rotee Māa-tulun* روٹي معہ تلن—or leavened bread, baked in an oven, but using leaven instead of yeast.

Bāqurkhānee Nān باقرخاني نان—differing from the preceding merely in shape.

Gāoodeeda گاودیدہ—of a round shape.

Gāoozubān گاوزبان—of a long shape, resembling neat's tongue.

Sheermāl شیرمال—a sweet bread.

Girda گردہ or *Nān Dākhilu* نان داخلہ—of a large and round form.

Qoors قرص—likewise round.

P'hoolkay پہلکي *Khumeer P'hoolkay* خمیر پہلکي or *Nān Pāoo* نان پاو—small and flat.

Khumeeree Rotee خميري روٹي—the bread, used by Europeans, made with yeast.

b. Unleavened:

Rotee روٹي—wheaten cakes toasted on an earthen or iron dish or plate. The term is generally, but improperly, applied to leavened as well as unleavened bread.

Chupāteeān چپاٹیاں—thin wheaten cakes; the same as *rotee*, but considerably thinner.

Sumosay سموسي—three-cornered *rotee.*

Meethay Pooreeān میٹھا پوریاں.

P'heekay Pooreeān پھیکي پوریاں.

Poorun kay Pooreeān پورن کي پوریاں.

K'hujoorān کھجوران—sweet bread: wheat flour, poppy seed, sugar, and *k'hoprū*, mixed up with water, cut into small pieces and fried.

Sutpoortee Rotee ستپرتي روٹي—made of layers of *chupāteeān* one upon another, with every alternate one besmeared with *ghee* and sprinkled with sugar, united at the edges and fried in *ghee*, or toasted on an earthen or iron dish.

P'hayneeān پھینیاں—as the preceding, but smaller in size and without sugar.

Pārātay پاراٹي—like *chupāteeān*, but somewhat thicker.

Mootkoolay مٹکلي—wheat flour paste, sweetened and formed into a long shape by pressing with the closed fist, boiled in steam, *i. e.* placed on straw in a pot with water, (boiled dumplings).

Buldār بلدار—wheaten cakes with *ghee* in separate layers, like our pastry.

Sohālee سہالي—wheat flour kneaded with water, made into very thin cakes and fried in *ghee.*

Pooreeān پوریاں—a kind of cakes fried in *ghee*; three varieties, viz. fruit, meat, and *dāl* patties.

Loong Chirray لونگ چڑي or *Baysun-kee Rotee* بیسن کي

روتي—a kind of cake made of powdered Bengal horse-gram, either fried or not.

Bhayjeeay بهجئي—fried cakes.

Muthee Rotee مثهي روتي or *Qowaymāq* قويماق—made of flour, white of eggs, and onions, fried in *ghee*.

Other varieties are :

Chulpuck چلپک.

Cheela چيلا.

Khārā or *Meethā Rotee* كهارا يا ميتها روتي.

Undon kee Rotee انڈون كي روتي.

Goolgoollay گلگلي.

Duhee Burray دهي بڙي or *Māūsh Duhee* ماش دهي.

Row-gundar روغندار—with plenty of *ghee* in it.

Seekh Rotee سيخ روتي—(vide p. 267.)

5. Kubab كباب Kabobs—Cut meat into thin long pieces, dry them in the sun, and roast them by placing them on live coals, or fry them in *ghee*.

Kooftay kay Kubāb كوفتي كي كباب—meat hashed. Add all the warm and cold spices (Gloss.) except tamarind, and pound them well in a wooden mortar, then form them into flat cakes, and fry them in *ghee*.

Tikkay kay Kubāb تكي كي كباب—lumps of meat, with spices and without tamarind, as in the preceding, fried in plenty of *ghee*.

Moosumun مسمن.

Hoseinee Kubāb حسيني كباب—pieces of meat with salt and lime juice toasted over a fire.

Shāmee Kubāb شامي كباب—chopped meat, with all the aromatics, and all *thundā* (Gloss.) spices (except *chillies* and tamarind) green ginger and lime juice, made of a particular shape a finger thick, fried in *ghee*.

Kulleejāy kā Kubāb كليجي كا كباب—liver, heart, and kidneys, cut into small pieces, trussed on skewers, with salt, and roasted.

Luddoo Kubāb لدّو كباب — chopped meat, with all *gurm* and *thundā mussāla* (Gloss.) or aromatics and spices, green ginger and lemon juice, formed into balls and roasted on the fire. To be surrounded with thread, to prevent their falling asunder.

Seekh Kubāb سيخ كباب—like *luddoo k.* but with more *kyan* pepper, cut into thin long pieces like dried dates, fried in *ghee*.

Putthur kay Kubāb پتهر كي كباب—used on a journey: they light a fire on a stone and remove it when the latter is well heated, and then roast slices of meat on it.

Much-ch'hee kay Kubāb مچهي كي كباب—or fish kabob.

Quleeu قليه—broiled flesh or meat dressed with any thing, usually eaten with *polaoo*.

6. SALUN سالن or *Sālnā* سالنا—curries. Put any meat, properly washed in water, into an earthen or metallic vessel, and either let it boil in its own juice (which will be sufficient if the meat be tender), or add a little water; then add *ghee* and spices, and stir it well.*

---

* The following is a more general recipe for making good curries: Take of *ghee* or butter, 2 *ch'huttaks* (or 4 ounces; or half that quantity if the meat be fat, or the curry wanted dry); onions, 1 *ch'huttak* (2 ounces); garlic, 2 or 3 cloves; turmeric, cummin seed, coriander seed, of each 1 *tola* (3 drams); red chillies (cayenne pepper), 3 in number; black pepper, 4 or 5 corns; green ginger, $\frac{1}{4}$ *ch'huttak* ($\frac{1}{2}$ ounce); salt, a tea-spoonful. The spices are all to be separately ground on a *sil* (a stone in use for the purpose, resembling an oil-man's grinder and muller, but rough), adding a little water when the substance is dry; the coriander seed to be previously toasted a little to impart to it an agreeable smell. Put the *ghee* into an earthen pot, or a tinned copper sauce-pan, and fry half the quantity of the onions, sliced lengthways, in it, and when they have acquired a yellow-brown colour take them off and set them aside. Then add to the remaining *ghee* the meat mixed up with all the spices, and cover it up. Occasionally uncover it, and (before the meat is sufficiently done) as the *ghee* evaporates, sprinkle a table-spoonful of water on it; if much gravy be required, a proportionate quantity of water is to be added, but the drier a curry is the nicer it tastes. *Do-peeaza*, and others, have no

Sālun of *Qoormā* قورما—use chopped meat, add some water, all *gurm* and *thunda mussalas*, (Gloss.) tamarind and *ghee*.

Do. of *Do-peeāza* دوپيازه—meat cut into pieces; in other respects as the preceding.

Do. of *Nurgis* نرگس.

Do. of *Bādāmee* بادامي.

Do. of *Shubdayg* شبديگ.

Do. of *Dālcha* دالچه—meat, *dāl* (*chunna* or *moong*), with or without *brinjal*.

Do. of *Kut ka Sālun* كٹ كاسالن—decoction of Madras-horse-gram (*kooltee ka kut*): boil it until it be a good deal evaporated; if still too thin add some pounded rice, and all the aromatics and spices. Fry onions in *ghee* seven or twelve times, and add them successively to the decoction. This among the great is boiled till it becomes sufficiently consolidated to form balls, which keep good six months or a year; and when required for use, a ball is placed on hot *polaoo* or rice, which causes it to melt and run over the rice. It is very rich, but delicious.

K'huttā كهٹا *K'hārā* كهارا or *Meethee Much-ch'hee ka sālun* ميٹهي مچهي كا سالن—put all the different aromatics and spices into tamarind water, add the fish to it, and cook as other *curries*. A second method is to add the *ghee* after instead of before.

Koolmā كلما.

Cheelā چيلا—omelet, with all the spices (no tamarind).

Baysun kee Birreeān بيسن كي پڑيان—*toowur*, *moong*, *hur-*

---

gravy at all. The addition of the following articles is sometimes had recourse to to increase the flavour, *viz*. dried cassia leaves (*tejpat*), dried kernel of the cocoa-nut, or the essence of the cocoa-nut, procured by rubbing rasped cocoa-nut with water through a coarse towel, tamarind water, green or dried mangoes and other fruits, lemon-grass, fenugreek (*matyhee*) seed, the leaves of which likewise, if added, improve a curry amazingly.

burra (or *chunna*), or *lobay-sāg*, add to them (no aromatics, but) all the spices (no tamarind), onions and its leaves chopped ; put into a mortar and pound them, form balls and dry them. When required make curry of them.

Sirrā or *Kullay* or *Nuhāree ka Salun* سرا يا كلي يا نهاري كا سالن—sheep's head, made as *do-peeāza*.

Kuleejay ka Sālun كليجي كا سالن—sheep's head, along with the liver of the sheep.

Meethāy Gosht ka Sālun ميٹهي گوشت كا سالن يا قليه سادة—as *do-peeaāz* but without tamarind, يا تركاري ڈالا هوا or with the addition of vegetables.

Botee ka or *Antree ka Sālun* بوتي كا يا انتري كا سالن—as the preceding, using tripes and the mesentery, &c. instead of the flesh.

Meethee Dāl ميٹهي دال—*dāl* boiled soft, with the addition principally of cinnamon and cardamoms as well as the other aromatics and spices (without tamarind), *bugar* as other curries.

K'huttee Dāl كهٹي دال—as the preceding, but with tamarind.

Khāgeena or *Khāriz* خاگينه يا خارز—melt *ghee* in a pot, add all the varieties of aromatics and spices, plenty of onions, and breaking eggs one by one add them to it, stirring them well together.

Burrā بڑا—all kinds of *dāl*, and flour, with aromatics and spices (not tamarind), made into balls and fried in *ghee*.

Chumkooree kee birreeān چمكوري كي بريان.

Qeemu قيمه.

Jhingay ka Sālun جهنگي كا سالن—or shrimp curry.

Kurway K'heeree, or *Kuporay ka Sālun* كروي كهيري يا كپوري كا سالن.

Tullay Muchch'hee تلي مچهي—or fried fish.

Sālun تركاري كا سالن—curries made of *turkāree* or esculent vegetables; such as garden stuffs, large legumes, small pulses, &c., and a number of pot vegetables but little known to Europeans; and of *bhājee* بهاجي or *sāg* ساگ greens. First fry the onions in *ghee*, then add the vegetables or greens and spices. N. B. If there be too much salt, tamarind, or *chillies*, they do not keep good long; as for other spices being more or less, it does not signify.

Sālun of *Bygun* بيگن يا بينگن کا سالن—or *brinzal.* Solanum melongena, *Lin.* or egg plant.

Do. of *Torāee* ترئي کا سالن or توراي—cucumis acutangulus, *Lin.* or acute-angled cucumber.

Do. of *Chichoonday* چچونڈي کا سالن or چچنڈا يا چيچوندا or *Pottōl* (Beng.), *Pulwul* (Hind.)—trichosanthes anguina, *Lin.* (trichosanthes dioica, *Roxb.*) or common snake gourd.

Do. of *Kuraylay* کريلي کا سالن—momordica charantia, *Lin.* or hairy momordica; three varieties in use.

Do. of *Gownwār* or *Mutkee kay P'hulleeān* گنوار يا مٹکي کي پهلي کا سالن—dolichos sabæformis, *Lin.*

Do. of *Saym kee P'hulleeān* سيم کي پهلي کا سالن—dolichos lablab, *Lin.* or black-seeded dolichos; several varieties used.

Do. of *Bhayndee* بهينڈي کا سالن—hibiscus esculentus, *Lin.* eatable hibiscus, or bandaky.

Do. of *Aloo* آلو—solanum tuberosum, *Willd.* or potatoe.

Do. of *Rut Āloo* رتآلو کا سالن—dioscorea sativa, *Lin.* or common yam.

Do. of *Pend Āloo* پنڈ آلو کا سالن—convolvulus batatas, tuberous bind-weed, country or sweet potatoe; skirrets of Peru, or Spanish potatoe.

Do. of *Māt kee Bhājee* مات کي بهاجي—amaranthus tristis, *Lin.* roundheaded amaranth, (amaranthus oleraceus, *Heyne*), or eatable amaranth.

Do. of *Āmbāree kee Bhājee* انبارٹکي بهاجي—hibiscus cannabinus, *Lin.* or ozeille greens, (hibiscus sabdariffa, *Willd.*) Indian hibiscus or red sorrel.

Sālun of *Maythee kee Bhājee* میتھي كي بهاجي—trigonella fœnum græcum, *Lin.* or fenugreek greens.

Do. of *Sooee Chookay kee Bhājee* سوي چوكيكي بهاجي—anethum graveolens, *Lin.* or dill greens.

Do. of *Ghōl* or *Khoorfa kee Bhājee* گهول يا خرفه كي بهاجي—portulaca oleracea, *Lin.* purple, garden or small purslane.

Do. of *Kurrum kee Bhājee* كرم كي بهاجي—or cabbage curry.

Do. of *Ārwee* اروي كا سالن—caladium esculentum, *Ventenat.* or esculent caladium.

Do. of *Hureea Kuddoo* هريا كدو كا سالن—cucurbita lagenaria, *Lin.* green pumpkin, or bottle gourd.

Do. of *Meethee Kuddoo* ميٿهي كدو كا سالن—cucurbita hispida, *Thunb.* (cucurbita melopepo, *Willd.*) red pumpkin, or squash gourd.

Do. of *Shulgum* شلغم كا سالن—or turnip.

Do. of *Peeāz* پياز كا سالن—or onion.

Do. of *Mirch* مرچ كا سالن—capsicum frutescens, *Willd.* or chilly.

Do. of *Chiggur* چگر كا سالن.

Do. of *Chowlāee* چولائي كي بهاجي—amaranthus polygamus, *Lin.* or hermaphrodite amaranth.

Do. of *Āmbotee* انبوتي كي بهاجي—oxalis corniculata, *Lin.* procumbent oxalis, or yellow wood sorrel.

Do. of *Poklay* پوكلي كي بهاجي.

Do. of *Kāhoo* كاهو كي بهاجي—lactuta sativa, *Lin.* or lettuce.

Do. of *Kāsnee* كاسني كي بهاجي—chichorium endivia, *Lin.* or endive.

Do. of *Jumkooray* جمكوري كي بهاجي.

Do. of *Lāl Sāg* لال ساگ—amaranthus gangeticus, *Roxb.*

Do. of *Pāluk ka Sāg* پالك كا ساگ—or a species of spinage.

Sālun of *Chundun Butway* چندن بتوي كي بهاجي .

Do. of *K'huttee Chun-wul* كهتي چنول كي بهاجي .

Do. of *Kuchchoo* كچو كا سالن—arum colocasia, *Roxb.* or Egyptian arum ; and innumerable others.

The following is an excellent receipt for *curry powder* : Take of powdered *huldee* or turmeric twenty tea-spoonfuls, red dried *chillies* or Cayenne pepper eight tea-spoonfuls, *dhunneea* or coriander seed, *zeera* or cummin seed, *tayjpāt* or dried cassia leaves, of each twelve tea spoonfuls, and mix them together.

7. SHEERNEE شيريني Sweets.

Meetha Pooreean ميٹها پوريان—between two thin wheaten cakes insert pounded *sohaleean*, *khoprā*, *goor*, *khush-khush*, and kernels, and fried in *ghee*.

Khara Pooreean كهارا پوريان—meat chopped with *gurm* and *thunda mussala* between two cakes as above, and fried in *ghee*.

N. B. If one cake be folded double it is called *kunola* كنولا , and not *pooree* پوري .

Feernee فيرني—*soojee*, sugar, milk, *ghee*, cardamoms, cloves, aniseed, boiled in syrup made of the milk and sugar (or *goor*), and fried in the *ghee*.

Sheerbirrinj or *K'heer* شيربرنج يا كهير—rice parboiled in water, is again boiled in milk, adding sugar, spices, and kernels.

Mulāee ملائي or *K'howā* كهوا—cream or milk inspissated by boiling.

Hulwā حلوا—*soojee*, one *seer* fried in *ghee* (q. s.) half *seer*, add syrup two or three *seers*, *k'hopra* three *tolas*, and spices (not quite one *tola*), viz. cinnamon one stick, ten cloves, ten cardamoms, and a little aniseed, and mix over a fire.

Fālooda فالوده—same as *hulwū*, except that the *soojee* is boiled in milk, and when still somewhat soft, poured into a dish. As it cools and hardens, it is cut into square pieces.

Punbhutta پن بهتا—a kind of drink made from rice.

Moorubbā مربا or *Goor-āmba* گرانب—cut mangoes into thin slices and boil in syrup (adding water if required); when soft put them into melted *ghee*.

Āfshoru or *Ābshoru* افشره یا ابشوره commonly called *Āb-shola*—lemonade, or a species of negus without the wine, made with the juice extracted from pomegranates, quinces, lemons, oranges, and other fruits or plants. *Batāsha* is sometimes substituted for the sugar. Some dissolve in it perfumed cakes made of the best Damask fruit, containing also an infusion of some drops of rose-water. Another kind is made of violets, honey, juice of raisins, &c. It is well calculated for assuaging thirst, as the acidity is agreeably blended with sweetness. It resembles, indeed, those fruits which we find so grateful when one is thirsty.

Shurbut شربت—sugar and water, or eau sucré, with sometimes the addition of aniseed and cardamoms.

Sheera شیره—or syrup, made of sugar, with sometimes the addition of wheat flour, milk, *ghee*, and dried cocoanuts, resembling thick treacle, and is eaten with bread dipped into it.

Seekunjebeen سکنجبین—oxymel of vinegar and honey; or lime juice, or other acid, mixed with sugar and honey.

Goolgoollay گلگلي—wheat flour, sugar (and *tyar* or *duhee*), with anise and cardamom seeds made into dumplings, and fried in *ghee*.

Muleeda or *Māleeda* مليده يا ماليده—pounded *rotee*, or wheaten cakes, with *ghee*, sugar, aniseed, and cardamoms, all well mixed up.

Hurreera حريره—*soojee*, sugar, milk, and water, aniseed, and cardamoms, boiled to a thin consistence.

Meethee Thoollee ميٹهي تهولي—as *hulwā*, but with the addition of milk, and of a thinner consistency.

Surrolay سرولي—wheat flour, *ghee*, sugar, poppyseed, dates, and almonds, made into a paste and formed into little pieces between the fingers, and boiled in milk.

Sayweeān سيويان—or vermicelli boiled in milk,&c. as *surrolay*.

8. Meethaee مٹهاي or Sweetmeats.

Luddoo لڈو—a kind of sweetmeat made chiefly of sugar, with the addition of cocoanut kernel rasped and cream, and formed into the shape of large boluses or grape shot.

Doodh payra دوده پيڑا—a sweetmeat made of sugar, milk (or cream), and rice or wheat flour.

Julaybee جليبي.

Butāshā بتاشا—a kind of sweetmeat or sugar cakes of a spongy texture (or filled with air, as the word implies).

Khājā كهاجا—a sweetmeat like piecrust.

Eelāchee Dānā الاچي دانا
Rayooreeān ريوڑيان.
Burfee برفي.
Nookteeān نكتيان or
Bondeeān بونديان.
Dur-bayhaysht دربهشت.
Meethay Sayoo ميٹهي سيو.
Shukur-pāray شكرپاري.
Sāboonee صابوني.
Nuqōl نُقل or *Nuqoldana*.
Imrutee امرتي.
Hulwā-e-Sohun حلواسوهن.
Pup-ree پپڑي.
Undursā اندرسا.
Puttee پٹي.
Goordhānee گڑدهاني.
Gōnd گوند.

9. Toorshee ترشي Acids.

Āchār اچار or pickles, *Āām** *kā Āchār* آم كا اچار or mango

---

* Or, rather Ambuh, as in the following couplet:

انب فرستاد حسن خان بمن *Ambuh firristad Hussun Khanbumun*

انبتہ اللہ نباتاً حسن *Ambutuhoollah Nubatun Hussun.*

a play upon words, of which the following version will convey an idea:

A *man-go* Mr. Fair did send to me,
Go-man, thank Him who made so *fair* a tree.

pickle—mangoes (green) about three hundred, divide into two, take out the stones and dry in the sun for three days. Take turmeric nine *pice* weight (four ounces and a half), garlic nine *tolas* (three ounces and three drams), salt three *pukka seer* (six pounds), mustard seed three *pice* weight (one ounce and a half), coriander seed, toasted, three *pice* weight (one ounce and a half); mix the spices together, and lay the mixture in alternate layers with the mangoes, and add *gingilie* oil twenty-four *tolas* weight (nine ounces), or as much as will cover them.

Duhee دهي—curds, or curdled milk. Warm milk on a slow fire (so as not to boil) till the cream which collects on the surface acquires a reddish hue, then take it off the fire, and while still lukewarm add a little stale *duhee* (or tyar), tamarind, or lime juice.

Meethee Chutnee میٹھي چٹني—or a condiment made of green *chillies*, salt, garlic, *kotmeer* (or the leaves of the coriander plant), and green ginger. The following are most excellent receipts for preparing two varieties of it.

1. Dehli, or celestial *Chutnee*: Take of green mangoes one *seer*, raisins one *seer*, mustard seed one *seer*, green ginger one *seer*, garlic one *seer*, onions (none) or half a *seer*, dried red *chillies* half to one *seer*, moist or soft sugar one to two *seers*, salt one *seer*, white wine vinegar four *seers* (or bottles). The ginger, garlic, and onions are to be peeled, and together with the *chillies* are to be cut into thin slices previously to being pounded; the mustard seed to be washed and dried, then gently bruised and winnowed; the raisins to be washed and freed from the stones; the sugar to be made into a thick syrup; the mangoes to be picked of their rinds, cut into thin slices (some boil them in three bottles of the vinegar, adding the fourth when mixing them up with

the other ingredients) and pounded; the remaining articles are to be separately pounded, and then the whole is to be incorporated, put into a stone jar, well closed, and placed in the sun for a month or two. If put into a glass bottle, it is occasionally to be put out in the sun. It will keep good for years.

2. Love-apple *Chutnee*: Take of love-apple (solanum lycopersicum, *Lin.*) a large platefull, the rinds and seeds to be rejected, and only the pulp used; dried salt-fish cut very fine (as if rasped), a piece about two inches square; six onions cut into thin longitudinal slices; eighteen green *chillies* chopped fine, dried tamarind two *pice* weight (or one ounce), mashed up in about three or four ounces of water (stones and fibres to be rejected); salt a teaspoonful, *ghee* or butter five *pice* weight (or two ounces and a half). First put the *ghee* into a tinned copper vessel placed on the fire, when it is melted add the onions, and as the latter begin to assume a reddish hue add the *chillies*, stirring them well for five minutes; then add the salt fish, and continue stirring the whole: when the *ghee* has nearly evaporated add the love-apples, and stir it about for a good while; lastly, add the tamarind water and salt, and mix the composition well until it acquires a pretty dry consistence (like that of *brinzal-chutnee* or *sāmbāl*). This *chutnee* is only for immediate use, and will not keep above a day or two.

K'huttee Chutnee كهتي چتني—dry *chillies*, salt, tamarind, onions, garlic, and *kotmeer*.

Boorānee بوراني—a kind of food consisting of the fruit of the egg plant (*byn-gun*) fried in sour milk.

Ch'hāch kee Kurree چهاچ كي كڙي—soak rice in water, pound it, mix it with *tyar*; add cold spices, and stir about till it acquires a thick consistence.

K'huttay Ch'hāch kee Kurree كهتي چهاچ كي كڙي—add tamarind to melted *ghee*, one or two kinds of *dāl* flour, as that of *chunna* or *toowur*, and the cold spices as in the preceding.

Baysun kee Kurree بيسن كي كڑي—mix three or four kinds of *dāl* flour with water, add tamarind and spices, &c. as in the preceding.

Unday kee Kurree انڈي كي كڑي—as *khuttay kurree*, wtih the addition of eggs previously fried in *ghee*.

Noor Quleea نور قليه or *Kurug* كرگ.

Rāeetā رايتا—boil pumpkin in water; take *duhee*, break it up a little, mix with all the varieties of (cold) spices and mustard seed, and add the pumpkin. This is what is called *kuch-chā rāeetā*; if *bugar* be given it becomes *pukka rāeetā*.

Chār چار—or *moloogoo-tunny* Tam., *lit.* pepper-water (corrupted into *mullikatawny*).

VI. MUSICAL BANDS AND INSTRUMENTS.

1. Nutway ka Taefa نٹويكا طايف.

This *tāefa* or band consists of male performers, commonly employed by great men, as kings, princes, and the nobility, to attend them when they promenade or take an airing. It consists of the following instruments:

Seetār ستار—or a sort of guitar made of wood, without any holes on the board, and mounted with from five to seven steel wires, all of which are used in playing, and that with both hands. (Vide *Sārungee*).

Moor-chung مرچنگ—or jew's harp.

Duff ڈف—which consists of a wooden dish or plate, covered with leather, and is about a foot (or somewhat less) in diameter.

Theekree ٹهيكري—consists of two pieces of wood, one held between the fore and middle finger, the other between the middle and ring finger of the left hand; while with the thumb and middle finger of the right hand the ends of the sticks on the outside of the hand are made to strike against each other, producing the same sound as castanets.

2. Kunchnee ka Taefa كنچني كا طايفہ.

This band is employed by princes and the nobility on feast days, &c. All the instruments are played upon by men, except the fifth, which are worn by women, who dance and sing; and their number is never less than three, nor more than five. The instruments are as follows:

Poonggee پونگي—or drone, consisting of a dried pumpkin (cucurbita lagenaria, *Willd.*), with a single or double bamboo tube attached to it, having eight holes, and played upon as a flageolet. The tone is altered to a higher or lower pitch by stopping the holes with wax, or by means of the fingers; in the former case occasioning a momentary pause.

Meerdung مردنگ or *Nurgă*—a kind of long drum, differing from the common *d'hol* (or drum) in being much longer, and broader in the centre than at either end.

Jhănjh جہانجہ or *Munjeera* منجيرا—consists of two small brass cups tied together with a string, and played upon by striking one against the other.

Ghugree گہگري—resembling the rings used by *tappal* or *dawk*-men and bearers on their sticks. They are fitted on the right thumb, are made thick and hollow, containing shots, which by shaking produce a rattling sound. If large, only one is used; if small, two.

Ghoongroo گہنگرو—consists of numerous small brass jingling bells or hollow balls fastened to a string, which is twisted round both the ankles of female dancers.

Sărung سارنگ or *Sărungee* سارنگي, also called *Tumbooră* تنبورا—much resembling the *seetăr*, with this difference, that although it has seven strings only one is played upon, and that with the right hand, the left not being used at all; and there are holes on the board.

3. Baja ka Taefa باجا کا طایف.

This band, commonly called *bājā-bujuntur*, is an indispensable one at weddings: no marriage can take place without it; the poorest are obliged to engage it. It consists of the following instruments:

D'hōl ڈھول—or drum, one foot two inches long, and eight inches in diameter.

Shuhnāee شہنای—two of different kinds are invariably used together; the first, without finger holes, two feet long and half an inch in diameter at the upper part of the tube, and four inches below, producing one tone, and serving as a bass; while the other, a foot and a half long, three-quarters of an inch in diameter above, and four inches and a half below, with holes, is played upon like a clarionet.

Bānkā بانکا—a kind of trumpet made of brass.

Qurnā قرنا—a kind of French horn, made of brass.

Jhānjh جہانجھ or *Munjeera* منجیرا—as beforementioned.

The preceding are the principal *tāeefas* (or bands), but there are others which have different appellations, though the performers make use of some of the abovementioned instruments; such as

Bhānd ka Tāefa بہانڈ کا طایف—or mimic's band, which consists of men dancing (in women's clothes), clapping their hands, and several making an uniform sound as a bass, while others sing. The only instrument they use is a *dholuk* ڈھولک or small drum, sometimes adding the *munjeera*.

Bhugteeon ka Tāefa بہگتیونکا طایف—as used by *bhāgōte* (or stage actors). They use the *meerdung* or *nurgā*, the *sārungee* or *tumboora*, and the *munjeerā*.

Quwal قوال—a set of male musicians, who sit, sing, and play on the *sārungee* or *tumboora* or *dholuk*.

Domneeān ڈومنیان or *Meerāshneeān* میراشنیان—females who only sing in presence of women, and play, sitting, upon the *dholuk* and *munjeerā*. They only use one *dholuk*, while the *munjeerā* may be increased to four in number. They receive a rupee a piece for their performances. They are of a particular caste, and follow that profession from generation to generation. This band is likewise termed *mooshāta ka tāefa* مشاط کا طایفہ .

Hijron ka Tāefa ھجڑونکا طایفہ—or band of eunuchs. A set of eunuchs dance and sing, playing on the *dholuk* and *munjeerā*.

Zunnāna ka Tāefa زنانہ کا طایفہ—or seraglio-band. Men personifying women dance and sing, playing on the *meerdung*, or *dholuk* and *munjeerā*.

Lowndon ka Tāefa لونڈونکا طایفہ—handsome boys (sometimes of respectable people) dressed up in women's clothes, whom they personate, and from whom they are with difficulty distinguished, dance and sing, while male performers play on the *meerdung*, *nurgā* or *dholuk*, and *sārungee*, *tumboora* and *munjeerā*.

Arbānee عرباني—or men who sing and play on the *duff* and *surōde*, or on the *rubāb* and *duff* or *dāirā*.

A List of Musical Instruments from the Keetab-e-Moosuqee کتاب موسقي .

Wind Instruments.

Zufeeree زفیري .

Puttee پتي—a leaf of the *cholum* (holcus saccharatus, *Lin.*) held between the lips and sounded.

Moorchung مرچنگ—or jew's harp.

Shuhnāee شہناي—a kind of clarionet, a cubit long, and having a leaf mouth-piece, vulgarly called *soornāee* سرناي

Soor سر—a bass or drone to the *shuhnāee*.

Algoza الغوزه—a small flageolet, a span long.

Nāgaysur ناگیسر .

Poonggee پونگي—of this there are two varieties, one made of leather, and sometimes accompanies the *kunchnee ka tāefa*; the other of pumpkin, usually played upon by jugglers and snake dancers, &c.

Qurnā قرنا—a straight or curved horn, twelve feet long. (Vide *bājā ka tāeefa*).

Toorree ترُي or *Toortooree* ترُترُي—commonly denominated by Europeans *collery horn*, consists of three pieces fixed into one another, of a semicircular shape.

Bānkā بانکا—as the preceding one, but the upper piece turned from the performer, forming it into the shape of the letter S.

Bāns-lee بانسلي—or flute.

Sunkh سنکھ—or conchshell. It is frequently used by devotees; also as an accompaniment to the *tumkee*. Sometimes they play trios and quartettos on the shells alone.

Nursingā نرسنگا—a sort of horn.

DRUMS, GUITARS, CYMBALS, CASTANETS, &c. &c.

Chitkee چٹکي—or snapping the fingers.

Tālee تالي—or clapping the hands.

Khunjuree خنجري—a sort of small tambourin, played upon with the fingers.

Duff دف or *Duffrā* دفڑا—or tambour de basque; "tympanum," according to Gentius, *Sadi Rosar. Polit.* p. 303. A sort of bass tambourin played upon with a stick.

Dāeerā دایرا—the largest variety of tambourin, being from a foot and a half to two feet in diameter, played upon with a stick.

Dhōl ڈھول—a larger drum than the following, both sides covered with leather, and played upon with the hands.

D'*holuk* ڈھولک or D*holkee* ڈھولکي—smaller than the preceding, and only one side covered with leather.

Meerdung مردنگ—the kind of drum which is an accompaniment to the *kuncheeān ka tāefa*, q. v.

Pukhāwuj پکھاوج—a kind of drum, a timbrel.

Tubla طبلہ—a couple of drums, played upon at the same time, one with each hand.

Nurgā نرغا.

Nuqāra نقارہ—or a kettledrum.

Ghurreeāl گھڑیال—a plate of brass for beating time.

Tukkoray تکوري or *Zayrbum* زيربم—or small kettledrums; one is called *zayr*, the other *bum*.

D*unkā* ڈنکا—or a bass kettle drum, middle size, between the *nuqāra* and *tukkoray*.

Tāsa طاسہ or *Tasha Murfā* طاشہ مرفا—a drum of a semicircular shape, played upon with two sticks, and invariably accompanied by the next (*murfā*).

Murfā مرفا—a drum like a *d'hōl*, covered at both ends with leather, but played upon only on one side with a stick.

Tubul تبل—an enormously large variety of drum, used in the field of battle.

Tumkee ٹمکي—a small circular brass plate, played on by striking it with a piece of wood, having a knob at the end.

Dhubboos دھبوس—consists of a rod of iron about a foot long, with a knob at one end and a sharp point at the other, having from fifty to a hundred hollow rings, which when shook rattle against one another: used by *fuqeers*, who wield it about, striking their abdomen of a sudden with the sharp point.

G'hurrā گھڑا—or empty earthen vessels, or water-pots, played upon with the hand.

ستار or *Yek Tāra* يکتارا—when with one steel wire, called by the latter name: sometimes it has nine or eleven steel wires; but generally three, whence its name, from سه three, and تار string.

Tumboora طنبورہ—a sort of *seetār* (guitar), having catgut strings instead of wire.

Sārung سارنگ or *Sārungee* سارنگي—a musical instrument like a fiddle, played upon with a bow.

Rubāb رباب—a kind of violin, a rebeck.

Been بين or *Vina*—a sort of *seetār*, but having two dried hollow pumpkins (cucurbita melopépo, *Willd.*) fixed to the end of it, with five or seven steel strings; described by Sir Wm. Jones in the Asiat. Res.

Keenggree كينگري—as the preceding, but having three or four pumpkins, and only two steel strings; generally used by Hindoos.

Qānoon—a species of dulcimer, or harp.

Urgunoon ارغنون—a kind of organ.

Rāgmālā راگ مالا.

Chukārā چكارا—a kind of violin.

Thālee تهالي—a flat earthen dish, on which they rub and rattle a stick with both hands.

Theekree ٹهيكري—two bits of sticks or fragments of earthen vessels used as castanets.

Doroo دورو—a small double-headed hand drum.

Surod سرود—a kind of guitar (or *seetār*), having catgut or silk strings.

Dupprā ڈپرا.

Munjeera منجيرا or *Jhānjh* جهانجه—a kind of small cymbals in the shape of cups, struck against each other, and accompanying most bands.

Tāl تال—cymbals used by devotees, and frequently an accompaniment to the *tāefus*.

Ghugree گهگري—one or two hollow rings with pebbles in them, worn on one or both thumbs, and rattled.

Ghoonghroo گهنگهرو—little bells fastened to a string, which is wound round the wrists and ankles, and which jingle at every motion of the limbs.

Sāz ساز.

Seekhān سیخان—a piece of iron about a cubit long, with which *fuqeers* pierce their necks and cheeks.

An Arab musical instrument, used by the Arabians who frequent the Malabar coast.

VII. BAZEE بازي OR GAMES.

1. *Shutrunj* شطرنج—or chess.
2. *Chowsur* چوسر or *Tukhta-e-Nurd* تخته نرد—as *pucheesee*, but using *pāsa* (or dice) instead of cowries. The dice are four or six-sided, four inches long and half an inch thick on every side, and are thrown by the hand, not from boxes, and fall lengthways.
3. *Chowpur* چوپڑ—as the preceding, differing merely in the form of the game.
4. *Geeān-chowsur* گیان چوسر.
5. *Gunjeefā* گنجفه or *Tās*—or cards.
6. *Pucheesee* پچیسي— This game is the most popular and celebrated in India (next to chess).*

* It is thus played; the board consists of four rectangles, with their narrow sides so placed as to form a square in the centre (as shewn in plate vii. fig. 2.) Each rectangle is divided into twenty-four small squares, consisting of three rows of eight squares each. It is usually played by four persons, each of whom is furnished with four ivory or wooden cones (called *got* or *gotee*) of a peculiar colour for distinction, and takes his station opposite one of the rectangles. His pieces (or *gotee*) start one by one from the middle row of his own rectangle, beginning at the division next to the large central space. They thence proceed all round the outside rows of the board, passing, of course, through those of the adversaries' rectangles, travelling from right to left (i. e. contrary to the sun) until they get back to the central row from which they started. Any piece is liable, however, to be taken up and thrown back to the beginning, as in backgammon, by any of the adversaries' pieces happening to fall upon its square; except in the case of the twelve privileged squares, which are marked with a cross (see plate); in that case the overtaking piece cannot move from its position. Their motion is determined by the throwing of six or seven cowries (i. e. shells) as dice, which count according as the apertures fall uppermost or not; one aperture up, counts 10; two, 2; three, 3; four, 4; five, 25; six, 30; seven, 12; and if none be turned up, it counts 6. A throw of 25 or 30 gives an additional move of 1. At the last step the

7. *Āthā Chumuk* اتها چمک.
8. *Tāq-jooft* طاق جفت—or the game of odd or even.
9. *Nukk'hā-moot'h* نکها موٹھ or *B'hur-moot'h* بهر موٹھ—somewhat like odd or even.
10. *Chitput* چت پٹ—or wrestling.
11. *Lyay* لئي
12. *Chow-gān* چوگان—a game resembling cricket (or tennis), but played on horseback.
13. *Mudrunggum* مدرنگم—like *mogol putthān* (four tigers and sixteen sheep).
14. *Pāsay* پاسي—or dice of a square and oblong shape, numbered much in the same way as the European dice.
15. *Mogol Putt'hān* مغل پٹهان—played like the game of draughts on a diagram sketched on the ground, or on a board or paper, using sixteen cowries or gravel, pebbles, &c. on each side for men.
16. *Mogdur* مگدر—they frequently make use of violent exercise within doors, with dumb-bells or heavy pieces of wood, not unlike the club of Hercules, weighing from eight to twenty pounds, which they whirl about the head so as to open the chest and strengthen the arms, which may account for their being excellent swordsmen. They stretch themselves at full length upon their hands and feet, kissing the ground hundreds of times, and and nearly touching it with the chest, but without suf-

---

throw must amount exactly to one more than the number of squares left to enable the piece to go into the central space; that is, as we would say, off the board. If it happen to stop on the last square, therefore, it cannot get off until you throw a 25 or 30. The players throw in turns, and each goes on until he throws a 2, 3, or 4, when he loses the lead. If the same number be thrown thrice successively, it does not count. The game is generally played with six cowries, making the highest throw 25 (the six apertures up then counting 12), hence it is termed *pucheesee* (from *puchees*, 25); and the board used is a carpet, ornamented and marked with different colours of cloth sewed on it. It is sometimes played by two persons, each taking the two opposite rectangles with eight pieces, and playing them all from the rectangle next to him: the game continues till three of the players get out. They never play for money.

fering the body to come in contact with it; which occasions a great exertion to the whole frame. This is called *Dund.*

Among the respectable classes, Nos. 1, 2, 3, 4, 5, 6, 11, and 16 above are much played; among the vulgar, Nos. 8, 9, 10, and 13; among the children of the former, Nos. 12, 13, and 14; and among the children of the latter, Nos. 6, 7, 9, and 15.

VIII. لڑکیونکي کهيل CHILDREN'S PLAYS.

Ānk'h-moochānee آنکهہ مچاني—or blindman's buff.

T*ālum-tolā* تالم تولا.

Bāgh-bukree باگهہ بکري lit. Tiger and sheep; Second var. 3 *baghs* (tigers), and 13 *bukrees* (sheep).

Cheel jhuptā چيل جهپٹا—not unlike our "rules of contrary." If a person raise his hands at the call of the word *Guddā p'hurpur* (when he should not do so), he is most immoderately tickled by all the party.

Undhlā bādshāh اندهلا بادشاه—lit. the blind king.

Gillee dundoo گلي ڈنڈو—the game of tip-cat. *Gillee* is the short stick, which is struck by the longer one called *dunda.*

Jhār bāndrā جهاربا ندرا—(*lit.* the tree-monkey; so called from the circumstance of one being mounted on a tree.) or Dab-*dubolee* ڈاب ڈبولي.

Bhooroo ch'hub-ja بهڑو چهب جا or *Ek tārā* or *Do tārā* يک تارا يا دو تارا—something like blindman's buff.

Gulgul kooppay گلگل کپي or *Kooppay-māee* کپي مائي.

Ageel-jhup اگيل جهپ— or marbles; a second var. called *Ekpurree subsurree* consists of chucking a number of marbles into a hole.

Goleeān گوليان—or marbles, played into two holes, the player winning a *pice* or two each time his ball strikes another ball or enters the hole.

Ekkul khwājay اكل خواجي—also played with marbles and two holes, the player counting one each time his ball strikes another ball or goes into a hole; and whoever first counts ten is the winner. The loser is punished in various ways.

Sut k'hooddee ست كهڐي.

Lōn-pāt لون پاٹ.

Hoordoo or *Kubuddee* حرڐو - كبڐي *Torā* or *P'hullā* تورا - پهلا—a game among boys, who divide themselves into two parties, one of which takes its station on one side of a line or ridge called *pala* پالا made on the ground, and the other on the other. One boy, shouting "*Kubuddee kubuddee*," passes this line, and endeavours to touch one of those on the opposite side. If he be able to do this, and to return to his own party, the boy that was so touched is supposed to be slain; that is, he retires from the game. But if the boy who made the assault be seized and unable to return, he dies, or retires in the same manner. The assault is thus made from the two sides alternately, and that party is victorious of which some remain after all their opponents are slain.

Thikkree-mār ٹهكري مار—throwing a *thikkree* (or a fragment of an earthen vessel) so as to glide along the surface of the water.

Boojha-boojhoo بوجها بوجهو—one's eyes are bound up, and he is desired to guess who it was that touched him, and is not unbound till he does guess.

Tookk'hay ٹكهي.

Ghoom گهوم a stick buried in the earth to which a string is previously fastened, and by holding which they run in a circle.

Boontee or *Chundoo* بونتي - چنڈو—2 var. 1st. *Oorān Chundoo* اڑان چنڈو— a cap is thrown up, and whoever gets it pelts the others with it, and they run away. 2d. *Bumā Chundoo* بما چنڈو—a stone is set up against a wall, at which a *chundoo* (or cap) is aimed by each three times; whoever succeeds in throwing it down takes it up and pelts it at the others.

Luttoo لٹو—or tops.

Chukkree or *Chukkee* چکري - چکي—a bandalore; a small reel with a cord fixed to its centre, which winds and unwinds itself alternately by the motion of the hand.

Qāzee moollā قاضي ملا.

Kān chittee or *Suwāree* کان چتي - سواري—or holding by the ears, while the adversary strikes a piece of wood supported on two stones and attempts to throw it down.

P'hissul-bundā پهسل بنڈا—sliding down the smooth banks of a *tank* or river, a sloping stone, or hill.

Ooree mārnā اري مارنا—jumping from a height into a *tank*, well, or river.

Puttung Oorāna پتنگ اوڑانا—*lit.* Flying kites; which latter comprise three varieties. 1. *Kun-kowā* کن کوا in raising which they use silk line. Mrs. M. H. Ali justly observes, vol. ii., p. 14, "they fly kites at all ages. I have seen men in years, even, engaged in this amusement, alike unconscious that they are wasting time, or employing it in pursuits fitted only for children. They are flown from the flat roofs of the houses," (by the lower orders more frequently from a plain or common, or, in fact, from any place) "where it is common with the men to take their seat at sunset. They are much amused by a contest with kites, which is carried on in the following manner. The neighbouring gentlemen, having provided themselves with (silk) lines previously rubbed with paste and covered with pounded glass" (mixed up with any glutinous substance, generally the juice of the pulp of the small aloe plant, aloe perfoliata, *Vera. Lin.*) "raise their kites, which, when brought in contact with each other by a current of air, the topmost string cuts through the under one" (usually the reverse in the hands of an adept in the art, as I know from personal experience), "when down falls the kite, to the evident amusement of the idlers in the streets or roadways, who with shouts and hurrahs seek to gain possession of the toy, with as much avidity as if it were a prize of the greatest value: however, from the numerous competitors, and their great zeal to obtain possession of it, it is usually torn to pieces. Much skill is shewn in the endeavours of each party to keep his string uppermost, by which he is enabled to cut that of his adversary's kite." 2. *Tookkul* تکل—is raised by means of a thin string, and resembles (except in shape) the European kite. 3. *Puttung* or *chung* پتنگ یا چنگ is a large square kite, four feet by five, bent back by thin rattan stays, which produce pleasing sounds, not unlike that of the Æolian harp; it can only be flown in very windy weather, when it sometimes requires more than one person to hold it. It is raised by means of a thin rope instead of twine, and sometimes flown at night, with a lantern fastened to its long tail.

Gop'hin گوپہن—or sling.

G'hirkā گہرکا—a little pole fixed in the ground with another across resting on a pivot; a boy sitting at each end, with his feet touching the ground, whirls round, whereon it makes a creaking noise.

Guddhā guddhee گدھا گدھي—*lit.* jack and jenny-ass.

IX. ATUSHBĀZEE آتش‌بازي OR FIREWORKS.

These in the East are superb. They are of various forms, representing animate and inanimate things; such as trees, tigers, elephants, men, sea-fights, eclipses of the sun and moon, &c.

Putakhā پتاخا—or crackers.

Ch'hooch'hoondree چهچهوندري—a sort of squib held in the hand.

Mahtab مهتاب—or blue lights. 2d. var. *Nuktee Mahtab* نكتي مهتاب.

Goolrayz گلريز or *Kurrayla* كريلا—or matches, with or without stars.

Ahunee Nulla اهني نلا or *Bhooeen Nulla* بهوين نلا—or Roman candle, made of iron, buffalo-horn, or bamboo, placed on the ground. 2d. var. *Dum Nulla* دم نلا—ditto, but with occasional globes of bright light bursting up.

Huth'-nulla هتهه نلا—ditto, but small, held in the hand. 2d. *Phool-jhurree* or *Phukna* پهولجهري يا پهكنا—ditto, with flowers.

Tara Mundul تارا منڈل—like the *Dumnulla*, but ever and anon stars burst up of a sudden.

Huwāee حوائي or *Bān* بان—the common rocket.

Holuqqay حلقي—or rockets with stars.

Hinggun هنگن—a rocket with a small staff.

Nurree نري—rockets without staffs, which run on the ground.

Chukkur-ban چكر بان 1. *Asmanee Ch:* اسماني چكر بان—a piece of bamboo placed horizontally on another fixed in the ground, or held in the hand and whirls round on a pivot. 2d. var. *Bhooeen Ch:* بهوين چكربان—is placed on the ground, and whirls round first to the right and then to the left alternately.

Gotta-khōr غوط خور—or diver; so called, because, being lighted, it is thrown into water (river or tank) when it dives, and every now and then shows itself above water.

Undā انڈا—*lit.* an egg; so called because the composition of the following is put into an egg-shell.

Ānār انار—*lit.* a pomegranate; or *Toobree* توبري flower-pots.

Totā ٹوٹا—or a straight squib. 2d. *Jungee* Totā جنگي ٹوٹا or a bent (serpentine) squib.

Gujga گجگا or *Mayndhul* مینڈھل—a fruit (Guilandina bonduccella, *Lin.*) so called, filled with composition; when lighted it is thrown amidst the crowd. It bursts with an explosion.

Nāriel ناریل—*lit.* cocoa-nut; or *Kuweet* کویٹ—*lit.* wood-apple; so called from the shells of these fruits being filled with the powder. They burst with the report of a gun.

Bich-ch'hoo بچھو—*lit.* Scorpion.

Kāntā کانٹا—a large hollow species of thorn filled with powder and exploded. 2d. var. *Hāthee Kāntā* هاتهي کانٹا—a larger thorn. If a stick be fastened to it it ascends in the air: otherwise it remains on the ground.

Sowkunā kee joree سوکناکي جوڑي—*lit.* rival wives. Two tubes like those of rockets fastened together, which strike each other alternately on the ground.

Dhān دهان— or rice husks filled with powder, with a small staff attached to them.

Erundee ارنڈي—or the shell of castor-oil seed, filled with the powder.

Ungoor kā mundwā انگور کا منڈوا—in imitation of clusters of grapes hanging from a shed.

Shoala شعلہ.

Asman kay Kuweet اسمان کي کویٹ.

Bhoeen champa بهوین چمپا.

Besides these there are many others such as those already alluded to, formed in imitation of natural objects, of which it has not been thought necessary to give any particular description.

GLOSSARY.

A.

Aba عبا—a cloak or habit worn by dervises, &c., very loose and open in front, not unlike a boat-cloak.

Abeer عبير—a grateful perfumed powder. The simplest, and what is most generally used, is composed of rice flour, or the powder of the bark of the mango tree (mangifera indica, *Lin.*) or of the *deoodar* (uvaria longifolia, *Roxb.*) camphor, and aniseed. A superior kind is prepared with powered sandalwood or *uggur* (wood aloes), *kuchoor* (curcuma zerumbet, *Roxb.*) or *ambi huldee* (curcuma zedoaria, *Willd.*), rose flowers, camphor, and civet cat perfume, pounded, sifted, and mixed. The dry powder is rubbed on the face or body, and sprinkled on clothes to scent them. Beejapore is famed for its *randa* or *abeer*.

Abjud ابجد—the name of an arithmetical verse, the letters of which have different powers, from one to one thousand, as follows:

قرشت	سعفص	كلمن	حطي	هوز	ابجد
400 300 200 100	90 80 70 60	50 40 30 20	10 9 8	7 6 5	4 3 2 1

ضظغ	ثخذ
1000 900 800	700 600 500

Ajwaeenee اجوايني vulgo *uchwanee*—is prepared of the following ingredients, viz. *kalee mirch*, piper nigrum, *Lin.* (or black pepper); *pipplee*, piper longum, *Lin.* (or long pepper); *piplamore*, rad. piper long. *Lin.* piper dichotomum, *Rottl.* (root of the long pepper plant); *huldee*, curcuma longa, *Lin.* (or turmeric); *sont*, amomum zingiber, *Lin.* (or dry ginger); *luhsun*, allium sativum, *Lin.* (or garlic); *khoolinjān*, or *kooleejun*, alpinia galanga major, *Rottl.* (or greater galangal); *baee-burrung* (a kind of medicinal seed); *long*, eugenia caryophyllata, *Lin.* (or cloves); *ghōr-butch* or *attivussa* (or a kind of medicinal root); *khorasanee ajwaeen*, hyosciamus niger, *Lin.* (or black henbane); *chooree ajwaeen*, cleome viscosa, *Lin.* (or viscid cleome), of each an equal weight; *ajwaeen*, sison ammi, *Lin.* (or Bishop's weed seed), a weight equal to all the above put together. These, reduced to a fine powder, is given mixed with warm water.

Amal-namu عمال نامہ—from *amal* actions, and *namu* history, (God's) book of remembrance, in which all the good and evil deeds of men are written by the recording angels, *Keeramun* and *Katebeen:* the former, sitting on the right hand of Jehovah, notes down all the good actions; the latter, on the left hand, records the evil deeds.

Arfāt عرفات—a mountain near Mecca, from which, among other ceremonies, the pilgrims make a procession to the holy monument situated on another mountain at a little distance. It was on mount *Arafāt* where the Mohametans imagine Adam, conducted by the angel Gabriel, met Eve, after a separation of two hundred years, in consequence of their disobedience and banishment from Paradise, whence he carried her afterwards to Ceylon. Eastern writers make Adam of a prodigious size; the most moderate giving him the height of a tall palm-tree, whilst others say that his foot was seventy cubits long, and the rest of his body in proportion.

Ātā آٹا—pounded wheat. When sifted it affords *myda* the finer part or wheaten flour, and *soojee* the coarser, q. v.

Azān اذان—or summons to prayer, proclaimed by the *mo-*

wazin (or crier) from the minarets or towers of the mosques. It is the same as the *tukbeer*, q. v. except omitting the sentence *qud qamut sulat.*

B.

Beera or *Beeree* (*pan kay*) پان كي بيڙا يا بيڙي—a parcel made up of betel leaf, &c. called *pansooparee*, q. v.

Bhung بهنگ—the name of an inebriating preparation, made with the leaves of the *ganja* or *bhung* (cannabis sativa, *Willd.* or hemp). It is in a liquid form, and chiefly drank by the Mohummudans and Mahrattas. The following is a recipe for the same.

Take of *siddhee* (hemp) leaves, washed in water, one *tola* (three drams), black pepper four *annas* weight (or forty-five grains), cloves, nutmeg, and mace, of each one *anna* (or eleven and one-fifth grains) weight: triturate the leaves and other ingredients with one *pao* (eight ounces) of water, milk, or the juice of water-melon seed, or cucumber seed, strain and drink the liquor. It is usually employed without the spices; the latter rendering it highly inebriating. It is a very intoxicating draught.

Bismilla بسم الله—or "In the name of God;" an ejaculation frequently used by Mohummudans, especially when going to commence any thing. At the beginning of the chapters of the *Qoran*, and indeed prefixed to almost every Arabic, Persian, or Turkish book, is the following line:

بســــــــــــــــــــــــــــــــــــم الله الرحمن الرحيم

Bismillah hirruhman nirruheem, "In the name of God, the merciful, the compassionate," generally extending, either for ornament or mystery, the connecting stroke between م and س to an uncommon length.

Boza or *Boja* بوزا يا بوجا—is the name of a fermented liquor obtained from a grain called *ragee* راگي, alias *munruwee* منڑوي (cynosurus corocanus, *Lin.*), or *juwar*, alias *jaree* (holcus saccharatus, *Lin.*) great millet, fermented with *neem kay ch'hal* (bark of the margosa tree (melia azadirachta, *Lin.*), and further made intoxicating by the addition of *bichnag* بچناگ or poison root. It somewhat resembles country beer, and is chiefly used in the higher provinces of India.

Bundugee بندگي—a mode of salutation. Vide *Sulam*, in Gloss.

C.

Chiksu چکسہ—a perfumed powder, composed of a variety of odoriferous substances. The following is an elegant recipe for the same:

Take of *surson kay beej* سرسونکي بيج or sinapis dichotoma, *Roxb.* a kind of mustard seed; or *kown-ar kay beej* کنوارکي بيج aloe perfoliata, *Lin.* or aloe plant seed; or *bunnolay*, or *kupas kay beej* بنولي يا کپاس کي بيج gossypium herbaceum, *Lin.* or cotton seed; of any one of these a quarter of a *seer* or eight ounces: of *gayhoon kay ata* گيهونکي آٹا triticum *Lin.* or wheat flour; or *chunnay ka ata* چنيکا آٹا cicer arienatum, *Lin.* or powdered Bengal horse gram, of either a quarter of a *seer* or eight ounces: *maythee* ميتهي trigonella fœnum græcum, *Lin.* or fenugreek seed; and *gheoonla* or *gewla* گهيونلا, of each a quarter of a *seer* or eight ounces: *ambee-huldee* انبي هلدي curcuma zedoaria, *Roxb.* or turmeric-coloured zedoary, one-eighth of a *seer* or four ounces: *nagur-motha* ناگرموتها cyperus juncifolius, or cyperus pertenuis, *Roxb.* or rush-leaved cyperus, four *tolas* or one ounce and a half: *khush-khush* خشخش papaver somniferum, *Lin.* or poppy seed; *sundul* سندل santalum album, *Lin.* or sandal wood; *sundul ka putta* سندلکا پتا folium santal. alb. *Lin.* or sandal wood leaves, of each two *tolas* or six drams: *kuchoor* کچور curcuma zerumbet, *Roxb.* or zerumbet zedoary; *putchapan* پچپان; *bawuncheean* باونچیان; *balay kee jur* بالیکي جر andropodon muricatum, *Kœnig.* or cusscuss root; *ubruk* ابرک or mica (erroneously called talc); *bagnuk* or *nuckholay* باگنک یا نکھولي; *put'hur kay phool*, بتھر کي پھول lichen rotundatus, *Lin.* or rock lichen, of each one *tola* or three drams: *kafoor* کافور laurus camphora, *Lin.* or camphor, quarter of a *tola* or forty-five grains: *sonf* سونف pimpinella anisum, *Lin.* or aniseed, half a *tola* or one dram and a half: *ood*, عود styrax benzoin or benzoin (vulgo benjamin); *eelachee* الاچي amomum cardamomum, *Lin.* or cardamoms; *long* لونگ eugenia caryophylla, *Lin.* or cloves; *darcheenee* دارچیني laurus cinnamomum, *Lin.* or cinnamon, of each a quarter of a *tola*, or forty-five grains; *jap'hul* جاپھل myristica moschata, *Wood.* or nutmeg: *jowtree* جوتري myristica moschata, *Wood.* or mace, of each two *masha*, or thirty grains. The *maythee* is first to be toasted with any of the first three kinds of seed, then well dried, pounded and sifted, and mixed with the other ingredients, which are likewise to be previously reduced to a fine powder and sifted. In using this powder it is generally mixed up with *phool-ail ka tail* (or sweet scented oil), instead of water. The poorer classes of people, when many of the above substances are not procurable, prepare the *chiksa* with only a few of them.

Choorway چُڑوي—paddy, (*i. e.* rice in the husk), well soaked in water, is dried in the sun; then toasted in an earthen pot till one or two begin to burst open, after which it is pounded in a wooden mortar and winnowed.

Chukkur چکر—a weapon, resembling a quoit in size and shape, used principally by the Sikhs, consisting of an iron ring with a sharp edge, which they throw with great dexterity, and usually carry several of them on the head, fastened to the hair.

Chukoleean alias *Sootreean* چکولیان یا ستریان—a dish consisting of wheat flour made into paste, formed into small cakes, and boiled in water together with meat, *gurm* and *t'hunda mussala*,* and salt.

Churus چرس—the exudation of the flowers of hemp collected with the dew, and prepared for use as an intoxicating drug. A man covers himself with a blanket and runs through a field of hemp early in the morning; the dew and gum of the plant naturally adhering to it, these are first scraped off, and the blanket afterwards washed and wrung. Both products are boiled together, and an electuary formed. The quantity of five grains, placed above the *goorakoo* (q. v.) and smoked, proves speedily intoxicating.

Circumcision—The operation, as practised by natives in India, is performed in the following manner: a bit of stick is used as a probe, and carried round and round between the glans and prepuce, to ascertain that no unnatural adhesions exist, and to ascertain the exact extent of the frœnum; then the foreskin is drawn forwards, and a pair of forceps, consisting of a couple of pieces of split bamboos (five or six inches long and a quarter of an inch thick), tied firmly together at one end with a string to the extent of an inch, applied from above in an oblique direction, so as to exclude about one inch and a half of the prepuce above and three-quarters of an inch below: the forceps severely grasping it, occasions a considerable degree of pain; but this state of suffering does not continue long, since the next thing to be done

* *Gurm mussala* گرم مصالح or warm spices, includes pepper, cloves, mace, cinnamon, cardamoms, *shah zeera* (cuminum cyminum, *Var.*), and *cubeb cheenee*, cubebs; *Thundu mussala* ٹھنڈا مصالح—or cold spices, comprises chillies, onions, garlic, ginger, turmeric, coriander and cummin seed, tamarind, &c.

is the removal, which is executed by one stroke of the razor (drawn directly downwards). The hæmorrhage which follows is inconsiderable, and readily stopped by the application of burnt rags or ashes; over this is put a pledget, with an ointment prepared of *dammer* (or country rosin) and gingilie oil. (Ol. Sesam. Oriental.) I have seen adults undergoing this operation for phymosis, who were required by the native practitioners to confine themselves to their beds for ten or fifteen days. The applications to the wounds in these cases were various. The most common practice was to fumigate the wound daily with the smoke of benjamin, and apply the ashes of burnt rags, which were sometimes kept on for three days. I found the wound heal much more kindly and rapidly by our common dressings of white ointment or Turner's cerate.

D.

Daee داي—there are four kinds of *Daees*, viz. 1. *Daee junnaee*, a midwife; commonly called simply *Daee*. 2. *Daee doodh-pillaee*, a wet-nurse; commonly denominated by the familiar term *Anna*. 3. *Daee k'hillaee*, a dry nurse, or a nursery maid; commonly called *Ch'ho-ch'ho*. 4. *Daee asseel*, a maid servant, or a lady's maid; commonly called merely *Asseel* or *Mama*. A midwife generally receives as her fee for attending upon a woman at her lying-in, from the nobility, jewels to the value of twenty or twenty-five rupees; a suit of clothes, consisting of a *lungga*, a *saree*, and a *cholee*, or an *eezar*, a *peshwaz*, an *unggeean*, a *koortee*, a *doputta*, and about ten or twelve rupees in money: from the middling classes, a *saree*, a *cholee*, and five or ten rupees: and from the poorer classes, one and a quarter to two and a half rupees, and sometimes a *cholee* in addition; or, in addition to a rupee, her lap is filled with *pansooparee*, as a trifling recompense in return for, and emblematic of, her having filled the mother's lap with the infant. Another statement, more especially applicable to a particular part of the country (Hydrabad). 1. Nobility :—A suit of clothes, value from twenty-five to one hundred rupees; cash, fifty to one hundred rupees; jewels, one to one hundred rupees worth, with sometimes a pension of ten or twelve rupees per mensem for life. Her salary, during the period of suckling, is from four to ten rupees per month, exclusive of food, which among the great is very sumptuous, that is, so long as the infant enjoys good health; the moment, however, it becomes ill, they get displeased with her, and make her live as low, comparatively, as she lived high before; a change which is very little relished. They are very particular in the choice of a *wet nurse:* they take none but a respectable woman of their own caste, and one who is married; for they suppose the child to acquire the temper and disposition of the nurse. She has three meals a day, which, though constituting part of the dinner cooked for the family, costs from seven to ten rupees per month extra. She moreover receives presents at different feasts, such as at the two great ones, viz. *Eed-ool-fitr* and *Buqr-eed;* and at the minor ones of *Akhree char shoomba* and *Shub-e-burat*, as well as at the anniversary of the child's birth, and at his marriage. The present consists of four or five rupees, with or without victuals, a *saree* and a *cholee*, to the value of four or five rupees. 2. Middling class :—Salary, six or seven rupees per mensem; plenty of the daily food of the family. On dismissing her, a suit of clothes of from ten to twenty rupees, and in cash eight or ten rupees: no ornaments. 3. Poorer orders, have also nurses from among people of the lowest caste. Moosulman children are generally suckled till they are two years and a half old, which, agreeably to the *Shurra*, is the period within which the wet nurse is considered as the child's foster-mother. (Vide p. 145.) If a child suck another woman during that time, she is not his foster mother. It is not unusual to see children of three and four years hanging about their mother's breasts. The females among the nobility scarcely ever suckle their own offspring, but employ a nurse, for they consider it weakening, and detrimental to the beauty of their form. The diet which is considered wholesome for the wet-nurse consists in the following: *polaoo*, *birreeanee*, fish, *khoorfay ka bhajee* (portulaca oleracea, *Lin.* or purslane), *ambotee kay bhajee* (oxalis corniculata, *Lin.* or yellow wood sorrel), *paluk kay bhajee* (or spinage), *chookay kee bhajee* (rumex vesicarius, *Lin.* or country sorrel), and cabbage. Those which are considered unwholesome, and to be refrained from, are the following: *bygun* (solanum melongena, *Lin.* brinjal or egg plant), *ambaree kee bhajee* (hibiscus cannabinus, *Lin.* or ozeille, erroneously called in Bengal sorrel), *maat kay bhajee*, or *sada noteea* (amaranthus tristis, *Lin.*), *kurayla* (momordica charantia, *Lin.*), *maythee kee bhajee* (trigonella fœnum græcum, *Lin.* or fenugreek greens). None of the *dals* (or peas) are good except *moong* (phaseolus radiatus, *Lin.* phaseolus aureus, *Roxb.* green gram, or rayed kidney bean), and cooling articles, such as cucumbers, carrots, turnips, and potatoes.

Dal ڈال—a round flat ornament, of the size and shape of a crown piece, made of stone, bone, or mother-of-pearl, worn by *fuqeers* round the right ankle, suspended by means of silk thread, which is passed through a couple of holes. The ornament itself hangs immediately below the outer ankle-bone.

Domneean ڈومنیان—the females of a low caste of Moosulmans called *dom* دوم, who sing and play in the company of females only. The instruments they play on are the *dhōl* (or a kind of drum), and *munjeeray* (or a kind of cymbals).

Dozanoo bythna دوزانو بیٹھنا—*lit.* sitting on two knees, or kneeling; it is different, however, from the European mode of kneeling: they rest the body, or sit upon the left foot placed horizontally with the sole turned upwards, while the right foot is placed perpendicularly, with the great toe touching the ground and heel up, the hands resting on the thighs. In repeating prayers in this position, the eyes are directed to the region of the heart. I may observe, that the right foot is never moved from its original position, while the left is altered to the vertical in the act of making *sijdah* (or touching the ground with the forehead), and placed again in its horizontal posture, when the person praying sits on the sole of it.

Dumree دمڑي—a small copper coin current in the Carnatic, four of which go to a *pice*.

Dur-gah درگاه—a tomb or shrine. There are two noted ones of this kind near and at Mangalore. The first is situated at the village of Cuddry (two miles off), and called *Sheikh Furreed ka Durgah.* It consists of a hole in the centre of the side of a perpendicular rock composed of laterite, which is said to lead to a considerable distance (they say all the way to Hydrabad, 450 miles). The opening is square, about six feet above the ground, ascended by a flight of stone steps rudely constructed, and just large enough to allow of a person to crawl in. The cavern is very dark, and no one knows the exact size of it, as none dare venture in. Adjoining is a chasm in the rock, and of inconsiderable size, which at its entrance has been built up with stone, and an opening left for people to creep in by as in the other; but this is found open within (or exposed to the air) after it is once entered. Tradition states that, about one hundred years ago (this being A. D. 1832), there was a peer named *Sheikh Furreed*, who likewise made another similar *chilla* (*i. e.* neither speaking, eating, nor drinking for forty days, but worshipping God and living retired from the world) in Hindoostan. He resided at Cuddry for twelve years, during which time he used to observe *chillas*, remaining for forty days together in the cavern, seeing and speaking to nobody, eating and drinking nothing; after the forty days were over, he was wont to come out for four or five days, but partake of no other food but the leaves of a plant (since named after him), *furreed-bootee* (the latter word signifying a medicinal herb), a sort of shrub which grows wild in the surrounding jungles, and has a sweetish taste: he drank water, spoke during these days, said prayers in an adjoining stone building, and then retired again to this cavern to perform another forty days *chilla*, and so on. At the end of twelve years he disappeared, and it is said, this being the road to Mecca, that he set out for that town by this subterraneous route, and has never been heard of since. Moosulmans resort hither occasionally, and on Fridays (their sabbath) cook victuals, and having offered *fateeha* over them while burning incense in his name, distribute them among the *fuqeers* resident there, as well as those who have accompanied them. If a *durgah* be situated in a place where no food can be dressed (from want of materials or otherwise), they take sweetmeats with them, which they substitute in its stead. This *durgah* is in the charge of a *fuqeer*, who receives (or rather helps himself to) the offerings that are made by visitors, and which are placed at the entrance of the cave. When he dies (the office not being hereditary) another is appointed, the one best qualified from his known piety and zeal. The committee for electing a successor consists of the four principal *mukkanwalay* (peers), residing at the four principal *mukkuns* (or houses of peers), spiritual guides (so called) at Mangalore, and six or ten of their *mooreeds* (or disciples). On such occasions numerous *fuqeers* are likewise present. The four peers having come to an unanimous conclusion, appoint either one of their disciples, or the son of the deceased, if he be found duly qualified. In the days of the Sooltan (Tippoo), the individual in charge of this *durgah* used to receive (by order of the Sooltan) rupees corresponding to the number of masts of the vessels that entered the roads or harbour; for every ship three rupees, *pattamars*, &c. two rupees, *munjee*, &c. one rupee: this rule has been abolished since the place has fallen into the hands of the British. Here is likewise a pagoda (or Hindoo place of worship) where a grand annual festival takes place, on which occasion an immense concourse of people assemble.

The second *durgah* is situated at Mangalore, on the banks of the river, and consists of a large long tomb with minarets at each extremity. *Low Lungur Shah* (a *fuqeer*) is buried here, whose name it bears. Lamps are burned here every night, and it is chiefly visited by Malabars (a Hindoo caste), but also by Moosulmans and other Hindoos. Most Hindoos, however, frequent *Sheikh Furreed's durgah*. These *durgahs* are resorted to when people are desirous of being freed from any distemper, misfortune, &c. If the individual who is enshrined in the *durgah* have been wealthy, large dinners are provided, *fateeha* offered, and the food distributed to any who choose to partake of it; there being sometimes *kunchnee ka taefu* (bands of dancing girls) to entertain the guests. Among the great this takes place on every night of the year (and is never observed in the day time); but among the poorer classes of people, every Monday and Thursday, or once a week or month.

E.

Eed-gah or *Numaz-gah* نمازگاه - عیدگاه—*lit.* a place of festival or of prayer: a building generally situated without the walls of a town (often amidst gardens), erected on a platform or a pediment three or four feet above the level of the ground, and on an eminence, consisting of a square wall with two or more minarets, and having in the centre, on a level with the ground, three steps, which forms the *mimbur* منبر (or pulpit), from which the *khootba* خطبہ (or sermon) is read on particular occasions, or on particular feast days, such as those of *buqr-eed* and *rumzan kee eed*, which occupies from an hour and a half to two hours. It is said that the Prophet, in addressing the congregation, stood on the uppermost step; *Abu Bukur* (his successor) on the second; *Oomur* on the third or lowest; but *Oosman*, observing that at this rate we might descend to the bowels of the earth, fixed upon the middle as the one from which to deliver the sermon; since then it has continued so. This building is merely intended as a signal post for people to assemble at to hear the *khootba* read. A bamboo, or any other post, might answer the same purpose, but a brick building is usually preferred, as being more durable, and affording individuals an opportunity of handing down their names to posterity, by being at the expence of erecting them. It is by no means a sacred edifice.

Ehram احرام—putting on the pilgrim's habit when at a certain distance from Mecca. While they wear this mean habit they interdict themselves all worldly enjoyments, &c.

F.

Fanam—a small silver Madras coin, value about twopence.

Fateeha فاتحہ—the offering up of prayers to the Almighty for the remission of the sins and the acceptance into Heaven of the individual in whose name it is desired, be he a saint or sinner, rich or poor, old or young. It consists in saying, " For such or such a one I offer " this prayer;" then repeating the first chapter of the *Qoran*, which comprises the following short prayer: " Praise be to God, the Lord of all creatures, the most " merciful, the King of the day of judgment, Thee do " we worship, and of Thee do we beg assistance. " Direct us in the right way, in the way of those to " whom thou hast been gracious; not of those against " whom thou art incensed, nor of those who go astray." It is called also the *fateeha* chapter, followed, when praying for the souls of the dead, by the hundred and eleventh chapter, termed *Qoolhoo-oollah*; which latter, if read thrice over, is considered equivalent to having read the whole *Qoran*; for all the blessings will be derived from the one as from the other. Sometimes merely these prayers are offered, at other times oblations are also made at the same time. Reading or performing *fateeha* over any kind of food previous to distribution, which is so commonly done, is not enjoined in the *Qoran*; consequently an innovation. *Fateehas* are of various kinds. (Vide Index.)

Fateeha, Neeut khyr kee فاتحہ نيت خيركي—from *neeut* intention, and *khyr* good; *i. e. fateeha* offered in the name of the living, in contradistinction to other *fateehas*, which are performed for the dead.

Fateeha, Suhnuk, vulgo *Sanuk* فاتحہ صحنك—*sanuk* is the name of a small earthen pot, seven of which are used at this offering. They are filled with boiled rice, which is completely covered with *duhee* (or curds), sugar, and *ghee* (or clarified butter), and sweetened (not acidified), *moong* (phaseolus radiatus, *Lin.*) or *chunnay kay dal* (cicer arienatum, *Lin.*) and *fateeha* being offered over them in *Beebee Fateema's* name, they are distributed to the seven respectable women invited to partake of them, for it is not every woman that is allowed the honour of eating of so sacred a dish. (Vide p. 108.)

Fitr or *Iftar* افطار - فطر—the breaking of fast, which takes place every evening during the Mohummudan Lent; or on the last day of the month *Rumzan*, called *eed-ool-fittur*, عيدالفطر, or the festival of breaking up Lent.

Fitra فطره—alms given upon the *eed-ool-fittur* abovementioned.

Flowers or *P'hool* پهول—whenever flowers are mentioned as being sent or used on any occasion, it is invariably meant to allude to garlands, nosegays, &c., not to single loose flowers. The different forms into which they are manufactured are thus distinguished: 1. *Sayhra* سهرا tied on the forehead, covering the eyes as a veil, worn by men as well as women; 2. *Jalee moeebund* جالي موي بند representing a network tied to the forehead and covering the forepart of the head, worn only by women; 3. *Surpaynch* سرپينچ a string of flowers wound round the head in the form of a turban by women; 4. *Har* هار or a wreath of flowers, worn as a necklace, and hanging down on the breast; 5. *Buddhee* بدهي or wreaths of flowers, crossing each other on the breast and back like a soldier's belt; 6. *Toorru* طُرّه a nosegay or bouquet; 7. *Pak'hur* پاكهر an ornament of flowers (intended to represent an armour) thrown over the horse's head and body; 8. *Gujra* گجرا flower bracelets; 9. *Gend Guhwara* گيند گهوارا or flowers formed like the scale of a balance tied on to images. Vide *Mohurrum*. 10. *Chuddur, P'hool kay* پهول كي چدر or flowers worked in the form of a sheet, spread on graves.

Furz فرض—the word signifies God's commands, and those of two kinds: 1. *Furz* فرض or injunctions, which, in delivering them, he has repeated thrice; 2. *Wajib* واجب or injunctions, which, in delivering them, he has repeated twice.

G.

Ganja گانجا—the leaves or young leaf-buds of the hemp plant (cannabis sativa, *Willd.*), which are frequently rubbed between the hands, added to tobacco and smoked, to increase its intoxicating powers, or smoked by itself. Vide *Bhung*.

Ghurra گهڙا—a large earthen pot, a waterpot, a pitcher.

Gold-*mohur* or *Ashrufee* اشرفي —a gold coin, equal, in Bengal, to sixteen *sicca rupees;* in Madras, to fifteen *Arcot rupees;* and in Bombay, to fourteen *sonaut rupees.*

Gool-ab گل اب—or rose-water; it is contained in a *goolab-pash* گلاب پاش or a kind of long-necked silver bottle, perforated with holes at the mouth in the form of a muffineer, out of which the rose-water is sprinkled on the guests.

Goorakoo گڑاکو- گڈاکو prop. *Goodakoo*—from the Sanscrit word *good* (Hindoostanee *goor*) raw sugar, and the Teloogoo word *akoo*, leaf. It is the name given in the Deccan to the tobacco for the *hooqqa** (called in Bengal *tambakoo* تنباکو), in the preparation of which these enter as chief ingredients. The following are two very valuable formulas for this composition:

1. Take of tobacco leaves four *seers;* common treacle four *seers*, preserved apples, or as a substitute either preserved pine-apple or *byer* بير, zizyphus jujuba, *Lin.* jujubes or Indian plum, half a *seer;* raisins, half a *seer;* *gool-qund* گل قند or conserve of roses half a *seer:* these are to be well pounded together in a large wooden mortar, put into an earthen pot, the mouth of which is to be made air-tight, and buried under ground for three

* *Hooqqa* حقّه—the pipe and its apparatus used in the East-Indies for smoking tobacco through water.

months previous to being used. If it be desired to have the tobacco spiced, add Pegu cardamoms one *ch'huttack; cubab cheenee* كباب چيني piper cubeba, *Lin.* or cubebs, one *ch'huttack;* sandal wood one *ch'huttack*, putchapaut or *pas ka pan*, two *ch'huttacks; auneck* or *juttamasee* جتاماسي cyperus stoloniferus, *Kœnig.* valeriana jatamamsi, *Roxb.* or spikenard, and mix them all well together before you proceed to the burial ceremony.

N. B. The tobacco without the spices is reckoned by far the most wholesome, and if it has been allowed the prescribed time of fermentation under ground, will be found very mellow and agreeable. If the smoker cannot bear strong tobacco, the leaves must be washed in cold water from one to five times, and as often dried in the sun, then pounded.

2. Recipe (of *Mooneer ool Moolk*). Take of good tobacco leaves twenty *seers* (forty pounds); *tar ka goor* تاڑ كا گڑ or raw sugar of the palmyra tree (borassus flabelliformis, *Lin.*) twenty *seers; sad-koofee* سعد كوفي (Arab.) *nagurmotha* (Hind.) ناگرموته (cyperus juncifolius) or root of the rush-leaved cyperus, two *tolas* (six drams); *kayla* كيله or ripe plantains (musa paradisiaca, *Lin.*) twenty in number; *kaweet* كاويت (feronia elephantum, *Roxb.*) or wood-apple, ten in number; cloves two *tolas* (six drams). Pound all separately except the two first, then mix them with two *seers* of each of the two first; make eight divisions of the remaining tobacco and sugar, triturate one at a time well with the mass; then add them all together, and knead them again well with the hands; afterwards bury them (as above) for a month in a dunghill.

Gurm mussala, see note p. lxv.

H.

Hoomā هما (or همای)—a fabulous bird. The phœnix of the East.

Huddees حدیث—properly a saying, but generally applied to the sayings which tradition has attributed to Mohummud. These are divided into two classes; the first is called *Huddees-e-nubuwee* حدیث نبیوی or the sayings of the Prophet; the other *Huddees-e-qoodsee* حدیث قدسی or the holy sayings, which they believe the angel Gabriel brought from heaven.

Huj حج—the pilgrimage, to Mecca. *Ameer-e-huj*, the chief or commander of the pilgrims (an officer of great dignity during the splendour of the Khaliphat, and generally filled by the son or declared successor of the reigning sovereign).

Hundee هنڈی—a small earthen pot.

I.

Ispund اسپند—the seeds of the *Maynhdee* (q. v.), which is burnt at marriages to drive away evil spirits. It is also burnt as a charm for the like purpose during the forty days of the puerperal state; particularly at the door, whenever a visitor retires, as well as when the infant is taken out of the room to be bathed, and brought in again. It is generally thrown into the fire along with some *benzoin* (or benjamin), or with mustard seed and *putchar ka putta.*

J.

Ja-e-numaz جای نماز vulgo. *Janeemaz* or *Moosulla* مصلا— or a place of prayer. The term is applied to the carpet, mat, or cloth on which they stand while praying.

Jibbreel جبریل—or the angel Gabriel. The Mohummudans reckon four great angels, viz. 1. *Jibraeel, Jibreel*, or *Jubra-ueel* جبرایل - جبریل - جبرعل — the archangel Gabriel, who is God's messenger. The protector of the Mohummudans. 2. *Meekaeel* میکائیل (Michael)—

the angel who presides over water (rain), whom the Moosulmans acknowledge to be the protector of the Jews. 3. *Israfeel* اسرافيل—or the angel who presides over the wind, and will sound the last trumpet at the resurrection. 4. *Izra-eel* عزرائيل—or the angel of death. The Mohummudans affirm, that when a dead person is buried two evil spirits, named *Moonkir* منكر and *Nukeer* نكير, of a frightful aspect and black colour, make the dead sit upright in the grave and arraign him: if he be found innocent, they suffer him to lie down again and rest in quiet; if not, they give him several blows with a hammer between the two ears, which occasions incredible pain, and makes him cry out terribly. Vide Sale's *Qoran*, Prel. Diss., sect. 4.

K.

K'hana كهانا—food or meals. Moosulmans use three meals a day: 1st. *Nashtā* or *Hazree* حاضري - ناشتا or *breakfast;* at nine or ten A.M., which consists, among the great, of rice, *k'hichree*, or wheaten cakes with curries, fried fish, preserves, pickles, omelet, eggs broken up into lumps while frying, *duhee* (or *tyar*), buttermilk, *chutnee* (*shubdeg*), carrots, *haleem* made of meat, wheat flour and *ghee*, *moosummum*, fried fowl in *ghee*, milk, and sugar, with *sayweean*, *dal*, *char* (or *mooloogoo tunny*, literally pepper water), *goorday ka pooray* (sheep's testes). Among the middling orders, of rice, *k'hichree*, or wheaten cakes, eggs, pickles, *chutnees*, *duhee*, *dal*, *char*, and fried or boiled fish. Among the poorer classes, of *basee k'hana*, or stale rice which has been kept overnight in water and acquires a slightly acid taste, with *kyan* pepper, *chutnee*, or *dal* and rice, with *char* or fish. 2d. *Khana* كهانا or *dinner*, which they partake of at three or four P.M., the lower orders generally at 1 P.M.; it consists, among the nobility, of rice, occasionally *polaoos*, curries, *moosummun*, *chut-*

nees, shurbut, *kubabs*, and occasionally fruits: among the middle ranks, of rice, occasionally *polaoos*, wheaten cakes, with curries, fruits, and water: among the poor, of rice and *dal*, or fish, with *chutnee*; occasionally meat. In most places they eat *ragee* (or *munruwee*, cynosurus coracanus, *Lin.*) cakes, instead of any of the foregoing. 3d. *Rat ka k'hana* راتکا کہانا or *supper;* at seven or eight P.M.; this consists, among the nobility, of milk, *mulleeda*, and fried sweetmeats; sometimes *polaoo*, with a variety of fruits, wines, and coffee; among the middling classes, of milk with *rotee*, rice, curry, and sweetmeats: among the poor, of the same as dinner or breakfast.

K'hich-ree کھچري—a dish made of rice and a species of pea called *dāl*, together with *ghee* and spices. (Vide Append., p. xxx.)

Khootba خطبه—an oration or sermon delivered every Friday after the forenoon service in the principal mosque (in which they praise God, bless Mohummud and his descendants, and pray for the king or reigning monarch,)* with exhortations. This was generally pronounced in former times by the reigning *Khuleefa*, or the heir apparent.

K'hopra کھوپرا—is the kernel of the *nariel* (or fresh cocoa-nut), when fully ripe, taken out, divided in the middle, and dried. This is very generally eaten by the natives, and is esteemed not only superior in flavour to the *nariel*, but more wholesome, being considered more digestible, and less apt to create flatulence or generate worms. Its price is double that of the other. It is frequently used as an ingredient in curries and in medicine.

---

* This, in the author's opinion, should at present be the Honourable East-India Company, but that is not done; they pray for the king of Delhi, he being the titular sovereign of the Indian empire.

Khuleefa خليفه—(Caliph) a title given to Mohummudan sovereigns or successors of the Prophet; to which was annexed the most absolute authority both in religious and civil government.

K'hullee كهلي—oil cakes; the dregs of the seeds which remain after the oil is expressed.

Koossoom كسم—carthamus tinctorius, *Lin.* or safflower. The beautiful red dye called *koossoom ka rung*, so much in use on all occasions, and so frequently referred to in this work, is prepared as follows: Take of *koossoom ka p'hool* (or the dried flowers of safflower) one *seer* (two pounds), put them into a towel suspended by its four corners to sticks fixed in the ground, pour cold water on them, rubbing at the same time the flowers well with the water, and continuing the washing as long as the strained water remains yellow. When it begins to acquire a red colour, squeeze the water out of the flowers and spread them out; then having sprinkled four *pice* weight (two ounces) of *soojeekhar* سجي كهار, or an impure carbonate of soda, mix them well together. Put the flowers again on the suspended cloth, and pour on them three gugglets of cold water, and keep the strained liquid of each gugglet separate; add to these the juice of as many lemons (about twenty or twenty-five) as will the change the colour of the fluid into a most beautiful hue. In dyeing cloth, it is first soaked in the faintest coloured liquid, then in the darker, and lastly in the darkest, leaving it in each for a few seconds or minutes.

Kufnee كفني *Alfa* or *Alfuh* الفه - الفا—it consists of a piece of cloth about fifteen feet long, and about a yard wide. In the centre of its breadth a slit is made through which the head is passed, where a collar is sewed on; one-third of the cloth hangs behind, reaching down to the calf of the leg, and two-thirds before; the superfluous quantity in front is tucked up by means of the *kummur-bund*, which at the same time forms a sort of bag to receive the contributions of the charitable.

Kulma كلمه—the two members of the Mohummudan confession of faith, *i. e.* لا اله الا الله *la illaha illaylah*, "There is no God but God;" ومحمد الرسول الله *wo Mohummudoor russool Oollah*, "And Mohummud is the messenger of God."

Kunchneean kay nach كانچنيان كي ناچ—or dancing girls. These dancing women and their musicians form a separate kind of caste, and a certain number of them are attached to every Hindoo temple of any consequence. The allowance which the musicians receive for their public duty is very small, yet morning and evening they are bound to attend at the temple to perform before the image; they must also receive every person travelling on account of the government, meet him at a distance from the town, and conduct him to his quarters with music and dancing. All the handsome girls are instructed to dance and sing, and are all prostitutes, at least to the Brahmuns. In ordinary sets they are quite common; but under the Company's Government, those attached to temples of extraordinary sanctity are reserved entirely for the use of the native officers of the temple, who are all Brahmuns, and who would turn from the set any girl that profaned herself by communication with persons of low caste, or of no caste at all, such as Christians or Moosulmans. Indeed almost every one of these girls, that is tolerably handsome, is taken by some native officer of revenue for his own special use, and is seldom permitted to go to the temple except in his presence. Most of these officers have more than one wife, and the women of the Brahmuns are very beautiful; the dancing girls are sought after by all natives with great avidity. The Moosulman officers in particular were exceedingly attached to this kind of company, and lavished on these women a great part of their incomes. The women very much regret their loss, as the Moosulmans paid liberally, and the Brahmuns durst not presume to hinder any one who chose from amusing an *asoph*, or any of his friends. The Brahmuns are not nearly so liberal of their money, especially where it is secured by the Company's Government, but trust to their authority for obtaining the favours of the dancers. When a Moosulman called for a set of dancers, it procured from twenty to two hundred *fanams*,* according to the number and liberality of his friends who were present; for in this country it is customary for every spectator to give something. They are now seldom called upon to perform in private, except at marriages, where a set does not get more than ten *fanams*. The girls belonging to this caste who are ugly, or who cannot learn to sing, are married by the musicians. The *nutwa*, or person who performs on two small cymbals, is the chief of the troop, and not only brings up the boys to be musicians, and instructs all the good looking girls born in it to sing and dance, but will purchase handsome girls of any caste whatever which he can procure. When a dancing girl grows old, she is turned out from the temple without any provision, and becomes very destitute, unless she have a handsome daughter to succeed her. If she have this, the daughters are in general extremely attentive and kind to their aged parents. In the opinion of some Europeans nothing can be more silly and unanimated than the dancing of the women, nor more harsh and

* A Madras small silver coin, value about twopence.

barbarous than their music; while others perhaps, from long habit, have acquired a relish for the latter, and have even been captivated by the women.—F. Buchanan's Journey through Mysore, Canara, and Malabar, Vol. II. p. 267.

Kuntha کنٹھا—a necklace of large beads made of the basilar process, or button of the conch-shell, worn round the necks of all the Bengal sepoys.

L.

La-howl or *Lahowl-o-la qoowuta illa bil lahil alli-il azeem*, i.e. "There is no power or strength but in God, who is great and mighty;" or, in other words, they mean there is no striving against fate. NISI DOMINUS FRUSTRA.

Lota لوٹا—a small metallic pot, generally made of brass or tinned iron.

Luddoo لڈو—a kind of sweetmeat, made chiefly of sugar, with the addition of rasped cocoa-nut and cream, and formed in the shape of large boluses.

M.

Majoon معجون—this electuary is much used by the Mohummudans, particularly the more dissolute, who take it internally to intoxicate and ease pain, and not unfrequently, from an over-dose of it, produce a temporary mental derangement. The chief ingredients employed in making it are *ganja* (or hemp) leaves, milk, *ghee*, poppy seeds, flowers of the thorn apple, the powder of the nux vomica, and sugar: or, take of milk four *seers* (eight lbs.), put into it a *seer* of *ganja* leaves, and boil until three *seers* remain; take out the leaves and coagulate the milk by putting into it a little *duhee*: next day churn it and separate the butter, to which add *junglee long*, nutmegs, cloves, mace, saffron, of each one *tola* pounded, and sugar-candy five *tolas*, and boil to an electuary. Or simply the leaves of the hemp are fried in *ghee* (or clarified butter) and strained, and to the liquor some sugar is added, and the beverage drank; or the liquor is boiled with the sugar until is acquires a consistence sufficiently thick to form cakes on cooling.

Maleeda or *Muleedu* ملیده - مالیده—wheaten cakes, dried, pounded, and mixed up with *ghee* and sugar.

Maynh'dee مینهدي—(Lawsonia spinosa, *Lin.*, Lawsonia inermis, *Heyne*, Ligustrum indicum) prickly Lawsonia, Ivenie, or Eastern Privet. The leaf, triturated with rice gruel or water, is much used by the Mohummudan women in staining the nails, palms of the hands, and soles of the feet, of a red colour. The plant forms a fine hedge, and perfumes the air with a delicious fragrance. Few shrubs are more esteemed throughout India, Persia, and Arabia than this. Its seeds, called *ispund* (q. v.), are likewise used on various occasions.

Meesee مسي—a powder (made of vitriol) with which the teeth are tinged of a black colour. The following is a good recipe for preparing the same: Take of *maphul* ماپهل or *majoophul* ماجوپهل (quercus robur, *Lin.*) or gall-nuts two ounces; *neela toota* نیلا توته or *neela thotha* نیلا تهوتها or *tooteea* توتیا (sulphas cupri), or blue vitriol two drams; *beer* بیر or steel filings one ounce; *hulla*, vulgo *hurla* هلّا یا هرلا (terminalia chebula, *Willd.*) or chebulic myrobolan, half an ounce; *keekur kee phullee* کیکر کي پهلي (acacia Arabica, *Lin.*) pod of the Indian gum Arabic tree half an ounce; lime juice, q. s.; pound and sift the vitriol, mix it with the steel filings, add the lime juice to them, and put them in the sun to dry, *i. e.* until the mixture becomes black, which colour it will have acquired in about a couple of hours; then pound this as well as the two other ingredients, sift, and preserve the powder for use.

Miswak مسواك—a twig of a tree, of which several kinds are in use, as that of the *neem* نیم (melia azadirachta,

Lin.) or the margosa tree; the *agara* آگاڙا (achyranthes aspera, *Lin.*) or the rough achyranthes; the *peeloo* پيلو (salvadora persica, *Vahl.* careya arborea, *Roxb.*) or the toothpick tree; the *kala mahmud* كالا محمد (phyllanthus multiflorus, *Klein.*) or the many-flowered phyllanthus; and the *khujoor* كهجور (phœnix dactilyfera, *Lin.*) or the date tree; or the *mulsayree* alias *bokool.* It is used as a substitute for a toothbrush. It is about a span long, split at one end and chewed to render it softer. In using it it is held in a particular way; the end not to be used, is to be held between the ring and little finger, the three great fingers are to grasp the middle, and the nail of the thumb to press against the other extremity.

Moocheewalay موچي والي—*Moocheemen*, a class of people of a particular caste, whose profession on the peninsula of India (Deccan) is painting, bookbinding, making saddles, palankeen bedding, caps, &c. and not shoemakers, who have this appellation in Bengal.

Moosulla مصلا—vide *Jae-numaz*.

Mudud مدد—betel leaf q. s. (previously toasted a little in a brass or iron cup) is chopped and mixed with forty-five grains of opium, made of a proper consistence to form pills of the size of a pepper-corn, and smoked, one at a time, in a broken *kulkee:* in a few minutes the pill bursts and evaporates.

Muhdee مهدي—or the director and leader, is the surname of the last or twelfth *Imam*, whom the Persians believe to be still alive; and that he will appear again with Elias the prophet on the second coming of Jesus Christ. (Vide p. 14 and 259.)

Munja منجا—same as *nayoota*, q. v. Also the rubbing the body over with turmeric, &c. on particular occasions; such as circumcision, *bismilla*, virginity, and marriage.

Munjun منجن— or dentrifice. Tooth-powder is frequently

made of burnt almond shells, or *gool*,* i.e. burnt *goodak*, (the residuum of a *chillum*, or the tobacco of a *hooqqa* burnt to cinders) with black pepper and salt; but what is used by the generality of people is merely common charcoal, which in my opinion is the best dentrifice in existence. It is not unusually made by burning *hulla* هلا (terminalia chebula, *Willd.* or chebulic myrobolan), or *soopeearee* سوپياري (areca catechu, *Lin.* or betel nut) into cinders, and pounding it fine; which probably is the next best.

Murseea مرثه—properly any funeral eulogium, but applied particularly to those sung during the *Mohurrum*, in commemoration of *Hussun* and *Hosein* (the sons of *Allee*).

Musjid مسجد—a mosque, or Mohummudan place of worship. All mosques are square, and generally built with good stones. Before the chief gate there is a square court paved with white marble, and low galleries round, the roof of which is supported by marble pillars. In these they wash themselves before they go into the mosques. The walls are all white, excepting some few places, on which the name of God is written in large Arabic characters. In each mosque there is a great number of

---

* A recipe for making the best *gools* (or fireballs) for the *hooqqa*: take of

	Seers.	Chh.
Charcoal of the Tamarind tree (tamarindus indica, *Lin.*)	6	12
Ditto *Peepul* پيپل (ficus religiosa, *Lin.*)	2	4
Ditto common Rice (coryza sativa, *Lin.*)	2	4
Gum of the *Bubool* or *Keeker* كيكر يا ببول (acacia arabica, *Roxb.*)	1	2
Goor گُر Molasses or raw Sugar	2	4
Rice gruel or *Conjee* كانجي..........................	2	0
	16	10

The charcoals should be thoroughly burned, reduced to a fine powder, and sifted. The gum and molasses to be dissolved in the *conjee*, mixed with the former, and well beat up in a large wooden mortar, then formed into balls and dried in the sun. The more they are beat up the better.

lamps, and between the lamps hang many crystal rings, ostrich's eggs, and other curiosities from foreign countries, which make a fine shew when the lamps are lighted. About each mosque there are six (generally two or four) high towers, each having three little open galleries, one above another. These towers, as well as the mosques, are covered with lead, and adorned with gilding and other ornaments: they are called *minarets*, and from them, instead of a bell, the people are called to prayers by certain officers appointed for that purpose, whom they call *mowazins*. Most of the mosques have a kind of hospital belonging to them, in which travellers, of what religion soever, are entertained during three days. Each mosque has also a spot which is the burying-place of its founder; within it is a tomb of six or seven feet long, covered with velvet or green satin: at each end are two wax tapers, and round it several seats for those who read the *Qoran*, and pray for the souls of the deceased. It was not lawful to enter the mosques wearing shoes or stockings, for which reason the pavements are covered with pieces of stuff sewed together in broad stripes, each wide enough to hold a row of men kneeling, sitting, or prostrate. Women are forbidden in the *Qoran* to go into the public mosques; therefore the great and wealthy have frequently a mosque in their own compound (or area), where females perform their devotions. Some of the women are taught Arabic, and are able to read the *Qoran*. The different officers attached to mosques are the following: viz. 1st. a *qazee* (or ecclesiastical judge); 2d. a *khuteeb* (or priest); 3d. a *moolla* (or schoolmaster); 4th. two *naibs* (or his deputies); 5th. a *furash* (or sweeper, called also *moojawir*, i. e. devoutly employed); 6th. a *gussal* (or one whose business it is to wash the bodies of the dead); 7th. two *dowrahaburdar* (guides or messengers). In inferior mosques we merely find a *moolla* and a *mowazin;* and the latter has no pay, but lives upon what he can earn by carrying messages of invitation, or acting as a servant at marriage ceremonies.

Mussala, *gurm*, and *thunda*, see note p. lxv.

Mussuh مسح—drawing the hand over any part, or over the surface of any liquid.

Myda ميده—vide *Ata*.

N.

Nadulee نادلي—a stone having generally a verse or certain sentences of the *Qoran* exquisitely engraved on it, and worn, suspended to a string, round the necks of children.

Nayoota نيوتا—*lit.* presents which are sent along with invitations to the individual invited; also erroneously applied to the invitation itself. *Nayoota ka chittee*, a letter of invitation.

Nufil نفل—a voluntary act of devotion, which may be omitted innocently as not being prescribed, framed by the Prophet's companions, other theologians, and the four *Imams*.

Numaz نماز—prayers; i. e. those only offered to the Almighty; and especially those prescribed by law, said five times a day.

Nuzur-o-nyaz نزر و نياز—vide *Oors*.

O.

Ood (dukh.) عود—Styrax Benzoin, Benzoin, or Benjamin. This is the substance intended when the term *ood* is used, and not lignum aloe or wood aloes, which the Persians term *ood;* the latter being denominated *uggur*, q. v.

Ood-buttee عود بتي—more properly *uggur kay buttee*, q. v.

Oors عرس—oblations. Offerings to a saint.

Oors, *i.e.* oblations or *fateeha* offered, 1. in the name of the Prophet, as *bara wufat* (p. 233): 2. in the name of the *Peers*, or spiritual guides,* as *peeran-e-peer* (or saint of saints, *i. e. dustugeer*, called *geearween*), observed in all places (p. 237); *shah mudar ka oors*, observed in all places (p. 241); *qadir wullee sahib*, observed at Nagore (near Negapatam) (p. 243); *rujub salar*, observed in all places (p. 249); *khwaja bunday nuwaz*, observed at Bhuraich (p. 265); *mowla allee*, observed near Hydrabad (p. 268): 3. in the name of all *Wullees*, or saints,* as *bawa shurf ood deen*, observed at Shaban, four or five miles S. of Hydrabad; *syed shah jummal buhar*, observed at Bhowangeer, two marches from Hydrabad.

Nuzur-o-Nyaz, or vows and oblations, 1. in the name of God; 2. in the name of the Prophet; 3. in the name of his companions; 4. in the name of the saints. These are not observed on any fixed day, but each performs them according to the vow he has made. (Vide Chap. XXVII.) The offerings used on the above occasions consist of fruits, flowers, and boiled rice.

P.

Palkee پالكي — palankeen or palanquin, litters or sedans. These are of four kinds, viz. 1. *Palkee* پالكي or palankeen, is carried on the shoulders by four men, who support it by a pole at each end; double or treble sets of bearers generally attend it, to render the burden as light as possible, and they are relieved every five or ten minutes by fresh relays. 2. *Chowtha* چوتہہ is a kind of palankeen of frame work covered with canvas, and is carried by four men, commonly used in the

---

* An ordinance (not enjoined either by God or the Prophet) but observed by almost all Moosulmans, and fixed on particular days. The observance is optional.

army. 3. *Meeana* میانہ used on marriage occasions, and solely by natives. 4. *Doolee* ڈولي the most common kind, generally used by the lower classes of people in Bengal.

Pansoopeearee پان‌سوپیاري—abbr. *pansooparee* (from *pan* betel leaf, and *soopeearee* areca nut); the term, however, comprehends all the other ingredients, some or all of which are eaten in combination with them: it includes betel leaves, areca or betel nut, catechu, quick-lime, aniseed, bishop's weed seed (*ajwaeen*), coriander seed, cardamoms, and cloves. These folded up in the leaf or leaves, and made up into a parcel, are termed *pan ka beera* (q. v.), and it is in this form that it is generally employed on occasions of ceremony, consequently it is in this sense that it is to be understood, when merely *pan sooparee* or betel is mentioned.

Phool-el-ka tail پہولیل کا تیل— or odoriferous oil, obtained from sweet-scented flowers, prepared thus: Take off the husks of *til* تل or gingilie oil seed, place alternate layers of any fragrant flowers with it in a covered vessel, let it stand for a week; throw away the flowers, and put fresh ones in their place, and repeat this operation from three to five times; then express the oil from the seeds, which will have acquired a delightful odour.

Pice or *Pysa* پیسا—a copper coin, value about two farthings.

Pool-surrat پل صراط—a bridge, finer than a hair and sharper than the edge of a sword, situated between heaven and hell, on which all mankind will have to go on the resurrection day. The righteous will pass over it with ease, and with the swiftness of a horse or of lightning; while the wicked will miss their footing, and fall headlong into hell, whose flaming jaws will be gaping wide beneath them.

Punjayree پنجیري—or a caudle, given to puerperal women, is prepared thus: Take of *ajwaeen* اجواين sison ammi, *Lin.*

or bishop's-weed seed, eight *pice* weight (or four ounces); *soojee* (vide *Ata*), one *pukka seer* (or two pounds); country gum arabic, one-eighth of a *seer* (or four ounces); raisins, eight *pice* weight (or four ounces); poppy seed, sixteen *pice* weight (or eight ounces); co-coanut sliced, sixteen *pice* weight (or eight ounces); blanched almonds, eight *pice* weight (or four ounces); dates, eight *pice* weight (or four ounces); sugar (soft), one *pukka seer* (or two pounds). With the exception of the sugar, fry all the ingredients in *ghee* (or clarified butter), and lastly add the sugar.

Q.

Qaf قاف—mount, a fabulous mountain supposed to surround the world and bound the horizon. It rests on the stone *sakhrat*, an entire emerald, which imparts the azure hue to the sky.

Qeeam قيام—or the standing position in prayer, when the person stands with his feet parallel to each other, and either four or eight fingers apart. The *sheeahs* place them a foot and more distant from one another, the hands resting upon one another over the navel.

R.

Rooa روا—a small copper coin, more of a globular form than flat, three of which are equal to a *pice;* current in the Mysore country.

Rookoo ركوع—in prayer, consists in bending the body forwards and resting the palms of the hands on the knees, with back and neck horizontal, and eyes fixed on the great toes.

Rookoo kee tusbeeh ركوع كي تسبيح—viz. *Soobhāna, Rub'bee-ool' Azeem, i.e.* Praised be the great God, our preserver. Vide *Tusbeeh.*

Rozu روزه fasting, fast; Lent. *Rozu k'hōl'na,* to break fast.

Rukat ركعت—reading a certain number of prayers and

chapters of the *Qoran* in conjunction with a certain number of inclinations of the head, or of bendings of the body, or of genuflexions (as prescribed in the *Qoran*), constitute a *rukat.*

Rukat Soonnut ركعت سنّت—are prayers established by the Prophet, of which there are two varieties: 1. *Soonnut mowukkeeda*, or prayers which he offered himself, and has enjoined others positively to observe, consequently, the neglect of which is sin: 2. *Sonnut gyr-mowukkeeda*, or prayers which, though he performed himself, he has not insisted upon others performing; the observance of these, however, is a meritorious deed, though the omission of them is not regarded as sinful.

Rupee روپيه or روپيا—a silver coin, varying in value in different parts of Hindoostan, from one shilling and eightpence to two shillings and sixpence.

S.

Sheeah شيعه—a sect of Mohummudans who believe *Allee* to have been the successor of Mohummud. They reject *Aba Bukur*, *Oomr*, and *Oosman ;* and hence the *Soonnees* call them *rafzee* رافضي or heretics.

Shola شوله or *Bhend* بهيند—æschynomene aspera, *Lin.*, æschynomene paludosa, *Roxb.*, commonly called *pith* in India by Europeans. The root of this plant is white coloured, and very light and spongy, with which a variety of toys, artificial flowers, birds, &c. are made, and garlands, which latter are used in marriage ceremonies. Fishermen use it to float their nets and lines with. A bundle of it held under each arm is used to learn to swim with, and to cross rivers. The turbans of the servants of Europeans are made of it. When charred it answers the purpose of tinder. I have no doubt but what is called rice-paper is nothing more than this pithy substance, cut in circular folds with a very sharp instrument.

Shurbut شربت—in the Deccan, is merely a solution of sugar in water (or sugar-candy in rose-water, substituted by the great), without the addition of lime-juice; the latter (or lemonade) being termed *abshola; Gilchrist, ubshoru;* probably both a corruption of *abshorah* ابشوره water cooled with saltpetre: but in Bengal, as well as Persia, they give to lemonade the term of *shurbut*, where the celebrated Eastern mode of preparing this beverage is by dissolving perfumed cakes, made of the best Damascus fruit, in water, lemon or orange juice, and sugar; adding also a few drops of rose-water. A different variety is made of violets, honey, juice of raisins, &c. It is well calculated for assuaging thirst, as the acidity is agreeably blended with sweetness: it resembles, indeed, those fruits which we find so grateful when thirsty.

Shurra شرح—law. The precepts of Mohummud.

Sijdah سجده—or prostration. A position in prayer, consisting in stooping forwards while in the sitting (the Mohummudan kneeling) posture, and touching the ground with the forehead; the eyes at the same time directed to the tip of the nose.

Sijdah tyhet سجده تحيت—nearly similar to the preceding; the only difference is, that instead of touching the ground with the forehead, he is to kiss his own thumbs, the two fists being in contact, with the thumbs directed upwards, and placed on the ground.

Sohagin سہاگن—women whose husbands are living; so called from their wearing their *sohag* سہاگ, (ornaments which are dispensed with when they become widows), viz. the *nuth*, *boolaq*, *baysur*, *pote*, *gulsayree*, and *bunggree*. Widows, moreover, never wear red clothes.

Sohagpoora سہاگ پڑا—some nutmeg, mace, cloves, catechu, poppy seed, and one or a half rupee piece, enclosed in a piece of red paper folded up, with a bit of mica tied on the outside of the parcel with red thread.

Sontana سونٹانہ—is composed of pounded *sohaleean* سہالیان or thin wheaten cakes fried in *ghee*, *tilleea gond* تلیاگوند a species of gum, sugar, *khopra* کھوپڑا (or the dried kernel of the cocoa-nut), and *ghee* گھي or clarified butter.

Sook'hmook'h سُکھمُکھ—Vide Index.

Soonnee سني—orthodox Mohummudans, so called because they believe in the *Soonnut*, q. v. They revere equally the four successors of Mohummud, viz. *Aba Bukur*, *Oomr*, *Oosman*, and *Allee*. These are nicknamed by the *Sheeahs* (whose mortal enemies they are) *Kharjee* خارجي or outcasts, because they say the latter do not allow *Allee* to have been the legal successor of the Prophet; which is however erroneous, for they really do consider all four as legal successors, in the order in which they stand.

Soonnut سُنّت—the traditions of Mohummud, which by the orthodox Moosulmans (thence called *Soonnees*) are considered as a supplement to the *Qoran*, and of nearly equal authority. These are however rejected as an apocryphal book by the *Sheeaites* (or sect of *Allee*).

Soonnut rukat, vide *Rukat*.

Soorma سُرمہ—*lit.* antimony. It is applied in a very subtile powder to the eye, or on the inside of the eyelids, which answers the same purpose, to improve the brilliancy of that organ, and not to the eyelashes and eyelids as some state it to be, which latter application is *kajul* or lamp-black. That usually sold in the bazars in Hindoostan is not the real grey ore of antimony, but a galena or sulphuret of lead. The origin of the use of antimony to the eye is thus stated: when God commanded Moses to ascend *Koh-e-toor* (Mount Sinai) to shew him his countenance, he exhibited it through an opening of the size of a needle's eye, at the sight of which Moses fell into a trance. After a couple of hours, on coming to himself, he discovered the mountain in a blaze, when he, and the people who accompanied him descended immediately. The mountain then addressed the Almighty thus: "What! hast thou set me, who am the least among all mountains, on fire!" Then the Lord commanded Moses, saying, "Henceforth shalt thou and thy posterity grind the earth of this mountain, and apply it to your eyes." Since then this custom has prevailed; and some of the earth or rock (or rather mineral) brought from Mount Sinai, (which at least it should be, and is intended to represent, though frequently an ore of antimony or lead is substituted) is to be had in most bazars under the name of *soorma*, which is brought from Arabia to this country (Hindoostan) by the Arab merchants.

Subzee سبزي vulgo *Subja* سبجا—an intoxicating liquor, prepared from *ganja* or hemp leaves, and chiefly used in the higher provinces. The following is a recipe for making it: Take of dried *siddhee* leaves (*ganja* or hemp) two *tolas*; black pepper, ten or twelve corns; cardamoms, two or three; *post ke dana* پوست كي دانه *i. e. khushkhush* خشخش or poppy-seed one tea-spoonful; *kukree* ككڙي cucumis utissimus, *Roxb.* cucumis sativus, *Lin.* or a kind of cucumber-seed, one tea-spoonful. All the ingredients are to be well rubbed down in a mortar with a wooden pestle, and then gradually pour a quart of milk or water, as you like best, upon it: you may also put an ice-cream into it if you please, and having stirred the whole well together, serve it up in tumblers. This makes a fine beverage, and exhilirates whilst it has not the bad effects of liquor and wines.

You may sweeten it to your palate, but then it is intoxicating in the extreme.

Sudqa صدقہ—or propitiary offerings; had recourse to in order to get rid of any distemper, &c. There are several ways of doing it: 1. They take four or five kinds of grain, peas, or seeds, such as *kooltee* کلتي glycine tomentosa, *Lin.* or Madras horse gram; *moong* مونگ phaseolus radiatus, *Lin.* phaseolus aureus, *Roxb.* green gram, or rayed kidney bean; *oorood* اُرود phaseolus mungo, *Lin.* or black gram; *til* تل sesamum orientale, *Lin.* or gingilie oil seed, &c. put into separate baskets, and place on the contents of one of them a cup filled with oil, into which having looked (as into a mirror) they drop into it a *fanam* or two, or more, according to their means, and distribute them to the poor. 2. or they pour two or three bags of *chawul* (unboiled rice) over the head of the patient, and distribute it to the poor, having used the oil also as in the preceding case. 3. or they give away some cloths of the length of the body (*i. e.* four cubits long) in charity to the poor, not omitting to use the cup of oil, as above: to constitute this a complete *sudqa* forty pieces of cloth should be distributed, but in this particular they are generally guided by their means. 4. or they also give animals, such as cows, elephants, &c. Among the great they have artificial ones of these, made of gold or silver; for instance, Hyder Allee (Tippoo's father) presented to the Brahmuns a calf made of silver, weighing about two or two and a half *maunds* (one hundred and sixty or two hundred pounds).

Suhnuk and *suhnuk*, vulgo *Sanuk fateeha*—vide *fateeha*.

Sulam سلام—or salutation; *sulam kurna;* to salute. These are of different kinds, viz. 1. *sulam* سلام consists in merely touching the forehead with the *right* hand. It is considered highly disrespectful to use the left hand on this occasion, (or in fact on any other) that hand being employed for a particular ablution. 2. *Bundugee* بندگي as above, but meeting the motion of the hand with a gentle inclination of the head forwards. 3. *Koornish* كورنش as the preceding, but bending the body also. 4. *Tusleem* or *tusleemat* تسليمات consists in touching the ground with the fingers and then making *sulam;* sometimes repeated thrice.* *Kunch-nees* (or dancing girls) invariably use the two latter modes when they enter into the presence of those who hire them to dance, at the same time saying "*bundee koornish buja latee,*" or "*bundee tusleem kurtee;*" i. e. your slave makes her obeisance. 5. *Qudum-bosee* قدمبوسي or *Zumeen-bosee* زمين بوسي which consists in kissing the foot, or touching it with the hand, or touching the edge of the carpet on which the person sits, and either kissing the latter or making a *sulam.* Done only to parents and great people. 6. *Ushtang* اشتانگ (vulgo *sashtung* ساشتنگ) consists in prostrating themselves on the ground, with the arms stretched out, and the palms of the hands joined together. Only done by Hindoos, never by Moosulmans. 7. *Gullay-milna* گلي ملنا or *manuqa* مانقه—a mode of salutation performed by embracing each other, throwing the arms across each other's necks, and in that position inclining the head three times, first on one shoulder and then on the other, alternately.

Suna ثنا—praise.

سبحانكَ اللّهمّ بحمدكَ و تبارك اسمكَ و تعالي جدُّكَ و
لاالٰه غيرك

* In the *Qanoon-e-Adab* it is somewhat differently stated, *viz.* that which is here described as *bundugee* is called *tusleem,* and what here stands for *tusleem* is *koornish.*

i. e. *Soob-ha'nayka, Al'lahoom'ma, bay-hum'-day-ka, o tuba'rukis moka, o ta'alla jud'doka, o la-illa'ha, gyr'oka :* or, "I thank and praise thee, O God, and bless thy name, and extol thy glory; for there is no other God but thee !"

Sundul صندل—*lit.* sandal wood. Whenever this word occurs throughout the work, it does not allude to sandal wood itself (which it literally means) but to a perfumed embrocation obtained by rubbing a piece of sundul wood with water on a stone called a *sundlasa* صندلاسہ (p. 119). Again, in using it, a particular mode is observed; it is applied with the right hand, and invariably to the right side of the neck first, drawing the fingers (which are apart) from behind forwards, so as to leave four distinct streaks; then the same to the left: afterwards the abdomen is merely touched with it with the forefinger (meaning to signify, may your offspring enjoy good health) !): lastly, the back in like manner is touched with it (as much as to say, may all your relations continue well!).

Sutwara, vulgo *Suthoora* ستوارا - ستھورا—is a preparation made of *gayhoon ka ata* گیہوں کا آٹا or wheat flour, *sonth* سونٹھ or dried ginger, *shukur* شکر or soft sugar, and *ghee* گھی or clarified butter, mixed together over a fire : particularly given to puerperal women.

T.

Tukbeer تکبیر—repeating the Mohummudan creed (or only saying *Allaho akbur*, "God is great," on particular occasions), viz. repeating four times, *Allah-ho akbur* الله اکبر, "God is great;" twice, *Ush'-huddo-un', lah'-illah-hah il'laylah'* اشہدان لااله الا الله "I bear witness" (addressing himself to the recording angels) "that there is no other God but Him, the (one) God :" twice, *Wo ush'-hud-do-un'na Mo-hum'-mudoor Russool ool'lah* واشہدان محمد

الرسول الله "and I further bear witness that verily Mohummud is the messenger of God:" then turning to the right side (as if addressing the people), twice, *Hy'-ah' lus sulwat'* حي علي ال صلواة "come, enliven your prayers;" to the left, twice, *Hy'-a-lul ful'lah* حي علي الفلاح "come for refuge to the asylum;" twice, *Qud-qamut-sulwat* قد قامت الصوات "stand up to prayers;" twice, *Allāh-ho ak'bur* الله اكبر "God is great;" lastly, once, *Lah'-illah'-hah, il'laylah', Mohum'mudoor, Russool oollah* لا اله الا الله محمد الرسول الله "there is no God but the (one) God, and Mohummud is HIS messenger."

Tu-ooz تعوز—having recourse to God against evil. اعوز باالله من الشطان الرجيم *A-oo-zo billahay minnush-shytan nir-rujeem*, i. e. I solicit the protection of God against Satan the accursed.

Tusbeeh تسبيح—the Moosulman *tusbeeh* (i. e. rosary or chaplet) contains one hundred beads, and are made of the following different materials, viz. 1. *K'hujoor ke beej* كهجور كي بيج or date stones; 2. *Mahee dundan* ماهي دندان or fish-bones; 3. *Uqeeq* عقيق or cornelians; 4. *Uqeeq-ool-buhur* عقيق البحر or Mocha stones; 5. *Motee* موتي or pearls; 6. *Goollee* گلي or corals; 7. *Uqqul-bar* اقل بار (vulgo *Uqqul buhur*) canna indica, *Lin.* or the seeds of the shot plant; 8. *Zytoon* زيتون or olive stones; 9. *Sudduf* صدف or mother-of-pearl; 10. *Solaymanee* سليماني or onyx; 11. *Peer puttaree* پير پتاري or agate; 12. *Abnoos* آبنوس or ebony; 13. *Ryhan* ريحان beads made of the wood of the ocimum pilosum, *Lin.*, or the basilic basil; 14. *Bujjur buttoo* بجر بتو or seeds of the corypha umbraculifera, *Lin.*, or umbrella bearing palm; 15. *Khak-e-shuffa* خاك شفا *lit.* the curative dust (meaning the earth of *Kurbulla*, p. 171, or field where *Hosein* suffered martyrdom), and greatly venerated; 16. *Lyl-o-nuhar* ليل و نهار *lit.* day and night. A kind of red wood spotted with black; 17. *Sundul* صندل or sandal wood; 18. *Hurfa-leooree* (dukh.) هرفاليوڑي or the stones of the cicca disticha, *Lin.* or chilimillie; called also the country-gooseberry, and churmayla, *Hind.*

Tusbeeh تسبيح—the act of praising God, e. g. سمع الله لمن حمده ربّنا الكَ الحمد *Sum'mee alla'ho lay'mun hum'meda rub'buna luk'ulhumd*, or "the great God hears whatever praises I offer to him. Oh my Protector, I thank thee!"

Tushfee-ool wittur تشفي الوطر—forms of prayer instituted by *Beebee Aaysha* (the wife of the Prophet Mohummud.)

Tusmeeu تسميه—*lit.* nomination, appellation, giving a name. The following is so termed: بسم الله الرّحمن الرّحيم *Bismillah hirruhman nirruheem*, i. e. In the name of the compassionate and merciful Jehovah.

Tuwaf توّاف—turning or encompassing; making the circuit of any holy place, such as that of the *kaaba* (vide p. 63), &c.

Tyammoom تيمم—purifying, or rubbing the hands, face, and other parts of the body, with sand or dust (agreeably to the Moosulman law) where water cannot be got, previous to performing religious duties, in the same manner as if they were dipped in water.

U.

Ubeer عبير—vide *Abeer*.

Uggur اگر—lignum aloes, wood-aloes, or aloe wood; a species of wood which, on being thrown into the fire, smokes, and emits a delightful odour.

Uggur-kee-buttee اگر كي بتي—wood aloes, or aloe-wood pastils, erroneously called *oodbuttee;* they are composed of *uggur* اگر or wood aloes, *sundul* صندل or sandal wood, *ood* عود benzoin or benjamin, *ch'hureela* چهڑيلا or a kind of rock lichen (lichen rotundatus, *Rottl.*), *puchapat* پچاپات, *sillarus* سلارس or *sullajet* سلاجت a beautiful crystallized foliated gypsum, *talisputtree* تالس پتري a fragrant smelling plant, *roomee mustukee* رومي مصطكي or gum mastich, sugar candy, or gum; these are pounded fine, mixed up with rose-water, and formed into pastils. The best come from Beejapoor, in the Mahratta country.

Urgujja ارگجا—name of a perfume of a yellowish colour, and compounded of several scented ingredients. The common kind is a mixture of sandal wood, wood-aloes, and some odoriferous oil. The following is a superior recipe for its composition: Triturate sandal wood and wood-aloes with rose-water, then add *choa* چوا or the oil of aloes-wood, *suntooka* سنتوکا, *zoobad* زباد or civet-cat perfume, of each two *mashas;* otter of roses, or *chumbaylee*-oil چنبيلي or the oil of jessamine, of each a quarter of a *tola;* mix all well together, and rub the body over with this delightful perfume.

Uttur or *Utur* (prop. *Itr* عطر)—or otter, of roses, &c. This, on ceremonial occasions, is invariably offered to the guests on a little cotton, twisted at the end of a bit of stick four or five inches long.

W.

Wajib-ool-wittur واجب الوطر—prayers enjoined in the *Qoran* and *Huddees*, *but* of the authenticity of which there is some doubt.

Z.

Zoobuh ذبح—a sacrifice, slaughter; *zoobuh kurna*, to sacrifice, to kill (animals for food, agreeably to the Mohummudan law), to slaughter. Any individual (Hindoo or Christian) may perform the *zoobuh*, which consists in repeating the words *bismillah Alla ho akbur*, "in the name of the great God," while drawing the knife and cutting across three particular parts, which are essential to the operation, viz. the windpipe, the carotid arteries, and the gullet (or the *rug* called *mirree*), on which such slaughtered animal becomes lawful food to Mohummudans. If only two of these be divided, it is unlawful.

Zukat زکات—or alms; the Mohummudan law recommending it to every person to give to the poor, or for other religious uses, a certain portion of their possessions, by way of purifying or giving a blessing to the rest. This is called by some writers a tenth, but erroneously, as it varies according to the description of a man's estate, to its value, and to the piety of the donor; some giving one-fifth, one-fourth, one-third, and even a half of all they have to the poor. *Hussun* (the son of *Allee*, and grandson to the Prophet) gave away his whole property twice during his life, for the relief of the indigent.

INDEX,

CONTAINING

A List of the Subjects treated of, and general Definitions of numerous Oriental Terms occurring, and some of them more particularly explained, in the foregoing Work.

Aba. Append. p. xi.
Abbas Allee Ullum-burdar (Hosein's step-brother), 276.
Abdar-khana, the place where water is kept for drinking, 187, 223.
Abd-ool-qadir, a saint venerated, 433.
Abeer, a perfume. Gloss.
Abee Soofeean, a proper name, 169.
Abil Hoonnooq, the name of an author, 166, 169.
Abjud ka hissab. Gloss. 308.
Abkhora, a water or drinking cup, 424.
Abnoos, ebony. Vide Tusbeeh, Gloss.
Abroo, char; eyebrows, moustaches, beard, and hair of the armpits, 284, 289.
Adalut Shah, a Mohurrum fuqeer, 191.
Adum (Adam), his origin, &c., 132, 325.
Aeeam e nuhur, the season of sacrifice. Vide Ayyam, 69.
——— e qur, the day of rest. Vide Ayyam, 69.
Aet e Footooh, a verse of the Quran used in exorcism, 323.
——— ool Koorsee, ditto, 334, 383.
Afgan, or Putthan, one of the four Mohummudan tribes, 8.
Afshan, or Zur-afshan, paper sprinkled over with gold-leaf-powder, 125.
Afsoon, incantation, 329.
Aftabgeeree, a kind of parasol or umbrella used over the ullums at the Mohurrum. Vide pl. ii. fig. 8, 181.
Agara kee jur, root of the achyranthes aspera. Lin. 377.
Ahmud Khan, vows made to him, 276.
Ahud, or Ohud, q.v. where a noted battle was fought, 234.
Ajwaeen Sison Ammi, Lin. bishop's-weed seed, 3.
Ajwaeenee, vulgo Uchwanee. Gloss. 3.
Akhara, the fairy assembly, 384, 387.
Akhir muheena, the sixth month, 243.
Akhree char shoomba, a feast, 49, 96, 229, 230, 268, 425.
Alfa, or Kufnee, a fuqeer's dress. Gloss. 190, 285, 298, 412.
Algunnee, a line or rope for hanging clothes on, 305.
Al-hookm e Lillah, a Mohurrum fuqeer, 191.
Allawa, a pit dug in front of the Ashoor-khanas, 173, 186, 222. A hole dug within doors or out, over which they wash their hands and throw refuse in, 249.
Allee, son-in-law of Mohummud, 10, 257.
Alms, on whom to be bestowed, 59.
Al-oomr-e-Lillah, a Mohurrum fuqeer, 191.
Alope Unjun. Vide Unjun, 377, 378.
Alweeda, or Ulweeda, q. v., a discourse on the Rumzan separation, 225, 257.
Amal-nama. Gloss.
Ambaree, a howda with a canopy or umbrella cover, 125, 219.
Ameen, amen, 80, 263.
Ammama. Append. p. ix. 299.
Amows, the day on which the conjunction of the sun and moon takes place, 357.
Ang-gaythee, a chafing dish, 196.
——— Shah, a Mohurrum fuqeer, 196.
Anjun. Vide Unjun, 376.
Anna, an Indian silver coin equal to two pence, 37, 94, 116.
Ansurs, the four elements, 308.
Antee, or Sylee, q. v., a necklace made of coloured threads worn by fuqeers, 96, 189.
Anwut, a toe ornament. Append. p. xxvii, 118.
Aorad, repetitions (plur. of Wird), 294, 302.
Araish, artificial flowers, 44, 126.
Arbanee, a kind of musicians, 99.
Arfa, a feast, accompanied with oblations offered to saints, 251, 252, 260.

Arfat, or Jubbool Arfat. Vide Gloss. 70.
Asa, or Sonta, a club carried by devotees. 295.
Asan (lit. easy), a fateeha, so called, 270.
Asar-e-moobarik, or the blessed token, alias Asar-e-shurreef, or the sacred emblem, *viz.* a hair of the Prophet's beard or moustaches, 236.
Asayb-walee, a demoniac, 384.
As'hab e-kuhuf, i. e. the companions of the cave, or the seven sleepers, 276, 340.
Ashoora, the ten first days of the month Mohurrum, 148, 172, 269.
Ashoor-khana, or Astana, the ten-day house, 172, 186.
Asman, the seven firmaments, 149.
Asmangeeree, a cloth fastened to the ceiling of a room, 119.
Asoph ood Dowlah, oblations offered at his shrine, 280.
Astana, the same as Ashoor-khana, 172, 268, 279.
—— Mudar ka, 243.
Astrological Tables, 19, 85.
Ata, pounded wheat. Gloss.
Attaran, perfumers, 189.
Attributes of the Deity, 358.
Attu-hyat, 79.
Atush-bazee, fireworks. Append. IX. p. lvii, 44, 254.
Aysha, night. Vide Numaz, 55, 78.
Aytaykaf bythna, the being engaged in constant prayers at the mosque, 255, 257, 262.
Ayyam-e-nuhur, season of sacrifice, 69.
—— e-qur, day of rest, 69.
Ayzeed, he who caused Hussun to be poisoned, 150.
Azad (solitary, or free), a class of devotees, 297.
Azan, the summons to prayer, 75, 239, 257, 258.

Baba-Boodun, alias Hyat Qulundur, or Hyat-ool-Buhur, 246, 281.
—— Lal, oblations offered at his shrine, 280.
Badeea, bowls, generally made of brass or bell metal, 120.
Badkush, or Mirwaha, a fuqeer's fan, 295.
Badla, brocade, or variegated silken stuff, 40, 176.
Bagh, or Tiger, a Mohurrum fuqeer, 201.
—— nuk, or Tiger's nails, used as charms, 356. Append. xxiv.
Baja-bujuntur. Mus. Instr. Append. p. xlvi.
Bajra, holcus spicatus, Lin. panicum spicatum Roxb., 277.
Bandee, a female slave, 120.
Banuwa, or Banwa, prop. Bay-nuwa, q. v., 190, 288.
Baoolee, ear ornament. Append. p. xxi, 220, 275.
Bara-masa, real fuqeers so called. Vide Fuqeers, 192.
Bara-wufat, a feast so called, 189, 233, 425.
Ba-shurra (lit. with law), a class of fuqeers, 296.
Bawa, a mode of address among fuqeers, 193.
—— Boodun, alias Hyat Qulundur, 246, 281.
—— fuqur ood Deen, a venerated saint, 246, 281.
—— peearay kay fuqeeran, a class of devotees, 294.
Bay-aj khora, an usurer, a Mohurrum fuqeer, 205.
Baygur, tinsel or tinfoil, 194.
Baylun, a rolling-pin, 119.
Bay-nuwa, a class of fuqeers, 190, 288, 289.
Bayra, a raft or float, a feast so called. Vide Juhaz, 273, 430.
Bayree (lit. fetters), a ring worn round the ankle, 237, 239, 275.
Bayr ka pat, leaves of the Indian plum-tree, zizyphus jujuba, Lin., 410.
Bay-shurra (lit. without the law), a class of fuqeers, 296.
Baysun, powdered chunna, q. v., 112.
Baz, the falcon, 406.
Bazoobund, a kind of armlet. Vide Append. p. xxiv.
Beebee Fateema, the daughter of Mohummud married to Allee, 2, 108, 253.
—— ka basun, a ceremony, 108, 277.
—— ka Sanuk, ditto, 108, 277.
—— kee kundoree, ditto, 277.
Beebeean, a ceremony so called, 147.
Been, or Vina. Mus. Instr. Append. p. li, 293.
Beera, or Beeree. Gloss. 278.
Beer-e-zumzum. Vide Zumzum, 64.
Beg, an honorary title signifying brave or valiant, 9.
Begum, the wife of a Syed, 16.
Bhajee, greens. Append. p. xxxvii, 27, 374.
Bhand, a mimic, an actor, 43.
Bhanda, or Ch'hutthee ka, a dish of food so called, 6, 26.
Bhend, or Shola, q. v. in Gloss., a kind of pith, 125.
Bhoojbund, an armlet. Append. p. xxiv.

Bhoojputur, Epidermis of the Betula Bhojpatra, Wall., 356.
Bhoora, a ceremony on the third day after Shubgusht. Vide Chowthee, 139.
Bhoot-unjun. Vide Unjun, 377, 378.
Bhow*n*ra, a species of large black bee, said to be enamoured of the lotus, 302.
Bhubhoot, cow-dung ashes, 196, 329.
Bhugna, corr. Baghnuk, q. v.
Bhu*g*teea, a dancing boy dressed up as a dancing girl, 43.
Bhugwee, cloth dyed with red ochre, used by fuqeers, 294.
Bhun*d*ara, or Mudar ka ch'han*d*a, q. v., 101.
Bhundaree Shah, a Mohurrum fuqeer, 190.
Bhung, an intoxicating drink. Gloss. 45.
Bhungee, or Bangy, a stick with ropes hanging from each end for slinging baggage to, which is carried on the shoulder, 217.
Bhuranch, name of a town or village about thirty miles north-east of Lucknow, 249.
Bhurla, or Bulla, terminalia bilirica, Roxb., or belleric myrobolan, 52.
Bhurrung, a Mohurrum fuqeer, 195.
Bhyree, a hawk, 406.
——— Shah, a Mohurrum fuqeer, 198.
Bich'hway, a toe ornament. Append. p. xxvii.
Bichnâg, poison root. Vide Boza, Gloss.
Bidaut-e-hoosna, 254.
Bihisht, or Heaven, the seven heavens, 149.
Birreeanee. Vide Cookery, Append. p. xxix, 96.
Bisk'hopray kee jur, trianthema decandra, Willd., or trianthema pantandra, 377.
Bismilla. Gloss. 111, 326, 425.
——— or Bismilla-khwanee, the ceremony of teaching children to repeat the name of God, 39, 40.
Boolâq, a nose ornament. Append. p. xxi, 118, 220, 275.
Boo*d*dha, Boo*d*dhee, Mohurrum fuqeers, 201.
Boojputthur. Vide B'hoojputur.
Bookhoor, perfumes burnt in exorcising, 308.
Booraq, the animal on which Mohummud is said to have passed from Jerusalem to heaven. Vide Pl. I, fig. 4, 172, 186, 235, 251.
Boorboorook (prop. Boorboorqa), a small double hand-drum, 215.
——— Shah, a Mohurrum fuqeer, 215.
Booroojan, the signs of the zodiac, 307.
Boo*tt*ee, a mixture of duhee (tyar) and rice, 224.
Boqcha, a cloth for wrapping up clothes in, 119.
Bosu-gah, lit. the place for kissing on; *viz.* the neck, 168.
Boza, or Boja, a kind of beer. Gloss. 296, 407.
Buddhee, or Heemael, q. v. See Flowers, Gloss.; made also of gold, silver, leather, &c., 237, 239, 242, 275.
Budhna, or Budhnee, a kind of pot with a spout to it, 46, 411, 416.
Bugla, or Bugola, paddy birds; also, a Mohurrum fuqeer, 186, 198, 406.
Buglee-qubur, a particular kind of grave, 416.
Bujjurbuttoo, corypha umbraculifera, Lin., or umbrella bearing palm. Vide Tusbeeh, Gloss.
Bukht-kholna, or changing one's bad luck, 383.
Bullaeea*n* layna, taking another's evils on one's-self, 92.
Bullayr kay dana, dolichos lablab, Var. 378.
Bun*d*aree Shah. Vide Bhundaree Shah, 190.
Bunda Nuwaz kay churagan, a feast, 265, 426.
——— kee muheena, the eleventh month so called, 265.
Bundugee. Vide Sulam, Gloss.
Bunggree, glass bracelets. Vide Append. p. xxv, 118.
Bungurharon, manufacturers of bunggrees, 293.
Buqal, a shopkeeper, 207.
Buqr-eed, the twelfth month, 49, 252, 264, 266.
——— qoorbanee, the sacrifice, a feast, 266, 425.
Burat, the night of record, 251, 252.
———, assignment, 128.
Burchee, a spear or lance with a wooden stock carried by fuqeers, 295.
Bu*rr*a, a kind of cakes made of ground pulse. Append. p. xxxvii, 107.
Burree, wedding gifts, 106, 109.
Burus ga*n*th, birthday anniversary, 38.
Bussunt, lit. spring, a festival, 429.
Butasha. Vide Sweetmeats, Append. p. xlii, 50, 167, 333.
Butun-e-Muhasurah, a valley so called, 66.
Buzul, a gift or present to avert calamity, 310, 312.
Byât, the becoming a mooreed or disciple, 281, 299.
Byraga, or Zufur-tukeea, a small crooked stick or piece of iron which the by-

ragee or devotee places under his armpit to lean upon as he sits. Vide pl. IV, fig. 3.
By*t*huk, a particular nocturnal assembly of women, 278.
Byt-oollah, the house of God, the temple of Mecca, 63.

Chadur P'hool kay, a flower-sheet spread on graves, 235, 413, 420.
Chah-e-Zumzum. Vide Zumzum, 64.
Chandnee, a canopy, 115, 119.
Char-paee, four legs, an Indian or country cot, 10.
Char Peer-chowda khwanwaday, four spiritual guides and fourteen households, 287.
Char-yar, the four friends, 191.
Char-yaree, the soonnees, so called, 9.
—— abroo, the beard, moustaches, eyebrows, and hair on other parts of the body, 284, 289.
Char-zanoo, lit. on four knees, i. e. sitting cross-legged, 385.
Chawul. Vide Rice.
Cheerownjee, or Chironjee, nut of the chironjia sapida, Roxb., 264, 270.
Cheroot, or Choo*tt*a, a segar, 114.
Ch'hach'h, butter-milk, 418.
Ch'hay-paee, six-legged, a country cot made with as many legs, 10.
Ch'hee*n*ka, a network made of strings or cords, to place any thing on the cords of a bhungee. q. v. Pl. IV, fig. 7.
Ch'heet, chintz, 119.
Ch'hulla (vulg. Chulla), a thin wiry metallic ring, 46, 275, 412.
Ch'hurree, or Ch'huttee, q. v., 141, 285, 295.
Ch'hurree-romal, a twig of a tree with a handkerchief wound round the upper end of it, 285, 295.
Ch'huttee, alias Churree, q. v., a switch or wand, 141, 285, 295.
Ch'hutthee, a ceremony, 4, 23, 24, 425.
Ch'hutthee ka Bhan*d*a, a kind of dish, 6.
Ch'hutthee-mah, a particular dish of food so called, 6.
Chiksa. Vide Glossary, 97, 104.
Children's Plays. Append. VIII, p. liv.
Chilla, or Astana, a fuqeer's residence, 268.
——— the shrines of reputed saints, the period of forty days after childbirth, 4, 27.
——— a forty-day abstinence, 306, 318, 425.
Chillubdars, a class of devotees, 292.
Chillumchee, or Sylabchee, a washhand-basin, 120.
Chindur-Shah, a Mohurrum fuqeer, 214.
Chippa; Tambeel ka, a calipash carried by devotees, 195.
Chironjee. Vide Cheerownjee, 270.
Chistee, a subjunction to names of fuqeers, 301.
Chishteea, a class of fuqeers or devotees, 288, 289.
Choba, a dish of polaoo mixed with slices of cocoa-nuts, dates, and almonds, 103, 134.
Chogod, a large species of owl, 378.
Cholee. Dress, Append. p. xv.
Cholera (*Wuba*, lit. plague), 238.
Cholna, alias Kach'ha, q. v., 202, 214.
Chon*d*a, hair braided on the top of the head, 109.
Choona, vulg. Choonam, quicklime, 306.
Choonggay, fried cakes, made of wheat flour, sugar, and ghee, 224.
Choon*t*ee, or Chootee, the plait or tie of hair behind, cue, 91, 109.
Chooraeel, the ghost of a woman who died while pregnant. Vide Puleeta lamp charm, No. 10, 338.
Chooreean, a female ornament (Append. p. xxv.) worn by fuqeers, 91, 293.
Choorway, a dish prepared from parched rice. Gloss., 253.
Choo*t*ee, or Choontee, q. v., tufts of hair left on children's heads unshaved, dedicated to saints, 32, 272.
———- Pooreean kee, pincers for ornamenting poorean, q. v., 120.
Chor-huldee, a ceremony so called, 97.
Chow-ghurray, a small box with four partitions for holding spices, &c., 118.
Chowk-bhurna, a ceremony, 97, 124.
——— by*t*hna, to sit in a circle, a technical phrase among fuqeers, 245.
Chowkee, a stool, 119.
Chown-ur, or Chown-ree, an instrument for driving away flies. Vide Pl. III, fig. 4, 213.
Chowtha. Vide Palkee, Glossary.
Chowthee, the ceremony of untying the kunggun on the fourth day after the Shubgusht, so called. Vide Bhoora, 139.
Chubootra, an elevated seat or platform. Vide Mayzunna, 77, 186.
Chuddur, corrupt. of Chadur, q. v.
——— P'hool kay. Vide Flowers, Gloss., 235, 413, 420.
Chukkee, a hand mill, 108, 186.
——— nama, a song sung while grinding at the mill, at weddings, 108.
——— nowree, a ceremony so called, 109.

Chukkur, a weapon. Gloss., 195.
Chukoleean, or Sootreean. Gloss,, 254.
Chulla, prop. Ch'hulla, q. v.
Chumbaylee, jasminum grandiflora, Lin. jessamine, 382.
——— kay mundway, 184.
Chundoo, a kind of hanging lamp made of bamboo frame-work covered with mica, 175.
Chundun Suffeid, sandal-wood, 308.
——— har, a necklace, neck ornament. Append. p. xxii, 101.
——— lal, logwood, 308.
Chundur Buddun and Mohy Yeear, oblations offered at their shrines, 281.
Chunna, Bengal horsegram, cicer arienatum, Lin., 112, 202.
Chupa*t*eean, very thin wheaten cakes. Append. p. xxxiii.
Churagan, lit. lamps, oors or illumination, 238, 241, 268.
Chura*g*dan, niches for lamps on tombs, 419.
Chura*g*ee, a present made to the Moolla for offering up oblations at the tomb of a saint, &c., 190, 218, 236.
Churawa, presents of jewels and dresses to the bride, 90, 93.
Churkhee Fanoos, revolving shades; or Fanoos-e-kheeal, q. v., Pl. I, fig. 3, 185.
Churrus, or Churs, an inebriating electuary, Gloss. 296, 407.
Chu*tt*ana, (lit. causing to lick) a ceremony, 33.
Chutnee, a condiment. Append. p. xliii.
——— Shah, a mohurrum fuqeer, 202.
Circumcision. Vide Glossary, 43, 425.
Compound, an area or enclosure round a house, 5.
Cookery, Moosulman. Append. V, p. xxvii.
Congratulations, 264.
Cot, country or Indian. Vide Charpaee, 10.
Cowries. Vide Kowra, 206, 222.
Curries. Vide Cookery, Salun, Append. p. xxxv, 3, 134.
Curry Powder. Append. p. xxxix.

Dad-muhal (lit. palace of justice). Vide Pl. I, fig. 2, 185.
Daee junnaee. Vide Gloss. 2.
—— doodh pillaee. Gloss.
—— k'hillaee. Gloss.
—— asseel. Gloss.
Daeera kee Fateeha. Vide Fateeha, 417, 422.
Daeeraywalay, or Muhdee-walay, a subsect of Moosulmans, 13, 260.
Damnee, or Daoonee, dress. Append. p. xvi, 412.
Dâl, a pulse, phaseolus radiatus, Lin. phaseolus aureus, Roxb. green gram, or rayed kidney bean.
*D*al, an ornament worn by fuqeers. Gloss. 196, 285.
Dant neekulna, teething, 33, 34; or Dant ghoongnee, ditto, 34.
Daroo, ardent spirits of any kind.
Data, a mode of address among fuqeers, 193.
Dawut, invitation, 35.
Dawut Elm-e, the science of exorcism, 294, 303, 309, 316.
Day*g*', a large, or Day*g*'cha, a small copper caldron, 120, 376.
Death, when created, 149.
Deed, viewings or beholdings of the deity, or of some part or other of the body, pointed out by the Moorshud, 302.
Deen, religion, 45, 263.
Deenar, a Persian coin. In Hindoostan, equivalent in value to two and a half rupees, 59.
Deewargeeree, tapestry or cloth for adorning a wall, 119.
Demons, 312.
Dewankhana, a hall, a parlour, 110, 112.
D'hal sahib, a Mohurrum ullum (lit. Mr. Shield), 177.
D'han kay K'heeleean, or K'hoee, swollen parched rice, 282, 333, 383.
D'hayleez K'hoondlana (lit. treading the threshhold), a ceremony, 89, 95.
Dhingana, vulgo Dheegana (lit. a forfeit), a demand of it at a ceremony, 126.
——— Budhnee, the earthen pot used at this occasion, 127.
*D*hol, the common drum. Vide Mus. Instr. Append. p. xlix.
D'holkee, or *D*'holuk, a small drum. ditto, p. l., 278.
D'honee, a fire lighted by fuqeers, over which they sit, imbibing its smoke, 290.
D'hotee, a cloth worn round the waist, passing between the legs and tucked in behind, 190.
D'hummul koodana, a ceremony, 241, 242.
Dhunna, or Dhun Unjun. Vide Unjun, 377, 378.
Dhunneea, coriander seed (coriandrum sativum, Lin.) 330.
Dhu*tt*ee, the cloths or dresses, with which ullums are bedecked. Vide Pl. II. fig. 7, 177, 221, 227, 280.
Dinner, a moosulman, 110.

Dirrum. Vide weights, Append., 59, 406.
Divorce, 144.
Doa-e-Masoora, supplication for the remission of sins, 49.
—— Qoonoot, prayer of praise, 81, 130.
Do-gana Rukat. Vide Rukat, 63, 259.
*D*ola, bier, 413.
—— Run ka, the war-bier, 226.
*D*omneean, a class of musicians. Gloss. 33, 43, 384.
Dona, a leaf folded up so as to hold any thing, 272.
Doodh payra, sweetmeats. Append. p. xli., 270.
——— ka Muheena, the tenth month, so termed, 261.
*D*oolee. Vide Palkee. Gloss. 27.
Dooneeadar, a mode of address among fuqeers, 193.
Door, or Hulqa, female ornaments. Append. p. xxi., 220, 275.
Do-paee, a variety of magic squares, 347.
Do-pu*tt*a, dress. Append. p. xii., 117.
Do-shala, a pair of shawls. Vide Dress, Append. p. xii., 299.
Dost, a Mohurrum fuqeer, 191.
Downa, artemesia austriaca, Lin. lad's love, old man or southernwood, 382.
Dowr, circle; implying repetition, 310, 312.
Dowry, 130, 135.
Do-zanoo bythna. Gloss. 385.
Dozukh, hell (the seven hells), 149.
Dresses. Append. III. p. ix.
Duff, a kind of tambourin. Mus. Instr. Append. p. xlix., 194.
Duff and Surode players, 99.
Duffalees, a class of wandering devotees, 289.
Duhee, or Tyar, curdled milk, 107, 121, 276, 401.
Dulleea, rice and milk made of a very thin consistence. Vide Kheer, 100, 273.
Dum Mudar, lit. the breath of Mudar. Vide Zinda Shah Mudar, 242.
Dumree, a copper coin. Gloss., 3.
Dungul kurnaywala, (lit. assembler of a crowd), the master of ceremonies, 228.
Durgah, the sacred shrines of saints. Gloss., 32, 44, 178.
Durood, blessing or benediction, 172, 316.
Durwaysh or Fuqeer, a religious mendicant or devotee, 296.
Dusmasa. Vide Fuqeers, 192.
Dussayra (prop. Dush'hra), the chief Hindoo festival in the Deccan, answering to the *Doorga pooja* in Bengal, 187.
Dustar or Puggree. Vide Dress. Append. p. ix. 300.
Dust-bosee, shake (lit. kiss) hands, 264.
Dusth-bulla or Kurb-bulla, q.v., 163.
Dust-punna, a pair of tongs carried by fuqeers, 196.
Dustugeer. Vide Peer e Dustugeer, 237, 425.
Dustugeer-walay, an appellation given by the Gyr-muhdees to all other sects, 260.
Dustur-khwan, a table-cloth; or rather a floor-cloth, one spread on the ground, 111, 119.
———— lord of the, 326.

Earths (the seven), 149.
Eeboodee, the ashes of the Ood-dan, q.v., 180.
Eed, feast, 49, 268, 427.
—— ka Muheena, 261.
Eed-ool-Fittur (or Fitr), the feast of alms, 261, 268.
———e-Rumzan, the Rumzan feast, 261, 266.
———, Zoha or Qoorbanee, the feast of sacrifice, 96, 266, 268.
Eedee, a verse, or something relating to the eed (or feast), written by schoolmasters on coloured or illuminated paper, given to their pupils to exact presents from their parents, 47, 49, 96, 232, 254, 264, 268.
Eedeeana, holiday presents, 268.
Eed-gah, or Numaz-gah, (Gloss.) 57, 261, 266, 268. Vide Pl. III, fig. 2.
Eelachee, cardamoms; a ceremony, 35.
Eemamein, or ullums, (lit. standards,) 176, 289.
Eemameins, the Sheeahs, so called, 269.
Eemam, a priest, 132, 175, 414.
——— azum, (lit. the great priest) i. e. Huneefa, q. v.
——— Jaffur Sadiq, 238, 277.
——— Muhdee. Vide Muhdee, 260, 431.
——— Shahee, a class of fuqeers (or devotees), 298.
——— Zamin, a saint, in whose name vows are made, 275.
——— Zaday, or ullums, q. v., 176.
Eenam (lit. a gift), land given by government as a reward for services, or as a fee, a pension in land, 300.
Eeranee, Persians who are all Sheeas, the Sheeas so called, 9.
Ees, or Esau, 9.
Eezar. Vide Dress, Append. p. xiii, 117, 404, 411.

Ehram, the pilgrim's or the sacred habit. Gloss. 61.
Enchanters, 336.
Ehsan, thanks, 326.
Elements (the four), 84, 86, 308, 349, 351.
Emambara, a sacred building for the celebration of the Mohurrum, 174.
Executor, 407.

Fairies, specimens of their names, 387.
Fanam, a silver coin. Gloss. 5.
Fanoos-e-kheeal, or Churkhee Fanoos, q. v. Vide Pl. I, fig. 3, 185.
Farayqa, the night of discernment, 252.
Fateeha, prayers offered up over oblations, &c. made to saints, &c. Gloss. 172, 253, 270, 422, 425.
——— Daeera kee, the cemetery oblation, 417, 422.
——— Huzrut Shah kay, or Mowla Allee, 275.
——— Asan, 278.
——— Neeut khyr kee, prayers offered for the welfare of any one. Gloss. 91, 94, 417.
——— Kundoree kee, 249.
——— Sanuk. Gloss. 2.
——— Geearween, 240.
Feernee. Vide Cookery, 3, Append. p. xl.
Fireworks, 254. Append. IX, p. lvii.
Firmaments (the seven), 149.
Fitnee, rice and milk made of a thicker consistence than k'heer, q. v., 100.
Fitr, or Iftar. Gloss.
Fittra, fast offerings. Gloss. 57, 261, 262.
Flowers of various kinds—for these, vide the word in the Gloss.
Food, lawful and unlawful, 405.
Foorat, the river Euphrates, 162.
Fujur kee Numaz, 55, 78.
Fuqeer, alias Durwaysh, a devotee, 264, 281, 284, 296, 301.
——— Bara-masee, real fuqeers, 192.
——— Dus-masee, the Mohurrum fuqeers so called, 192.
———s, Mohurrum, 180.
——— e-Rufaee, or Goorz-mar, 241.
Furash, a sweeper and spreader of carpets, 378.
Furreed ood Deen, Shukur Gunj, a saint, 280.
Fursh, carpeting, mat, any thing spread, 97.
Furz, God's commands. Gloss. 49, 189.
——— Wajib. Gloss.
——— Kufaeea, 258, 420.
Futthan (a victor), corrupted into Putthan, 12.
Fyz-e-Billah, *i. e.* God's grace or bounty ships, 61.

Gadee, bedding, any thing stuffed, spread on the galeechu to sit or lie on, 119.
Gaee-lootana, a ceremony so called, 241, 242.
Gaeen-*en*, singers, girls brought up by the nobility and taught dancing and singing, 17.
*G*aleecha, a small carpet, 119.
Games. Append. VII, p. lii.
Ganja. Vide Glossary.
Ga-*rro-rr*ee Shah, a Mohurrum fuqeer, 214.
Gaynd, tagetes erecta, Lin. Indian or African marigold, 382.
Gayroo-Lal, red ochre, 195.
Geearween (lit. the eleventh) Dustugeer's, a feast so called, 237.
Gend, or Gaynd, tagetes erecta, Lin. Indian or African marigold, 382.
Gend-guhwara. Vide Flowers, Gloss. 220, 275.
Genii, their origin, nature, food, names, king, &c., 324, 328.
G'ha*nt*ee, strips of different coloured cloths tied round the ankles by Mohurrum fuqeers, 195.
G'hee, stale butter clarified by boiling and straining.
G'hooghoo, the owl, 378.
G'hoomna, a dance of the Mohurrum fuqeers, 194.
G'hoongchee, a small red seed with a black spot, or entirely white, forming two varieties, called red and white goomchee, q. v.
G'hoonghroo. Append. ankle ornaments, p. xxvii, and Mus. Instr. p. xlvi.
G'hoongnee, wheat or Bengal horsegram boiled whole in water with sugar, 34.
G'horay (lit. horses), or K'hoolay G'horay (lit. loose horses), a ceremony, 250, 275, 279.
G'huggree. Mus. Instr. Append. p. xlvi. Vide Pl. IV, fig. 2, 213.
G'huggree-walay, a Mohurrum fuqeer, 213.
G'hurra, a large earthen pot. Gloss.
G'hurree, twenty-four minutes, two and a half making one hour, 37, 378, 395.
Gilla, or Gulla, q. v. money, 240.
Gingilie oil, ol. sesam. orient., Lin., country (Indian) sweet oil, 25.
Girday, or Gul-tukeea, a small round pillow placed under the cheek in bed, 119.
Goga, or Zahir peer, a saint, 432.
Gol, society; whence Mogol (Mogul), 9.

*G*olam, a male slave, 56, 120.
Gold mohur, or Ashrufee, a gold coin. Gloss.
Gom, a flag, a ceremony, 246.
Goochee, a bundle of one hundred betel leaves, 274.
Gool, fire-balls for the hooqqa. Gloss. p. lxxxvi.
Gool-ab, rose-water. Gloss 412.
Gool-ab-pash, a bottle from which rose-water is sprinkled, 118.
Gool-cheenee, chrysanthemum Indicum, Lin. Indian chrysanthemum, *vulgo* Christmas-flower, 382.
Goolgeean, Goolgooleean, or Goolgool-lay, swollen rice mixed with molasses formed into balls. Append. Cook. p. xxxiv, 96, 210, 270, 278.
Goollee, coral. Vide Tusbeeh, Gloss.
Gooloobund, any thing worn in any way about the neck. Dress, Append. p. x, 196, 215, 293.
Goomchee, or Ghoongchee kee jur, abrus precatorius, Lin. or wild Jamaica liquorice, 377.
Goor, jaggree, raw sugar, treacle, or molasses, 401.
Goor-akoo, or Goodakoo, the tobacco for the hooqqa. Gloss. 284.
Goorgee. Dress, Append. p. xiii, 194, 195.
Goorz, a sort of iron club, pointed at one end, and having a knob at the other covered with spikes. Vide Pl. IV, fig. 5, 291, 417.
——- mar, a class of fuqeers, 241, 291.
Goruk-dhun*d*a, an iron instrument resembling a Chinese puzzle carried by fuqeers. Vide Pl. IV, fig. 6, 295.
Gosaee*n*, or Suneeasee, a class of Hindu devotees, who go about almost naked, 290.
Gosha-nusheen, in retirement, contemplating the Deity, 258.
*G*osool, baths, or purifications of divine command, 53, 72, 75, 258.
——— bathing or washing, 405, 411.
Go*t*e, presents given at the birth of a child, 6.
Go*t*ha, *narrow* gold or silver lace. Vide Kinnaree, 195.
*G*ows-ool-Azum, (the great contemplative) or Dustugeer, q. v., 237, 432.
—— oos Sumdanee, or Dustugeer, 237.
Guava, or Jam, Umrood, or Sufree-am, psidium pyriferum, Lin., 141, 382.
*G*udeer, a feast celebrated by Sheeahs, 10, 269.
Guhwara, a (swinging) cradle, 27, 32.
Gujra, or Soomurrun, bracelets made of coloured thread, worn at the Mohurrum, 184, 188.
Gujra, formed of flowers. Vide Flowers, Gloss. 41.
*G*uleez-Shah, a Mohurrum fuqeer, 214.
Gulla, lit. grain or corn, but here money, 240.
Gullay-milna. Vide Sulam, Gloss.
Gul*t*ukeea, or Girday, a pillow for the cheek, 119.
Gun*d*a, a knotted string tied round the neck of a child, &c. as a charm, 374, 389.
——— four of any thing. 274.
Gurdonee, a silver neck ring, 39.
Gurm-mussala. Vide Mussala.
Guroh, a band or troop (of fuqeers), 190.
——— sur, leader of ditto, 190, 214, 245.
*G*ussala, or Moorda-sho, persons whose office it is to wash the bodies of the dead, 409, 419.
*G*yr-muhdee. Vide Muhdee, Gloss. 1, 13, 14, 259, 260.

Hafiz, a celebrated poet, at whose shrine oblations are offered, 281.
——- one who knows the whole Qoran by heart, 21, 69, 256.
Hajee, a pilgrim.
——- Ruhmut oollah, oblations offered at his shrine, 281.
Hajee Ahmuq, and Hajee Bay-wuqoof, Mohurrum fuqeers, 200.
Hajrah (Hagar,) 64.
Halalkhor, the lowest caste of people in India. Vide Hulalkhor, 230.
Hanee, a proper name, 158.
Har. Vide Flowers, Gloss.
Haris, a proper name, 161.
Hat'h-burtana, a matrimonial ceremony, 142, 147.
Hat'h-kutoray-wala, a Mohurrum fuqeer, 198.
Hazaree, a ceremony, 251.
Hazirat, the flame of a charm-wick, 376, 379, 382.
Hazree, (lit. breakfast) a ceremony, 276.
Heavens, the seven, 149.
Heemacha, a bag made of the skin of a lamb, used by fuqeers, 295.
Heemael, or Buddhee, q. v., 194.
Hells, the seven, 149.
Hijray, eunuchs, 28.
Hijron ka Taefa, 29. Append. xlviii.
Hijree, or Hijrah, the flight of Mohummud; hence his era (16 July, A. D. 622), 12, 171.
Hindoos turned Mohurrum fuqeers, 187, 218, 239.
Hooma, a fabulous bird. Gloss.
Hoonnoor-hosein kay Fuqeeran, Mohurrum fuqeers, 212.

Hooqqa, the pipe and apparatus in which tobacco is smoked in the East, 114, 211.
Hoor (e-shudeed, the martyr), 163.
Hooroof-e-Tuhjee, the Arabic alphabet, 307.
Horoscope, 19, 371.
Hosein, a son of Allee, 8, 148.
Hosein's martyrdom, 150.
Hosein Abdool, or Baba Wullee, a saint, 280.
Hoosnein, meaning Hussun and Hosein, 156, 221.
Howda, an open litter fixed on the back of an elephant, in which people ride, 218, 219.
Howz-e-Kowsur, a fountain in Paradise, 404.
Huddeea, a ceremony, 47, 49.
——— Qoran kee, ditto, 48, 284.
Huddeearoo, a kind of ring used at marriages. Append. p. xxvi, 91.
Huddees, the traditions of Mohummud. Gloss. 329.
———e-Nubuwee, the traditions of the prophet. Gloss. 135.
———e-Qoodsee. Gloss.
Huj, a pilgrimage. Gloss. 60.
—— Mukkay ka. Vide Mukkay (Mecca), 60.
Hujooloha, an epithalamium, 136.
Hujr-ool-uswud, the black stone at Mecca, 63.
Hukeem, a physician, a Mohurrum fuqeer, 203.
Hulal-khor, outcasts, to whom all sorts of food are considered lawful, 230.
Huldee, turmeric; a ceremony, 97, 124.
——— Maynhdee, a ceremony, 102.
——— bythna, sitting in state, alias Munja bythna, q. v.
——— chor, a ceremony, 97.
——— saoo, ditto, 97.
Hullah, or Neembolee, neck ornament. Append. p. xxii, 118.
Hullah, Hurla, Huldah, or Zungeehur terminalia chebula, Willd. chebulic myrobolan, 52.
Hulqa, or door, ear ornament. Append. p. xxi, 239.
Hulwa. Append. Cook. V, p. xl, 6, 276.
Humbulee, one of the four principal Mohummudan sects, 244.
Hundee, a small earthen pot. Gloss.
Hunnoman, the Hindoo monkey-god, 373, 383.
Hunslee, or Towq. Append. Orn. IV, neck 15, 275.
Hunufee, one of the four principal Mohummudan sects, 244, 406.
Hurla. Vide Hullah.
Hurreebayl (lit. a green creeper), or Shookrana, a ceremony, 93.
Hurreera. Cookery, Append. p. xli, 3, 46.
Hussun, a son of Allee, 148.
Hussun's martyrdom, 150.
Huwa, Eve, 132, 326, 349.
Huzrut-shah, a name of Mowla Allee, 275.
——— Baba Fuqr-ood-Deen Gunj ool Israr, a saint, 281.
Hyât, life, said to be created on the tenth day of Mohurrum, 149.
——— Qulundur, or Baba, or Bawa-Boodun, a saint. Vide Oors, 246.
Hydur Wullee, a saint, 281.

Iblees (Satan), one who despairs of God's mercy, 325.
Ibraheem (Abraham), 67, 132, 267.
Iftar, the evening meal during Lent, so called, 255.
Ink (Indian), receipts for making it, 231.
Is-haq (Isaac), 9, 266.
Islam, the proper name of the Mohummudan religion, 162.
Ism, a name, or attribute, 303, 304, 310.
——e Azum, the great attribute of the Deity, 259.
—— Jullalee, the terrible attributes, 304.
—— Jumalee, the amiable attributes, 304.
Ismaeel (Ishmael), 67, 266, 267.
Ispund, the seed of the Maynhdee, q. v. and Gloss. 4, 7, 46.
Israfeel, the name of an archangel. Vide Jibbreel. Gloss.
Istugfar, deprecation. Vide Ustugfar, 78.
Iznee, a fuqeer who acts as a messenger, 284.
Iznee Shah, a Mohurrum fuqeer, 191.
Izraeel, the name of an archangel. Vide Jibbreel, Gloss.

Jae-numaz, a place of prayer; vulgo Janeemaz, or Moosulla. Gloss. 78, 119, 263.
Jaffur-bin-Tyar, a proper name, 166, 380.
Jageer, land given by government as a reward for services, or as a fee, a pension in land, 131, 300.
Jalee-moeebund. Vide Flowers, Gloss.
Jam, any vessel for drinking out of, 304.
—— Vide Guava, 117.
Jama. Append. Dress III, p. xi, 11, 117, 189, 404.

Jamdanee, a sort of leathern portmanteau, 119.
Jam-khana, or Shutrunjee, a large carpet, 119.
Jan (lit. life or soul), an expression of affection, 16.
Jaree, or Juwar, holcus saccharatus, Lin. or great millet, 57.
Jayhez, bridal paraphernalia, 106, 116, 147.
Jeeb-ch'hilnee, a tongue scraper, 119.
Jhan*d*a, a banner (mudar ka), 243.
——— (Dustugeer ka), 239.
Jhar-Shah, a Mohurrum fuqeer, 207.
Jewels and ornaments. Append. IV, p. xvii.
Jhola, a swing. Vide Guhwara.
Jhol-p'horana, a matrimonial ceremony, 106, 120, 147.
—— kay ghurray, ditto, 107, 121.
Jhoo-*th*a, leavings of food, that which has touched food and is thereby defiled, 285.
Jhun*d*a, a flag (Dustugeer ka), 239.
————— (Mudar ka), 243.
Jibbreel, the angel Gabriel. Gloss.
Jin, genii, 324.
Jin-noonee, 324.
Joada, a proper name, 156.
Jogeean, Hindu devotees, 207, 376.
Joobba. Append. Dress, III, p. xi, 5, 200, 294, 300.
Joolwa, a matrimonial ceremony, 98, 128, 135, 147.
Joomagee, ditto, 142, 144, 148, 425.
Jootee ka jora, a pair of shoes, 117.
Jooz, a section, what printers technically term a sheet, 420.
Jora, a suit of clothes, 144.
Jotee, a large lamp made of paste, 374.
Jubbool Arfât, a mountain near Mecca, 70.
Juch-chee, a lying-in woman, 1.
Juddee, a class of Mushaekhs, 299.
Jugglers, 214, 223.
Juhad Fee-subeel-illah, or holy war, 162.
Juhaz (lit. a ship), or Bayra, a ceremony, 31, 97, 99, 272, 273, 425.
Jullaleea, or Khakeea, a class of fuqeers, 199, 293.
Jullalee Isms, the terrible attributes, 304.
Jullal-ood-Deen's Koondon, a ceremony, 250.
Jumadar, a native officer, 263.
Jumal choon*t*ee, or Jumal bal, a ceremony, 32.
Jummadee-ool-Akhir, the sixth month, 243.
————— Awul, the fifth month, 101, 141.
Jummalgo*t*a, or croton nut, 204.
Jummalee Isms, the amiable attributes, 304.
Jumma-Oollah, or Jumma Allah, God's assembly, 245, 293.
Jummaut-khanu, a meeting-house, 259.
Jummun Juttee, the founder of a sect of devotees, 290.
Jumra, gravel or small stones thrown at pillars representing the Devil in the valley of *Mina*, q. v., 66.
Jun-bhât, a ceremony, 108.
Junnut-ool-buqqeea, the name of the cemetery at Medina where Hussun was buried, 157.
Juwahir-e-Khumsa, a work alluded to, 305, 310.
Juwar, great millet, holcus saccharatus, Lin. 277, 333.

Kaaba, the temple of Mecca, 62.
Ka-ch'ha (or Cholna), a cloth worn round the hips, passing between the legs, and tucked in behind, 202.
Kafir, an infidel, 9.
Kajul, lamp-black, 5, 23, 118.
——— Dan, or Kujlotee, a box for holding Kajul or lamp-black, 118.
——— Mohnee ka, the philter lamp-black, 342.
Kakool, the tufts of hair left on both sides of the head, the middle part being shaved from the forehead to the neck, 289.
Kakra, a large wick, 332.
Kalik, the soot which collects under pots, 23.
—— ka tuwa, an iron plate on which wheaten cakes are toasted, or kalik collected, 4.
Ka*n*-chee, a ceremony, 143.
Kan-ch'haydana, boring the ears, 33, 34.
Kara, webera tetrandra, Willd., or the thorny caray, 374.
Karwa Owleea, a saint, 281.
Karwan, caravan, 159, 269.
Kat-Bawa-Sahib, the name of a saint, 272.
Khadeema, servants in charge of tombs, mosques, &c., 69.
Khakeean, or Jullaleea, q. v., 199.
Khak-e-Shuffa. Vide Tusbeeh, Gloss.
Khalee muheena, the tenth month, 261.
Khan, a title of the Putthans, q. v., 12, 15.
Kharjee, schismatics; the Soonnees so called by the Sheeas, 9, 10.
Kharwa, a kind of coarse red cotton cloth, 119.
Khas-burdar, a matchlock-man in a great man's retinue, 218.

Kheelafut, deputyship, the dignity of khuleefa (Caliph), 281, 284, 300.
K'heelecan. Vide Dhan kay K'heeleean.
K'heer, or Sheerbirrinj. Cook. Append. p. xl, 100, 212, 387.
——— kay hundee, the kheer pot, a ceremony, 244.
K'hichra. Append. p. xxxi, 227.
K'hich-ree. Append. p. xxx.
——— kay Rusum, a ceremony, 28.
Khidmutee, the sweeper, an attendant of a mosque, 132.
Khilaut, a dress, a robe of honour, 144, 263, 282.
K'hind-rray shah, a Mohurrum fuqeer, 214.
Khoaja (com. Khaja), a man of distinction, a gentleman.
——— Bunda nuwaz, q. v., the name of a saint, 288.
——— Khizur, the saint of waters, 31, 100, 273, 431.
——— Buha-ood-deen Nuqshbund, the founder of the Nuqshbundee fuqeers, 294.
——— Zaday, 15.
Khoan, a large tray, 28.
Khoancha, a small tray, 394.
Khoan-posh, or Toraposh, a tray-lid, 119.
Khoan-waday (com. Khanwaday), lineage, or household of fuqeers, so called, 287.
K'hodon-garon, a Mohurrum fuqeer, 211.
Khogeer, a native saddle, a pack-saddle, 209.
——— Shah, a Mohurrum fuqeer, 209.
Khomasee, a particular kind of magic square, 347, 351.
K'hoolay-ghoray. Vide Ghoray, a ceremony, 250.
Khoolee, a proper name, 168.
Khoolfaee, a class of Mushaekhs, 299.
Khooshka. Vide Rice, 4.
Khootba, an oration or sermon, 170, 257, 262, 263.
K'hopra, dried kernel of the cocoa-nut. Gloss.
——— ch'hilnay kee chowkee, an instrument for rasping the kernel of the cocoa-nut, 120.
K'hujoor. Vide Tusbeeh, Gloss.
Khuleefa (vulgo Caliph), a deputy or successor. Gloss. 301.
———, a Mohurrum fuqeer, 190.
K'hullee, oil cakes. Gloss. 39.
Khun, the date of the moon, 172.
Khunjuree, a small tambourine. Mus. Instr. Append. xlix, 207.
K'hurran-wan, wooden pattens, 61.
K'hurray-pan bantna, a ceremony, 88.
K'hurree, pipeclay, 194.
Khuttab, the father of Oomur, 10.
Khuteeb, a priest, 132, 170, 262.
Khutna, circumcision, 43, 425.
Khutum, the seal or conclusion, a term in the science of exorcism, 310, 312.
——— e Qoran, reading through of the entire Qoran, 177, 238, 421.
Khwaja Moyeen ood Deen chishtee, 243.
Kibla. Vide Qibla.
Kinnaree, *broad* gold or silver lace. Vide Gotha, 195.
Kishtee, a kind of tray, 28.
——— or Kuchkole, a cup or bowl (generally of beggars), a fuqeer's wallet, 285, 295.
——— Elias ka, a boat, ship, vessel, bark. Vide Juhaz, 431.
Kneeling. Vide Dozanoo bythna, 385.
Kodalee, a spade, 173.
——— marna, to dig with the spade, a ceremony, 173.
Kolsa, a king crow, 378.
Koofee (Cufa), name of a town, 154.
Koolsoom, Hosein's sister, 156, 168.
Koolthee, Madras horse-gram, Glycine tomentosa, Lin. Dolichos biflorus, Roxb. xxxv.
Koondon, or Koonday, a large earthen pot, 250, 275, 374.
——— Syed Jullal ood Deen's, a ceremony, 250.
Koondul, or Pogool, large Hindoo ear-rings, 208.
Koornish. Vide Sulam, Gloss. 69.
Koorsee, the eighth heaven, 149.
Koorta. Vide Dress, Append. X, 412.
Koossoom, safflower, or bastard saffron, carthamus tinctorius, Lin. Gloss. 117.
Kordulla, or Kurdora, a string tied round the waist, to which a lungotee is fastened, 208, 290.
Korla, or Kora, cat-o'-nine-tails (or rather of one tail), 194.
Kothmeer, the coriander plant. Append. p. xxviii, xliii.
Kot-wal, a Mohurrum fuqeer, 191, 203.
Kown-ul, the two outsides of the house on either side of the door, so called. Vide Kuwn-wul, 4.
Kowra, a large shell; Kowree, a small one, 206, 222.
Kowra-kowree, by fuqeers meant for money, 193.
Kubab. Append. Cook. V, xxxiv, 267.
Kubeer Punthee, a saint, 280.
Kuch-kole, or Kishtee, a fuqeer's wallet, 285, 295.

Kuchoor, curcuma zerumbet, Roxb., or zerumbet zedoary. Vide Abeer, Gloss.
Kuffun, a shroud, 411.
Kufgeer, a skimmer, 120, 219.
Kufnee, or Alfa, a fuqeer's dress. Gloss. 190, 285.
Kujlo*t*ee, or Kajul-Dan, q. v., 118.
Kuleeja, the liver, 339, 374, 383.
Kuleejee, the pluck; *viz.* the heart, liver, lungs, spleen, and kidneys of animals, 25, 333.
Kulma, the creed.
——— purhna, to repeat the creed, one of the points relating to practice. Gloss. 54, 192.
——— e-Shuhadut, the martyrdom-creeds, 285, 408, 411.
——— e-Tumjeed, 285.
——— e-Towheed, 285.
——— e-Rud-e-Koofoor, 285.
——— e-ty-ub, or ty-eeb, 285, 408, 414.
Kulmay Shureeut, the five creeds, 285.
Kulundur. Prop. Qulundur, q. v.
Kulus kay mât'h, or Jhol kay g'hurray, a matrimonial ceremony, 106, 107, 142, 144, 147.
——— oo*t*hana, ditto, 142.
Kumkhwab (vulg. Kingcob), silk interwoven with gold or silver flowers, 40, 344.
Kumeez. Vide Qumees.
Kummul-shah, a Mohurrum fuqeer, 209.
Kummurbund. Dress. Append. p. xii, 180.
Kunch-neean kay nâch. Vide Gloss. 93.
——— taefa. Mus. Instr. Append. p. xlv.
Kundoree, a ceremony, 249, 275.
——— Beebee Fateema kee, ditto, 277.
——— Fateeha kee, ditto, 249.
——— Rujub kee, ditto, 249.
Kunggun, bracelets, 109, 117, 139, 142.
——— kholna, a ceremony, 139, 147.
Kunghy, a comb, 118.
Kungooray, small triangular lumps made of Thoollee. Vide p. 3, 143.
Kunjur, a hawker of fruits and vegetables, 35.
Kunkee, ground rice, or the scraps that fly off in pounding rice to separate it from the husks, 3.
Kun*t*ha, a necklace or rosary of large beads made of silver, crystal, or the earth of Kurbulla. Gloss. 190, 213, 285.
Kunz-ool-Gurraeb, the title of a work, 166.
Kurb-bulla (err. Kurbula), the name of a place in Iraq where Hussun is buried, 71, 163, 221.
——— ka mydan, the plain where Hosein was slain, 221.
Kurdora. Vide Kordulla, 208.
Kureem ood Deen, oblations offered at his shrine, 281.
Ku*rr*a (pl. Kurray), a ring worn on the wrists, ankles, &c. Orn. Append. p. xxiv and xxvii, 196, 343.
Kurrahee, a flat vessel of iron, brass, or earth, in which food is boiled or fried, 278, 376.
Kurrunj kay tayl (Ol. dalbergiæ arboreæ, Willd.), 337.
Kussub, penance, a term used in the science of exorcism, 302.
Kussur ka *gh*ur (lit. fractional house), a term used in forming magic squares, 348.
Kusund ka ku*t*ora, a cup made of bell-metal, 394.
Ku*t*ar, a dirk or dagger carried by fuqeers, 194, 295.
Kuwway shah, a Mohurrum fuqeer, 198.
Kuw*n*-wul. Vide Kow*n*-ul, 273.

Lahowl. Vide Gloss. 66, 335.
Lakh', a hundred thousand, 129.
Lemonade. Append. p. xl.
Libas, a suit of clothes, 144.
Life, when created, 149.
Liffafa. Vide Luffafa.
Lodee, or Lot, from whom a description of Putthans have descended, 12.
Loong, or Loonggee. Vide Dress, Append. p. xii.
Lo*t*a, or Tumbaloo. Gloss. 274, 378.
Lowh, the tablet on which the decrees of the Deity are written, 149.
Lubbay, a class of people who sell beads, precious stones, &c., 244.
Luch-ch'ha, a necklace worn tight round the neck, Orn. Append. p. xxii. 118, 131.
Luch-ka, or Mohur-punkhee, alias Juhaz, q. v., Pl. IV, fig. 8, 273.
Lu*dd*oo. Cook. sweetmeats. Append. p. xli, 41.
——— bandhna, folding hands, a ceremony, 33.
Luffafa, a sheet used in shrouding the dead, 412.
Luggun, a large flat hollow utensil in the form of a basin, 120.
Luhud-bhurna (lit. filling the grave), a ceremony, 423.
Lunggot, Lunggota, or Lunggotee, a cloth worn between the legs. Dress, Append. p. xiii, 290, 297.

Lunggree, a large shallow pan used for kneading dough, and at meals for serving rice, &c., 120.
Lunggur (lit. anchor), a string of flowers or leaves, a ceremony, 217, 275.
——— nikalna, a ceremony, 217.
Lutkun-muhbun, a silk twist for the Choontee, 109.
Lyla, a Mohurrum fuqeer, 195.
Lyl-o-nuhar. Vide Tusbeeh, Gloss.
Lylut ool moobarik, the blessed night, 252.
——— Qudur, the night of power, 258, 259.
——— Qudur's shub-baydaree, a ceremony, 255.

Mahee Dundee, fish bones. Vide Tusbeeh, Gloss.
——— Mooratib, insignias denoted by the figure of a fish and two balls carried as ensigns upon elephants before kings and nobles, 176.
Mahtabee, cloth on which is pasted devices of the heavenly bodies in gold or silver, 234.
Majoon. Vide Gloss. 45.
Maleeda, or Mulleeda. Append. p. xli, 235.
Malik Ryhan Sahib, oblations offered at his shrine, 281.
Malukee, one of the four principal Mohummudan sects, 244.
Manda, a kind of bread, 30.
Mangnee (lit. asking), *i. e.* in marriage, a ceremony, 88, 89, 93.
Mangoe pickle. Append. p. xlii.
Mapullay (Moplays), a class of Mohummudans who inhabit the Malabar coast in the Peninsula of India, 244, xii, xiii.
Mareea, the jungle (err. plain) of Kurbulla, 162.
Marij (lit. flame without smoke, *i. e.* wind), genii formed of it, 324.
Marijin nuboos, the title of a work, 251.
Maroo, two antelope horns in opposite directions joined at their bases; carried by fuqeers, 194, 295.
Marriage, 83.
Martyrs, twenty descriptions of persons become so, 71.
Marwaree, a class of Hindoos inhabiting Marwar. A most industrious race of merchants, 215.
Mash, phaseolus max, black gram, 383.
Masha. Vide Weights, Append. II.
Mata (lit. the small-pox), a Hindoo deity who is worshipped for averting the small pox, 279.
Mât kay bhajee, amaranthus tristis, Lin. a green, 271, 277.
Maweea, a proper name, 150, 169.
Maykh Shah, a Mohurrum fuqeer, 211.
Mayla (lit. a fair), an assemblage of fuqeers so called, 221, 241, 284.
Maynhdee, or Henna (Gloss.), 102, 104, 382.
——— called Taboot or Musjid, 102, 110, 235, 240.
——— night of, 179.
Mayraj, ascension (the Prophet's), 249.
Maywa, *viz.* Choorway, Sugar, and Phootanay, 190.
Mayway ka Tubuq, the fairy fruit-tray, 384, 387.
Mayzuna, higher than a chubootra, with steps to mount by, 77.
Meals, Moosulman. Vide Khana, Gloss.
Measures. Append. II, p. vii.
Meean, master or friend, an address expressive of kindness, 16, 278, 386.
——— kee kurrahee, a ceremony, 278.
Meeana. Vide Palkee, Gloss. 110, 138.
Meehree, a woman's side locks, 141.
Meekaeel, the archangel Michael. Vide Jibbreel, Gloss.
Meena-bazar, or Mina Bazar, q. v., 61, 67.
Meer, a title by which Syeds are called, 9.
Meeran Mohy-ood-Deen, or Dustugeer, 237.
Meerza, or Mirza, a chief or prince, 15.
Meer-zada, a title of Moosulmans, 16.
Meesee, dentifrice. Gloss. 44, 118, 122, 124, 125.
——— Dan, a box for holding Meesee, 118.
Meetha Polaoo. Vide Polaoo, Cook. Append. xxvii, 88.
Mica, or Ubruk, 109, 172, 185.
Mimbur, a pulpit, the minarets of a mosque, 77, 175, 262.
Mina Bazar, Mina a valley near Mecca, 61, 67.
Miracles related, 246.
Miraj. Vide Mayraj, 249.
Mirwaha, or Badkush, a fan, 295.
Mishqal, a weight. Append. Weights II, 59.
Miswak, a kind of toothbrush. Gloss. 72, 101.
Moashur, a variety of magic squares, 347, 354.
Mogol (Mogul), 1, 8, 9, 14.
——— a Mohurrum fuqeer, 205.
Mohnee ka kajul, the philter lampblack, 342.
Mohummudanism, 55.
Mohur punkhee, Bayra, Kishtee, or Juhaz. Vide Pl. IV, fig. 1, 273, 430.

Mohurrum, the first month, 148, 229, 425.
——— festival, 96, 148, 172.
——— fuqeers, 189.
——— Nuzur-o-Nyaz, 219.
Moobariz khan, a ceremony, 276.
Moochee-walay, or Moocheemen. Vide Gloss. 110.
Mooduwir, a circle, implying repetition, 310, 312.
Moogra, jasminum undulatum, Lin. the many-leaved jessamine, 382.
Moojawir, a proprietor or landlord of Ashoor-khanas (lit. a sweeper of, or one attached to a mosque), 180.
Moolhid-nooma, lit. resembling infidels, 289.
Moolla (impr. Moolna), a doctor or learned man, 84, 373, 382.
Moonajat, supplication, 80, 82, 263.
Moon*d*un, shaving, a ceremony, 27, 31, 425.
Moong kay Dâl. Vide Dal.
Moonkir and Nukeer, two angels who examine the spirits of the departed in the tomb. Vide Jibbreel in Gloss. 417.
Moonshee, a secretary or teacher (the celestial, Mercury so called), 20.
——— or registrar, the Eternal (the Almighty so called), 150.
Moonuqa, a species of raisins, 264.
Mooraqibba, contemplating the Deity, with the head bowed down between the knees.
Mooratib. Vide Mahee, 176.
Moorch'hul, a fan for driving away flies, especially of peacock's feathers. Vide Pl. III, fig. 3, 177, 181, 220, 386.
Moorda furosh, a caste whose business it is to carry the dead, 206.
——— sho, or Gussala, persons who wash the bodies of the dead, 409.
Mooreed, a disciple (male or female), 281, 425.
Moormoora, a kind of food; rice pressed flat and eaten raw (Shakesp.), 34.
Moorshud, an instructor or spiritual guide, 282, 299.
Moortooza Allee, a name of Allee, q. v., 253.
Moorubba, a kind of magic square, 347, 350.
Moosa (Moses), 133.
——- Sohag, the founder of a sect of devotees, 293.
——- Ushuree, a proper name, 152.
Moosafir Shah, a Mohurrum fuqeer, 205.
Mooshahidda, the contemplation or vision of future, absent, or invisible things.
Mooshata, a female jester, 136.
Mooslim, a proper name, 157.
Moostussa, a variety of magic square, 347, 354.
Moosubba, a variety of magic square, 347, 352.
Moosuddus, a variety of magic square, 347, 352.
Moosul, a long wooden pestle, 122, 198.
Moosulla, or Jae numaz, q. v., 78, 318.
Moosulman dinner-party described, 110.
——— cookery. Append. V, p. xxvii.
Moosummum, a variety of magic square, 347, 353.
Moo*t*koolay, balls of paste boiled (dumplings), 333.
Moo*tt*'hee band'hna, crawling on all fours, 33, 34.
Mootuwullee, superintendent or treasurer of a mosque, 132.
Moozafur. Cook. Append. p. xxix, 96.
Moozduluffa, an oratory between Arafat and Mina near Mecca, 66.
Moplays, see Mapullay, 244, xii, xiii.
Moqbirra, a mausoleum, 416.
Moqeish, gold or silver thread, 117, 124, 125.
Motee, pearls, rosaries made of them. Vide Tusbeeh, Gloss.
Mousul, the name of a city on the western bank of the Tigris, 154.
Mowazin, a public crier to summon to prayers, 75, 132, 257.
Mowla Allee, a name of Allee, q. v., 251, 268, 426.
Mowlood, poetry chaunted before the bier of a deceased person when carried out, 414.
Mowluwee Meer Askaree, oblations offered at his shrine, 281.
Mowzeean (lit. noxious things), or vices, 302.
Mozurriq, gilt or illuminated paper on which are pasted devices in gold leaf, 49.
Mudareea, or Tubqateea, a class of fuqeers, 289.
Mudar ka Astana. Vide Astana, 243.
——— ch'handa, alias Bhun*d*ara, 97, 99, 101.
——— j'hun*d*a, a ceremony, 243.
Mudawutnee, an internuncio, or a go-between, 83.
Mudeena nuqsha, Medina-picture, 184.
Mudh-e-Hosein, the praises of Hosein, 227.
Mudud, an intoxicating beverage. Gloss. 296, 407.
Mugrib, sunset. Vide Numaz, 255.
Muhboob-e-soobhanee, or Dustugeer, 237.

Muhdee. Vide Glossary, 259, 431.
——— walay, the name by which the Gyr-muhdees call themselves, 260.
Muheena, doodh ka, 310.
——— eed ka, 310.
——— khalee, 310.
Mujnoon, a Mohurrum fuqeer, 194.
Mujzoob (lit. abstracted), a class of fuqeers, 297.
Mukkay ka huj, the Mecca pilgrimage, 54, 60.
Mukkroo, any thing which the Prophet abstained from himself, without enjoining others to do so, 406.
Mulleeda. Vide Maleeda, 235.
Mullung, a Mohurrum fuqeer, 195.
——— fuqeers, an order of devotees, 244, 290.
Mumat or Death, created on the tenth day of Mohurrum, 149.
Mun, or Maund, forty seers or eighty pounds, 276, 406.
Munday, a kind of sweetmeat, 276.
Mundeel. Dress, Append. p. ix, 117.
Mun*d*up, a canopy, 103.
Mundwa, a pandaul, a temporary shed constructed of bamboos and mats, 106.
Mun*d*way kay Beebeean, a ceremony, 106, 107, 117.
——— kay K'hana, a ceremony, 108.
Munja, or Nayoota, presents, a ceremony. Gloss. 28, 35, 37.
——— by*t*hna, sitting in state, a ceremony, 40, 97.
Munjeera. Mus. Instr. Append. p. li, 29, 33, 34.
Munjun, tooth-powder. Gloss. 72.
Muqna, a veil, 125, 130.
Murdan-ool-gyb, or Rijal-ool-gyb, q. v., 395.
Murseea, an elegy, dirge, or funeral eulogium. Gloss. 173, 228.
——— nowh, lamentations, mourning over the dead, 178, 221.
——— Khwanee, repeating or singing the Murseea, 178.
Murwa, a mountain near Mecca, 63.
———, origanum marjoram, Lin. sweet marjorum, 382.
Murwan, a proper name, 155.
Musah, or Mussuh, q. v., 73, 410.
Musan, the place where Hindoos burn their dead, 346.
Mushaekh, holy men, divines, 281, 299.
Mushroo, stuff of silk and cotton, 40, 387.
Musical Bands and Instruments. Append. VI, p. xlv.
Musjid, a mosque. Gloss.
Musjid ool Haram, the sacred or inviolable temple; *i. e.* the Kaaba, 63.
——— or Taboot, or Maynhdee, q. v., 235.
Mussala Gurm. Vide Chukoleean, Gloss.
——— Thunda. Ditto. p. xlv.
Mussoor, a kind of pulse, ervum lens, Lin., 417.
Mussuh. Vide Gloss.
Mu*t*kee, a small earthen pot or jar, 126, 240.
——— shah, a Mohurrum fuqeer, 202.
Mutloob, the object or thing wished, 316.
Muzar-ool-Huram, the holy monument near Mecca, 66.
Muzhubee, the Sheeahs so called, 9.
Myda. Vide Ata, Gloss.

Nadulee, a kind of stone worn round the neck. Gloss. 356.
Naet, or Nuwaet, a sub-sect among Moosulmans. Vide Nuwa-ay-tay, 14.
Naftulna (lit. shifting of the navel), a disease, 366.
Nahown, the fairy bath, 376, 381, 382, 383, 388.
Nakhoda (from Naoo, a vessel, and Khoda, lord or master), a ship captain, 246.
Nâl-sahib (lit. Mr. Horse-shoe), an Ullum, q. v. Vide Pl. II, fig. 9, 177, 181, 225.
Namum, the marks Hindoos make on their foreheads, 374.
Nan, leavened bread. Cook. Append. p. xxxii, 421.
Nanuk-shah, or Nanuk Pun*t*hee, a Mohurrum fuqeer, 212, 280.
Naqoos, a bell or conch-shell. Vide Note, 76.
Nara, the tape or band for the trowsers, 117, 122.
Nariellee, juice (or toddy) of the cocoanut tree, 296.
Narsinga, or Nursoo, q. v., a Hindoo deity. Vide Diagram No. 10, 338.
Nayoota, or Munja, *i. e.* presents carried in state, a ceremony. Gloss. 28, 35, 37.
Neekah, the solemnization of matrimony, 128, 135, 147.
——— ka seegah, the marriage contract, 130.
Neema. Dress, Append. p. xi, 117.
Neembolee. Orn. Append, xxiii, 118.
Neeut, a vow, 78, 255, 414.
——— kheyr kee Fateeha. Vide Fateeha, 91, 94, 417.
Neeza, a lance; carried about at the Mohurrum, 180.
Nekmundun, a saint, venerated, 200.

Nisbut, or Mangnee, q. v , 93.

Nissab (lit. alms), the repeating an attribute of the Deity a certain number of times, 303, 310, 311.

Nowbut, instruments of music sounding at the gate of a great man at certain intervals, 57, 98, 126.

Now-roz, new year's day, 428.

Nufil (pl. Nuflen), a voluntary act of devotion. Vide Gloss. 55, 78, 258.

Nuhur, a fast so called, 266.

Nukeer, name of an angel. Vide Moonkir and Jibbreel in Gloss., 417.

Numaz, prayer. Gloss. 72.

—— 1. Fujur kee, morning prayer, 55, 78.

—— 2. Zohur kee, mid-day prayer, 55, 78.

—— 3. Ussur kee, afternoon prayer, 55, 78.

—— 4. Mugrib kee, sunset prayer, 55, 78.

—— 5. Aysha kee, evening prayer, 55, 78.

—— Ishraq, at 7½ A. M.
—— Chasht, at 9 A. M.
—— Tuhujjood, after 12 P. M.
—— Turaweeh, after 8 A. M.
particular forms of prayer not of Divine command, 55, 56.

—— e-Junaza, the funeral service, 168

—— gah, or Eedgah. Vide Pl. III, fig. 2, 57, 261.

—— kurna, praying, one of the points of the Mohummudan religion, 54, 55.

Numuk chushee, a ceremony, 89, 96.

Nuqara, a kettle drum. Mus. Instr. Append. p. I, 57, 126, 273.

Nuqarchee, a small drum, 218.

Nuqday ka jora, or Chooreean. Wrist ornament, Append. p. xxv, 105, 387.

Nuqeeb-ool-Foqra, a Mohurrum fuqeer, 191.

Nuqlee shah, a Mohurrum fuqeer, 209.

Nuqol. Cook. Append. p. xli, 222, 421.

Nuqshbundeea, a class of fuqeers or devotees, 294.

Nuqshabundee, a Mohurrum fuqeer, 200.

Nurseea, a Hindoo deity, 279.

Nursoo, alias Narsinga, fourth Aootar of Vishnoo. Vide Diagram No. 10, 338.

Nuth'. Vide Nose Orn. Append. p. xxi, 118, 210.

Nuth'-nee, a small ring worn in the nose, usually by children. Ditto, p. xxii, 275.

Nuwa-ay-tay, or Naet, q. v., a sub-sect among Moosulmans, 1, 12.

Nuwwab (Nabob), a governor of a town or district, 211, 266.

Nuzur o Nyaz, vows and oblations. Gloss. 269.

——, the Mohurrum, 219.

Nyaz, Mohurrum kee, the Mohurrum oblations, 219.

—— Oollah, offerings in the name of God, 270, 275.

—— Russool, offerings in the name of the Prophet, 270, 275.

Ohud, a mountain about four miles to the north of Medina, where a memorable battle, in which the Prophet was engaged, took place, 234.

Oobala Chawul. Vide Rice, 4.

Ood, Benzoin or Benjamin. Gloss. 98, 409.

—— dan, a box for holding the frankincense, 180, 239.

—— buttee, frankincense pastiles (prop. Uggur kee buttee, q. v.), 190, 409.

—— ka ekka, a metallic receptacle for pastiles, 120.

—— ka jhar, a tree formed of Benjamin pastiles, 217.

—— soz, a censer to burn ood in, 177.

Oogal, or Peek, q. v., that which is spit out after chewing betel-leaf, 278, 386.

—— dan, a spittoon, 120.

Oollah Ruhum kay Pin*deean*. Vide Ruhum, a ceremony, 270.

Oon*t* Shah, a Mohurrum fuqeer, 216.

Oors, oblations or offerings to a saint; also called Churagan (lit. lamps or illuminations). Gloss. 189, 235, 238, 243, 244, 245, 265, 268, 280.

—— e Tubbur-e-Ullum, a ceremony, 246.

—— Baba Boo*d*un, alias Hyat Qulundur, a ceremony, 246.

—— Bawa Fuqqur-ood-Deen, a ceremony, 246.

Orhnee. Dress, Append. p. xvi, 28.

Ornaments. Append. IV, p. xxvii.

Paddy, or Dhan. Vide Rice, 416. Append. xxxii.

Paee-jama. Dress, Append. p. xiii, 105.

Pagodas, a Madras gold coin equal to three rupees and a half, 376.

Pak'hur. Vide Flowers, Gloss. 124.

Palampore (correct. Pullung-posh), q. v., 119.

Palkee, or Palankeen. Vide Palkee, Gloss. 120, 140.

Pan, betel-leaf, piper betel, Lin.

—— dan, betel-box, 118.

—— kee Beera, betel-leaf-parcel. Gloss. 120, 122.

—— k'hurray, ban*t*na, a ceremony, 89.

Pan oothana, a ceremony, 90.
—— soopeearee, betel. Vide Gloss.
Paoon minut, or Paoon mayz, the measuring for the wedding garments, 105, 147.
Paootee, a kind of lamp, 253.
Paysh-qubz, a particular kind of dagger carried by fuqeers, 295.
Paytara, a large, or Paytaree, a small rattan box, 119, 224.
Peek, or Oogal, q. v., 278, 386.
——- dan, or Oogal-dan, q. v., 120.
Peepul, ficus religiosa, Lin. the poplar-leaved fig tree, 181, 230.
Peer, a spiritual guide or saint, 282, 299.
—— Deedar kay koondon, a ceremony, 272.
—— Julal, oblations offered at his shrine, 280.
—— e-Dustugeer kay Geearween, ditto, 237.
—— Millaoo kay pindeean, ditto, 271.
—— Shittab kay pindeean, a ceremony, 271.
—— Puttaree, an agate. Vide Tusbeeh, Gloss.
Peeran, or Ullums, q. v., 176.
—— Char, the fourteen saints from whom all fuqeers have descended, 287.
—— e-Peer, the saint of saints, *i. e.* Dustugeer, q. v., 237.
Peetalee Sheernee, cakes of raw sugar, 274.
Peshwaz, or Tilluck. Dress, Append. p. xv, 28, 105.
P'hayta, a small turban. Dress, Append. p. ix, 295.
P'hool. Vide Flowers, Gloss.
—— churhana, alias Zeearut, or Teeja, q. v., 421.
—— kee chuddur. Vide Flowers, Gloss. 235, 413, 422.
—— el ka tail, odoriferous oil. Gloss. 51.
—— peehnana, a ceremony, 44.
—— ka Tubuq, the (fairy) flower tray, 384.
—— Soongnee, any sweet-scented flower, enclosed in a piece of cloth for the bride to smell, 117.
P'hootanay (err. Poothanee), parched Bengal horse-gram, 50, 190.
Pice, corrupt. of Pysa, a coin. Gloss. 2.
Pindeean, 270, 271.
Planets (the seven), 18, 308.
——, their dispositions, 20.
Plays (Children's). Append. VIII, p. liii.
Pogool, alias Koondul, large Hindoo ear-rings. Vide Append. p. xxi, 208.
Polaoo. Moos. Cook. Append. V, p. xxvii.
Pool-sirat, the bridge between Heaven and Hell. Gloss. 267.
Poonggee. Mus. Instr. Append. p. xlv. Vide Pl. V, 214.
Poor (lit. full), a ceremony so called, 236.
Pooreean, a ceremony, 89, 95.
——. Cook. Append. p. xxxiii, 95, 143.
—— kay choontee, 120.
Poorun, a ceremony, 277.
Post-khar, an artificial hand with a long handle for scratching the back, 295.
Pote, glass beads. Orn. Append. p. xxii, 133.
—— ka luch-chha, a necklace of strings of black glass beads, 131.
Presents, made on particular occasions, 37.
Puberty (male), ceremonies observed at, 53.
—— (female), ditto. Vide Virginity, 51.
Puchar ka putta, 7.
Pucheesee, a celebrated game. Append. p. lii, Pl. VII, fig. 2.
Pudduck. Orn. Append. p. xxii, 101.
Puggree. Dress, Append. p. ix, 117, 404.
Puk'hal, a large leather bag for holding water, carried on bullocks, 219.
Pukhawuj. Mus. Instr. Append. p. l, 278.
Puleeta, a charm, 330, 337, 347, 379.
Pulas ka p'hool, butea frondosa, Kœnig. 140.
Pulgoond'hun, the plaiting of a girl's side-locks, a ceremony, 39.
Pullung, a cot, 119.
—— posh (corrupt. Palampore), a coverlet, 119.
Punchee, a cloth worn by Hindoos about the loins, 208.
Punja-e-Hyduree. Vide Pl. II, fig. 10, 176.
Punjaet, a part of a chapter in the Qoran, 48.
Punjay, alias Ullums, q. v., 176.
Punjayree, or caudle. Vide Gloss. 5.
Punjutun, the five, *viz.* Mohummud, Allee, Fatima, Hussun, and Hosein, 8, 191.
Punk'ha, a fan carried by fuqeers, 295.
Purda, a curtain, 119.
Purree-walee, a fairy woman, 382, 384.
Purree kay Tubuq, the fairy tray. Vide Tubuq, 376, 381, 384.
Purree Nahown, the fairy bath, 384, 388.
Purrud, borrowed clothes, 5.

Pushmee, or wool. Sylees made of it, worn by fuqeers, 293.
Putka, a cloth worn as a kummurbund, not so long, but richer. Dress, Append. p. xii, 117, 282.
Put kay chawul ch'hurana, a ceremony, 106, 122, 147.
Putra, a board on which dough is kneaded and moulded, 119.
Puttara (err. Paytara), a large rattan or bamboo close basket, 119, 224.
Puttee, a ceremony, 23, 97, 99.
———, the side locks over the temples, 116, 123.
Putt'han, a tribe, 1, 8, 12, 16, 260.
Putwa, a braider, a maker of fringe and tape, 189.
Pyal, or Chironjee, q. v., 270.
Pyruhun. Dress, Append. p. xi, 299, 412.

Qadiree, a subjunction to names of fuqeers, 301.
Qadireea, an order of devotees, 288, 289.
Qadir wullee Sahib's oors, a ceremony, 243, 265, 425.
Qaf, a fabulous mountain. Gloss. 327, 388.
Qafeela, a body of travellers, 159.
Qamut, part of the *Tukbeer*, or creed, 171.
Qazee, a judge, civil, criminal, and ecclesiastic, 128, 257, 262.
——— Lyn and Qazee Bay-Deen, Mohurrum fuqeers, 210.
Qeeam, the standing position in prayer. Gloss. 79.
Qibla, the temple of Mecca, 78, 282.
Qoofool, lit. a lock, *i. e.* for resolving mysteries, 310, 312.
Qool-hoo-Allah. Vide Soora, 191.
Qools (The four), 130.
Qoorbanee, the sacrifice, 67, 96, 266.
Qoottoob Sahib, or Qoottoob-ood-Deen, oblations offered to him, 280.
Qoran, 11, 117.
——— kee Huddeea, a ceremony, 48, 284, 425.
——— Khutum-e. Vide Khutum, 177, 238, 421.
Qowl-beera, the betel contract, a ceremony, 91, 94.
Qudum-bosee, or Zumeen-bosee. Vide Sulam, Gloss. 283.
Qudum-e Ibraheem, the footstep of Abraham, 63.
——— Russool, the footstep of the messenger, Mohummud, 177, 234.
——— Moobarik, the blessed footstep, 234.
Quleea. Cook. Append. p. xxxv, 233, 277, 284.
Qulum, the pen (of record), 149.
Qulundur, a class of fuqeers (or devotees), 298.
Qumees. Dress, Append. p. x, 299, 412.

Rafzee, heretics; the Sheeahs so called by the Soonnees, 10.
Ramjunnee, a variety of dancing girls, 17.
Randa, or Abeer, q. v., Glossary.
Raootee, a kind of tent, 223.
Raykabeean, saucers, 120.
Rayooreean. Cook. Append. xlii, 222.
Reeazut, penances, mortifying the flesh, 294, 302.
Reech Shah, a Mohurrum fuqeer, 215.
Reetha, sapindus emarginatus, Vahl. or sapindus detergens, Roxb. soap nut, 24, 410.
Relationship. Vide Append. I.
Relatives, unlawful to marry, 144, 145.
Rengna, crawling as a child, on all-fours, 34.
Rice, unboiled or raw, Chawul, 4.
——— boiled, Khooshka or Bhat, 4.
——— in the husk, D'han or Paddy, 416.
——— parboiled in the husk, Oobala chawul, 4.
Riddles, &c., 113.
Rijal-ool-gyb, or Murdan-ool-gyb, 395.
Robaee, a variety of magic square, 322, 347, 349.
Rooa, a coin. Gloss. 3.
Rooh, or spirit, 234.
———. e-Siflee (lower), alias Rooh-e-Jaree, travelling spirit, 234.
———. e-Moqeen, the resident spirit, 234.
———. e-Oolwee, the lofty spirit, 234.
Rookn-e-Yemenee, 63.
Rookoo, the stooping posture in prayer. Gloss. 70, 79.
———kee tusbeeh. Vide Gloss. 79, 82.
Rote, sweetened wheaten cakes besmeared with sundul, 220, 224, 230.
Rotee, bread, properly unleavened bread. Vide Nan. Cook. Append. p. xxxii.
——— meethee. Cook. Append. p. xxxiv, 100.
——— row-gundar, wheaten cakes with a superabundance of ghee in them, 46.
Rowzut-ool Athar, the title of a work, 163.
———-oosh Shohuda, Book (praises) of the Martyrs, 162.
Roza, a fast (Rumzan ka). Gloss. 255, 426.

Roza ruk'hna, fasting, a point of the Mohummudan religion, 54, 56.
—— ka fittra, fast offerings, 57.
Rubee-ool-awul, the third month, 233.
———oos-sanee, the fourth month, 189, 237.
Rufaee, an order of devotees, 241, 291.
Ruhmut, the night of mercy, 252.
Ruhum, or Ruhum kay Pindeean, a ceremony, 270.
Rujub, the seventh month, 229, 249, 268.
——— salar kay kundoree, a ceremony, 249.
Rukat. Vide Gloss. 61, 79.
——— Dogana, two rukat prayers, 63.
——— Furz, 78.
——— Soonnut, 78.
——— Wajib, or Wajib-ool-wittur, q. v. Gloss. 78.
Rukhtunee, a douceur, a vail or vale, a perquisite, 23.
Rummee ool jumar, the throwing of gravel, a ceremony, 66.
Rumnay-walay, Mohurrum fuqeers, 213.
Rumzan, the ninth month, 229, 255.
——— kee eed, or eed ool fitr, the feast of Lent, 49, 57, 96, 261.
——— ka Roza, or the Mohummudan Lent, 255, 426.
Rung-burree kay k'hana, the dinner for the bridegroom sent from the bride's, 116, 121.
Rung k'helna, the bespattering with colours, a ceremony, 141.
Run ka *Dola* (lit. the war-bier), a ceremony, 226.
——— Shurbut, lit. the war-lemonade, 179.
——— Taboot, or Run ka *Dola*, q. v., 226.
Russool-nooma (lit. displaying the messenger), a class of fuqeers so called, 289.
——— shahee, a class of fuqeers (or devotees), 298.
Rutjugga, nocturnal vigils, 2, 271.
Ruzaee, a quilt, 119.
Ryan, one of the portals of heaven, 56.
Ryhan, Vide Tusbeeh, Gloss.

Sachuq, or Burree, 109.
Sachuq kay mutkeean, earthen pots painted, in which the Burree apparatus are conveyed, 110.
Sahib, an address expressive of affection or respect subjoined to names, 16.
Sahiban, the Ullums (q. v.) so called, 176.
Sahib e-Nissab, one who has eighty rupees in his possession for a year, 58, 267, 300.
Saints, Moosulman, 433.
Salar Mussuood *Gazee*, or Rujub Salar, q. v., 99, 249.
Sal-girub, or geera, the birth-day-anniversary, 38, 425.
Salik (lit. a traveller or pilgrim), a class of devotees, 296.
Salna (pl. Salnay), or Salun, curries, 108. Vide Cookery, Append. p. xxxv and xxxvii.
Salun kay kutoray, curry cups, 120.
Salutation (verbal) and its reply, 286.
——— among fuqeers, 286.
——— to fuqeers, 287.
Sang, a spear or javelin formed wholly of iron, carried by fuqeers, 214, 295.
—— burdar, spearsmen, 214.
Sanuk fateeha. Vide Fateeha.
Saoo-huldee, a ceremony, 97. Vide Huldee.
Sara (Sarah), 132.
Saree, 28, 37. Dress, Append. p. xv.
Sarung, or Sarungee. Mus. Instr. Append. p. xlvi. Vide Pl. V, 293.
Satan, his names, deputies, wife, and nine sons, 325.
Sayhra, 41, 117, 124, 130, 136, 240. Vide Flowers, Gloss.
Sayjbund, silk cords, with gold or silver tassels, for fastening the bedding or mattress to the bedstead, 119.
Sayla, muslin, 28.
Saynd'hee, the juice or toddy of the date-tree, 296.
Sayweea*n*, vermicelli, which the natives usually prepare between the hands instead of using a press, 119, 261, 264.
——— ka tukhta, a board for making sayweea*n* on, 119.
Seeanas (lit. cunning, artful), conjurors, 334, 338, 373, 382.
Seekaykaee, mimosa abstergens, Roxb. 24, 410.
Seekh rotee. Vide Note P., 267.
Seekundur (Alexander the Great), vows made to him, 279, 281.
Seen, or Thalee, a brass dish, 141.
Seena-bund (lit. breastband), used in shrouding the dead, 412.
Seena-zunnee, lit. breast-beaters, 174.
Seepahee (Sepoy), a native soldier, 90, 132, 233.
Seetar. Mus. Instr. Append. p. xlv, Vide Pl. V, 207, 293.
Seetaray, stars, planets (the seven), 18, 307.
Shaban, the eighth month, also a feast so called, 49, 96, 229, 251, 426, 430.
Shadee (lit. rejoicings), marriage, 128, 147, 425.
Shafaee, one of the four principal Mohummudan sects, 243, 244.

Shah (lit. a king), a title given to fuqeers, 286, 301.
—— Ahmud Abd-ool huq, 276.
—— Buddee-ood-Deen, or Zindu Shah Mudar, 241.
—— Dawul kay roteean, a ceremony, 277.
—— Shurf Boo Allee qulundur, a ceremony, 276.
——— ood Deen, yeheea Moonayree, 276.
—— Abd-oollah Shootar-e-nak, 289.
—— Mudar. Vide Zindu Shah Mudar, 196, 241.
————'s churagan, a ceremony, 241.
————'s fuqeers, 242.
—— Shums ood Deen Dariai, oblations offered to him, 280.
—— nizam ood Deen owleea, oblations offered to him, 280.
—— Dola, a saint, at whose shrine oblations are offered, 280.
—— Arzanee, ditto, 280.
—— Lohaunee, ditto, 280.
—— Selim Chishtee, ditto, 280.
—— nusheen, or Dad Muhal, 172, 185, (lit. royal seat). Vide Pl. I, fig. 2.
Shameeana, a canopy, 103, 219.
Shaving, propitious days for, 405.
Sheeah, partisans or followers of Allee, and opposed to the Soonnees, (q. v. Gloss.) 1, 9, 70, 174, 238, 251, 256, 257, 262, 269, 276, 289, 419.
Sheen, a cover for pots, 120.
Sheerbirrinj, or K'heer, 236. Vide Cook. Append. p. xl.
Sheernee, sweets, 329. Vide Cook. Append. p. xxxix.
Shees kay basun, a ceremony, 108.
Sheikh, 1, 8, 9, 13.
——— farooqee, Sheikhs descended from Oomr, 9.
——— Siddeeqee, Sheikhs descended from Aboo Bukr Siddeeq, 9.
——— Qorayshee, Mohummud and all his companions and descendants, 9.
——— Mohummud Ali Hazin Gillanee, a saint, 280.
——— Suddoo, a Moosulman who became a demon. Vide Diagram, No. 10, p. 338.
——— Suddoo kee kuraee, a ceremony, 279.
——— Furreed, oblations offered at his Durgah, 281.
——— Buha ood Deen Zakaria, oblations offered at his shrine, 280.
Shijra (prop. Shujra, q. v.) a list of saints or holy predecessors given by moorshuds to their disciples, 283, 300.
Shikra, a hawk, 406.
Shola (vulgo Sola), or Bhend, 125. Gloss.
Shookr, thanks, 326.
——— e-yeldooz, a planet so called, 395.
Shookrana (prop. Shukur-ana), a ceremony, 88, 89, 91, 93.
Shookree, or Sheernee, q. v.
Shookreea, thanksgiving, 126, 262, 283.
Shoomur-zil-Jowshun, a proper name, 167.
Shootaree, a subjunction to names of fuqeers, 301.
Shootareea, an order of devotees, 289.
Showbala, a Mohurrum fuqeer, 208.
Shub-baydaree, watching all night, and repeating Murseea, &c., 178.
Shub-e-Burat, a feast, 49, 251, 268, 425.
Shub-gusht, lit. the nocturnal perambulation (matrimonial), 44, 106, 124, 147.
———— (Mohurrum), 182, 220.
Shudday, or Ullums, q. v., 176.
Shugul, occupation, employment, a technical term in the science of exorcism, 302.
Shuhab, safflower, 102. Vide Koossoom.
Shuhadut ka roz, lit. the day of martyrdom, a ceremony, 221, 226.
Shuheed, martyrs, twenty grades, 71.
Shuhurbano, the wife of Hosein, 168.
Shuhur-gusht, city perambulation, 124.
Shujra (vulgo Shijra, q. v.), 283, 300.
Shukur-bhât, lit. sugar and rice, 88.
——— khoree (lit. eating sugar), or Shookrana, a ceremony, 93.
Shuma, a brass lamp, also one carried by devotees, 120, 294.
Shumbaylee, the vitex trifolia, Lin., three-leaved, or vitex negundo, Lin., five-leaved chaste tree, 25.
Shumla, the worked or embroidered end of a turban or kummurbund left flying loose, 180, 404.
Shurab, wine, 296, 333, 407.
Shurabee, a Mohurrum fuqeer, 210.
Shurbut, (eau sucré), sugar and water. Gloss. and Cook. Append. p. xli.
——— khoree (lit. drinking lemonade), or Shookrana, a ceremony, 93, 94.
——— Run ka (war-lemonade), 179.
Shurra, a proper name, 159.
——— the precepts of Mohummud, 27, 235, 286.
Shurra-e-kurkhee, the title of a work, 76.
Shurraee, 202. Dress, Append. p. xv.
Shurreef, (lit. noble, eminent), an affix to names, 15.
Shutrunjee, or Jamkhana, a large carpet, 119, 174.
Shuwal the tenth month, 57, 229, 260.

Shytan, or Satan, 325.
——— his four Khuleefay, or deputies, 325.
Sibbel (lit. gratis), water offered at any time gratis to any person, dispensed "in the name of God," 223, 407.
Siddee (prop. Syedee), an African or Æthiopian, 197.
Sift-e-Eemam, articles of belief, 130.
Signs of the Zodiac, 363, 372.
Sijdah, prostration in prayer. Gloss. 69, 260, 388.
——— e-tyhet, 70. Vide Gloss.
Sil, a stone on which spices, &c. are ground, resembling an oilman's grinding-stone and muller, but their surfaces are rough, 334.
Silsilla, the descent of a family, pedigree, 244, 282, 294, 300.
Singar-dan, a toilet bag, for containing a looking-glass, comb, tongue-scraper, meesee, soorma, &c., 109, 118.
Skies (The seven), 149.
Sneezing, 420.
Sohag, such ornaments as are worn by married women while their husbands are alive, 116. Vide Sohagin.
Sohageea, a class of fuqeers, 293.
Sohagin, a married woman, 107, 122. Gloss.
Sohagpoora. Vide Gloss. 109, 118.
Sohaleean, thin wheaten cakes, 107.
Sohurwurdee (fuqeers), an order of devotees, 288.
Sojna, or Dawut, the science of exorcism, 313.
Solasee, a variety of magic square, 322, 347, 348.
Solaymanee, the onyx stone. Vide Tusbeeh, Gloss.
Sonta, or Asa, a club carried by devotees, 293, 295.
Sontana, 23. Gloss.
Soobah-dar, a native officer (lit. a holder of provinces), 263.
Soofees, mystics of the East, 296.
Soojee. Vide Ata, Gloss.
Sook'ha, dry tobacco eaten with betel leaf, 284.
Sook'hmook'h, dried coffee, 96, 223, 228.
Sooltan Surwur, oblations offered to this saint, 280, 433.
Soombool (arsenic), food of devotees, 193.
Soomurun, or Gujra, bracelets made of coloured thread, worn at the Mohurrum; and of flowers worn on other occasions, 189, 299.
Soonnee, orthodox Mohummudans, 1, 9, 174, 238, 257, 259, 262, 419. Vide Gloss.
Soonnut, the traditions of Mohummud, 49, 405. Gloss.
——— Jummaut, the Soonnees so called, 9, 71.
——— Mowukkeeda. Vide Rukat, Gloss.
——— Gyr mowukkeeda, 78. Ditto.
——— Rukat, q. v. in Gloss. 80.
Soontan, circumcision, 43.
Soop, a winnowing basket 28.
Sooparee (prop. Soopeearee), betel or areca nut. Vide Pan-sooparee, Gloss. 274.
Sooplee, a kind of basket for winnowing corn with. Vide Soop, 212.
Soora-e-Alhumd, or Soora-e-Fateeha, the 1st chapter of the Qoran, 41, 47, 413.
——— Alum, or Ullum-turkyf or Feel, the 105th ditto, 256, 345.
——— Buqr, or A. L. M., the 2d ditto, 47.
——— Char Qool, the 109th, 112th, 113th, and 114th ditto, 130.
——— Chayhul Qaf, the 40th ditto, 346.
——— Easeen, the 36th ditto, 47, 383, 393, 408.
——— Eezaja, or Nussur, the 110th ditto, 91.
——— Fateeha, or Alhumd, the 1st ditto, 41.
——— Feel, or Ullum-e-turkyf, the 105th ditto, 256, 345.
——— Innafut-huna, or Inna, the 48th ditto, 383.
——— Iqra, or Ulluq, the 96th ditto, 41.
——— Qool hoo Allah, the 112th ditto, 191, 413, 415.
——— Mozummil, the 73d ditto, 383.
——— Ruhman, the 55th ditto, 47.
——— Tubut, the 111th ditto, 346.
——— Ullum turkyf, or Feel, the 105th ditto, 256, 345.
——— Ulluq, or Iqra, the 96th ditto, 41.
Soorma, an application for the eye to brighten vision. Vide Gloss. 118, 148, 192, 261, 412.
——— dan, a box for holding Soorma, 118.
Soorwal (prop. Shilwar), Dress, Append. p. xv., 105.
Soosee Eezar, trowsers made of a particular kind of cloth, 387.
Sootreean, or Chukoleean, q. v. 101, 254.
Sorahee, gugglet, or goglet (prop. goblet), 120.
Sowaree Ullums. Vide Ullum, 176.
Subza, ocimum basilicum, Lin. the basilic basil, 217, 382, 417.
Subzee, an intoxicating liquor. Gloss. 45.

Sudduf, mother of pearl. Vide Tusbeeh, Gloss.
Sudqa, propitiatory offerings. Gloss. 60, 261, 373.
Sudqee, or Sudqee jana, to become a sacrifice for the welfare, &c. of another, 278.
Suffa, a mountain near Mecca, 63.
Suffeid Goomchee kee jur. Vide Goomchee, 377.
Suffur, the 2d month, 227, 229.
Sufoora (Moses' wife), Zipporah, 132.
Suhnuk, or Sanuk-Fateeha. Gloss. 2.
——— k'hanay walay, partakers of the lady's dish, 108.
Suhur, or Suhurgahee, dawn of day-breakfast during Lent, so called, 57, 255.
Suhur-gusht, or dawn-of-day-perambulation, 124.
Sulaee, a tent, probe, needle, or piece of wire, used for applying Soorma to the eyes, 118.
Sulam (The), *viz.* Ussulam-oon-allyhoom Ruhmut-oolahe, i.e. The peace and mercy of God be with you all! 80, 258.
——— or saluting. Vide Gloss.
——— 1. Sulam, 95, 283.
——— 2. Bundugee, 116.
——— 3. Koornish, 69.
——— 4. Tusleem, or Tusleemat, 69, 116.
——— 5. Qudumbosee, or Zumeenbosee, 69, 116.
——— 6. Sash*t*ung. (prop. Ushtang.)
——— 7. Gullaymilna, or embracing.
——— Female, 116.
——— among Fuqeers, 287.
Sulams, the seven, 230.
Sulamee, a present given on particular occasions to persons making a sulam, 95, 138.
Sumdeean, or near relatives, *viz.* the fathers and mothers in law, 102, 133.
Sumunnee (alias Shah Shurf boo Allee qulundur), 276.
Suna. Gloss. 79.
Sundlasa, a flat circular stone on which sandal-wood is ground down, 119.
Sundooq (lit. a chest or trunk), a coffin, 119, 412.
Sundooqcha, a box, 119.
Sundul, a ceremony, 235, 238, 243, 244, 268.
——— an embrocation of sandal-wood. Vide Gloss. 264, 337.
——— bâth', a ceremony, 133.
——— ka k'hor, or sandal-wood core, 119.
Sunk'h, a conch shell. Mus. Instr. Append. p. xlix. Vide Pl, VI, 213.
Sunneeasee, Hindoo devotees, 344, 376.
Sunud, a grant (of land, &c.) 300, 313.
Surburah, stewards at an entertainment, 112.
Sur-e-bay-tun, tun-e-bay-sur. Mohurrum fuqeers, 208.
Sur-o-tun, a festival, 227.
Sur-guroh, a leader of a troop of fuqeers, 190, 244.
Surpay*n*ch. Gloss.
Surposh, dish covers, 119.
Surreeool Eejabut, a speedy answer, 310, 312.
Surso*n*, a variety of mustard seed, 184.
Surode. Mus. Instr. Append. p. li. 99.
Surwa Unjun. Vide Unjun, 377, 378.
Suthoora (prop. Sut'hwara), q. v. 4.
Suttra (lit. mark of defence), 81.
Sutwara. Vide Gloss. 4.
Sutwasa (lit. the 7th month), a ceremony, 1.
Syed, one of the four Mohummudan tribes, 1, 8, 9, 275.
——— Abd-ool-qadir, a saint, 281.
——— Abd-ool Qadir Jillanee or Peer-e-Dustugeer, 237, 288.
——— Ahmud Kubeer, the founder of the Rufaee class of fuqeers, 241, 291.
——— Alleewee, the descendants of Allee, by his other wives, not by Fatima, 8.
——— Hussunee and Hoseinee, the descendants of Allee, by Fatima, 8.
——— Jullal-ood Deen, Bokharee, 293.
——— Jullal ood Deen's Koondon, 249, 250.
——— Shah Zouhour, a saint venerated, 280.
——— Zein-ool-Abaydeen, a saint venerated, 280.
——— ool-taam, the prince of food, 236.
Sylabchee, or Chillumchee, a wash-hand basin, 120.
Sylee, or A*n*tee, q. v. 188, 189, 298.
——— wala (vulgo Suhaylee wala), 189.

Taboot (or Tazeea), bier or coffin. Vide Pl. I, fig. 1. 70, 172, 183, 234, 257, 273.
——— Bunggreea*n*-ka, ditto formed of glass bangles, 183.
——— Mom-ka, ditto of wax, 184.
——— Run-ka. Vide Run, 226.
——— or Maynhdee, 102, 235, 240.
Tafta, a kind of silk cloth. Taffeta, 94, 176.
Tahbund, or Loonggee. Dress, Append. p. xii, 294, 298.
Tail churbana, a ceremony, 106, 122, 147.

Tail ghurray, oil pots, a ceremony, 106, 107, 122, 147.
Taj, dress, Append. p. ix, 285, 299.
Talib, an inquirer or wisher, 301, 316, 321, 344.
Tambukhs, a large spoon to serve out rice with, 120.
Taree, the juice (or toddy) of the Palmyra tree, 296.
Tasa-Murfa. Mus. Instr. Append. p. l.
Tasay, small drums played upon by children, 253.
Tash, cloth interwoven with gold or silver thread, 40, 176.
Tattoo (corrup. of Tuttoo), an inferior species of Indian horse, 203.
Taweez, a flat square monument, 416, 419.
——— an amulet. Vide Orn. Append. p. xxiii, 335, 343, 347, 356, 379.
——— for the cure of incontinency of urine, 366.
——— the warding off of demons, fairies, enchanters, &c. 366.
——— Naftulna, q. v. 366.
——— the itch, 367.
——— the piles, 368.
——— the small-pox, 368.
——— all purposes, 369.
——— a haunted house, 369
——— casting out devils, &c. 370.
——— scrofula, 357.
Tayra Tayzee, a ceremony, 189, 229.
Tayzee, date of the moon, only in the month Suffur, so called, 229.
Tazeea (or Taboot), q. v. the representation of the tomb of Hussun and Hosein, 175, 184.
——— khana the house of mourning, or Ashoor-khana, q. v. 172.
Teeja or Zeearut, visiting the grave, 421.
——— of the Ullums, 226.
*T*eeka, a spot made on the forehead with lamp black, 212.
Teen, (lit. earth, dust, or clay), Adam created from it, 324.
Teen eearee, the Sheeahs so called, 9.
Thala, a large flat metallic dish, 120.
Thalee, a small ditto, a salver, a platter, 120.
*T*heekree, a piece of a broken earthen pot. Vide Append. p. li. lv., 374.
Thoollee, Cook. Append. p. xxx, 3, 143.
*T*hunda-kurna (lit. to cool), but here meaning laying the ullums, &c. away, 221.
——— mussala. Vide Mussala, Gloss.
Thup-*t*ee, a musical instrument, 93.
Til, Sesamum orientale, Lin. Gingilie oil seed, 229, 387.
Til kay tayl, gingilie or country sweet oil, 271.
Tilluck or Peshwaz, q. v.
*T*ippoo Pad-Shah, oblations offered at his shrine, 281.
Tola, (a Sicca rupee weight), equal to three drams. Append. p. v., 37, 59.
Tombs, 419.
Tooranee (or Turkish). The Soonnees so called, 9.
Toorra, a bouquet. Vide Flowers, Gloss, 213.
Toortooree, Mus. Instr. Append. p. xlviii, 93.
Toowur kee Dal, Citysus cajan, Lin. or pigeon pea, 112,
*T*opee, Dress. Append. p. ix., 28, 298.
To-*rr*a, Orn. Append. p. xxv, xxvii, 111, 275.
Tora, a number of trays, containing various dishes of food, presented to others by great men, or the dishes set before guests at meals, 111.
——— posh, a covering for dishes, 119.
Tosha, a vow or oblation, 276.
Toshuk, a mattress, 119.
Towq, a collar, a ring worn round the neck. Orn. Append. p. xxiii, 237, 239, 275.
Tubbul, or drum (of peace or war), 165.
Tubqatee, a subjunction to names of fuqeers, 301.
Tubqateea or Mudareea, an order of devotees, 242, 288, 289.
Tubuq, a tray, 28, 120, 384.
——— Mayway ka, or fruit-tray, 384, 387.
——— P'hool kay, or flower-tray, 384.
——— Purree kay, or fairy-tray, 376, 381, 384.
Tubur-e-Allum, a saint in whose name they perform oors, q. v., 246, 281.
Tubut. Vide Soora-e-tubut. 346.
——— makoos, the chap. Tubut read backwards, 346.
Tufseer, a commentary on the Qoran, 329.
——— e Hoseinee, 163.
Tug*t*ee from tugut. Vide Tukhtee, 234.
Tukbeer, the Mohummudan creed. Gloss. 81, 266, 414.
——— e-tushreek, q. v., 69, 267.
Tukeea (lit. a pillow), a fuqeer's stand or residence, 119, 298.
Tukhtee, any thing covered with gold-leaf, or tin, &c. -foil, 227.
Tukht-e-ruwan, (proper. travelling thrones), in which dancing girls and musicians are carried, on men's shoulders. Vide Pl. III, fig. 1, 126.

Tukseer, Elm-e-, the science of numbers, 347, 354.
Tulaq, a divorce, 144.
—— e-Byn, the husband's *once* saying to his wife, "I have divorced you." 145.
—— e-Rujaee, ditto repeated *twice*, 145, 146.
—— e-Mootuluqqa, ditto *thrice*, 145, 146, 152.
Tulqeen, the becoming a moreed or disciple, 281.
Tulwar, a sword, carried by fuqeers, 295.
Tumbaloo or lota, a small metallic pot, 101, 120, 240.
Tumboora. Mus. Instr. Append. p. li. 293.
Tumkeean. Mus. Instr. Append. p. l. 253.
Tuooz, having recourse to God against evil. Gloss., 79.
Tuqdeer, Fate; created on the 10th day of Mohurrum, 149.
Turaweeh, prayers offered daily at 8 A.M. 56, 255, 256, 262.
Tureequt, the path (*i. e.* to Heaven), 281.
Turkareean, vegetable curries. Cook. Append. p. xxxvii, 218.
Turweeah, the 8th day of Zeehuj, so called, 65, 267.
Tusbeeh, chaplet or rosary. Gloss. 285, 299.
—— act of praising God. Gloss.
—— Rookoo kee. Vide Rookoo, 79, 82.
Tusheeah, the Sheeahs so called, 9.
Tushfee-ool-wittur, Gloss. 78.
Tushreek, days of communion, 69.
Tushtureean, small plates, 120.
Tusleem. Vide Sulam. Gloss., 69.
Tusma, Dress. Append. p. xiii, 245, 285, 299.
Tusmeeu, Gloss., 79.
Tussanoon, the Soonnees, so called, 9.
Tussawoof, theology of the Soofees, or mystics of the east, 299.
Tuttee, a skreen or frame, 172, 185, 211.
Tuttoo, or tattoo, q. v., 203.
Tuwaf. Vide Gloss., 212.
Tyammoom, ablution with sand. Gloss. 68, 72, 75.

Ubeer. Vide Abeer. Gloss.
Ubruk or Mica, (not Talc, which mineral is never used), 185.
Ubjud. Vide Abjud ka hissab and Gloss., 308.
Uchwanee, (prop. Ajwaeenee, q. v.), 3.
Uggur, wood-aloes. Gloss., 239, 330.
—— kee buttee. Gloss., 190.
Ujjum, every country in the world except Arabia, 165, 305.
Ullum, standards or representations of the crests of Hosein's banners. Vide, Pl. II. fig. 3, 5, 6, and 7; 70, 172.
—— Suwaree, mounted ullums, 176.
Ulweeda, or Alweeda, q. v., 225, 257.
Unggooshtan or Huddeearoo, q. v., Orn. Append. p. xxvi, 91, 118.
Unggothee or Ch'hap, ditto, p. xxv, 118.
Ungurkha, Dress. Append. p. xi., 189.
Unjun, the magic mirror, 376, 382.
—— Alope, 377, 379.
—— B'hoot, 377.
—— D'hunna or Dhun, 377, 378.
—— Surwa, 377, 378.
—— Urth, 377.
Uqeeqa, a ceremony, 27, 30, 425.
Uqqeeq, or cornelian. Vide Tusbeeh. Gloss.
—— ool-buhur or Mocha stone. Vide Tusbeeh. Gloss.
Uqqul-buhur. Canna indica. Lin., or shot plant. Vide Tusbeeh. Gloss.
Urgujja, a perfumed powder. Gloss. 235, 421.
Ursh, or the 9th Heaven, 149.
Urth Unjun. Vide Unjun, 377, 378.
Ushur, tithes, a term in exorcism, 310, 312.
Usma e-hoosna, the glorious attributes, 304, 314.
—— e-Oozzam, the mighty, 304, 310.
—— e-Azum or Ism-e-Azum, q. v. the greatest attribute of the deity, 259.
Ussulam-oon-Allykoom, "Peace be unto you," 111, 286.
Ussur, afternoon. Vide Numaz, 267.
Ustugfar, deprecation, 130, 282, 285.
Uttur, otto of roses. Gloss., 118, 264.
—— dan, a perfume-box or receptacle for perfume, 118.

Virginity, puberty in females, 51.

Wajib-ool-witur. Gloss. 78, 81.
Weaning, 34.
Weights and Measures. Append. II. p. v.
Wird, repeating perpetually; *i. e.* something out of the Qoran, or a supplication or blessing. Vide Aoorad, 294.
Wives, the number authorized, 144.
Wufat-nama, the history of one's death, 234.
Wukeel, an agent, 129.
Wullee, a saint who can perform miracles, 237, 281, 301, 302, 322.

Wuseeqa, a bond or written agreement, 407.
Wusseeut-nama, a will or testament, 407.
Wuzaet, a daily performance of duty, 294.
Wuzoo, ablutions before prayer, 72, 407, 410.

Yeaqoob (Jacob), 12,
Yezeed, 151.
Yusoof (Joseph), 12, 132.

Zain Shah, oblations offered at his shrine, 281.
Zeearut (Teeja, or P'hoolchurhana), visiting the grave, 172, 421, 422.
——— of Ullums, 226.
Zeehuj, Zeehujja, Zilhuj, or Zoolhuj, the 12th month, 65.
Zeeqaeda, the 11th month, 265.
Zein-ool-Abaydeen, a proper name, 164, 170.
Ziffaf, leading a bride home, 142.
Zikkirs, reminiscences, repeating the attributes of God, or the creed, 298, 300, 302.
Zilhuj, or Zilhujja. Vide Zeehuj, 265.
Zinda Shah Mudar. Vide Shah Mudar, 101, 241, 289, 290, 425.
Zohur, noon. Vide Numaz, 55, 78.
Zooba, or Zoobuh. Vide Gloss. 187, 242, 407.
Zoobayr, a proper name, 151.
Zool-fuqqar, An Ullum, a representation of the double-bladed sword of Allee. Vide Pl. II, fig. xi, 177, 181.
Zoolhuj. Vide Zeehuj, 65.
Zooljunna, the name of Hosein's steed, meaning a winged wolf, 164.
Zoonnar, the Brahminical thread, 208.
Zuee, 12.
Zufur-tukeea, or Byraga, q. v. Pl. IV. fig. iii, 295.
Zukat, legal alms. Gloss. 67, 300.
——— dayna, alms-giving, a point of the Mohummudan religion, 54, 58.
——— of Isms, the prescribed offerings, or the attributes of the Deity, 303, 310, 312.
Zuleekha, Potiphar's wife, 132.
Zumeen, earth (the seven do.), 149.
Zumeenbosee. Vide Sulam. Gloss.
Zumzum, Hagar's well, at Mecca, 64, 407, 409.
Zung, a small bell, 195.
Zunjeer, chains, or fetters, 275.
Zur-afshanee, or Afshan, q. v. 49.
Zur-baf, cloth of gold, or gold tissue, 176, 234.
Zurda. Cook. Append. p. xxix, 96.
Zureeh, a tomb in the shape of a taboot, 257.
Zurwuruq, gold leaf, or tinsel, 126.
Zynub, Hosein's sister, 168.
Zytoon, olives. Vide Tusbeeh. Gloss.

CORRIGENDA.

Page. Line.
3, the last, *for* Vide Glossary, *read* Vide Index.
4, 4, *referring to* Glossary, *read* †Vide Index.
4, 20, *for* in a corner, *read* in the kown-ul."
5, 9, *for* large, *read* small.
5, 10, *for* small, *read* large.
17, the last, *for* 20 and 22, *read* 18 and 20.
19, 3, *for* Geneathliacal, *read* Genethliacal.
20, 34, *for* formed, *read* famed.
24, 33, *for* Gootlee, *read* Ghoontees.
32, 5, *for* Chap. XXXII, *read* Chap. XXVII.
42, 27, *for* set, *read* sit.
46, 3, *for* it, *read* them.
— 30, *for* Ch'hilla, *read* Ch'hulla.
51, note 1, *for* Vol. II. p. 349, *read* Vol. I. p. 349.
68, line 9, *omit*, not even excepting.
69, the last, *after* Vide Glossary, *read* Sulam.
74 2, *after* the water that remains, *add* i.e. in the lota or utensil in which they usually take up the quantity sufficient for performing the Wuzoo.
79, 9, *omit* (four.)
88, 18, *for* 1, *read* 3.
97, 7, *for* Muelleda, *read* Mulleeda.

Page. Line.
112, 29, *for* Alkumd-o-lillah, *read* Alhumd, &c.
— 27, *for* drunk, *read* drank.
123, 33, *for* by the application, *read* by the daily application.
124, 28, *for* Sohag, *read* Sohagin.
134, 27, *for* p. 117, *read* p. 103.
185, 31, *for* fig. 2 and 2, *read* fig. 2 and 3.
229, 2, *for* kae, *read* kee.
256, 9, *for* Eeman, *read* Eemam.
261, 17, *for* fitr, *read* fittra.
— 24, *for* just detailed, *read* about to be detailed.
271, 25, *for* (p. 173), *read* (p. 249).
278, 29, "Vide Plate," to be omitted.
285, 6, *for* Kulmay-e-Shureeut, *read* Kulma-e-Shureeut.
288, 4, *for* Aboo-Oollah-Huqeeqee, *read* Abd-Oollah-Huqeeqee.
293, 6, *for* sear, *read* scar.
294, 34, *for* rend, *read* bend.
300, 32 and 33, *for* Khuleefut, *read* Kheelafut.
329, 32, *for* Vide Glossary, *read* Vide Note, p. 296.
334, 21, *for* (p. 372), *read* (p. 373.)
378, 14, *for* lavigate, *read* levigate.
382, 27, *for* Vitex, &c., *read* Jasminum grandiflora. Lin. Catalonian Jasmine, or Jessamine.
391, 27, *for* skulls, *read* skull-caps.
395, 26, *for* note vide, *read* vide note.
407, 13 and p. 409, l. 13, *for* (p. 61), *read* (p. 64).

APPENDIX.

xxvii, 5, *for* cub, *read* curb.
xxxvi, 34, *for* matyhee, *read* maythee.
xxxix, 28, *for* lactuta, *read* lactuca.
xl, 13, *for* insert, *read* are inserted,
xlii, 17, to be *read* across as one line.
xlii, 28, *for* ambuh, *read* ambh from the Persian Ambuh.
xliii, 13, *for* cream, *read* scum.
xlix, 7, *for* twelve feet, *read* six feet.
l, 12, *add* or treble and base.
l, 33, *insert* Seetar *before* ستار
li, 10, *for* end *read* ends.

GLOSSARY.

lxii, 15, *for* one-fifth *read* one-fourth.
lxxxv, 7, *after* Bookol *read* or Bholsuree, Mimusops Elengi, Lin.
lxxxvi, 11, *for* مرشہ *read* مرثیہ
xcv, 27, *for* utissimus *read* utitatissimus.

THE END.

Pl. I

Fig. 1.

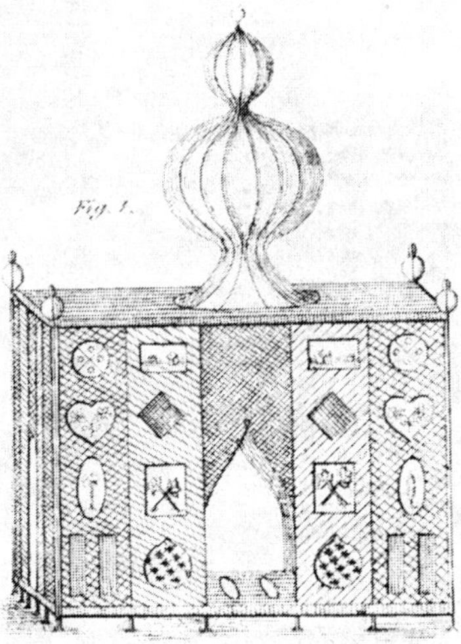

Taboot, or Tazea

Fig. 2.

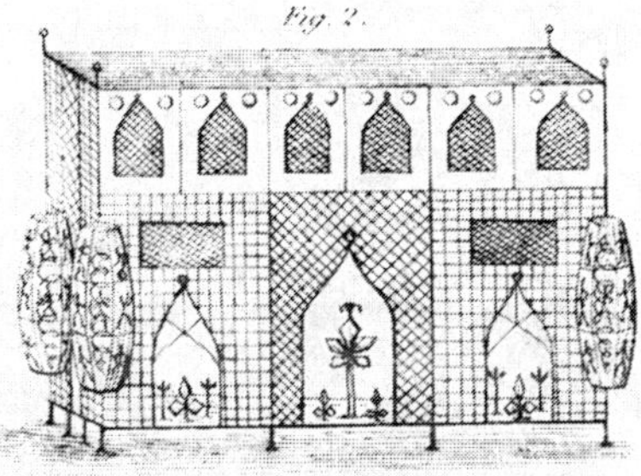

Shah-Nusheen, or Dalt-mahal

Fig. 4.

Fig. 3.

Churkhee-fanoos, or Fanoos-e-kheal.

Booraq

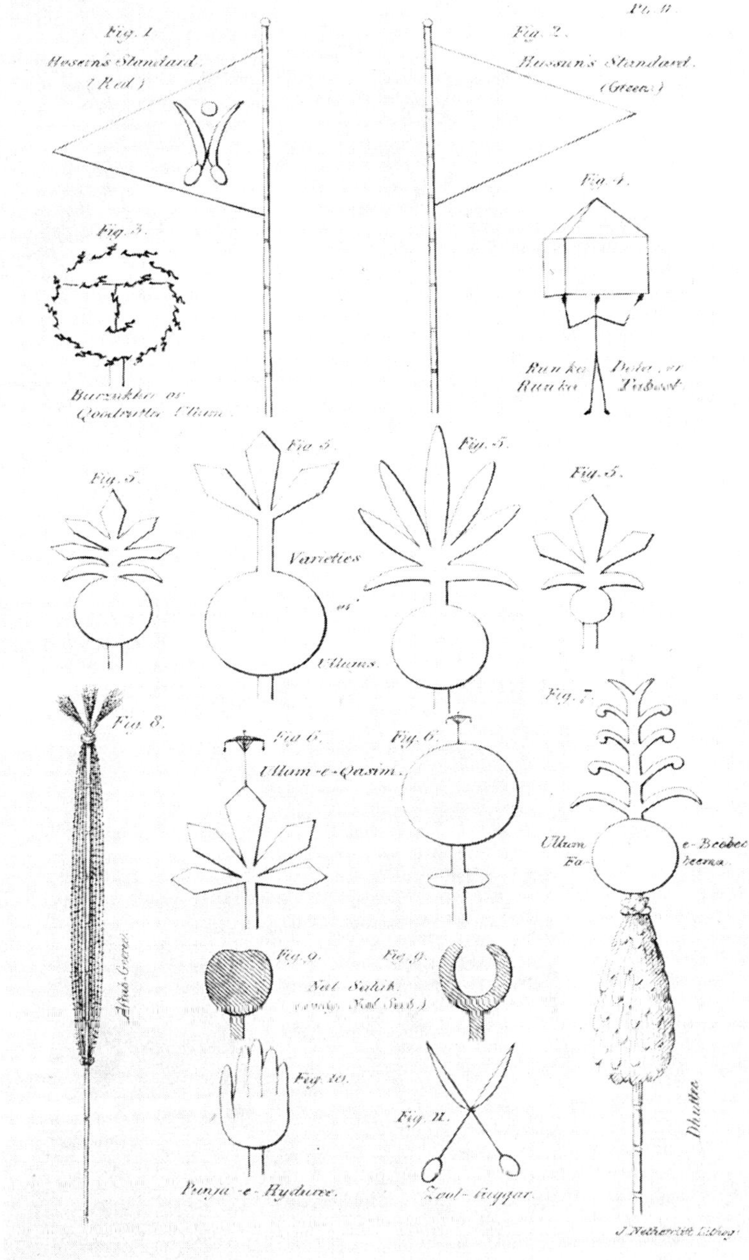

J. Netherclift Lithog.

PL. III.

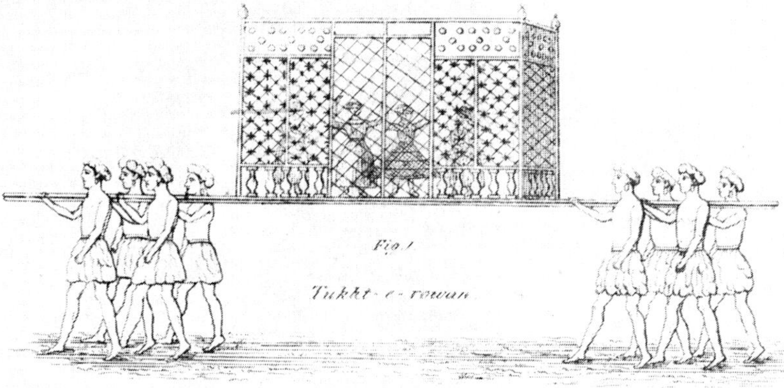

Fig. 1

Tukkt-e-rowan

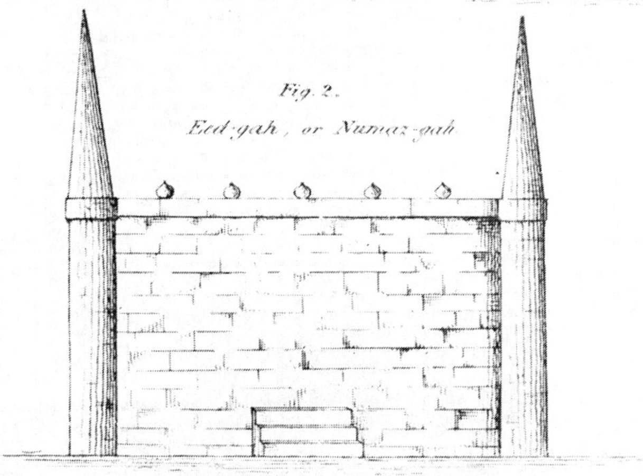

Fig. 2.

Eed-gah, or Numaz-gah

Fig. 3.

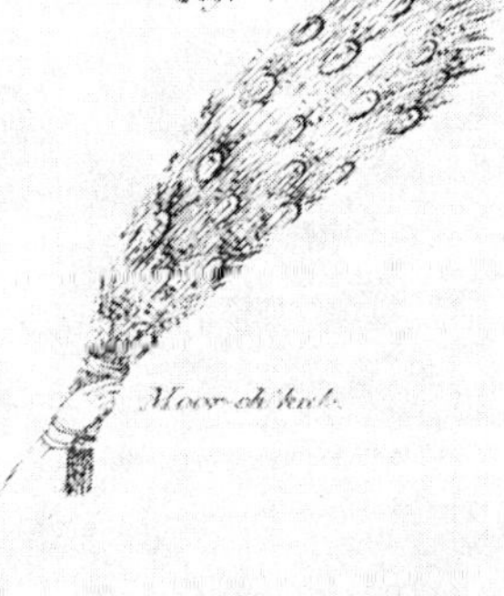

Moor-ch'kul.

Fig. 4.

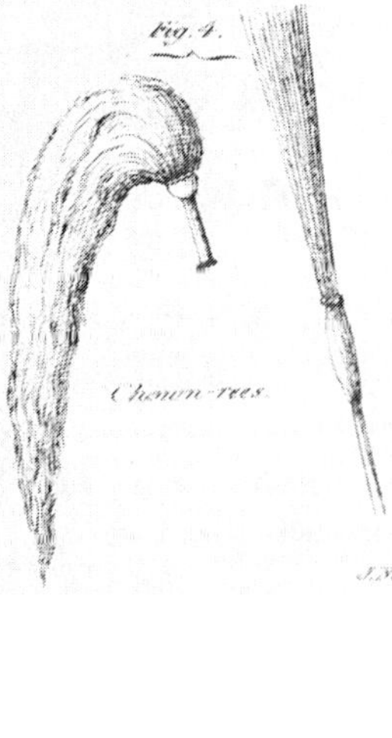

Chowr-rees

J. Netherclift Lithog.

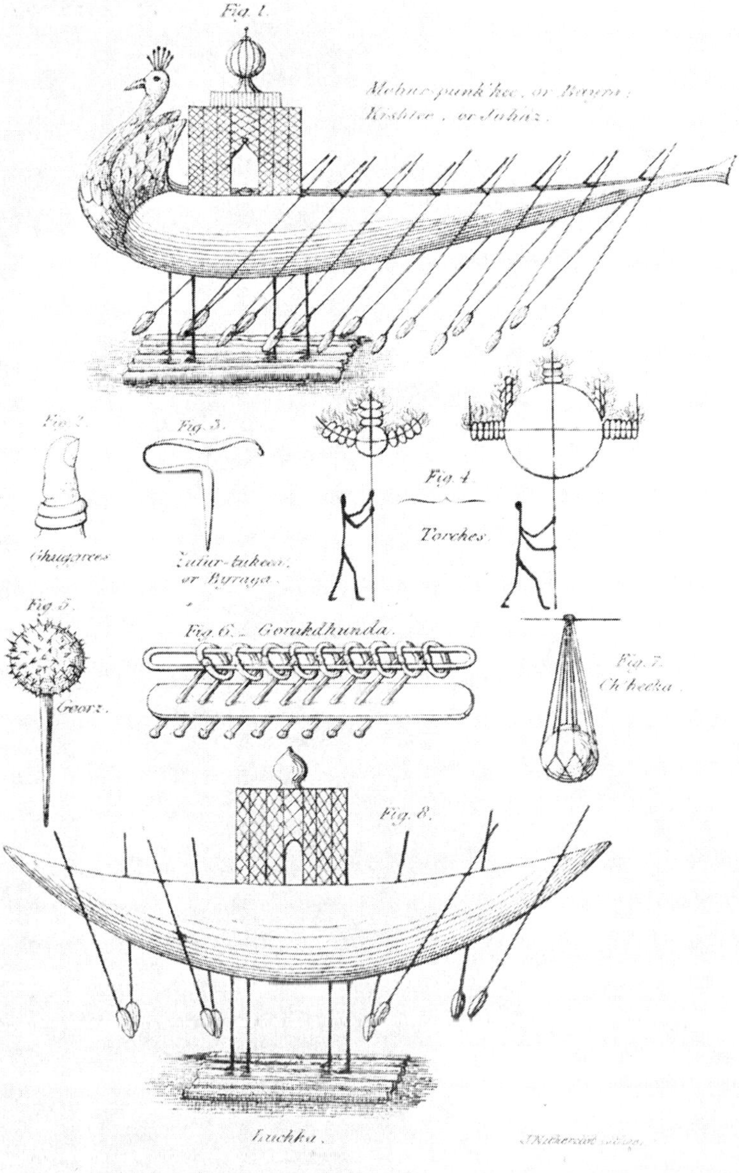

J. Netherclift lithog.

Musical Instruments.

I. Nutway ka Taefa. (Vide Appendix, p. 45.)

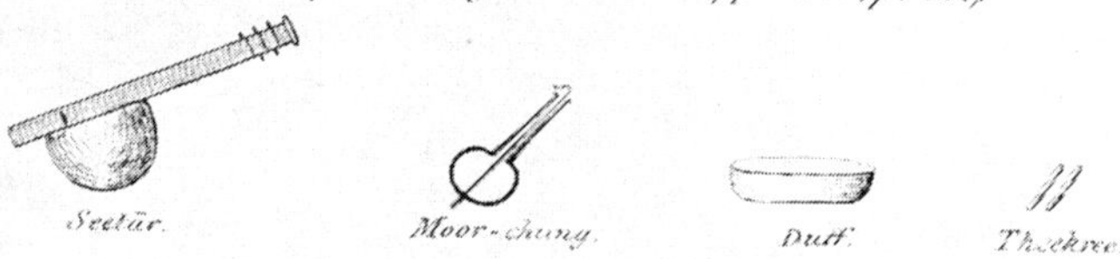

II. Kunchnee ka Taefa. (Vide Appendix, p. 46.)

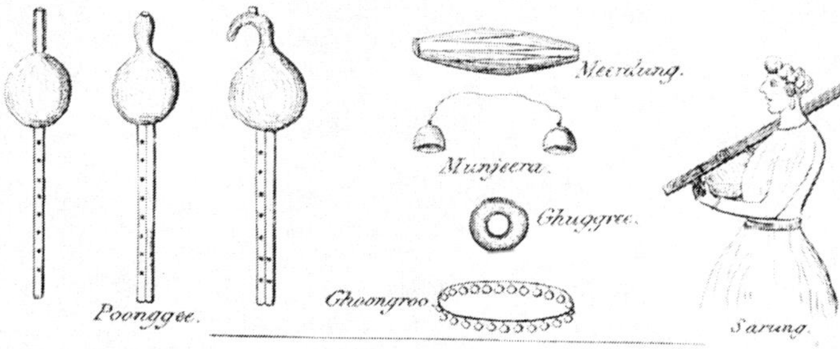

III. Baja ka Taefa. (Vide Appendix, p. 47.)

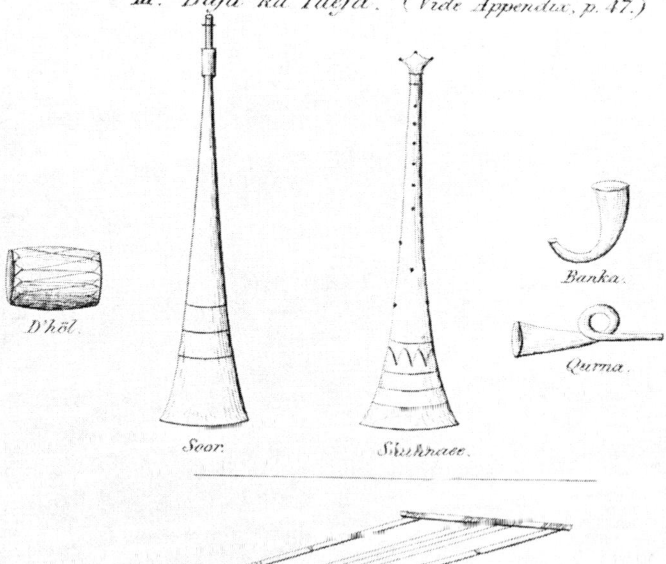

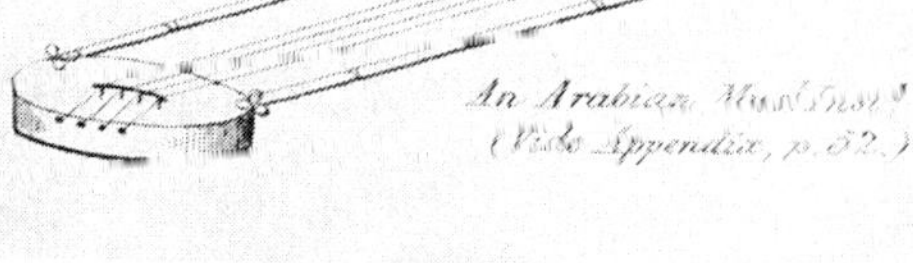

An Arabian Mus! Inst!
(Vide Appendix, p. 52.)

J. Netherclift Lithog.

Musical Instruments.

(Vide Appendix, p. 48.)

J. Netherclift Lithog.

Miscellaneous.

Pl. VII.

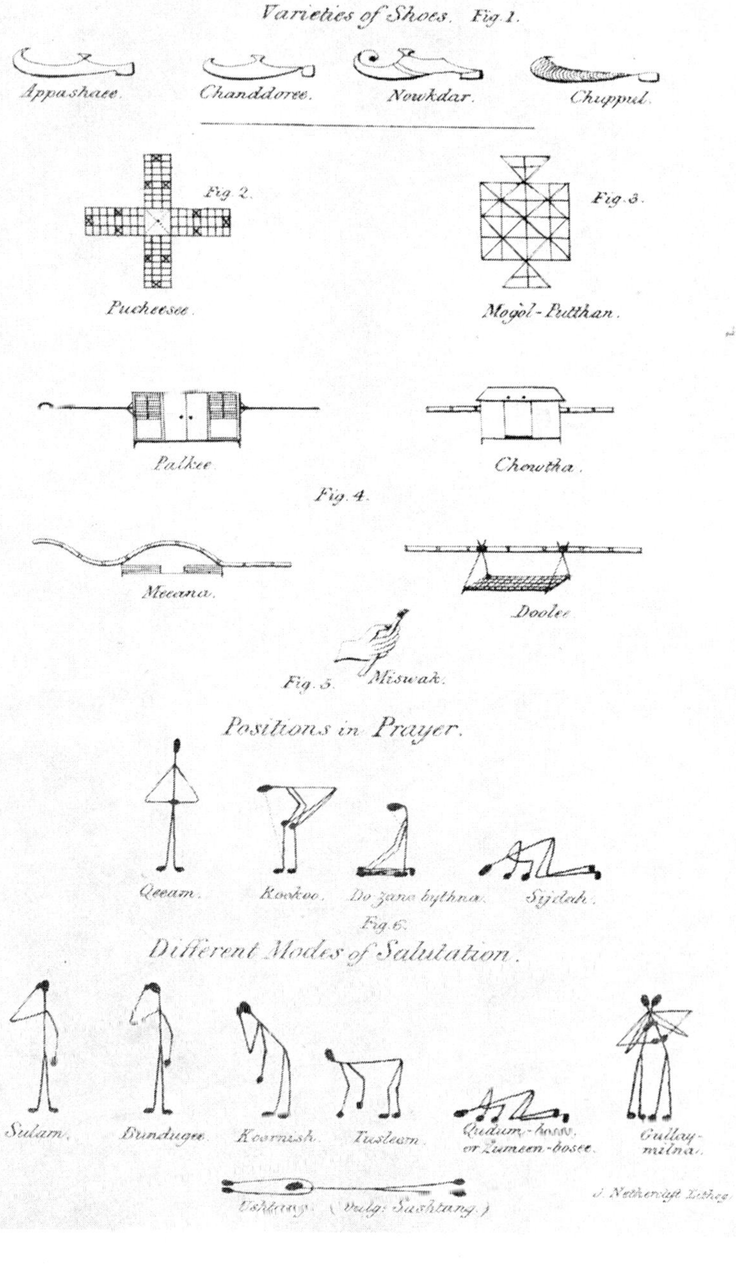